ARMENIANS
IN
INDIA

ARMENIANS IN INDIA

FROM THE EARLIEST TIMES TO THE PRESENT DAY

A WORK OF ORIGINAL RESEARCH

MESROVB JACOB SETH

GYAN

Published by

Gyan Publishing House
5, Ansari Road
Daryaganj, New Delhi-110002
Phone: 011-47034999, 9811692060
E-mail: books@gyanbooks.com

Distribution Network
gyanbooks.com
India, USA, Canada, UK, Australia, France

ISBN : 978-81-212-4495-4 (HB)
First Published, 1937

2nd Impression 2020

Printed at: Gyan Press, Delhi.

Armenians in India
Author: Mesrovb Jacob Seth

ARMENIANS IN INDIA

FROM THE EARLIEST TIMES TO THE PRESENT DAY

A WORK OF ORIGINAL RESEARCH

BY

MESROVB JACOB SETH

(Gold Medalist, Armenian College, Calcutta.)

Member, Royal Asiatic Society of Bengal; Royal Asiatic Society of Great Britain and Ireland; Indian Historical Records Commission; Calcutta Historical Society; Numismatic Society of India; The American Numismatic Association; Bengal Library Association; and Examiner in Classical and Modern Armenian to the University of Calcutta.

PUBLISHED BY THE AUTHOR

9, MARSDEN STREET

CALCUTTA

1937

TO

THE CHERISHED AND EVERLASTING
MEMORY
OF
MY DEAR AND REVERED FATHER.

JACOB SETH MACKERTICH AGAZAR SETH
(1820—1900)

who instilled into my youthful heart a taste for historical and antiquarian knowledge and an ardent love for the rich classical Armenian literature.

These pages are reverently and affectionately
DEDICATED
AS A SMALL TOKEN OF GRATITUDE
BY
HIS YOUNGEST AND ONLY SURVIVING SON.

MESROVB J. SETH.

"Part a zavakatz.
Zanoon tznoqatz.
Araviel hargele.
Khan uzkianus euriantz."—*Thaliadian*

Translation.

"It is the duty of children to honour the names of their parents more than their own lives."—*Thaliadian.*

Mesrovb J. Seth

PREFACE.

As a small contribution to the history of India and as a supplement to Armenian colonial history, we have succeeded, under great difficulties, in publishing a complete history of the Armenians in India, a work of original research, which we trust will supply a long-felt want.

We have laboured ceaselessly in the thorny fields of historical and antiquarian research for 45 long years, for the sake of an ideal. We have borne the heat of the day and have toiled fearlessly in deserted and snake-infested cemeteries, where we have, so to speak, opened old graves, gathered the dried bones, breathed life into them and made them speak. We have, during the past 45 years, travelled extensively in India, from Lahore in the Punjab to Madras in the Deccan, and from Surat in Guzerat to Dacca in East Bengal, practically from North to South and from East to West of this great Continent.

We have, under great physical difficulties and discomforts, succeeded in rescuing from oblivion, thousands of old Armenian epitaphs from deserted cemeteries and churchyards. These will be published, *Deo volente*, in a separate volume, with illustrations, historical and biographical notes, under the title, *Armenian Obituary of India*. Those valuable landmarks tell the sad tale of colonies, once flourishing, which have disappeared with the shifting of trade from old commercial centres to new. As is well known, the once important trade of Surat was captured by Bombay, and that of Dacca, Saidabad and Chinsurah by Calcutta, by reason of the favourable geographical position of the two great ports, Bombay and Calcutta.

In 1895, we published, a short history of the Armenians in India, the *first* work of its kind, as no attempts had been made, previous to that, to place on record the achievements of the Armenian settlers in India.

The work was received very favourably by the public and the Press. It was dedicated to the late Mr. Gladstone, the "Grand Old Man" of England, in recognition of his strongly-expressed sympathy for oppressed Armenians in Turkey which had endeared him to every Armenian throughout the world. The veteran statesman, in an autograph letter, thanked us for the work saying that he was "gratified by the honour we had done him". The views which he expressed in his letter, anent the massacres of Armenians in Turkey, are published on page 183 of the present work.

The work had some shortcomings, for it was prepared in great haste, during the sultry nights of the summer of 1895, as we were anxious to place before the British public, an authentic record of the valuable services rendered by the Armenians to the British cause in India, in the fond hope that the chivalrous British nation, the champions of liberty and justice, would come to the rescue of oppressed Armenians in Turkey, who were being ruthlessly massacred for their Christian religion, by the blood-thirsty Turks, during the never-to-be forgotten barbarous regime of Sultan Abdul Hamid of cursed memory, justly called the "Great Assassin" by the greatest British statesman of the 19th century, referred to above.

We are glad to state that since the publication of our first edition, we have had ample and unique opportunities of collecting much valuable data relating to the early Armenian settlers in India, from musty old records, from well-nigh obliterated inscriptions, and lastly from the letters of the Jesuit priests who resided at Agra, Delhi and Lahore during the glorious days of the mighty Moguls. Our object in collecting fresh and hitherto unpublished materials, was to bring out a new and an enlarged edition, as the first one, published 42 years ago, was out of print. For want of leisure, the bane of literary workers, the work was unavoidably deferred till last year when an event occurred, which though highly vexatious, yet it proved to be a blessing in disguise, for it made us more determined than ever to publish the fruits of our labours, without any further delay, since time and tide wait for no man and procrastination is verily the thief of time.

We have endeavoured, with the rich materials at our disposal, the accumulations of many years of patient search, to make the present edition as complete as possible, as those who have read the former edition can testify. For instance, we had in our first edition, referred to the famous Mirza Zul-Qarnain, in a few words, for want of materials, whereas in the present work we have devoted 87 pages to the life and work of that illustrious Armenian, thanks to the valuable researches of the late Father Henri Hosten, S.J. of blessed memory.

We had in our first edition given the translations of only nine Armenian inscriptions, from Agra, which we had found in the pages of the "Azgasare", an Armenian weekly published in Calcutta by the immortal Mesrovb Thaliadian, from 1845-1852, but in the present work we have published a complete list of the Agra inscriptions, to the number of 125, with biographical and historical notes. The achievements of several distinguished Armenians, who flourished at the Court of Akbar, were not recorded in our former edition, for want of materials, as we were a novice then and moreover had no time for research work. The reader will see, in the course of this work, that the Armenians, apart from being eminent merchants in India, have given to the country of their adoption able governors and administrators like Mirza Zul-Qarnain and Markus Erizad, clever diplomats like Khojah Israel Sarhad, Margar Avag Sheenentz and Khojah Petrus Arathoon, distinguished military Commanders like Gorgin Khan, and Colonel Jacob Petrus, skilled artisans and manufacturers of huge pieces of ordnance like Gorgin Khan and Shah Nazar Khan, renowned poets like Mirza Zul-Qarnain and Sarmad who composed beautiful odes and poems in a language (Persian) which was not their own. And this forcibly reminds us of what a great English writer once said of the late Bengalee orator, Sir Surendra Nath Banerjee, that what Cicero was to Rome, Demosthenes to Greece, Burke and Sheridan to England, so was Surendra Nath Banerjee to India, with this exception that whereas the former orators spoke and fired the imagination of their hearers in their own language, the Indian Demosthenes spoke, with equal if not greater force, in a language which was not his own, namely English.

Armenians though members of a small minority community, have nevertheless rendered valuable services to the British cause in India. We shall give but a few instances. When Calcutta which to-day occupies the proud and the enviable position of the "second city" in the wide British Empire, over which the sun never sets, was still in its infancy, an Armenian merchant-diplomat, the famous Khojah Israel Sarhad, secured from the Mogul Government certain important rights and privileges for the early British Settlers in Bengal, without which the settlement founded by Job Charnock in the village of Sutanati in 1690, after his expulsion from Hugli, could never have existed and attained its adolescence, for according to the verdict of that renowned research scholar and historian, the late Professor C. R. Wilson, "if Job Charnock be the Founder of Calcutta, the author of its privileges and early security is the great Armenian merchant, Khojah Israel Sarhad". And it was this merchant-diplomat who secured for the English, the historic "Grand Farman" from the Mogul Emperor Farrokh Siyar in 1715.

In the dark days succeeding the sack of Calcutta and the tragedy of the "Black Hole", a humane Armenian merchant, Khojah Petrus Arathoon, secretly supplied the British fugitives who had taken refuge in their ships down the river at Fulta, with boat loads of provisions for six months, before the arrival of the Army of Retribution from Madras, under Admiral Watson and Colonel Clive in December 1756. And in the momentous days before the famous battle of Plassey, which made the English absolute masters of Bengal, the same Armenian was employed by Clive to negotiate with Mir Jaffar for the overthrow of Nawab Suraj-ud-dowlah, the author of the "Black Hole" tragedy. It was the same Armenian, whom Clive calls the "Armenian Petrus", who was again instrumental in the removal of the imbecile Nawab Mir Jaffir in 1760, when his son-in-law, Mir Kasim was placed on the *masnad* (throne) of Murshidabad as the Nawab Nazim of Bengal, Behar and Orissa.

Before we conclude, we must record our thanks to the Government of India for the honour they did us by appointing us in 1925, a member of the "Indian Historical Records Commission", which was inaugurated in 1919, for unearthing and bringing to light unknown and hitherto unpublished records of historical interest relating to India. It may be mentioned, *en passant,* that for reasons of economy, the Commission suspended its annual Meetings and historical Exhibitions in 1931, but we are glad to see that they are to be resumed this year, in December, as in former years.

In the Papers which we read before the Commission at Lahore, Lucknow, Rangoon, Nagpur, Gwalior and Patna, from 1925-1930, we were able to place on record the achievements of some illustrious Armenians who had achieved fame and found a niche in the history of India during the 17th and 18th centuries. These were published in the *Proceedings* of the Commission by the Government of India and they have been incorporated in the present work.

And as historical works are now-a-days published with illustrations to make them more interesting, we intended also to have the present work illustrated, and with that object in view, we had secured, with much difficulty, a large number of old pictures and photographs of places and persons connected with the work, but we had, most reluctantly, to abandon the idea, as the illustrations would have made the book exceptionally heavy, it being somewhat unwieldy already, without illustrations. These will be published in a separate volume, printed on art-paper, with the usual letter press, under the title *Armenian Album of India*. It will contain, among others, the portraits of such celebrities as Khojah Petrus Woskan, Agah Shameer, Rev. Arathoon Shumavon, Colonel Jacob Petrus. Edward Raphael, Samuel Moorat, Sir Gregory Charles Paul, Sir Apcar Alenxander Apcar, Sir Catchick Paul Chater, Deputy Surgeon-General Dr. J. M. Joseph, M.D., Arratoon and Gregory Apcar, Joseph Emin and Sarmad, the martyred Armenian poet of India.

We trust this work will serve some useful purpose as a book of reference to the future historian of India and the antiquarian, and we shall be greatly gratified if it acts as an incentive to the present generation of Armenians in India to emulate the strong piety and patriotism that animated their illustrious ancestors. Then we shall feel rewarded, for in the words of our mentor, the immortal Mesrovb David Thaliadian, "it is the duty of the true patriot to revive the spirit of the children by the example of the noble deeds of their ancestors."

MESROVB J. SETH.

No. 9, Marsden Street, Calcutta.
1st June, 1937.

SECTIONS.

The book is divided into 17 Sections, as under :

Note :—Some Sections contain several chapters, the contents are given in the pages that come immediately after.

We extremely regret being unable, owing to ill health, to prepare an Index, for which we crave the indulgence of our readers, as the spirit is willing, but the flesh is weak.

We have however given in the following List of Contents the names of all the important places and persons which are recorded in these pages.

CONTENTS

CHAPTER XLVI.

CHAPTER XLVII.

CONCLUSION.

APPENDIX.

WORKS BY THE SAME AUTHOR.

1. HISTORY OF THE ARMENIANS IN INDIA ... 1895
2. IS CLASSICAL ARMENIAN DEAD? ... 1923
3. THE REPUBLIC OF ARMENIA 1924
4. THE SOCIETY OF MEKHITHAR 1924
5. *ARMENIANS AND THE EAST INDIA COMPANY ... 1926
6. *HINDOOS IN ARMENIA 150 YEARS BEFORE CHRIST 1927
7. *GORGIN KHAN 1928
8. *KHOJAH PETRUS 1929
9. *ARMENIANS AT AGRA AND GWALIOR ... 1930
10. *AGAH CATCHICK ARAKIEL 1931
11. *ARMENIANS AT CHANDERNAGORE ... 1931
12. *THE OLDEST CHRISTIAN GRAVE IN CALCUTTA 1932
13. *THE SECOND OLDEST CHRISTIAN CHURCH IN BENGAL 1936
14. *ARMENIANS AS POLITICAL STEPPING-STONES (Khojah Israel Sarhad) 1936
15. GRICH VOSKEGRICH MATENAGRIN, (The pen of the author with a golden pen) being a biographical sketch of the immortal Mesrovb David Thaliadian, in classical Armenian, printed and published by the Mekhitharists at Venice, with a Foreword by the Rev. Father Vardan Hatzuni, Rector of the "Raphael-Moorat College" ... 1926

Those marked with an *asterisk* have been incorporated in the present work.

SOME RARE ARMENIAN PUBLICATIONS FOR SALE, SUITABLE FOR MUSEUMS AND LIBRARIES.

		Rs.
1.	A beautifully illustrated BIBLE in classical Armenian, in the original binding, printed and published by Mekhithar at Venice, in 1733	250
2.	A complete copy of the AZDARAR, the *first* Armenian journal in the world, edited, printed and published at Madras from 1794—1796, by Rev. Arathoon Shumavon, (vide p. 597). There are three complete copies in existence	1,000
3.	A Latin-Armenian DICTIONARY (Dictionarium Novum Latino-Armenian) by Jacobo Villolle S. J. printed at Rome in 1714 ...	100
4.	Mosis Chorenansis HISTORIAE ARMENIACAE, translated into Latin from the original Armenian by the brothers William and George Whiston, and printed, with the Armenian text, at London, in 1736	50
5.	A complete copy of the AZGASARE, edited, printed and published by Mesrovb David Thaliadian, at Calcutta, from 1845—1852 ...	500
6.	HISTORY OF ARMENIA, in classical Armenian,by Father Michael Chamchian of the Mekhitharist Society, printed at Venice in three large volumes, from 1784—1786	150
7.	The BIBLE in classical Armenian,without illustrations, printed by the Calcutta Auxiliary Bible Society at Serampore (Bengal) in 1817	50
8.	HORDORAK (Exhortations) printed at Madras by Jacob Shameer in 1772. This is the *first* Armenian publication in India (vide p. 596)	50
9.	VOROGYTHE PHARATZ (Code of Laws for Armenia) compiled by Jacob Shameer, and printed at Madras in 1773 ...	50
10.	TRUTHS OF THE CHRISTIAN RELIGION, in classical Armenian, by the monk Johanness of Julfa, printed at Calcutta by Rev. Joseph Stephen in 1797 (vide p. 601)	50

ARMENIANS AT AGRA

MIRZA ZUL-QARNAIN

CHAPTER I

AN ARMENIAN GRANDEE OF THE MOGUL COURT

There are few who are acquainted with the history of the Armenians in India, their condition, their traditions and the sphere of their activities. Many are ignorant of their past, and the influence they exerted for good in those olden days of turmoil and unrest. It may not be generally known that the Armenians have been connected with India as traders, from the days of remote antiquity. They came to this country by the overland route, through Persia, Bactria (Afghanistan) and Tibet and were well established in all the commercial centres long before the advent of any European traders into the country. It may be noted however that the early Armenian traders formed no permanent settlements or planted any colonies in India. They were merely birds of passage who came all the way from the land of Ararat of Biblical fame, to purchase the spices and the fine muslins for which ancient India was famous. It was Akbar, the Marcus Aurelius of India, who induced them to come and settle in his dominions instead of being mere sojourners in the country. He was well aware of the intelligence of the Armenians and their integrity in commercial matters and wished to improve the trade of the country through their agency.

It is recorded by Thomas Khojamall, the Armenian historian of Bengal, that during one of his *incognito* tours in

Cashmere, Akbar met an Armenian merchant, Hakobjan (Jacob) by name, who had his son, a handsome lad, with him. Akbar invited the Armenian merchant to come and settle at Agra and at the same time to induce his countrymen in the Punjab and elsewhere in India to come and reside at the imperial city where they would be given permission, by their royal patron, to build a church for the worship of God in their own way, as Akbar knew that the Armenians were a religious race of ancient Christians and would not settle in a place where they could not have and enjoy the free and undisturbed use and exercise of their own religion.

Akbar's invitation to the Armenians had the desired effect, for a flourishing Armenian colony soon sprung up at Agra and at the express wish of the Emperor, an Armenian Church was erected there in 1562. Akbar, who could appreciate true worth and reward real merit, took a great liking to his Armenian subjects whom he regarded as valuable assets. One of his queens, Mariam Zamani Begum, was an Armenian.

Abdul Hai,* the Chief Justice (Mir Adl) was, according to the *Ain-i-Akbari,* an Armenian. The lady doctor in the royal Seraglio, was an Armenian, Juliana by name. It

---

* Abdul Hai is mentioned in some MSS. of the Akbarnama (Vol. III) as taking part in the religious discussions of Akbar. His full name was Mir Abdul Hai, Mir Adl. The *Tabaqat* calls him Khwajah Abdul Hai and says that he was an Amir. In the *Ain-i-Akbari* he is mentioned as "the Qazi of the Imperial Camp" (Ordu).

That Abdul Mai, the Armenian, was the Chief Justice of Akbar's Court, is evident from the following episode in the *Ain-i-Akbari.* "In the 35th year, at the feast of Abanmah, the Court witnessed a curious spectacle. The Sadr [Miran, better known as Sadr Jahan Mufti] and Abdul Hai, the Chief Justice of the Empire, took part in a drinking feast, and Akbar was so amused at seeing his ecclesiastical and judicial dignitaries over their cups, that he quoted the well-known verse from Hafiz—

در دور پادشاه خطا بخش جرم پوش

حافظ قرابه کش شد و مفتي پياله نوش

was this Lady Juliana, who was given by Akbar in marriage to Prince Jean Philipe de Bourbon of Navarre of the royal house of France, when that *debonair* adventurer appeared at the Court of Akbar in 1560. A daughter of the Armenian Abdul Hai, the Chief Justice, was given in marriage by Akbar, the royal match-maker, to an Armenian at his Court in 1590. Iskandar (Alexander) by name, who had come originally as a merchant from Aleppo to Agra and entered the service of Akbar.

Iskandar had two sons. The elder, Alexander, born in 1592, was given the name of Mirza Zul-Qarnain by Akbar and by that august name he was known all the days of his life. Zul-Qarnain means the two-horned, the title of Alexander the Great.*

Mirza Zul-Qarnain, the subject of this memoir, rose through sheer merit, to be a Grandee (Amir) of the Mogul Court during the glorious reign of Jehangeer and Shah Jehan, the worthy successors of the great Akbar. As a lad, Mirza Zul-Qarnain was a great favourite with the Emperor Akbar and was brought up in the royal palace as the adopted son of Akbar's Armenian queen, whose nephew he is supposed to have been, for it is a moot point whether Akbar's Armenian wife was a daughter of Abdul Hai, the Armenian Chief Justice, or some other lady.

In the letter of Fr. Jerome Xavier, 1596 we read, "Last year (1595) before the whole people, the King (Akbar) had a reliquary of Our Lady attached with a gold chain round his neck and he gave it to a small boy, a Christian, the son of an Armenian Christian, whom he had about his neck, and kissing it with his lips and eyes he gave it to the boy to kiss and put it on his eyes and finally he hung it on his breast and gave it to him and this while at the window before the whole people."

---

* Our readers will find, in the third chapter of this work, a very interesting Foot-note by Father Hosten about the origin of this curious title of Alexander the Great.

That well-informed royal chronicler, the Emperor Jehangeer, gives the following account of Mirza Zul-Qarnain in his Memoirs, called *Tuzak-i-Jehangeeri* :—

ذوالقرنین بفوجداری سانبهر دستوری یافت او پسر اسکندر ارمنی است
پدرش در خدمت عرش آشیانی سعادت پذیر بود حضرت صبیه عبد الحی
ارمنی را که در شبستان اقبال خدمت می نمود باو نسبت فرمودند از او دو
پسر بوجود آمد یکی ذوالقرنین که بفهم و دانش آگاهی و خدمت طلبی داشت
و در عهد دولت من دیوانیان عظام خدمت خالصه نمکسار را بعهده او
مقرر نمودند و این خدمت را بفهم سرانجام میکرد درینولا بفوجداری آن
حدود سرفراز گشت به نغمه هندی سری دارد سلیقه اش درین فن درست
رفته و تصنیفات او مکرر بعرض رسیده و بپسند افتاده

It can be translated thus :—

"Zul-Qarnain obtained leave to proceed to the *Faujdar*-ship of Sambhar. He is the son of Iskandar, the Armenian, and his father had the good fortune to be in the service of Arshashyani [Akbar], who gave him in marriage the daughter of Abdul Hai the Armenian, who was in service in the royal harem. By her he had two sons, one was Zul-Qarnain, who was intelligent and fond of work, and to him, during my reign the chief *diwans* had entrusted the charge of the Government Salt Works at Sambhar, a duty which he performed efficiently. He was now appointed to the *Faujdarship* of that region. He is an accomplished composer of Hindi songs. His method in this art was correct and his compositions were frequently brought to my notice and were approved."

Apart from being an accomplished composer of Hindi songs, Mirza Zul-Qarnain was a singer of repute and a poet of great merit, who composed verses in elegant Persian, which was then and for a long time afterwards the language of the Mogul Court.

It is mentioned in Waris's continuation of the Padishah Nama (page 392 of British Museum MSS.) that Mirza Zul-Qarnain came from Bengal and presented poems which he had composed in Shah Jehan's name on the occasion of his accession, and got a present of four thousand rupees. We have still to discover the famous poem which he composed on the occasion when Shah Jehan removed his capital from Agra to Shah Jehanabad, or Delhi, in 1648. A Jesuit Father refers to this remarkable poem as follows: "The King at great expense had built a most magnificent city to which he gave the name of Ganabad [Shah Jehanabad] in praise therefore of the vast city he had founded, the King asked Mirza [Zul-Qarnain], by far the best poet of those regions, to write a suitable piece of poetry. Mirza summoned up all the power of his talent, he wrote in verse that was perfect; but in it he sang, not the praises of the King, but the power of God alone: Mirza's only object was to show to the King that the glory of the city and its perfection were attributable to God alone. The King, who, in his greed for flattery, expected his own praises, indignantly rejected the panegyric. Afterwards, he submitted his name where that of God came in, so that what was said to God's praise would be attributed to him. In this you see how Mirza's intrepid piety came into conflict with the intolerable arrogance of the King."

It may be mentioned that Mirza Zul-Qarnain, had been brought up in Akbar's Court with the future Shah Jehan. They had been playmates, and Shah Jehan had to allow Mirza Zul-Qarnain many things which he would have suffered from no one else.

That Shah Jehan was very friendly with Mirza Zul-Qarnain, the following extract from "Tavernier's Travels in India," will show. Writing in 1665, Tavernier says: "There are some who wonder that Cha-Jehan against the practice of the Mahumetans, who abhor images, did permit of carving, but the reason conjectured at is, that it is done upon the consideration that his father and himself learnt from the Jesuits certain principles of mathematics and astrology. Though he had not the same kindness for them [the Jesuits] at another time, for going one day to visit an Armenian, that lay sick, whose name was Cotgia, whom he loved very well and had honoured with several employments, at what time, the Jesuits who lived next to the Armenian's house, rang their bell; the sound thereof so displeased the King, as being a disturbance to the sick person, that in a great fury he commanded the bell to be taken away, and hung about his elephant's neck. Some four days after, the King seeing his elephant with that great bell about his neck, fearing so great a weight might injure his elephant, caused the bell to be carried to the *Couteval,* which is a kind of a railed place, where a Provost sits as a judge, and decides differences among the people of that quarter, where it has hung ever since. This Armenian had been brought up with Cha-Jehan, and in regard he was an excellent wit, and an excellent poet, he was very much in the King's favour, who had conferred upon him many fair commands, though he could never either by threats or promises win him to turn Mahometan."

Although Tavernier gives Cotgia as the name of the sick Armenian, whom Shah Jehan visited, yet it is evident from the concluding portion of his account that the sick friend of the Emperor was nobody else but the famous Mirza Zul-Qarnain, who had been brought up in the royal seraglio with Shah Jehan, as can be seen hereafter.

Probably Tavernier could not recollect his name when writing his Travels and simply mentioned Cotgia, as Cojah or Khojah was then a common title of honour among eminent merchants and others.

But how could Tavernier have called him a "Khojah", for Zul-Qarnain bore the distinctive honorific title of "Mirza" all the days of his life.

And as a good Christian, Mirza Zul-Qarnain must have been deeply grieved and greatly perturbed in his sick bed at the sacrilegious action of Shah Jehan in removing the bell from the home of the Jesuits whom he honoured and respected always.

We have seen the origin and the parentage of this noble Christian lad, brought up from his infancy in a Mohammedan palace, with all its luxuries, temptations and blandishments, yet remaining true and loyal to the faith of his ancestors, despite the threats of Jehangeer and the persecution of his erstwhile playmate, Shah Jehan, for in the words of an American divine, the Rev. Frederick Davis Greene, M.A. for several years a resident in Armenia, "by nature the Armenians are deeply religious, as their whole literature and history show. It has been a religion of the heart, not of the head. Its evidence is not to be found in metaphysical discussions and hair-splitting theology, as in the case of the Greeks, but in a brave and simple record written with the tears of saints and illuminated with the blood of martyrs."

It will be interesting to follow the life history of Mirza Zul-Qarnain whose achievements and meteoric rise to fame have not been surpassed by any Armenian in India during the last three hundred years. He was the greatest and the most remarkable Armenian that lived and died in this country, the land of his adoption.

His father, Iskandar, enjoyed the *jagir* of Sambhar where he had been in charge of the government salt monopoly at the Salt Lake.

Shortly after Jahangeer's accession to the throne, at the end of 1605, Iskandar came from Sambhar to Agra to pay his respects to the Emperor and give an account of his administration, Jahangeer pressed him to become a Mahomedan. The circumstances, which led the Emperor to prove false to the good advice he had himself given to Iskandar in 1598, were as follows: There was at the Court a young Hindu nobleman, who had allowed himself to be circumcised. He was the son of a great Captain, who had been high in Akbar's favour. One day, Jahangir represented to him that, as he was no longer a heathen, he ought to make choice of another religion and become either a Mahomedan or a Christian. "If you choose to become a Christian," he said, "I shall call the Fathers, who will baptize you." The young man chose to become a Mahomedan, and the King to mark his satisfaction had him paraded on an elephant throughout the city.

Seeing that what he had done delighted the Mahomedans, Jahangeer now wished to obtain the same from Iskandar "a distinguished Armenian gentleman," who had stood high in the favour of the late King, and who had his two sons brought up at Court with the King's own nephews. The King (Jahangeer) took it into his head that he would get this Christian to accept the law of Mahomed; but, he remained steadfast in his religion, to the great consolation of the Fathers. He kept them constantly informed of what happened, and, one day, speaking with them, said :—"What do I desire more here on earth, than to die for the faith of my Saviour, in forgiveness of my sins and in expiation of the scandal I gave." (Long before, he had, contrary to the law of the Church and the representations of the Fathers, married the sister of his deceased wife). But this Christian (Iskandar, Zul-Qarnain's father) together with his two children escaped the danger.

Subsequently, the King asked for the two children, and, hearing that their father had taken them with him he had them brought back to the palace and received them in the most friendly manner. A few days later, he asked them what religion they belonged to. The children answered that they were Christians. "Well, then," said the King "if you are Christians, eat pork." They answered that there was no precept among Christians enjoining them to eat pork, though, on the other hand, there existed no prohibition." The King's proposal ended there for the time being.

The next day, in the morning, these children came to see the Fathers, and related to them all that had occurred. The Fathers encouraged them and taught them how they should conduct themselves, in case the King should urge them further. Indeed, so it happened : for, as the Mahomedans did not cease sitting near the King's ears to get him to pervert these children, the King forbade them to go out of the palace, and kept them in confinement. When this had lasted some time, he had them brought again before him, and, placing pork before them, he wished to force them to eat it, but the younger of the two said that, if the Fathers should tell them they must eat it, they would do so. This had been pre-arranged, in the hope that the King would have the Fathers called, in which case they would assist the children and keep up their courage. The King wished to call for the Fathers, when one of his favourites grew so vexed at the answer of this little child that he slapped him once or twice in the face, saying angrily : "What hast thou to do with the Fathers here, when the King commands?" Seeing this the King left the Fathers and the pork alone, and said to the children : "There is nothing to be done. You must become Mahomedans. Recite then the "Calima," (i.e., the profession of faith of the Mahomedans). The children refused to comply. Hereupon, the King had many rods brought and gave orders to scourge them, as is done to malefactors. Terrified at the impending torture, the poor children muttered in a whisper between their teeth what the Mahomedans taught them. And so they were conducted sad and disconsolate to their room.

The next day, the King sent in someone to circumcise them, but, they would in no way allow it, and started crying so piteously that they were left unmolested this time, until the King had been informed. Not long after, they were brought before the King. He asked them why they refused to be circumcised. The poor children answered: "We shall never allow it, because we are Christians." The Fathers, who went daily to visit the King, had instructed them thus.

The King, hearing their bold answer, tried them first with great amiability, and next with grievous threats. Encompassed on every side and seeing that their words were of no avail, one of them approached the King, and joining his little hands said: "Lord King, we beg of thee for the love of Alazareth Jeam (Hazarat Isa, that is, of the Lord Jesus), not to have us circumcised." But the King refused to listen, and, ordering them to be bound hand and foot, he caused them to be forcibly circumcised. This done, "Recite now," he said, "the Calima" (or profession of faith of the Mahomedans). They refused with great firmness, whereas the King became so angry that he commanded them without pity to be most cruelly scourged. The elder boy, being only fourteen years old, yielded under the pain; but the younger one, who was eleven years, kept firmer and would not comply. The blows were redoubled; yet, he was heard to say only: Ah Alazareth Jeam!" that is, "Oh Lord Jesus!" To strengthen himself he held continually a reliquary in his hands. Matters had now come to such a pass that the King was moved to pity and relented: but one of his favourites still gave the lad thirty blows, so hard and cruel that it was enough to make a stout man flinch. In fact, the poor child lost courage under this barbarous treatment and recited what they wanted him to.

Triumphant, as it were, at his victory, the King left orders to dress their wounds. The same night, the Fathers came near the children entirely unaware of what had passed. They found them stretched on the floor, quite disconsolate and not uttering a word. But, as soon as they perceived the Fathers, "We are Christians," they cried out,. "we were circumcised against our will." The Fathers inspired them with courage to remain steadfast. They did so with such intrepidity that they loudly abused Mahomed in the presence of the Mahomedan priest, and cared no longer for what the King commanded; nay, the elder boy, who had been the weaker one under sufferings, seized a poniard and cut through the skin and flesh of his right arm a cross about a palm's length to triumph with these scars to the spite of the Mahomedans. As they behaved now openly as Christians and cared for nothing, the King, without molesting them further, left them alone.

Iskandar, the father of Mirza Zul-Qarnain, died in 1613 being at the time of his death in possession of a *jagir* and the farm of the government salt monopoly at Sambhar Lake, in Rajputana, worth annually from five to six lakhs of rupees.

He was succeeded in his office by his son, Mirza Zul-Qarnain, then 18 years old, who proved to be an able and a skilful administrator. In 1620, Jehangeer praised his administration and made him *faujdar* of Bahraich in Oude When Shah Jehan who had been Zul-Qarnain's playmate in the palace became intolerant of non-Mahomedans, he recalled Zul-Qarnain from Bahraich and in 1633 mulcted him of so much money (estimated at 8 lakhs of rupees) that he was practically ruined. About 1640 he was again favoured. In 1645 he served in Bengal with Sultan Shuja, one of Shah Jahan's sons, leaving his "jagir" of Sambhar to be administered by an uncle, called Jani Beg, on a salary of Rs. 50,000 per annum. In 1649 he was back on his "jagir", in 1651 he was in Kashmere and in 1652 at Lahore, on both occasions with the Emperor Shah Jahan.

The heroism of these brave lads had conquered Jahangeer. He acknowledged it soon after. The King, seeing one day the two children, whom he had caused to be circumcised, called them to him and asked whether they wished to be Mahomedans or wanted to remain in the religion of their father. The children answered they would live and die in the faith of Jesus Christ, which they had sucked in with their mother's milk. Hearing this, the King turned to some of his favourites and remarked, 'It is a shame not to remain in one's faith," and to the children he added, "Remain free in your religion."

Although the two brothers, Zul-Qarnain and Iskanderus were forcibly circumcized in 1606 by Jehangeer's orders, when the elder was fourteen and the younger eleven, they always resisted all efforts to convert them to Islam.

The Fathers always spoke well of Zul-Qarnain's religious fervour and charitable principles. In an Annual Letter it is stated: "At all the most solemn Feasts of the year, Mirza sends to the Fathers a large sum of money to be distributed in alms among the poor Christians. His kindness towards those who came from paganism is beyond words. He helps and assists them in all their needs, that they may be confirmed in the Holy Faith. He does the same for orphan girls, who otherwise would be in danger. He presents them with dowries, and marries them according to their rank, thus placing their virtue beyond the reach of temptation. In a word, Prince Mirza is among these Mogores, another Apostle, a second St. Paul, who becomes "omnibus omnia, ut omnes Christo lucrifaciat" (all things to all men, that he may save all). Kind to all, the pillar of Christianity, the only refuge of all the afflicted, he not only procures to all the bodily assistance they want, but ministers with even greater successes to their souls. An old woman had for more than sixty years remained stubborn in her idolatry. She followed the superstitious sect of what they call here "jogin." Hearing Prince Mirza's preaching and his pious exhortations, she resolved to become a Christian. And so, after a year's trial, in order to confirm her in the Faith, she was solemnly baptized, to the great satisfaction of all, and with the hope of converting others. Another, a lady of rank, wished to become a Christian, chiefly, she said, because the religion of that Father of ours whom she saw daily assisting people in dying well and burying the poor, could not be false. Such then is the power, even on the heart of barbarians, of the example of Christian piety and mercy."

Michel Angelo Lualdi summarizes the Annual Letter of Goa for 1619, when he says: "The Faith was propagated most in a certain province of Mogor, where Mirza Zul-Karnain a native of Armenia and a Christian from his birth ruled since 1619 with the title of Governor. Greatly in favour with the King, and therefore very powerful, he promoted largely our religion. He built a church in his province, where the faithful would assemble and acquit themselves of the observances of their religion. The number of the poor having greatly increased, he took some two hundred of them into his palace and supported them with great generosity. This example of his faith and charity drew many away from the impious persuasion of Mahomed, and the unhappy thraldom of idolatry; hence, he obtained the name of Father of the Christians of Mogor. Extending still further the bounds of his great charity, and in order to keep up the care of our Redeemer's Sepulchre in Jerusalem, he sent thither from the remote banks of the Ganges rich presents and a goodly sum of money for the maintenance of the religious entrusted with the custody of the Holy Places. He wished to have a Sodality established under the patronage of the Mother of God, and he was the first to have himself enrolled and to profess his allegiance to the great Queen. When the exercise of the Friday scourging was introduced, he distributed himself the chords to the congregation, and to induce them to chastise the unruly senses for their rebellion against reason he would forestall them in taking the discipline. Every day he assisted with great reverence at the Sacrifice of the Mass, beseeching the Lord of all things to keep and augment his Christian flock. So lively and unfaltering was his faith that, when human means failed to avert from his consort the dangers of parturition, he had recourse to help divine. Full of trust in a crucifix containing sacred relics which he wore round his neck, he took it off placed it round the neck of the lady, and presently she was happily delivered of a lovely boy. The pious Armenian considered himself beholden to God for this heavenly favour, and in token of his gratitude to the Eternal Monarch he restored all his prisoners to liberty. But, lest clemency should get the better of justice he paid their creditors from his own purse, leaving criminal cases to be judged in another Court."

Besides his many other benefactions, Mirza Zul-Qarnain gave a handsome sum of money by which the Jesuits bought landed property near Salsette, Bombay. With his help the Jesuits founded the College at Agra. The Superior of the Mission was the Rector of the College as well. Similarly a Mission was formed in Tibet, with funds from the Mirza, but it was destroyed in 1640.

Then followed a period of persecution. Fr. Francis Corsi, writing to the General of the Order, from Agra, on the 5th October, 1633, states that in September 1632, the Mirza's step-mother and his two half-brothers had been seized their property taken and the two half-brothers had of their own accord become Mahomedans, hoping thus to save their lives. Then the Mirza was recalled from Bengal and Shah Jahan wished to make a Mahomedan of him too, or else seize his treasures. He began, however, by molesting the Fathers. On the day of the Epiphany 1633, their house was invaded by armed soldiery. and the three bells, one of them a present from Jahangeer, were removed from the steeple. Even one of their great friends, a former pupil of theirs, turned against the Fathers. Fr. Francis Corsi going to his house on February 18 was severely ill-treated. On February 23, the Fathers were suddenly ordered to leave their house and were kept four days in prison. On being allowed to go home they found everything in such disorder that it took them eight days to fit it up again. On March 6, they said Mass again; but the judge came that day, sat down, called the Mirza and began tormenting several persons to know where his treasures were. Fr. de Castro received, on three occasions, fifty lashes. After the fourth or fifth blow he fell senseless to the ground. That night the Mirza was taken to the palace and the four Fathers were then next day conducted to prison. On the 13th March they were released together with the Mirza when the latter promised that he would pay the sum they wanted, 400,000 "scudi" (8 lakhs of rupees) Afterwards they wanted more and both the Mirza and the Fathers were left alone for the time being. The Mirza subsequently paid 3 lakhs of "scudi," but he had still to pay one lakh more. From the position of a rich man he was reduced to poverty though the Fathers hoped that the King would sooner or later reinstate him.

In spite of it all Zulkarnain to the day of his death enjoyed a unique position which many envied.

In 1654, Mirza Zul-Qarnain gave up his *jagir* and retired to Delhi on a pension of rupees one hundred per diem and there it is presumed he died in 1656. His wife Helena died in 1638 and was buried in a fine garden he had at Lahore. She left three sons and a daughter Clara who married well. The sons had all the title of Mirza and were named respectively Observam (John Baptist), Eres, Irij, Irich (Gasper) and Daniel (Michael). They all predeceased their father, except Daniel. A great grand-daughter of Mirza Zul-Qarnain, was Bibi Anna Dessa who died at Delhi on the 12th March, 1736, and was buried at Agra where her grave can be seen to this day. We have made a careful search at Agra, Delhi and Lahore for the graves of Mirza Zul-Qarnain and the members of his family, but have found no traces of them.

We have not yet been able to discover the exact date of Mirza Zul-Qarnain's death, but we fancy it was about 1656 when he would have been about 64 years old. If he died at Sambhar, in Rajputana, it is likely that he was buried there. We should expect that there was something like a family graveyard at Sambhar, since the Iskandar family resided there so long. At any rate there must have been a Christian Cemetery at Sambhar and a number of Armenian, Syrian or Portuguese inscriptions might still be discovered there if a search were made by the Archaeological Department. It is more likely, however, that Mirza Zul-Qarnain did not die at Sambhar. The last years of his life appear to have been spent at Delhi where Shah Jehan held his court. It is possible that he was buried at Lahore in the grave erected to his wife Helena.

Between 1670 and 1678 we hear also of one Nurulla, "a relative of our Brother Mirza Zulcarnen, the founder of the College at Agra", who while at Delhi, took into his house a sick Hindoo woman, the slave of a Rajput, and was instrumental in having her baptized before she died.

CHAPTER II

THOMAS KHOJAMALL'S ACCOUNT OF MIRZA ZUL-QARNAIN.

Despite the fact that Armenians lived and died in fairly large numbers at Agra and other large cities in India during the halcyon days of Mogul supremacy in the 16th and 17th centuries, yet they left no written records of their activities, traditions and social condition. As a mercantile community they were deeply engrossed in commercial pursuits and had evidently no time for recording events, communal or general, possessing social or historical value.

A business man, with very rare exceptions, cannot be a historian. A historian, worthy of the name, must be a scholar. The Armenians of that period were not men of letters. They were shrewd business men and had not the tastes or the aptitudes of a historian. They were simply concerned with trade, current events and local politics. Their only ambition in life was to amass wealth being born with a commercial genius like the Jews and the Marwaris.

And to unearth their history and bring it to light, the historian of 20th century has had the uncanny task of opening their forgotten graves, collecting the dry bones and breathing life into them make them speak after a silence of 300 long years.

With one solitary exception, and that too of a very poor type, the Armenians in India have had no historian in the past. Thomas Khojamall, a merchant and the only Armenian with some pretensions to historical knowledge wrote a short history of Bengal, from the commencement of the 18th century to the conquest of Bengal by the British after the epoch-making battle of Plassey in 1757.

As a contemporary, Khojamall, be it noted, records with true national pride, the achievements of Gorgin Khan, the Armenian Minister and Commander-in-chief of

Nawab Mir Kassim, the last independent Nawab-Nazim of Bengal, Behar and Orissa from 1760-1763.

Khojamall wrote his history, in Armenian, at Allahabad, in 1768, in the reign of Shah Alam, from Persian sources, according to the Preface. The manuscript which was badly worm-eaten, was found at Agra in 1822 in the possession of one Satoor Arrathoon of that place. It was copied afresh by one Gabriel Andreasian at the instance of the Armenian bishop Pogose who was proceeding to Gwalior at the request of Colonel Jacob, the Armenian Brigadier-General of Scindia's army. The good bishop brought down the copy with him to Calcutta and it remained here in manuscript until 1849 when it was edited and published by the well-known Armenian poet and journalist, *the late Mesrovb David Thaliadian*.

As an Appendix to his history, alluded to above, Khojamall gives an account of Mirza Zul-Qarnain, founded, no doubt, on traditions that may have been current among the Armenians of Agra or Calcutta during the second-half of the 18th century.

In the light of recent discoveries amongst Jesuit and other irrefutable records, Khojamall's* account of Mirza Zul-Qarnain, is full of inaccuracies, being exaggerated and out of focus historically, yet it throws a deal of sidelight on the career of the Armenian Grandee of the Mogul Court, as can be seen, from the translation of the narrative which we give below, for what it is worth, with our remarks.

THE ADOPTION BY KING AKBAR OF THE SON OF HAKOBJAN† OF JULFA WHOSE NAME WAS ZUL-QURNELL.

"Akbar Shah the Great, Emperor of India, son of Nasiruddin Humayon, ascended the throne in the year of our

---

* Thomas Khojamall, the merchant-historian, died at Delhi in 1780 and his body was brought down and buried in the old Armenian Cemetery at Agra, where his grave, with a tombstone, bearing an inscription in Armenian, erected by his faithful Indian servant Chichroo, can be seen to this day.

† Hakob is the Armenian name for Jacob, *jan* being a Persian affix, meaning life, a pet.

Lord 1554. In his days there came from Julfa,* a Mr. Jacob,† with his wife, and he resided at Kashmir engaged in trade. There a son was born to them; but, unfortunately, not finding a priest at that place to baptize the child, they named him, according to their own wishes, Zul-qurnell.

"The mighty Emperor about this time goes to Kashmir to visit his subjects, and, whilst going about incognito, he comes across the child of Mr. Jacob and is much pleased with his beauty. He orders some of his chiefs to stay there and ascertain whose child he was and to take him with the parents to him. The chiefs, having found out, took the parents with him to the Emperor. When Akbar heard that he was of the Armenian nation, he became very glad. He liked the child very much, and, turning to the father, said: 'Oh, Mr. *moosafir* [traveller] and respected merchant, will you give me your son or not, so that I may adopt him, for I have no son?' Mr. Jacob having bowed replied: 'My lord King, live for ever. Although I and mine are your servants, yet I shall not give him willingly, for I am an Armenian by nationality and a Christian, and you are a Turk and a Mohammedan; if I were to give you my child and you made him a Mohammedan, I shall be disgraced amongst my own people and they will upbraid me by saying that either for money or through force I gave my son to the King.' The King was greatly pleased at this pious and fearless reply, and he swore that he would never interfere with the religion of either the child or the parents.

---

* Julfa was an Armenian city of great commercial importance on the bank of the river Aras (the Araxes of the ancients) in Armenia. It was destroyed in 1605 by the order of Shah Abbas the Great of Persia who forcibly removed the entire population of 12,000 families to Isfahan, his capital, where they built a beautiful city, which they styled New Zulfa, in everlasting memory of the one abandoned in Armenia.

† There is, in the possession of an Armenian curio-collector at Constantinople, a unique antique jar, of beautiful workmanship, made of brass, bearing an inscription in Armenian of which the following is a translation :—

> "Made in the city of Lahore in the year 1616 for the use of Khojah Minas, the son of Khojah Yaqoob [Jacob]."

Could he have been a son of the Armenian merchant Jacob whom Akbar met at Kashmir?

'Remain firm in your religion,' he said, 'I shall be exceedingly glad; but, as I have no child, I shall adopt this child.'

"Then he ordered that, dressed in regal robes, they should be taken to his palace and that the child be kept in every kind of comfort as his son as long as he remained in Kashmir. Then, when he returned to Akbarabad [Agra], he took with him this very adopted Zul-qurnell with his parents and there gave Mr. Jacob for his residence a place near the Selahkhana (or Armoury) of the King. He then ordered that they should build a Church, have an Armenian priest brought out and follow their ancestral faith. Hearing this, there came to Akbarabad from Julfa an Archimandrite, a priest and many Armenian families, who were very well received by the King, who granted them 5000 bigahs of land at Akbarabad for building houses, gardens, farms and other important places. But Zul-qurnell, the adopted son of the King was always in the Palace, where he was a great favourite with the King and the Queens, and you may say he was being taken from the arms of one to another.

"God knows how to make his beloved respected before foreign nations, because the King was kind enough to allow an Armenian child to remain pure in his religion and for his sake show respect to his nation; therefore God too was pleased to reward him according to his wishes; hence, in the year 1563, on the 17th of Rabi-ul-avval, He gave the King a male child, from his favourite Queen, and he was called Mir Salim Salathin, that is to say, heir-apparent. The mighty Emperor too was not unaware of this divine favour, for it is said that he would always say, 'God looked at me and gave me this my second child through the coming of the Armenians and my favourite son Zul-qurnell." And thus the two children growing up together were very fond of each other, and the King seeing their innocent love was exceedingly pleased.

"When Zul-qurnell came of age, Akbar gave him landed properties, namely Jagirs, the town of Hooghly in Bengal, the province or pergannah of Samar [Sāmbhar] in the district of Akbarabad, whence comes good salt, and the country of Punjab in Lahore. Then Zul-qurnell commenced building himself grand palaces with shops all round, and he had jewellers, that is Johurris, whom he occupied, for they say he himself was very fond of buying and selling precious stones. It seems he was by nature a very humble and meek person, but the King Akbar liked him so much that without his order nobody could do anything, either rich or poor. It is said that whoever wished to go to him was allowed freely and boldly, and he never allowed the request of those who went to him to remain ungranted. He would neither eat nor drink, not that he wished to show himself off with pride, but that he had made a habit of it. But they say he had the Mansab [rank] of seven thousand and paid much attention to it.

"In the year of our Lord 1605, King Akbar died and Mirza Salim Salathin succeeded him and was called Nur-ud-din Jehangeer. When the whole world were going to congratulate the King on his accession, Zul-qurnell trembling through fear would not come out of the house and would not go to offer his felicitations to the King. Several times he sent word to him and invited him to come, but his false fear compelled him to run away by himself and go to his jagir at Hooghly. This escape made the King very, very sorry, so he ordered that all the Armenians be watched. Afterwards when he learnt that the escape was more through fear than anything else, he wrote on oath, 'Fear not, I and you are brothers. Do you not know my love from my youth? Come to me, and, whatever may be your requests, I shall grant you the same. Is it likely that I should be ungrateful towards my father's behest and think of harming you? If you do not come willingly, I shall have you brought in bonds.' In like manner, our own people [the Armenians] beseechingly wrote to him to come.

"When he came and presented himself, the King loved him much and said, 'Why do you now keep aloof, brother? Am I going to take back from you the properties presented to you by my father, or is there anything wanting which I will not make good? Ask, even half of my kingdom, and I shall grant it to you.' Our hermit king-to-be fell on his face to the ground and said, 'My Lord, I verily know your love and favour, but I beg of you to allow me to stay at home like a poor man and pray for you.' The King said, 'Since that is your wish, I am glad; do as you like, but come and see me sometimes.'

"Henceforward, having retired from all important affairs, he gave himself up to singing, which in the Indian language is called *Rāg*, and he made so much progress that he was not inferior to the very best singers of olden times. His name is mentioned in the Indian work called *Rāgmālā*.* Following such trivial pursuits, he neglected himself, his children (of whom, they say, some are still to be found at Chandernagore in Bengal), as also his properties and his own nation."

There are many points in Khojamall's account of Mirza Zul-Qarnain which are entirely wrong and cannot stand the acid test of stern historical facts. In the first place, Akbar ascended the throne in 1556 and not in 1554. Mirza Zul-Qarnain's father's name was Iskandar and not Jacob, according to the Tuzuki-i-Jehangeeri. He came from Aleppo and not from Julfa. Akbar did not meet him in Cashmere, as Iskandar came to Akbar's Court at Agra. Jehangeer was born in 1568 and not in 1563. The grant by Akbar of 5000 bigas of land to the Armenians at Agra is highly incredible. Mirza Zul-Qarnain's *mansab* of 7000 is exaggerated, for according to the *Ain-i-Akbari, mansabs* above 5000 were reserved for His Majesty's "august sons", unless it can be averred that Mirza Zul-Qarnain was classed with the royal princes being a great favourite of Akbar. His disappearance from Court on the accession of Jehangeer in 1605 is a palpable anachronism, as he was a lad of 13 years at that time and not in a position to retire from active service. As we have seen, Mirza Zul-Qarnain served the Mogul government faithfully and loyally till the time of his death which occurred in 1656, or 50 years after Jehangeer's accession. When Iskandar, his father came from Sambhar to Agra at the end of 1605, or beginning of 1606, to congratulate Jehangeer on his accession, the king tried to tamper with his religion, and Iskandar, fearing

---

* We have tried, without success, to find the *Ragmala* containing some of Mirza Zul-Qarnain's Hindi or Hindustani compositions and songs. Will students of Indian music, conversant with the history of Hindi songs of the Mogul period, throw light on the subject?

probably that he would do the same with his two children then at the Court, took them away with him to Sambhar.

When at Lahore in 1606, Jehangeer remarking the absence of the boys, had a search made for them. They were brought back and shortly after, forcibly circumcised, as stated in the preceding chapter. The father of the boys on hearing of this was inconsolable and for three days he wept and refused all food. He sent one of his servants to Lahore for information and the Jesuit Fathers wrote back to say it was not safe for him to go there himself. According to Father Botelho, Mirza Zul-Qarnain disappeared from the Court after his forcible circumcision but after a diligent search he was found and brought back.

As we have said, Khojamall wrote his account of Mirza Zul-Qarnain from traditions and it was probably this event which he relates as the reason for the sudden disappearance of the Armenian lad from the Court on the accession of Jehangeer in 1605.

It is not likely that the descendants of Mirza Zul-Qarnain could be living at Chandernagore, in Bengal, as stated by Khojamall, for the Armenian grandee lived most of his life at Agra and Delhi, where the Great Moguls resided and held their Court.

A great granddaughter of Mirza Zul-Qarnain lived and died at Delhi as stated before.

And lastly, the active, the energetic and the highly intelligent and talented grandee who was given successively the *Faujdarship* of the provinces of Sambhar, Bahraich, Lahore and Bengal by the mighty Mogul Emperors could not have been the visionary, the recluse and the singer, as depicted by Khojamall, who as an unreliable historian and a pessimist has unknowingly done a great injustice to the memory of his great and noble countryman, Mirza Zul-Qarnain, who was loved by Jehangeer for his able administration, respected and rewarded by Shah Jehan for his poetical talents and lauded by the good Jesuit Fathers as "the pillar of Christianity in India."

CHAPTER III.

THE JESUITS AND MIRZA ZUL-QARNAIN

In the preceding chapters, we have given a summarised account of the life and career of Mirza Zul-Qarnain, culled from an illuminating and a highly interesting article published by the late Father H. Hosten, S.J. in the Memoirs of the Asiatic Society of Bengal in 1916. The erudite scholar had for years collected, with great assiduity, all the information available on the subject from Jesuit and other sources, which but for his indefatigable efforts and consuming zeal, would never have seen the light of day.

As the historian of the Armenians in India, and a humble admirer of the distinguished Armenian who has found a niche in the history of the Mogul Empire, I am deeply indebted to the learned Jesuit for saving from oblivion and placing on record the valuable fruits of his researches concerning the achievements of his hero, the patron of the early Jesuits at the Mogul Court and the benevolent Founder of the "Agra College."

And whereas the good Jesuit Fathers have left interesting accounts of the golden deeds of their Armenian friend, the Armenian bishops and priests who came to Agra to minister to the spiritual needs of their flock, have left no records at all to remind the future generation of the existence of a flourishing Armenian colony at Agra during the glorious reign of the great Moguls—Akbar, Jehangeer and Shah Jehan.

It may be mentioned, *en passant*, that the following seven Armenian priests died at Agra between the years 1614 and 1675, and were buried in the old Armenian Cemetery of that historic city, where many of their countrymen lie buried.

1614. Rev. Asatoor.
1616. Rev. Mekhithar.
1630. Rev. Sookias.
1656. Rev. Zacharia.

1668. Rev. Johanness.
1671. Rev. Bagdassar.
1675. Rev. Arrathoon.

The first four of these priests were, successively, contemporaries of Mirza Zul-Qarnain and must have witnessed the meteoric rise to fame of their distinguished compatriot, but they wrote nothing about him, owing probably to the religious bigotry of the time, because the grandee was a staunch friend of the Jesuit Fathers at the Mogul Court.

What an incalculable harm religious fanaticism and intolerance have done to the nation in the past !

It is gratifying however to see, that, with the spread of education and enlightenment, the Orthodox Armenians of the present day, and their name is legion, fraternise with their separated brethren, the Roman Catholic and the Protestant Armenians. A hopeful sign of the regeneration and the advancement of the ancient race with a glorious past.

We shall now proceed giving some very interesting extracts from the letters of the Jesuit Fathers, published, *in extenso*, in Father Hostens' Memoir alluded to above, as many of our readers could not possibly have had an opportunity of seeing the Memoir which was published, 20 years ago, by the world-renowned Asiatic Society of Bengal, the parent of all Asiatic societies and the patron and the torch bearer of learning, of historical and antiquarian research, of scientific investigations, and learned studies in linguistics, anthropology, ethnography epigraphy and the allied subjects for the past century and half.

Mirza Zul-Qarnain's father, Iskandar, is mentioned clearly for the first time in a letter of Fr. Jerome Xavier to the General of the Society (Lahore, August ?, 1598).

"Quite recently," he wrote, "a violent storm fraught with danger burst over us, and little more was needed for the pestilential and baneful sect lately started by the King [Akbar] to gather fresh strength and overwhelm us. It came about thus. After the death of his Christian wife, a certain Armenian, a Christian,—if a man in such dispositions can yet be called a Christian,—was bent on a sacrilegious marriage with his niece* (*ex ea neptem volebat sacrilegiis nuptiis sibi copulari*). I refused to agree to these incestuous nuptials; whereupon, he tried by soliciting the interference or an order of the King to make me consent to, or at least wink at, his union. The King had us called for, and, as we suspected the motive of this exceptional summons, we commended ourselves to God, offering Him such prayers and vows as the little time at our disposal allowed, and determined to lay down our lives rather than allow an incest and a crime. Leaving our Brother Benedict [Goes] at home, I went with Father Emmanuel Pigneiro [Pinheiro] to the Court. Benedict rarely set foot in the palace, but that night he longed to accompany us, in the hope of sharing the sufferings and crown which our vindication of the truth was likely to gain for us. Accordingly, he remained a long time hanging about the palace, expecting to be informed of our sufferings and torments, and prepared to associate himself in our glorious triumph; but, when he saw that matters took a different turn, he called the Christian children and catechumens together, and in a stirring exhortation encouraged them bravely to die for their faith; then, disciplining

---

Note :—The footnotes in this Chapter are by Father H. Hosten, S.J. Those by the author bear the initials M.J.S.

* Iskandar married his deceased wife's sister and not his niece, as wrongly stated by Fr. Jerome Xavier. No Armenian, whether Orthodox, Roman Catholic or Protestant, will marry his niece, as it is considered an incest and a sin to enter into such a matrimonial alliance. If Iskandar married his deceased wife's sister, it was for the sake of his two motherless children who, he knew, would be looked after, with a motherly care and affection, by their aunt, which could not be expected from a strange step-mother. A similar case happened in Bombay some 36 years ago, when an American gentleman of good social position, Alexander Agabeg by name—another Iskandar—wished to marry his deceased wife's sister. The Armenian priest of Bombay could not possibly celebrate the marriage, it being against the rites of the Armenian holy Apostolic Church, whereupon the gentleman who wished to marry his deceased wife's sister for the sake of his only child then two years' old, applied to His Holiness the Catholicos of all Armenians at Etchmiadzine, in Armenia, and the supreme head of the church was graciously pleased to sanction the marriage by granting special dispensation. The widower married his deceased wife's sister in the Armenian church and it proved a very happy marriage. The writer of these times knew them well, being related to the wife.—M. J. S.

himself, he besought Our Lord in a long and fervent prayer to give us strength and courage to resist the impious machinations of our enemies, because the King insistently urged us to yield to the Armenian's criminal and incestuous designs. After expostulating with us, the King asked us what harm there would be for the Armenian in marrying two sisters and following his [the King's] sect, which he had embraced, that so he might obtain as a Moor what he was as a Christian forbidden to do. My answer was that by doing so he relinquished the path leading to Heaven to tread the road which would bring him to hell; wherefore, the Armenian and whosoever embraced such a Law was devoting himself to certain destruction. My bold and intrepid answer was unpalatable to the King. Before the whole of his Court it condemned his new fangled teaching. Still, he tried to dissemble his annoyance and displeasure, and composed his countenance to conceal the pain and chagrin he felt. Great as was the surprise which my liberty of speech caused among the bystanders, the prestige which it conciliated to the Gospel was greater still, when they saw us willing and eager to shed our blood in its assertion and vindication, an example of constancy little familiar to the Moors, who shrink from the slightest discomfort which the profession and defence of their law may entail. When the Prince [Salim, Jahangeer] heard of these proceedings, he was indignant at the Armenian's denial of Christ, and showed by unmistakable signs how he wished to visit upon him the punishment which his dereliction of his faith richly deserved."

In another letter of Fr. Jerome Xavier, dated Agra, September 6th, 1604, we are told that Akbar liberated at the request of the Fathers fifty shipwrecked Portuguese captives. They started from Agra southwards, at the beginning of December (1603), and a certain Armenian, called Iskandar, through whose villages they passed, supplied them with a few rupees each, which enabled them to reach Goa, travelling by way of Ahmadābād and Cambay.

We learn from Father Corsi that Sikandar, Mirza Zul-Qarnain's father, died in 1613, and we may suppose from the same source that the eldest son, Zul-Qarnain, then 20 years old, was appointed to the office of collector of the salt revenues at Sambhar. Anyhow, Zul-Qarnain appears to have been in charge there in 1616, when Tom Coryate went from Ajmer to visit the place. "After I had been with the King," he says, "I went to a certain noble and generous Christian of the Armenian race, two days' journey from the Moghul's court, to the end to observe certain remarkable matters in the same place. To him by means of my Persian tongue I was so welcome that he entertained me with very civil and courteous compliments and at my departure gave me very bountifully 20 pieces of such kind of money as the King had done before." A two days' journey would have brought the English traveller to the Sāmbhar Lake, and the salt-pans would have proved a sufficiently attractive sight.

Coryate goes on to relate the following story about one Sikandar, an Armenian who must have been Zul-Qarnain's father :—

[P. 492.] "The King likes not those that change their Religion, hee himselfe being of none but of his owne making, and therefore suffers all Religions in his Kingdome. Which by this notable example I can make manifest : The King had a Servant that was an Armenian, by name Scander ; to whom upon occasion of speech of Religion, the King asked if hee thought either hee or the Padres had converted one Moore to be a true Christian, and that was so for conscience sake, and not for money : who answered with great confidence, That hee had one which was a perfect Christian, and for no worldly respect would bee other, whom the King caused presently to be sent for : and bidding his Master depart, demanded why hee was become a Christian, who rendered certaine feeble, implicite, Jesuiticall Reasons, and avowed that hee would never be other : whereupon the King practised by faire speeches and large promises, to withdraw him to the folly of Mahomet, offering him Pensions, meanes, and command of Horse, telling him hee had now but foure Rupias a Moneth Wages, which was a poore Reward for quitting his præpuced faith : but if hee would recant, hee would heape upon him many Dignities : the Fellow answering, it was not for so small Wages hee became Christian, for hee had limbes, and could earne so much of any Mahometan, but that hee was a Christian in his heart, and would not alter it. This way not taking effect, the King turned to threatnings, and menacings of Tortures and Whippings; but the Proselyte manfully resolving to suffer anything, answered, hee was readie to endure the Kings pleasure. Upon this resolution, when all men expected present and severe castigation, the King changed his tune, highly commending his constancie and honestie, bidding him goe and returne to his Master, and to serve him faithfully and truely, giving him a Rupia a day Pension for his Integritie. About two Monethes after the King having been a hunting of wild Hogges, a beast odious to all Moores, and accustomed to distribute that sort of Venision among Christians and Razbootes, sent for this Armenian, Master of this converted catechumen or Mahometan, to come and fetch part of his Quarrie. The Armenian not beeing at home, this his principall Servant came to know the Kings pleasure, who commanded him to take up a Hogge for his Master, which no Moore will touch; which hee did, and being gone out of the Court-gate, was so hooted at by the Mahometans, that hee threw downe his Present in a Ditch, and went home, concealing from his Master what had passed. About foure dayes after the Armenian coming to his watch, the King demanded of him whether the Hogge he sent him were good meat or no; who replyed, hee neyther heard of, nor see any Hogge: whereat the King remembering to whom this Hogge was delivered, caused the fellow to be sent for, and examining the matter, had it confessed how he threw away the Hogge, and never carryed it home: the King pressing to know the reason, the poore fellow answered how he was mocked for touching it, and it being a thing odious to the Moores for shame he threw it away: at which he replyed, By your law there is no difference of meats, and are your ashamed of your lawes? or to flatter the Mahumetans, doe you in outward things forsake it? Now I see thou art neither good Christian, nor good Mahumtan, but a dissembling knave with both. While I found thee sincere, I gave thee a pension, which now I take from thee, and for thy dissimulation doe command thee to have a hundred stripes, which were presently given him in stead of his money, and bade all men by his example take heed, that seeing hee gave libertie to all Religions, that which they choose and professe, they may sticke unto."

This story appears to be the same as that related by Father Jerome Xavier, S.J., in a letter from Agra, September 6, 1604 : "To show favour to some Portuguese who had arrived, the Prince [Salim, later King Jahangir] asked them if they would like some pork to eat, and they said they would. The Prince ordered a pig to be fetched, and, when it was brought, he gave it to a young Christian and bade him take it to his master, but the young man was ashamed and let the pig escape. At supper, the Prince, remembering the pig, asked the young man's master if he had received it, to which he answered: 'No, my Lord, and I have neither seen nor heard anything of it.' The Prince thereupon sent for the young man and rated him soundly as a disgrace to his religion, dismissed him from his service, took away what he gave him for his daily maintenance, and ordered that two or three months' arrear of pay owing to him should be forfeited."

The Annual Letters of Goa for 1619 mention the Mirzā as the Governor of a province over which Jahāngir has appointed him. He had in his service more than 200 Christians, and two of the Fathers resided at his court. The name of the province is not given in the Annual Letters of 1619 and 1620, but we find Sāmbhar mentioned in Letters of 1621 and 1624. We read in the Annual Letter for 1619 :—

Mission of Mogor.—[P. 131] "Of the four Fathers employed on that Mission, two reside at Agra, the ancient Capital of the King, and two accompany him wherever he goes, because he wants it so. . . . . . .

[132] "Our harvest of new Christians was largest in a certain Province over which the King has appointed as Governor an Armenian Christian, a man of singular virtue, whom all the Christians worship as their Father. His name is [133] Mirzè Zulcarnen Mirza Zul Qarnain. He has taken at his Court some two hundred poor people, whom he maintains without regard to expense. His largesses—a bait wherewith he conceals his hook—attract the Gentoos and Maomettans so strongly that he fishes up many into the Church of Jesus Christ, who then abjure their vile Maomet. Having been installed Governor of that Province, he secured at once the services of one of our Fathers, and when he had taken

possession of his Province, he called still another. Both have reaped plentiful fruits ; so necessary is it for the propagation of the Gospel that it should first pass through the ears of the body. Hence many Gentoos and Maomettans have been regenerated through baptism, and these Neophytes are drawn by the Governor's good example to assist with great devotion at Mass and the divine offices, and they show great fervour in frequenting the Sacraments. He asked the Fathers to establish a Sodality of the Holy Mother of God, and was the first to give his name. Like a bright glowing torch, he leads the way in the observance of the rules, hears Mass daily, takes the discipline on Fridays, and distributes himself the disciplines to the brethren. The women have grown jealous of the piety of the men. To our astonishment they lock themselves up on a certain day of the week in a certain apartment, where after the example of the Governess and her court-ladies, they go through the same practices.

"Mrizè did not allow the fire of his charity to remain pent up within the confines of his Province ; it blazed forth beyond those limits and reached far-off Palestine. Besides the alms which he assigns every month to the Fathers for their upkeep, to needy Neophytes, widows and orphans (all of whom would certainly have been in extreme want [134] now that the King has withdrawn the allowance which he used to grant to Fathers Jerome Xavier and Manoel Pinheiro [Pinheiro], his great friends), he sent to Jerusalem valuable presents and a big alms for the maintenance of the Religious in charge of the Holy Places.* Moreover, on hearing of the above-mentioned hurricane, and how the churches had been badly damaged all over the North, he sent six thousand rupees, a kind of silver money, for repairing the Church of the Blessed Virgin.

"Our Lord does not allow Himself to be outdone by the Mrizè's great liberality. The following will clearly show

* He sent to the Armenian Fathers of Jerusalem Rs. 6,000 ; to the Franciscans at Jerusalem. Rs. 1,000 ; to the Franciscans of Aleppo, Rs. 500; to the Franciscans of Bethlehem, Rs. 500. I think I have read in one of the MS. letters that he sent valuable lamps to be put up in the Church of the Holy Sepulchre at Jerusalem

how He pours by torrents into his soul virtue upon virtue. He had a son, the heir to all his riches, temporal and spiritual, a boy richly gifted in body and soul, the Court's delight. He fell dangerously ill, and only those who know how much he and father were loved by all, can say how deeply all were concerned. All felt aggrieved ; the mother was inconsolable, while the father's heart was rent asunder, on the hand by his love for so sweet a boy, one so well deserving of his love, on the other by his supernatural desire to please God, desire not a whit inferior to his natural affection for his child. Understanding that the disease was making progress, he made to God —like another Abraham—a heartfelt sacrifice, and bathed in tears burst forth in the following prayer : 'Lord, Thou gavest me this son ; to Thee I return him, to Thee I offer him and consecrate him. Receive him, I beseech Thee, clothed in the white garment of innocence with which he was vested in baptism. I know well how much more happy he will be in Heaven than in the Mogor's Royal palace.' And to show that he spoke from the heart, he forbade severely all his people to call in [135] the aid of sorcerers, and let the child be contaminated by their pagan superstitions : anyone acting to the contrary must lose his head in the attempt. God accepted the Mrizè's prayer. The child died, and the father gave thanks to God from his inmost heart, because He had been pleased to accept the dearest pledge of love which he could offer after himself. Nor did he show less joy when he heard that the chief Maomettan's little son, who lay mortally ill, had with his father's consent received baptism from our Father. Mrizè ordered to bury the child in the church, and, to surround the ceremony with all possible pomp, he made it a point to be present with all the Christians then in that town. This gave the followers of the false Prophet so much to talk about and wonder at, that they formed a much higher opinion of baptism than theretofore.

"This faithful servant of God is so greatly favoured by the Divine Majesty that all the affairs of his government are daily crowned with increased success. Plenty has chosen his house as her abode, as a treasure-house wherein she pours and empties out her cornucopia. He is the eye of the King; for him to ask is to obtain; his name is famous everywhere; in fine, he is so full of heavenly grace that it redounds marvellously on those of his household.

"His wife was in the throes of a dangerous parturition. Mrizè, taking from his neck the cross studded with relics which he used to wear, had it hung from the neck of his consort, and behold! presently she gave birth to a most pretty boy. The good Mrizè recognized in this a special favour of God, a reward for the generous oblation he had made of his other son to the Divine Majesty. To celebrate [136] so happy an event, not merely the birthday of an heir, but a great miracle obtained through the Holy Cross, he began the festivities by releasing all the prisoners and paying off their debts.

"The followers of Maomet dare not, under so powerful a protector of the Christian law, set their face against it: on the contrary, they respect it, and many are the Gentoo slaves whom they restore to liberty on condition of their becoming Christians."

Mission of Mogor.—[P. 161]—"Five of our Fathers are cultivating this vast kingdom. One of them is always following the King and his army; another resides at Agra, the capital, with a great part of the Christians. The other three are near Prince Mirza Zulcarne, the father, pillar and mainstay of this Christianity. All have had ample occasion to labour for Christ, one excepted, who for reason of illness was sent back to [Portuguese] India. . . . .

'The Christians who live under Prince Mirza make daily [165] marvellous progress in holiness and virtue. The Sodality of the Blessed Virgin, instituted last year at his request, goes on better and better. The members of it are already every month approaching the Sacraments of Confession and Holy Communion, whereas formerly they did so only once a year. Their example provokes among the rest of the Christians a greater frequentations of the Holy Sacraments. Foremost in all works of piety is the good Prince Mirza. Not only does he by his edifying example excite all his people to every kind of good work, but he assists them liberally and lavishly with frequent and copious alms. He does not allow that those of the Sodality should miss the Saturday and Sunday meetings. He is never absent himself from the Sodality meeting, or from the exercise of the discipline, which he takes with the rest every Friday in honour of Our Lord's Passion. He insists that the children be twice a day at the Catechism, we mean the Christian Doctrine, and to excite them to fervour in an exercise so holy and so beneficial to their souls he proposes fine pious prizes. The Lent he obtained from the Father who is with him and takes care of all those Christians that the exercise of the discipline should take place twice a week, so that during this more season they might doubly mindful of the Saviour's sufferings. It happened at that time that for necessary reasons the Father was called away by the Superior of that Mission. This departure grieved the good Prince [166] deeply, because he would now be deprived of the opportunity of frequently going to confession, as was his custom. When the Father had gone, he took the resolution of abstaining from meat during two months (the time of the Father's absence), and he observed this resolution so strictly that even the Saracens wondered, when they saw him, even at solemn banquets, regularly refusing to touch meat. Nay, happening to travel in Lent, he kept the fast most punctually, and during the many days that the journey lasted he would eat only once a day, at noon. He continued likewise his usual bodily penances and mortifications, and when Holy Week had come, he celebrated it with all the ceremonies and devotions which he would practise at home.

"No sooner was the good Prince apprised of the arrival of the two Fathers sent from Goa, than he sent fifty persons on horseback to escort them and serve them during the rest of the journey. When they had come nearer, he went himself a great part of the way to meet them with his ordinary body of cavalry and infantry, a large number, not to speak of his elephants and other things of truly regal pomp. Presently, when he came within sight of them, this Christian Prince dismounted, cast himself on the ground, and, kissing reverently the hands of the two Fathers, asked their blessing; [167] after which he conducted them to his palace with every demonstration of honour and pleasure. Too great for words was the ecstasy of this good Lord when the Fathers presented him from the Father Provincial of Goa with the patent giving him a share in the good works of the Society. At once he placed it on his head, saying with incredible joy that he valued that present more than any earthly treasure. The number of our spiritual labourers having increased, the good Prince bestowed on the Father Superior of the Mission an alms of fifteen hundred scudi, and five hundred more for the other Fathers in Mogor.* But our Fathers are not the only recipients of the liberality of this Christian Prince. He extends it to the rest of the Christians, and even to the poor Gentoos.

"A Christian, one of the chief citizens, lying near death, wished to make his will ; but he found his debts were so considerable that, if he wanted to satisfy his creditors, he must deprive his children of much which they could not miss. The poor sick man was in sore perplexity. When this most liberal Prince came to hear of it, he went to see him, consoled him and promised that he would pay off his debts, even if he survived. And so he did, thus showing how strong a hold charity and compassion can take of a Christian heart.

"At this time a great scarcity and penury of food [168] harassing the Gentoos. For the last five years the rain had failed. The sky had seemed of brass. A great number of people flocked to the city of our Mirza, and the good Prince, moved with pity, ordered a rich Gentoo to distribute daily to his people a sufficient quantity of food, with which he would regularly supply him. This man did so for many days, when Mirza began to scruple whether he could in conscience perform, through a barbarian, an enemy of Christ, this pious work of feeding the famished. He sought the advice of the Father who is with him, and was asked on that occasion why he used for so holy an object the services of a Gentoo rather than of a Christian. 'Because, Father,' was the pious Prince's answer, 'there is not a single man among the Christians rich enough to make people believe that he exercises this charity towards the poor at his own expense. If a Christian were to give such alms in this city, all would at once think that evidently I am behind it. Therefore, to avoid vain glory in this matter, I thought

---

* The *scudo*, like the *cruzado*, was then valued at Rs. 2. In 1633, Mirza Zul-Qarnain was made to pay Shāh Jahān Rs. 800,000, and this sum is converted by the Jesuits into 400,000 *scudi* or *cruzados*. Hence, the *scudo* has been reckoned too low in Sir R. C. Temple's edn. of *Travels of Peter Mundy*, II. 379.

of employing this rich Gentoo whom many will probably imagine to be the giver of these alms.

"Last June one of our priests was sent to Goa in order to negotiate with the Superiors the foundation of a College of the Society [170] at Agra, the capital of Mogor, which Prince Mirza wishes to found on a yearly revenue of fifteen hundred scudi.

"During his journey, the Father did not neglect to labour for Christ and make himself useful to the souls of the Barbarians among whom he passed. God grant for his glory, for the confusion of Maomettan obduracy, and the good of those idolaters, that affairs of the Agra College may go on improving." . . . . . .

Mission of Mogor and its Residences—[P. 336] "We continue cultivating the Christianity of this great Empire. It grows and would grow still more, if we had labourers, the want of them being greatly felt in this premier Province of the East. For just reasons, a Father has again been stationed in the Residence of Laor [Lahore]. At Sambar and at Agra they have laboured as much as these places admit of........

"Last year two sons of the Seraphic Father St. Francis came to Sambar [Sāmbhar], and this year two others came with their Commissary, a Religious of great talents, and one who has well merited of his office........*

[341] "Mirza Zulcarnen continues to give much edification, and to show much zeal for the cause of Christianity. We hope of him that he will promote much the new Christianity of this country, and that of [Portuguese] India."

* The Commissary's name alone is found—Father Francis of Madrid. In a letter dated 14th July 1624, he writes his impressions of Sāmbhar and Agra to the Provincial of Goa. "Before penetrating further into the interior," he says (*op. cit.*, p. 337), "I met at Sambhar Fr. Francis Corso [Corsi], whose Christian community is so well instructed that one could desire nothing better. The rare virtues displayed by that Father in that ministry drew from my eyes tears of joy and the charity with which he received us was equal to all his other virtues. From there I went to Agra, where I found two other Fathers........." The object of these five Franciscans in visiting Mogor does not appear; but, we understand that coming to Agra, they would not neglect to pay a visit to Mirza Zul-Qarnain at Sāmbhar and thank him for his liberalities to their Order.

Fr. Hosten writes :—"In May 1628, Father Francisco Corsi, S.J., who had been in Mogor since February 1600, wrote to the General of the Society of Jesus in Rome a statement regarding the benefactions made to the Mission of Mogor by Mirza Sikandar and Mirza Zul-Qarnain since 1613. One of the Mirza's chief titles to the everlasting gratitude of the Fathers was that he had donated in 1619 a large sum of money with which to buy landed property in the "North," *i.e.*, near Salsette, Bombay. The Missionaries and their Christian poor were thus made independent of the King, by whom chiefly they had until then been maintained. The Mirza's foundation was called the *Collegium inchoatum* of Agra. As in the case of the "College" of Hugli, the term "College" applied to the Jesuit House of Agra has led to many misunderstandings. The organisation of the Society did not then know residences not dependent on a "College"; hence, when the Order established itself in a new country, a "College" was founded, around which secondary houses were grouped. Agra under the Jesuits (1600-1773) never had a College worth speaking of. At most there was a small school for elementary education. The "Rector" of the Agra College was merely the Superior of the Mogor Mission, the Agra, "College" being the chief Jesuit House in Mogor with two or at most three other mission-stations dependent on it. About 1628, Zul-Qarnain made another foundation for a "College" in Tibet. Evidently, there was no question of a big school to be conducted in Tibet, but of a Mission in want of regular subsidies to carry on its work. The headstation would have been called a "College," and its branch-stations, "Residences." On the destruction of the Tibet Mission about 1640, the Superior of the Mogor Mission asked that its funds should be applied to the Agra College, the revenues of which had become inadequate. One of the first acts of the English authorities of Bombay was to confiscate the estates of the Agra College."

From Fr. Corsi's account written in 1628 :—

"Of the origin of the foundation of the Collegium Inchoatum in the city of Agra, made by Mirza Zul-Carne, and accepted by our Revd. Father Mutio Vitellesqi in the year 1621."

"When King Acbar [Akbar] was reigning in Mogor,

there came to this Court an honourable man, an Armenian, called Mirza Scander [Mirza Sikandar = the Lord Alexander] a native of Halepo [Aleppo], whom the King esteemed highly, as he was a young gentleman and possessed of good parts, among others a knowledge of various languages, in particular Portuguese, because he had been living some years as a merchant in the cities of India. Hence, the King not only admitted him as a cavalier (*criado de cavalo*), but married him with a damsel called Juliana, the daughter of another honourable Armenian, Koja Abdellahi (whom I also knew).* Owing to this connection, M. Escander was much more esteemed at Court. M. Scander's first-born son by the said Juliana was our Founder Mirza Zulcarnen, a name given him as a favour by King Acbar himself, this being the name of Alexander the Great, whom they call Scander Zulcarnen.† A year later, Bibi Juliana gave birth to another son, named M. Scanderus,‡ who died lately.§ The King, of his || special affection for Bibi Juliana, gave both the boys to one of the Queens, who was childless, to be adopted and educated as her own children. She did so, and brought them up in the royal palace until they were twelve years old, when, the laws of the women's quarters not allowing them to continue there any longer, they left and went to their father's house. King Acbar tried to marry M. Scander with a sister of Bibi Juliana now dead,|| but, as Fr. Jeronimo Xavier and the rest of the Fathers objected, the good King, understanding that it could not be done without a dispensation from the Holy Father, resolved to ask this favour from His Holiness through Our Father General. The Supreme Pontiff granted it him by word of mouth (*vivae vocis oraculo*),

---

* Khwāja 'Abdu-l-Havy. He died therefore after 1600.

† Sikandar Zul-Qarnain = Alexander, the two-horned. The marriage must have taken place about 1590. Zul-Qarnain was born in 1592, considering that he was 14 years old in 1606, and 20 in 1613.

‡ Mirza Iskandarus. Both the father and his two sons had names representing Alexander. The Relation of 1606 makes M. Iskandarus three years younger than his brother M. Zul-Qarnain. He was born in 1595, therefore.

§ *Pouco depois se morreo* might mean; he died shortly after. We translate as above in view of certain remarks which follow.

|| Bibi Juliana must have died before 1598, since it was in 1598 at the latest that Mirza Sikandar, senior, married Juliana's sister.

and gave orders to write that he granted this dispensation, because the request came from so high a King, one who so greatly favoured in his Kingdom Christianity and the ministers of the Holy Gospel. It was at this time, in February of the year 1600, that I arrived at this Court.

"Shortly after the two boys had left the Queen's house, King Acbar died. His son, King Jahangir, succeeded him, and, at the instigation of some Grandees of his Court, he tried to make the two boys renounce the law of Jesus Christ and embrace the law of the Moors. In fact, he ordered them to be circumcised by force, and first he had so many lashes given to each that the bodies of both were covered with blood and with the marks of the cruel stripes, as I myself saw ; for I accompanied Fr. Jeronimo Xavier, who, on hearing of the case, went at once to visit, console and encourage them. And, though the two, mere children yet, showed some weakness in this encounter (*auto*), by pronouncing under the lashes certain words of the creed of the Moorish law, still I am of opinion that we may regard them as Confessors of the law of Jesus Christ. Indeed, during this same tragic affair, after the boys had uttered the said words, they strongly resisted when they tried forcibly to circumcise them. Amid tears, M. Zulcarnen clamoured to the King : 'Sire, tell them to cut off our head, not the foreskin !' What strengthens me in this belief is what happened shortly after; for the King, regretting already what he had done, told both the boys to live in the law of Jesus Christ like their father; and so they have been doing until now, through the Lord's mercy.* M. Zulcarnen, in particular, worthily redeemed his weakness as a child. When he was come to man's estate, and had become one of the King's nobles (*fidalgo*), charged with important commissions, the King gave him many times occasion to discuss in his presence and before the whole Court about the things of our Holy Law against the highest and wisest Moors in the King's entourage. He would do it so ably that the King himself *applaudebat et approbabat quae dicebat* (would applaud and approve what he said), and

---

* This compared with the statement *pouco depois se morreo* shows that Mirza Iskandarus, Zul-Qarnain's brother, had died shortly before Father Corsi wrote, *i.e.*, before May 1628.

he showed such zeal that Fr. Jose de Castro, who was always present, wrote to me several times, and related to me orally, that he could not have done it better himself.

"In 1613, when M. Zulcarnen was twenty years old, his father M. Scander died.* He left a very large fortune, which was distributed among the four sons he left behind (two by his first wife, and two by his second), in conformity with the testament which he had drawn up through Fr. Jeronimo Xavier. In the said testament M. Scander left twenty thousand Rupees to be distributed as follows for the good of his soul :—

	Rs.
For the Armenian Fathers who are in Jerusalem	6,000
For the Fathers of St. Francis in Jerusalem†	1,000
For the Fathers of St. Francis in Halepo‡	500
For the Fathers of St. Francis at Bethlehem§	500

* We do not know where Mirza Sikandar (senior) and Bibi Juliana were buried.

† From the 13th century Catholicism was upheld in the Holy Land almost exclusively by the Franciscans. The Order has a special province, the *Custodia Terræ Sanctæ,* the head of which, till 1847 the supreme authority for Catholics in Palestine, is the Franciscan Provincial, the *Custors Terræ Sanctæ*. The Franciscans have at Jerusalem the little Convent of the Holy Sepulchre with the Chapel of the Apparition, that forms the northern part of the group of buildings at the Anastasis. This has been Franciscan property since the 13th century.

The Gregorian Armenians possess at the Holy Sepulchre the Chapel of St. Helena, of St. John, of the "Division of Garments," of St. James (behind the Anastasis), and "the Stone of the Holy Women." They have further the right of walking in procession about the Anastasis, and take their turn to celebrate their offices at it. They have other establishments in Jerusalem. Cf. ADRIAN FORTESCUE *in Cath Encycl.,* New York, VIII.

It would seem that Zu-l-Quari'n benefactions to the Armenian Fathers of Jerusalem went to the Gregorian Armenians, non-Catholics, which makes us suppose that his father Sikandar was not originally a Catholic.

‡ The Christian population of Aleppo is now 19,000 Catholics (Greeks, United or Melchites, Syrians, Armenians, Maronites, Chaldeans and Latins), 2,800 non-Catholic Christians (mostly Gregorian Armenians). Four Catholic Archbishops govern the Melchites, the Syrians, the Armenians, the Maronites. The Gregorian Armenians are administered by a Vartabet appointed by the Catholicos of Sis. Cf. S. PETRIDES in *Catholic Encycl.,* New York, *s.v.,* Aleppo.

§ Bethlehem counts to-day 5,000 Latins, 100 Catholic Melchite Greeks, 4,000 Greeks and a few Armenians. The Franciscans govern the Latin

For the Church and the Christians of Lahor	2,000
For the Church and the Christians of Agra	4,000
For his grave with a chapel	3,000
For widows and marriage dowries for orphan girls	2,000
For saying Masses at Goa	400
For arranging (*pera concertar*) a cemetery for the deceased Christians of Lahor*	600
Total ...	20,000

"M. Scander ordained further that, as to the specified property which he left to the King, four portions should be made of whatever the King might not take, but leave to his sons; three-fourths of this to be divided among his children, and one-fourth to be given to the Fathers of the Society at Agra and spent by them in pious works at their discretion. In fact, the King left to the sons of M. Scander many of the things they offered him from their late father; and, as it was very difficult to verify from reliable accounts (*averiguarse por contas certas*) how much the said one-fourth amounted to, Fr. Xavier and Mirza agreed that, so long as the matter was not ascertained more clearly, the said fourth part would be seven thousand rupees. Besides, as M. Zulcarnen was nearly sure that, after the division of the property, his three brothers would not pay their share of the alms, he took upon himself of his own accord, and with the consent of his brothers, the whole of this obligation, and gave Fr. Jeronimo Xavier a voucher to the effect that he owed twenty-seven thousand Rupees, left by his father for the rest of his soul.† And, according as Mirza kept paying, it was noted down in the said voucher, as follows:—

parish. The greater part of the Church of the Nativity is now shared by different Communions; while the choir belongs to the Greeks alone, the Grottoo of the Nativity is open to the Latins, the Greeks and the Armenians, who hold services there each in turn. Cf. S. VAILHE in *Cath. Encycl.*, New York, s.v., Bethlehem.

* Where was that cemetery? It must have contained Armenian tombs.

† *i.e.*, Rs 20,000, as shown by the total in our list above, and Rs. 7,000 agreed upon between Fr. Jerome Xavier and M. Zul-Qarnain as constituting one-fourth of what did not belong to Jehangeer.

"*Memo of payments made by M. Zulcarnen in compliance with his obligation towards his father's will.*

	Rs.
We received from M. Zulcarnen six thousand Rupees sent to the Armenian Fathers in Jerusalem	6,000
Other one thousand Rupees sent to the Fathers of St. Francis in Jerusalem	1,000
Other one thousand Rupees, of which Rs. 500 were sent to Halepo, and Rs. 500 to Bethlehem, to the Fathers of St. Francis ...	1,000
We sent to Goa for Masses	400
Mirza gave for sundry marriages	620
He gave again to Fr. Jeronimo Xavier, when he went to Goa at the King's order	490
He gave again for his father's tomb and chapel	3,000
Fr. Jeronimo Xavier also gave Mirza a paper good for one thousand Rupees to be spent at [his] discretion on pious works, by the terms of the above-said will	1,000
Fr. Antonio Machado, being Superior, also gave Mirza a paper in the said form to the value of	500
Total of the above ...	14,010

" In the year 1614, the Portuguese having seized at Surat a ship belonging to the King's subjects, they ordered us to close our churches in these parts,* and took from us the alms which the King used to give us; hence, to maintain ourselves and the poor Christians, we were obliged to melt down (*desfazer*) and sell two gold chalices and the candlesticks and other silver furniture of the church, and we were, so to say, constrained to stop giving the ordinary alms to many widows and poor

* The Jesuit Letters of the period (MSS.) and the letters of the English factors contain much information on this incident. Cf. *e.g.*, W. NOEL SAINSBURY, *Calendar of State Papers* (1513-1616), London, 1862, pp. 251, 258, 259, 260, 316, 321, 327, 331, 333, 334, 346, 349, 357.

Christians. M. Zulcarnen, on learning this, said to Fr. Jeronimo Xavier that he would keep on his establishment all the Christians who would be willing (in fact, he kept many, both foot and horse), and that he would give to all the widows and other poor Christians the same alms as they used to receive daily. To this effect, he began from the month of July of the year 1614 to give us every month two hundred rupees deducible from his debt, and we received it monthly and put it down in the aforesaid voucher for twenty seven thousand rupees. With this alms we maintained ourselves and gave charity to the poor Christians. Mirza told us that he gave us the said alms to fulfil his duty as executor of his father's will.

"On the ground of this ordinary allowance which Mirza gave us, we received the following :—

		Rs.
In the year 1614, from the month of July	...	1,200
In the year 1615, we received	...	2,400
In the year 1616, we received	...	2,400
In the year 1617, we received	...	2,400
In the year 1618, we received	...	2,400
Total of the above	...	10,800
Which with the aforesaid sum of	...	14,010
Makes	...	24,810

"At this time, being Superior of the Mission in the place of Fr. Antonio Machado, deceased at Agra, I proposed to Mirza that, though the King was giving us now again the ordinary allowance, which for the present was sufficient for our upkeep and that of the poor Christians, he should give us once for all, instead of his monthly donation of Rs. 200, a goodly alms with which to buy in India immovable property, so that, if at any time the King's alms failed us, || we might therewith maintain ourselves and our Christian poor, thus precluding the necessity of our leaving the country for want of means. This plan pleased Mirza so much that he promised at once, and shortly after gave us, twenty thousand rupees. Even then he did not cease giving us his monthly donation of Rs. 200. Fr.

Jose de Castro took this sum to Goa, whither he went chiefly to negotiate this affair, which thanks to God, was concluded. By means of our Fathers, we bought the two *aldeas* (villages) which we have in the North. They cost twenty-seven thousand rupees. So, we had a debt of seven thousand rupees ; but, we paid off at once four thousand rupees which Mirza gave us, and the rest was repaid. But, as at that time Fr. Andre Boves was Superior and had this matter in hand, I do not well remember how the sum was paid.* However, I always considered it certain that it was paid, either from the extraordinary alms Mirza gave us, or from the revenues which the *aldeas* were already yielding for us. When these *aldeas* were bought, our Fathers in India, knowing Mirza's good heart and how great and munificent a benefactor he was to us, resolved in the Congregation then held to petition our Father General in behalf of the whole Province || to accept Mirza as a founder†. Our Father General granted the favour, as appears from a letter of our Father Assistant, dated the 31st December 1621, in answer to one of Fr. Jose de Castro. He says :—

" 'The foundation of the Prince Mirza is accepted with the gratitude due to one so great and so devoted to the Society and to the Christian weal ; and the examples of his life, which your Reverence described, well show how much God has imparted Himself to him. Doubtless, He has chosen him to be the pillar of that small church, and the foundation of the

* "The first founder of the Agra College and of its Mission was Senhor Mirza Zulcarne, who gave a sum sufficient to buy the village (aldea) of Parela in Bombaim and another called...in Salcete of the North. From Parela that Mission received eight thousand xerafins, and from 4 to 5 [thousand] from...[the other *aldea* (?) ; the name of the aldea is missing in the original, as above]. But, as the English took Parela, the College and the Mission were much crippled and in debt, until the Senhora Juliana Dias da Costa offered to become a second and new foundress; she gave 50 thousand xerafins, which being profitably placed partly met with the revenues of the *aldea* and other values (*estimacoes*) the necessities of the Mission, which costs yearly from 9 to 10 thousand xerafins, owing to the great dearness in those lands and the enormous expenses incurred by the journey of the Fathers and sending up their provisions." (*L. o das Moncoes*, No. 79, fol. 331). Extract from Annual Letter of Fr. Antonio de Azevedo, Provincial S.J., Goa, 1714. Cf. *O Oriente Portuguez,* Nova Goa, Vol. VII, 1910, pp. 182-183.

great one we hope to see raised in those Provinces. Let your Reverence assist him and try to serve him in everything, as is due to so noble a heart in return for the favours he bestows on us.

"After this announcement and good news, we hoped that the [diploma of the] foundation would come at once from Rome; but, in the year 1625, seeing that it was so long delayed, I, being again Superior of the Mission,* wrote lengthily about this affair to the Fr. Visitor, Andre Palmeiro,† and complained lovingly that there should have been so much forgetfulness in a matter of such moment. The Father answered me by the present letter here appended :—

"'TO FR. FRANCISCO CORSI OF THE SOCIETY OF JESUS.

"'With regard to making Mirza Founder of a College, which Your Reverence spoke to me about, this matter was referred to Our Reverend Father General years ago, and it was done also at the last Congregration, [the proceedings of] which Fr. Maoel Mendez has now brought us with its answers.‡ There is a special answer to your Reverence's petition. I shall put it down here, both the application and the answer to it.

"'It was represented on behalf of the Mogor Mission that the noble Mirza Zulcarnen—such is his devotion and charity towards the Society and the whole of that Mission—was offering willingly to invest the sum of money required for a yearly revenue of one thousand five hundred xerafins,§ a sum

* Fr. Corsi must have succeeded as Superior of the Mission to Fr. Antonio d' Andrade, who went a first time to Tibet in 1624 and returned thither in 1625.

† He had come to India in 1627.

‡ Fr. Manoel Mendez came to India in 1625 with eleven companions; ten Portuguese, and one a Pole. The date of their embarking at Lisbon and of their arrival at Goa is not stated in A. FRANCO, S.J., *Op. cit.*

§ The xerafin is calculated as equivalent to somewhat less than 1*s.* 6*d.* in *Hobson-Jobson.* Its value has varied. In one of the quotations of *Hobson-Jobson* (1st edn., p. 743) it is equal at Bombay to 5 tangas (A.D. 1675); (*ibid.*, p. 867) it is equal to a cruzado (A.D. 1540); in 1653, at Goa, it represents 6 tangas; and I find in FARIA Y SOUZA, *Asia Portuguesa,* III, 363, No. 12, that it was equal to about a real of eight in 1636. Now a real of eight or a peso was worth Rs. 2 of the then currency.

sufficient for maintaining the labourers of that Mission and supporting the poor Christians. This had been done heretofore with the King's alms, now greatly reduced. It is asked that he be received as founder of a *Collegium inchoatum* for that Mission. The whole Congregation therefore petitions Our Reverend Father to comply with the wishes of so great a man, one who has so well deserved of the Society, and to have regard to the interests of that Mission.'

"'The answer is as follows :—

"'We complied long ago with the pious wishes of that excellent gentleman. May the All-Good God *increase the growth of the fruits of his justice* * and finish what He has begun in him and through him. The interests of the Mogor Mission, one of the most glorious to the Christian Religion, lie very near to our heart, nor shall we ever neglect anything that may tend to protect and promote it.'

"'Now, both this application and the fact that an earlier application had been presented to him [the General], allusion to which is made in the beginning of this reply, was unknown to me until I received this reply and Your Reverence's letter. And since, as you see in the beginning of the answer, in the word *annuimus* (we complied) Our Reverend Father refers to the first letter written to him, I have looked for that answer to know in what form the concession was made; but, so far I could not trace it among the letters of that time; still, I shall examine more carefully the moment I find leisure, and I hope to send you a clear solution before my departure for China. From Goa, the 28th of November [1]625. ANDRE PALMEIRO.'

"It seems, however, that his many occupations made the Father lose sight of this affair of ours ; for, he left Goa and bade us good-bye in a special letter without a word about this matter.† Accordingly, I wrote about it to Our Father General ; for I considered it a great blemish on our part that we should have received the foundation, and should be enjoying

* 2 Cor. ix. 10.

† Fr. Andrew Palmeiro is shown as having arrived in China in 1628. He died at Macao on April 4, 1635. Cf. *Catalogus Patrum ac Fratrum S.J. qui . . . . in Sinis adlaboraverunt,* Chang-hai, 1892, pp. 6-7.

the revenues of it, Fr. Assistant's letters being there to certify that the foundation had been received, and yet, years after it, our Superiors knew nothing of it. I wrote to the same effect || to Fr. Valentin Caravalho, as soon as he became our Provincial. In June [1]627 he wrote to me in answer to this point :—

"'With reference to the foundation of the Senhor Mirza, I say that it is accepted by our Reverend Father General, and in the letter now sent herewith in answer to the said Senhor's letter to me, I reply to him in that sense. Your Reverence may tell Mirza the same. Still, we shall write to Our Father asking him to acknowledge in due form the acceptance of the *Collegium inchoatum* founded by Mirza. I am of opinion that it was sent five years ago in the ships in which the Count Viceroy came, because no post reached Goa that year and all the letters were lost.'*

"On receipt of these letters of the Fr. Provincial, I presented to Mirza the one intended for him and told him by word of mouth what the Father directed me in mine to do, and, from that time, by order of Holy obedience, Mirza was here held by Ours as the Founder of the *Collegium inchoatum* of Agra, as it is called.

"The accounts given above show that Mirza owed by the terms of his father's will .... Rs. 27,000, of which he has paid .... Rs. 24,810.

"This at the end of the year [1]618, when the accounts were made. I shall now show how he has satisfied the remainder of his obligations.

"When I proposed to Mirza that he should give us in a lump sum twenty thousand Rupees, I meant that he should give the said sum insteaed of the Rs. 200 which he gave us monthly ; but the Holy Ghost granted him grace to make him do more than what I dared ask. 'Father,' he told me, 'I

* The allusion must be to the armada of four ships which left Lisbon on March 18, 1622. Count de Vidigueyra, Don Francisco de Gama, for the second time appointed Viceroy of India, was Captain-in-chief. The ship of the Admiral, D Francisco Mascarenas, fought the Dutch at the entrance of Mozambique and was lost. The Capitana, the *S. Teresa,* was also lost at Mozambique. Cf. FARIA Y SOUSA, *Asia Portuguesa,* III, 381, 382, 554, 555.

cannot know exactly how much I owe towards my father's legacy, and it is impossible to ascertain the matter from account-books (por contas), as Your Reverence knows. Hence, I wish to continue giving Rs. 200 every month, and God Our Lord, Who knows it all full well, will accept whatever I owe for the good of my father's soul, and what I give over and above He will accept for the good of mine.' Mirza continued to give the said alms ; he continues still up to the present month of May of [1]628, when I write this ; so that, between the end of the year 1618, when the accounts were made, and the end of the current month of May of [1]628, *i.e.*, during nine years and four months, we received, merely on account of this monthly allowance of Rs. 200.........Rs. 22,400,

[*The top of foll. 678r and 678v is somewhat damaged ; but the sense can be made out.*]

which, added to the aforesaid sum of...........Rs. [24,810],
makes in all ....Rs. [47,210],

or much more, it is clear, than what his father left to be given for his soul's welfare. And besides the said sum of Rs. 47,210, he gave us in a lump sum twenty thousand Rupees and the rest on other occasions, with which sum we purchased, as mentioned above, the *aldeas* for the foundation of the *Collegium inchoatum.*

"Besides, if it were necessary, I could draw up a list of other large extraordinary alms which Mirza gave us, both in gold and silver plate for the Church, and in cash for good works, the whole amounting, I should think, to forty thousand Rupees. Again, Mirza maintained since 1614, and is still maintaining at Sambar in the present year [1]628, when I am writing, many widows and poor Christians ; he took also into his service many other Christians, not so much because he stood in need of their services, but because they were Christians. You may guess from this how much money he must have been spending. He did the same for many of his relatives, persons of rank, but poor, many of them. Considering that they lived and live as Mirza's retainers and draw large salaries, he spent also much on them. I omit the many . . . .other sums which Mirza always gave [in alms] to others, non-Christians. In one day alone he gave five thousand Rupees for ransoming captives taken in a certain war in which, by the King's order, he had also taken part, and he ordered that none of his captains should [keep? ransom?] any of them. I omit all this, because it is foreign to my purpose, which is :—

"1st, to show clearly and to evidence how Mirza complied with what his father ordered in his will should be given for the good of his soul, since he gave much more;

"2nd, how he gave us, the Fathers of the Society of Jesus, enough to provide for the foundation of the *Collegium inchoatum* of Agra; hence, it is our clear duty to give him the title of Founder;

"3rd, how, besides being a real Founder, he is also a munificient benefactor of the Society and of this small Christainity of Mogor; therefore, we owe him Masses and prayers, not only as to a Founder, but also to a munificient benefactor. We particularly who belong to this Mission, and all the Christians of it, must pray in a special manner to God Our Lord for the safety and welfare of Mirza and all those of his household; we must ask God to save him many years for his greater glory and the good of this Christianity.

"Agra, in May of the year 1628.

I. H. S.
FRANCISCO CORSI."

Fr. Hosten writes :—

There must exist in printed books, accounts of travellers, letters of merchants and factors, or even in the Muhammadan historians a number of interesting entries about Mirza Zul-Qarnain. We shall quote those we have come across, and we hope that more will be found.

Between 1627 and 1632, Zul-Qarnain was in charge of a Province in Bengal, the capital of which was 200 miles from Agra and 300 from Hugli. He had about 200 Christians in his service, a number sufficiently large to justify the presence of a chaplain. Fr. Joseph de Castro had followed him. Fr. Francisco Morando was there also some time.

Father de Castro wrote from 'Mogor' on August 8th, 1632, to Father Joseph Baudo, S.J., Turin, that he had been with the Mirza those last three years. The Mirza had all that time been Governor of some Provinces of 'Bengala,' but the capital is nowhere mentioned in de Castro's letters.

In 1632 the difficulties between the Portuguese of Hugli and Shāh Jahān came to a crisis. One of Shāh Jahān's grievances was that they had sent him no embassy of congratulation on his accession to the throne. Hugli was invested on June 24th, 1632, and taken at the end of September of the same year. Fully 4,000 Christian prisoners arrived from Hugli at Agra in July 1633.

Meanwhile Zul-Qarnain and the Christians of Agra were also to taste the gall and wormwood of persecution.

On November 24th, 1632, Father de Castro wrote from Agra to the General of the Society that he had arrived from Bengala eight days before. The King had recalled the Mirza, and received him with much honour, so that the Fathers hoped he would receive some other honourable commission. On the other hand, the events then taking place in Bengal were ominously shaping the situation at Agra, and it was feared that the King, who had from the beginning of his reign shown himself hostile to the Christians, was preparing worse days for them.

The Muhammadan historians are not altogether silent about some of these events. As it is quite rare for them to go out of their way to notice Christians, we must not lose anything of what they have to say of Zul-Qarnain.

The '*Amal Sālih,* a big MS. history dealing with the reign of Shāh Jahān, narrates under the 5th year of the reign (1632) that Zul-Qarnain, whom it calls Zul-Qarnain Feringhi, came from Bahraich in Oudh, where he was Faujdār, and paid his respects to Shāh Jahān, presenting five elephants as his nazr. Bahraich was then a likely place to get elephants from. The MS. adds that Zul-Qarnain had been attached to the Court from childhood and that he was a favourite on account of his rare knowledge of Hindustani music and melody.*

---

* The substance of this paragraph and its reflections was kindly communicated to me by Mr. H. Beveridge. (May 5, 1913). The passage occurs in Vol. I, fol. 178v of the India Office copy of the '*Amal Salih,* after an account of the taking of Hugli and just before the betrothal of Dārā Shikoh to Sultan Parviz's daughter. Mr. Beveridge also points out

A note in the translation of the *Tuzaki-i-Jahangiri* (II. 194n.) states that M. Waris's continuation of the *Padishah-nama*, p. 392, of Brit. Mus. MS., mentions that Zul-Qarnain Farangi came from Bengal and presented poems which he had composed on Shāh Jahān's name, for which he got Rs. 4,000.

Mr. H. Beveridge favours me with several interesting observations concerning the Mirza's return from Bahraich and his removal from office.

"Father Joseph de Castro says that they arrived at Agra on November 16th, 1632. The native writers, Muhammad Salih and 'Abdu-l-Hamid, do not specify the corresponding date of Zul-Qarnain's arrival. But the *Badshahnama*, on the same page that it records his presenting five elephants, has the date 12th Jamād*-l-awwal 1042, which corresponds to 15th November, 1632. The entry of Mirza Zul-Qarnain's presentation precedes this by a few lines; so we may suppose it occurred a little earlier in November. This would not, I think, conflict with Father de Castro's statement that they arrived eight days before the 24th November, for I fancy that the Father's dates are according to the Gregorian Calendar, that is, they are New Style, whereas Gladwin's Tables, which I use, are, I believe, Old Style. So, the corresponding Hijra date would be ten days earlier according to the Gregorian Calendar and so would correspond to 5th November or so. All Catholics, I believe, accepted the Gregorian Calendar in the 16th century, whereas England adopted it two centuries later.* The difficulty about the date may be got over by the difference of Calendars, or, as the *Badshahnama* does not give the date of Mirza Zul-Qarnain's arrival, it may be that we must not press the question of the exact dates too closely. It may also be that there is an error of a day or two in Father de Castro's statement.

"The entry of the 15th November in the *Badshahnama* is a curious one. It gives an account of a discussion about

---

that a shorter entry about Zul-Qarnain's return from his faujdarship of Bahraich and his presenting five elephants to the King is found in the *Padishah-nama*, Bibl. Ind. edn., I. 446.

* The Gregorian Calendar came into vogue in India in Oct. 1583. Cf. de Souza's *Oriente Conquistado*, Lisbon edn., II, 184.

Alexander the Great. Asaf Khan extolled the character of Alexander the Great, and said no one had ever shown that he did or said anything bad. Shāh Jahān replied that, of course, if Alexander the Great was a Prophet, nothing could be said against him. But, this was not proved, and so Shah Jahan thought exception might be taken first to a saying of Alexander's and secondly to an action of his. The saying was that when Darius's ambassador asked Alexander for tribute, Alexander replied that the hen was dead that had laid the golden eggs. This, in Shah Jahan's opinion, was an unworthy remark, for Alexander meant his father Philip, when he spoke of the hen. Now, it was very disrespectful to compare one's father to such a paltry thing as hen! The other exception he would take was that he thought Alexander had done an imprudent and even wicked thing in going to Nostraba, the Queen of Barda, disguised as his own ambassador.

"It has occurred to me that it would not be too fanciful to suppose that this discussion about Zul-Qarnain might have arisen from the coincidence of Mirza Zul-Qarnain's arrival in Agra. He might even have been present at the discussion!

"Another curious thing about the entry of Zul-Qarnain's presentation in the *Badshahnama* is the fact that it is immediately followed by a statement of Shah Jahan's resolve to give a preference to Muhammadans in making appointments. This would give colour to Father de Castro's statement that the Mirza was removed from office."*

Mr. H. Beveridge expresses his surprise that, if Mirza Zul-Qarnain was Governor of Bahraich. Fr. de Castro should say he was in Bengal, and Sir Richard Carnac Temple (*The Travels of Peter Mundy*, II. 380n. 1) remarks that, if he was

* Letter of July 21, 1913. Two days later, Mr. H. Beveridge wrote: "I see from the *Badshahnama,* Vol. I, Pt. I, p. 195, that one Salih, a brother's son of Jāafar Beg Asaf Khān, was made faujdar of Bahraich in the year of the accession 1037 (A.D. 1628). Mirza Zul-Qarnain was perhaps his successor. I have a doubt in my mind, however, if the place mentioned in p. 195 be Bahraich. It is spelt Bahraij, and possibly Broach in Gujarāt is meant. Before that Salih was faujdār of Pilad, which is Gujrāt.

at Bahraich, the distance from Hugli would be twice as great as stated. I have found lately in a letter by Fr. d'Azevedo, Agra (undated letter, but belonging to the first months of 1632), that Don Goncalo, as the Mirza was called, was at "Gorepur" in 1631, which we should indentify with Gorākhpur in the United Provinces. This brings the Mirza nearer to Bengal and Hugli, but produces, perhaps, a discrepancy between d'Azevedo and the Muhammadan authors. In the *Ain*, Bahraich appears as a Sarkār of 11 mahals, while Gorākhpur contained 24-parganahs.

On February 6th, 1633, Fr. J. de Castro wrote from Agra that the bell of their church had been removed on the day of the Epiphany (January 6th, 1633); four *piyādās* had been posted in the house to keep watch day and night, and the Fathers had been forbidden to make any converts. The Mirza had shown himself firm in certain demands of the King touching the faith. As for Hugli, the news had reached them that the town had been sacked.

On October 8th, 1633, Fr. J. de Castro wrote from Agra to Fr. Nuno Mascarenhas, the Assistant of Portugal, that the Mirza had to pay 8 lākhs of rupees, or about 400,000 cruzados. To help him as much as they could, they had given back to him the golden chalice which he had presented to the Church in the days of his opulence.

Peter Mundy, a servant of the E. I. Co., who held office at Surat and Agra, and had been sent on a commercial mission to Patna in 1632, was not far wrong when he remarked on March 11th, 1633, while at Mozābād, on his way from Agra to Surat *viâ* Ajmer: "Seven Course Northward lyes Sambar [Sāmbhar], the Jaggueere (*jagir*) of Mirza Zilkurne [Zu'l-kārnain, Alexander] of 1000 horse pay, each horse 25 rupees per moneth, whoe is now putt out [from his governorship in Bengal] and made Tagguere [*taghir,* dismissed], himselfe, wife, Children and servants in prison, because the King is informed hee hath store of money and demaunds of him 60 lack, haveing sent Pioneers [investigators] to search and digg his howse. Before I came away [from Agra] hee offers 5 lack, which will not bee accepted, soe remains still prisoner.

Hee is a Christian and the Chiefest in all India, formerly in favour."*

Zul-Qarnain was not long molested. He paid 8 lakhs of rupees, was reduced for a time to extreme penury, and then gradually rose again to favour. Many of the Portuguese captives from Hugli were "released," says Manucci, "through the petitions of some persons at court, chiefly an Armenian, who was a great favourite, or through the money paid by a Venetian, my compatriot, called Hieronomo Veroneo, a man ransomed by the Portuguese." The reference belongs to the period between 1633 and 1640, since Veroneo died in 1640.

On November 2nd, 1633, Zul-Qarnain assisted at the burial of Fr. Matthew de Payva, S.J., and helped in carrying the coffin from the Church to what is called the Martyrs' Chapel in the actual Catholic cemetery of Agra. In 1634 he was with his chaplain at Lahore in the King's suite. The end of that year was marked with a new outburst of bigotry on the part of the King; the Fathers of Agra were ejected from their house the images and pictures in their Church were broken or torn, and the whole of 1635 the Fathers were in imminent danger of being expelled from the country. At last, thanks to Asaf Khān's never-flagging friendship, they were allowed on December 8th, 1635, to return to their College, but on the iniquitous condition that their Churches of Agra and Lahore be pulled down. This was done. Even the Church of Sind (Tatta) was destroyed. The persecution had now done its worst, and, though the Fathers never grew to favour with Shāh Jahān, they were at least tolerated after this.

We next hear of Zul-Qarnain in 1636. John Drake wrote to the President and Council of the E. I. Co. at Surat (June 4th, 1636) that he had arrived at "the *lasker* which nowe is at Kerkey [Kharki or Kirki, *i.e.*, Aurangābād] six course wide of Dowletabad," and he had delivered their letter to the Padre, who was living with "Mirza Zulkerne." The

---

* Note communicated by Sir Richard Carnac Temple. Cf. his *Travels of Peter Mundy*, vol. II. 240-241.

latter had given Drake good advice and proffered his services with Asaf Khān.*

Father J. de Castro announced to the General of the Society in Rome (Agra, Sept. 1st, 1640) that Mirza Zul-Qarnain was again in the King's favour. His two eldest sons were pages of honour in the King's service. The Mirza's Christian name was Gonsalvo; his three sons were called Gioa Baptista (the eldest), Gasparo, and Micaele (the youngest. Clara, his daughter, was 19 years old; she ought to have been married already, but it was difficult to match her with a Christian of her rank.†

On January 1st, 1642, de Castro informed the General that the Mirza had asked the King's permission to join the service of his second son (Sultān Shujā'), then Governor of Bengal [1639-60]. He had left Agra with his three sons, while his daughter Clara, and Magdalen, the nurse and governess of the household, stayed behind.

In 1645, the Mirza was still in Bengal with his three sons and Father Francis Morando, his Chaplain. The Captain of the Christians at Sāmbhar was the Mirza's uncle, Janibeg, a "Chaldean." Janibeg's salary was Rs. 50,000 a year; he had to pay to the King an annual revenue of five lakhs of rupees. Father de Castro was Chaplain to the family at Sāmbhar.‡

We should not be surprised if Mirza Zul-Qarnain had been instrumental in obtaining from Sultān Shujā' in 1646 the confirmation of the ancient privileges and exemptions of the inhabitants and Augustinians of Hugli.§

Bernier states that Sultān Shujā', while at Rājmahal; sent out "of the inferiour *Bengala* for many pieces of Canon, and a good number of *Portugals* that were retired thither, because of the fertility of the Country: For he much courted all those

---

* Cf. W. Foster, *The English Factories in India* (1634-36), Oxford, 1911, p. 262. Reference communicated by Sir Richard Carnac Temple.

† MSS. in the author's possession.

‡ Letter of Fr. J. de Castro, Sāmbhar, July 20, 1645 (MS.).

§ See our paper *A Week at Bandel*, in *Bengal: Past and Present*, Calcutta, Vol. X, Pt. I, pp. 107-111.

Portugal Fathers Missionaries, that are in that Province, promising them no less than that he would make them all rich, and build Churches for them wheresoever they would. And they were indeed capable to serve him, it being certain, that in the Kingdom of *Bengala* there are to be found no less than eight to nine thousand Families of *Franguis, Portugals,* and these either Natives or Mesticks."*

Among the remarks which Father Alexander de Rhodes, S. J., makes on Mogor, we find: "Our society has a large college in the town of Agra, which a very honourable (*honnête*) Armenian, named . . . . [*a blank*], founded about 30 years ago."†

In 1648 the Mirza was back at Agra, for he watched from a balcony, with Father Antonio Botelho, Shāh Jahān's magnificent progress towards Delhi, his new capital.

"These last years," wrote Father John Maracci, S.J., in April 1649, "while a distinguished Christian Lord, called Mirza, was Governor of Bengala, in the King of Mogor's name, Fr. Francis Morando, and Italian of the Province of Goa, being confessor to him and the whole of his family, the propagation of the Faith was marvellous in that Kingdom."‡

One of Father Morando's converts in Bengal was a young Englishman, John Damont, "& the Father of the Christians [Fr. James d'Abreu (?), of Murmugao, near Goa] made use of this Neophyte for the conversion of several other Heretics of his country, who come to traffic in those parts of Murmugano & of Pardes, & last year [1648] at least fifteen were reconciled to the Church."§

---

* Cf. F. Bernier, *The History of the late Revolution . . . ,* London, 1671, pp. 193-194.

† Cf. *Voyages et Missions du P. Alex. de Rhodes,* Paris, 1854, p. 397. The remark occurs in the chapter on Surat, where the Father was from September 30, 1647, to February 3, .1648. The first edition of his travels appeared in 1653. There are other editions of 1666 and 1685.

‡ Cf. Jean Maracci, S.J., *Relàtion de ce qui s'est passé dans les Indes Orientales,* Paris . . . . S. Cramoisy, MDCLI, pp. 65-66.

§ *Ibid.,* pp. 38-39. This relation was written at Rome in April, 1649. Fr. Maracci had come as Procurator of the Goa Province, probably in the beginning of 1648 or 1649.

In a list of Shāh Jahān's grandees, belonging apparently to the end of the 20th year of his reign (1648), the name of Zul-Qarnain, the Armenian, appears as holding the rank of 500 with 300 horse.*

In 1648 Mirza Zul-Qarnain is reported as Governor in the Kingdom of Lahore. "Fr. Anthony Ceschi from Trent . . . . must reside at present in the Kingdom of Laor as confessor and preacher to the Governor of it, who is called Mirsạ, which means Alexander the Great, a Christian prince in great favour with the King. His house is composed of more than four hundred persons, the greater number of them Christians."† Father Maracci added: "Father Francis Morando, a Bolognese, and a great scholar in the Partian [Persian] and Industanne [Hindustāni] tongue, remained sixteen years at a stretch with the said Lord and his children, accompanying him to all the Kingdoms where he has been Viceroy and Governor."‡

Father Anthony Ceschi di S. Croce, S.J., wrote to his parents a *Brief Relation on the state of affairs in the Indies in the year* 1649, dated Agra, September 15th, 1649.

"The Mission of Mogor, he says, is at present at peace with the Prince § and the Governors of the Kingdom. Only this year are matters of the Christian faith being discussed; but, though they hear them, they do not for that matter open their heart to the call of God. Many of those people are baptized this year, and Mirza Lucarne (*sic*) [Zul-Qarnain] has made a generous profession of the faith. When asked by the King—as being the chief of the courtiers—whether he believed that after the Christian Prophet another was still to come, he answered intrepidly no; and yet he thought that his well-

* Note by Mr. H. Beveridge. Cf. *Bādshānama*, Bibl. Ind. edn., I. 748(top of page).

† Cf. Jean Maracci, S.J., *op. cit.*, p. 22.

‡ Cf. *ibid.*, p. 23. If Fr. Morando had by 1648 remained 16 years with the Mirza, he would have been with him from 1632. Fr. de Castro, the Mirza's chaplain, writing from "Mogul" [Gorākhpur?] on August 28, 1632, says, indeed, that Father Francis Morando is with him, pending his departure for Tibet. Cf. *J.A.S.B.*, 1910, November, p. 531.

§ Dārā Shikoh, Shah Jahan's eldest son.

weighed answer would cost him his head; but the King dissembled and changed the topic of conversation."

We hear of the Mirza again in 1651. The Patriarch of Ethiopia, Don Alfonso Mendez, S.J., writing with apostolic freedom to the Cardinals of Propaganda (Goa, December 20th, 1651) once more denounces the Bishop of Chrysopolis, Don Matthew de Castro, for his extravagances. We have seen only the summary of that letter. "An *aper exterminator* [ravaging boar] has penetrated into Mogor. I should abstain from speaking about it, knowing that near Your Eminences I am held per mendace [as untruthful]. But the truth is one . . . . Disedifying conduct of the Bishop of Chrysopolis among the Mogorins and Turks. Scandal taken by the Christians, Catholics, English and Dutch alike. His effronteries towards Mirzâm Zulkarnem, a Christian, the friend of the Jesuits, who calls to his help Father Buseo [Busi]. The Fathers of Mogor have recourse to the King against the accusations made in public by the Bishop of Chrysopolis, especially against their being spies of the King of Portugal and having usurped the property of Portuguese deceased in Mogor. But the Bishop of Chrysopolis boasts before all of the instructions he had received from Rome.

"Let Your Eminences weigh the damage done by him to Christianity, and restore peace to the Mission. If the Jesuits of Mogor are at fault, why does he not denounce them to Rome? Why does he instead make a Maomettan Prince judge in this matter? Is this the way to defend the Apostolic See?"

Father Botelho will tell us more anon about the vagaries of Don Matheus de Castro, a Brahman of Divar (Goa), educated partly in Rome and created a Bishop and Vicar-Apostolic first of Ethiopia, then for the Bijapur and Gulkandah Kingdoms, whose immoderate zeal disturbed West, South and East for many years.

Two other passages in Father Ceschi's printed life and letters may be quoted here. On September 5th, 1651, he wrote from Agra to his parents :—

"A certain Christian was disputing with the Moors, when, inspired by Heaven, he said that the faith he was preaching must be true, if a bird should presently appear and repeat the song he would sing first. They were under tents in a treeless plain, and lo! a little bird came flying presently, which imitated very well the song the Christian sang . . . ." We know from other unpublished Jesuit letters that this Christian was no other than Mirza Zul-Qarnain.

In another letter to the Rector of the College of Trent (Delhi, August 24th, 1654) Father Ceschi says:—"The Prince is extremely fond of the Fathers. He called me lately, though against my wish, to his palace and presented me with a dress of honour (*munusculo insigni cuisdam panni*). Mirza, one of our Christians, is one of the grandees at Court. At the Prince's request, the King condoned to him lately 50 thousand gold mohurs (*aurei*). The Mirza (*Mirzatius*) came to thank his patron.* 'This is not my work at all,' he answered. 'You owe it all to the help of Christ and the prayers of your Fathers. Thank them.'"

We have from Father Anthony Botelho's pen a very important paper on the religious and political situation in Mogor during the six years that he was a Missionary there (1648-54). The account was not, however, written before 1670 (cf. our article in *J.A.S.B.*, 1910, p. 453, *n.* 5). Though the good Father had at his disposal the Archives of the Mission of Goa, he found it too troublesome to hunt up and consult the original documents on sundry points, with the result that many of his statements regarding the beginnings of the Mission under Akbar and Jahangir must be received with caution.†

---

* I understand that the patron was the Prince Dārā Shikoh.

† Father Anthony Botelho went from Surat to Mogor at the end of 1647 or in January 1648. "Before the English ship was got in readiness," writes Fr. Alexander de Rhodes, S.J., "God greatly consoled me by the arrival [at Surat] of our Fathers, who came from Goa and stayed some time with me in Surate. Three of them left, a few days later, for the College of Agra, a distance of 40 days from Surate; the first was Fr. Anthony Botel [Botelho], a Portuguese, a man of great merit and influence, who was sent as visitor and Rector of the College which is in that town, the capital of the whole kingdom; the two others were Fr. Anthony Ceski [Ceschi], a German, and Fr. Henry [Uwens, *alias*] Buscé [Buseo, Busil], a Fleming, both of them young men, already in priest's orders, with aptitudes for learning the languages of the country. The letters I received lately in Rome [1651-52?] tell us of the great fruits which accompany the labours of these three Fathers in the King-

We publish here only the last portion of Father Botelho's account, viz., his

Relation on the Christianity which We have in the Kingdom of the Great Mogol.*

"I could enlarge very much and write a very long account on the origin and beginnings of this Christianity in the Kingdom of the Great Mogol, but that I know that everything has been very well related and written in the Archives of the Secretariat of the Province of Goa. Whereas, however, it is there, so to say, cast into a well, and there are many good things and chronicles of the doings of the Fathers of the Society in this Province,—and I do not know when this chronicle will see the light,† owing to the great indifference of the Superiors and their not setting aside someone to continue this chronicle with the view of publishing and printing it, I am obliged to say briefly how our Fathers entered that Great Kingdom about a hundred years ago. That great Empire of Mogol was then governed by King Hacabar—"Hacabar" means "immortal" in Persian,‡ and "Patxâ Hacabar" means "Immortal King," —the great-grandfather of King Elamguir § now reigning. As

dom of Mogor." Cf. de Rhodes, *Voyàges et Missions,* Paris, Julien, 1854, p. 399. He is mentioned in 1647 in C. Beccari, S.J., *Notizia e saggi di opere . . . . ,* Roma, 1903, p. 20, and in Jean Maracci, S.J., *Relation de ce qui s'est passé . . . . présentée . . . . au mois d'Avril* 1649, Paris, MDCLI, p. 21, where it is said that, as Rector of Diu, therefore before his going to Mogor, he tried to penetrate into Ethiopia, but could go no further than Suakim.

* Brit. Mus. Add. MSS. 9855, fol. 41*r*—45*v*. Title: *Rellacao da Christandade quet emos no Reino do Gram Mogol.* There is in the beginning of the same volume (fol. 14) a Latin abridgment. Cf. *J.A.S.B.,* 1910, pp. 448, 459, and 459 n. 1.

† He alludes probably to the history of the Society in the East by Fr. Sebastiao Gonsalves, whose death is announced in the Annual Letter of 1619. Fr. Francis de Sousa used Gonsalves' materials for his *Oriente Conquistado,* the two printed volumes of which contains the history of the Jesuit Missions in the East from 1542 to 1585. The third volume, a MS., must be still in Portugal. Gonsalves' *Historia da Companha na India,* ff. 252, written between 1593 and 1619, is now at Lisbon, Ajuda Library MSS. $\frac{49}{80}$ Fr. Cros utilised if for his life of St. Francis Xavier. Cf. A. Brou, *S.Francois Xavier,* Paris, G. Beauchesne, 1912, I, p. ix.

‡ *Akbar* means great, not immortal.

§ Aurangzeb took the title of 'Alamgir on his accession in May 1659.

I have said in my Relation on the greatness of the King of Mogol, this King was very warlike, and it is he who brought under his sceptre the whole of Mogol up to Bengala, Bisnagar [Vijayanagar], Vizapur [Bijāpur], and other Kings of lesser importance throughout Industao. He was very intelligent and desirous to know about all the sects, whether of the Heathen or of the Moors, many of whom follow Muhammad [regularly: Mafamede], others Ali, Muhammad's son-in-law. This King Hacabar, going to parts of Bengala, found there a priest of the country and started arguing with him and examining into many things of our holy law and faith.* The priest answered to everything, as far as he knew, and finished by telling the King that, if His Majesty wished to have a deeper knowledge of, and be better grounded in, the things of the faith of the Firinguis (*i.e.*, of the Portuguese), there were in Goa some Fathers, called Fathers of St. Paul,† and that he should call some to his Kingdom. Learned as they were, they would solve all his doubts and explain to him the mysteries of the faith of the Portuguese. So said, so done. The King despatched at once and in all haste a messenger with a [*farmān*] for the Fathers of St. Paul, and this *formao* is kept to this day in our Secretariat of Goa.‡ In it he said; 'Masters of the law, come to my Kingdom with all your books, and be quite sure that I shall treat you with much love, and have no fear.' The Holy Martyr Rodolfo Aquaviva and Father Antonio de Monserrate had then come from Europe. Both were sent,§ and they were the first who, about a hundred years ago, entered the Kingdom of the Great Mogol. When the

* We gave a more accurate account of what happened in *J.A.S.B.*, 1912, pp. 216-218. Akbar did not go to Bengal, but called a priest from there.

† As the Jesuits were popularly called from the name of their College of S. Paolo da Santa Fé, Goa.

‡ The original does not appear to exist among the Marsden MSS. in the British Museum.

§ There was a third one, Francisco Henriques. The beginnings of the Mission under Akbar are ably exposed in *J.A.S.B.*, 1896, pp. 38-113, and in Fr. F. Goldie's *First Christian Mission to the Great Moghul.* Fr. Goldie was not aware of the article in *J.A.S.B.* Our last and best authority is Father Antonio Monserrate. Cf. *Memoirs A.S.B.* (1914), III, No. 9, pp. 513-704.

Fathers arrived, King Hacabar was in the City of Phatepor [Fatehpur Sikri] with his Court. He rejoiced much at the Fathers' arrival, ordered them to lodge in an apartment of his Palace, and presently he entrusted to them one of his sons to be taught Portuguese and good manners.* Little by little, the King was informed by the Fathers about the mysteries of our holy faith and law, and he assigned for the Fathers' daily maintenance a certain sum of money, besides which he gave the Fathers continually so many gifts in money and in kind (*e pecas*) that the letters of the said Fathers, still preserved in this Secretariat, show the money was so ample that they did not know what to do with it, for there were not yet then Christians among whom to dole it out. The Superiors wrote to them from Goa to take only as much of the money as was necessary for their daily wants, and to explain to the King that we were poor. They did so, and the King was much edified.†

"In spite of the religious discussions that were held, the King remained as much a Moor as before. Great was the Fathers' patience; they wrote repeatedly from there to the Superiors that they were losing time in inaction, and asked them for orders to return to Goa and to go where they might do more good. From Goa they encouraged them to have patience; for patience and long-suffering surmounted all obstacles. King Hacabar fell into another folly. He said to the Fathers that he had heard whatever pertained to our law, and that with the knowledge* he had of the various religious schools among Muhammadans, he wished to make a religion which would combine our and his. When the Fathers saw his extravagance, they undeceived from there the Fathers Superiors and said they wished to leave the place. They were told from there to come at once, but not without the King's

---

* Prince Murād.

† Mrs. F. A. Steel in her *A Prince of Dreamers*, as she calls Akbar, identifies the Provincial of Goa with greed of money, and Blessed Rudolf Aquaviva with greed of souls! And she goes out of her way to insist upon the truth of her descriptions, implying that they are result of a careful study of her subject. C. H. Thurston, S.J., on *Once more the Jesuit in fiction* in *The Tablet*, London, January 5, 1910, pp. 88-90.

permission and good pleasure. The Fathers laid the matter before the King, and he told them he had no hold on them: if they wished, they could go back to their country; but they should know that, if they left his Court, he would be much displeased and chagrined. The Fathers continued to have patience still some time, until the King resolved to send an Ambassador to the Sovereign Pontiff with Fr. Antonio de Monserrate. The Ambassador came to Goa, whence he was to go to Rome; but he died at Goa,* and Fr. Antonio de Monserrate remained on this side, while Fr. Rodolfo Aquaviva, too, returned to Goa after some months. I do not know what was his pretext, but he had the King's leave. A few months after his return, Fr. Rodolfo Aquaviva went to the Christianity of Salcete, where he obtained afterwards at Cunculy [Cunculim] the crown of a glorious martyrdom. A few months later, the King heard how the Holy Martyr Rodolfo Aquaviva had been so cruelly killed for the faith; and, speaking to his courtiers, he said that God had thus chastised him for not wishing to remain in his Kingdom and Court.† Such is the preposterous judgment of those who are ignorant of our holy faith! They take as a punishment from the hands of God the reward He bestows on His elect. The Superiors of Goa, knowing how King Hacabar had been unwilling to let our Fathers depart from his Court, however just their reasons, thought proper that we should return to that Court and send others again, seeing that we were treated there with so much respect that the King kept us at his expense, and that, even if the conversion of the King himself did not follow, our residing at the Court of the greatest Monarch of the whole of Asia redounded to the greater glory of God,

---

* Monserrate (*op. cit.*, p. 637) does not state that 'Abdullah died at Goa, neither does Father Goldie, nor Francisco de Sousa, S.J., *Oriente Conquistado,* II. C. I. D. II. §§ 43-48, 53-64, 74 *sqq.* Fr. DANIEL BARTOLI, S.J., *Missione al Gran Mogor,* Roma, 1714, p. 73, says he returned to Court. We hear of him still in 1595 and later (MS. letters).

† According to Monserrate, Akbar, on hearing of Rudolf's death, put his finger in his mouth and said, deeply moved: "Woe to me! Father, I told you timely enough not to go, but you did not wish to listen to me!" Cf. *op. cit.*, p. 637. See also Bartoli, *op. cit.*, p. 149.

while it made the world wonder.* It was thought in the beginning and at the Court of King Idalxâ, up to the time that I was there by order of obedience, that King Hacabar had died a Christian. King Idalxâ himself told me these very words: '*Antonio Botelho, sache he qui barâ Patxâ.Hacabar Christao muhâ, qui nã?*† That is: 'Antonio Botelho, is it true or not that the great King Hacabar died a Christian?' I answered: 'Would to God it had been so; but he kept us deluded with such hopes, and died in your sect of Muhammad.' I do not now remember which Fathers repaired then to the Court of the Mogol in the place of the Holy Martyr Father Rodolfo Aquaviva and Antonio de Moncerrate. What I am sure of is that it was still in King Hacabar's lifetime that Fr. Hieronimo Xavier of happy memory went also to that Court.‡ He was an apostolic man, and King Hacabar esteemed him much, and so did always, too, King Janguir, Hacabar's son, who succeeded him to the throne. Fr. Hieronimo Xavier was many years at King Janguir's Court, and he composed a very big book in Persian dedicated to King Hacabar and entitled in the dedication: "Mirror of Princes." He composed other very good works in Persian, which are kept in our College of Agra and in this Secretariat of Goa. The book I speak of is also written in Persian, as are many others composed by the same Fathers.§

---

* The fact is that Akbar recalled the Fathers in 1590 and 1595.

† *Sach hai ki bara Padshah Akbar Khristan mua ki na?*—Some parts of the abridged Latin translation of Fr. Botelho's memoir were quoted by Sir Edward Maclagan in *J.A.S.B.*, 1896, p. 93 *n.* 2, p. 107. Fr. Botelho must have been at the Court of the Idal Shah of Bijapur some time between 1654 and 1670.

‡ This was in 1595.

§ On Jerome Xavier's literary labours, cf. *J.A.S.B.*, 1896, pp. 110-113; *ibid.*, *erome Xavier's Persian Lives of the Apostles*, 1914, pp. 65-84; H. Beveridge, *J.R.A.S.*, 1901, pp. 78-79, on the *Samrat-al-flasafa*, one of Jerome Xavier's works, made in collaboration with 'Abdu-s-Sattar (compare *J.A.S.B.*, 1896, p. 93, and see the *Tuzuk-i-Jahangiri*, A. Rogers, and H. Beveridge's transl., I, 389; II, 82, 82 *n.* 3). C. Sommervogel, S.J., (*Bibl. de la C. de J.*, VIII, col. 1339, No. 4) mentions *Directorium Regum ad Regni gubernationem*. This must be the *Mirror of Princes* referred to by Botelho, unless he refers to the *Mirror of Holiness, i.e.*, the *Miratu-l-Quds* otherwise called the *Dastan-i-Masih* (Life of Christ), which was dedicated to Akbar, while the *Mirror of Princes*, if it is the

"While Father Hieronimo Xavier was at King Janguir's Court, great was the prestige enjoyed by him and other Fathers, who joined him, such as Manoel Pinheiro, nick-named the Mogol,* Fr. Joseph de Crasto [*sic*], Francisco Corci, and others nearer to our times, whose names I omit. King Janguir granted Father Hieronimo Xavier the boon of a certain number of Christians, whom he had taken prisoners in certain wars and whom he kept shut up in a prison whence they could not escape.† These being instructed again in the faith, together with others, adult heathens, men and women, whom he baptized, the Mission of Mogol derived its origin from them. They multiplied among themselves, and this was the beginning of that Christianity,‡ and the zealous labours of the other Fathers of that Mission added to their numbers in after years. When I was Superior of it, I baptized twenty-one pagans, and from time to time there are always some *quos Deus elegit et praedestinavit* (whom God chose and pre-destinated) to be brought within the fold. In my time, the number of those Christians who received Holy Communion and went to Confession rose to seven hundred. I could not say with certainty how the numbers stand at present. The ordinary Annuals will tell us, if they do not forget. The Fathers Missionaries devote themselves to this small flock as much as if the Christians were many. Hence it is that they are well instructed in the Catechism,§ and in the mysteries of

---

same as the *Guide of Kings,* would have been dedicated to Jahangir in 1609, according to the *Bibl. Marsdeniana,* p. 305. Cf. *J.A.S.B.,* 1896, p. 113.

* His obituary is in the Annual Letter of Goa for 1614. "He died aged 67 years, of which he had spent 46 in the Society, and 20 near the King of Mogor, to whom and to whose subjects he had endeared himself. He knew Persian so perfectly that he astonished the Mogorese." Cf. our translation of the passage in *The Examiner,* Bombay, 1912, p. 57. Probably it was the Fathers who playfully called him the "Mogor," meaning that he had thoroughly acquired the Indian habits and ways.

† An allusion to the Portuguese captured at Asirgarh, some of whom enlisted under Akbar as *ahdis,* 'soldiers with 2 horses apiece,' while others were left dependent on the Mission (1600-1604). Cf. *J.A.S.B.,* 1896, pp. 83, 90.

‡ Adapted from Rom. viii. 30.

§ A Persian-Hindustani catechism was composed by the Fathers in or about 1611.

our holy faith; and rare is the Christian who misses Mass on days of obligation. Many hear it even on week-days; and, besides going to confession annually, they confess and communicate many times, chiefly on the feasts of Christ, Our Lady, the Apostles, and other chief Saints of the year.

"For many years that we were in that Mission, up to the death of our Brother Mirza Zulcarne, the Fathers were four in number, because one was always accompanying him wherever he was going with the King, while the other three were fixed in our College of Agra. Every Sunday and Feast-day, one of the three, who managed the things of the Church, explained the Doctrine,* not only to the children, but to the rest as well, instructing them in the mysteries of our holy faith. The three days of Holy Week are very devoutly kept in the Church there. The Church is situated within our enclosure, and the men enter by the common gate, while the women enter by a private door (*porta falça*) opening near the sanctuary (*capella mor*).† On those days there are two sermons (*estaçoens*): one on Maundy-Thursday, the other on Good Friday; and it happened, when I was there, that a Father preaching in Portuguese on the Descent from the Cross, all the Christians were so deeply moved in consequence, and there was such a flood (*lit.* monsoon) of tears, that the Moors living near our gate were attracted by their sobbing and came running to the gate to ask what the weeping was for, to which the Porter answered that it was a certain custom of ours, and of the Christians when they were within doors. On all Fridays of Lent, in the evening, an instruction on the Doctrine adapted to their intelligence, is given to those Christians; this is followed by [considerations on] some mystery of the Passion, and the proceedings conclude with a very devout procession in which a crucifix is carried along within our garden and enclosure (*cerca e crastas*). And I assure you that, when I saw this the first time, my eyes filled with tears, and inwardly I said to

* *i.e.*, the Catechism.

† The Fathers must have lived in the actual compound of the Catholic Cathedral of Agra; the Church in Fr. Botelho's time must have been the old Cathedral (now the Native Chapel); as for the house, I fancy it is embodied in the present house of the Capuchin Fathers.

God : 'O Lord, how this small procession (moving along to the singing of the litanies of the Saints) must please Thee more than the pompous Friday processions of Goa, which so many people run to see. (What is most remarkable is that we do all this to the beard and in the Court of the Mogol King.) The glory be to Thee, O Lord, who allowedst this in the very midst of those who profess the law of Muhammad.' The greater part of the Christians of this Christianity are very poor. Possessing no lands to cultivate,—for everything belongs to the King,—they get their living by serving some Christian Armenian merchants, Englishmen, and Dutchmen, or by following some trade which they know, as that of embroiderers, surgeons, etc. The costume of the Christians of Mogol is that of the country : the *cabaya,* reaching down to the knee ;* trousers up to the heels, and a turban. As a mark and token of the Christian law which they profess, all wear their beads around their neck. The Christians of the Christianity of Mogol are the best, and the most solidly grounded in our faith of the whole of this East. This conclusion—absolute as it is—was reached by the late Fr. Thomas de Barros. He was some time in Mogol, and Rector of the College of Agra, and he would say : 'The Christians are so poor, and yet they prefer to live in poverty, and, though they could say to the Fathers : 'Take away your Christian ; I am dying of hunger, and want to go to the Cassiz † and tell him I wish to belong to the law of Muhammad, and he will give me *rosina* at once, *i.e.* my daily sustenance,' yet no ; they do not do so. Hence, I say none are so firm in the faith.' To understand this, you must take it as certain that whoever goes to the Cassiz, be he heathen or Christian, and tells him he wishes to embrace the sect of Muhammad, is sure of a daily ordinary ration, in proportion with his rank. I do not deny that some do at times fall away ; but they are very rare, and it was when the Moors convicted them of other crimes and threatened them with some grievous punishment. They apostatised *ad tempus* (for a time) ; because, *data occasione* (finding an opportunity), they would acknow-

* The surcoat or long tunic of muslin. Cf. *Hobson-Jobson,* 1886, p. 105.

† From *qasis* : priest, rather than from *qazi* : judge.

ledge their error, and presently come to the Church to be reconciled and protest their faith in the law of Christ.

"King Janguir gave our Fathers a garden near the City of Agra, used as a *Gorastao,* or cemetery, where we might bury our dead. He did the same in the City of Laor, where we have a house. In this garden, or *Gorastao,* which is entirely blest, we have also a small vaulted chapel, where our dead Fathers lie buried very neatly; there are stones above the tombs with the names of the deceased Fathers and the year of their death.† And when some Christian dies, all the others assemble to accompany him to the grave. He is carried in a coffin, after our manner; before him goes a procession of small boys vested in their white *opas,* and singing the prayers; in front is carried a copper crucifix surmounting a small staff and covered with a black veil. *Et hoc est mirum* (and this is wonderful) that even some Moors, who were friendly with some Christians, accompanied their corpses to the grave, helping the Christians in carrying the coffin on their shoulders. And Fr. Francisco Morando told me that he was in the College of Agra when Father Matheus de Paiva died there,‡ and that the concourse of the Moors who accompanied him to the grave and carried the coffin on their shoulders was such that it was wonderful; and by this service which they rendered to Fr. Matheus de Pavia, the Moors wished to testify to the Father's great charity, when alive; for, having some knowledge of medicine, he would help them with remedies in their illnesses. On All Soul's Day, the Fathers of that Mission are in the habit of going with all the Christians to that garden or cemetery, and to say Mass in that small chapel At the end, there is a sermon on the souls in Purgatory, and

---

* *Qabaristan*: cemetery. The Portuguese of Calcutta at the beginning of the 19th century pronounced the word in the same corrupt way. They do so still. I cannot imagine that *gorastao* stands for *gora* (white, a European) and *sthan* or *stan* (a place).

† The place of the Jesuit house and cemetery at Lahore has not yet been determined. Sir Edward Maclagan and Fr. Felix, O.C., of Antwerp, told me that they had made a diligent search. No old European inscriptions appear to have been found; but has sufficient attention been paid to Armenian ones?

‡ Nov. 2 (All Souls' Day), 1633.

the Christians lay on the graves in that garden fine napkins whereon they deposit offerings of eatables, which the Fathers at once distribute among countless *Jogues* and *faquirs* who flock thither.* Besides them, many Moors assemble there to witness the solemnity, to see the Father going along in his cope (*capa d'asperages*),† sprinkling holy water and reciting the responses over the graves. I did it several years while I was at Agra, and, when performing this ceremony, I felt the greatest pleasure and spiritual consolation, considering that we enjoyed this liberty in spite of Muhammad and under the Great Mogol's beard. The Armenian merchants (who were fifty or sixty in my time) were much surprised at the freedom we had at the Great Mogol's Court. It was a privilege not enjoyed by the other Religious settled in Constantinople, where the Turks molested them in a thousand ways, going at times as far as beating them severely.

"The College we have in Agra is built in the City itself, not much in the centre of it, but towards the western third of it (*nao muito no meyo della, senao pera a terceira parte que cae pera o Occidente*). Fr. Antonio d'Andrade, of happy memory, built this College in the form of a Z. It has eight rooms and two storeys (*andares*). And as it was small, we had not lodgings enough to receive guests and some distinguished Moors who came to speak with us, or Dutchmen and Englishmen, who have their factories in the Town and are very kind to us. I, being Visitor of that Mission, added to it two small rooms and a hall for guests, and the Dutch and English themselves gave me for the purpose six or seven hundred rupees in alms. In olden times, we had a very fine church within the walls and precincts ; it was entirely vaulted and had cost eleven or twelve thousand rupees the greater part of which sum had been donated by an Armenian, a rich

---

* *Jogis* are Hindu ascetics ; *Fakir* (*lit.* poor) is a Muhammadan mendicant, the word being frequently used by the old European writers as synonymous with *jogi.*

† The cope used for the *Asperges,* or sprinkling with holy water before the parochial Mass on Sundays, is violet ; the cope used for the blessing of graves is black.

Christian merchant;* but, King Xajan [Shāh Jahān] ordered to destroy the Church on the occasion which I shall relate. King Xajan was very much disturbed by the insults he had received from the Portuguese of Bengala and the natives of the country at Ogoly [Hugli], a sea-board district of those parts. He sent against it a powerful army, destroyed its buildings and the ships in the harbour ; but, all those who escaped death, whether Portuguese or natives, women and children, were caught by the Moors,† and Fr. Morando, who was in our College of Agra on that occasion, told me that they numbered upwards of four thousand souls. All entered that City as prisoners to be presented to the King, and the greater number of them, of the men at least, came two by two, with iron rings round their necks and chains.‡ The King took as his slaves many of the chief men, and the white women he ordered to be taken to his Mal,§ or women's quarter; the rest of the men he distributed among various Umbraos,|| and the greater number of these people fell away, and he ordered to circumcise them, to which some consented for fear of the various kinds of death they threatened them with, others out of love for their wives, who were scattered about in the Mal of King and of the Umbraos. Even so, there were many who

---

* Khwaja Martinus. This gift of money for the church is not alluded to in Fr. Joao de Velasco's letter. At any rate, Fr. Botelho does not say that John Philip de Bourbon and Lady Juliana built the Agra Church of 1604. Tradition says, moreover, that John Philip de Bourbon and Lady Juliana were both buried in the Agra Church. Cf. Fr. Felix, O.C., p. 204 *n.* 26, in *Catholic Calendar* for Agra. . . .1907. The tradition must be utterly wrong, for Lady Juliana died before 1598, *i.e.,* before any church is heard of at Agra. Lady Juliana da Costa, her namesake, was buried in the present Agra Church, having died in 1732. (Cf. GENTIL, *Memoires sur l'Indoustan,* Paris 1822, pp. 367-380). This appears to be the cause of the confusion. There is no inscription over Lady Juliana da Costa's grave.

† Some 3,000 escaped to Saugor Island, at the mouth of the Hugli, but many of these may have been caught, like the rest, subsequently.

‡ In the beginning of July 1633.

§ Not an unusual form of the word *mahal*: mansion, seraglio. *Mahal-sara*: the inner or female apartments of a mansion.

|| For *umara,* the Arabic plural of *amir.* In old European accounts it is used as a singular for a lord or grandee of the Moghul Court Cf. *Hobson-Jobson,* s.v. omrah.

did not renounce their faith, because they were not pressed so much. And there were so many of those of Bengala who, on Sundays and Feast-days, assembled near the College to enter the Church and hear Mass, and they made such a noise and quarrelled so much among themselves before entering, that as Fr. Morando told me, even at the door of the *Misericordia* or in the *Rua Direita* (Straight Road) of Goa, they did not quarrel or shout as much as there. Seeing this, the Cassiz and the Mulnas [*sic*],* the masters of the law of Muhammad, went to King Xajan, asking him to remedy such disorders. The Firinguis, they said, were living in his own court with as much freedom as if they had been in their own country, all of which brought contempt upon the law of Muhammad professed by his Majesty and his vassals. Hereupon the King felt roused to action. He ordered at once his officers to destroy our Church, and the Fathers were told to leave the College.† They lodged for some months in a *sarai* [mansion, inn] near the City, and the King would have sent them all to Goa but for the intervention of the King's father-in-law, Acafacan [Asaf Khān], our friend, as I said in its own place. The Church destroyed, the King signed a new *formao* [far-mān] thanks to Acafacan. It allowed the Fathers to return to the same College, but not to build a Church. It granted us only to make a house within our compound, where we might teach the Doctrine and instruct our Christians, as we did in our country ; but it forbade our making Christians of the Moors ; otherwise, we should be considered *gunegares*,‡ or liable to any penalty the King might decree. As for the Church, the Fathers built in the place of

---

* *Qashish* or *qasis*, a Muhammadan priest ; *maula* (Arab.), *mulla* (Hind.), a learned man, a teacher, a doctor of the law. Perhaps the word *mulna* (in the text) represents *maulana* (*lit.* our lord), a title given to persons respected for learning, a doctor. But, is likely that a long *a* would be slurred over?

† Cf. Bernier (Constable's edn., p. 287) : "Chah-Jehan . . . .depriv-ed them of their pension, and destroyed the church at *Lahor* and the greater part of that of *Agra*, totally demolishing the steeple, which contained a clock heard in every part of the city." This is not quite accurate. The church at Agra was entirely destroyed. Was there a clock or a bell?

‡ *Gunahgar* or *gunahkar*=criminal.

old one, a ground-floor with a terrace above, something quite big enough to have in it the Divine Offices, Mass, etc., as I have said.* Concerning the King's order in his *formao* that we should make no Christians of the Moors, we are in no danger of falling under such sentence, because, even without the King's order, no Moor becomes a Christian in those parts, however much the Fathers may speak to them—as they always do, when occasion offers—about the things of our holy faith, or the errors of their accursed sect. Many come to our College at times out of curiosity, not from any wish of discussing with us. And I shall tell here in passing what answer a distinguished and intelligent Moor gave to one of our Fathers after a long discussion and explanation of the mysteries of our holy faith. 'Padre Gi,'† *i.e.*, Senhor Padre, I see very well by what you have told me that your law is better than ours; but I find it impossible for me to keep, and so, good-bye.'

"Both from a spiritual and temporal point of view, this destruction of Ogoly and the large number of captives brought to Agra was like a thunderbolt lighting upon our Christianity of Mogol. From a temporal point of view: because a large number of the common sort was without means, the Umbraos

---

* This must be the old Cathedral of Agra, now the native chapel, *minus* the additions made under Father Francis Xavier Wendel (1769, 1772) and Bishop Pezzoni (1835), additions attested and traceable by the inscriptions on the walls. The cupola over the sanctuary must be one of the later improvements.

Fr. J. de Castro writes to the General (Agra, Apr. 16, 1637): "It is true that he [Shah Jahan] obliged us to destroy the two churches of Lahor and Agra; still he gave us leave [Dec. 8, 1635] to erect for our use another house in the above-said place of the Church of Agra, as in fact we have done, building two or three rooms which serve us very well for our purpose. There we celebrate at present the divine offices, and say Mass in such a way that the men on the one side, and the women on the other, hear it without being seen by one another. Every day, after the Masses, we collect the sacred vestments and whatever might give a clue to this." The new building referred to served as chapel. The first Mass was said in it on Sept. 8, 1636. (*MS. Letter of Fr. de Castro to the General,* Sept. 17, 1636). The openings still seen in the walls may have been used as hiding-places, and the rings in the ceiling may have held the curtains hiding the women.

† *Ji* : sir.

taking only the captives from Bengala, both men and women, who could be of use to them. Therefore, as they were so many and the Fathers could not help our poor Christians and the new arrivals, misery and poverty drove many of the latter to become renegades, while the others were helped by the Fathers. From a spiritual point of view : because so many of them apostatized, nay—for our sins, alas !—Portuguese of the flower of Portugal. All these were a bad example to our Christians. Add also to the Kings's and Mulnas' fury in destroying the Church that, one Holy Saturday morning (through the imprudence of the Christians of Bengala, who fancied they were at home) there was to be seen hanging in the street of our College an effigy of Judas, a mannikin of straw with turban and *cabaya*, when, lo ! in came without delay the Cassiz and the Mulnas, fuming with anger, and saying that the Christians had hanged their Muhammad. Reason as we might, there was no persuading them that the figure was that of Judas, and that some thoughtless Christian* had done it, whom they were welcome to punish soundly. And I have said why King Xajan got so angry, and which were his reasons for ordering the destruction of the Church of the Agra College.

'We have also in the City of Laor a very large house containing two small halls, a room, and a very fine *varanda*. Below the *varanda*, on the ground-floor, the place is very convenient to allow the Christians, who are found in that City, to hear Mass, when now and again one of Ours goes there, or while he resides there, when the King goes there with his Court.† We are very well known in the City of Laor, for King Janguir held his Court there ; here lived Fr. Jeronimo Xavier and others, his companions, and King Janguir was so familiar with the Fathers that he would at times come to our house, and during the Christmas season grand cribs were erected with many figures and hydraulic inventions,‡ the King spending much money on it.—At times the Fathers sent to Goa for one of our Brothers to manage the crib. The last who was sent for it was one Martis,§ a very expert lay-brother,

* It will be remembered that the Jesuit Church built at Lahore by Akbar was destroyed at the end of 1635.

† Fountains?

‡ Martins.

who was at Dio [Diu] and thence went to Mogol, when I was a novice.* During his lifetime, Janguir paid for the Fathers' maintenance. Each had daily from him so many rupees: Fr. Hieronimo Xavier had ten rupees a day; another five, another seven, another three, so that the Fathers had plenty for themselves and for giving alms to the poor Christians. King Xajan, his son, continued to pay daily the same sum to the Fathers, until he caused the destruction of the Church we had in Agra †; and he would have continued the expense, if the Fathers of those days had asked him or reminded him of it; but they had very good and just reasons for renouncing it if they received already at Goa the revenues of the foundation for the College of Agra made by our Brother Mirzâ Zulcarane.‡

"To finish this relation, I wish to speak awhile of our Brother Mirzâ Zulcarane, the founder of the College of Agra, and the column of that Christianity; and, if Fr. Morando had lived after the Mirzâ's death,§ he might have written a relation of many pages on the life and exemplary conduct of this good Christian. I shall mention and relate here only some things, which, while I was in the College of Agra, I heard sometimes related by Fr. Francisco Morando, who during 22 years, when Mirza Zulcarane was in the King's *lascar*,|| followed him to Bengala, Cabul, Laor and Multan, and twice he was many years with him at Sambar.¶

---

* This would show that Fr. Botelho entered the Society in India. His name is not in Franco's list of the Jesuits who embarked at Lisbon for the East.

† End of 1635.

‡ The title "brother" is explained by his participation, as founder of the Agra College, in the spiritual merits of the Cociety.

§ Father Morando appears then to have predeceased the Mirza, but we do not know the year of the death of either. Morandi's tomb is not at Agra. If we suppose that he came to Mogor in 1631, it would follow that, as he was 22 years the Mirza's chaplain, he left Mogor in 1653, a year before Fr. Botelho. How many years did he live after that? The Mirza is still heard of in 1652.

|| *Lashkar*: army.

¶ An allusion to his serving under Sultan Shuja in Bengal. Probably, he followed Shah Jahan to Afghanistan in 1648. I do not remember any

"Our Brothêr Mirza Zulcarne was not, as some thought, of Armenian parentage, but the son of a very honourable and powerful Christian merchant, of Alipy nationality and born at Alepo [*sic*], who came with his merchandise to Mogol, to the Court of the Mogol King Hacabar, during the last years of his Reign and Empire. This merchant, during King Janguir's reign, found the climate of the country to his taste, and settled in that Court, and King Janguir married him with one of the Ladies of his Palace, who, it was said, had some Armenian blood in her. She became a Christian with her husband, and bore him two or three sons, who were also baptized by Fr. Hieronimo Xavier, as appears from my calculations.* As this woman could freely enter into the Palace of the King's wives, since she had lived there many years, she took with her Mirza Zulcarane, her first child, a love of a baby, they say, whose baptismal name was Belchior.† The King obtained from the mother that she should leave him in his Palace to be brought up with he young Prince Corrao [Khurram], later Xajan [Shāh Jahān], both being of the same age. However, young Mirza would often speak with his father and mother, who instructed him in the faith, and King Janguir was as fond of this little Mirza as of his own son Corrao, and many times, when he went out, he took him with him in his palanquin. Years rolled by and young Mirza continued to be the object of the King's favours. When Mirza was now 14 years old, the King, in his love for him, wished to make him a Moor and get him circumcised ; but the youth would not agree, saying that he had to keep the law of his father and mother, and that he was a Christian

---

other reference to his having been in Multan. If Fr. Morando was twice with Zul-Qarnain at Sambhar, he must have been there between 1633 and 1642, since the Mirza was in Bengal from 1642 to 1648, and Morando was with him (the second time?)at Sambhar in 1649-51.

* Melchiir : was this an additional baptismal name to that of Goncalo?

† Fr. Botelho is incorrect in many of these details, *e.g.*, when he fancies that Sikandar (senior) came to Mogor at the end of Akbar's reign, that Lady Juliana was alive in Jahangir's reign, that she and her husband were not Christians (does he mean Catholics?) at the time of their marriage, that Fr. erome Xavier baptized them. Like Bernier, he differs from the *Tuzuk-i-Jahangiri* and the earlier Jesuit accounts in stating that, not Akbar but Jahangir influenced Sikandar's marriage with Lady Juliana.

like them. Before the youth's resolution the King's caresses changed to grievous threats. These proving unavailing, there followed cruel strappings and lashes with thongs of camel-hide. The boy was in such a pitiful plight after this scourging that he was brought to death's door.* When he came to and recovered, he disappeared from King Janguir's Palace when they were least on their guard ; but, as the King was so fond of him, he ordered to search for him with every diligence. His parents were dead by this time. At last they found him and brought him back to the King's Palace. The King, taking compassion on him, told him to live happy in his law, since he was so much pleased and satisfied with it.* And Fr. Francisco Morando told me, when relating this, that Mirza was not only a good Christian, but that he had been also a Martyr for Christ. Mirza had aptitudes and talents of a high order. He became such a great poet in the Industane tongue that he had among the Moors the same reputation as a poet as Camois [Camoens] has here with us. He was also a good singer, and he himself put to music the songs which the King made [*sic*].† So, King Janguir was so delighted with him that he kept him always at Court and gave him a very large monthly salary, which allowed him to have his suite and cavalry accompanying him. He grew older, and was upwards of thirty years old, when the King appointed him *Divao* [Divān], or Viceroy of the *Praganâ* [Pargana] of Sambar, of which I have spoken at length in my Relation on the Mogol's greatness.‡ At Sambar, Mirza had a thousand horse and fifteen elephants of his own, and many Christians of Mogol were making large profits under Mirza, because he assisted them in their poverty, favoured them and helped them in everything he could. And he was so liberal that when

* From the* there are several anachronisms. The boy was taken away in 1605 and brought back to Lahore in 1606. Only his mother was dead then.

† Instead of "que fazia ElRey," we expect "que fazia por ElRey" = which he made for the King.

‡ He was *not* upwards of 30 years old when he was appointed to the Parganah of Sambhar, whether the fact occurred in 1614 or in 1619, or, as we have it in the *Tuzuk-i-Jahangiri* (transl. by A. Rogers and H. Beveridge), II. 194, in the beginning of 1621.

one of the King's singers caught the conceits or the tune of the songs he composed, he would there and then present him with a horse. It happened once that he was so pleased with a singer that he gave him an elephant, and, Fr. Morando expressing his surprise at such a grand present, Mirza said: 'Father, reflect that for me to give a horse is like giving a goat, and giving an elephant, like giving a horse.'

"In King Janguir's reign our Brother Mirza Zulcarane lived. many years at Sambar. (Mirza means Lord, and Zulcarane means some arms or badges of Alexander the Great; therefore to say Mirza Zulcarane is as if you said: Lord of Alexander's badges.* This lasted until his son Xajan succeeded him. One of the first acts of the new King was to deprive Mirza Zulcarane of that *Praganâ* and confiscate all he had.† The reason for it was that when Xajan, formerly Corrao, had revolted against his father Janguir, and was passing by Sambar, he told Mirza that he was in need of money, and that he should give him at once a certain number of *leques* [lakhs] of rupees with which to cover his expenses. Mirza refused, on the plea that he had no leave from his father Janguir, to whom he had to give an account of all the money and revenues of the lands under him. Xajan took occasion of this recall him from that place.‡ Mirza

* Zul-Qarnain means two-horned, *bicornutus*. The horns of the bull, not only among the Hebrews and other Semitic races, but in some of the classical Latin authors, are symbolical of strength, power, courage. Col. Jarrett (*Ain,* III, *377n.* 1) says that, according to Tabari, Alexander received this name, because he traversed the world from end to end, the word qarn signifying a horn, a term also applied to the extremities of the universe. The epithet is given to Alexander in the Qoran (Sur. xviii, vv. 82, 84, 92). According to Sale, other opinions of the derivation are that he had two horns to his diadem, or two curls of hair. (On these curls of hair, called *cornua*, see Facciolati—Forcellini's *Totius Latinitatis Lexicon, s.v.* cornu). Scaliger supposes the epithet arose from Alexander's being represented in his coins and statues with horns as the son of Jupiter Ammon, or as being compared by the prophet Daniel (viii. 6) to a he-goat, though there represented with only one horn.

† Perhaps, a confusion with his recall from Gorakhpur is 1632.

‡ During the first five years of Shah Jahan's reign Zul-Qarnain was in favour. Shah Jahan may have raked up in 1632 the grievance here mentioned by Fr. Botelho.

came away to Agra, where he possessed a very fine house along the River.* Mirzâ's enemies represented to the King that, though he had given a good account of himself and paid whatever belonged to the King's crown, he had brought with him his profits amounting to many *leques* of rupees. The King's officers went to his house and dug in many parts of it and of his garden, to find out whether he had hidden any money. Mirza left his house (*se sahio de sua corte*), and came to our College of Agra, whither the King's officers followed to dig with the same diligence our garden and cloisters (? enclosure, *crastas*). Finding nothing, they went away. Mizra was many years in disfavour with the King. Nevertheless, he accompanied him wherever he went, to the hunt or any other enterprise; and, as King Xajan had been as a child brought up in the Palace with Mirza, his suspicions vanished, and, in the year 1649, when I was at Agra, the King reinstated Mirza in the government of Sambar, on condition that he [Mirz] should pay him every year six *leques* of rupees from the salt-revenues. Mirza went back, taking with him, as always, Fr. Francisco Morando. He remained there two years, at the end of which Mirza told King Xajan that, as he was now old † and had no longer the strength to conduct the management of those revenues, he must, if he wished to enhance them, appoint in his place some one more able than himself. The King did as requested. He called Mirza to his Court, assigned a hundred rupees a day as his salary, and dispensed him, as a privilege, from going with him when he travelled. As to Mirza's two sons, the King gave one seven rupees a day, and to the younger five.‡

* If the Mirza's house was close to the river, how could it have been near the house of the Jesuit Fathers, as Tavernier says? Would not this show that Tavernier is mixing up Zul-Qarnain's story with that of another Armenian? The distance to the river is not, however, very great, and Zul-Qarnain's garden may have come close to the Fathers' property.

† He was only sixty. The above passage gives an answer to a remark my friend Mr. H. Beveridge made in one of his letters. He could not, he said, find in the Muhammadan authors any allusion to the Mirza's having been re-employed.

‡ Was his youngest son, Mirza Daniel, born in or before 1638, too young in Fr. Botelho's time (1648-54) to take service under the King?

Even in the poverty to which he now found himself reduced, and though the pay he now received from the King was so small compared with what it used to be, he kept fifty horsemen in his service to accompany him when he went outside. And as he was so devoted to poetry, he composed at every step verses in the King's honour; and, first calling the King's singers to his house, he taught them and sent them to the Palace to sing that night what he had composed. On one occasion, as the King had come from Laor, Prince Darâ Xecut * called Mirza, with whom he was very friendly, and told him: '*Mere bhay, mere bhay,* i.e., my brother, my brother, my father has just come from Laor ; make a *Torpet,*† *i.e.*, a composition in his honour.'—'I am not now in the mood for it,' Mirza answered; 'but, if your father were to become a Christian, I should make a very fine hymn in his honour.' The Prince laughed heartily at the supposition. Eventually, however, Mirza made the song. King Xajan ventured to tell Mirza Zulcarane through a third party that, if he wished to follow the sect of Muhammad, he would let him have Sambar for life. Now it yielded eight *leques* of rupees a year.* To this Mirza answered, 'Go and tell the King that my religion is not so cheap in my eyes that I should barter it against any number of *leques* of rupees.' A good example for those who write with their own blood that they sacrifice their life to the devil in return for a treasure, and in the end they find themselves in a bonfire.

"Fr. Francisco Morando would speak at length about Mirza's Christianity. He knew him very intimately, having

---

It is said further that Zul-Qarnain saw his (three?) sons and daughter honourably married in his lifetime, and that the youngest Daniel, survived his father.

* Prince Dara Shikoh, Shah Jahan's eldest son. Possibly, Fr. Botelho refers to a song composed by the Mirza, at Dara Shikoh's suggestions in 1651, when Shah Jahan returned from Kashmir. *to* Lahore.

† *Dhurpad*: a kind of song in the Hindi or Braj bhasha dialect (*Forbes*). "The Dhdrpad (Dhrdva-pada) consists of four rhythmical lines without any definite length of words or syllables." *Ain,* Jarrett's transl. III, p. 251 and 251 *n.* 2.

‡ Therefore, it left Zdl-Qarnain in 1649-51 a profit of 2 lakhs, and a larger margin of profit during his earlier tenures of administration.

been 22 years his companion. Every day Mirza recited Our Lady's rosary, heard Mass, and, what is more, when he was travelling about with the King, Fr. Mòrando had to say Mass daily in his tent. And it happened often that the King's *lascar* was already moving when the Mass began; still, they would not touch Mirza's tent before Mass was finished. His intelligence was very sharp and keen. Sometimes he spoke to Fr. Morando about predestination in a way which astonished him. Once, for instance, a poor *basar* [bazar] woman passing near him, he said: 'Father, how have I deserved that God should make me a Christian in preference to that poor woman who passes there, and who, if she dies without baptism, will surely go to hell?' Fr. Morando said sometimes that Mirza had never known any other woman than his own wife; as a young man and a widower, he was without reproach, a rare thing for one who lived all his life at the Court of so mighty a King and a Moor too, where liberty is so great and the occasions of offending God are so many. It is the custom, as I said above, that all the Umbraos and noblemen (*fidalgos*) should go twice a day to pay their respects to the King. Mirza did it often too, not that he was obliged—since the King had dispensed him—but when he liked. One day as some of the Umbraos were in the King's presence (one of them saw Mirza entering the court of the Palace Gate. 'Sire,' he said to the King, 'Mirza Zulcarane is coming along there; but he looks as if he had drunk wine to-day.'—'Then,' said the King, "tell the head porter (these are always persons of high rank) that he must not let him in, and let him tell him to come another day, for we have no time to-day.' The porter obeyed, and Mirza returned home. But, a few days later, when Mirza was in the King's presence with other nobles, the one who had accused him to the King for being drunk, happened to enter at the Palace Gate, and a noble, a friend of Mirza's, having related the story, told him: 'Here comes the fellow who, some days ago, said to the King that you were drunk. From his ways it seems that he has indulged in wine, himself. So, tell the King, too, that such a one looks tipsy.'—'You people are blind,' answered Mirza. 'You do not know the law of the Christians. My law teaches me that, if one strike you on the one cheek, you must offer him also the other.* You must not be vindictive, but must do good to those who do you evil.' Mirza was well read in our Gospels, the Psalms and Holy Scripture,† which he had in Persian ; and, when occasions offered themselves, he would often, and to good purpose, make use of those weapons.

"A certain ecclesiastic placed in authority went to the City of Agra, while I was in that Mission, to see whether he could expel us from it. He made every effort for this purpose, went to the other chief towns, as Laor and Dely, where the King then already, was with his Court, and interested some Umbraos to get them to influence the King and convert him to his evil intentions through defamatory papers and letters against us. It was, perhaps, one of the most violent storms that burst over us from the time that we settled in that Great Kingdom. What happened, and what he did against us, God knows, and we who bore it. It is a very long story, and, if I tried to put it in order in writing, I should fill more than four sheets of paper. Suffice it to say that finally, by means of a quite baseless calumny, he succeeded through some one else in getting the King to imprison for more than a month and a half, say about two months, Fr. Henrique Buzeu [Buseo, Busi] (God rest his soul !) ; but God, who defends the cause of truth, allowed that everything should become clear, and the Father came out of prison with great credit to himself and honour to the Society, the King considering as a base slander the charges brought against the Father. After this ecclesiastic had done what he could, he happened to speak at Agra with one born at Cochy [Cochin] and married at Ogoly [Hugli], who, as I said, came with the other captives. He was a half-caste, but of good extraction (? character, *de bom natural*) ; and, though the King's prisoner, his pay was big enough to let him live in comfort. I do not name him, because he is well known and my story does not require my naming him.

* The reference is either to St. Matth. v. 39 or to St. Luge vi. 29.

† *J.A.S.B.*, 1896, pp. 95, 113, shows what parts of the Old and New Testaments Zul-Qarnain may have possessed in Persian. In 1912 I found in the Catholic Cathedral Library of Agra a copy of Fr. J. Xavier's Persian translation of the four Gospels.

6

This ecclesiastic went often to the renegade's house, and once he told him: 'Senhor so-and-so, do you think that with four fellows of my pluck I could get rid of those Paulists?' The apostate replied very sensibly, 'But, since you see that the Fathers are four, why do you try what you cannot succeed in?'—'I should worst them,' said the ecclesiastic, but for the help they get from Mirza Zulcarane.' Another person from Bengala, who had been circumcised, and was intimate with Mirza, told him the above story. 'Tell this ecclesiastic,' was Mirza's answer, 'that, if we had not the help of the cross, the devil would get the better of the whole world.' What is worse in this story is that, when this clergyman came to Dely, Mirza gave him an alms of a hundred rupees.

"King Xajan was in the Kingdom of Cassimir [Kashmir], where, owing to the said clergyman's false and slanderous information, he ordered to seize Father Buzeu, then with Mirza.* The King started from Cassimir for Laor, and the roads were so bad that he left the greater part of the army in Cassimir with orders to follow the next day. Father Buzeu was yet in prison, and Mirza Zulcarane came to speak with His Highness. Immediately the King told them to stop his state-conveyance or *Tactarabandi*,† as it is called,—a very large litter, *andor*) carried by 16 to 20 men, on the top of which is a silver *cherola.* To the Umbraos near him, among others Alimardan ['Ali Mardan Khan] (about whom I said much a propos of the Mogol King's greatness), he said, '*Sastao,*' *i.e.*, stop, 'and let it be said that King Xajan orders to stop his train in order to speak with Mirza Zulcarane. The latter coming in the King's presence, said loudly and angrily, for he was naturally irritable, 'Sire, how can you, on so glaring a lie, leave my Padre in prison? Say that he must be free, and here I give you my head to cut off any time that they prove what they accuse the Father of.' Mirza was so much in earnest that the King told him, 'Go back to Cassamir, and tell Sadulacan [Sa'dullah Khan], the King's chief Umbrao, *et secundus a Rege* [and next in power to the King], to bring

* Events of 1651.

† *Takht-i-rawan*: a kind of sedan chair.

the Father with him to Laor, when he comes.' The moment Mirza had turned to go away, the King said to the Umbraos near him, 'Did you not notice how angry and vexed Mirza was when speaking to me? Don't be surprised; I know the man, and I must bear with him, while life lasts, since we were brought up together as boys in the Palace.*

"Mirza Zulcarane was married with Dona Ilena [Helena], whose grave—a very fine one—I saw at Laor in a garden which Mirza owned there.† She bore him three sons and a daughter. The eldest was called Mirza Observam; the 2nd, Mirza Eres ; the 3rd and youngest, Mirza Daniel.‡ Mirza saw his sons and daughter very honourably married during his lifetime. One day, speaking to one of his great friends, a certain Umbrao, who had easy access to the King, Mirza Zulcarane asked him, 'Will you get the King to appoint my sons *Mancebdares* [mansabdars], *i.e.*, captains of three

---

* Fr. Busi says in a letter to the General (Lahore, 17th December 1651) that he had left prison some days before and that, as the Rector [Fr. Anthony Botelho] had written on the subject, he did not enlarge on it. A letter of Fr. Botelho's (Agra, 20th January 1652) to Fr. Bento Ferreira, Goa, states that he had left Agra for Lahore on November 8th, 1651, to obtain Fr. Busi's liberty. Much prudence was required. Bishop Dom Matheus was still in Lahore, ready to leave for Agra, Surat, Mocha. Fr. Botelho had to conceal himself in the suburbs of Lahore until Bishop Matheus was gone. Prince Dara Shikoh suggested to Mirza Zul-Qarnain, then at Lahore, to compose a piece of poetry to soothe Shah Jahan. The result was obtained. Fr. Busi was restored to liberty on the feast of St. Francis Xavier, 1651 (*i.e.*, December 3rd).

† Her death is announced in a letter by Fr. Francis Morando, S.J. (Agra, September 15th, 1638) as having taken place some days before. May not Mirza Zul-Qarnain's mother, Lady Juliana, have been buried there too? She had died at Lahore in 1598.

‡ Mirza Observam would be John Baptist, Mirza Eres (Irij, Irich) would be Gaspar, and Mirza Daniel (Danyal) would be Michael. The Mirza's son, who is mentioned in the Annual Letter of 1619 as having died, could not have been Mirza Observam, as Sir R. C. Temple suggests (*Travels of Peter Mundy,* II 376); he would be rather the boy who is spoken of in 1619 as born after the death of the Mirza's then only child. I do not know what Christian name Observam represents. It may have something to do with the visit to Sambhar in 1624 of the Franciscans or Observantines. Clara, too, the name of Zul-Qarnain's daughter, recalls a Franciscan Saint. Irij is a Muhammadan name (see *e.g.*, BLOCHMANN, *Ain,* I. 339, 491, 511).

hundred horse, a dignity leading to that of Umbraos?'* The Umbrao answered, 'I shall ask the King to appoint your sons not only Mancebdares, but even Umbraos, provided they are willing to embrace the law of Muhammad',—'then don't' said he, and get away! Our law is so precious that not all the riches of the whole world can be compared with it!' The Umbrao stood confounded. Mirza's two eldest married sons died during his lifetime ; the last survived him ; but (either deception or lack of judgment, for he seemed at times eccentric and ill-balanced) he let himself be circumcised to follow the sect of Muhammad. It did not last long, however. Recognising the error, which he, the son of such a great Christian, had fallen into, he felt intensely grieved, and, making a very big cross, he took it upon his shoulders, and, with a rope around his neck, dragged it about the streets of the City of Dely, confessing his sin aloud, and begging God's mercy. He was reconciled to the Church, and died shortly after in the faith, and I doubt not that God granted him this grace through his father's praying in heaven that his house and family might be spared such a slur.

"I have not said all I could about the Mission of Mogol. I leave the rest to the usual Annuals which relate things of great glory to God and credit to that Christianity. Comparing it with many others of the Society throughout this East, we can say of it : *Pusilus* [*sic*] *grex* [little flock], as far as numbers go, but we can give it the first place for fidelity to the practices of our holy law. May Our Lord in His infinite mercy open the eyes of that so vast heathenism and Moordom, and bring them into the way of the true salvation."

The Latin abridgment of Fr. Botelho's *Rellacao da Christandade que temos no Reino do Gram Mogol* is evidently the work of a scholar in Europe, who, striking the panegyrical note, indulges in some oratorical embellishments of his own.

* *Mansabdars* were of many ranks. "From the remarks and quotations of Blochmann it would seem that *Mansabdars*, from the commandant of 1,000 upwards, were styled *umara-i-kibar, or umara-i-'izam*, "Great Amirs"; and these would be the omrahs properly." *Hobson-Jobson*, *s.v.* omrah.

It was natural that he should seize upon the similarity of name between the Mirza and Alexander; but, "a Numa in peace, an Alexander in war, and a Cæsar in both" are flourishes which the sober historian would have avoided. In the light of the documents we have handled Zul-Qarnain appears to us a good administrator, and a great Christian hero, not as a great soldier.

For the sake of completeness, let the latinist speak.

"But, as all the success we have had in Mogor, the flourishing condition of the Christian religion, all the revenues possessed by the Agra College, are (after God) due entirely and solely to Mirza Zulcarnem, whom the Society adopted as one of its brethren, it behoves us to dwell awhile in just praise of him. This man, I mean Mirza Zulcarnem, was as noble in birth as illustrious by his deeds and renowned for his Christian piety. An Amir (*Umbraus*) in dignity he was a Numa in peace, an Alexander in war, a Cæsar in both, brave in warfare, meek in peace, upright in his conduct, a model of valour, a pattern of gentleness, a champion of religion ; the Mogors honoured him for his greatness, the world for his renown, and religion for his virtue. The Mogor Kings owe him a thousand victories, a thousand nobles thank him for his benefits, while the Society of Jesus owes him great affection. For the Mogul he was a strenuous leader, for the faith a powerful champion, for the Society a faithful friend and brother. Through him warlike courage flourished, the Christian religion increased, and the Society had cause to rejoice. This is the man who, although sprinkled with holy water in his cradle, became the delight of King Janguir for his foreign beauty, so that the King himself, a thing that is rare among the Mogors, had the boy at his own table. He, at the age of twelve, saw the King's affection turned into wrath and endured many and severe stripes because he obstinately refused to abjure the Roman faith, so much so that Father Francisco Morando called him a glorious martyr of Christ. As a young man he possessed a very subtle wit and wrote verses in his mother-tongue with such elegance that the King was greatly delighted thereby. In rewarding singers he was so liberal that he frequently gave them as recompense a horse or an elephant. He was wholly of a noble nature, ready to forgive injuries and yielding to the wishes of others. He was offered by the King the highest honours and a million a year, if he would abjure the true religion. But he preferred to be afflicted with the people of God and to live less rich, so that he might win the wealth of heaven and become a partaker and heir of everlasting life. He it was who turned back upon their author the poisoned darts aimed against the Society by an ecclesiastic high in honour, and delivered the Mogor Missionaries from grievous punishment. It is he, lastly, who freed Father Henry Busi (*Buseum*) from undeserved bonds, and with Christian freedom addressing the King, offered his head to the sword if the sentence on the Father were to be carried into effect.

"He married Helena, a distinguished lady, and had three sons by her, Mirsa [Mirza] Observam [John Baptis], Mirsa Eres [Irij, Irich, Gaspar], Mirsa Daniel [Danyal, Michael], and he might have seen them all advanced to high honour during his lifetime, to the dignity of Mancebedars and Umbraos, if they embraced the law of Mahomet. This the King firmly promised him."

Fr. Manoel Figueredo, S. J., a Missionary in Mogor and a contemporary of Bibi Anna Dessa, the great grand-daughter of Mirza Zul-Qarnain, has left us a short account of Zu-l-Qarnain. Written as it was 75 years or so after Zu-l-Qarnain's death, it distorts already considerably the real facts. It must rest on the traditions current in 1735, since, as the Father remarks, the earliest documents of the Agra Mission had been plundered.

"On the death of Akbar, Joanquir [Jahangir] ascended the throne and reigned 23 years. During his reign, a young

* "The Latin has *ad millionem annui reditus*, which may be read to mean a *koti* (crore) a year (really 10,000,000), which at that time, as a monetary expression, meant Rs. 2,500 in cash. Whatever may have been at times in India the meaning of a *koti* of rupees, our latinist had in view "a million of annual revenue." A million of what? It matters little : we understand that the 8 lakhs a year which passed through the Mirza's hands (1649-51), 2 or 3 lakhs of which were his balance of profits, represented a million in European parlance, and 8 lakhs seem to have been offered him as the price of apostacy.

Armenian, born of Christian parents and called Tulkarnet [*sic*; Zul-Qarnain] was brought up at the court. As the boy advanced in years, his zeal for the faith grew greater, although the Emperor often tried with manifold caresses and repeated menaces to gain him over to his sect. Once, pointing with his finger to the highest tower of the Royal Palace he threatened the youthful Christian athlete that, unless he abandoned the law of Christ, he would have him thrown from the top. The boy immediately ran away from the Emperor and mounted the tower. After some hours the Emperor asked for his Tulkarnet; and, being told that he had run away for fear, he ordered to make a search for him and bring him to his presence. They found him on the said tower, and, as the Emperor wished to know why he had fled thither, the boy said quite eagerly, 'To be the quicker ready for Heaven, when Your Majesty would give the order to throw me down.'—Are you not afraid of death, then?' asken the King. 'No,' answered the youth, 'for who dies for God lives for ever in Heaven.'* This answer pleased the King so greatly that he prevailed on his sons to accept Tulkarnet as their brother; as for him, he made him later an Amire or Ombrau, that is, a Lord of the first rank, and gave him quite generously the revenues belonging to that dignity.

"Now, Tulkarnet received some information about the zeal of our Missionaries; he asked, therefore, the Reverend Fr. Provincial of the Goa Province to send him some Priests. His request was willingly granted and he received them with the greatest affection.† Tulkarnet founded for them from his income a College at Agra, whence soon many Apostles were sent through the Kingdom, who laid the foundation-stone of the Mogor Mission; all this with the Emperor's consent, which the cherished courtier‡ had obtained from him.

"After Joanquir's death, his son Sachajan ascended the throne. He was as well inclined towards Tulkarnet as his

* This story of the tower is not to be found in the very ample letters of the Jesuits between 1600-1610.

† A flagrant anachronism, as we know.

‡ The cherished courtier (*der beliebte Hoff-Herr*) was either Zul-Qarnain or 'Asaf Khan, the former rather.

father had been. Once this Emperor sent a Jesuit from the town of Lahor into misery because he had disputed too hotly with the Mahometans on religious matters. As soon as Tulkarnet was informed of this, he went to the Emperor and asked him where was his Birtzadak (which means a son of the most just). The Emperor answered that he had fled from the country. Thereupon Tulkarnet shook a pillar of the Emperor's throne and said with great earnestness: 'What is this throne of Solomon at last coming to?'* Hereupon the Emperor marvelled, remarking full well that Tulkarnet refused him his help for the protection of his throne. He promised him therefore at once that the Missionary would come back as soon as possible to the kingdom.† What I have just related happened in the presence of the Ombraus, or chief Courtiers, and they seized this opportunity to accuse the good Tulkarnet of leze-majesty. But the Emperor told them, 'Tulkarnet has at heart the welfare of the kingdom; hence, he takes the liberty to warn us of danger; no one else is allowed to do this.'

"As long as this pillar of the faith was standing, Christianity too stood firm; but no sooner had Tulkarnet descended into the grave, advanced in years and redolent with the perfume of his excellent virtues, than the fabric of the Church began to shake, and the Grandees of the Kingdom who were devoted to Mahomet dared again to harass us: one of them went so far as to take possession of our College at Agra, on the plea that all Tulkarnet's property reverted to the Emperor's exchequer. To avoid a greater evil, the Fathers were obliged to submit to this injustice and to hide for a time in secret corners. However, they trusted always in the Providence of Almighty God, and soon they experienced its effects. For the Ombrao, against all expectation, called the Fathers and told them to occupy their College again. The Mother of God, he said, to whom the Church of Agra is dedicated, had appeared to him and had threatened him with death, unless he restored their house to the Missionaries. The College had

* The meaning seems to be: "What has become of the Emperor's wisdom and justice?"

† The story may be a reminiscence of what happened to Fr. Busi (*alias* Uwens), as we saw in Fr. Botelho's narrative.

been robbed of many things, but the Fathers had to keep silent about the plunder and consider themselves happy that they had recovered a fixed abode."*

With this narrative, we bring to a close the interesting life history of Mirza Zul-Qarnain, the greatest Armenian that lived and died in India during the glorious reign of the great Moguls —Akbar, Jehangeer and Shah Jehan. By his integrity, uprightness, intelligence, high sense of duty and administrative powers of a very high order, the Armenian lad, brought up in the royal palace, endeared himself to his royal masters and found a niche in the history of the Mogul Empire. The Armenians in India should be justly proud of such an illustrious countryman who with the characteristic tenacity of his race, remained loyal to the faith of his ancestors, despite the persecutions of Jehangeer and Shah Jehan, living and dying a good Christian in the service of a non-tolerant Mohammedan government.

* This story of the occupation of the College may be a corrupt account of what happened, during the Mirza's lifetime, in 1635.

CHAPTER IV.

DOMINGO PIRES *

THE ARMENIAN INTERPRETER AT THE COURT OF AKBAR

Very little is known about this Armenian linguist, who played an important part at Akbar's Court as a Portuguese interpreter, Portuguese being then the only European language prevalent in India. But where could he have acquired that language? Probably at Goa which was the seat of the Portuguese government in India, or at Mylapur, a Portuguese town near Madras on the Coromandel Court, since there were Armenians in both the places, engaged in trade, during the reign of Akbar and his predecessors. He was employed by Akbar as the interpreter to the embassy he sent to Goa in September 1579, inviting Jesuits to his Court, for the purposes of religious discussions.

Akbar addressed letters to the Portuguese Viceroy, Don Lewis d' Athaide, to the Archbishop and to the Provincial Roderich Vincente, to the following effect :—

"To the Chief Padri, in the name of the Lord.
Letter of Jalal-ud-din Mohamad Akbar,
King by the honour of God.

Head Father of the College of St. Paul, know that I am very well disposed towards you. I am sending Abdullah, my ambassador, and Dominic Perez (an Armenian Christian, the interpreter) with the request that you will send me two learned Fathers and the books of the Law, especially the Gospel, that I may know the Law and its excellence. For I desire to know it. I beg, therefore, earnestly that they may come with these envoys, and bring the books of the Law. And the Fathers may be sure that I shall receive them most

---

* Domingo is not an Armenian name, neither is Pires. He must have assumed that name, which is Portuguese, when living either at Goa or at Mylapur which in those days were two important centres of commerce in Portuguese India.

courteously, and entertain them most handsomely. When I have learnt the Law sufficiently to appreciate its excellence, then may they depart at their pleasure, with an escort, and honoured with abundant rewards. Let them come in perfect security. I take their defence on myself."

The Father Provincial was delighted at the invitation, and Father Rudolf Aquavira (son of the Duke of Arragon and Atria) and Father Anthony Montserrat, a Catalan, were appointed to accompany the embassy. To these it was thought well to add Father Henriquez, a Mohammedan convert from Ormuz, in the Persian Gulf, a man of great piety, but of slight learning, whose knowledge of Persian, however, though not very extensive, would be of great use, Persian being the language of Akbar's Court. Father Rudolf was appointed Superior.

The caravan left Goa for Surat on the 17th November 1579 and after a tedious journey of over three months, it reached Fatehpur Sikri, the residence of Akbar, on the 28th February 1580. The Fathers were received in audience immediately with all cordiality and after they had gone to their lodgings, Akbar sent them plates full of gold Mohurs for their acceptance, but they declined the present with courtesy.

The following day, the Fathers were again admitted to audience in the magnificent Diwan-i-Khass, which is still standing amongst the ruins of the deserted capital (Fatehpur Sikri) and they brought as a present to Akbar the new Royal Polygot Bible of Plantyn, printed for Philip II of Spain (1569-1572) magnificently bound in seven volumes. Akbar accepted this valuable present with great respect and taking off his head dress (turban), he kissed the sacred volumes and placed them on his head one after another, showing greater reverence for those containing the Gospel. The books were then carefully taken away and placed in his private chamber.

Abdul Fazl, the learned author of the *Ain-i-Akbari,* (the Institutes of Akbar) gives the following account of the first arrival of Christian Missionaries to Akbar's Court, in the *Akbar Nama* (History of Akbar):

> "1580 At this time Padree Farmatiun (sic) arrived at the Imperial Court from Goa, and was re-

> ceived with great distinction. He was a man of much learning and eloquence. A few intelligent youngmen were placed under him for instruction, so that provision might be made for procuring translations of Greek authors, and of extending knowledge. With him came a number of Europeans and Armenians who brought silks of China and goods of other countries, which were deemed worthy of his Majesty's inspection."

It can be clearly seen from the above that there were Armenian merchants in Goa at that time engaged in the China silk trade and "goods of other countries".

But we have digressed. Domingo Pires, the Armenian, continued to act as interpreter to the Jesuit Fathers at Akbar's Court before they became conversant with the Persian language.

It appears from the Jesuit letters of the period that the Armenian interpreter was a great favourite with Akbar for he took an active part in the marriage service of Domingo Pires when the matrimonially inclined Armenian, breaking the barriers of the strict conservatism of his race, married an Indian woman contrary to the custom then prevailing amongst the Armenians.

According to the Jesuit letters, Akbar assisted at his marriage on the 24th September 1582, the Emperor translating to the Indian woman Father Rudolf Aquaviva's Persian Sermon, and sitting down afterwards with his children and two of his principal chiefs at a banquet *a la Portugaise,* in the Fathers' house.

In 1595, Domingo Pires accompanied from Goa to Lahore the Fathers of the third Mission. As the Fathers of the third Mission were still ignorant of Persian, he acted as their interpreter before the King.

In 1596, we find him at Lahore with his daughter. The Jesuit Fathers, Jerome Xavier, Pinheiro and Brother Benedict Goes, were living in 1595-1596 near Akbar's Palace, within the Lahore Fort. The Fathers' house was along the river, and, when the King went to his pleasure-boat, he passed sometimes that side with his daughters, one of them a marriageable girl ; and, what is more, he would call the Fathers and converse with them, while in his daughter's company, a breach of Moslem etiquette. "In this matter", the Fathers write, "the King and the Prince [Celim, later Jehangeer] have great confidence in us, and, when we go to see the Prince, we go with his permission along the river, under the window of his wives, and sometimes, when we come back, the daughter of the King [Akbar] calls out to us from above, 'Oh, Padri, Padri ! By the sign of the Holy Cross, God deliver us' ! And it seems she learned this from a small girl, the daughter of Domingo Piz [Pirez], an Armenian, who brought us from Goa, and who [the girl] is with the Queen the greater part of the year."

It is pleasant however to see that the young daughter of Domingo Pires, from his Indian wife, was brought up as a good Christian and taught to have a deep and a reverential love for the Holy Cross.

In this connection it may be mentioned that the Armenians are, by nature, deeply religious, as their whole history and literature show. It has been a religion of the heart, not of the head. It may be remembered that during the past forty years, over a million Armenians have laid down their lives in Turkey for the love of the Holy Cross and the Christian religion, whilst Christian Europe witnessed the organised wholesale massacres of poor and defenceless Armenians with perfect equanimity and apathy. And this forcibly reminds us of the fulminations of that single-handed champion of freedom and justice, the late William Ewart Gladstone, the "Grand old Man" of England, who in an autograph letter addressed to the writer of these lines, dated Hawarden, May 1, 1896, gave expression to the following vehement sentiments of righteous indignation. The veteran statesman wrote :—

"I continue to regard with acute pain and shame the thiumph of wickedness in Turkey over the whole civilised and Christian world. I know of no similar disgrace upon record.

The only and limited mitigation of these feelings is found in a deep reverence for all those Armenians who have preferred their faith to their life."

And it was this great Englishman who had once said that "to serve Armenia is to serve civilization."

CHAPTER V.

PRINCE JOHN PHILIP BOURBON
AT
THE COURT OF THE GREAT MOGUL

During the reign of the illustrious Akbar, justly styled the Great, a contemporary of Queen Elizabeth of England and of Shah Abhas the Great of Persia, there arrived at the Mogul Court, between the years 1557 and 1559, a French prince, John Philip Bourbon of Navarre, a scion of the royal house of France. He told the Emperor that having been taken captive by Turkish pirates, during a voyage he had made in company with his family priest, who was his preceptor, he had been taken to Egypt as a prisoner. This happened in 1541 when he was fifteen years old. Once in Egypt, the young prince soon gained, by his affable manners, the esteem of the sovereign of the country who took him in his service and gave him a command in his army. He was again made a prisoner in a war with the Abyssinians, but his Christian religion, his noble lineage, his lively intelligence and his great learning soon raised him to a high position in that Christian country, which a highly civilized Christian nation of to-day is trying to crush and subjugate by sheer force of superior arms.

By reason of his high position in that country, he succeeded, under certain pretexts, to sail to India in one of those Abyssinian vessels which at that time kept up continued relations with the Konkan coast.

Landing at Broach, he heard of the splendour and the magnificence of the Court of the Great Mogul and deserting the Abyssinian fleet, he went forthwith to Agra.

Akbar, who always welcomed distinguished foreigners at his Court, was struck by his gracious manners, his noble bearing and his vivid intelligence. He immediately offered him a command in his army and a little later he appointed him master of the guns and conferred on him the title of a *Mansabdar*, and being desirous of keeping the prince at his court permanently, Akbar gave him in marriage an Armenian lady, Juliana by name,* who was employed at that time as a lady doctor and in medical charge of the Emperor's seraglio.

This lady, who according to some writers was the sister of Akbar's Christian wife, built the *first* Christian Church at Agra, where according to a well-founded tradition in the family records of the Bourbons in India, both Lady Juliana and her husband, John Philip Bourbon were buried.

The above is confirmed by a note in the Agra Mission Archives in which it is stated that "the old Church was built by Philip Bourbon of the House of Navarree and his wife Juliana, an Armenian lady who was in medical charge of the Emperor's Harem. They are both buried in the Church itself, probably the epitaphs are in Armenian."

This Church was pulled down in 1636 by the order of the Mogul Emperor Shah Jehan and rebuilt afterwards. The present Native Chapel, in the compound of St. Peter's Roman Catholic Cathedral, stands on the site of the old Church erected by Philip Bourbon and his Armenian wife, Lady Juliana, in 1562.

We have searched for their graves both inside and outside the Church, but they are not there, although they are said to have been buried in the Church they built.

There must have been other graves in that old Church with tombstones bearing inscriptions in Armenian, which have disappeared, with the exception of one which has been used as a wisdom-sill in the dome, partly embedded in the mall. The date on that tombstone is 1671. It is to the memory of one Sookias, the son of Thariguleh, from the great city of Valarshapat in the district of Erivan in Armenia.

---

* Juliana seems to have been a favourite name among the Armenian lady doctors in Akbar's seraglio. The wife of Iskandar, Mirza Zul-Qarnain's mother, as we have seen, was also a Juliana, and she too was a lady doctor in Akbar's seraglio according to the Jesuit accounts.

We are inclined to think that many such stones were utilised in rebuilding the Church, otherwise how could a tombstone find its way into the dome of the present Church.

Now let us revert to the history of the Bourbons.

Colonel W. Kincaid, late of the Indian Political Service, writing in the *Asiatic Quarterly Review* for January, 1887, says—

"In the latter half of the sixteenth century, about the year 1560, John Philip Bourbon of Navarre, who was a member of the younger branch of the family of Henri VI, sailed for India, having, tradition relates, been obliged to leave France because he killed a relative of high position in a duel. He landed at Madras * a priest and two friends accompanying him. The two latter died on the voyage, and the priest remained at Madras, but John Philip Bourbon, sailing on to Bengal went thence to Delhi and sought an interview with the Emperor Akbar. On hearing of the high rank of the exile, the Emperor sent for him, and being interested in his story, treated him with much favour and distinction, eventually appointing him to a post at his Court. Not long afterwards the Emperor being much pleased at his courtly bearing and conduct, and desiring to retain his services, offered him in marriage the Lady Juliana, sister of the Emperor's Christian wife, who on account of her skill and her knowledge of the European system of medicine, had charge of the health of the imperial ladies. This marriage was duly solemnised, whereupon the Emperor conferred upon his brother-in-law the title of Nawab and placed the imperial seraglio under his care and the Lady Juliana was included in the select band of the imperial sisters. The honourable office conferred on Bourbon remained in the possession of the family until the sack of Delhi by Nadir Shah in the year 1737."

The descendants of Prince John Philip Bourbon, after passing through many vicissitudes and thrilling adventures during

* This is an anachronism, as the town of Madras was not in existence in 1560. Bourbon must have landed somewhere in the neighbourhood of the present city of Madras and thence sailed for Bengal and then gone overland to Agra.

the decadence of the Mogul Empire, are still to be found in Bhopal. Several members of the family lived and died at Agra where their graves can be seen to this day in the old Armenian cemetery of that place. The Bourbons kept up the family tradition of marrying Armenian wives, for we find in the above cemetery, near the gate on the left side, the grave of an Armenian lady who had married a Bourbon. Her name was Anna, according to the Armenian inscription. The Persian inscription gives her name as Anna Khanoom of the Armenian nation. She died on the 5th January 1855, aged 18 years.

According to Col. Kincaid, Francis de Bourbon a great grandson of Prince John Philip Bourbon, came to Narwar with all his clan to the number of about 300 souls not long after the plunder of Delhi in 1739. Three miles from there lies the now ruined Fort of Shergarh which was entrusted to him. Father A. Strobl says a mission station and a church, with a resident priest, were opened at Narwar in 1743. Fr. Tieffentaller, who was at Narwar between July 1747 and the beginning of 1750 and again between December 1751 and 1765, as the chaplain of the Bourbon family, writes that, after the Rajah's palace, one of the finest buildings within the Narwar Fort, "was the palace of a certain Christian, born of Armenian parents, whom the gentoo [Hindoo] Raja admitted to the government of this province, and whom the Mogol Emperors loaded with honours and favours. He had houses built for all his family, and a chapel to God, where he and the other worshippers of Jesus Christ, whether relatives or servants, assemble on all Feast-days and Sundays, one of the Jesuit Fathers saying Mass."

According to Fr. Tieffentaller, the Bourbons were then living at Narwar, near Shergarh, which their tradition speaks of as the hereditary fief received from Akbar, yet the head of the family at Narwar at that time is said by the Jesuits to be of Armenian parentage and Col. Kincaid states that Francis de Bourbon, born in 1680, had married in 1710, an Armenian lady, "a relative of his own."

For a fuller account of the Bourbons in India, see Major-General Sir John Malcolm's *A Memoir of Central India*, Vol. II p. 341, and Colonel Kincaid's *Tales of the Tulsi plant*.

CHAPTER VI

CAPTAIN WILLIAM HAWKINS

An Envoy from James I to the Mogul Court

We have seen in the preceding Chapter how a French Prince, John Philip Bourbon, found his way to the Mogul Court in 1560 and was kindly received by the Emperor Akbar, who being struck with the remarkable personality of the royal adventurer conferred on him the little of a *Mansabdar* and in order to retain his services permanently he gave him an Armenian lady in marriage.

And by a strange coincidence, a *debonair* Englishman, Captain William Hawkins, who appeared at the Court of his son Jehangeer, in 1609, not as an adventurer however, but as the envoy from King James I of England, was given an Armenian lady in marriage by Jehangeer, the royal matchmaker, as a token of the high esteem in which the British envoy was held by the Emperor who saluted Hawkins by the lofty title of *Inglis Khan* "swearing by his father's soule that if I would remayne with him," writes Hawkins, "he would grant me articles for our Factorye to my Hearts' desire and would never go from his word."

Hawkins arrived at Agra on the 16th April 1609, after encountering many obstacles during the long and tedious journey of 40 days from Surat. He had arrived at Surat with his ship, the "Hector", on the 24th August 1608, and left that port on the 1st February 1609, for Agra. Whilst at Surat, the Governor of that place had pillaged the seaman's goods, only paying "such a price as his owne barbarous conscience afforded." The avaricous Governor, writes Hawkins, "came to my house three times, sweeping mee cleane of all things that were good." These were the valuable presents he had brought for the Emperor Jehangeer.

On his arrival at Agra he was sent for by the Emperor who was so eager to see this ambassador from a new country that he scarcely gave him time to put on his "best attyre".

Hawkins delivered the letter bearing the King's (James I) seal which the monarch for sometime carefully examined. An old Portuguese Jesuit priest acted as interpreter in making the contents of the letter known to the Emperor, but doing his best to prejudice him. The Emperor "with a most kinde and smiling countenance bade mee most heartilye welcome," says Hawkins, and reached down from the throne to receive the letter. The Emperor then promised "by God that all that the King of England has written he would grant and allow with all his heart and more."

Jehangeer then invited the Envoy to visit the palace daily and held long discourses with him, in the Turki language, about England and the countries of Europe. The Emperor not only requested him to stay at Agra until he could himself send an Embassy to England, but urged him, in true oriental fashion to accept a wife, in addition to many other valuable presents. This strange offer Hawkins could not possibly refuse, for policy's sake, but he hoped to be able to evade the same, without displeasing the Emperor, by telling him that his religious convictions would not allow him to marry any one but a Christian, thinking that no Christian girl could be found in that remote quarter of the globe, but in the words of Hawkins, "the Emperor's search was so diligent that he produced a young Armenian mayden of noble birth" whom he gladly married in 1609.

Hawkins gives a graphic account of this interesting episode in his journal which is published in the pages of "Purchas his Pilgrimes". He writes :—

"The King was very earnest with mee to take a white Mayden out of his Palace, who would give her all things necessary, with slaves, and hee would promise mee shee should turne Christian : and by this means my meates and drinkes should bee looked into by them and I should live without feare. In regard shee was a Moore [Mohammedan] I refused, but if so bee there could bee a Christian found, I would accept it. At which my speech, I little thought a Christian's Daughter could bee found, so the King called to Memorie one Mubarique Sha his Daughter, who was a Christian Armenian, and of the Race of the most ancient Christians, who [Mubarique Sha] was a Captaine, and in great favour with Ekbar [Akbar] Padasha, this King's Father.

This Captaine dyed suddenly, and without will, with a Masse of Money, and all robbed by his Brothers and Kindred, and Debts that cannot be recovered, leaving the Child but only a few Jewels. I seeing shee was of so honest a Descent, having passed my word to the King, could not notwithstand my fortunes, therefore I took her, and for want of a Minister, before Christian witnesses, I marryed her, the Priest was my man Nicholas, which I thought had beeene lawfull, till I met with a Preacher that came with Sir Henry Middleton, and hee showing mee the error, I was now marryed agayne. For ever after I lived content and without feare, shee being willing to goe where I went and live as I lived."

It may be added that it is a national characteristic with Armenian wives to "love, honour and obey" their husbands during their wedded life.

Jehangeer tried to induce Hawkins to make India his home, promising to make him an officer (*Mansabdar*) of 400 horse, with an allowance of the equivalent of £3200 a year.

The permission for an English factory at Surat * was first granted, and then, under pressure from the Portuguese Viceroy, withdrawn. The Portuguese were the masters of the Indian seas at that time, and a Portuguese naval officer had told Hawkins that "these seas belonged unto the King of Portugal

* In 1612, Jehangir permitted the English Company to establish factories at Surat, Ahmedabad and Cambay and these purely commercial houses became, in the course of time, the solid foundations of British rule in India.

and none ought to come here without his license". The Portuguese Captain—Major had gone even further in his insolence and "set to vilely abusing His Majestie, tearming him King of Fishermen and of an Island of no import and a fig for his Commission."

After a struggle of four years, trying to obtain permission from Jehangeer for the English to trade in India, Hawkins was obliged to return to England, his Mission having proved a failure, through the intrigues of the Portuguese, notwithstanding the Emperor's kindly feeling towards him, yet his journey to Agra and his residence at the Mogul Court, may be looked upon as the opening scene in the history of the British connection with India, as he was the first Englishman ever received by the Emperor of Hindoosthan as the official representative of the King of England.

It appears from Hawkins narrative in "Purchas his Pilgrimes," that his wife had her mother, brother and relatives living at Agra at the time of their departure from that city on the 2nd November 1611.

They got safely on board Sir Henry Middleton's ship in January 1612 and proceeded to Bantam, whence they sailed for England in the "Thomas," arriving at Saldanha Bay on the 21st April 1613. The "Thomas" sailed from Saldanha Bay on the 21st May 1613, but Hawkins was not fated to see his native land again, for he died at sea on the passage from the Cape and his body was carried home and buried in Ireland. His Armenian widow was left in a very forlorn condition, alone amongst total strangers in a strange land, but she had a very fine diamond worth £2000 and some smaller ones worth £4000, so that she had no difficulty in finding another English husband. In 1614, she married Gabriel Towerson, who had been in the voyage of Captain Saris and had brought home the "Hector"—the ship in which Captain William Hawkins had sailed to India in 1609.

In 1617, Captain Gabriel Towerson and his Armenian wife went out to India again and visited Agra, where the lady remained with her relatives.

Towerson went home and in 1620 he was appointed principal Factor at the Moluccas Islands where he was murdered, after suffering inhuman treatment from the Dutch on the 27th February 1623. He was the chief victim of the wholesale massacre of the English by the Dutch at Amboyna.

It may be mentioned that the Honourable East India Company presented the Armenian lady from Agra, on the death of her first husband, with a purse of 200 Jacobuses;* "as a token of their love", upon a general release being given by her.

It may be observed that the romantic matrimonial alliance of Hawkins with an Armenian maiden of Agra in 1609, was the first Anglo-Armenian marriage in this country where, during the past 300 years, several † Englishmen of high birth and position have married Armenian wives, actuated, no doubt, by the same sentiments that prompted the Envoy of King James I of England to accept an "Armenian Mayden" as his legal wife, the lady being "of the Race of the most ancient Christians" according to the testimony of Captain William Hawkins, the *first* Englishman to get married in India.

This Armenian lady, born and bred at Agra, was the *first* person to visit England from India. We mention this because, some three years ago, a certain correspondent wishing to know who was the *first* Indian to visit England, started a controversy in the columns of a Calcutta daily. The controversy

---

* A "Jacobus" was a good coin of the value of 25 shillings, struck in the reign of James I.

† In 1813, an English doctor, James Short, of the Honourable East India Company's service, married at Patna an Armenian lady, Mary by name, the widow of an Armenian merchant named Minas. One of their daughters, named Mariam, became one of the queens of Ghaziuddin Hyder (the first King of Oude) and was called Nawab Sultan Mariam Begum Saheba. She received a monthly pension of Rs. 2,500 from Ghaziuddin Hyder during her lifetime, and as she had no issue, a pension of Rs. 833-5-4 per month was allowed after her death to her younger brother, Joseph Short, and it is being paid to this day to the descendants of Joseph Short from the Government Wasika office at Lucknow. (Vide *Aitchison's Treaties*, Vol. II).

Nawab Sultan Mariam Begum Saheba lived and died a Christian in 1849 and was buried at the cemetery near the Roshan-ud-dowlah's Kothee at Lucknow The beautiful marble tombstone over her gave was broken and destroyed by the mutineers in 1857. There is a mural tablet to her memory in the R. C. Church (St. Joseph's) at Hazratganj, Lucknow, erected by her sister-in-law, Amelia Short.

continued for some time, but none of the correspondents could prove conclusively that the persons mentioned by them were the *first* visitors to England from India.

The controversy was dying a natural death when a Eurasian pedagogue entered the arena, armed with a valuable discovery he supposed he had made, and which he thought would settle the question once for all and he would win laurels for his historical knowledge. And with a flourish of trumpets he pronounced the *dictum*, by announcing that one Mir Muhammad Husain Fazlal, who visited England in 1775-76, with a Mr. Elliott, was the *first* Indian to visit England. Although we held the trump card, when the controversy started, yet we had remained reticent in order to gauge the historical knowledge of the self-styled historical students, but when the self-opinionative pedant tried to pass himself off as an authority on matters historical, we had to place our card on the table immediately by announcing in the pages of the same journal, (on the 10th May, 1933), that the Armenian lady from Agra, the wife of Captain William Hawkins, was the *first* person to visit England from India in 1612.

CHAPTER VII.

MARTYROSE'S CHAPEL

THE OLDEST CHRISTIAN EDIFICE IN NORTHERN INDIA.

Few visitors to Agra know of the existence in that historic city of an old Christian mausoleum which has for over three centuries withstood the ravages of Time and the elements, to say nothing of the vandalism of the Jats or the fanaticism of Shah Jehan, who, at the instigation of his favourite queen, Mumtaz Mahal of Taj fame, laid sacrilegious hands on the places of Christian worship which had been erected at Agra and Lahore by the good Jesuit Fathers during the halcyon days of the tolerant Akbar and his equally liberal-minded son Jehangeer.

This Mausoleum which is not built of marble, like the world-famed Taj, is nevertheless the *oldest* Christian structure in Northern India, having been erected in 1611 at the old Armenian Cemetery* of Agra over the grave of a very wealthy, and a highly pious and charitable Armenian merchant, Khojah Martyrose by name. And as the name Martyrose means a *Martyr* in the Armenian language, the place has been called "Martyr's Chapel," which is a misnomer, if not misleading,

* In this extensive Christian cemetery, lies buried, amongst other notable Europeans and Jesuit Fathers, John Midnall or Mildenhall, the *first* and the *only* Englishman that saw Akbar the Great. Midnall died at Ajmere in 1614 and as there was no Christian cemetery in that place, his body was removed by the good Jesuit Fathers and interred in the Armenian graveyard at Agra. The Portuguese inscription on the red sandstone tablet at the head of his grave is as follows: "JOA DE MENDENAL, INGLES, MOREO AOSI............E. JUNHO 1614." When we last visited the cemetery in December 1929, on our return from the Gwalior Session of the "Indian Historical Records Commission," we were pleased to see that the Archæological Department had at last placed a white marble slab over his grave with a suitable inscription in English. This was not there in 1919, when we were deciphering and copying the large number of Armenian inscriptions in that historic cemetery.

as the Armenian merchant Martyrose who lies buried in that Mortuary Chapel, did not win a martyr's glorious crown.

It is an octagonal building of masonry surmounted by a beautiful dome with a cross on the cupola over the dome.

As you enter the chapel, you will find, on the right hand niche, two mural tablets of sandstone, one with an inscription in Armenian at the head, and the other with a Persian inscription at the foot of the grave of the pious Armenian merchant, both being in a fairly good state of preservation despite their great age. The Persian inscription is as follows :—

اینجا مدفونست خواجه مرتینس ارمنی مقدسی

که خود را غلام کریستس می گفت و چون

صاحب خیربود هرچه با خود داشت بنذر

آنحضرت بفقرا ایثار کرد

یک هزار و ششصد و یازده از تولد حضرت عیسی

The transliteration of the Persian inscription is as follow :—

> "Inja madfoon asth Khwajeh Martinus Armanee moqdesee khe khod ra qolam a Christhus me gofth va choon saheb a khair bood har cheh ba khod dashth beh nazr a an hazrath beh foqera isar khard. Ekh hezar shish sad o yazda az thavallode a hazrath a Isa."

The Armenian inscription is as follows :—

ՀԱՆԳԱՒ Ի ԱՅՍ ՏԱՊԱՆՍ
ՓԻՐԲԱՇԻՆ ՈՐԴԻՆ
ՄՂՏԵՍԻ ՄԱՐՏԻՐՈՍ ՋՈՒ
ՂԱՅԻ ՎԱՂՃԱՆԵՑԱՒ
Ի ԱԿՌԱՑ ՔԱՂԱՔԻ ԵՒ
ԱՊՐԱՆՔՆ ԵՏ Ա̅Յ Վ̅Ս ԻՒՐ
ՀՈԳՈՆ. ԹԻՎ ՀԱՅՈՑ ՌԿ։

The Armenian epitaph can be romanized, thus :—

> "Hangav e ais tapanus Phirbashin wordin Muqdesi Martyrośe Juqaie vakhtzanetsav e Akra khaqakhee ev aprankhun yet Astutzo vasun yiur hogon.
>
> Thiv Haiotz 1060.

There have been several translations of the Persian inscription since 1876 by Dr. Fuhrer and others, but none of them have been rendered into English correctly, as will be seen presently, but the Armenian inscription, is being translated here for the *first* time and it is as follows :

> "In this tomb rested the pilgrim Martyrose, son of Pheerbashee of Julfa. Died at the city of Agra and gave his goods to God for his soul, in the year 1060 of the Armenian era."

The Armenian era commenced in the year 551 A.D. so that the year 1060 of that era will be equivalent to 1611 A.D. which corresponds with the date gicen in the Persian inscription.

In this connection we may mention that the Archæological Department have, in the interests of archæology, placed a white marble slab over the grave of the Armenian Martyrose, with the following inscription, which is a translation, though not a correct one, of the Persian inscription at the foot of the grave and it runs thus :—

> "Here lies holy Khwaja Mortenepus, Armenian, who was a professed disciple of Christus and who was a righteous man, whatever he had he gave in charity to the poor, in token of fidelity to his adored master. In the year one thousand six hundred and eleven from the birth of Christ."

As there are some glaring mistakes in the above translation, we shall therefore give a correct rendering of the original Persian inscription, as copied by us in 1919 and it will be thus :—

> "Here lies interred the Armenian Khwajeh Martinus, the pilgrim, who called himself the slave of Christus, and as he was of a charitable disposition,

> he gave whatever he possessed, in charity, to the poor out of respect for the Lord. [In the year] one thousand, six hundred and eleven from the birth of the Lord Jesus."

It will be observed that in the translation of the Archæological Department, the name of the deceased, which is the most essential part of the epitaph, has not been translated correctly, for instead of the Persian "Martinus"—the Latin name for Martin or Martyrose—the erudite translators of the Archæological Department have got, we cannot understand how and wherefrom, the jaw-breaking name "Mortenepus", which is not an Armenian name at all. Then again, the Persian word "moqdesi", which means a pilgrim in Armenian, (one who has visited the Holy Sepulchre at Jerusalem) has been wrongly translated as "moqaddasi" which means a holy man and in the same arbitrary manner the Persian word "qolam" (a slave) has been translated as a "disciple". What a faithful translation !

Now a person who humbly called himself the "Slave of Christus"—Christus being the Armenian name for Christ—would turn in his grave if he were called a "holy man," so that the incompetent translators have done a great injustice to the memory of that humble and devout Christian by calling him "holy."

We would in this connection, humbly suggest to the Agra Archæological Department to remove the rather misleading inscription that appears on the present marble slab, replacing it by another one with the correct translations of both the inscriptions, Armenian and Persian, as given above.

Now let us see who this pious and charitable Armenian merchant was and where he hailed from.

In his "Annual Letter" to Rome, Father Joao de Velasco, S.J. writing from Agra on the 25th day of December, 1612, says :—

"The King [Jehangeer] granted us for burying the Christians a convenient and ample ground, whither the remains of the Christians were transported amid solemn prayer on the

2nd of November [All Souls' Iay]; the presents offered by the Christians for the dead were distributed amongst the poor, whether of the faithful or of the pagans; whatever remained was carried to the jail to comfort the prisoners, which act of charity astonished and edified the Moors [Mohammedans] not a little. Lately this place [cemetery] was adorned with a Chapel (templum), erected with the alms of a pious Armenian, who, free from the bonds of wedlock after the death of his wife, went to Rome and Jerusalem on a pilgrimage to the holy places of our Redemption. From there he went back to his country (patria) and bestowed on the two sons, left him after his wife's death, whatever they had a right to, after which he devoted himself so wholly to God that he called himself only the Lord Jesus' little slave (mancipiolum), and did not allow others to call him by any other name. However, he travelled diverse countries as a merchant, buying and selling goods, and making profits amounting to many thousands of gold pieces (Aurei). But all his gains he gave away to the poor or spent in other works of piety and charity, and that so faithfully that he was loath to subtract anything for his own sustenance: for, he would say repeatedly that these goods were no longer his, but the Lord Jesus', to whom he had consecrated himself.

Once, after a long time, five thousand gold pieces [gold Mohurs] were adjudged him at last in a law suit, when, to the judge's wonder, he presently distributed among the needy the money he had received; he ransomed very many captives from his own purse, relieved many in their wants, gave dowries to poor women of good character, and thus, like the Lord Jesus' very faithful servant, he spent his goods and his life. Doubtless, he deserved to enter into the joy of his Lord. He was buried in the Chapel (in templo) he had built, and he asked Father Xavier to write over his tomb: 'Here lies Martin (Martinus), the slave of the Lord Jesus'. This was done, and after his death all that remained of his goods was partly spent in building and adorning the Chapel, as he had ordered, partly given to the poor, whom he had appointed heirs to his property."

The above testimony from the pen of a good Jesuit priest, who evidently knew the pious Armenian merchant personally, is eloquent proof of the goodness of my noble countryman.

The late Father H. Hosten, S.J., who brought to light the above highly interesting letter, comments on it, in his interesting account of Mirza Zul-Qarnain, as under :—

"Is it not pathetic that the inscription on that good man's grave should have been so long a puzzle to antiquarians, or that his good deeds should be made public again after an oblivion of three centuries? The inscriptions on his tomb, both in Armenian and Persian, are near the right-hand recess of the octagonal Chapel, as one enters. These lines, the *oldest* in the cemetery, will have been read at times with incredulity, as a piece of vain boasting. How modest an expression they are of great realities and of the gratitude of the poor!"

This is the history of the oldest Christian structure in the United Provinces and the Punjab and it is to be hoped that future compilers of Guide-Books to Agra will include that venerable edifice in the itinerary of the places and sites of historical and archæological interest which are visited annually by hundreds of tourists and globe-trotters who flock to Agra during the winter months from all parts of the civilized world to see, study and admire the master-pieces of Mogul architecture—the beautiful Taj, the most magnificent tomb of Itmad-ud-dowlah, the matchless Pearl Mosque of Shah Jehan, and the majestic Fort of Akbar which bear silent testimony to the glorious achievements and the unparalleled magnificence of the Great Moguls.

There is a mural tablet* in the above chapel on the right

---

*Blunt, in a note on page 38 of his *List of Christian Tombs and Monuments,* relating to the inscriptions in Martyros's Chapel, says, "All the Armenian inscriptions, (save that of Khwaja Mortenepus) were on the walls and are now hidden behind a veil of whitewash from which I hope that some day they will be rescued." We wrote to the Archæological Department at Agra, some years ago, protesting against this act of vandalism, but nothing was done in the matter, we are sorry to say. Should we visit Agra again, we shall try to rescue from oblivion the valuable inscriptions which, according to Blunt" are now hidden behind a veil of whitewash". There are in the chapel the graves of twenty-six Jesuit priests who died at Agra between the years 1633 and 1767 and were buried there.

Fr. Felix, in his *Notes on the Jesuit Missions to the Mogul Emperors,* 1907, gives a list of the epitaphs with a plan showing the position of the graves in Martyrose's Chapel.

hand side, facing the gate, with a laconic Armenian inscription of six words, which can be translated thus :—

"I, Reverend Zachariah of Tabriz, came in 1105." The date, as in most of the inscriptions in that cemetery, is in the Armenian era, corresponding to the year 1656 A.D. Incorrect and rather misleading translations of the above inscription have been published from time to time by different investigators, all of whom, blindly following each other, have given the year 1615 A.D. as the date of the inscription, and as if that glaring error was not enough, the translators have called the *priest* from Tabriz a "bishop" !

Dr. A. Fuhrer, in his *List of Christian Tombs and Monuments,* Allahabad, 1896, has "Episcopus Zachar from Tabrez, 1615".

Frederick Fanthome, in his *Reminiscences of Agra,* Calcutta, 1895, has "Father Zakur, Bishop, died 1615."

Fr. Felix, in the *Catholic Calendar and Directory for the Archdiocese of Agra,* for the year 1907, gives the following translation :—

"Father Zachar, Bishop, I am from Tabrez, 1615."

Blunt, in the *List of Inscriptions on Christian Tombs and Monuments in the United Provinces of Agra and Oudh,* Allahabad, 1911, blindly follows Fr. Falix and reproduces his translation, as he has done with *all* the Armenian inscriptions at Agra.

This is how incompetent translators distort historical facts through ignorance.

Now let us see when Rev. Zachariah died and where he was buried.

In January 1917 whilst the convicts in the Central Jail at Agra were digging the vegetable garden, they came upon a rectangular stone, about four feet high with a cross carved on it and an inscription in Armenian, in a very good state of preservation, despite its age. The inscription, which is in relief, can be translated thus :—

"This holy cross* is in memory of the Reverend Zachariah

* It was a time honoured custom among Armenians in the olden times to erect perpendicular stone slabs in cemeteries, with a cross,

and of his parents, Joseph and Mariam and Sargiss. In the year 1106."

The Armenian date in the inscription is equivalent to 1657 A.D.

The stone seems to have been the pedestal of an altar or a baptismal font, as the top portion has been cut into a square to fit into the socket of something heavy which may have been placed over it. Now the question arises, how did this memorial pillar come to be buried in the jail compound? Was there an Armenian church standing there in 1657? We feel certain that if the Archaeological Department at Agra, were to make further excavations in the vegetable garden of the Central Jail, some more valuable finds may be brought to light which may unravel the mystery surrounding that stone.

The late Fr. Hosten requested us to furnish him with a translation and a transliteration of the Armenian inscription on that *Kachkhar,* (cross-stone) and he published a very interesting article in the Journal of the United Provinces Historical Society for 1919 (Vol. II) under the caption, "The Armenian inscription of the Central Jail compound, Agra."

The stone had been removed from the jail garden, and in October 1919, we found it lying in the compound of St. Peter's Cathedral, which is facing the Central Jail.

We were afterwards, informed by the Rev. Fr. Hyacinth of St. Peter's College that the stone had been erected as a monument in the cemetery behind the old cathedral, now known as the Native Chapel.

A great grandson of Rev. Zacharia, who died in 1801 at Delhi, lies buried in the D'Eramao cemetery of that city. The inscription on his tombstone can be seen in Chapter XII.

The cemetery, as we have seen in the preceding chapter, was opened in 1611 and the first person to be buried there was Khojah Martyrose who was interred in the Chapel which he had built in his lifetime, yet there are two inscriptions in that cemetery which bear dates outerior to 1611.

---

carved, in relief, on them, in memory of their departed parents and relatives. These memorial tablets were called *Kachkhar* (cross-stone) in Armenian, hence the words—"this holy cross" in some of the inscriptions.

One of the inscriptions is on the tombstone of one Carapiet, the son of Mackertich of Julfa, who died in the year 1006 of the Armenian era, or 1557 A.D. The other is on a *Kachkhar* (cross-stone) erected to the memory of one Gundaqb, the son of Martyrose, who died in the year 1009 of the Armenian era, corresponding to the year 1560 A.D. Father Joao de Velasco, S.J. in his "Annual Letter", written from Agra on the 25th December, 1612, (published on p. 105) says :—"The King [Jehangeer] granted us for burying the Christians a convenient and ample ground, whither the remains of the Christians were transported amid solemn prayers on the 2nd of November." [All Souls' Day, 1612].

It appears from the above that prior to the opening of the new cemetery, there was another Christian burial ground at Agra and the remains of the Christians were removed from that place to the new cemetery amid solemn prayers on the 2nd November, 1612.

It is therefore quite possible that these two tablets, the oldest in the cemetery, came from the old burial ground with the remains of the Christians, as stated by Fr. Velasco who was an eye witness to the removal of the remains. We have always held the opinion that the Armenians who flocked to Agra in fairly large numbers during the long reign of Akbar (1556—1605) had a church and a cemetery of their own and many must have died there between the years 1556 and 1605, yet there are no other tombstones or memorial tablets of that period with the exception of the two referred to above and which have fortunately survived the ravages of Time and the elements for about 400 years.

We have seen in Chapter VI that the Emperor Jehangeer gave the daughter of Mubarique Sha, an Armenian, who had been in the military service of Akbar, in marriage to Captain William Hawkins, the envoy from King James I of England, in 1609. According to Hawkins' narrative of the marriage, the Armenian Captain was dead before his daughter was married, but his grave cannot be traced. Where could he have been buried? We have not been able to trace the graves of his widow or his widowed daughter and the other members of his family who lived and died at Agra after the new cemetery was opened in 1611. The grave of Domingo Pires, the Armenian interpreter of the Portuguese language at the Court of Akbar, cannot also be traced.

There must have been a fairly large number of Armenians at Agra during the reigns of Akbar, Jehangeer and Shah Jehan, judging from the number of graves that can still be seen in the old Armenian cemetery of that historic city, amongst which there are graves of many eminent merchants from New Julfa—the Armenian suburb of Ispahan.

It appears from Manrique's Travels (1629-1643) that the Armenian merchants had a *Caravan Serai* of their own at Agra and Fray Sebastian Manrique who arrived at Agra on Xmas Eve, 1640, writes as follows:—"After entering the City, I made my way to the Caramossora [Caravan Serai] of the Armenians in order to obtain information there about a rich merchant there to whom I had been directed to apply. On hearing that he was at Biana,* three days journey from Agra,

* Biana or Bayana lies S. W. of Agra on the railway to Kotah. It has always been famous for its indigo, a fact which is mentioned by Abul Fazl in the *Ain-i-Akbari* and it is constantly referred to in the Surat Factory Records (1634—36). There was a great competition between the English and the Dutch in purchasing that commodity and the shrewd Armenian merchants of Agra played a prominent part in raising the prices, as can be seen from the following extract from the *Remonstratie* of Francisco Pelsaert, a Factor of the Dutch East India Company at Agra from 1620-27. Writing of the indigo trade, the enterprising Dutchman says:—

"From repeated personal experience then my opinion is that such times (indigo season) it is more profitable for the Honourable Company that buyers should keep quiet than they should run about the country from one village to another. Goodness knows the Armenians do quite enough of that running and racing about like hungry fellows whose greedy eyes show that they are dissatisfied with the meal provided, who take a taste of every dish and make the other guests hurry to secure their portions, but directly they have tasted each course, they are satisfied and can hold no more. In the indigo market they behave just like that, making as if they would buy up the whole stock, raising prices, losing a little themselves and causing great injury to us and to other buyers who have to purchase large quantities."

In closing the Chapter on "Indigo," the well-informed Hollander writes:—

"I have now written at length of the Indigo bearing the name of Baynana which for the last four years has been very closely brought up and also that, as it was the season for purchasing Indico anil [indigo], he would be detained there longer than I could spare, I arranged to hire a cart for a week hence to go and see him." On his arrival at Biani, Maurique says "I got into touch with the merchant whom I had gone to see. He completed my business next day to my satisfaction arranging for a relative of his own to accompany me, who, being well instructed in such matters, would be able to guide me in dealing with any occasion which might arise, especially with regard to my business with Father Antonio de Christo—an Augustinian who had been a Prior at Hugli and was imprisoned in 1632-3 at Agra by Shah Jehan's orders."

Father Maurique was an Augustinian Friar himself and had come to Agra to obtain the liberation of Father Antonio de Christo and some Portuguese prisoners who were incarcerated at Agra. He had evidently brought a letter of introduction from an eminent Armenian merchant of Bengal to the Armenian merchant at Agra whom he went and interviewed at Biana and who most nobly placed the services of his relative at the disposal of the Augustinian Prior in his dangerous mission to appease the wrath of Shah Jehan.

Although the once flourishing Armenian Colony of Agra had almost died out by the middle of the last century, yet when the Mutiny broke out, an Armenian of Agra, Major John Jacob, the second son of Colonel Jacob of Gwalior, fought against the mutineers and laid down his life for the British cause. Another Armenian, Mr. Parsick* (Barsegh—Basil) who was the Deputy Collector at Agra, was sent to Fatehpur Sikri and did good service in repressing an outbreak on the part of the

---

both by us, by Armenians and by Moguls, the latter classes (Armenians and Moguls) export it to Ispahan whence some of it goes to Aleppo. In six years the English have not bought more than 600 bales, because owing to bad luck, adversity and mismanagement, their commercial position has greatly deteriorated, but if they began to buy against us, as they would like to do if they had the money, indigo is likely to rise in price.

* 'Parsick's father, Petrus, died at Agra in 1826, aged 43 years and his mother, Magdalena died in 1831, aged 30 years and they are both buried in the Armenian cemetery of Agra where their graves can be seen to this day.

turbulent characters of the place and with the aid of the *tahsildar*, Irshad Ali, managed to keep the road open between Agra and Fatehpur Sikri. He organised an armed force to prevent disorder and derived much assistance from the friendly Zamindars of Nagla Sarai, Dabor, Basahra Raja Nagar, Santha Singharpur and Abhnapura, driving off the marauding Gujars on more than one occasion and preventing a large number of the disarmed mutineers from occupying Fatehpur Sikri.

It is sad to reflect that the once flourishing Armenian community of Agra is now extinct after an existence of 300 years from the days of Akbar up to the middle of the 19th century. The only landmarks which are left in that historic city, are the numerous graves * in the old Armenian cemetery where some great men lie buried.

The last Armenian, one Avetis Galstaun, who was born and bred at Agra, died there about 16 years ago.

There was an Armenian at Agra some years ago who bore the Jewish name Zachariah.† He had two sons, named Joseph and Thomas. The former had two sons, David and Alick, and a daughter. These remnants of the Agra Armenians wishing to become Anglicised, renounced the family name and assumed Molton as their surname. This is how several Armenians in India and elsewhere, mostly in the United States of America, have changed their ancestral names out of sheer vanity. We shall give another instance. Some fifty years ago, an Armenian who had amassed great wealth in the domestic service of the late Nizam, Avietick Satoor Hyrapiet by name, had assumed the name of Albert Abid—a silly combination of European and Mohammedan names !

And before we conclude this Chapter, we would suggest that in view of the great antiquity of the sacred edifice—the

---

* The translations of the Armenian inscriptions in that old cemetery are given in Chapter IX of this work.

† Armenians being a religious race, have, from the commencement of the 4th century, when they embraced the Christian religion *en masse*, adopted a large number of Biblical names, from both the Testaments, with the exception of such odious names as Cain, Ham, Lot, Herod, Caiaphas, Pilate, Barabbas and Judas.

oldest in Northern India—a marble slab be placed by the Archæological Department at Agra, on the right hand side of the iron gate of the Chapel, with the following inscription for the information of the many visitors to that historic cemetery.

> MARTYROSE'S CHAPEL
> THE OLDEST CHRISTIAN EDIFICE
> IN NORTHERN INDIA.
> ERECTED BY A PIOUS ARMENIAN
> MERCHANT IN 1611 A.D.

We make this suggestion because the Archæological Department, have, in the interests of Archæology, placed a white marble slab over the grave of the Armenian Khojah Martyrose, who lies interred in that Chapel, with an inscription, in English, as stated on page 104. But if the worthy custodians of ancient tombs and monuments at Agra cannot see their way to comply with our humble request, we shall be pleased, with their kind permission, to place a tablet there to perpetuate the revered memory of our illustrious compatriot, who gave all that he possessed to the poor, irrespective of caste, colour or creed, being a firm believer in the precept that "he that giveth to the poor, lendeth to the Lord."

CHAPTER VIII

SHAH NAZAR KHAN

AN ARMENIAN KRUPP IN INDIA.

In the opening chapter of *Kim*, Kipling says :—"Who hold Zamzamah, that fire-breathing dragon, hold the Punjab, for the great green-bronze piece is always first of the conqueror's loot."

It would be interesting to follow the history of this remarkable gun, which is to be seen at the Central Museum, Lahore, facing the Sadr Bazaar, in which position it was placed on the occasion of the Duke of Edinburgh's visit to Lahore in 1870.

But when, where, by whom and for whom was this great gun cast?

In the old Armenian cemetery at Agra (opened in 1611 A.D.) there is the grave of an Armenian who, according to the inscriptions in Armenian and Persian on his tombstone, was an expert in the art of casting cannons and it was he who cast the famous gun called "Zamzamah" for Ahmad Shah Durrani, the Afghan invader of the Punjab, after Nadir Shah, in the second half of the 18th century.

The Armenian inscription on the slab which covers the mortal remains of the expert gun-maker, can be translated as follows :—

> "This is the tomb of Ostad [Master] Shah Nazar Khan, the son of Allaverdy of Qaiquli, who was an expert in the casting of cannons and who departed to the Lord with a good faith on April 25, in the year 1784."

On a perpendicular white marble slâb fixed at the head of the grave, there is an inscription, in beautiful Persian verse, the following being a copy :—

شاه نظر خان آنکه نامش شهرهٔ آفاق بود
صنعتش در توپ ریزی عزت لقمان فزود
چونکه اورا با مسیحا بود حسن اعتقاد
رفته در بهر سجودش جانب چرخ کبود
هاتف غیب از سر حسرت پی تاریخ او
گفت پا بوسي جناب حضرت عیسا نمود

It can be romanized thus :—

"Shah Nazar Khan ankhe namash shohreh a afaq bood,
Sanathash dar thooph reezee ezzath a loqman fozood,
Choonkhe oora ba Mesiha bood hosn a aythegad,
Rafthe dar bahr a sojoodash janeb a charkh khabood,
Hathef a qaib az sar a hasrath phey a thareekh oo
Gofth phaboosee a jenab a hazrath Isa namood."

It can be rendered into English, thus :—

"Shah Nazar Khan, he whose name was world-famed and in the craft of casting cannons, he added even to the excellence of Loqman*, since he was a believer in the Messiah, he went for obeisance to the blue sky [heaven]. A voice from the unknown mournfully said the following verse, giving the date of his death.

"He has kissed the feet of Jesus."

According to the *Abjad* system of reckoning, the date of the death of Shah Nazar Khan is to be found in the word *Isa* (Jesus) which, when calculated gives the year 1784 A.D.

* Loqman is supposed to be the inventor of cannons, according to the Persians.

There is an inscription in Persian, round the muzzle of the gun, as under :—

بامـــر دُر دوران شه ولـــی خـــان وزیر
ســـاخت توپ زمـــزمه نام قلعه گیـــر

عمل شاه نظرخان

It can be translated thus :—

"By order of the Emperor, Dur-i-Durran Shah Wali Khan, the Vazir, made this gun, named Zamzamah, the capturer of strongholds. The work of Shah Nazar Khan."

And on the back of the gun, right in the middle, there is a long Persian inscription, of which the following is a translation :—

"In the reign of the Emperor, possessing the dignity of Feridoon,
Dispenser of Justice, robed in equity—
In the reign of his present Majesty, Ahmad Shah Dur-i-Durran
A Prince occupying a throne mighty as Jamshed's
There was issued unto the Chief Vazir,
From the threshold of His Highness
An order to have cast, with every possible skill,
A gun, terrible as a dragon, and huge as a mountain,
(Yea, an order was given) to his heaven-enthroned.
Majesty's devoted servant,
Shah Wali Khan Vazir.
So in order to effect this great achievement.

The Master workman [Shah Nazar Khan] called up his endeavours.

Till with consummate toil was cast
This wondrous gun Zamzamah.
A destroyer even of the strongholds of heaven.
Under the auspices of His Majesty
I enquired of reason for the date of this gun,
Reason angrily replied,

'If thou wilt give thy life in payment I will repeat to thee the date.'

I did so and he replied :—

'What a gun is this!
The form of a fire-raining dragon.'

According to the *Abjad* system of reckoning, the last two lines give the chronogram of the date of the casting of the gun, which is 1174 A.H. or 1761 A.D.

The "Zamzamah"* is made of a mixture of copper and brass, obtained by *jazia*, a metal vessel having been taken by force from each Hindoo house at Lahore. The gun is 14½ feet in length, exclusive of the casemate, the aperture of the bore being 9½ inches.

The "Zamzamah" was used by Ahmad Shah Durrani in the famous battle of Panipat in 1761. After the battle, the Afghan invader on his way back to Kabul left it at Lahore with his Governor, Khwaja Ubed, as the carriage to take it to Kabul was not ready. The other gun he took with him but it was lost in his passage of the river Chenab. After the departure of Ahmad Shah Durrani, the great gun came into the possession of the Sikh Sardars of the Bhangi Misl, hence its name "Bhangianwali toph." It came to be regarded as a talisman of supremacy among the Sikhs. Eventually it came into the possession of the famous Ranjit Singh and it was used by him at the siege of Mooltan in 1818.

And about the same time that Shah Nazar Khan, the Armenian Krupp of India, was casting terrible guns at Lahore for his master, Ahmad Shah Durrani, his equally famous countryman, Gorgin Khan, the Armenian Minister and Commander-in-Chief of Nawab Mir Kassim of Bengal (1760-1763) was casting equally formidable guns for his master at Monghyr, which clearly shows that the Armenians, apart from being eminent merchants in India, have in the past achieved success in the art of war and in the manufacture of large and unique pieces of ordance like the "Zamzamah." This shows that the martial spirit of the race was still alive in them, despite

* Zamzamah means "hummer" or "applauder". It also means a 'lion's roar".

the terrible and the unheard-of persecutions in the land of their ancestors at the hands of the bloodthirsty Tartars, Saracens, Persians and Turks.

Of the many big guns cast by Shah Nazar Khan, the Armenian "Master Workman" at Lahore and at Agra the only one in existence at the present day is the "Zamzamah."

Kipling seems to have been quite impressed with this 18th century unique gun, for he has used an illustration of it as a frontispiece to his *Kim*.

CHAPTER IX.

OLD ARMENIAN INSCRIPTIONS AT AGRA.

LANDMARKS OF A ONCE FLOURISHING COLONY.

"Let's talk of graves, of worms and epitaphs."
—*Shakespeare.*

In the old cemetery at Agra which contains the *oldest* Christian tomb in the United Provinces and the Punjab, as shown in Chapter VII of the present work, there are a large number of Armenian graves bearing inscriptions in ancient Armenian. The late Father Felix,* O.C. during his incumbency at Agra, some twenty years ago, had these inscriptions translated into English by one Jacob David, an illiterate Armenian, the son of a blacksmith of Julfa (Ispahan) who being ignorant of the ancient language in which the epitaphs are written, translated them incorrectly and they were accepted by Fr. Felix as true and faithful translations. These were published by Fr. Felix first in the *Calendar and Directory for the Capuchin Missions in India,* 1908, and afterwards in his highly interesting *brochure* on the *Historical and Traditional Records of Early Christianity in Northern India.*

Fr. Felix evidently thought that any Armenian, no matter of what degree of intelligence, could translate those old inscriptions, but he did not know that a fair knowledge of the ancient language would be necessary to do the work efficiently.

---

* Father Felix, a Capuchin priest, was an erudite research scholar and has left some valuable records of the labours of the early Jesuit Missions to the Mogul Court during the 16th and 17th centuries. The late Father Hosten, a Jesuit priest, worked in the same field with great zeal and devotion. The former died at Lahore four years ago and the latter was laid to rest at Brussels on April 16 last year, in his sixty-third year having been connected with the Society of Jesus for 44 years.

Peace to their souls, rest to their ashes, as they were, in the words of St. Paul to Timothy, "workmen that needeth not to be ashamed." (Timothy II, Chapter II, 15.).

Unfortunately his Armenian translator did not possess the requisite knowledge, being, as we have said, an uncultured plebeian.

And this reminds us of what happened in 1894 in the Bengal Secretariat where a highly cultured Armenian, since dead, held an important post in the Public Works Department, but was ignorant of his mother language. One of the Registrars, who was placed on special duty, for collecting materials from the different churches and cemeteries in Bengal for the late Professor C. R. Wilson's *List of Tombs and Monuments in Bengal, possessing Historical and Archaeological interest,* had taken an estampage of the long inscription * on the tombstone of Khojah Johanness Margar in the Armenian Church at Chinsurah for the List, and knowing that his superior was an Armenian, he naturally thought of requesting him to be kind enough to translate the Armenian inscription for him. But great was his surprise when the Armenian official flew into a rage and told him, in a very angry tone, that he did not know Armenian at all. The nervous Registrar, who was trembling in his shoes, had to apologise to his irate superior officer for his unintentional discourtesy. The good and godly Registrar, worthy son of a worthy clergyman, had unknowingly offended the Anglicised Armenian by disturbing his equanimity, for which he was very sorry afterwards.

It is sad to observe that the Armenians who are born and bred in British India, with very rare exceptions, do not know their national language, history and traditions.

In 1911 when Blunt was compiling his *List of Inscriptions on Christian tombs and tablets of historical interest in the United Provinces of Agra and Oudh,* he blindly followed Fr. Felix's translations, copying them *verbatim,* with the note, "Translation from Armenian." It has been a case of the blind leading the blind and making confusion worse confounded.

---

* That interesting inscription, with many others, were subsequently translated and annotated by us for the List of Tombs and Monuments which the Bengal Government was compiling at that time. The translation can be seen in the Chapter on the Armenians at Chinsurah.

Some seventeen years ago, we were urged both by Fr. Hosten and Fr. Felix, to publish the correct translations of the Agra inscriptions, with historical and biographical notes, but as we intended, and still intend, publishing a complete list of all the Armenian inscriptions, to the number of five thousand, which we have collected, with great difficulty and at considerable cost, from the various Armenian churchyards and deserted cemeteries in India, during the last 45 years, we could not possibly accede to their wishes then.

We are glad to have the opportunity, at long last, of placing on record the valuable landmarks of the Armenians at Agra, which were rescued from oblivion by the writer of these lines in October 1919. There being no Armenians left at Agra to-day, these mute inscriptions tell eloquently the tale of the once flourishing Armenian Colony in that historic city.

Translations of the Armenian Inscriptions in the Cemetery at Agra (1611—1927).

1. This holy cross is in memory of Agah Murad son of Leon of Bitlis. Died in the year 1060 of the Armenian era [1611 A.D.]
2. Bashkhoom son of Satoor. Died at Agra in the year 1062 of the Armenian era [1613 A.D.]
3. Zachariah, son of Amir Khan. Died at Agra in the year 1062 of the Armenian era [1613 A.D.].
4. This holy cross is in memory of Rev. Astwatzatoor, son of Thasaleh of Julfa. Died at Agra in the year 1063 of the Armenian era [1614 A.D.].
5. This holy cross is in memory of Egath, son of Atir Asath. Died at Agra in the year 1064 of the Armenian era [1615 A.D.].
6. Rev. Mekhithar. Died at Agra in the year 1065 of the Armenian era [1616 A.D.].
7. This holy cross is in memory of Sookias, the son of Aqoob of Julfa. Died at Agra in the year 1065 of the Armenian era [1616].

8. This holy cross is in memory of Khamalbeg son of Khojah Soolthanoom of Julfa. Died at Agra in the year 1065 of the Armenian era [1616 A.D.].
9. Zachariah, son of Amir Khan. Died at Agra in the year 1069 of the Armenian era [1620 A.D.].
10. This holy cross is in memory of Petrus son of Pogose. Died in the year 1072 of the Armenian era [1623 A.D.].
11. This is the resting place of Safar who died in the year 1076 of the Armenian era [1627 A.D.].
12. This is the tomb of Safar, son of Mackertich. Died in the year 1076 of the Armenian era [1627 A.D.].
13. Rev. Sookias. Died in the year 1079 of the Armenian era [1630 A.D.].
4. This is the tomb of Eldood son of Booniath who departed to Christ in the year 1090 of the Armenian era [1641 A.D.].
15. This is the tomb of Johanness of Astabad who died in the year 1091 of the Armenian era [1642 A.D.].
16. This is the tomb of Khojah Murad who departed to Christ in the year 1093 of the Armenian era [1644 A.D.].
17. This is the tomb of Avetick, the son of Malijan who departed to Christ in the year 1094 of the Armenian era [1645 A.D.].
18. This is the resting place of Aslan of Amat. Died in the year 1095 of the Armenian era [1646 A.D.].
19. This is the tomb of Margar son of Baqoom who departed to Christ in the year 1096 of the Armenian era [1647 A.D.].
20. This is the tomb of Kirakose who departed to Christ in his young age in the year 1098 of the Armenian era [1649 A.D.].
21. This is the resting place of Murad, son of . . . . . . who died at Agra in the year 1099 of the Armenian era [1650 A.D.].
22. This is the tomb of Alexan the son of Aqniath of Julfa who died at Agra in the year 1100 of the Armenian era [1651 A.D.].

23. This is the tomb of Ayad the son of Amirphajeh. Died in the year 1100 of the Armenian era [1651 A.D.].
24. In this city, which is Agra, I Zachariah, son of Edgar, trusted in my Lord and found a resting place in the year 1100 of the Armenian era [1651 A.D.].
25. This is the tomb of Agazar, son of Martyrose of the Mamikonian family. Died in the year 1100 of the Armenian era [1651 A.D.].
26. This is the tomb of Galoost who died at Agra in the year 1103 of the Armenian era [1654 A.D.].
27. This is the tomb of Hyrapiet, the son of Mathews of Julfa. Died in the year 1104 of the Armenian era [1655 A.D.].
28. This is the tomb of Agah Samuel of the Delakhian family who was murdered by the Jats in the year 1104 of the Armenian era [1655 A.D.].
29. This is the tomb of Hakobjan the son of Khojah Murad. Died in the year 1106 of the Armenian era [1657 A.D.]
30. This is the tomb of Agah Qarzeh of the Khojentz family. Died in the year 1107 of the Armenian era [1658 A.D.].
31. This is the tomb of Franc, the son of Gregory, the Master mason. Died in the year 1107 of the Armenian era [1659 A.D.].
32. This is the tomb of Hovanjan of the family of Qalandar who departed to Christ, in the year 1108 of the Armenian era [1659 A.D.] Aged 20 years.
33. This is the tomb of Bashoom of the Khoobentz family. Died in the year 1109 of the Armenian era [1660 A.D.].
34. This is the tomb of Vardan of Lunjan. Died in the year 1109 of the Armenian era [1660 A.D.].
35. This is the tomb of Eaqoob [Jacob] the son of Safar. Died in the year 1110 of the Armenian era [1661 A.D.].
36. This is the tomb of Agazar of Julfa. Died in the year 1111 of the Armenian era [1662 A.D.].

37. This is the tomb of Johanness of Julfa, a merchant, who died in the year 1114 of the Armenian era [1665 A.D.].

38. This is the resting place of Rev. Johanness, the son of Jacob of Lunjan. Died in the year 1117 of the Armenian era [1668 A.D.].

39. This is the tomb of Khamal, the son of Jacob. Died in the year 1119 of the Armenian era [1670 A.D.].

40. This is the tomb of Rev. Bagdassar. Died in the year 1120 of the Armenian era [1671 A.D.].

(This grave is near the Chapel).

41. This is the tomb of Mibjan, son of Murad of Julfa. Died in the year 1120 of the Armenian era [1671 A.D.].

42. This is the tomb of Johanness of the Turjamentz family. Died in the year 1122 of the Armenian era [1673 A.D.].

43. This is the tomb of Hovanjan, the son of David of Julfa. Died in the year 1122 of the Armenian era [1673 A.D.].

44. This is the tomb of Soolthanoom of the Qalandar family. Died in the year 1122 of the Armenian era [1673 A.D.].

45. This is the tomb of Phanus [Stephen], the son of David who departed to God at Agra in the year 1121 of the Armenian era [1672 A.D.].

45A. This is the tomb of* (name obliterated), the son of Gregory, the Master mason. Died in the year 1125 of the Armenian era [1676 A.D.].

46. This is the tomb of Manook who is from the city of Venice. Died in the year 63 of the era of Azaria [1678 A.D.].

47. This is the tomb of Mackertoom, the son of Samuel. Died in the year 63 of the era of Azaria [1678 A.D.].

---

* His brother Franc died in 1659. See No. 31. Their father, the master builder, may, as a contemporary, have taken part in the building of the world-famed Taj and the other architectural master-pieces of Shah Jehan.

48. This is the tomb of Mackertoom, the son of Arbab Johanness who departed to Christ in the year 63 of the era of Azaria [1678 A.D.].
49. This is the tomb of Agazar, the son of Martyrose. Died in the year 1128 of the Armenian era [1679 A.D.].
50. This is the tomb of Mackertich, the servant of Christ and the son of Joakim. Died in the year 1130 of the Armenian era [1681 A.D.].
50A. This is the tomb of Jacob of Samson. Died in the year 1133 of the Armenian era [1684 A.D.].
51. This is the tomb of Arakiel of the Chinikentz family. Died in the year 1134 of the Armenian era [1685 A.D.].
52. This is the tomb of Agah Carapiet of the family of Ekaz. Died in the year 1137 of the Armenian era [1688 A.D.].
53. This is the tomb of Pogose, the dyer. (Undated).
54. This is the tomb of Agah Zini, the son of Petrus of the family of Zinentz who departed to God in the year 1137 of the Armenian era [1688 A.D.].
55. This is the tomb of Hovanjan, the son of Pogose of the Jrookentz family of Julfa who died in Christ in the year 1150 of the Armenian era [1701 A.D.].
56. This is the tomb of Catchick, the son of Arakiel. Died in the year 92 of the era of Azaria [1707 A.D.].

Note.—No burials seem to have taken place between the years 1707 and 1774. Could they have been buried elsewhere, we doubt, as there was plenty of space in that cemetery for burials. We know however that with the removal of the Imperial capital to Delhi, the population of Agra dwindled down completely and the Armenians, who were great merchants and military men, may have followed the Imperial camp, hence the non-occurrence of deaths at Agra between those years.

Another strange thing is that we do not find any Armenian ladies buried in that cemetery from 1611—1777. Evidently no Armenian ladies came out to India, with their husbands, in those days.

57. This is the tomb of Samuel, son of the late Zorabbeg. Died in the year 159 of the era of Azaria [1774 A.D.].

58. This is the tomb of Nazar, the son of Baboom of Charsoq who departed from this world in the year 1774.

59. This is the tomb of Petrus, the son of Astwatzatoor of Arabkir who departed to the Lord in the 26th January, 1775.

60. This is the tomb of Pogose, the son of Booniath of Astabad who departed from this world in the year 1225 of the Armenian era [1776 A.D.].

61. This is the tomb of Rev. Arathoon who died in Christ in the year 1776.*

62. This is the tomb of Zorababel, the son of Gorgin of Tiflis. Died in the year 1776.

63. This is the tomb of Mariam Khanoom, the daughter of Lazar who departed to the Lord on the 13th June, 1777.

64. This is the tomb of Malcom of Astrakhan who departed to the Lord on the 30th May, 1778.

65. This is the tomb of Gabriel, the son of Moses of Tiflis who departed to the Lord on the 12th January, 1779.

66. This is the tomb of Elina, the daughter of David Khan of the family of Arqoothentz who departed to the Lord on the 6th December, 1779.

67. This is the tomb of Anna, the wife of Martyrose who departed to the Lord on the 13th April, 1780.

68. This is the tomb of Anna, the daughter of David Khan of the family of Arqoothentz, who departed to the Lord on the 23rd April, 1780.

69. Thomas, the son of Khojamall † of Julfa, who departed to the Lord at Delhi in 1790. His servant Chichroo placed this tablet over his grave.

---

* We regret that through a printer's mistake, the date of Rev. Arathoon's death has been wrongly recorded on page 23, in the list of the seven Armenian priests who died at Agra between the years 1614 and 1776. The date should have been 1776 and not 1675 A.D.

† He is the Armenian historian referred to in Chapter VIII, page 15, of this work.

70. This is the tomb of Anna, the daughter of Satoor, who departed from this world in the year 1783.

71. This is the tomb of prince Simon Khan, the son of Arathoon, who died by a bullet in war and was buried here at Agra on the 31st January, 1783.

72. This is the tomb of Ustad [Master] Shah Nazar Khan *, son of Allavery of Qaiquli, who was an expert in the art of casting cannons. He departed to the Lord with a good faith on the 25th April in the year 1784.

(There is also an inscription of six lines in beautiful Persian verse, on a perpendicular white marble slab fixed at the head of the grave. For a translation of the Persian inscription and the skill of the Armenian Krupp see Chapter VIII.)

73. This is the tomb of Azaria, the son of Arathoon of Kars, who was called Haghverdibeg. He departed to the Lord at Agra on the 22nd September, 1786.

74. This is the tomb of Captain Agazar, the son of Jacob of Maragh. He died in the Lord at Agra on the 5th January, 1793, aged 61 years.

75. This is the tomb of Anna, the wife of the late Michael of Julfa, who departed from this world in 1794.

76. This is the tomb of Gorginbeg Orosti, who died in the Lord at Agra in the year 1798.

77. This is the tomb of Merine, the daughter of Manook Khalam of Julfa and the wife of Galoost, who departed from this world at Agra on the 30th March, 1801, on a Saturday, leaving her son Agah Michael as a remembrance. May God preserve him. Amen.

78. This is the tomb of Marooth Joseph Marooth. Died in the Lord at Agra on the 3rd January, 1802, aged 41 years.

---

* Shah Nazar Khan's son, Mackertich, known as Shah Mirza, died at Gwalior in 1823 and was buried in the Armenian cemetery at Agra near his father's grave. See No. 94.

There is also an inscription in English as follows :—

Here lies the body of Marooth Joseph who died 3rd January 1802, Aged 41 years.

79. This is the tomb of Joanna*, the daughter of Elchee [envoy] Johanness of Julfa and the wife of Petrus of Erivan, who departed this life at Agra on Thursday, the 6th February, 1802, leaving her son, Captain Jacob, as a remembrance, whom God may preserve. Amen.

(There is also an inscription in Persian).

80. This is the tomb of Johanness of Qaiquli, who is called Aivazbeg Khan. He was a Commandant and died at Agra on the 17th December, 1803, aged 52 years.

81. This is the tomb of Anna Khathoon, the daughter of Gorginbeg, the Georgian, who died in the Lord at Agra on the 11th January, 1804, aged 15 years.

82. This is the tomb of Stephen, the son of Melik Petrus of Erivan, who departed from this world in the 6th March, 1805.

83. This is the tomb of Hripsimah, the wife of Gorginbeg, the Georgian, who died in the Lord on the 8th August, 1809.

(There is also an inscription in Persian).

84. This is the tomb of Kirakose,† the son of Arathoon of Kars, who was called Novroozbeg. He departed from this world on the 19th July, 1809.

85. This is the tomb of Pheri,‡ the daughter of the late Petrus of Erivan and the wife of Satoor Arathoon of Julfa, who departed this life at Gwalior on the 13th January, 1815.

---

* She was the mother of Colonel Jacob Petrus of Gwalior.

† His widow died in 1817. See No. 90.

‡ She was the sister of Colonel Jacob Petrus of Gwalior and as her mother, Joanna Petrus (See No. 79) was buried in the Armenian cemetery at Agra, she was also buried there, the body having been brought down from Gwalior.

86. This is the tomb of Satoor,* the son of Arathoon of Julfa, who departed this life at Gwalior on the 17th August, 1817.

87. In this tomb lies interred the body of Rev. Petrus, the son of Sarkies of Karabagh in Armenia. He died in the Lord in this city of Akbarabad [Agra], on the 15th June, 1816. Aged 57 years.

Fathers and brothers in Christ pray for him and may the Lord God have mercy on you.

(This grave is near the Chapel).

88. This is the tomb of Meherban Khanoom, the daughter of Davidbeg of Georgia and the wife of Michaeljan Thomas. Died in the Lord in 1816. Aged 32 years.

(There is also an inscription in Persian).

89. This is the tomb of Gabriel, the son of Daniel Agabab of Tiflis, who died in the Lord at the city of Agra on the 26th October, 1816. Aged 81 years.

90. This is the tomb of Annakhathoon, the wife of Kirakose who was known as Novroozbeg. She died in the Lord in ripe old age, on the 1st February, 1817 at Agra.

91. This is the tomb of Khathlina, the daughter of Jooan and the wife of Astwatzatoor, who died in the Lord at Agra on the 15th November, 1818. Aged 19 years.

92. This is the tomb of Thagoohi Khathoon † [Regina], the daughter of Petrus and the wife of Mackertich, known as Shah Mirza, who died in the Lord at the city of Agra on the 1st June, 1821. Aged 62 years.

93. This is the tomb of Petrus, the son of Gorginbeg Khan of Tiflis, who died in the Lord on the 4th August, 1822 at Agra. Aged 85 years.

(There is a long inscription in Persian).

---

* He was the husband of Pheri, the sister of Colonel Jacob Petrus of Gwalior (See No. 85). His body was also brought down from Gwalior and interred next to his wife's grave in the Armenian cemetery at Agra.

† She was another sister of Colonel Jacob Petrus of Gwalior. Her grave is next to her mother's grave in the Armenian cemetery at Agra. (See No. 79.) Her husband died in 1923. (See No. 94.)

94. This is the tomb of Mackertich,* the son of the late Shah Nazar Khan. He was known as Shah Mirza. He died in the Lord at Gwalior on the 25th December, 1823 and his body was brought down to Akbarabad [Agra]. Aged 65 years.

95. This is the tomb of Sophia Khanoom, the daughter of Arathoon and the wife of David George. Died in the Lord on the 16th May, 1823 at Agra. Aged 22 years.

96. This is the tomb of Astwatzatoor, the son of Johanness, who died in the Lord on the 21st June, 1825 at Agra. Aged 25 years and 22 days.

97. This is the tomb of Petrus, the son of Barsegh, who died in the Lord on the 2nd April, 1826 at Akbarabad [Agra]. Aged 43 years.

There is also an English inscription thus :—

Petruse Parsick died 2 April, 1826.
Aged 43 years.

98. This is the tomb of Elina Khathoon, the daughter of Kirakose and the wife of Johanness Jacob of Constantinople. Died in the Lord at Akbarabad [Agra] ,on the 3rd August, 1827. Aged 35 years.

(There is also an inscription in Persian).

99. This is the tomb of Captain Simon Gregory of Hamadan, who died at Gwalior on the 27th May, 1828 and his body was brought down to Agra. Aged 53 years.

100. This is the tomb of Captain Johanness Gregory of Constantinople, who died in thé Lord at Gwalior on the 1st July, 1829 and his body was brought down and buried at Akbarabad [Agra].

(He was known as Gregory Khan).

101. In loving memory of Magdalena, widow of Petrus Parsick, died 21st January, 1831. Aged 30 years.

---

* He was the son of the famous Shah Nazar Khan (See No. 72) and the husband of Colonel Jacob Petrus' sister Thagoohi Khathoon who died in 1821. (See No. 92.)

This slab erected by her grandson in January, 1902 replaces an upright one of sandstone showing signs of decay.

(Her husband, Petrus Parsick, died in 1826, see No. 97.)

102. Sacred to the memory of Master Petruse Parsick, who departed this life on the 12th August, 1832. Aged 6 years. The remains of his parents are also deposited underneath :—

Happy Petruse early blest
Rest in peaceful slumber rest,
What is life? A vapour past
What is death? A dream the last.
Removed to heaven by God your King
Will angels joined his praises sing.

(Inscriptions Nos. 101 and 102 are in English only.)

103. This is the tomb of Anna Khathoon the wife of Manook of Kabul. Died in the Lord on the 4th January 1833 in the Porsa village and the body was brought down and buried at Agra. Aged 55 years. (Adjoining this grave there is one with an inscription in Persian).

104. This is the tomb of Zorab Simon of Kabul, who died at Agra on the 12th January 1849. Aged 42 years.

There is also an inscription in English as follows :

Sacred to the memory of Mr. Zorab Simon of Cabul, Armenian merchant, who departed this life on the 12th of January 1849. Aged 42 years.

(This is an isolated grave in the cemetery far away from the others).—

105. This is the tomb of Mariam Khanoom the daughter of Thomas and the wife of Johanness who died in the Lord at Agra in the year 1849. Aged 75 years.

There is also an inscription in English as under :—

Sacred to the memory of M[ariam Khanoom] J. Johannes. Died 22nd August 1849. Aged about 75 years.

106. This is the tomb of Anna Bourbon, who died at Agra on the 5th January 1855. Aged 18 years.

(There is also an inscription in Persian).

107. Sacred to the memory of D. David, the wife of the late Captain David Shafraz who died on 18th November 1852.

108. This is the tomb of James the son of Mackertich of Agoolis who died at Agra on the 1st November 1855. Aged one year and 10 months.

There is also an inscription in English as under:

Sacred to the memory of James Mark' [Mackertich] who departed this life on the 1st November 1855. Aged 1 year, 10 months.

109. This is the tomb of Mariamjan the daughter of Mackertich Aviet of Agoolis who died in the Lord on the 27th March 1867. Aged 19 years.

There is also an inscription in English as under:—

In memory of Mary, daughter of Mackertich Aviet Died 27 March 1867. Aged 19 years.

110. Sacred to the memory of Mr. John David Jacob. Age 25 years and 5 months. Died on the 4th October, 1881.

111. In loving memory of Pherine Reghelini, daughter of Colonel David Jacob of Scindia's Army. Died on 20th February 1919. Aged 83 years and 3 months.

112. In loving memory of Phelomina Reghelini, grand daughter of Colonel David Jacob of Scindia's Army and Major Reghelini of Sumru Begum's Army. Died on 5th July 1927. Aged 76 years. Deeply mourned by her sorrowing son.*

---

* Mrs. Phelomina Reghelini's only son, Mr. John Michael Reghelini, was until recently, the popular Munsarim (Registrar) of the Chief Judge's Court at Agra. He is a great grandson of Colonel Jacob Petrus of Gwalior, from his mother's side. His paternal great grandfather, an Italian, was an officer in Begum Sumru's Army. He was the architect of the Cathedral at Sardhana which the Begum Sumru built at a cost of about four lakhs of rupees.

A word of explanation is necessary regarding the two different eras used in the old Armenian inscriptions at Agra and elsewhere in India. The great Armenian era commenced in the year 551 A.D. and the small, or the new era of Azaria, was started in 1615 A.D. and was used by the Armenians of Julfa and India only. The dates in these eras are not given in Roman figures, but in the letters of the Armenian alphabet, which like the Latin and the Arabic, have numerical value.

For instance, the date in the Armenian epitaph on the tombstone of Khojah Martyrose, (at the bottom of page 103) is given in two letters of the Armenian alphabet, namely RA and KEN, the numerical value of the former being 1000 and that of the latter 60, in all 1060. And as the great Armenian era commenced in 551 A.D. the year 1060 of that era is therefore equivalent to the year 1661 A.D.

In the same way, the date in the inscription on the tombstone of Manook from Venice, who died at Agra in the year 63 of the new era of Azaria, can be converted into the Christian era by the addition of 1615, which will give the year 1678 A.D. (See inscription No. 47). Fr. Felix's Armenian translator, being an unlettered man, was not conversant with the working of these eras, hence the serious blunders he has made in the translations of the Armenian inscriptions at Agra. One instance will suffice. The date of the death of Rev. Petrus of Karabagh who died at Agra in 1816 (see No. 87), is recorded, in Fr. Felix's list of inscriptions, to have occurred in the year 1683. What a faithful translation!

ARMENIANS AT GWALIOR

CHAPTER X

COLONEL JACOB PETRUS.

FOR 70 YEARS A COMMANDER OF SCINDHIA'S ARMY.

During the decadence of the Moghul Empire in India, in the second-half of the 18th century, Upper India was the happy hunting ground of European Military Adventurers, some of whom like De Boigne and Perron, achieved fame in the service of the Mahratta Chiefs.

In those days of stress and turmoil, when soldiers of the type of George Thomas and the notorious Sumru were carving out kingdoms and principalities for themselves, a young Armenian, Jacob Petrus, son of a merchant, possessing in no small measure the martial spirit of his race, decided to follow the military profession and through sheer merit he rose to be a Brigadier in the service of the Scindhia (Gwalior) whom he served loyally and faithfully for an uninterrupted period of seventy years and died, full of years and honours, on the 24th June, 1850, at the ripe old age of 95 years and 3 months.

Colonel Jacob was born of respectable Armenian parents at Delhi in 1755. His father Petrus (Peter) was a merchant from Erivan in Armenia and his mother Joanna, was the daughter of Elchee (Envoy) Johanness, an Armenian from Julfa, the Armenian suburb of Ispahan, the former capital of Persia, where a large Armenian colony was settled by Shah Abbas the Great in 1605. Colonel Jacob's father died at Delhi, but his grave cannot be found, as all the old Christian cemeteries and churches in that city were destroyed by the mutineers in 1857. His mother died at Agra on the 6th February, 1802 and lies buried in the old Armenian cemetery at Lashkarpur. He had two sisters, both of whom lived and died at Agra and are buried in the same cemetery where their mother is interred.

After the death of his father at Delhi, Colonel Jacob inherited, from his father's estate, a sum of five thousand rupees, which in those days was considered a fairly good heritage. A similar sum was given to his mother and his two sisters received jointly the residue of the estate amounting to five thousand rupees, according to the Armenian law of inheritance.

With the money inherited from his father, young Jacob, who evidently had no love for commerce or trade, turned his attention to military pursuits in which he was destined to achieve much greater success than in the prosaic field of commerce in which his father had laboured for several years at Delhi. It was the golden age of foreign military adventurers in India and young Jacob conceived the happy idea of following in their footsteps. He formed a military Corps and fought for the different native Chiefs on the remuneration system then prevailing in the dominions of the decadent Mogul Empire. Having attached himself to the Rajah of Burtpore, his Corps grew up daily in strength under the auspices of that Chief and for a period of three years he did well. He then fell seriously ill and was obliged to make over the control of his Corps to one of his brothers-in-law, who being a merchant with no knowledge of military affairs, allowed the Corps to get demoralised with the result that many of the soldiers deserted and took up service elsewhere. On his recovery, Jacob with the remnants of his Corps, entered in 1780, the service of General De Boigne, who was then in command of Scindhia's army. He fought at the battle of Oojein and for his bravery, he was made a Colonel by Dowlat Rao and given the command of the 1st Brigade which was composed of 12 Regiments of infantry, 4 Cavalry, 1 Brigade artillery with 150 guns. His pay was 3,000 rupees a month besides the revenue of the village of Jagsowlie and Soosara which was designated "Nankar" at Gwalior. The troops under his command were paid out of the revenues of the three "illaqas" (districts) known as Ambah, Kutwall, Bhind and Attair, computed at about 18 lakhs a year, which sum was collected by him and distributed among the troops. And because he paid the troops under him regularly they held him in the highest respect and served him most faithfully, whereas the troops that were under the command of Colonel John Baptiste Filose, were always in a state of mutiny as will be seen from the following extract from the "Letters from a Maharatta Camp during the year 1809," in which it is stated that "In justice, however, to the Hindoo character, I must repeat, that where they are well treated, no people on the face of the earth are more obedient, or are more easily governed, this is even here exemplified, in the difference of behaviour between the Sipahis of the two regular brigades : those of Jacob being rarely guilty of any disturbances or excesses, while those of Baptiste are as seldom out of a state of absolute mutiny : a difference attributable chiefly to the different modes in which they are paid, Jacob holding certain lands in *jaedad*, for the payment of his corps while Baptiste is entirely dependant on the Sarkar, and obliged to have frequent recourse to Dhurna, mutiny and other Mahratta expedients, to extort the smallest portion of the dues of himself and his troops."

Colonel Jacob held the highest and the most important position in the formidable army of the Scindiah before the memorable battles of Maharajpore and Punniar which sealed the doom of the Scindhias "irrepressible army in 1843. In the "Rambles and recollections of an Indian official," Major-General Sir W. H. Sleeman writes of the Gwalior army in 1833, as follows :

"The present force at Gwalior consists of three regiments of infantry, under Colonel Alexander, six under the command of Apaji, the adopted son of the late Bala Bai, eleven under Colonel Jacob and his son, [David], five under Colonel Jean Baptiste Filose, two under the command of the Mamu Sahib, the maternal uncle of the Maharajah, three in what is called Babu Baolis' campo, in all thirty regiments, consisting, when complete, of six hundred men each, with four field pieces. The "Jinsi," or artillery consists of two hundred guns of different calibre. There are but few corps of artillery and these are not considered very efficient I believe."

The following is from "*The Englishman*" (Calcutta), of August 21, 1843 :—

Gwalior.—The affairs of the State are in great confusion, indeed. The night before last a Battalion of Colonel Jacob's Brigade mutinied through the instigation of the usurper Dada Khasgeewala ; all other regiments of that Commandant have remained under arms, but quiet ; they yet appear attached to their old Brigadier. Our relation with this Government has ceased since the day the Regent Mama Sahib was expelled from the camp. The young Rajah is not imprisoned. The Maharanee, the widow of the late Maharajah Jankoojee Rae, is yet a girl of 11 or 12 years of age and is entirely guided by the advice of the usurper Dada who, in her name, conducts all the affairs and does all sorts of mischief. The poor Ranee, who is yet a child, is not aware of the consequences which will follow such misrule and bad management as are now in progress in this extensive dominion. Military preparations are being made with great expedition. 300 bags of grape shot each weighing 5 lbs. are daily being prepared in the arsenal in camp, and the gunpowder which had, perhaps, been stored in Dowlat Rae's time, and remained for ages untouched, is taken out for examination; the cannons long neglected and deemed unfit for use, are undergoing complete repair. All the affluent Chiefs are highly dissatisfied with the usurper for disregarding British council, and acting in opposition to the advice of the Governor-General; they seem to dread the result of such a line of conduct. But the usurper, who openly disacknowledges the supremacy of the British Government, is determined to oppose all opposition from our Government and to resist the British force should he be attacked by it."

Colonel Jacob's *campoo* consisted of 12 *pultans* of 1000 men each, the officers, about 40 in number, being Armenians.

He was held in such high esteem by the Scindhia that the whole city of Gwalior went into mourning at his death and during the funeral which was largely attended by the nobility and the military officers of the State, 95 minute guns, equal in number to the years of the veteran soldier, were fired from the ramparts of the historic Fort.

His grave as in the Armenian cemetery of Gwalior with a beautiful tombstone, bearing inscriptions in Armenian, Persian and English. The epitaph in English is as follows:—

> "Sacred to the memory of Colonel Jacob. Born 24th of March, 1755, obeit 24th of June, 1850. Aged 95 years and 3 months. He commanded the first Brigade of Scindhiah whom he faithfully served for 70 years.
> May he rest in peace."

There is in the possession of Mr. John Michael Reghelini of Agra, a great grandson, in the female line, of Colonel Jacob, a beautiful oil painting, in military costume, of the distinguished soldier. The painting was, at our request, exhibited by Mr. Reghelini, at the Historical Exhibition, held at Gwalior in December, 1929, in connection with the Gwalior Session of the "Indian Historical Records Commission."

The portrait, also in military costume, which is reproduced on the opposite page, is from a painting, in water-colours, which we found in the possession of an old Mahratta gentleman at Gwalior, whose father had been the *diwan* (manager) of Colonel Jacob's large estates.

And in this connection we would humbly suggest to the Gwalior Darbar, should these lines meet their eyes, to pay a tribute to the revered memory of Colonel Jacob by placing a portrait of the veteran soldier either in the State Museum or in the Hall of the Gwalior Municipality at Naumahalla, where the "Grand Old Man" of Gwalior lived and died 86 years ago.

Peace to his soul, rest to his ashes, and may the revered memory of the distinguished Brigadier be cherished and kept green for ages to be, in the progressive State of Gwalior, the pride of the Mahratta nation, which has given a Sivaji, a Mahadji and a Dawlat Rao to India.

From an Armenian journal published at Calcutta in 1850, I find that Colonel Jacob left, after his death, an estate worth 6 lakhs of rupees in hard cash and government Securities, besides his palatial house at Naumahalla.

Colonel Jacob had two sons, David and Owen the former held the rank of a Major under his father on a salary of Rs. 1,800 per month, whilst the latter held the post of a Captain under his brother, Major David Jacob, on a salary of Rs. 900 a month.

Major David led an extravagant, luxurious and licentious life, surrounded by noted musicians and dancing girls and his stables of valuable horses and tame tigers were noted at Gwalior. He died of phthisis on the 19th September, 1848, aged 35 years, and lies buried in the Armenian cemetery at

Gwalior. His widow Salbi by name, who died at Gwalior in 1893, was the daughter of an Armenian merchant of Calcutta, Pogose Carapiet by name. They had two daughters, Pherine, known as Mutrujan, who married Major Stephen Raghelini of Begum Samru's army, and Sarah, known as Chuttrujan, who married an Armenian, Shafraz Warden, of Agra. Gregory Warden, late Head Translator of the Allahabad High Court, was a brother of Shafraz Warden referred to above. Both the daughters of Major David Jacob are dead. They were alive in 1919 when we first visited Agra. A lineal descendant, in the female line, of Colonel Jacob, is Mr. John Michael Reghelimi, until recently the popular Munsarim (Registrar) of the Agra Chief Judge's Court. Mr. Raghelini is a grandson of Mrs. Pherine Reghelini, the granddaughter of Colonel Jacob, as stated above.

In this connection we may mention that both the grand daughters of Colonel Jacob were in receipt of pensions from the Gwalior Darbar in recognition of the valuable and meritorious services of their grandfather and we are pleased to hear that our esteemed friend, Mr. John M. Raghelini, has been granted, 1928, a *muafi* or pension of Rs. 75 per month for life, in recognition of the long and meritorious services of his great great grandfather, Colonel Jacob to the Gwalior State.

Verily merit has its reward in this progressive State, for whereas in British India and other countries, pensions die immediately with the pensioners, it is continued for generations in the enlightened Gwalior Raj.

The second son of Colonel Jacob, Captain Owen or John Jacob, left Gwalior after the death of his father in 1850 and went to reside at Agra in the large Kothi (house) in the Cantonments which is visible from the ramparts of the Agra Fort. He was very partial towards Mohammedans with whom he associated mostly. When the Mutiny broke out at Agra in 1857, he was persuaded by all his English and Armenian friends to take refuge in the Agra Fort with them, but his confidential Mematie servants dissuaded him from doing so and by acceding to their wishes, he fell into the trap cleverly laid for him by those robbers, who killed him and sacked his palatial house.

For his loyalty to the British cause in India, Major Owen Jacob, the worthy son of a worthy father, laid down his precious life. His name should be recorded in letters of gold in the annals of the Indian Mutiny which severely shook the British Indian Empire to its foundations. In this connection we beg to suggest to the Military authorities at Agra to place a memorial tablet either in the Agra Fort or in the Martyrose's Chapel, which as we have seen, was erected by a pious Armenian and it is therefore nothing but right that the murdered Armenian officer should have a memorial in that sacred edifice, where divine service was held in the days of yore, as is evidenced by the existence of an altar to this day.

Major Owen Jacob was commanding the loyal Agra troops against the mutinous Neemuch Brigade at the village of Susseva on the plain beyond Shahganj, on the 6th July, 1857, when alas ! he was the *first* to fall by the hands of his Mematie confidants, in whose integrity and valour to defend him to the last, he had unfortunately every confidence. His body which was mutilated beyond recognition by the blood-thirsty mutineers, was brought down to Agra and buried in the compound of his Kothi and over his grave, his widow erected a marble monument which can be seen to this day, bearing an inscription as follows :—

> Sacred to the memory of Major John Jacob, late of Scindiah Army, son of the late Colonel Jacob Petruse of Gwalior. Killed at Agra by the rebels on the 6th July, 1857. Aged 43 years.
>
> This monument is respectfully erected by his disconsolate widow and daughter. It is better to trust in the Lord than to put any confidence in man.

He had an only daughter who married a Frenchman, Debeneau, who was distantly related to General Ventura of Ranjit Singh's Sikh Army. Their son, James Debeneau, with his wife and children lived at Sirdhana with their grandmother, Major John Jacob's widow, in rather crippled circumstances.

Major Owen (John) Jacob was not the only Armenian who lost his life during the outbreak of the Mutiny at Agra. Two other Armenian residents of that city, Zacharias Parsick, a clerk in the Secretariat, and his aged mother, were both murdered by the rebels on the 5th July, 1857.

Helen,* the pious widow of Colonel Jacob, died at Gwalior on the 3rd July, 1871, aged 86 years, and was buried in the Armenian cemetery of that place next to her husband. Their only daughter, Merinjan, who had married an Armenian from Basra, Johanness Menatsakan Pogose, died at Gwalior on the 14th October, 1875, leaving an only son, by name Sarkies, who died at Gwalior, without issue, in 1897. Johanness M. Pogose, the son-in-law of Colonel Jacob, died at Gwalior in 1892, aged 85 years.

Helen, the widow of Colonel Jacob gave, in 1865, a donation of Rs. 6,000 to the Roman Catholic Mission at Agra, towards the erection of a chapel at Simla, as can be seen from the following letter of the Superintendent General of the Catholic Institutions.

Agra Catholic Cathedral House,
14th January 1865.

To
Mrs. Colonel Jacob,
Gwalior.

Dear Madam,

I was duly favoured with your letter of the 9th instant enclosing receipts and amounts on the Agra Bank to the amount of Rupees Six Thousand (6,000) and am very glad to say in reply that after communicating your wishes to the Manager, he has transferred the amount to my name with instructions that I

---

* Helen was the daughter of one Johanness, known as Noroz Bahadoor, who, like his father, had been the governor of the Fort at Delhi in the reign of the Mogul emperors. She had two sisters, one of whom, known as Shahzadi Bisab, had married Major Johanness, of Scindia's Army, who had constructed the artificial tank at Gwalior, known as "Waness Sahih ka talao" and which is in existence to this day.

may withdraw the same on the 1st January 1866, according to the Rules of the Deposits in the Bank.

It is needless to say that the above sum shall be scrupulously applied towards the building of a Chapel at Simla. I shall also take care that your name shall be recorded as a grand benefactress of the Mission and I trust that the prayers that will be offered in the said house of God, which is expected to be erected with your charitable donation, will call on you a due reward in this and in the world to come.

Imploring you the blessing of God.

I remain,
Dear Madam.
Yours faithfully,
F. LEWIS,
Superintendent General, Catholic Institutions.

Prior to her death, Helen, the pious widow of Colonel Jacob, sent to the Armenian Church at Calcutta and to the Cathedral at Julfa (Ispahan), all the sacred vessels and vestments, of great intrinsic value, which had belonged to the Gwalior Armenian Church erected by Colonel Jacob, who maintained for many years an Armenian priest at his own expense to attend to the spiritual wants of the Armenian colony at Gwalior, which at one time numbered thirty families all of whom were in the military service of the Gwalior State.

A number of Armenians served under Colonel Jacob as officers—commissioned and non-commissioned—of whom some built up considerable fortunes. One, Major Johanness, left a fortune of Rs. 500,0000; another, Woskan, returned to his native town of Erivan in Armenia, and there enjoyed a life of luxury and ease. After the battles of Maharajpore and Punniar in 1843, which resulted in the disabandonment of the huge army of the Scindhia, most of the Armenians quitted Gwalior and gave up their martial occupations for good.

Major Johanness, better known as "Waness Sahib," had constructed an artificial tank and a well, both of which are in existence to this day at Gwalior and are known as "Waness

Sahib ka talao and kooa." Major Johanness had married a sister of Colonel Jacob's wife by name Shahzadi Bisab. He died, without issue, at Gwalior on the 1st July, 1829, aged 60 years and his body was removed to Agra and buried at the Armenian cemetery there.

There are no Armenians now left at Gwalior and the only vestiges of the once flourishing colony are the Armenian cemetery and Colonel Jacob's Campoo, Parade and Garden. His palatial house at Naumahalla where the Armenian Church was located, is now in the occupation of the Gwalior Municipality.

Gwalior, where in the palmy days of Colonel Jacob, several Armenian families resided and had a Church of their own with a resident priest, has, in the natural order of things, shared the sad fate of Agra, Delhi and Surat, there being no Armenians left to tell the tale of the doings of their illustrious ancestors. The only landmarks of the Armenian colony at Gwalior are the few tombstones in the cemetery which was opened by Colonel Jacob in 1825. It is a walled place, with a gate, making the consecreted ground safe from desecration.

The following are the translations of the inscriptions in that small but beautiful cemetery :

1. This is the tomb of Carapiet, the son of Gaspar Bazrganbashi of Diarbekir who died in the Lord at the city of Gwalior on the 20th April, 1825.
2. This is the tomb of Mahtesy Alexan, the son of Khoodaverdi of Salmast who died in the Lord on the 16th May, 1834 at Gwalior.
3. This is the tomb of Anooshka, the daughter of Stephen and the wife of George Agabeg who died in the Lord on the 29th November, 1837 at Gwalior. Aged 14 years.
4. This is the tomb of Mariam Khanoom, the daughter of Mackertich, who is known as Shah Mirza,

---

* She was a niece of Colonel Jacob Petrus. Both her parents, Shah Mirza and his wife Thagoohi, are buried at Agra. Simon Gregory was a Major in Scindia's Army.

and the wife of Simon Gregory of Hamadan who died in the Lord on the 18th May, 1837 at Gwalior.

(There is also an inscription in Persian)

5. This is the tomb of Gregory Pogose who died in the Lord on the 30th January, 1839.

6. This is the tomb of the late Rev. Martyrose David of New Julfa who died in the Lord on the 2nd February, 1839 at the city of Gwalior. Aged 75 years.

(There is also a Persian inscription).

7. This is the tomb of the late Major David Jacob* who died in the Lord on the 19th September, 1848 at Gwalior. Aged 35 years.

(There is also a long Persian inscription).

8. This is the tomb of Phiarikhanoom the beloved daughter of Joseph Owen, who died in the Lord on the 20th August, 1849, at Gwalior. Aged 2 years.

(There is also an inscription in Persian).

9. This is the tomb of Anna, the widow of Aviet Johanness of Bayazid, who died in the Lord at Gwalior on the 18th November, 1849. Aged 30 years.

(There is also an inscription in Persian).

10. This is the tomb of the late Colonel Agah Jacob Petrus who died in the Lord on the 24th June, 1850, at Gwalior. Aged 95 years and 3 months.

(There is also an inscription in Persian. The English inscription is given on p. 138.)

11. This is the tomb of the late Moses Manook who was a Colonel in Hyderabad, Sind. He died

---

* Major David was the elder son of Colonel Jacob Petrus of Gwalior. He died during the lifetime of his aged father.

in the Lord at Gwalior on Monday, the 4th June, 1851. Aged 55 years.

(There is also a long inscription in Persian).

12. This is the tomb of Waness [Johanness] Gabriel, who died on the 2nd January, 1853 at Gwalior. Aged 90 years.

There are besides the above, 17 tombstones in the Armenian cemetery at Gwalior, 12 of which have no inscriptions and the remaining 5 are without tombstones. In a covered place are to be seen the beautiful tombstones of Colonel Jacob and of his elder son, Major David, with bilingual inscriptions, as recorded above, but the one over the grave of Helen, the widow of Colonel Jacob, who died at Gwalior on the 3rd July 1871, and was buried next to her husband, has no inscription.

Such is the irony of Fate, a person who gave large sums in charities to her own people, and to others, in her lifetime, is to be left uncommemorated after her death. Verily in the words of the poet, some great people die "unwept, unhonoured and unsung". Will the enlightened Gwalior Darbar that is still keeping the memory of Colonel Jacob green, by allowing a life pension to his great grandson, pay a tribute to the revered memory of the noble and pious lady by having a suitable inscription engraved on the existing beautiful tombstone which covers the mortal remains of the widow of the veteran soldier who served the Scindhia faithfully for a period of 70 years.

Should these lines meet the eyes of the Archæological Department of Gwalior State and the above suggestion be viewed with favour, in the interests of archæology, we shall be pleased to supply the requisite inscription, either in Armenian or English, there being no need for Persian in these days. It was different in the good old days when the language of the immortal Firdosi was the *lingua franca* in India.

CHAPTER XI.

ARMENIANS AT NARWAR.

Two Interesting Epitaphs.

It appears that prior to the Armenian settlement at Gwalior, with a church and a priest of their own, under the auspices of Colonel Jacob Petrus, towards the end of the 18th century, there have been Armenians in Gwalior State during the first half of the 18th century. There exist to this day two tombstones bearing Armenian inscriptions at Narwar. One dated 1743, marks the resting places of an Armenian military officer and the other is to the memory of an Armenian priest who died at Narwar in 1750, at the ripe old age of 72 years. The presence of an old Armenian priest at Narwar, which was an important city and the seat of a governor in those days, goes to prove the existence of a fairly large Armenian community in that place in the middle of the 18th century. This is confirmed by two contemporary Catholic priests who lived at Narwar from 1743—1765.

Fr. A. Strobl who was there between the years 1743 and 1751, writes as follows :—

"In the year 1742, a rich Christian, who is held in great esteem by the King of the place, built a new Chapel for the gathered Christians."

This is confirmed by Fr. J. Tiefentaller, who after travelling all over Hindustan, proceeded to Narwar about the end of 1747. He writes :—

> "There lived at that time at Narwar a Christian of Armenian descent who stood in high favour with the Great Mughol and was subsequently appointed Governor of that Province. He resided in one of the first palaces of the city and had houses built for his numerous relatives and employees, as well as a Chapel, in which he and all his Christian retinue attended divine service on Sundays."

> He further states that "the Armenian governor, the only supporter of the church at Narwar, having died, the small Christian community there dwindled away, soon to disappear altogether."

Fr. Tieffentaller left Narwar in the beginning of 1765, because we find him at Jhansi on the 11th February, 1765.

Translation of an Armenian inscription on a tombstone in Sikandarpura Ward of Narwar town in the Gwalior State.

> This is the tomb of Simon, son of the late Nazar of Julfa. Died in the year 128 of the era of Azaria [1743 A.D.].

There is also an inscription of two lines in Persian, which can be translated thus :—

> Solaiman Beg, the Armenian,
> son of Nazar Beg.

The Armenian name Simon has been converted into Solomon (Solaiman) in the Persian inscription, evidently for the sake of euphony.

Both father and son have the title of *Beg,* which clearly shows that they must have been in military service to have earned that title.

The inscription in Armenian, is beautifully carved and is in a fine state of preservation despite its great age. There is a figure of the Cross carved at the top of the bilingual inscriptions.

There is a large tombstone, in a fine state of preservation, near the Dak Bungalow, Narwar town, Gwalior State, with a long inscription of 26 lines, in ancient Armenian verse, of which the following is a literal translation.

"If you were to ask my tomb. I am a priest of the Armenian nation. I died at Narwar aged 72 years. I was a widower for 30 years. My name is Reverend Arakiel. I am a native of Julfa*, the son of a good and a pious man whose

---

* Julfa, or New Julfa, as it is called to distinguish it from the Old, is the Armenian suburb of Ispahan, the former capital of Persia. A large Armenian colony of 12,000 families from Julfa on the Araxes, in Armenia settled there in 1605, during the glorious reign of Shah Abbas the Great, the ornament of the Saffavi dynasty, which founded by

name is Pogose. My end came on the 13th day of the month of May in the year1750 of the Christian era and in the year 135 of the era of Azaria, on the day of the feast of the Apparition of the Cross.

Do not think he is here, his body was interred in this place for six months and then removed to Bengal and his mark was left here. He was taken and buried in the Armenian church at Chinsurah. I became a stranger in a stranger land. The sins of those who pray for him will be forgiven in the terrible day of judgment."

Narwar was an important town and the seat of a Governor during the days of Mogul supremacy.

The descendants of Prince John Philip Bourbon and his Armenian wife, Lady Juliana, to the number of about three hundred souls, came to Narwar from Delhi shortly after the plunder of that city by Nadir Shah in 1739.

There must have been a good number of Armenians amongst them, as the Bourbons were closely connected with the Armenians by marriage ties, for following the example of their princely ancestor, several members of the family married Armenian wives, the last being Anna Bourbon who died at Agra in 1855 and lies buried in the old Armenian cemetery of that place.

Shah Ismail in 1500, continued to rule in Persia till the year 1722, when the Afghans invaded the country during the reign of the imbecile Shah Sultan Hossain, committed untold barbarities and enormities on the peaceful inhabitants of Ispahan, made a prisoner of the mollah-worshipping king, whom they carried into captivity and ultimately put him to death in 1724.

The Afghans were driven out of Persia by the great warrior, Thahmaz Kuli Khan, who assumed the sovereignty of the devastated country in 1736, under the name of Nadir Shah. It was this cruel monarch who invaded India in 1739 and sacked Delhi, carrying off the famous "Peacock" throne of Shah Jehan and the historical diamond, the "Kohinoor", with a large booty, after making the streets of the Imperial City run with blood. Nadir's invasion of the Punjab was the death blow to the once glorious Mogul dynasty founded by Babar, of the house of Tamerlane, in 1524.

ARMENIANS AT FATHEPUR SIKRI

CHAPTER XII

AKBAR'S CHRISTIAN WIFE.

MARIAM ZAMANI BEGUM.

In the deserted and ruined city of Fathepur Sikri, the favourite capital of the Emperor Akbar, twenty two miles from Agra, founded in 1568-9, there still exists the beautiful palace of Akbar's Christian wife, known as the "Armenian Princess' Palace".

It is a well-known historical fact that one of Akbar's queens was an Armenian, known as Mariam Zamani Begum, That well-known Indian historian, Henry George Keane, in his *Sketch of the History of Hindustan,* says :—

> "Akbar subsequently married at least two other foreign ladies, an Armenian and a princess of Marwar. Preserving unmolested in the palace their Chapels and their Chaplains, these ladies would necessarily have their share in promoting the Catholicity of the Emperor's mind and predisposing him to regard with favour Hindus and Christians."

William Hunter, a great authority on Indian History writing of Akbar's wives says, in his *Indian Empire,* that "another of his wives is said to have been a Christian." Louis Rousselet, says in his *India and its Native Princes*: "Near Akbar's mausoleum beyond the enclosure, stands a vast ruined cenotaph enclosing the tomb of the Emperor's Christian wife, the Begum Maria."

De Laet, who wrote his *Empire of the Great Maguls* in 1631, that is only 26 years after the death of Akbar, when the slightest circumstance connecteed with him was fresh in the memory of all, mentions in his description of the palace "one set belonging to Mary Makany, the wife of Akbar."

Henry Blochmann, in his translation of the *Ain-i-Akbari* mentions in one of his notes that there is not the least doubt of

"Akbar having an Armenian wife." Fanthome, the author of *Reminiscences of Agra,* says: "I have in my possession information which leads me to believe that there is a great deal of truth in the assertion that Akbar had a Christian wife whose name was Mariam."

Some 20 years ago, the late F. Hosten S. J. read a learned Paper on Akbar's Christian wife before the Asiatic Society of Bengal and exhibited an artistic painting, in water colours, of the Emperor with his Christian wife. There was a Persian superscription which can be rendered into English thus: "Jalal-ud-din Akbar with Mariam Zamani Begum." In the painting Akbar is seated on a rich sofa, holding in his right hand the mouthpiece of his *hookah*; his left arm is thrown round the neck of the girl, who stands half reclining against him and supports his left-hand with her left.

Fr. Hosten's Paper, with the photographic illustration of the painting, were published in the "Statesman," on the 14th November 1916. The following is a copy:

AKBAR'S CHRISTIAN WIFE.

Two Interesting Pictures.

Two months ago, I was completing the proof-reading of my paper on "Mirza Zu-l-Qarnain, a Christian Grandee under three Great Moghuls, with Notes on Akbar's Christian Wife and the Indian Bourbons" (shortly to be issued by the Asiatic Society of Bengal) my conclusion being that Akbar appears to have had a Christian wife, an Armenian, when the unexpected discovery was made of a painting in the European style of art, representing Akbar with a Christian girl in partly European attire, and the Persian superscription "Jalal-ud-din Akbar ma Maryam Zamani Begum" (Jalal-ud-din Akbar with Maryam Zamani Begam).

The picture had been bought by Mr. A. Stephen, of Camac Street, Calcutta, from the estate of the late Prince Muhammad Bakhtiyar Shah, of the House of Tippu Sultan of Mysore, together with three other paintings. When Mr. A. Stephen mentioned casually to one of his friends, Mr. Mesrovb J. Seth, the author of "The Armenians in India" (Calcutta, 1895), that one of the paintings exhibited Akbar with a lady wearing a cross, Mr. Seth, who had helped me for my paper on Mirza Zu-l-Qarnain, naturally concluded that she must be Akbar's reputed and elusive Christian wife. An examination of the picture could not but strengthen him in this opinion, especially as the Persian superscription was plain. He communicated at once with me, and an examination of the picture, I made in his company, caused me also for my part, to concur in the view that the picture was intended to represent Akbar's Christian wife.

I confess that the name Maryam Zamani Begum was a surprise to me, not that the name is not connected in some traditional accounts with Akbar's Christian wife, but because it appeared to take so readily for granted a point which to prove is so extremely difficult, the best authorities being agreed that Maryam Zamani Begum was most probably the daughter of Raja Bihari Mal, and very probably Jahangir's mother. Considering, however, that these two points were not absolutely settled, we could feel less uneasy about the name.

If the picture was to speak for itself, it was evident that it was meant to represent Akbar's Christian wife. Opinions may differ as to the correctness of Akbar's likeness; but there will not be two opinions about the portrait being intended as a likeness of Akbar; only he and his son Jahangir shaved their beard, keeping only the moustache; the *takauchiyah* or cabaya is tied on the right, according to Akbar's own directions in the *Ain* (Blochmann, I. 88), whereas formerly it was tied on the left. Even the *huqqa,* of which Akbar holds the mouthpiece in his right hand, was meant to show that he smoked or presided at the invention of the *huqqa*. As for the girl, the first thing that strikes the beholder is that she wears a plain cross from her necklace of pearls. Now, no one has ever advanced that Maryam Zamani Begum was a Muhammadan. Therefore, the girl in the picture could be only a Hindu or a Christian. A Hindu she could not be: the dress, the *decolletage,* the absence of *tika* or beauty-mark, the amorous attitude of the pair, especially the cross, were against it. She was a Christian then. Of what nationality? Here again opinions could differ. The type of the girl is somewhat vague; but the arguments to prove that Akbar's Christian wife was Portuguese are extremely weak, while the Bourbon tradition that she was an Armenian compared with certain events of 1590-1600, appeared plausible. To me the face looked more Eastern than European, and some of my Armenian friends felt rather strong on the point that she had Armenian features. Various other characteristics of the picture seemed to favour this view. A European lady, on seeing the painting, compared Maryam's dress to that of a Circassian girl.

What led us further to emphasise the importance of the discovery was that at first we could not get beyond the information that the picture had been from time immemorial in the possession of its former owners. We might even have concluded that the picture had come to Calcutta by way of the Dekkan.

There were, however, two facts which called for reflection. First Akbar was represented smoking a *huqqa*. We have shown that Akbar smoked at least on one or two occasions, and that one of his doctors is credited by a certain tradition with having invented the *huqqa*. Be the latter point as it may, we could *a la rigueur* wink at the fact that the painter had tried to combine in one picture the idea that Akbar smoked sometimes, together with the tradition that he had a Christian wife. It was enough for our purpose if the picture antedated the late written evidence on Akbar's Christian wife. In fact, a good argument could be made out of a picture of Maryam dating from 1770-1800 because we still find at that date other descendants of Juliana than the Bourbons, and the Bourbons maitain that Juliana was the sister of Akbar's Christian wife. But, how old was our picture?

Secondly,—With the picture of Akbar's Christian wife there were three others of a different kind, but of the same size and style, all showing scenes of regal life at the Moghul Court: (1) dancing amusements of Princes in the Fort of Delhi in the time of Akbar II (reigned 1806-1837); (2) Nadir Shah and Muhammad Shah seated on the Peacock Throne not corresponding at all, except for the two Peacocks, to the gorgeous description of Tavernier and many others; (3) a darbar of Ahmad Shah (reigned 1748-1754). Now, not long before, I had come across a picture exactly similar to that of Nadir Shah and Muhammad Shah on the Peacock Throne, and it did not take long to re-discover it in the Loan Exhibition of Antiquities, Coronation Durbar, 1911, published by the Archæological Department of India, p. 134, Plate LIX, where it is described as the property of L. Bulaqi Dass of Delhi.

Further repeated investigations elicited the information that the picture of Maryam had been presented in 1902 to the widow of Prince Bakhtiyar Shah by her grandfather, the late Nawab Mirza Akbar Ali Beg, Prime Minister of Karauli, who died at Delhi some five or six years ago.

Expert knowledge was required to pronounce on the provenance and age of the picture. Mr. Percy Brown, the Principal of the Government School of Arts, went to inspect it and declared it to be late Lucknow or Oudh work, and that the European conception of it was not beyond an Indian painter imbued with the European methods of the Oudh school of art. One of his assistants, an Indian, studied it at the Government School of Arts, where it was sent for inspection, and said that the colours used—it is not an oil-painting—were European; hence, the picture might not be more than 50 or 70 years old. Possibly, it was an enlargement of an earlier miniature by a European. He even thought that, "some 24 years ago, in the time of Lord Curzon" (therefore not before 1899), he had seen in the shop of a Muhammadan painter at Delhi three or four oval pictures, like ours, but he could not be positive that the subject was the same. This was making our picture very young, indeed; and we might have tried to cavil about the period when the colours indicated as European were introduced into India, but there is no need for that now.

I then wrote to the papers describing our picture summarily, and asking whether similar pictures or miniatures were known to exist in India; also, what oral traditions were still current on the subject of Akbar's Christian wife. I had collected a good number of statements from printed books. To what extent had the wear and tear of time influenced them? In particular what was Maryam's nationality? Was she Portuguese or of some other nationality?

My letter appeared in the papers of September 16th, 1916, and, on September 20th, "Forty-Seven" informed us through *The Statesman* that he was told there was a painting of

11

Akbar's Christian wife in Nana Earnavis' Wada at Menavlii in the Satara District. I invited "Forty-Seven" to continue his investigations, and, if possible, to procure us a photo. If necessary, a photo of our picture will be sent for comparison; but I have not heard of "Forty-Seven" since, and the fact that Menavlii is not given in the "Imperial Gazatteer of India" or in the old Satara District Gazetteer is somewhat discouraging. Will "Forty-Seven" be so good as to send us his address? We cannot, of course, come to a conclusion so long as a copy of that picture is not obtained.

THE SECOND PICTURE.

A few days later, very definite information reached me privately from Delhi about a picture similar to ours. Mr. I. W. Bowring, I. Police, Delhi, wrote on September 24th that the "original" picture of Akbar and the Christian girl was in the possession of Munshi Bulaqi Dass, Proprietor of the Muir Press, Delhi, a gentleman who has hundreds of pictures in his albums. "He bought it with other pictures many years ago in an unfinished condition in pencil, and he has since had it painted. The picture, as far as he knows, came from the studio of the descendant of some court-painter. Mirza Akbar Ali Beg died here in Delhi five or six years ago. His sons (three) are here now. They live in the Farash-Khana quarter. Mr. Bulaqi Dass tells me that Mirza Akbar Ali Beg may have had a photo taken of his pictures, as he used to send for them to look at." (By the way, Mr. A. Stephen's picture in not a photo but a painting.) Mr. Bulaqi Dass was kind enough to send me his picture for inspection. It turns out to be identical in substance with that of Mr. A. Stephen. The conception is exactly the same. Only the coloration, the floral designs on the costumes and tapestry, and some trifling other details are different. Which of the two pictures is superior in execution, I leave to art-critics to decide. Nor does it matter, for Mr. Bulaqi Dass' statement that he bought his picture as a pencil-sketch "some 25 years ago" (as Mr. Bowring wrote on Oct. 4), and had it painted later, also the frequent visits to his house and borrowing of pictures by Mirza Akbar Ali Beg, can leave no reasonable doubt as to Mr. Bulaqi Dass' picture being the original one. The doubt is still less since Munshi Bulaqi Dass is, I am told, the same as L. Bulaqi Dass, who exhibited at the Darbar of 1911 a picture of Nadir Shah and Muhammad Shah on the Peacock Throne, for a copy of it, once in Mirza Akbar Ali Beg's possession, was bought by Mr. A. Stephen along with the picture of Maryam. The reason why the two pictures of Maryam remained unknown all through the oft-repeated discussions on Akbar's Christian wife, is that Munshi Bulaqi Dass did not exhibit his at the Durbar of 1911, while the other was kept in Prince Bakhtiyar Shah's *zenana*.

The discussion must now be transferred from Mr. A. Stephen's picture to that of Munshi Bulaqi Dass; and I am afraid it will yield little or nothing. A number of points in Mr. A. Stephen's picture, which we might have laid stress on to prove Maryam's Armenian parentage, are missing in the earlier picture. She looks more European in the latter, her complexion being fairer and rosier. Perhaps, the idea of the painter was that she was Portuguese. Again, and this is not less important, the Persian superscription is wanting in Munshi Bulaqi Dass' picture. Hence, the authority for its insertion in Mr. A. Stephen's picture appears to be simply that of Mirza Akbar Ali Beg, who may have borrowed the name from the current tradition.

We ought to be able to prove that the Munshi's picture is an original conception or a copy of something earlier. In the first case, we prove nothing unless we show that there exists among Hindus or Muhammadans a tradition running on parallel lines to, and independent of, that current among Christians. Both Hindus and Muhammadans seem to have such a tradition, but how shall we show that it is not borrowed from the Christians? It is not feasible. That the Muhammadans own to such a tradition, we might conclude from the statements of some of the letters that have appeared in the papers, *e.g.*, one by A. F. M. Abul Ali of Mymensingh in which the writer expresses, however, his scepticism regarding its truth. We might perhaps infer it also from the action of Mirza Akbar Ali Beg in labelling his picture as he did. Hindus, too, appear to believe in her existence. One of the prominent Maharajas of Bengal wrote to me that he has "always known Mariam

Zamani to be a non-Muhammadan woman, at least in the beginning; for whether she was subsequently converted to Islam, I cannot say." A Hindu painter, in whose family painting is a hereditary profession, volunteered the statement that he had heard his mother's father, Babu Shivlal of Patna, say that Akbar had a *vilayati Bibi,* not from Europe, but from Armenia. The man had nothing to expect from me, however, as he might have communicated with others who had heard me express my opinion about Maryam's Armenian extraction, his statement may be regarded by some as not unprejudiced. Then, there is the action of the Delhi Court-painter or one of his descendants who sketched the Munshi's picture; whether he was a Hindu or a Muhammadan remains to be learned.

Doubtless, all this proves next to nothing. I hope that my Delhi correspondent will succeed in finding out whether the Delhi painters have a tradition about Akbar's Christian wife and her nationality. Perhaps, he will discover the descendants of the Court-painter, and so learn whether the Munshi's picture is original or a copy of something earlier. If it is original and therefore fanciful, or nothing further is discovered, it would be some consolation if a picture of a new type, or at least older than Mr. Bulaqi Dass', were found at Menavlii, the place pointed out by "Forty-Seven."

And, if nothing turns up, what then? Then matters stand as they were. We have no new argument. That is all.

H. HOSTEN, S. J. "

The publication of Fr. Hosten's Paper led to a controversy and several letters, pro and con, appeared in the columns of the two English dailies in Calcutta—the "Statesman" and the "Englishman."

On the face of solid historical evidence, which cannot be challenged, some sceptics disputed the existence of a Christian queen in Akbar's seraglio.

Fr. Francisco Corsi, a Jesuit priest, writing on the 15th October, 1626, refers to Mirza Zul-Qarnain, who was brought up in the palace, as follows :—

> "The King [Jehangeer] loves him, as brought up in the Royal House at King Akbar's order by one of

> the queens, whom he called mother, and King Akbar he called father."

This clearly shows that Akbar had an Armenian wife, who was the childless aunt of Mirza Zul-Qarnain, whose mother had died when he was young, and according to Jesuit records, both he and his younger brother, Mirza Scanderus, were brought up in the Palace by their maternal aunt.

We had, prior to the publication of Fr. Hosten's Paper, published in the columns of the now defunct "Englishman," the following letter on the 20th September, 1916 :—

AKBAR'S CHRISTIAN WIFE.

THE ARMENIAN TRADITION IN INDIA.

Sir,—In his interesting letter which appeared in *The Englishman* on the 16th instant, my learned friend, Father Hosten, S. J. wishes to know if the "Armenians have no traditions in the matter." As the historian of the "Armenians in India from the earliest times to the present day" I have no hesitation in stating that Akbar's Christian wife was an Armenian lady from the banks of the Aras and her name was Mariam, which is the Armenian nomenclature for Mary. There is in Calcutta at the present moment in the possession of a well-known Armenian gentleman, a beautiful and highly artistic painting, in colours, of Akbar and his Armenian wife, nay Queen, as we shall see presently. The lady is depicted in semi-Asiatic, semi-European costume, without any of those rich and highly gaudy ornaments on the head which characterise the paintings of Hindoo or Mahomedan Queens of the time, but she has a beautiful double-row pearl necklace with a plain Armenian gold cross, with a diamond in the centre, hanging from the necklace. Let it be remembered that she wears a plain "cross" and not a "crucifix" and this fact goes to prove conclusively that she was an *Armenian,* for a crucifix is never worn by Armenians either as an ornament or as an amulet, a plain gold or silver cross being invariably worn by orthodox Armenians as an amulet. Then again, Akbar's Christian wife is seen in the painting wearing a beautiful and exquisite gold belt which is a specimen of ancient Armenian art. She wears a "Mantilla," hanging gracefully from her hair downwards and in old Armenian paintings the mantilla or "mandill" as it is commonly called, is always a prominent feature of their head gear. But all this is not perhaps sufficient evidence to prove her nationality as my critics will no doubt require something more tangible and reliable as regards the identity of Akbar's Christian wife. The late Professor Blochmann of the Calcutta Madrasah in his translation of the "Ain-i-Akbari," mentions in one of his notes that there is not the least doubt of "Akbar having an Armenian wife." Mahomedan historians make several references to one "Mariam" as one of the few wives of Akbar and her grave is to be seen at Sekundra to this day and known as 'Bibi Mariam ka Rowza." If it can however be proved that this *Mariam* of the Mahomedan historians is the Christian wife of Akbar, it can at the same time be proved that she was the Armenian wife of the great Mogul, as Akbar is known to have had but *one* Christian wife.

Let us lift up the veil over the painting of Akbar and his Christian (Armenian) wife and see what the picture has to say for itself. In the left corner of the painting there is the following inscription in Persian :—"Jelal-ud-din Akbar ma Mariam Zamani Beigum", which can be translated thus :—The glory of the Faith, Akbar, with Mariam Zamani Queen." Let us not lose sight of the fact that Mariam is called the *Queen* and it is not likely that the great Akbar—the Napoleon of the East—would have had his portrait painted with any other lady of the harem but the Queen, so that the Armenian-Christian Mariam was the Queen amongst Akbar's 8 wives, as enumerated in Abul Fazl's "Ain-i-Akbari."

Now the question arises. How did an Armenian lady from far-off Armenia find her way into Akbar's seraglio? As merchants, Armenians have been seen in India from time immemorial, and in my "History of the Armenians in India" published in 1895, I have dwelt at great length on the early Armenian colonies in this country but the limited space at my disposal will not permit me to go into details. Suffice it to say that they found great favour in the eyes of Akbar and held high and responsible posts under him in the Government of the country, the Chief Justice or Mir-Adl of the Imperial Camp being an Armenian by the name of Khwaja Mir Abul-Hai—Hai being the Armenian nomenclature for a native of Armenia. Then again, the famous Mirza Zul-Qarnain, who was a Grandee of the Mogul Court during the reigns of Akbar, Jehangir and Shah Jehan, was, I am proud to say, an Armenian. His father Mirza Sikandar had the salt monopoly of Sambhar in Rajputana and they all professed the Christian faith although at a Mahomedan court.

Now let us hear what Armenian traditions have to say regarding Akbar and his adoption of a handsome Armenian boy, who however is no other but the famous Mirza-Zul-Qarnain referred to above. An Armenian, Thomas Khojamall by name, who lies buried at the Agra Armenian cemetery (where he died on the 22nd January, 1789) wrote a History of Bengal in Armenian, from Mahomedan sources, at Allahabad, in 1768. In an appendix to the above work, he mentions of Akbar having adopted the beautiful son of an Armenian merchant, Hakobjan by name, whom he met in Kashmere, and at the same time invited the parents of the boy to go and settle at Akbarabad (Agra) and which they did, as was natural, and thereby laid the foundation of a flourishing Armenian colony at the capital, of which more hereafter. The handsome Armenian boy grew up in the Palace, beloved by all, and in the Jesuit records it is stated that on one occasion, of which the good Jesuit Fathers at the Court of Akbar were eye-witnesses, Akbar was seen at the window with the Armenian boy in his arms and with a cross hanging from his neck and which (cross) Akbar kissed and made the boy kiss too before the public gaze downstairs. It will no doubt occur to many that a Christian child would not have been cherished, fostered, nay tolerated in a Mahomedan seraglio had there not been a Christian lady behind the scenes and this Christian lady could be no one else but the Armenian "Mariam Zamani Begum"—Akbar's Christian (Armenian) wife.

MESROVB J. SETH.

We have seen on page 91 that the little girl of Domingo Pires,* the Armenian interpreter at Akbars' Court, was with the queen the greater part of the year. Now had there been no Christian queen in Akbar's seraglio, no Christian girl would have been allowed to enter the palace and become a companion of Akbars' daughter, spending the greater part of the year with the queen, according to the testimony of the contemporary Jesuit Fathers, but the sceptics say there was no Armenian queen in Akbar's seraglio, and the sceptics are "honourable men." Shade of Mark Antony!

Unfortunately in these days of improved audition and vision, thanks to the advance of science, (historical research) the disbelieving Thomases have ears, yet they cannot hear, they have eyes, but they will not see, being blinded by prejudice and racial antipathy.

It was at Fathepur Sikri that Domingo (Dominic) Pires, the Armenian interpreter at the court of Akbar, married, in 1582, an Indian woman, with the approval of Akbar, who assisted at the marriage service. The Jesuit priest, Fr. Rodolf Aquaviva writing from Fathepur Sikri on the 27th September, 1582, gives an account of the marriage as follows :—

"On Tuesday, the 24th of September, the Emperor [Akbar] came in the afternoon to see the marriage of Domingo Pires, in our Chapel. We decorated the Chapel very well and painted two trophies in his honour, and Domingo Pires ordered a Portuguese banquet to be prepared for him at our house. The Emperor was delighted with everything and showed me much affection for entertaining him to the best of my power. At the marriage I preached a sermon to the couple, the woman did not understand me, and the Emperor interpreted to her in her own language what I was saying in Persian. The Emperor remained in our house till nearly eight O'clock at night with great pleasure he brought to the house all the principal chiefs of the Muhammadans and the heathen. One of the heathen, a ruler in these lands was much amazed and made a jest of the chapel. Others, children of the Emperor, were present and dined at

* For an account of Domingo Pires, whose Armenian name we have not been able to trace, see Chapter IV.

the house, as well as two of the principal Muhammadan chiefs whom the Emperor sent for."

A short account of the origin of Fathepur Sikri may be of interest to our readers.

Fathepur Sikri, now a ruined city, is interesting only from an architectural point of view. It was founded by Akbar in 1570 as a thanks offering for the birth of his son, Selim, afterwards the Emperor Jehangeer, obtained through the intercession of a famous Mohammedan saint, named Shaikh Selim Chisti. Fathepur Sikri, the Windsor of Agra, was a favourite residence of Akbar throughout his reign and his palace was one of great magnificence.

Adjoining the Emperor's palace is the dwelling assigned to his Christian wife. It is exquisitely carved, and unlike other Moslem buildings, is covered with paintings in fresco. They represent the adventures of the Persian hero Rostam, as related in Firdosi's *Shah Nama*. Certain niches however, over the doors and windows contain pictures of a different character, and certainly have a religious significance. On one side are the Hindoo gods and goddesses—the elephant-headed Ganesh Mahadeva and Lakshmi—and the other, two tablets, almost obliterated by vandals, but still sufficiently distinct to show that one of them is intended for the Annunciation. Akbar's latitude in religious matters is well-known. Among the ornamental designs of this palace, the Armenian cross is not unusual, and it is related that when the Jesuits once solicited the Emperor's protection, he replied to them :—

"What would you have? See! I have more crosses* on my palace than you have in your churches."

The figures of an Armenian cross, which is similar to the Greek cross and is of the same shape as St. George's Cross, show clearly that the occupant of that beautiful palace was an Armenian lady, Akbar's Christian queen.

---

* Both Akbar and his son Jehangeer had great veneration for the cross. It is related by the Jesuits that Jehangeer once, rebuked an Armenian for omitting to wear a cross on his head or on his breast. It was an ancient Armenian custom to have the cross tattooed on the forehead or on the arm.

Although Akbar went to the enormous expense of building this splendid residence and capital, he did not long occupy it. The saint (Chisti) found his devotions interfered with by the bustle of the busy city and the gaieties of the court. At last, when the Emperor (Akbar) wished to surround the hill with a chain of massive fortifications, the holy man could no longer restrain himself. He told his royal master that he had gone twenty times on pilgrimages to Mecca and never before had had his comfort and quiet so much disturbed, accordingly he said that either the Emperor or he must depart. "If that be your Majesty's will," replied the Emperor, "that one should go, let it be your slave I pray."

Amongst the majestic ruins of Fathepur Sikri, Akbar's city of victory, special mention must be made of the Boland Darvaza, or High Gate, which was erected by Akbar in 1601, to commemorate his victories in the Deccan. It is the highest gateway in India and ranks amongst the biggest in the world. It is about 175 feet high from the road way and is visible from a great distance. It is said that on a clear day, the Agra Taj, which is at a distance of 22 miles, can be seen from the top of this gate. Fergusson calls it "noble beyond that of any portal attached to any mosque in India, perhaps in the whole world."

Across the front of this gate, Akbar, who had a great veneration for Christ, had the following inscription carved on it. "Isa [Jesus], on whom be peace, said: The world is a bridge, pass over it, but build not thereon. The world endureth but an hour, spend it in devotion."

It is strange however that Akbar, who was well acquainted with the teachings of Christ, could have ascribed the above saying to Jesus, for the divine Master in all his parables, which are peerless gems of thought, never compared the world to a bridge* although he impressed upon his followers the fickleness and the unstability of the world by advising them "lay not up for yourselves treasures upon earth, where moth and rust doth

* Christ never saw a bridge in his life time, as there were no big rivers in Palestine to necessitate the construction of bridges, and in the Hebrew version of the Bible, the word bridge is never used.

corrupt, and where thieves break through and steal, but lay up for yourselves treasures in heaven, where neither moth nor rust doth corrupt, and where thieves do not break through nor steal." (Matthew VI. 19-20).

With regard to Akbar's acquaintance with the teachings of Christ. We have seen on page 89 of this work that when the first Jesuit Mission came to Fathepur Sikri from Goa, in 1580, they presented Akbar with a beautifully illustrated copy of the Bible in Persian, bound in seven volumes, which the Emperor received with great veneration reverently kissing them and then placing the volumes on his head, one after another, showing greater reverence for those containing the Gospels. According to Sir Edward Maclagan, in his monumental work on *The Jesuits and the Great Mogul*, a polyglot Bible said to be the one presented to Akbar by the Jesuits was in the possession of a branch of the Bourbon family at Lucknow shortly before the Indian Mutiny of 1857. The Bourbons of Lucknow must have inherited that sacred volume from their remote ancestress, Lady Juliana, the sister of Akbar's Armenian wife, who was given in marriage to Prince John Philip Bourbon by Akbar in 1560. The polyglot Bible, according to the same authority, subsequently passed into the hands of a Father Adeodatus of Lucknow, and after passing through many strange hands during the past 350 years, it may now be resting safely on the shelves of some Catholic library, either in India or elsewhere. It is earnestly to be hoped that the sacred volume, with historic associations, did not find its way to the famous Louvain library in Belgium which the 20th century vandals with their much-vaunted "Kultur", looted, plundered and pillaged in 1914, with a rapacity reminiscent of the days of the Huns and the Tartars—Attila, Chengiz Khan and Tamerlane.

After Akbar's death in 1605* Fathepur Sikri was deserted, within fifty years of its foundation. The magnificent buildings

---

* Akbar was born on the 14th October, 1542, at Amerkote in Sind. He ascended the throne at the age of fourteen in 1556 and after a glorious reign of about fifty years, he died at Agra on the eve of his birthday, the 13th day of October 1605. He lies buried in the magnificent mausoleum, erected by his son, the Emperor Jehangeer, at Secundra, near Agra.

erected by Akbar are now more or less in ruins, the most striking being the beautiful tomb of the ascetic Shaikh Selim Chisti, referred to above. The sarcophagus containing the body of the saint is surrounded with an elaborate marble screen, as in the Taj, carved into trellis work of surpassing beauty. The tomb is covered with an arched canopy covered with mother-o-pearl, the floor is of jasper, the walls of pure marble, inlaid with cornelian, onyx and jasper, and the doors of solid ebony.

ARMENIANS AT DELHI

CHAPTER XIII.

SARMAD.

AN ARMENIAN POET IN INDIA.

Armenians and merchants have been synonymous words in India, for it was trade and commerce that attracted the Armenians to this tropical country from their homes in the delectable and snow-clad mountains of Armenia, from the days of remote antiquity.

Apart from eminent merchants, clever diplomats, great soldiers, able governors and administrators, casters of huge pieces of ordnance and manufacturers of firelocks, which, according to Marshman, "were superior to the Tower-proof muskets of the Company", the Armenians have given to India a poet of great merit whose fame spread over Mohammedan India as a saint and a scholar, in the middle of the 17th century, and to this day, his memory is revered and kept green by all lovers of the noble, the beautiful and the sublime, not only in this country, but in the countries where the charms of the beautiful language of the immortal Firdosi, Nizami, Saadi, Hafez, Jami and Khayyam, have captured and captivated the imagination of millions.

But who was this remarkable poet whom even the mighty Emperor Aurungzebe, the *last* of the Great Moguls, dreaded and ultimately beheaded, as can be seen later on.

Let us first tap the European sources for reliable information about this remarkable Armenian.

In the *Oriental Biographical Dictionary* by Thomas William Beale, revised and enlarged in 1894 by that eminent Persian scholar and historian, Henry George Keene,*

---

* Keene is the author of several learned works on Indian history, notably of the Mogul period. His *Turks in India* and *The Mogul Empire* are master-pieces. He has compiled interesting Guide Books to Delhi and Agra, replete with historical and topographical information. He was Judge at Agra in 1879.

M.R.A.S., we find the following authoritative account of Sarmad :—

"Sarmad, the poetical name of an Armenian merchant who came to India in the reign of the Emperor Shah Jehan. In one of his journeys towards Thatta, he fell so passionately in love with a Hindoo girl* that he became distracted and would go about the streets naked.

He was well versed in the Persian language and was a good poet. In the beginning of the reign of Alamgir [Aurungzebe] he was put to death on account of his disobeying the orders of that Emperor, who had commanded him not to go about naked. This event took place about the year 1661 (1072 A.H.). Some say that the real cause of his execution was a Rubai [quatrain] which he had composed, the translation of which is :

"The Mullas say that Mohammad entered the heavens, but Sarmad says that the heavens entered Mohammad." His tomb is close to the Juma Musjid at Delhi."

Following in the footsteps of his compatriots, Sarmad came out to India as a merchant from Persia by sea. He set up in business in the town of Thathah in Sindh, on the shores of the Indus, where his business thrived exceedingly and he spent his days in comfort and peace. During his sojourn in that city he contracted a close friendship with a Hindoo lad, Abhai Chand by name. This was the turning point in his life, for unlike his calculating and serious minded countrymen, he neglected his business, lost the equilibrium of his mind altogether and relinquishing his life of comfort and peace, he lived thenceforth the austere life of a naked Hindoo *fakir* (ascetic) and in this nude state he would go and sit at the door of his beloved Abhai Chand.

The following translation of a distich shows the true sentiment of the distracted Sarmad :

"I know not if in this spherical old monastery [the world]
My God is Abhai Chand or some one else."

The boy's father seeing the earnestness of the ascetic, and the purity of the attachment, allowed him to come to his house with

* According to Mohammedan historians and biographers it was a Hindoo lad of the Bunnia caste, Abhai Chand by name.

the result that his son Abhai Chand became so much attached to Sarmad that he could not bear to live apart from him. Soon after this, both left Thathah and went to Delhi. Shah Jehan was then the Mogul Emperor of India. People flocked round Sarmad and many found him to be a man of great sanctity and supernatural powers.

The eldest son of the Emperor, the unfortunate prince Dara Shikoh, whose devotion to Brahmanical dogmas and theosophical beliefs is well known, was one of Sarmad's constant visitors and staunch admirers. It was Dara Shikoh who brought the miraculous powers of the saint, (Sarmad) to the notice of his august father, the Emperor Shah Jehan. The prudent Emperor deputed Inayat Khan, one of the Umara (grandees), of his Court to ascertain the real facts. The grandee visited the naked saint and his report was most favourable if not reassuring. Prince Dara Shikoh was one of the many disciples of Sarmad and the tutor had predicted that Dara Shikoh would be the next Emperor after Shah Jehan, which prediction was not however fulfilled through the treachery of Aurungzebe who ascended the throne of the mighty Moguls by first imprisoning his father and then murdering his two brothers, Dara Shikoh and Murad Baksh.

Aurungzebe hated Sarmad for having been a partisan of Dara Shikoh on whom he had promised to confer the throne. When Aurungzebe had usurped the throne, he taunted Sarmad about the succession of his favourite disciple, Dara Shikoh, to the throne, which he had promised him. Sarmad calmly replied: "God has given him the eternal sovereignty and my promise is not falsified." Needless to add that the Emperor was greatly displeased and incensed with this sarcastic reply of the naked * saint and from that moment he decided to put an end to that poor man's life. The favourable moment was

---

* In a quatrain (rubai) addressed to his relentless persecutor, the Emperor Aurungzebe, Sarmad gives the reason of his nudity:

He who gave you the sovereignty of the world.
Gave me all the causes of anxiety.
He covered with a garment those who had any fault (deformity)
To the faultless he gave the robe of nudity."

not long in coming, as Sarmad, who was a Sufi,* had expressed sentiments of a heretical nature in the following distich, ridiculing the nocturnal journey of Mohammed to heaven.

ملّا گوید که بر فلک شد احمد سرمد گوید فلک به احمد در شد

It can be translated thus :—

"The Mullas say that Ahmad went to heaven,
Sarmad says that heaven came down to Ahmad".

According to the Sufis who believe in the unity of the creator and the created, there is nothing objectionable in this doctrine, moreover as in the opinion of certain *Ulama*, the *Miraj*, or the nocturnal journey of Mahomed to heaven was allegorical and spiritual, but a fanatic and a bigot like Aurungzebe, could not possibly tolerate such a blasphemy, open and palpable, that was likely to shake the foundation of the Mohammedan faith.

The supreme moment had at last arrived for Aurungzebe to wreak his vengeance on the harmless naked saint and scholar and he immediately ordered his execution.

It is said that when the condemned man was being led away from the tribunal to the place of execution, he uttered, *ex tempore*, 24 quatrains. The crowd was so dense that one could pass through it with great difficulty.

When the executioner, a low caste man of the sweeper class, approached him with his naked sword, he wanted, according to custom, to cover the condemned man's head, but Sarmad hinted not to do it, then he smiled and addressing the executioner said :—

"The friend with naked sword has now arrived
In whatever disguise thou mayst come,
I recognise thee,"

He also uttered the following distich :

" There was an uproar and we opened our eyes from the eternal sleep.

---

* For a history of the origin and the growth of Sufism in Persia, see the note at the end of this Chapter.

Saw that the night of wickedness endured, so we slept again".

Aqil Khan Razi, the court chronicler of Aurungzebe, writes that when the executionor was about to inflict the fatal blow, Sarmad uttered :

"The nakedness of the body was the dust of the road to the friend,
That too was severed, with the sword, from our head".

According to another version Sarmad uttered :

"My head was severed from the body by that flirt, who was my companion,
The story was shortened, otherwise the headache would have been too severe".

One of the companions of Sarmad, one Shah Asadullah, went up to him and told him

"Do cover your nakedness and utter the creed in full and you will be let off".

Sarmad looked up, said nothing in reply but uttered the following couplet :

"A long time since the fame of Mansur became an ancient relic,
I will exhibit with my head the gallow and the cord".

Sarmad died cheerfully and with complete resignation like every Armenian that has suffered martyrdom, for his religion, at the hands of the Mohammedans during the past 1300 years.

Prince Dara Shikoh, the disciple of Sarmad, and the rightful heir to the throne of the Moguls, was beheaded by the order of his younger brother, that consummate hypocrite and fanatic Aurungzebe, in the year 1069 A.H. (1659 A.D.) and two years later, Sarmad shared the fate of his royal pupil, "and from that day", says a native historian, "the house of Timour declined both in glory and power".

He was beheaded in 1661 near the Jama Musjid at Delhi, for heresy, in the midst of an imprecedentedly huge crowd and though not a Mohammedan, yet he was buried under the steps of the great mosque where his grave is venerated to this day, by Hindoos as well as Mohammedans, who make offerings of flowers, light candles and burn incense on the saint's revered grave, after his martyrdom 275 years ago. Sarmad was considered well inspired and a man of sanctity.

The people of India have not forgotten that the harmless naked saint was killed by the order of Aurungzebe because he loved Dara Shikoh and championed his cause.

It is recorded that on the day of the execution, the Emperor said to the ecclesiastics (*fudala*) that a man was not liable to be executed merely for his nudity but that he should be required to pronounce the Islamic creed. Addressing the saint, they said "How is it that inspite of your great learning, you only utter the first half of the *Kalima** or creed and not the remaining part"? Sarmad replied that "I am still absorbed in the negative part, why shall I tell a lie"? So, according to this version, Sarmad's execution, at the suggestion of the Emperor was made according to the Islamic Law. So far as can be seen, the execution, in the opinion of the fanatic Aurungzebe, was necessary from a religious point of view.

Living the life of a nude mendicant, composing delightful quatrains, some of which may well be compared with those of Omar Khayyam, yet Sarmad interested himself in politics by becoming a partisan of Dara Shikoh whom he predicted to be Shah Jehan's rightful successor. This was gall and wormwood to Aurungzebe. Sarmad was the centre of attraction to the public at Delhi. Dara was condemned and beheaded because of his apostacy and Sarmad was condemned and killed for having contributed partly to that apostacy. Deeply as he disliked his eldest brother Dara, for his politics and leanings towards the tenets of non-Muslims and mendicants, (majazib), his first act, as soon as he came to power, was to remove that arch heretic and those who had aided and abetted him in his apostacy and political activities. Sarmad who was a Sufi and

* The first part of the *Kalima,* which is in Arabic, can be translated thus: "There is no God but God" (La Ala Allalah) and the second part, "And Mohammad is his prophet" (Mohammad rasool Allah). It was quite natural that Sarmad refused to utter the second part of the *Kalima,* not being a Mohammedan.

a mystic philosopher was a great Persian scholar and had read science and metaphysics with such well known and distinguished scholars as Mulla Sadr-ud-din Shirazi, Mirza Abul Qasim Fandarsaki and other eminent scholars of the time.

Sarmad was so filled with divine love that to him the king, the judge, the executioner, the whole universe, including himself, were the same. The soul itself and the universe were merged into Divinity. He had no consciousness of himself.

The following letter which Prince Dara Shikoh addressed to Sarmad shows the high regard the royal pupil had for his saintly master:

"My Pir and Preceptor—

Everyday I resolve to pay my respects to you. It remains unaccomplished. If I be I, wherefore is my intention of no account? If I be not—what is my fault? Though the murder of Imam Hossain was the will of God: Who is (then) Yazid between (them). If it is not the Divine Will, then what is the meaning of "*God does whatever He wills and commands whatever He intends*"? The most excellent prophet used to go to fight the unbelievers, defeat was inflicted on the army of Islam. The exoteric scholars say it was an education in resignation. For the perfect what education was necessary?"

Sarmad's reply to the above epistle consisted of two lines, in verse, which can be translated thus:—

"My dear—

What we have read, we have forgotten,
Save the discourse of the Friend which we reiterate."

Sarmad's name stands prominent in the republic of letters. Daghistani calls him eminent in learning and Arabic scholarship. His impromptus are very popular in Delhi. His poems consist mostly of quatrains. In a quatrain* Sarmad says that he follows Hafez in *ghazal* and Omar Khayyam in *rubaiyat*.

---

* Sarmad pays a well-deserved compliment to Hafez and Khayyam, two of the greatest poets of Persia, in the following quatrain:—

"I have no business with the fancy and thought of others,
In composing a *ghazal* I adopt the manner of Hafez,
But in *rubai*, I am a disciple of Khayyam,
But do no quaff much of his wine."

All the biographical works of the Persian poets that have been written after him, contain appreciative and highly enlogistic notices of Sarmad.

His favourite companion and disciple, Abhai Chand, who was the son of a wealthy Hindoo rajah, according to Nasrabadi, left his father, mother, home and wealth and adopted the life of a mendicant and took to sitting on ashes like the Hindoo *faqirs*. According to the same writer, Abhai Chand, died soon after Sarmad was beheaded through intense grief.

As we have said, Sarmad was a Sufi poet and there are verses which he composed that might be construed by a bigot as being against Islamic religion and on account of such opinions he brought on his head the wrath of the Emperor Aurungzebe who was a stern puritan all his life and a bigoted champion of orthodoxy. His fanaticism, intolerance and his inordinate zeal for the Mohammedan religion were the main causes of the downfall of the glorious Mogul Empire in India.

Sarmad, who was a theist, taunted the fanatic Aurungzebe with the following caustic quatrain ; declaring his religious convictions and openly proclaiming, to the chagrin of the Emperor, that he was not a Mohammedan.

شاہ شاہا نیم زاهد چونتو عریان نیستم
شوق و ذوق شورشم لیکن پریشان نیستم
بت‌پرستم کافرم از اهل ایمان نیستم
سوی مسجد میروم امّا مسلمان نیستم

It can be translated thus :—

O ! King of Kings, I am not a hermit like thee, I am not nude.
I am frenzied, I am distracted, but I am not depressed,
I am an idolator, I am an infidel, I am not of the people of the faith,
I go towards the mosque, but I am not a Mussulman.

No complete collection of the quatrains of Sarmad have been published, though a few of them have been lithographed at Lahore, Delhi and Bombay, with biographical notices of the poet in the Urdu language.

According to Dr. Rieu, more than 400 of the quatrains of Sarmad are preserved in MS. in the British Museum. There is in the well-known Oriental Library of Rampur State a MS. copy of the *Diwan of Sarmad,* containing the portrait of the poet, with his disciple Abhai Chand.

Francois Bernier, M.D., a French physician at the Court of Shah Jehan, writing of naked Hindoo *faqirs,* in his *Travels in Hindusthan,* refers to Sarmad as follows :

> "I have seen for a long while a very famous one in Delhi, called Sarmet, who went thus stark naked along the streets, and who at length would rather suffer his neck to be cut off, than to put on any clothes, what promises or menaces soever Aurung Zebe might send to him."

On hearing of Sarmad's death, Bernier wrote as follows :—

> "I was for a long time disgusted with a celebrated Fakir, named Sarmet, who walked in the streets of Delhi as naked as he came to the world. He despised equally the threats and persuations of Aurungzebe and underwent at length the punishment of decapitation for his obstinate refusal to put on his wearing apparel."

Another European, Niccolao Manucci, in his *Storia do Mogor* (as translated by William Irvine; 1901) writes :—

Vol. I, p. 223 : Dara held to no religion, when with Mahomedans, he praised the tenets of Muhammad, when with Jews, the Jewish religion ; in the same way, when with Hindus, he praised Hinduism. This is why Aurungzebe styled him a kafir (infidel). At the same time, he had great delight in talking to the Jesuit fathers on religion, and making them dispute with his learned Mahomedans, or with Cermad [Sarmad] an atheist much liked by the prince. This man went always naked, except when he appeared in the presence of the prince, when he contented himself with a piece of cloth at his waist." And on p. 384, he says:

> "After the death of his brother, Dara, Aurungzib ordered them to bring to his presence Acermaad [Sarmad], the atheist, to whom Dara had been devoted, and asked him where was his devoted prince. He replied that he was then present, 'but you cannot see him, for you tyrannise over those of your own blood; and in order to usurp the Kingdom, you took away the life of your brothers and did other barbarities.' On hearing these words, Aurungzebe ordered his head to be cut off."

We have seen in the beginning of this Chapter, on the authority of that well-informed author of the "Oriental Biographical Dictionary", that Sarmad was an Armenian who, like his countrymen, had come to India for the purposes of trade, which in those days was the sole occupation of the Armenians in India. And in the prefaces to the Lahore and the Delhi editions of Sarmad's quatrains (rubayat) by learned biographers, he is called an Armenian by nationality and a Christian by religion, yet there are some Mohammedan historians and biographers who say Sarmad was a Jew* from Kashan in Persia and a convert to Islam.

There lived in Calcutta an eminent Persian scholar and a journalist, the late Syed Agah Jalaluddin-al-Hossaini, known as Muayyid-al-Islam, who was, by a strange coincidence, a native of Kashan, the supposed birthplace of the poet, Sarmad. In order to satisfy ourselves about the vexed question of the poet's nationality we thought of seeking his advice in the matter some eight years ago, as he was a great authority on Persian poets, their lives and their works.

---

* There are no records of Jews coming to India from Persia for the purposes of trade in the 16th, 17th or 18th centuries.

The Sassoons, the Jacobs and other merchant princes of Bombay came from Baghdad in Mesopotamia, so did the Ezras, the Gubbays and the Manassehs of Calcutta in the early part of the 19th century.

We called on the veteran journalist who had unfortunately lost his sight during the latter years of his life and found him lying on an easy chair, in the editorial office, dictating an editorial to his scribe for his favourite *Hablul-Matin.* After the usual salutations and compliments we asked the Persian sage about the nationality of Sarmad and the country he hailed from. He was greatly surprised that we, a countryman of the poet, should have any doubts in the matter, as Sarmad was known to be an Armenian from Persia. When we told him that a certain Mohammedan writer had said in a public lecture that Sarmad was a Jew from Kashan, he was highly amused and remarked sarcastically that it was not possible for a persecuted, miserable, unkempt, unwashed and unlettered Jew of Kashan to rise to the proud and enviable position of a famous Persian poet.

When we were wishing him good-bye and expressing our thanks for his kind courtesy, the good old man wished to know the reason of our enquiry about the poets' nationality. We told him that we intended writing an account of Sarmad in one of the leading Armenian journals and did not wish to commit ourselves, whereupon he said in an authoritative tone, "go and write that Muayyid-al-Islam says that Sarmad was an Armenian from Iran." (Bero benevis khe Muayyid-al-Islam meegooiad khe Sarmad Armanee bood az Iran).

Sher Khan Lodi, who was a celebrated poet in the reign of the Emperor Aurungzebe and had ample opportunities of seeing Sarmad, states, in his Life of poets, called *Maratal Khial*, that Hakhim Sarmad was an Armenian from Faranghisthan (Europe) and was originally engaged in trade when he came out to India.

Had Sarmad been a Jew of Kashan where his co-religionists had for centuries been persecuted and tyrannized by the fanatical Persians during the Seffevi regime, he would have, with the timidity of his race, covered his nudity and pronounced the *Kalima* when the supreme moment of losing his head had arrived, but the indomitable courage and the intrepidity of the martyr, in facing death with perfect equanimity, shows clearly that he was not of the race of that timid disciple of Christ, who in the hour of danger, forsook, abjured, renounced and denied his Master *thrice,* in the short space of a couple of hours, without the least remorse and compunction, despite the fact that he had for three years lived and worked daily with Jesus in the fond hope of becoming his Prime Minister, with Judas of Iscariot as the Minister of Finance, when that homeless and impecunious Nazarene became the temporal King of the Jews, as the simple fishermen of Galilee vainly expected.

Now that it has been conclusively proved that Sarmad* was not a Jew from Kashan, it will be interesting to know where he hailed from.

In the preface to the Lahore edition of Sarmad's quatrains, it is stated that Sarmad was born at Ganja, an important Armenian city in the Karabagh district, south of the Caucasus mountains. The famous Persian poet Nizami, was also born in that ancient city. Ganja is now called Elizabethpol.

The mountainous province of Karabagh in Eastern Armenia, came under the rule of Persia in 1620 by virtue of a treaty concluded between the Turks and Shah Abhas the Great of Persia. That far-seeing monarch entrusted the government of the province, which was solely inhabited by Armenians, to five semi-independent Armenian princes, known as *Meliks,* who kept up their quasi-independence until the beginning of the 19th century when the province was annexed by Russia.

A descendant of one of the Armenian *Meliks* of Karabagh, David Rreedone Melik Beglar, who came out to India in 1813 as a deacon and a chorister to the Armenian Archbishop Phillippos, an envoy from Etchmiadzine, lies buried in the Armenian churchyard at Chinsurah, where he died on the 22nd September, 1884, aged 89 years.

In the epitaph on his tombstone, he is called "the son of the late Freedone Melik Beglaroff, last independent Prince of Karabagh in the Province of Tiflis, Caucasus."

His eldest son, Joseph Beglar, the Executive Engineer, P. W. D., who died on the 24th April, 1907, aged 62 years, is likewise buried there.

---

* Sarmad, the poetical name (thakhallus) of the Armenian poet, is an Arabic word, meaning eternal, everlasting.

There are some interesting anecdotes, founded on traditions, about the supernatural powers of Sarmad, prevalent amongst the people of Delhi to this day, for the truth of which we cannot vouch.

It is said that the Emperor Aurungzebe who was a puritan, had strictly forbidden the use of *bhang* as a narcotic because of its deleterius effects. One of the many spies of the King reported to him that Sarmad, in defiance of the royal fiat, was addicted to the vice of smoking *bhang* and that he kept the drug in an earthen pot near him always wherever he sat. This was good news for Aurungzebe who was always trying to find fault with the poet whom he hated with a deadly hatred. He paid a sudden visit to Sarmad and found the poet lecturing to his disciples. He at once noticed the earthen pot and asked Sarmad what it contained. The poet suspecting that the Emperor had been apprised of the contents of the earthen pot, replied nonchalantly that it contained some milk and on the Emperor pressing him to show him the milk, Sarmad most unconcernedly uncovered the pot and lo and behold there was milk in it. His disciples who knew what the earthen pot contained originally were simply amazed and spread the news of the miracle performed by their master in converting the harmful *bhang* into harmless milk.

There is another ancedote equally interesting. One day Sarmad was watching a *mollah* praying earnestly and with great devotion in the Juma Musjid at Delhi. The poet told his followers that the *mollah*'s god was under his (Sarmad's) feet. A spy immediately carried the news to Aurungzebe who was praying in the mosque at the same time, it being a Friday. The irate Emperor came up to Sarmad and ordered him immediately to give a satisfactory explanation for his blasphemy. Sarmad who could never be intimidated by Aurungzebe, told him to send for the *mollah* and ask him to confess what he was praying for. The nervous ecclesiastic, who was trembling in his shoes in the presence of the stern monarch, *nolens volens* confessed that he was praying to God to grant him some money to enable him to get his daughter married.

Sarmad remarked that the *mollah* had spoken the truth for once in his life and asked Aurungzebe to get his men to dig the ground where he stood and on digging the place they found some gold coins buried there.

Sarmad was jubilant over the discovery and told the astonished Emperor in his usual cynical tone that he was not wrong when he said that the *mollah's* god was under his feet.

Aurungzebe was nonplussed and confounded but the news spread with lightning speed that Sarmad had worked another miracle.

Any wonder then that Aurungzebe hated Sarmad with the deadly hatred of a fanatic and wished to put an end to the life of an unbeliever who was looked upon as a saint and a holy man by the public in the early years of his reign of intolerance and religious persecution.

Whilst these lines were passing through the press, we were informed by the gallery assistant of the Delhi Fort Museum that there is an inscription on Sarmad's tombstone. We reproduce his letter which is as follows :—

> "In reply to your enquiry. I beg to inform you that at the head of Sarmad's grave, there is a masonry pillar with lamp niches and on it has been fixed an incised slab of stone containing the following inscription in Persian :—

شاه سرمد در عهد عالمگیر　　چو سفر ساخته بخُلد برین

گفت تاریخ اکـــبر مسکین　　لحد مرقد شهید سرمد این

Which can be translated thus :—

> When Shah Sarmad in the reign of Alamgeer [Aurungzebe] set out on a journey to Paradise. Poor Akbar said the date, 'This is the grave of Sarmad the Martyr'.

The people in Delhi greatly venerate the grave of Sarmad and daily burn lights and incenses and sprinkle fresh roses and flowers on it. The Mussulmans who come to Delhi from far and near never miss a visit to the grave of this saint. Besides, the musicians sing religious songs at the grave of Sarmad nearly every evening and particularly on Thursdays. A class of illiterate Mussulmans also celebrate the festival of *Basant* near his grave."

Peace to his soul, rest to his ashes and may the revered memory of the great poet be cherished and kept green, for ages to be, in the land where he suffered martyrdom for his open defiance of Islamic rituals and customs.

Aurungzebe, a lineal descendant of Chengiz Khan and of Tamerlane (Timur), was the incarnation of cruelty, bigotry and religious fanaticism, like his remote ancestors, who were monsters in human form.

He died at Ahmednagar on the 21st February, 1707, after an inglorious reign of forty-eight years.

When life was ebbing fast and his end was approaching he wrote from his death-bed to one of his sons : "The instant passed in power has only left sorrow behind. I have not been the guardian and protector of the empire. My precious time has been spent vainly." To another son he wrote :

"I depart, and carry with me the fruit of my sins. I came alone, alone I go, wherever I look, I see nothing but God. I have committed numerous crimes, and I know not with what torments they may be punished."

For his relentless persecution of the Hindoos, his memory is held up to execration by millions of Indians, although a certain Hindoo scholar of repute has spent much valuable time and energy in writing an exhaustive history of the Hindoophobe Emperor, in seven Volumes.

Would an Armenian historical scholar write a history of Sultan Abdul Hamid, the relentless persecutor of his race and religion? Never, because he would be anathematized by his countrymen for treason, if not heresy. In the same way, would a Jewish scholar and their name is legion, sing the praises of Hitler or an Abyssinian monk shower encomiums and invoke blessings on Mussolini?

Ja mais, as the French say, for fear of being pilloried by their countrymen as traitors to their race and country, but a Bengalee scholar, with much zeal and scholarly industry, immortalizes the avowed enemy of the Hindoos and their ancient religion.

Had he written a history of the great Akbar or of his equally tolerant son Jehangeer, he would have earned the everlasting gratitude of his co-religionists, because those Great Moguls, were favourably disposed towards the Hindoos, but to record the achievements of the fanatic Aurungzebe, the unworthy occupant of the throne of the noble and tolerant Akbar, was like "placing his money on the wrong horse," as Salisbury once said of the continued British support and friendship for the Sultan of Turkey during the Armenian massacres of 1896, when the streets of Constantinople ran red with the blood of thousands of defenceless and innocent Armenians, consequent on the ill-advised attack on the Ottoman Bank by a band of desperate Armenian revolutionaries who were forced to take that fatal step, to be able, perchance, to arouse Christian Europe from its morbid stupor and death-life slumber, but the Turkophil British premier of the day, the late Marquis of Salisbury, blandly said that they could not take their men-of-war to the mountains of Armenia to fight the Turks there. But enough of politics and the raking up of old memories, memories sad and sorrowful, of wholesale massacres, holocausts and pogroms before which Herod's massacre of the Innocents at Bethlehem and Nero's human torches of the early Christians in Rome sink into insignificance.

It will be remembered that both Herod and Nero lived nineteen centuries ago when the so-called civilization of the present day did not exist and tyrants could play with the lives of their helpless subjects, with impunity, but the organised and systematic massacres of defenceless Armenians in Turkey, of which, to their shame be it said, the Christian nations of Europe were passive spectators, were carried out in the last decade of the enlightened 19th century, when the Sultan, the highly vigorous "Sick Man of Europe," as he was then called, out-heroded Herod and Nero, counting on the international jealousies of the Europeaen powers.

It speaks volumes for the victorian civilization and the much vaunted Christianity of Europe on the eve of the 20th century.

When Italy, quite recently, invaded Abyssinia with the sole object of territorial aggrandizement as an outlet for her increasing population, she was immediately penalised by the European powers who imposed "sanctions" in the main hope of impeding her progress, although Italy was not found guilty of wholesale massacres in Ethiopia, but when the "Great Assassin," was annihilating an ancient Christian race, the torch bearers of the Christian faith in the East, not a finger was raised, by the Christian nations of Europe to stop the atrocities which had roused the just indignation of the "Grand Old Man" of England, that exemplary and highsouled Christian statesman, who in an autograph letter, dated the 1st May, 1896, addressed to the writer of these lines, gave expression to his strong views in the following memorable words:

" I continue to regard with acute pain and shame the triumph of wickedness in Turkey over the whole civilized and Christian world. I know of no similar disgrace upon record." Had he been in power at that time, matters would have taken quite a different turn, for was it not the plain, untitled, Mr. Gladstone who at the commencement of the infamous reign of the Red Sultan, raised his powerful voice and protested, with all the vehemence and oratory at his command, against the Bulgarian atrocities, committed by the Turks in that Christian country, the emancipation of which from the thralling yoke of the Turk, he accomplished through the military and active aid of Russia, the sole protector of Christians in those days.

Greece, the home of ancient civilization, culture and arts, when the world was young, owes her freedom from the galling yoke of the Turk to a noble and high-souled Englishman and Bulgaria, which was likewise groaning for centuries under the iron heel of the Turk, got her political independence through the strenuous efforts of another noble and great Englishman.

The revered names of Byron and Gladstone, will go down to posterity, emblazoned in letters of gold, as the liberators of those two Christian countries from the thraldom of Turkish misrule. And if Salisbury who was the British premier at the time of the Armenian massacres in 1896, had not callously abandoned the Armenians in Turkey to their fate, he would have earned the gratitude of the entire nation as the liberator of their helpless countrymen from Turkish tyranny, in view of the fact that he had been mainly instrumental in preventing Russia to occupy and administer the Armenian provinces of Turkey after the Russo—Turkish war of 1877-78.

But as it has been pointed out already, that astute British statesman had declared that it would be impossible for the British men-of-war to go and fight the Turks in the mountains of Armenia, yet when war broke out in South Africa, three years after, British troops were seen fighting the Boers in the mountains of the Transvaal simply because there were gold and diamond mines in the country!

But we have digressed, our only excuse being that "out of the abundance of the heart, the mouth speaketh."

Aurungzebe, the heaven-born hero of the Bengalee historian, ascended the throne of the Great Moguls in 1659, by first confining his father in the Agra Fort and then treacherously murdering his two elder brothers, the crown prince Dara Shikoh and Murad Baksh. Not satisfied with these political murders, which had paved his way to the throne, he filled the cup of his iniquities by murdering the harmless and innocent poet, because of his friendship for his hated brother, prince Dara Shikoh.

The murderer and the murdered were both laid to rest many many years ago, with this difference that whereas lights and incense are kept continually burning on Sarmad's humble grave at Delhi, nobody burns candles or incense on Aurungzebe's tomb at Ahmednagar.

The greatness of the tyrant invariably dies with him, but the fame of the humble saint and scholar lives after him for ages to be. The memory of the despot is cursed, but that of the martyr is kept green always.

According to Shakespeare, the king of British poets, "the good that men do, is oft buried with their bones, the evil remains after" and an Armenian proverb says, "the deprived liveth, but the depriver liveth not" (Apree zurkialn, chapree zurkogn.)

The following incident, which is still fresh in the memory of many people, proves the truth of the above proverb.

Some five years ago, the head of an educational institution in Calcutta, a scheming and an intriguing pedagogue with a shining cranium but without any academical qualifications, falsely and maliciously accused a member of the staff, a well-known scholar and a veteran national worker, of communistic ideals and activities in the school, misrepresenting nationalism for communism, and as he "was the monarch of all he surveyed and his right there were none to dispute", he had the nationalist removed from the institution without however giving the innocent victim of his intrigues a chance to defend himself, for the verdict of the tyrant was like "the law of the Medes and Persians which altereth not". (Daniel VI. 2).

But as God has said, "vengeance is mine", the tyrant, who was an adept in removing able teachers from the institution lest his position may be jeopardised, did not have the supreme gratification of enjoying the fruits of his villainy, for hardly a month had elapsed when he was struck down dead, as if by lightning, by the unseen hand of Providence, at a function on the Calcutta Maidan. We are thus forcibly reminded of the truth of the Armenian proverb that the deprived liveth; but the depriver liveth not, as in the present instance. The relentless persecutor who thought that he had won a great victory over his rival, died shortly after, but the persecuted, who was unjustly harassed and wronged, is by the grace of God, still living, in spite of physical infirmities, and may he live long to continue his useful and constructive work for the benefit of his nation.

Verily he who digs a pit for others, falls into it himself, so let those who harm innocent people, through sheer malice, remember that there is a just God above who sees everything and judges people according to their actions.

Hafez, the sweet-tongued nightingale of Persia, who was a good Mohammedan, and had committed the entire *Koran* to memory, hence his name, has said: "drink wine, burn the pulpit, throw fire into the Kaaba, dwell in an idol house, but harm nobody".

The following treatise on Sufism is from the *Encyclopædia Britannica*, (Ninth Edition).

"To conclude this sketch of the development of religious beliefs, it remains to say a few words on one of the most remarkable manifestations of Islam—its mysticism, or Sufism. In principle, mysticism is rather a mode of practising religion than a distinct religion; it depends on the character of the believer's mind, and adapts itself to all dogmas. It is the especial tendency of tender and dreamy spirits. Thus among the Moslems it is a woman who is considered to have founded mysticism. This woman, named Rabia, lived in the first century of the Hejira, and was buried at Jerusalem. Her doctrine was simply the theory of Divine love. She taught that God must be loved above all things, because he alone is worthy of love; and that everything here below must be sacrificed in the hope of one day attaining to union with God. These views were too similar to the Neo-Platonic ideas respecting the union of the human intellect with the Universal Reason not to have an attraction for the Gnostics, who abounded in the Shiite sects. Mysticism therefore made great progress in Persia, and assumed the character of a sect towards the year 200 of the Flight. A certain Abu Said, b. Abilkhair was the first who advised his disciples to forsake the world and embrace a monastic life, in order to devote themselves exclusively to meditation and contemplation; a practice which may very probably have been borrowed from India. The disciples of Abu Said wore a garment of wool (*surf*), whence they received the name of Sufis. Sufism spread more and more in Persia, and was enthusiastically embraced by those who wished to give themselves up undisturbed to philosophical speculation. Thus, under the colour of Sufism, opinions entirely subversive of the faith of Islam were professed. In its first form Sufism was quite compatible with Moslem dogma. It was satisfied to profess a contempt for life, and an exclusive love of God, and to extol ascetic practices, as the fittest means of procuring those states of ecstacy during which the soul was supposed to contemplate the Supreme Being face to face. But, by degrees, thanks to the adepts whom it drew from the ranks of heterodoxy, Sufism departed from the original purpose, and entered on discussions respecting the Divine nature, which in some cases finally led to Pantheism. The principal argument of these Pantheistic Sufis was that God being one, the creation must make a part of his being; since otherwise it would exist externally to him, and would form a principle distinct from him; which would be equivalent to looking on the universe as a deity opposed to God. In the reign of Moktadir, a Persian Sufi, named Hallaj, who taught publicly that everyman is God, was tortured and put to death. After this the Sufis showed more caution, and veiled their teachings under oratorical phrases. Moreover, it was not all the Sufis who pushed logical results so far as to assert that man is God. They maintained that God is all, but not that all is God. Sufism exists in Persia even in our own day."

For fuller information about the Sufi Mysticism, see *A literary history of Persia,* from the earliest times to Firdausi, in 4 Volumes, by the late Professor Edward G. Browne, M.A., M.B. (Vol. I. Chapter XIII.)

In order to give our readers an idea of the poetical genius of Sarmad, we give translations of some of his *ghazals* (odes) and *rubaiyats* (quatrains) which in point of elegance can vie with the best quatrains of the world-famous Omar Khayyam.

FARD

In the *Kaaba** and the idol temple, He became the stone, and He became the wood.
In one place He became the *Hajrul Aswad,* and in the other a Hindu idol.

GHAZAL (Ode)

He burnt me without cause, behold the spectacle,
He slew me without guilt, behold the Messiah,
A living being who has no soul, thou hast seen;
If thou has not seen, come and see me.
Ye, who care not to have a sight of Joseph,
Behold the agony of Jacob and Zuleikha !

---

* *Kaaba* is the inner part of the temple at Mecca. *Hajrul Aswad,* or the black stone, has come down from the time of heathenism in Arabia, and is venerated by the pilgrims who flock to Mecca every year from all parts of the Mohammedan world.

Ye, who wonder at my hapless days,
Behold for a moment this charming face.
Thou hast seen a Shah, a darwish and a qalandar,*
Behold Sarmad, the drunken and dishonoured.

RUBAIYAT (Quatrains).

1

Thou hast made thyself famous in winning hearts,
Also in the art of friendship and affection,
Those eyes which are vigilant are observant of thyself;
Every moment thou showest thyself in a hundred colours.

2

If I am a devotee, my object is the Friend,
What have I to do with the rosary and the sacerdotal thread!
This woollen garment wherein lie a hundred evils
Never shall I put on my shoulder : it is disgusting to me.

3

Our every-day avocation is villainy and wickedness.
Our flatterers and vessels have been filled with sins.
Creation is laughing and life is wailing
At our prayers, genuflexions and fastings.

4

Sarmad is a body, his soul is in the hand of another :
An arrow, but its bow is in the hand of another.
He wished to be a man in order to jump out of the nest,
He became a cow whose tether is in the hand of another.

---

* A qalandar is a darwish of a different sect.

5

Not only are these temples and sanctuaries His house
This earth and this sky are entirely His abode.
The whole world is mad about His fictions.
He is truly mad who is mad about Him.

6

His tyrannous passion, lo ! is Satan :
Always visible, yet hidden.
Thou art thyself the Devil, why are thou ill-disposed
to the Devil?
Before thy thoughts, he is bewildered.

7

Sarmad ! If He is true to his word, He Himself
will come :
If His coming is permissible, He Himself will come.
Why shouldst thou wander aimlessly after Him?
Sit down : if He be the Khud-a ;* He Himself will
come.

8

Sarmad ! the pang of love is not given to the
self-seeking,
The fire in the heart of the moth is not given to the fly.
It takes a life-time for the beloved to come to the lap :
This everlasting wealth is not given to every one.

9

Although a hundred friends have turned mine enemies,
Owing to the friendship of the one, my mind has
become contented.
I have accepted Unity and been freed from multiplicity
At last I became of Him and He of me.

---

* *Khuda* is here used in a double sense. *Khuda* is the Persian word for God and *Khud-a* means a self-comer.

10

He who gave thee the sovereignty of the world.
Gave me all the causes of anxiety.
He covered with a garment those with whom He found fault.
To the faultless He gave the robe of nudity.*

11

O King of Kings, I am not a hermit like thee, I am not nude,
I am frenzied, I am distracted, but I am not depressed,
I am an idolator, I am an infidel, I am not of the people of the faith,
I go towards the mosque, but I am not a Mussulman.

12

Pass on from the wordly fancy, thought and care.
Like the breeze of morn pass on from the garden and *field*.
Be not mad on the colour and smell of the rose and wine,
Be wise, pass on from these hallucinations.

13

Sarmad! thou shouldst shorten thy murmurings.
Thou shouldst adopt one course out of these two courses—
Either, thou shouldst give thy body for the pleasure of the Friend;
Or, thou shouldst sacrifice thy life in His way.

---

* Sarmad's clothes' philosophy or "Sartor resartus" is beautifully expressed in this quatrain.

14

To put trust in the promises of the man of the world
is wrong :
Yea wrong, verily wrong to-night wrong, to-morrow wrong.
Of the copy of the inquiry of our Book of life do not ask.
Its transcriptions are wrong, meaning wrong, composition
wrong, and spellings wrong.

15

I have no business with the fancy and thought of others.
In composing a *ghazal,* I adopt the manner of Hafez.
But in a *rubai* (quatrain) I am the disciple of Khayyam,
But do not quaff much of his wine.*

16

Sarmad ! speak not of the Kaaba and of the temple.
In the valley of doubt do not wander like the strayed
wayfarer.
Go and learn from Satan† how to worship.
Accept one *qebla* and do not bow before every stranger.

17

Say, who is in the world that has not committed a sin?
He who has sinned not : say, how could he live?
I do evil thou requitest with evil,
Then say, what is the difference between me and thee?

---

* Sarmad who himself was a great poet, pays a well-deserved compliment to two of the greatest poets of Persia—Hafez the master of *ghazal,* justly called the Anacreon of the East and Omar Khayyam, the tent-maker philosopher of Nishapur whose quatrains are greatly admired in the East and in the West.

† According to Mohammedan tradition, the Devil fell for refusing to pay homage to Adam at the command of God.

18

Sometimes thou are a cypress, sometimes a hyacinth and
sometimes a jasmine,
Now a mountain, a wilderness, and at another time a
flower-garden.
Now thou are the light of a candle, now the scent of a rose,
Sometimes thou art in a garden, and sometimes in an
assembly.

19

Sarmad ! thou hast done strange injury to the religion,
Thou hast bartered thy faith for one with an intoxicating eye.
With supplication and belief—thy entire wealth—
Thou didst go and squander on an idol-worshipper.*

20

He who believed in the secret of esoteric doctrine,
Became more expanded than the expanded heavens.
The Mulla [doctor] says that Ahmad [Mohammad]
went up to heaven,
Sarmad says that heaven came down into Ahmad
[Mohammed] †

In view of the beauty of Sarmad's poems, cannot an English scholar, well versed in the Persian language and possessing the poetical taste and aptitude of a Fitzgerald, be found to translate into English the beautiful quatrains of the

* In this beautiful quatrain, Sarmad apparently refers to his prosperous and happy days at Thatta, his love for the Hindoo lad Abhai Chand, his neglect of his flourishing business as a merchant and his renunciation of the esoteric religion of Islam, being a faithful follower of the esoteric doctrine of the Sufis

† This fatal distich brought on his head the wrath of the Emperor Aurungzebe,—the bigot, the fanatic and the assassin—and he was beheaded by the order of the Emperor for blasphemy, in 1661 A.D. at the capital city of Delhi where his grave can be seen to this day.

martyred poet? And we suggest that an Armenian scholar, walking in the footsteps of the late Joseph Zorab Mirzayiantz,* should render into Armenian the poems of the immortal Armenian poet who sang with great force, in a language not *his own—Persian being then the court language of the mighty* Moguls in India.

And before we close this Chapter, we have to record our grateful thanks to the late Maulavi Abdul Wali, Khan Sahib, for his interesting *Sketch of the Life of Sarmad*† from which we have derived some useful information regarding the life of the poet, but with due deference to his scholarship, we cannot accept the Maulavi's dictum that Sarmad was a Jew from Kashan in Persia.

In view of the authoritative statements of learned biographers and historians—European and Mohammedan—we are fully convinced that the martyred poet was an Armenian, for only an Armenian, inured to religious persecutions for centuries at the hands of the Mohammedans, could court death fearlessly in vindication of his ideals and convictions. The persecutions under which the Jews in Persia had groaned for centuries had made them very timid, it is not therefore likely that one of their co-religionists would have endangered his life by announcing in a Mohammedan country that the nocturnal journey of the prophet of Arabia to heaven was a myth.

The Kashani Jew is not an idealist, a religious fanatic or a mystic philosopher. He is out to make money to keep his body and soul together in a poor country. From what we have seen of the Jew in Persia in our younger days, he is a practical man of business and not a theorist or a dreamer. Sarmad was not however the only Armenian poet in India, as the illustrious Mirza Zul-Qarnain, the Armenian grandee of the Mogul Court, who was born and bred in India, was like-

* The late Mirzayiantz, the Armenian deputy in the Persian *Majlis* (parliament) and a Persian scholar of repute, rendered into Armenian verse the quatrains of Omar Khayyam with a learned treatise on the life and philosophy of the poet of Nishapur. It was published at Teharan (Iran) in 1923 and met with great success.

† A Paper read before the Asiatic Society of Bengal in 1924.

wise a poet of great repute. On the occasion of the accession of the Emperor Shah Jehan, the Mirza came from Bengal and presented beautiful poems which he had composed in Shah Jehan's name and got a present of four thousand rupees. And when the same Emperor had in 1648, removed the capital from Agra to Delhi, which was named Shahjehanabad after him, he asked Mirza Zul-Qarnain, by far the best poet of the day, to compose a suitable poem in praise of the new capital.

A Jesuit priest refers to this poem as follows:—

"Mirza summoned up all the powers of his talents, he wrote in verse that was perfect, but in it he sang, not the praises of the King, but the power of God alone: Mirza's only object was to show to the King that the glory of the city and its perfection were attributable to God alone. The King, who in his greed for flattery, expected his own praises, indignantly rejected the panegyric. Afterwards, he submitted his name, where that of God came in, so that what was said to God's praise would be attributed to him. In this you see how Mirza's intrepid piety came into conflict with the intore-able arrogance of the King".

And in the middle of the last century, an Armenian of Lucknow, named Johanness, wrote some beautiful poems in the Urdu language.

We cannot conclude this chapter without recording our grateful thanks to Hakim Habibur Rahman, the well-known Yunani physician of Dacca and a good Persian scholar, for having brought to our notice, some eight years ago, that the renowned poet SARMAD was an ARMENIAN.

CHAPTER XIV

VESTIGES OF ARMENIANS AT DELHI

GRAVES THAT HAVE ESCAPED DESECRATION.

In the absence of any information about the Armenians at Delhi from Armenian or Mohammedan sources, we have to rely on the casual references to them by English writers.

In the "Diary and Consultations of the Calcutta Council" for the 19th day of October, 1713, we find that an Armenian of Delhi, Khojah Manoor, was instrumental in getting two important *Hasbull Hookums* from the Mogul Emperor Farrokhsiyyar for the safe journey of the proposed English embassy to Delhi from Calcutta.

Let the records speak :—

"Cojah Surhaud [Khojah Sarhad] wrote last July to Cojah Manoor who formerly was chief eunuch to Mahomed Azeem, the father of King Furruckseer and is now entitled Nazar Cawne [Khan]. His present office is to attend Patshaw [Badshah] Begum the daughter of Aurungzeeb. This Nazar Cawne's intercession prevailed with the King to order a *Hasbull Hookum* to be given ordering all Subahs, Governors and officers whatsoever to guard our present for the King through their several Governments till it shall arrive with the English that shall accompany it and Cojah Surhaud at Court. This *Hasbull Hookum* being arrived under a cover to Cojah Surhaud at Dilly [Delhi], write him the King has ordered another *Hasbull Hookum* for us to pass all the English trade in his dominions with the usual freedom till the Royall *Phirmaund* [Farman] is obtained. Cojah Surhaud flatters us with hopes that the second *Hasbull Hookum* may be with us in a few days."

It is related in the history of the Sarman-Sarhad Embassy which was sent to Delhi from Calcutta in 1715 to obtain the Grand Farman from the Mogul Emperor Farrokhsiyyar that on their arrival at the Imperial city the envoys were met by an Armenian priest, Rev. Stephanus, (Stephen) who had brought dresses of honour for John Sarman and Khojah Israel Sarhad, the Armenian member of the delegation. Under date, Delhi, the 8th July ,1715, it is recorded :—

"We arrived at Farruckabad the 3rd instant (July) where we were met by Padre Stephanus bringing two *surpaws* [dresses of honour] which were received with the usual ceremony by John Surman and Khoja Serhaud. The 4th we arrived at Baorapoola, three coss from the city, sending the padre before to prepare for our reception, that, if possible, we might visit the King the first day, even before we went to the house which was got for us. Accordingly the 7th in the morning, we made our entry with very great order; there being sent a *mansabdar* of two thousand, with about 200 horse and peons, to meet us, bringing likewise two elephants and flags. About the middle of the city we were met by the Sallabat Khan Bahadur, and were by him conducted to the palace where we waited till about twelve o'clock till the King came out. We were very well received."

The presence of an Armenian priest at Delhi and that an ecclesiastic of distinction to have been entrusted by the Mogul Emperor with the delicate and responsible task of the reception of the English envoys from Calcutta, shows clearly that there was an important Armenian colony at the Imperial City in the early part of the 18th century and if there was a priest, there must have been a church too, far whereever the Armenians settled in India during the 16th, 17th and 18th centuries, the first thing they did was to erect a church of their own with a priest to officiate therein.

In the general devastation of the Imperial City which took place in 1739, their church and the cemetery were destroyed by the soldiery of Nadir Shah. And during the dark days of the Indian Mutiny in 1857, all the Christian churches and cemeteries that had come into existence since the sack of the city by the Persian invader in 1739 were likewise destroyed by the mutineers.

The only Christian cemetery which escaped destruction by the mutineers was the Deramao cemetery, which, being outide the city, was not desecrated by the ruffians in 1857.

There are in that isolated cemetery six tombstones with Armenian inscriptions, the following being translations.

1. This is the tomb of Zachar, the son of Lazar of Tiflis. Departed to God on the 31st December, 1787. (There is also an inscription in Persian, with the date 1202 A.H.)
2. This is the tomb of Qarib, the son of the late Lucas of Tiflis, who departed to God, on the 4th March, in the year of our Lord 1794 at Dilli [Delhi].
3. This is the tomb of Maqsood, the son of the late Mahtesy [pilgrim] Agameer of Van, who departed to God on the 5th January in the year of our Lord 1795.
4. This is the tomb of Gregory, the son of the late Malcom of Constantinople who departed to God on the 9th January, in the year 1248 of the Armenian era [1799] at Dilli [Delhi].
5. This is the tomb of Agah Thaddeus,* the son of the late Eleazar and the grandson of the late Rev. Zachariah of the Shahnazar family of the capital city of Tabriz.

   Departed to God on the 22nd January in the year of our Lord, 1801 at Dilli [Delhi].
6. This is the tomb of Anthony, the son of Khatin of the family of Dinibeg of Tiflis who departed to God on the 16th September 1801, in the city of Dilli [Delhi].

In the *List of inscriptions on Tombs or Monuments in the Punjab, N. W. F. Provinces, Kashmir and Afghanistan,* by Miles Irving, Lahore, 1910, incorrect translations of these inscriptions are given. For instance, the word *tomb* has been translated as *coffin,* which shows that the translator, which we understand was the late Dr. Führer, was not sufficiently conversant with the Armenian language. The Armenian word for a coffin is *dagagh,* whereas the word used in the epitaphs is *tapan,* which means a tomb.

---

* The grandfather of Agah Thaddeus, the Rev. Zachariah, came to Agra from Tabriz in Persia in 1656, according to a mural tablet in the "Martyrose's Chapel" in the old Armenian cemetery (opened in 1611) at Agra. He died there in 1657, as can be seen in the List of inscriptions.

The name Zachar, son of Lazar, in the inscription of 1787 (No. 1) has been wrongly translated as Karo, the son of Gazar. How "Zachar" became "Karo" is a mystery. We may mention, *en passant,* that in October 1919, when we were deciphering the Armenian and other inscriptions in that deserted and snake-infested cemetery, situated in a jungle about 15 minutes drive from the Ganesh Flour Mills in Subzimundi, we saw a huge snake coiled at the foot of a pomegranate tree in the lower portion of the cemetery where the graves had disappeared owing to the accumulation of water during the rains, and in trying to escape from the poisonous reptile, we almost fell into a deep well in the middle of the cemetery. Such are the risks and dangers to which research workers expose themselves sometimes in pursuit of a hobby.

But that was not the only ordeal. When we arrived at the cemetery, we found the gate locked, as the caretaker had gone to the city on account of a Hindoo festival. But as we had found the place with great difficulty after a long and tedious drive, over trackless fields, in a bone-shaking country carriage, called *ekka,* we were determined to see the place with the sole object of rescuing from oblivion the landmarks of the Armenians at Delhi, as we had been told by the Archælogical Department, that there were some Armenian tombstones in that cemetery. Nothing daunted, we scaled the wall and gained, burglar-like, access to the cemetery as if a great treasure was hidden there.

There are in all 24 graves, with tombstones, in that cemetery, the oldest bearing the date 1782. In that isolated cemetery lies interred the Carnelite monk, Fr. Gregorio who died on the 29th September 1807. It was this priest who baptised the famous Begum Sumru of Sardhana on the 7th May 1781, at Agra when she was given the Christian name Joanna Nobilis.

The late Fr. Felix, who was an authority on the history of the Christians at Agra, Delhi and Lahore, during the Mogul period, writes about the Armenians at, Delhi as follows :—

> "Delhi also had a fair congregation of Armenian Christians, but it gradually died away after Nadir

Shah had taken possession of Delhi in 1739, when the two churches and the residences of the Jesuit Fathers were burned down and the beautiful buildings of some noble Christians families totally destroyed by the flames. These two churches were built during Jehangir's reign. It was during this time of general devastation that the famous Christian cemetery, situated near the place where they kept the heavy artillery, was destroyed and so the Armenian epitaphs were effaced along with many other Christian inscriptions."

There is in the Archæological Museum at Delhi, located in Shah Jehan's beautiful Fort, a white marble slab, with a black border, bearing an inscription in Armenian, the letters being inlaid with black slate. The tablet bears No. C. 27.

It can be translated thus :—

"By [the grace of] God, this house is [to the memory] of Phanus [Stephen] the son of Joseph of Urumiah. In the year of our Lord 1781."

On enquiries we find that the above tablet came from the collection of the Delhi municipality when the Museum was inaugurated, but where did the municipality get it from originally, nobody can say.

The inscribed slab in the Delhi Museum is not a tombstone but a memorial tablet, commemorating the erection of an Armenian church or a chapel at Delhi in 1781. Whether that sacred edifice was destroyed before or during the Indian Mutiny, we cannot say, but the fact remains that there existed an Armenian church in that city since 1781.

ARMENIANS AT LAHORE

CHAPTER XV.

ARMENIANS AT LAHORE.

In the course of our investigations, we find that Lahore, an important commercial centre in the Punjab and the summer capital of the Mogul Emperors, had an Armenian colony in the beginning of the 17th century.

Fr. Jerome Xavier writing from Agra on the 6th September, 1604, says "the poorer Armenians in Lahore made their livelihood by selling wines, for which they often get into trouble, as the Viceroy holds their trade in detestation (though he drinks well himself) and it was when Pinheiro had persuaded these Armenians to desist from this calling that they were safe from persecution of the Viceroy. Owing to Akbar's Firman, the Christians might practice their religion quite openly."

The same Jesuit Father, in a letter from Lahore, dated the 25th September, 1606, says that when the city was in a turmoil in 1606, owing to the revolt of Prince Khusru, the son of Jehangeer, the Armenian merchants stored their goods at the Father's House, for safety.

At one time the Mogul Governor had threatened to exterminate the Christians in Lahore and the Armenian community were in such fear, writes Fr. Pinheiro, on the 12th August, 1609, that "some twenty-three Armenian merchants fled with haste, escaping through different gates, as it seems they have no mind to be martyrs, may God make them good confessors." It appears that the Armenian community of Lahore was a fairly large one at that time, judging from the number of merchants who found safety in flight when a storm of persecution was brewing and as they were men of business, they had therefore no desire of winning martyrs' crowns, much to the disappointment of the over-zealous Father Pinheiro.

It is stated in Fr. Pierre du Jarric's *Akbar and the Jesuits,* that Fr. Pinheiro persuaded several Armenians to join the Catholic Church. "The Armenians in this country" says Fr. Jarric, "as a whole, are less ready than formerly to scorn and insult the Church; for it is known that the Fathers enjoy the favour and support of the Viceroy, and that the officers of justice have orders to banish from the town, (Lahore) any whom they name to them. The behaviour of the Armenians was also influenced by the fact that their new Archbishop, on whose advent they had been counting, died on his way to India. Having reached Ormuz, he had been prevented from continuing his journey by sea and set out for Lahore by way of Persia in 1599. He perished on the road; unsuccoured by God or man. His books and all else he possessed were stolen. The former fell eventually into the hands of Father Pinheiro, which greatly annoyed the Armenians, who had desired to present them to the King. They thought that their prelate was coming to India to be Archbishop of Serre, that is of the Christians of St. Thomas in Malabar, but that office was filled in a different manner".

Our information of the Armenians in that city is very meagre and of a fragmentary nature. Their cemetery, from which we could have gained some valuable information, as at Agra, has unfortunately disappeared during the repeated Afghan invasions, in the middle of the 18th century, under Ahmad Shah. The only vestiges of the once-flourishing Armenian colony in that city are the four tombstones in the Central Museum, one of which, with a legible inscription, bears the date 1601 A.D.

That famous gun, the "Zamzamah", which was cast by an Armenian at Lahore, in 1761, is another valuable relic that has survived the ravages of Time and the loot and pillage of the invaders from the north. There is still another interesting relic of the once prosperous colony, in the shape of a unique brass jar of beautiful workmanship made at Lahore, in 1606, for the use of Khojah Minas, the son of Khojah Yaqoob (Jacob). (See the second foot-note on page 17).

By using the word *Khojah* in quick succession, we are again exposing ourselves to the criticisms of some of our hyper-critical Anglicised compatriots in Calcutta, who argue, with the oratory of a Demosthenes, that the use of that uncanny Persian word will leave an indelible impression on the minds of the English and Indian readers that the holders of that title were

Persians, and as staunch nationalists, burning with a zeal for the national prestige, the critics vehemently resent the idea of their ancestors being known as such. Our critics are unfortunately ignorant of the history of the Mogul times when that honorofic title (Khojah) which is equivalent to the present *Sir*, was invariably borne by Armenian merchants of distinction and high repute in India. And let the Ciceros and the Sheridans of the present day remember that as the titles of "Pasha" and "Sirdar" did not make the ill-fated General Gordon and the equally unfortunate Lord Kitchener, Egyptians or Turks, we fail to see how and by what force of argument, the Armenian merchants of the Mogul days, bearing the titles of "Khojah" or "Agah", can be mistaken for Persians.

The critics evidently do not know that in Mohammedan countries, Armenians of distinction and high social status, have always borne Mohammedan titles, civil and military. In India and Persia, they have been honoured with the titles of "Agah," "Khojah" and "Khan," and in Egypt and Turkey, they have been given the titles of "Effendi," "Bey" and "Pasha." A few instances will prove of interest. Nubar Pasha, the "Grand Old Man" of Egypt in the second-half of the 19th century, although an Egyptian Pasha, was a renowned son of Armenia. Prince Mirza Malcolm Khan, the Persian Minister at the court of St. James for several years, although a Persian Mirza and a Khan, was a distinguished Armenian from Julfa. Ephrem Khan, the commander of the Persian nationalists who struck the death blow to the Khajar dynasty, some twenty years ago, was likewise an Armenian. Artin Pasha, the trusted Minister of the Turkish government, some forty years ago, was an Armenian. Gorgin Khan (Khojah Gregory) the Minister and the Commander-in-Chief of Nawab Mir Kasim of Bengal, from 1760-1763, was an Armenian from Julfa. Shah Nazar Khan, the skilled artisan who cast the famous gun, the "Zamzamah," for Ahmad Shah Durrani, was an Armenian too.

The critics should know that as British titles cannot make the title-holders Englishmen, in the same way the Persian or the Turkish titles borne by the Armenians in the past, cannot possibly change their nationality or religion. It is to be hoped that the Armenians who will be living in India a hundred years hence, will not criticise and malign the contemporary historian for calling the Armenians of the 20th century by their English titles, namely Mr. and Sir, for the Armenians of those days, should there be any Armenians left then, will in the natural order of things, be called "Baboos" "Srijuts," and "Seths."*

History has a happy knack of repeating itself, for if the Armenians were called "Agahs" and "Khojahs" in Mogul India and were known as "Mister" and "Sir" in the days of British supremacy, it will not be at all surprising if they are called "Baboos," "Srijuts" or "Seths" when the Swaraj flag will be flying all over India, with the words, "INDIA FOR THE INDIANS," writ large on them.

The Armenian merchants who came out to India in the early part of the 17th century were from Armenia direct and not from New Julfa, as that Armenian suburb of Ispahan came into existence in 1605, as has been shown in a foot-note on p. 148. In a letter written from Armenia, in 1609, by an Armenian archimandrite, named Joseph, to a wealthy Armenian merchant at New Julfa, Khojah Woskan by name, the archimandrite says: "It is now eight years since my brother Sikandar [Alexander] has gone on a commercial journey to the country of Lahore." It appears that the Armenians had a special quarter of their own at Lahore, enclosed by a wall near the Fort. Fr. Tieffentaller relates that Ahmad Shah, the Afghan invader, overran the Punjab for the second time and conquering the province, took with him on his return to Kabul all the Christian gunners who were in the service of Mir Mannu, the governor of Lahore. The Armenian quarter still existed during the third invasion of the Punjab by Ahmad Shah, in 1757, because Fr. Tieffentaller says that the Armenian and Georgian soldiers in the service of Ahmad Shah protected it against the Afghan soldiers and it escaped the general pillage and devastation of which the unfortunate inhabitants of Lahore were the victims during those dark days of cruelty and barbarism.

Francois Valentyn relates in *Oud en Nieuw Ooost-Indien* (Vol. IV. p. 283) that on 10th December, 1711,

* Seth is the Guzerati word for Mr. or Baboo.

when the embassy of the Dutch East India Company, under Johan Josua Ketelaar, reached Lahore, an Armenian Bishop and some Jesuit priests came out to greet him.

The presence of an Armenian bishop at Lahore in 1711, is another proof of the existence of an important colony there, for as a rule, Armenian bishops reside in cities where there is a fairly big flock in need of spiritual ministrations. And if there was a bishop at Lahore, there must have been a church or a chapel for the worship of God in their own way, as in other large cities in India, but no traces of a sacred edifice can be found in that city which by reason of its importance and great wealth was always a prey to the avarice and cupidity of the invaders.

We have seen on p. 39 that Mirza Iskandar, the father of Mirza Zul-Qarnain, left in his will the sum of Rupees 2,000 "for the church and the Christians of Lahore," and a sum of Rupees 600 "for arranging a cemetery for the deceased Christians of Lahore."

According to the Jesuit records, Mirza Zul-Qarnain, who was the Governor of Lahore at one time, had a garden in that city and when his wife Helen died in September 1638, she was buried in a beautiful mausoleum in that garden.

Mirza Zul-Qarnain's mother, Lady Juliana also died at Lahore in 1598 and she may have been buried in that garden. In all probability, the Mirza himself, who died in 1656, may have found a last resting place in that family cemetery near his mother and wife.

There are no traces of these graves, or of any Armenian graves at Lahore where Armenians lived and died during the 17th and 18th centuries.

The Jesuit priest, Fr. Emmanuel de Figuieredo, writing in 1735 says that "beyond Delhi where we have two residencies, lies Lahore,* one of the greatest cities of this kingdom. Here

* The people of Ispahan, the former capital of Persia, who were justly proud of their beautiful city in the glorious days of the Saffavi kings, used to sing the praises of the ancient metropolis in a distich which can be translated thus :—

"Ispahan is half the world, provided there is no Lahore"—
Ispahan nesf a jehan. agár Lahore na bashad.

is generally stationed the elite of the Mughal Army, composed for the greater part of Christian officers, who by their fidelity and courage, in all dangerous attacks on the enemy, prepare the way for the Emperor's felicitous victories."

At present there are only a few Armenians residing at Lahore. They are the Arathoons, the Martyroses and the Jacobs, the former having settled there about the middle of the last century. The Armenian Archbishop Sahak Ayvadian, visited them in May, 1907, on his way to Peshawar, and confirmed their children who had been baptised in the Anglican Church for want of an Armenian priest. A brother-in-law of the ancestor of the Arathoons of Lahore, one George Joseph of the Creet family of Julfa, had settled at Jullunder in the middle of the last century. He was of a charitable disposition and knew the value of education, so he founded a school at his birthplace, Julfa, which a few years after his death was amalgamated with the C. M. S. school, founded there in 1870, by the late Rev. Robert Bruce, D.D. of revered memory.

There is a black marble tablet erected to the memory of the late George Joseph, in the Calcutta Armenian church, with inscriptions in the Armenian and English languages. The English inscription is as follows.—

> " Sacred to the memory of George Joseph Esq., born in Julfa, by whose beneficence a school is established in the land of his birth for the instruction of Armenian youths in the Armenian, English and Persian languages, and by whose liberality a fund is also provided for the relief of the poor. He departed this life in Jullunder on the 6th December, 1864."

Lahore with its beautiful climate, its majestic buildings and its great wealth was a strong rival of Ispahan in the days of Mogul supremacy.

ARMENIANS AT KABUL

CHAPTER XVI

ARMENIANS AT KABUL.

A CHRISTIAN COLONY IN AFGHANISTAN.

Although Kabul is outside the scope of this work, but as a large number of Armenian gunners were, according to Fr. Tieffentaller, taken from Lahore to Kabul, by Ahmad Shah, in 1755, it will be interesting to follow their fortunes in their new abode.

The Armenian gunners from Lahore were not however the first settlers at Kabul, for according to the traditions which had been handed down to the remnants of the colony which still existed in that city up to the close of the last century, a large number of Armenians had settled there during the reign of Nadir Shah two hundred years ago.

Sir Edward Maclagan, a great authority on the history of the Jesuit Missions in India, says, in his *The Jesuits and the Great Mogul,* that "Benedict Goes when passing the borders of this country [Kafiristan] in 1603, had heard accounts of Kafiristan which led him to believe that there might be Christians there, and this belief had been reaffirmed in Father Kircher's work, *China Illustrata,* published in 1667. A few years later the Fathers in Mogor learnt from some Armenians who had come to Agra from Kabul that the inhabitants of Kafiristan, (who were not Muslim) bore a cross traced (escripta) on their heads and had probably at one time been Christians. Fired with the prospect of this new opening for their efforts, the Jesuits at Agra obtained permission to undertake a Mission to Kafiristan, and the task was entrusted to Father Gregorio Roiz, then at Agra." From the above it appears that there were Armenians at Kabul in 1670, long before the days of Nadir Shah or Ahmad Shah.

Very little is known of the history of that isolated colony, although Kabul, in common with the other cities in India and the East, was under the ecclesiastical jurisdiction of the extensive

Perso-Indian diocese, the headquarters of which was at Julfa, the Armenian suburb of Ispahan. It appears that up to the thirties of the last century, priests were regularly sent to Kabul from Julfa, but owing to the apathy of the prelates who succeeded the Archbishop Carapiet, no priests were sent there, perhaps the spiritual welfare of that small community in the midst of a fanatical people, was not considered to be of sufficient importance by the worthy dignitaries who sat on the episcopal chair in the Cathedral at Julfa, with the result that the small flock, which had dwindled down to about thirty families by that time, was left without a shepherd, their dead being deprived of a Christian burial and their children of the sacrament of baptism, as can be seen presently.

In the Report of the Peshawar Mission, C.M.S., *for* 1870-71, there is an Appendix, under the captain "Some account of the Armenian Christians in the city of Cabul," which is reproduced here *in extenso*, as it is highly interesting.

"There are now eighteen Armenian Christians in the city of Cabul, six are males and twelve females. One of them was educated in our Peshawar Mission School and has a fair knowledge of English. One of the women became the wife of the late Ameer Azim Khan and the mother of Sardar Ishaq Khan, whose name has frequently figured prominently in the recent disturbances in Cabul. She is now a prisoner in Fort Ghuznee.

The Rev. Joseph Wolff* in 1832 when in Cabul ministered to the Armenians, and relates in his Diary that he preached to them in Persian in their Church. Then there were four Armenian men and nineteen ladies and children. In 1839 when Lord Keane marched to Cabul, the Chaplain, the Rev. G. Pigott, baptised two of the children. And in 1842 the Rev. J. N. Allen, Chaplain to General Nott's force, baptised three others. One of them is now a member of our Peshawar Church.

Since then two young men came to the Peshawar Mission for baptism and have since returned to Cabul.

This small Christian community has for many years been permitted by the Cabul Government to worship God in their

* *Joseph Wolff was a Jewish convert to Christianity. He was the first Missionary to go to Kabul.*

own little church. But they have frequently suffered from the numerous political changes which have taken place in that land of anarchy and bloodshed. Only last year several of them were imprisoned by the Ameer and were at last released through the intercession of the Missionary at Peshawar.

In such a position of uncertainty they have not been able to make much effect towards the spread of Christianity, but on two occasions they have sent enquirers to Peshawar, who were afterwards baptized, and whose names are still borne on the books of our Peshawar Mission. It is related by the Armenians that they once baptized a convert from Mohammedanism under the following remarkable circumstances.

An Afghan robber, having dug through the roof of the Armenian church, descended and collected all the silver vessels of the place with the intention of stealing them. But in attempting to ascend through the aperture of the roof of the church, he fell three times. Believing that the Almighty had arrested him in the very act of theft, this Afghan robber at once delivered himself up to the Armenians and begged for Christian baptism. This Afghan convert, *the first fruits of Afghanistan,* died only a few years ago. The Rev. J. N. Allen's account of his visit to the Armenian Church at Cabul in 1842 is particularly interesting, and we now give it, *in extenso,* with the hope that it may awaken an interest in a people who have for many generations maintained a Christian profession amidst Mahomedan bigotry and hatred.

"1842, October 1st. I went into the town and accompanied by Captain Boswell, 2nd Regiment, Bengal N. I. set forth to make inquiries respecting a small community of Armenian Christians, of whom I had heard from my friend the Rev. G. Pigott, who had babtized two of their children when he visited Cabul in 1839, as Chaplain to the Bombay Army under Lord Keane.

After some inquiry, we discovered them in a street in the Bala Hissar, leading from the Jellalabad Gate; their buildings were on the North side of the street. We went up an alley and turned into a small court on the left, surrounded by buildings and filled with the implements of their trade. A little door led from this court into their church, a small dark building, but upon procuring lights, I found that it was carpeted and kept clean, apparently with great care. Its aspect was due east and west, and an altar stood at the east end, surmounted by a small picture of the Holy family, much dimmed by smoke and dust. Upon the altar were six silver candlesticks, two small silver crosses and two copies of the Holy Gospels. In front, without the altar rails, was a small desk, on which lay a book of daily prayers in Armenian. The altar was not against the wall, but had a space behind, and stood on a raised step. Our guides showed me a volume containing the Gospels in Armenian and another with the Epistles, also a small English pocket Bible, with clasps, Oxford Edition, which I think was said to have been bought from a Hindoostanee. They stated that body came into Afghanistan with Nadir Shah, that they were then two hundred families, but were now reduced to four, comprising thirty-five persons, men, women, and children. They subsist by making Shiraz wine and distilling spirits. They said they endured much from the Afghans and were often subjected to heavy exactions.

Whether they have wealth or not, it is impossible to say. The place wore an air of poverty, but the men and women whom I saw were well dressed. If they are wealthy, which I think probable, they would be most unwise to make any show of it. I was much affected at finding this dim spark of Christianity in the midst of such utter darkness, and earnestly prayed that it might be fanned by the breathing of the Holy Spirit to a bright and pure flame, which might enlighten the nations around. When they understood that I was a Christian priest, the woman prostrated herself on the ground and would have embraced my feet; this I endeavoured to prevent and could I have spoken in her own tongue, would have addressed her in the words of St. Peter to the household of Cornelias, "Stand up, I also am a man."

The man, whose Afghan name was Timour, was less enthusiastic. He clasped my hand in both his, and bowing down, pressed it first to his lips and afterwards to his forehead. They told me they had had no priests for thirteen years, that one had come from Hindoostan and got as far as Peshawar, but was afraid to venture farther.

It was highly interesting to hear from the lips of these eastern Christians the names of our blessed Saviour and his holy evangelists and apostles.

October 3rd. I went to the town by engagement to baptize some children of the Armenians, who had joyfully availed themselves of the opportunity afforded by the presence of a clergyman, for procuring their admission into the Christian Church by this holy sacrament. I was accompanied, on this occasion, by Major Stopford and Captains Macduff and Adamson. H. M. 40 Regt. and Captain Button, 2nd Regt. Bengal N. I. On arriving at the Armenian church, I found them prepared, and a large basin of lukewarm water placed in front of the altar. The water I observed was transferred, with great reverence, to a large earthen jar, I presume to be preserved as holy. After service my friends wished to examine the picture, crosses etc. on the altar and asked whether they might be permitted to enter the rails. They were told that they might if they would divest themselves of their swords. These were immediately carried away by Timour and placed outside the door of the church. I was much struck with their deep reverence and love for the house of God. My friend Mr. Pigott, told me that when he asked them why they remained in Cabul in the depressed state in which they were, they replied: "How can we leave our Church." After the sacrament of baptism had been administered, there was a little entertainment of tea and cakes in an upper room. Here I saw Secunder and Miriam, the two children baptized by Mr. Pigott. They were remarkably pretty with very fair complexions, indeed both children and adults were very handsome and had most impressive features.

Farewell, I thought as I rode away, farewell brethren in Christ, amidst much that may be ignorant and superstitious, there is a cleaving to Christian ordinances and a reverence for Christian teachers, which encourages me to hope that there is a love to the Master, as well as to the house and the servants. We shall probably meet no more on earth, but I will indulge in the hope of meeting you, where we shall no longer see through a glass darkly, but shall know even as also we are known. May our one Lord, in whose one faith and one baptism we are united, watch over you and be your protector in the midst of the enemies of the Cross of Christ and cause that the blessed banner under which you and I are enlisted, may speedily be unfurled as a sign by which the kingdoms of this world shall be subdued and become the kingdoms of our God and of his Christ that he may reign for ever and ever."

The Armenians at Kabul told the Rev. J. N. Allen in 1842 that they had had no priests for thirteen years which was quite true, for as we have stated in the beginning of this chapter on the authority of that well-informed writer and journalist, Mesrovb Thaliadian, no priests were sent to Kabul from Julfa after 1830.

In this connection it may be observed that whereas scores of priests were sent annually to India and the East the Armenians living at Kabul were simply ignored and deprived of spiritual comforts and consolations, and the reason is not far to seek, because they were not rich and opulent like their more fortunate brethren at Bombay, Surat, Calcutta, Dacca, Madras, Rangoon, Singapore and Batavia.

Nothing eventful seems to have occurred in the history of that neglected and isolated small community from 1842 to 1896, when the late Ameer Abdur Rahman Khan, sent a formal invitation to the Armenian Community of Calcutta to send ten or twelve families to go and reside at Kabul in order to "relieve the loneliness" of their distant brethren and sisters, who, "feel very unhappy for want of the society of their own nationality."

The letter was sent through a trusted Armenian official, named Serwurdin Khan, a native of Kabul, whose Armenian name was Lucas A. Joseph, and who was the manager of the Ameer's gunpowder factories at Jelalabad.

The Ameer's letter, which was in the flowery Persian language, was translated and circulated among the Armenian Community of Calcutta in April 1896. It was as follows :—

CIRCULAR.

The following is a translation of a letter from H. H. the Ameer of Kabul addressed to the Armenian Community of

Calcutta handed to us and now published for the information of the Community. The bearer of the original letter is Mr. Lucas A. Joseph, an Armenian of Afghanistan, high in the service of the Ameer. This gentleman is for the present putting up at No. 6 Old China Bazar Street where he will be glad to see any one interested in the invitation held out by His Highness.

H. J. SHIRCORE,
C. M. ARATHOON,
Wardens of the Armenian Churches,
Calcutta & Chinsurah.

TO THE ARMENIANS IN CALCUTTA.

After many favours and kindness,—Be it well known to the Armenian Community in Calcutta that in the time of the late king, Nadir Shah, whom God rest in peace, a few families comprising nearly five hundred persons of the Armenian nationality came to this country and passed their days in comfort. At present only one family, consisting of 21 souls, young and old, male and female, survives. They feel very unhappy for want of the society of their own nationality, although during the rule of our predecessors, and, at present, under our rule they neither have experienced, nor will experience any harm or trouble; on the contrary, all of them, young and old, have held, and are still holding, posts and stipends under the Government of Afghanistan, so that they are well off in their living.

It is desirable that, from your national and religious feelings and sympathies, you should send ten or twelve families, men of education and of some profession, to live in the Dominions of Afghanistan, and so relieve their loneliness, and they themselves pass their days in comfort.

At this present one of them, our esteemed Serwurdin Khan, who is Manager of our Gunpowder Factories at Jelalabad, is starting for your parts for his marriage; and ten thousand rupees (British money) has been paid him from this illustrious court as a wedding present.

With reference to your coming to these Dominions we have given him our assurance, in all respects, that rank, allowances, and places to dwell in shall be given to every one according to his position and qualification; and that you shall live in peace and security; the above named will give (the) assurance to you. And the said Serwurdin Khan will describe to you our kindness and the style of his living.

Given on Monday the 13th of the month of Rajab 1313.

Written by
MIRZA ABDULLA.

Seal on the back of the original.

Ameer Abdur
Rahman Khan
&c., &c.

In May 1896, the Armenian Community of Calcutta, sent, through the Wardens of the Armenian church, a suitable reply to the Ameer, the following being a copy :—

TO HIS HIGHNESS

AMEER ABDUR RAHMAN KHAN,

The Sole Ameer of Afghanistan.

YOUR HIGHNESS,

It is with due appreciation of the high honour conferred on us, the ARMENIANS OF CALCUTTA, that we acknowledge the receipt of YOUR GRACIOUS FIRMAN by the hand of the respected SERWURDIN KHAN (MR. LUCAS A. JOSEPH) YOUR HIGHNESS' servant, whom we are most happy to welcome among us. Of YOUR HIGHNESS' KINDNESS to our countrymen settled in YOUR DOMINIONS we had some report; to have it now confirmed to us by such august authority, affords us much gratification, especially to be assured of the continued well-being of, and YOUR HIGHNESS' interest in, those few who are still enjoying YOUR HIGHNESS' beneficence, and the more so that YOUR HIGHNESS in your benevolence extends your kindness and generosity to embrace us, the ARMENIANS OF CALCUTTA, within the scope of YOUR HIGHNESS' feelings. We duly realise the isolated condition of our brethren and sincerely sympathise with them in their loneliness. The presence of their countrymen would indeed relieve this loneliness and afford them increased social happiness and contentment. It shall be our best endeavour to encourage ARMENIANS to go into YOUR HIGHNESS' DOMINIONS and settle down as loyal and worthy subjects, who will be of service to YOUR HIGHNESS and whose well-being will draw, we hope, not only from Calcutta, but from every part where their countrymen may be living and where the fame of YOUR GENEROSITY and KINDNESS towards the race shall reach, from far ARMENIA, TURKEY OR PERSIA, large numbers of hardworking industrious and staunch servants round YOUR HIGHNESS' THRONE which may GOD ever preserve. We regret much, however, that immediately no families are likely to remove from here, for the reason that they are established in business and in the practice of their several professions, having also all their connections of kinship with one another which they would be very loth to sever. After some intercourse, however, we are very hopeful that these difficulties will be got over and free communication established with YOUR HIGHNESS' DOMINIONS. In the meantime we would crave YOUR HIGHNESS' permission to offer to the ARMENIANS in all Afghanistan the opportunity for receiving for themselves the privileges of our Church and religion, which owing to their peculiar circumstances they do not possess. We propose for the present, with YOUR HIGHNESS' permission, to supply their urgent needs in this respect by sending one of our Priests to meet them in Peshawar and administer to them baptism and the sacraments, and supply any religious instruction that may be found essential for their spiritual well-being. For this purpose YOUR HIGHNESS may command them to come into Peshawur. We might mention that our Priests here cannot leave their jurisdiction, that is, go out of British India, without a reference to and the express sanction of our Bishop at Julfa in Persia.

We would also crave permission to suggest for YOUR HIGHNESS' consideration that the children of the ARMENIANS OF AFGHANISTAN be sent by YOUR HIGHNESS into India—to Calcutta it may be—for their general education and a professional training. On completing their terms they would return to their homes to render their true and loyal services to their Sovereign.

As to our esteemed and honourable friend, your servant, SERWURDIN KHAN (MR. LUCAS A. JOSEPH), we will do our best to help him towards realising his hopes. YOUR HIGHNESS will no doubt allow that the reluctance on the part of our maidens to sever themselves from their families by so great a distance is very natural and very difficult to overcome. It is also somewhat unfortunate that he arrived at the beginning of our season of Lent during which and for nearly two months after the festival of Easter (April 5th) no marriage can be solemnised in our Church.

We have to express our very great regret at the delay that has occurred in replying to YOUR HIGHNESS' GRACIOUS FIRMAN to us. We have endeavoured to acquaint the Members of our Community individually, as far as possible, with YOUR HIGHNESS' GOOD WILL towards us. We have also had to hold several meetings for the exchange of views which has necessarily taken up much time.

In conclusion we have to express our heart-felt gratitude to a Sovereign of YOUR HIGHNESS' might and enlightenment for the kindness shown to us all as a nation and especially to those who are still living secure under the shadow of your fatherly arm, and our confidence in YOUR HIGHNESS' liberal and protective sentiments towards a people that have been true to their faith and their honour, ever peaceful and loyal to the Governments under which they live. May GOD in His Universal goodness give you peace and happiness, contentment and health all the days that it may be His will to spare YOUR HIGHNESS to your people, and may the time be long is the prayer of YOUR HIGHNESS' most humble and grateful Servants the ARMENIANS OF CALCUTTA on whose behalf we beg to subscribe.

Calcutta, this the 25th day of May, 1896 A.D.

The Armenian officer from Kabul who was a widower, with three motherless children—two boys and a girl—did not, contrary to his expectations and the wishes of his august master, succeed in securing an Armenian bride in Calcutta, although a most amiable person, as no spinsters cared to go and reside in a God-forsaken and barbarous country like Afghanistan, and just as well they did not leave their comfortable homes to be driven into exile a year after as will be seen shortly.

The accredited agent of the Ameer could not induce any of the Armenians of Calcutta to accept the Ameer's invitation which though alluring was not good enough for those who had enjoyed the benefits and the blessings of British rule. They were not going to leave the substance and run after the shadow.

After a good deal of search, the disillusioned agent succeeded in inducing two superannuated Armenians of the never-do-well class to accompany him to the new Canaan, a land overflowing with milk and honey.

One of them was an adventurer who had found his way to Calcutta from Turkey and the other was a Calcutta Armenian, named John Sarkies who had been a teacher of the English language in the local Armenian College for a short time and had been dismissed for his violent temper. On their arrival at Kabul, the two emigrants from Calcutta, were weighed in the balance and were found wanting, as the astute Afghan autocrat required men of worth and merit and had no earthly need for worthless fossils. They were immediately repatriated at the Ameer's expense. But as wonders never cease and the unexpected always happens, the Ameer who in his solicitude for the communal welfare of his loyal and beloved Armenian subjects was anxious to augment the fast diminishing community at Kabul, banished, exactly a year after his cordial invitation, all the Armenians from his dominions and the unfortunate and hapless remnants of a once flourishing colony had to desert their church, their ancestral homes and the revered graves of their forebears and take refuge, under the British flag at Peshawar, carrying with them their sacred books, mostly in manuscript.

The reason of the wholesale deportation of the unfortunate Armenians, men, women and children, ranging between the ages of 5 and 63, was that the good friend of the Ameer, the accursed Sultan Abdul Hamid of Turkey, known as the "Great Assassin," had written to his brother despot and requested his Afghan co-religionist to banish from his dominions all the Armenians as a dangerous people—the manufacturers and throwers of deadly bombs, of which the Armenophobe Sultan had personal experience in his capital.

The Red Sultan had at the same time written to the late Nasir-ud-din Shah of Persia, who loved his loyal Armenian subjects with a paternal affection, to follow his example and persecute the Armenians in his dominions, but the good and God-fearing Shah, who sat on the historic throne of Anooshirvan the Just, replied curtly and told the blood-thirsty Sultan that the Armenians in Iran were his eldest children (*Aramen a farzand a arshad a man hasthand*).

Nothing was done by the wealthy Armenian community of Calcutta to relieve the distress of the unhappy refugees from Kabul who found an asylum at Peshawar in March 1897 where they have lived since in perfect peace and free from the molestations of their bigoted Afghan persecutors.

These people are the descendants of those brave Armenians who for two centuries kept the torch of the Christian faith burning in darkest Afghanistan suffering untold persecutions, and yet when they were asked by an English clergyman in 1841 why they remained in Kabul in the depressed state they were at the time, they pathetically replied, "how can we leave our church."

The following account of the Armenian refugees from Kabul appeared in the now defunct "Englishman" (Calcutta) of the 11th February 1907.

> "It is just possible that a very interesting discovery of ancient manuscripts will probably be made. As one result of the Ameer's visit to Calcutta, attention has been directed towards a small community of Christians from Armenia who had been living in Kabul for very many generations. These people in the time of the late Ameer Abdul Rahman had dwindled down to ten families. They were, for reasons unknown, banished to Peshawar

and brought down with them a collection of manuscripts said to be of immense antiquity. Indeed, they are so old that none of the families possessing them are able to read them. It appears that the priesthood had died out amongst these Christians in Kabul, and the community was too remote to be able to get priests from elsewhere. Hence the neglect of the sacred writings. In the traditional history of Armenia reference is made to an *Afghan* country, where the early Christians found a refuge from persecution. It has been hitherto thought that by *Afghan* country was meant the mountainous regions of Georgia, but it would be strange indeed if it were now discovered that it was in Kabul, supposed for so many years to be the very centre of fanaticism, that the flame of the Christian faith was kept alive when it was being ruthlessly trampled out elsewhere. In any case an examination by experts of the manuscripts now said to be in Peshawar, should yield some valuable results. The families themselves are unaware of the history of the first settlement in Kabul, except that it dates back to the very earliest times."

The publication of the above article roused some interest amongst the Armenians in Calcutta and the Armenian Archbishop Sahak Ayvadian, who was in Calcutta at that time, was induced to pay a pastoral visit to the refugees at Peshawar in the hope of securing some valuable ancient manuscripts.

The Archbishop on his arrival at Peshawar, early in May 1907, found that the children had been baptized already by an Anglican priest so he had them confirmed according to the rites of the holy Apostolic Church of Armenia. Another Armenian, Astwasatoor Hyrapiet Vardanian, born at Kabul and baptized at Peshawar, was confirmed by the late Rev. Psak H. Hacobian in the Armenian Church at Calcutta on the 20th May 1907. Whether the Archbishop was able to secure any ancient Armenian manuscripts, we cannot say, but he brought down to Calcutta some printed old Armenian books of not much value. These were placed in the library of the Armenian church of Nazareth in this city.

We remember having heard in 1890 from the late Rev. Johanness Catchick, the vicar of the Armenian church of

Calcutta from 1845—1897, who died at the ripe old age of ninety years in June, 1897, that an elderly Armenian from Kabul, Yusoph Khan (Joseph) by name had come to Calcutta in 1846 with a large number of Armenian manuscripts for disposal, but as there were no buyers at the fabulous prices he had set on them, he took them back to Kabul, having sold only one rare manuscript copy of the Armenian New Testament to the late Johanness Avdall for the sum of one hundred rupees, which in those days was considered a big price for a manuscript, when MSS. did not command the fancy prices which are paid now by Museums and art-collectors for rare pieces. These must have been the ancient manuscripts which the refugees from Kabul fetched with them to Peshawar when they were exiled from their homes in 1897, but what became of them ultimately, we cannot say, unless they came into the possession of the Armenian bishop who visited and confirmed the refugees at Peshawar in May 1907.

In the old Armenian cemetery at Agra, there are the graves of a few Armenians from Kabul who died and were buried there in 1833 and 1849.

Some ten years ago, one of the Armenian refugees at Peshawar named Vahan Daniel who was in the Indian Police, came down to Calcutta with his son whom he placed in the local Armenian College to learn the mother language. Such is the love of nationality amongst these patriotic remnants of the Armenian colony of Kabul.

The names of all the Armenians who received confirmation at Peshawar and Calcutta are recorded in the Register of Births and Baptisms kept in the Armenian holy church of Nazareth at Calcutta.

The story of the remorse-stricken Afghan thief who had gone to rob the silver articles in the Armenian church at Kabul should serve as an object lesson to those who feel no compunction to rob the church either as employees or as recipients of charity from church funds under false pretences. There are many people who on the plea of poverty, receive monetary help from a certain church regularly every month, yet they go about in taxis and are seen frequently at the cinemas, restaurants, races and other places of amusement.

And there are some unscrupulous employees of a certain church who while enjoying sinecures, do not hesitate to extort money from that church under false pretences. Apart from these plausible thieves, there are also some light-fingered gentry who rob the church in broad daylight by pilfering Prayer-Books, and this is no exaggeration, for in a certain church, thirty seven beautifully-printed and exquisitively-bound Prayer-Books were placed on the pews for the use of the devout congregation, but when an inventory was taken a year after, only sixteen torn copies were left. What became of the rest?—The second-hand bookshops and the ubiquitous *bikri-wallahs,* (buyers of old articles and rubbish)will be able to explain. Some twenty years ago, a certain person, of the *nouveau riche* class, wantonly demolished and razed to the ground a beautiful church, which would have stood for another two hundred years, at it was not a dilapidated building having been erected firmly in 1822. The vandal having got rid of the church of which he was the self-styled warden or custodian, placed the funds of the demolished church in his own business. But as nobody can rob a church with impunity, the vandal's flourishing business soon began to decline and it got so heavily and hopelessly involved that it passed into the hands of the creditors who eventually turned him out of the concern and in order to drown his sorrows, caused by the terrible fall, he drank himself to death.

We had warned the vandal, both privately and in the public press, when the sacrilege was committed, of the divine punishment that awaited him, but as he was arrogance personified and drunk with the highly intoxicating wine of transitory prosperity, he paid no heed to our friendly advice and admonition, on the contrary he showered invectives on our head for having dared to criticise his action since he was a rich man and therefore infallible and his actions were above reproach. Let those who rob the church or lay sacrilegious hands on church property, reflect and ponder over the condign punishment that sooner or later, is meted out to the bandits by the unseen hand of Providence.

The following account of the Armenian colony at Kabul was published in our *History of the Armenians in India,* in

1895, when we did not possess much data about the past history of that isolated community.

"The Armenian traders, who had penetrated as far as Manilla in the Far East, also formed a colony at Kabul situated on the old caravan route to India from Persia and the East. Afghanistan is regarded politically as the "Buffer State" and Kabul, its capital, has always been a commercial centre of considerable importance. At one time it contained a flourishing Armenian colony, consisting of thirty well-to-do families, who as colonists, built themselves a national church. Kabul, not unlike the many Indian cities where the Armenians had settled and erected churches, was included in the extensive diocese of the Armenian Archbishopric of Julfa, the jurisdiction of which extends from the north of Persia to the Far East, including India and the East Indies. The Archdiocese of Julfa, as far back as the thirties, sent priests to Kabul, and the Armenian colonists there, despite their reduced circumstances, managed to maintain the priest sent to them. For some years afterwards they were left without a priest, as the diocesan bishops of Julfa neglected their little fold in far-off-Kabul, where the Armenian colonists had for ages tenaciously preserved their nationalism and the faith of their forefathers isolated as they were in a Muhammadan country. They were therefore obliged to bury their dead without any religious ceremony. Their offspring were left unbaptised until the memorable year 1839, when the Indian Government, under Lord Auckland, the Governor-General sent an expedition to Afghanistan for political reasons, to place the Durrani Shah Shuja upon the throne of Kabul in the place of Dost Mahammad Barakzai, the usurper. The army escorting the exile Shah Shuja from Ludhiana made its way through the Bolan Pass to the Afghan capital, and Shah Shuja, in August 1839, was led triumphantly into the historical *Bala Hissar* at Kabul and enthroned. Dost Mahammad soon after surrendered to the British troops and was sent to Calcutta as a State prisoner. On the entry of the British troops into Kabul, the Armenian residents went in a body to the military chaplain with the forces. At their entreaties he accompanied them to their national church, where divine service had not been held for some years. There they brought forward their unbaptised children, whom he baptised in accordance with the rites of the Anglican Church. The Armenians of Kabul, in their priestless state, stood faithful to their national religion and survived the terrible persecutions of Ameer Shere Ali who tried to convert them to the Mohammedan faith and turn their church into a mosque."

We have seen that with British help, Shah Shuja, who had been driven out of Kabul and was an exile at Ludhiana, was restored to the throne of Afghanistan in 1839, in place of the usurper Dost Mohammad Barakzai. Shah Shuja, as every student of Indian history knows, was an Afghan of the Durrani house, which had ruled in Afghanistan since the days of Ahmad Shah, known as Dur-i-Durran or Durrani.

There is however a coin, struck in his name, with a strange legend* in which he is called an Armenian. How he came to be called an Armenian is a mystery which we have not been able to unravel all these years in spite of queries in the public press. In an able article on Indian Numismatics, which appeared in the *Journal of the Royal Asiatic Society of Bengal*, Vol. LVII, No. 1, of 1888, the late Chas. J. Rodgers, Honorary Numismatist to the Government of India, writing of the couplets on coins after Jehangeer, makes particular mention of the following interesting *baith* (couplet) on the coins of Shah Shuja of Afghanistan, copied from the pages of the Tharikh-i-Sultani, by Sultan Mohammad Khan; the son of Musa Khan Durrani.

The couplet is as follows :—

سکه زد بر سیم وطلا شه شجاع ارمني
نور چشم لارڈ برنس خاک پای کمپني

It can be romanized thus :

Sekkhe zad bar seem o thela, Shah Shuja Armanee,
Noor a cheshm a Lord Burnes, khakh a pha a Khomphanee.

* Inscriptions on coins, shields and medals are called "legends".

And it can be rendered into English thus :—

The Armenian Shah Shuja, the light of the eyes of Lord Burnes,* the dust of the foot of the Company, put his stamp on silver and gold. [Struck coins in silver and gold].

The coin or coins bearing that mysterious legend, which have baffled our investigations all these years, must have been struck at Kabul by the order of Shah Shuja after his restoration in 1839 hence the flattering allusions to Lord (Sir) Burnes and the Company through whose strong support he had regained the throne of his ancestors.

But the late Mr. Rodgers, than whom a greater Numismatist has not lived in India during the second-half of the 19th century, remarks that these coins "could never have been struck by the King's 'permission'."

With due respect to the scholarship of the late Mr. Rodgers and his intimate knowledge of Indian numismatics, we may point out that striking coins in those days was the King's prerogative and no private individuals could have dared issue counterfeit coins in the king's name, for fear of losing their heads, especially in a semi-barbarous country like Afghanistan, where human lives were of no value whatsoever.

There can be but one solution of the knotty problem of Shah Shuja's parentage. His mother may have been an Armenian lady in the same way that the wife of a subsequent Ameer, to wit, Azim Khan, and the mother of Sardar Ishaq Khan of Kabul, was an Armenian, who according to the Report of the Peshawar Mission for 1870-71, was responsible for "the recent disturbances in Cabul" for which she was incarcerated in Fort Ghaznee, as stated on page 208.

Will Indian numismatists, historical students, research scholars and investigators, and their name is legion, solve this problem in the interests of Afghan history and numismatics?

---

* Lord Burnes, mentioned in the interesting Persian couplet, is Sir Alexander Burnes, an accomplished Persian and Hindoosthani scholar, who was treacherously assassinated by the Afghans on the 2nd November 1841 at Kabul where he had been posted as a Political Agent after the restoration of Shah Shuja in 1839.

ARMENIANS AT SURAT

CHAPTER XVII

ARMENIANS AT SURAT.

Historic Surat, the birthplace* of British power in India and the most important emporium in Western India during the 16th, 17th and 18th centuries, prior to the rise of Bombay to eminence as the "Gateway of India," had an important Armenian colony in the 17th and 18th centuries, although there are traces of an Armenian settlement in that city during the 16th century.

In the Armenian cemetery at Surat, adjoining the cemeteries of the early British and Dutch factors, there is the tombstone of an Armenian lady who died there in 1579 A.D. The inscription, which is in ancient Armenian verse, can be translated thus :—

> "In this tomb lies buried the body of the noble lady, who was named Marinas, the wife of the priest Woskan. She was a crown to her husband, according to the proverbs of Solomon. She was taken to the Lord of Life, a soul-afflicting cause of sorrow to her faithful husband, in the year one thousand and twenty eight of our Armenian era, on the fifteenth day of November at the first hour of Friday, at the age of 53.
>
> Ye who see this tomb, pray to the Lord to grant mercy."

The year 1028 of the Armenian era is equivalent to the year 1579 A.D. (For the origin and the computation of the Armenian era, see p. 134).

The interesting epitaph tells us that the death of Marinas was "a soul-afflicting cause of sorrow to her faithful husband,"

---

* It may not be generally known that the first English Factory (commercial house and emporium) was opened in 1612, at Surat, the premier city then in Western India, by the permission of the Mogul Emperor Jehangeer, that devotee at the shrine of Bacchus who had left the reins of the vast Government in the able hands of his famous queen, the remarkable Persian lady, known to fame and history, as Noor Jehan (the light of the world).

Rev. Woskan, who must have been the spiritual head of the Armenians living at Surat during the reign of Akbar, the patron of their race.

And if there was an Armenian priest at Surat in 1579, there must have been a church or a chapel in that city for the worship of God in their own way. According to an Armenian geographer, the old Armenian church at Surat was destroyed by the Mogul governor (but he does not say when) at the instigation of the Turkish merchants who came to Surat, after their pilgrimage to Mecca, for the purpose of buying goods. During the interval between the destruction of the old church and the erection of a new one in 1778, dedicated to the Virgin Mary, the Armenian residents of Surat held divine services in a house set apart for the purpose.

The beautiful church built in 1778 was pulled down a few years by the wardens of the Armenian church of Bombay, as it had fallen into ruins, and the site is now being used as a play ground for school children.

In January 1907, when we paid a visit to the church, it was still standing, although a portion of the roof had fallen, but the altar, the sacristies (vestries) on either side of the altar, the gallery for ladies on the west side of the church, were in a fair state of preservation, as also the priests quarters on the left side of the main gate.

Alas for departed glory and the vicissitudes of Time! for by an irony of Fate, the beautiful church, with historical associations, was, in the absence of devout worshippers, found in the indisputable possession of thousands of owls, bats, crows, cats, rats, snakes and scorpions which howled, screeched and hissed ominously when the present writer, at the risk of his life, entered the sacred edifice where his revered grandfather, Seth Mackertich Agazar Seth, had worshipped during the last quarter of the 18th century.

There is a Mortuary chapel in the Armenian cemetery at Surat which is still standing and it will continue to exist as a valuable landmark of the once-flourishing Armenian colony in that historic city, because it has fortunately come under the control of the Public Works Department as a "Protected

Monument," thanks to the solicitude of the late Lord Curzon for the Preservation of Ancient Monuments in India.

We could find no date, either inside or outside the beautiful chapel, showing the year of its construction, but in all probability it must have been erected during the 17th century, because there is a grave inside that chapel, with a tombstone bearing the date 1695, of which more hereafter.

It was at Surat that the English first came in contact with the Armenians who were the premier merchants in that city during the 17th century, but before proceeding with the interesting history of the British relations with the Armenians in India, it will be necessary to make a digression and review the early connection of the Armenians with India long before the advent of the English or other European traders, adventurers and interlopers into the country.

It may not be generally known that the Armenians—sons of a noble but ill-fated fatherland—whose love of commerce has been proverbial, have, from time immemorial, traded with India, whither they were allured from their distant homes in the snow-clad mountains of Armenia, by the glamour of the lucrative trade in spices, muslins and precious stones which they carried on successfully with Europe long before the advant of any European traders, adventurers and interlopers into the country.

They were the principal foreign traders in India and carried on an extensive trade with Europe through the Persian Gulf, as also through the Gulf of Arabia, and the Portuguese, who were the first Europeans to exploit the trade of the country, tried to strangle by violence, as was their wont, the Armenian trade at the mouth of the two Gulfs but without any success, and what they failed to do by open violence and highhandedness, the cool-headed and the ever diplomatic English achieved by stratagem and non-violence.

The English merchants on their arrival in India in the early part of the 17th century, saw with grave concern that the Armenians—the pioneers of the foreign trade of India— were well established in the country and were carrying on an extensive, important and rather a lucrative export trade with Egypt, the Levant, Turkey and the Mediterranean ports, principally with Venice and Leghorn, through the Persian and the Arabian

16

Gulfs, in Arab sailing vessels, for as is well known, the Arabs were great navigators in those days and their ships known as "buggalows," crossed the vast Indian Ocean and called at Sumatra, Java, the Phillipines and as far as China, and it was through these very Arab ships that the religion of the prophet of Arabia penetrated into Malaya, Sumatra and far-off Java. The goods that were shipped by the Armenians to the Persian Gulf ports were sent from thence overland through Persia and Turkey in Asia and thence to Europe, *via* Trebizond and Alexandretta (otherwise known as Iskanderon) whilst those that were shipped to the Arabian Gulf were likewise exported to Europe through Egypt. In this connection it may be mentioned that the Cape route was not known then, as it came into prominence only when Vasco-de-Gama, the pioneer of European adventurers, found his way to India in 1498, although Columbus had set out with the same objective six years before, but had discovered America instead, so that it can be safely asserted that it was the glamour of India, which in the hoary past had loomed large in the expeditions of a Semiramis and an Alexander, that led to the discovery of the New World which has played such an important part in the politics, civilisation, culture and the material advancement of the old world. And yet by an irony of fate and a perverse destiny, that great and illustrious Spanish navigator, who in his futile attempt to reach the shores of India, had, by a mere chance found an unknown Continent, equally rich, was treated ignominiously by his unappreciative and unpatriotic countrymen steeped in ignorance and bigotry, but then was not the immortal Galileo treated similarly? But I have digressed.

The English as is well known, had come by the Cape route to capture the trade of the country, not by violence however, like their predecessors the Portuguese, but by peaceful penetration, so instead of being hostile and antagonistic towards the Armenian traders who were well established in the country and were at the same time great favourites at the Courts of the Moghul Emperors and their Viceroys, they saw the advisability, nay the absolute necessity of cultivating their friendship. The English merchants knew that by securing the collaboration and the help of the Armenians, they could thereby secure a footing in the country and it was to their advantage therefore to fraternise with them, with an ulterior motive of course, as later events will clearly show. They perceived that the Armenians, by reason of their old connection with the country, and their thorough knowledge of the different vernaculars and of the ways, the manners, the habits and the modes of thinking of the different races that inhabited India, could prove a veritable thorn on their side if they were not respected and treated gently, for only the astute sons of Albion know how to treat, nay handle, an Asiatic and their highly successful administration of this vast and rich country (India) with its millions of diverse races and creeds for the past 200 years is an eloquent proof of their being adept students of human nature.

And in order to avoid competition and rivalry with its concomitant evil effects, it was necessary therefore to gain the Armenians on their side as a valuable asset by peaceful methods of course, and they hit upon the right plan to achieve that end, and needless to add, they succeeded *par excellence*. The practical and the shrewd Britishers saw that the only superiority that they had over the Armenians in India was in their shipping, by reason of their being a purely maritime nation, and in virtue of that indisputable power, they soon set about to promulgate a scheme for alluring the unsuspecting Armenian traders into their net, and to their credit be it said, they succeeded *par excellence* as will be seen shortly.

The importance and the extensiveness of the Armenian trade with Europe was naturally detrimental to their interests, but how could they possibly impede or obstruct the same, as they were not in a position to oust them by violence, for they were only a handful of merchants and had no military power at their back like their predecessors the Portuguese.

And even if they had the requisite military strength to turn all the Armenians out of the country, they would not have attempted to run such a great risk for fear of bringing on their heads the just wrath of the mighty Moguls with whom the Armenians were great favourites, as is well known. In the circumstances they could not afford to jeopardise their position by being hostile and in any way antagonistic towards the Armenians who enjoyed the patronage, the protection and the friendship of the Mogul Emperors and their Viceroys and

Governors all over India from the days of the great Akbar downwards. And where open violence would have failed, and failed ignominiously, displomacy succeeded *par excellence*, thanks to the consummate skill of the few cool-headed but crafty gentlemen who presided over the destinies of the old East India Company, otherwise known as the "Company of the Merchants of London trading to the East Indies" which as every student of Indian History knows, was inaugurated on the 31st day of December 1599, during the reign of that truly great queen, Elizabeth.

CHAPTER XVIII

KHOJAH PHANOOS KALANDAR.

THE LEADING ARMENIAN MERCHANT IN INDIA.

As stated in the foregoing chapter the English hit upon the right plan, for we find the "Company of London Merchants," after mature deliberations, making overt overtures to the Armenian merchants of India in 1688, through their illustrious leader, the famous Khojah Phanoos Kalandar, who happened to be in London at that time with his nephew, the well known Khojah Israel Sarhad, the future merchant-diplomat of India, to enter into an agreement with them to divert their extensive trade with Europe from the old channel into the new one round the Cape, *exclusively* through British shipping.

The bait took and the unsuspecting and ever-confiding Armenians fell into the snare, for *a clevery-worded Treaty was* immediately *drawn up* between Khojah Phanoos Kalandar, representing the Armenian nation, and the Governor and the Company of London Merchants trading to the East Indies, and it was signed, sealed and delivered on the 28th day of June in the year 1688. Needless to add that the specious Treaty, or Charter, as it was called, in which British acumen is vividly shown, proved the *death knell* to the extensive and important Armenian trade in India, as future events clearly showed.

The benefits that would accrue to the Armenian nation under that memorable Treaty, seemed very alluring on *paper* of course, as the Armenians were to participate then and at all times in *all* the advantages that the Company granted to any of their own or other English merchants with respect to trade or otherwise within the Company's Charter. Great privileges were likewise allowed them for carrying their persons and their merchandise to and from Europe in the Company's ships. They were also allowed to reside and trade freely in the Company's towns and garrisons where they could hold *all* civil offices and employments, equally with the English. They were further allowed the free exercise of their own religion and the worship of God in their own way, and as a further inducement, the English stipulated to give the Armenians ground for a church, to be first built at the expense of the Company where-ever forty or more of the Armenian nation became inhabitants of any of the Company's towns or garrisons.

The benevolent and the ever-altruistic English even stipulated that they would not continue in their service any Governor who should in any way disturb or discountenance them (the Armenians) in the full enjoyment of their trade and privileges, which clearly shows that they were mortally afraid to offend them in any way, lest they should lose their esteemed friendship and valued collaboration in the furtherance of their *cause in the country. But later events proved conclusively the* truth of the German Emperor's pithy remark that a treaty was nothing but simply "a scrap of paper."

The specious terms of the Treaty, or better still the Death Warrant of the Armenian trade in India had the desired effect, as they resorted in large numbers from other places in India to the Company's Settlements where they established themselves, built churches, most of which exist to this date, and carried on their usual trade with Europe.

Being the leading merchants in Asia, they contributed considerably to the increase of trade in the respective Settlements where they resided, and thereby added to the population thereto. They were of the greatest service to the Company's Agents and Factors in the disposal of their goods from England, as also in providing them with Indian merchandise for export to England. This is clearly seen in a communication from the Court of Directors to their Governor in India, under date the 13th September 1695 in which it is distinctly stated that "Multan and Scindy are brave provinces for many sorts of extraordinary good and cheap commodities ; but whenever the Company shall be induced to settle Factories in those provinces, or any other way think to arrive at trade with them, otherwise than by *Armenians*, they would infallibly come off with great loss."

And with the gradual growth and expansion of the English trade in the country, it was deemed absolutely necessary to obtain further privileges from the Delhi Court, but how was that to be secured? Thanks to British acumen and resourcefulness, the valuable, nay indispensible, services of an Armenian were requisitioned and through him the historical and all-important "Grand Farman" which proved to be the "Magna Charta" of the English in India, was obtained from the Mogul Emperor Farrukh Siyar in 1717, of which more hereafter.

But before proceeding any further with the history of the cordial relations of the Armenians in India with their *confreres* the English, it will be necessary to publish the full texts of the Treaties, Agreements, Charters or better still, the Death Warrants, concluded by the astute Britishers with their formidable rivals, the Armenians, so that the unbiased readers may be able to form their own opinion and draw their own inferences and conclusions therefrom, since these so-called Treaties have never received the publicity they deserved, and at one time their very *existence* was denied and they were produced with much reluctance, in1772, when an honourable member of the House of Commons insisted on their immediate production. In this connection it may not be out of place to mention that a clever legal luminary, *Thomas Nuthall*, who happened to be the Solicitor to the Company, tried to prove by force of untenable arguments that the Treaties were null and void, inasmuch as they had been concluded by the *old* Company, although the *old Company had legally and by an Act of Parliament surren*dered all its rights, title, interests, assets and liabilities in India to the *new* Company formed in the reign of Queen Anne of England.

The following is a copy of the famous Treaty, the original of which can still be seen in the archives of the India House in London.

Copy of an Agreement made between the Governor and Company of Merchants of London trading to the East Indies, and the Armenian Nation, dated 22nd June* 1688.

"The Governor and Company of Merchants of London trading to the East Indies, to all to whom these presents shall come, send greeting.

---

* See Reports of the House of Commons, 1772 and 1773, vol. 3rd, page 283.

"Whereas representation hath been made to us by Sir Josiah Child, Baronet, our Deputy-Governor, that, upon long conferences by him had with Cogee Phanoos Calendar, an Armenian merchant of eminency, and an inhabitant of Isphahan in Persia, as also with Sir John Chardin of London. Knight, they had, on behalf of the Armenian nation proposed to him several particulars for carrying on a great part of the Armenian trade to India and Persia, and from thence to Europe, by way of England, which will redound greatly to his Majesty's advantage in his customs and to the increase of the English navigation, if the Armenian nation might obtain such license from this Company as will give them encouragement to alter and invert the ancient course of their trade to and from Europe. And we being always willing to increase and encourage the public trade and navigation of this kingdom, after a serious debate of all the propositions relating to this affair, have thought fit to agree and resolve as follows, *viz.* :

First.—That the Armenian nation shall now, and at all times hereafter, have equal share and benefit of all indulgences this Company have or shall at any time hereafter grant to any of their own Adventurers or other English merchants whatsoever.

Secondly.—That they shall have free liberty at all times hereafter to pass and repass to and from India in any of the Company's ships on as advantageous terms as any free man whatsoever.

Thirdly.—"That they shall have liberty to live in any of the Company's cities, garrisons, or towns in India, and to buy, sell, and purchase land and houses, and be capable of all civil offices and preferments in the same manner as they were Englishmen born, and shall always have the free and undisturbed liberty of the exercise of their own religion. And we hereby declare that we will not continue any Governor in our service that shall in any kind disturb or discountenance them in the full enjoyment of all the privileges hereby granted to them, neither shall they pay any other or greater duty in India than the Company's factors, or any other Englishman born, do, or ought to do."

Fourthly.—That they may voyage from any of the Company's garrisons to any ports or places in India, the South

Seas, China or the Manillas, in any of the Company's ships, or any permissive free ships allowed by the Company, and may have liberty to trade to China, the Manillas or any other ports or places within the limits of the Company's Charter upon equal terms, duties and freights with any free Englishman whatsoever.

But whereas all persons in England do pay for bullion outwards two per cent. for freight and permission, and three per cent. homewards for diamonds and other precious stones, it is hereby declared and agreed, that the *Armenians* shall pay three per cent. outwards for bullion and two per cent. homewards for diamonds; for coral and amber-beads they shall pay six per cent. for freight and permission and for coral, amber, raw-cohineal, quick silver, sword blades, fire arms of all sorts, haberdashery wares, iron of all sorts wrought or unwrought, paper, all sorts of stationery wares, English looking or drinking glasses and for all sorts of Norimbergh wares and merchandises, ten per cent. for permission and six pounds per ton freight.

That all sorts of leather and Venitian wares and merchandises may be shipped out permission free, paying only six pounds per ton freight. For all cloth or woollen manufactures of what kind or sort soever, they pay twelve and one half per cent. in lieu of all charges whatsoever, excepting in the freight and the Company's customs in India. For lead ten per cent. permission and three pound per ton freight. For provisions of all sorts for eating and drinking, six pounds per ton freight, but no permision. And for all sorts of goods homeward bound they shall pay in manner and form following, *viz.*, for diamonds, pearls, rubies, all sorts of precious stones, and ambergris, two per cent. for freight and permission as aforesaid. For musk of any kind six per cent. for freight and permission besides freight. For all raw silk of Persia, twenty-one pounds per ton freight, but no permission, custom or any other charges whatsoever, excepting only two and one-half per cent, towards demorage of our ships. For all goods whatsoever of the growth and manufacture of Persia (red Carmenia wool excepted, which is hereby totally prohibited) ten per cent. permission and the same freights as the Company themselves pay, without any other charges whatsoever. For all sorts of China and Bengal goods, during the Company's indulgence for those kinds of goods, and no longer, in what place soever laden, thirteen per cent. for permission and all other charges, whatsoever, over and above the same freight as the Company pay, and the customs hereafter mentioned, *viz.* All goods outward and homeward bound are to pay the Company in East India five per cent. custom on the first cost as per invoices of the said goods, whether they be laden from or delivered into any of the Company's ports or places, or into any other ports or places whatsoever, excepting only from this article all bullion, diamonds, and other precious stones, ambergris, musk and raw Persian silk. And it is agreed, that the permission money and freight for all goods outward bound to be paid in India as aforesaid shall be accounted for at eight and one-half rupees per pound sterling, upon hypothecation of the goods to the Company in London. And we do declare that for ease of accounts, the custom due to the Company in East India is to be included together with the other charges, *viz.* Freight and permission according to the premises and all inserted in one sum upon the respective bills of loading which sum is always to be paid before the delivery of the goods to the persons mentioned in the said bills of loading which is the true intent of the hypothecation before expressed. That all goods which have once paid custom are not to pay any again, either upon importation or exportation of the same goods to the place where they first pay it, or to any other port or place belonging to us in the East Indies. That every person that shall take passages on any of the Company's ships shall pay in East India twelve pounds sterling for his permission outwards, at the rate of eight rupees and one-half per pound sterling; and the like sum to be paid here for every person that shall take passage homewards, besides eight pounds per head for sea provisions, which it hereby agreed shall always be paid in London. And for such persons who shall board at the Captain's table, they shall pay ten guineas to the Captain for the same. But the servants shall be messed apart by themselves, and always have the same allowance of ship-provisions as the officers and the seamen of the ship have or ought to have. And it is also granted to the said Armenians that the passengers shall be allowed, both out and home, to carry with them their wearing clothes, furniture and provisions, not exceeding one quarter of a ton for each man, freight free. And whereas the said Armenians have used to drive a great trade from India to Turkey overland, by way of Persia and Arabia, and are now desirous to drive that whole trade by the way of England, it is hereby declared and agreed. That the said Armenians have liberty to send upon any of the Company's ship for England, any sorts of goods of East India consigning to the Company by true invoices and bills of loading, and not otherwise, paying ten per cent. permission on the value of the said goods in London, besides the same freight as we ourserves pay. And it is hereby declared that the Company have liberty to detain and keep in their possession all such goods as shall be consigned unto them as aforesaid, until they have shipped them off upon English shipping, bound to Turkey, Venice or Leghorn and taken security that they shall not be landed in any other ports or places of Europe except the place to which they shall be directed by the said Armenian proprietors or their agents. And, lastly, it is declared and agreed, that notwithstanding anything aforesaid it shall and may be lawful for the said Company to reserve and keep for their own use any of the said goods so intended for Turkey, as aforesaid, paying the proprietors one third part clear profit on the first cost as aforesaid; all freight, charges, and disbursements whatsoever being first deducted and foreprized, *eight rupees in India being in this case to be accounted for one pound sterling*. In witness whereof, the Governor, Deputy-Governor and three of the Committee of the said Company have hereunto set their hands and caused the larger Seal of the said Company to be affixed, this two-and-twentieth day of June, Anno Domini 1688, and in the fourth year of the reign of our Sovereign Lord James the Second by the Grace of God, King of England, Scotland, France and Ireland, Defender of the Faith etc."

BENJAMIN BATHURST,
Governor.

JOSIAH CHILD,
Deputy Governor.

WORCESTER.
JOHN MOORE.
GEORGE BOUN.

Simultaneously with the above, another Treaty, equally alluring, was concluded with the Armenians by the English, of which the following is a true copy :—

"The Governor and Company of Merchants of London trading to the East Indies to all to whom it may concern, send greeting. Whereas it had been represented to us, that the Armenian nation have a desire to carry on a trade and commerce with our people in the East Indies, we do for the better encouragement of that nation to settle and cohabit in the several garrisons, cities and towns in the East Indies under our jurisdiction, by these presents declare, grant and agree, that whenever forty or more of the Armenian nation shall become inhabitants in any of the garrisons, cities, or towns belonging to the Company in the East Indies, the said Armenians shall not only have and enjoy the free use and exercise of their religion but there shall also be allowed to them a parcel of ground to erect a church thereon for the worship and service of God in their own way. And that we will also at our own charge, cause a convenient church to be built of timber, which afterwards the said Armenians may alter and build with stone and other solid material to their own good liking. And the said Governor and Company will also allow fifty pounds per annum, during the space of seven years, for the maintenance of such priest or minister as they shall choose to officiate therein.

Given under the Company's larger Seal, as also under the hands of the Governor, Deputy-Governor, and three of the Committee of the said Company this two-and-twentieth day of June, Anno Domini 1688, and in the fourth year of the reign of our Sovereign Lord James the Second, by the Grace of God, King of England, Scotland, France and Ireland. Defender of the Faith etc."

BENJAMIN BATHURST,
Governor.

JOSIAH CHILD,
Deputy Governor.

WORCESTER.
JOHN MOORE.
GEORGE BOUN.

And in order to please the illustrious representative of the Armenian nation, through whose great influence and strenuous efforts the important negotiations had been so successfully concluded, the magnanimous English, in a fit of unexampled generosity, granted the sole Monopoly of the Garnet trade in India to Khojah Phanoos Kalandar and to his descendants after him, as set forth in the following Treaty, in which they naively say that it was granted in compliance with his "request." Here is the Treaty :—

"The Governor and Company of Merchants of London trading to the East Indies, to all to whom it may concern send greeting. Whereas Cogee Phanoos Calendar, an Armenian merchant of eminency, and an inhabitant of Isphahan, in Persia, hath taken great pains in making an agreement with the said Company for a great trade to be carried on in English shipping by himself and others of the Armenian nation; the said Governor and Company in consideration thereof do, by these presents (at the request of the said Cogee Phanoos Calendar) freely grant unto him and his family the sole trade of Garnet, he paying ten per cent. custom for the same, and the usual freight paid by the Company. And the said Company do hereby declare that they will neither trade in the said commodity themselves, nor suffer any other persons, English or stranger, for the future to trade or traffick in that commodity.

Given under the Company's larger Seal, as also under the hands of the Governor, Deputy-Governor, and three of the Committee of the said Company, this two-and-twentieth day of June, Anno Domini 1688, and in the fourth year of the reign of our Sovereign Lord James the Second, by the Grace of God, King of England, Scotland, France and Ireland. Defender of the Faith etc."

BENJAMIN BATHURST,
Governor.

JOSIAH CHILD,
Deputy Governor.

WORCESTER.
JOHN MOORE.
GEORGE BOUN.

Here again British suavity asserts itself in a most pronounced manner, for although they admit, and admit they must, that they were granting him the monopoly of the Garnet trade in India in consideration of the "great pains" he had taken "in making an agreement with the said Company for a great trade to be carried in English shipping by himself and others of the Armenian nation" yet at the same time and without any fear of contradicting themselves, they do not hesitate or blush to place him under an obligation to the Company by granting his request in a most magnanimous manner. Pray tell us gentle reader in what part of the civilized world can remuneration for valuable services rendered be at any time considered or construed as a favour or an act of grace, if not charity? Is not the labourer worthy of his hire, then why confound wages justly earned with charity? When you pay a labourer his wages, do you for a moment think that you have given him charity or done him a great favour? But then the *honourable* gentlemen who were signatories to the Treaty concluded with the noble and illustrious Armenian, say, without the least compunction, that it was "at the request of the said Cogee Phanoos Calendar" that the monopoly was granted as if he were an ordinary concession-hunter or a mercenary, simply striving for self-aggrandizement at his nations' expense, when as they admit, he was "a merchant of eminency and the head of the Armenians in India."

We are however inclined to think that instead of Khojah Phanoos Kalandar asking the English for any favour which would have been *infra dig.* for the proud and the magnanimous Armenian, the English Company, with a view to ingratiate themselves with the great Armenian, must have specially asked him to do them the honour of accepting a small present in the shape of an insignificant monopoly as a memento of the auspicious friendship just begun, if not for the valuable services rendered by that illustrious Armenian to the British cause in India. That the English greatly appreciated and valued the friendship of that remarkable Armenian magnate is evident from the fact that when they were sadly in need of soldiers for the protection of their several important factories in India, principally at Surat, they approached Khojah Phanoos Kalandar again for help and collaboration, as the following communication from the Court of Directors in London to their "Deputy and Council of Bombay" under date the 26th January 1692, will clearly show :—

"Stores of all kinds wee have sent you by this ship, the *Modona,* and what souldiers wee could procure. But it is very difficult to get any at this time while the King (William III) has occasion for such vast numbers of men in Flanders. Among those wee send great mortality has happened, as well in their passage out as after their arrival, which has put us on discourse with the Armenian Christians here, to see if by their means wee could procure some private souldiers of their nation from Ispahan, which wee should esteem, if wee could get them as good as English. Not that they have altogether the same courage which Englishmen have, but because by their conduct they are now so united to the English nation, and particularly to this Company, that in effect wee and they have but the common interest. They are very near to our national and reformed religion, as sober temperate men, and know how to live in health in a hot climate. Coja Phanoos Calandar tells us it will be difficult to get any considerable number of them to be souldiers : they are universally addicted to trade, but some few, he thinks, may be picked up at Surat and he will write to his friends at Julpa [Julfa] to see if they can persuade any from thence to come to you to make an experiment of their entertainment, and of their liking or dislike of the service."

The same communication, in which the original spelling has been carefully preserved, goes on to say :—"If you can procure any Armenian Christians to be souldiers, wee doe allow you to give them the same pay as our English souldiers and forty shillings gratuity and the charge of their passage from Gombroon [Bandar Abbas] to Bombay, wee would not have above fifty or sixty in our pay at one time, and if you had the like number of Madagassar slaves to teach the exercise of arms and to do some inferior duty under our English souldiers, being listed upon an English Captaine kept in a Company by themselves under the Dutch manner, and allowing them a competent proportion of rice, a red capp and red coat and some other trifles to please them, not having above fifty or sixty at a time, and they never to have a custody of their own armes, wee hope such a contrivance might be a good Auxiliary aid to our own garrison, especially when English souldiers are scarce and wee need some balance of power. For take it as an infallible constant rule, that the more castes the more safety and the less danger of mutiny. Wee know their is a necessity for increasing our English souldiers and wee will doe it as soone and as much as wee possibly can. In the meantime, Armenian Christians if you could have them *are the very best men to be trusted* and next to them Madagascar Coffrees." From this it will be seen that the Armenians, and Khojah Phanoos Kalandar in particular, were held in high esteem by the Court of Directors for their strong attachment to the Company and their unswerving loyalty to the British cause in India.

The Hon'ble East India Company was readily anxious to cultivate the friendship of the Armenian merchants, who, being acquainted with all parts of the country and having a thorough knowledge of the vernacular, were of great help to them in pushing on the Company's trade in the interior. This fact is illustrated by an extract from a communication to the Indian Governor from the Court of Directors, London, dated 13th September, 1695:

"Multan and Scindy [Scind] are brave provinces for many sorts of extraordinary good and chief commodities; but whenever the company shall be induced to settle factories in those provinces, or any other way think to arrive at trade with them, otherwise than by Armenians, they would infallibly come off with great loss."

As fellow-traders, the Armenians rendered yeoman services to the company, whose early records and proceedings teem with favourable references to them.

Khojah Phanoos Kalandar, the "Armenian merchant of eminency," as the English call him, was a native of Julfa (Ispahan) but had settled down at Surat, where his only son's grave, in the Mortuary chapel at the Armenian cemetery, can be seen to this day, bearing an inscription in classical Armenian, of which the following is a translation :—

"This is the tomb of Kalandar, the son of Phanoos Kalandar of Julfa, who departed this life on Saturday, the 6th day of March, 1695."

It may be mentioned that this is the only grave inside the chapel which shows the high esteem in which the deceased was held by the Armenian community of Surat, for only great men—national benefactors and philanthropists—are buried *inside* Armenian churches and chapels.

Despite ceaseless investigations, we have not yet been able to find either the time or the place of Khojah Phanoos Kalandar's death, for he is not buried at Surat. He may perhaps have died in London where he had gone in 1688 with his nephew—the future diplomat Khojah Israel Sarhad—or he may, most probably, have returned to Julfa, his birth place, and slept there with his forefathers.

His only son, Kalandar, who died at Surat in 1695, could not have left any male issue for we could find no other graves of Kalandars either in the Surat Armenian cemetery or in the dilapidated church in the city. There are in the old Armenian cemetery at Agra, the graves of two Kalandars (Qalandars) one of whom named Hovanjan of the Kalandar family, died in 1659, and the other, named Soolthanoom, also of the Kalandar family, was laid to rest in that historic cemetery in the year 1673, (See pp. 124-125. Nos. 32 and 44). In all probability these two Kalandars were either the brothers or the nephews of Khoja Phanoos Kalandar* of Surat fame. There are some Kalandars buried in the Armenian churchyard at Madras. Although there are no lineal descendants of Khojah Phanoos Kalandar in the male line, still there are, in the present day, several prominent and well-known Armenians in India and elsewhere who can claim descent from him, through his

---

* In the *Court Minutes* of the East India Company in London, for the 27th January, 1664, we find that "Jacob Callender [Kalandar] and Avietick, two Armenians, are given leave to take their passage to Surat, paying for it themselves, in one of the next ships and to carry two casks of refuse of amber, if no examination it is found to be the same as is now shown".

And on the 24th February 1664, we find the following entry in the *Court Minutes* :—

> "Callender [Kalandar] an Armenian, to pay 151. [£15] for his passage in the *London* to Surat, and [£251] for freight and permission for two vats of amber."

This Jacob Callender, [Kalandar] must have been a relation, if not a brother, of Khojah Phanoos Kalandar.

daughter, who had married Khojah Minas of the noble family of Khojah Emniaz of Julfa. Their only daughter, Hripsimah, married Satoor Tharkhan of the well-known Shookhoorean family of Surat. Satoor Tharkhan had come over from Surat to Calcutta, where he died in 1761, aged 36 years, and his grave can be seen in the Armenian churchyard of Nazareth to this day, with an inscription in ancient Armenian. His widow, Hripsimah, after marrying a second time, died in 1770, and was buried next to her husband in the Calcutta Armenian churchyard. Her second husband, Moses, who by the way was a relation of hers, survived her by three years and died in 1773, evidently of a broken heart, and was buried next to his wife in the same churchyard, so that by a strange coincidence, Hripsmah, the grand daughter of the illustrious Khojah Phanoos Kalandar, lies buried between her two devoted husbands, which should be a great consolation to her soul in the next world.

Satoor Tharkhan's daughter Begoom, by his wife Hripsimah, born in 1755, married the famous Agah Catchick Arrakiel of Calcutta in 1771.

CHAPTER XIX.

KHOJAH KIRAKOSE.

AN AGENT OF THE SHAH OF PERSIA.

In the *Court Minutes* of the Company in London, for 29th November 1667, we find the following entry :—

"Signor Kogeo [Khojah] Keriakos, a subject of the King of Persia (as it appears by his testimonial letters) acknowledges through an interpreter the favour shown to him about three years ago when he was permitted to lade some goods in the Company's ships bound for India and returns the thanks of the said King, and having some looking-glass, fifty pieces of cloth bought in Holland, and other things for the King of Persia's use, desires permission to lade these in some of the Company's vessels bound for Surat, with a parcel of amber bought for his own account ; he is told that the Court is ready to show favour to any one so recommended, but there is difficulty in acceding to his request, for no cloth, much less foreign cloth, is allowed to be laden in the Company's Ships, but he shall be offered any other accommodation, and, if he will send in a list of the goods he wishes transported to India, he shall know the Company's decision next Wednesday."

In the *Court Minutes* for the 4th December 1667, there is the following entry :—

"Signor Kogea [Khojah] Keriakos presents particulars of the goods he wishes to send to Surat, and permission is given him to lade them in the ships now bound for the Indias, *viz.* Venice wares and glass, looking-glass, English cloth, amber, one chest of guns, one of swords, one or musical instruments, one of several rarities, and one of gilded leather ; permission is also given for his brother, Signor Avedike [Avietic] with his three servants and three mastiffs to take their passage in the said ships upon such terms as shall be agreed".

In a long letter from the Directors of the Company in London to their President and Council at Surat, dated the 27th March 1668, which reached Surat by the ship *Constantinople Merchant* in the beginning of September of that year, we find the following reference to Khojah Kirakose who was deputed to London by Shah Sulaiman of Persia to purchase certain goods for him. He must have been an eminent merchant to have been entrusted with such an important mission.

"Here hath byn one Cojah Karickoes, with a letter of recommendation from the King of Persia to us, the French, and Dutch Company to assist him, as a person imployed by him with a stock to buy some goods and procure some rarities for him, and hath been very sollicitous with us for permission to carry out [blank] clothes of severall collours that hee bought in Holland, as hee saith for the King of Persiaes owne court ; which wee were very unwilling to graunt, doubting it was but a feigned thing or a writing that might bee easily there procured. Yet, least it should bee reall, and that by our refuseall wee should discontent the said King, and this person seeming to bee very desirous and promising to use his utmost endeavours to begett a good understanding betweene the King of Persia and us, either in the setling of an equall proportion for our halfe customes or an agreement for the selling thereof to the said King, we have condiscended for the shipping of the said cloth and his brothers passage on the ship *Constantinople Merchant*, provided that hee consignes the goods to you, that so you may see them unladen at Surratt and from thence reshipt for Persia, without making sale of any part of them at Surratt or parts thereabouts . . . . . which causeth us againe to put you in mind of setling our said customes as wee have before desired, or selling them to the King of Persia for the best rate you can ; in order to which, instruct Mr. Thomas Rolt, whome wee have entertained Chiefe for that implyment, and such others as you shall imploy in this affaire that they make use of the endeavours of this Cojah Karickoes for the begetting of a good agreement. This person himselfe is intended overland; but by his brother, and a writing from him which wee herewith send you, those which you imploy will be directed how and where to meete with him in Persia . . . . You speake concerning the ascerting of our right in Persia, that it may be best done before the Portugalls grow too powerful there. Wee thinck there is more cause of feare of interruption from others then from them. However, wee cannot give any sudaine [sudden] order therein, having only this yeare provided ships for out and home, and have given you directions to endeavour the composing and setling of that affaire without force, which wee earnestly desire may be done; which if you cannot effect, then advise us fully how you thinck wee may proceed by way of force, that wee may governe our selves accordingly."

In the *Court Book*, vol. XXVI, page 170, for the 2nd of January 1668, we find the following :—

"Certain Committees having discoursed with Signor Keriacos and found him very willing to improve his interest with the King of Persia to serve the Company in the settlement of their customs there, which he engages to do effectively, he is given permission to send in the Surat shipping fifty whole cloths, on condition that they are consigned to Sir George Oxinden and sent direct to Persia."

In the *Court Book*, vol. XXVI, page 240 for the 3rd April 1668, we find the following :—

"Sir Samuel Barnardiston reports that the goods of Signor Keriacos have been valued at 4300l. [£4300] the freight and permission amounting to 236l. [£236] which latter he will undertake to pay on notice of their shipment; order is hereupon given for the Commanders and master of the *Constantinople Merchant* and *Rebecca* to be instructed to sign bills of lading for such of these goods as they shall take on board, and Sir Samuel is requested to give in the report in writing."

And on page 251 of the *Court Book* for the 8th April 1668 it is recorded that "An Armenian priest, and a boy belonging to Signor Keriacos, to be allowed, on paying, to take passage in the Company's shipping to Surat and the Signor to be permitted to lade his goods in any of the Company's vessels."

In the *Court Book*, vol. XXVI, page 273 for the 26th June 1668 it is recorded that :

> "Signor Avedick Keriakos [a brother of Khojah Kirakose] is given permission to ship ten chests of glass (which he had leave to transport last year) in this next shipping and be allowed to send three servants, on paying freight and passage money."

In the *Court Book*, vol. XXVI, page 380, for the 27th January, 1669, we find the following entry :—

> "Signor Keriakos is given leave, in accordance with an order of June 26 last, to ship the remainder of his ten chests of glass, and three of his servants, on board the *Sampson* for Surat, freight and permission to be arranged by the Committee for Private Trades."

On page 398 of the same *Court Book* for the 24th February 1669, it is recorded that "Signor Keriakos to pay 75l. [£75] for the freight of ten chests of glasses and the passage of three of his servants in the *Sampson* for Surat."

And in 1676, we find the Surat Council writing to their Governor at Bombay to render every help to Khojah Kirakose and other Armenian merchants, as follows :—

> "These are at the entreaty of Khojah Karakuz and other Armenians concerned in the ship *S. Francisco* that is lately put into Bombay. As they have been very importunate with us to write in their affair, we do desire you to countenance and assist them, as merchants, with boats and other necessaries as also with convenient warehouses to protect them from the rains."

CHAPTER XX.

AGAH OWENJOHN JACOB GERAKH

AN EMINENT AND A PIOUS MERCHANT.

The decadence of the Armenians at Surat, after a long period of great prosperity, commenced when hostilities broke out between the English and the French in India. The war between these two rival powers in the Carnatic, (Madras Presidency) which broke out in 1783, gave the death-blow to their commercial pursuits in India, and at Surat in particular.* This fact will be seen clearly from the following translation, extracted from an original letter in Armenian written from Surat, under date the 28th April 1783, by one Agah Owenjohn Jacob, of the Gerakheantz family, to the Armenian Archbishop of Julfa :—

"We are having troublous times nowadays, as the English are engaged in war with the French and Hyder Ali, and at present they are fighting the Dutch, so that there is war on land and at sea. Our [Armenian] merchants lost two lakhs of rupees over a ship from China that was captured at sea, and lately the Maharattas captured a ship bound for Surat from Bengal, whereby we lost two and a half lakhs of rupees."

The same letter, after giving a minute account of a severe storm that had raged at Surat in the previous month, goes on to say :

"A ship bound for Busrah was lost at sea, in which our [Armenian] merchants lost goods worth one and a half

---

* We have in our possession a list, in the Armenian language, which comprises the names of 33 Armenian merchants who flourished at Surat during the short space of 20 years, *i.e.*, from 1780-1800, when the following individuals were eminent merchants :—Agah Owenjohn Jacob of the Gerakheantz family of Julfa, Agah Mackertich Melikhnazean, Agah Gaspar Johannes, Agah Marooth and Agah George Ter Arratoon.

lakhs. From Bombay the Armenians had sent us a consignment of forty-two bales of silk, but the ship was wrecked and the cargo lost. All these misfortunes befell us within the space of forty days: we are at a loss what to do. The entire loss sustained by our merchants at Surat alone amounts to more than six lakhs, of which the major portion belonged to me. God's will be done."

Writing on 18th February 1784, or about nine months after the previous letter, he wrote to the following effect, of which this is a translation:

"We are gradually declining and getting poorer, and dangers and calamities are on the increase daily. Many sustained heavy losses and became bankrupt owing to the severe storm that raged in March last, in which I alone lost Rs. 56,000. At present the Java ships are being either captured or wrecked at sea, whereby our merchants have already lost two lakhs of rupees, of which Rs. 13,000 belonged to me."

In another letter to the Armenian Archbishop Jacob of Julfa, dated the 28th March 1788, the Nestor of the Surat Armenians, who was piety personified, complains of the jealousy of his compatriots as follows:—

"We are our own ill-wishers, how is it possible that, with such hearts, we may receive good from God. As our numbers are decreasing, we are increasing the evils". He then pathetically refers to the evils—the ungodliness of some of the wealthy Armenians intoxicated by success, of which he gives full particulars but advisedly we refrain from mentioning them lest we offend the religious susceptibilities of our Armenian readers, because "by nature the Armenians are deeply religious, as their whole literature and history show", according to the eloquent testimony of an American Missionary, the Rev. Frederick Davis Greene, M.A. for several years a resident in Armenia.

We have in our possession an autograph letter, written from Surat by one Johanness Seth (connected with our family), dated 28th February, 1797, to our great-grand-father, Mackertich Agazar Seth at Julfa, Ispahan, of which the following extract is a translation:—

"You ask me earnestly with regard to our brother Seth's voyage, the details of which he has not written to you, but which are, however, as follows :—

Agah Marooth, my principal, had purchased a ship and named it *Arshak*, in which he loaded goods to the extent of Rs. 1,50,000 for export. He appointed Mr. Seth as super-cargo and gave him Rs. 8,000 as his share in the concern. He also gave him goods worth Rs. 20,000 for sale at Malacca,* and others had given goods for Rs. 15,000. Mr. Seth himself had invested *his all* in goods and loaded in the same ship of which he was the super-cargo. He started with others in the *Arshak* and safely reached Madras, and sailing from thence arrived in safety at Penang. There they sold a considerable portion of their goods, and after making

---

* Malacca was captured by the Portuguese, under Albuquerqe, in 1509, when Portugal was a great maritime power and had command over the eastern seas. It fell afterwards into the hands of their rivals, the Dutch, in 1642. They, in their turn, were expelled by the English in 1759, who retain Malacca to the present day. It was a town of considerable importance both from a political and commercial point of view, owing to its favourable situation. Commerce, that had given significance to the place, had allured thither Armenian merchants from India and elsewhere. There they formed a settlement and built for themselves a national church. Traces of their sojourn are to be seen to this day in the shape of tombstones inscribed in Armenian. The following is a translation of one of these rare and interesting inscriptions, of which we have a copy in our possession :—

"Hail thou that readst the tablet of my tomb ! wherein I now do sleep;
Give me the news, the freedom of my countrymen, for them I did much weep;
If there arose amongst them one good guardian to govern and to keep,
Vainly I expected in the world to see a good shepherd come to look after the scattered sheep;
I Jacob, the grandson of Shameer, an Armenian of a respectable family whose name I keep,
Was born in a foreign place in Persia, in New Julfa, where my parents now for ever sleep;
Fortune brought me to this distant *Malacca,* which my remains in bondage doth keep.
Separated from the world on the 7th July in the year of Lord 1774 at the age of 29.
And my mortal remains were deposited in this spot, in the ground which I had purchased."

further purchases embarked for Malacca. While at sea and within a short distance of Malacca they were attacked by three French frigates, who opened fire and captured them. After plundering them of all they possessed, the French put them ashore at Penang, from whence they returned to Surat deprived of all they possessed. This disastrous event was a source of great financial loss first to Agah Marooth, secondly to me, and last, though not least, to our poor brother, Mr. Seth, who thereby *lost all that he possessed,* and for which he had toiled for so many years. Under the circumstances, his loss is keenly felt by us. All these, our present misfortunes, are mainly due to the wars that are being waged between the English and the French and other European nations, for which we, as well as merchants of other nationalities, have suffered heavily during these few years. I may add that, in the present year alone, the merchants in the Fort here have lost fifteen lakhs of rupees. It is the same all over India. There is no more life in us. May God have mercy on our merchants, whose affairs are by no means in a healthy condition !"

The unfortunate Mr. Seth, referred to in the interesting letter from Surat, was the grandfather of the writer of these lines. He was the only son of Mackertich Agazar Seth, for many years the Mayor (Khalanthar) of Julfa, who died in 1822, aged 90 years, and was buried, as a mark of great respect, in the hallowed enclosure, (covered and railed) called "tapan", in the church of the blessed Virgin Mary, where Khojah Avietick, the son of Khojah Babakh, the founder of the church, had been laid to rest in 1649.

Seth, the victim of the French freebooters, had been a successful merchant at Surat for twenty years (1778-1798) but as we have seen, he lost his entire fortune at sea, off Malacca, in 1796.

At the earnest request of his aged father, he returned to Julfa where he married Nanajan, one of the daughters of the illustrious Jacob Malcom, in 1799. He died at Bushire in 1821 and was buried in the Armenian churchyard of that place where his grave can be seen to this day. He left four daughters, (one of whom named Thangkhatoon, married the immortal Armenian poet, Mesrovb David Thaliadian), and three sons. The youngest son, named Jacob, who died in December 1899, aged 80 years, was the writers' revered father. He is buried in the Armenian churchyard of Calcutta. Peace to his soul, rest to his ashes.

It appears that during the days of Agah Owenjohn Gerakh, there was a large Armenian community at Surat, because in one of his letters, he informs the Archbishop Jacob at Julfa that of the fourteen priests sent out by him in 1788 for the different Armenian churches in India, four were retained at Surat, for the spiritual ministrations of the community in that city. It is quite evident that there must have been at least 300 to 400 persons at Surat to need the services of four priests at a time. Agah Owenjohn Jacob, extracts from whose letters to the Armenian Archbishops Mackertich and Jacob of Julfa are given above, was one of the leading Armenian merchants of Surat during the second-half of the 18th century. He was both pious and patriotic, burning with a praiseworthy zeal for the moral and the intellectual uplift of his countrymen in the homeland. He gave, in 1790, the princely donation of Rs. 25,000 to a Rev. Stephen who had been deputed by the Armenian Archbishop Joseph Arghootheantz of Russia to collect donations from the Armenians in India in aid of the national institutions at New Nakhijevan, a city which had been recently founded in Russia by the said Archbishop who it may be noted was a great friend and a favoured protege of the Empress Catherine II of Russia. In addition to the above donation of Rs. 25,000 the patriotic Agah Owenjohn founded and endowed two schools in that new city, one in the name of St. Gregory the Illuminator and the other in the name of the blessed Virgin Mary. He also founded a printing press at New Nakhijevan for the publication of books in the Armenian language. From the colophons (hishatakaran) which are given at the end of the several useful books issued from that press, we find that the benefactor was the son of Khalanthar (Mayor) Jacob and his wife Mareban, the grandson of Agah Gherakh and his wife Thagoohi, and the husband of Goolistan. He had no male issue, but had young daughters, according to the colophons, whose names, strange to say, are not mentioned in the colophons. In 1790, he sent a remittance of Rs. 3,125 to the wardens of the Armenian church of Calcutta to be kept in trust for the benefit of St. Catherine's Nunnery at Julfa, the annual income only to be remitted to the nuns in that convent. And it was in this convent, founded in 1623, that the *first* school for Armenian girls was opened in 1858, through the munificence of the late Manook Hordanan (Jordan), an eminent Armenian merchant of Batavia (Java), and named "St. Catherine's national school for girls".

Agah Owenjohn Jacob Gerakh, that highly pious Armenian, had, in his lifetime, sent some valuable sacred vestments for the use of the church of the blessed Virgin Mary at Julfa, situated in the large parish, known as the "Great Maidan", where he had been baptised in 1718, and where his revered ancestors had worshipped.

These, together with some other rare and antique sacred vestments were sold by public auction some sixteen years ago at Julfa by the order of the late Archbishop Sahak Ayvadian, and they were purchased by a certain Armenian resident of Julfa for 1715 Persian thoomans and were brought out to Calcutta for disposal. Some eight rare prices, consisting of chasubles (shoorjar), helmets (sagavart) and amices (vakaz) were purchased jointly by Mr. J. C. Galstam, O.B.E. and the late Mr. A. Stephen, for Rs. 1,500, and were presented by them to the Armenian church of Nazareth, Calcutta, where they are carefully preserved among the valuable sacred vestments of that church, the oldest place of Christian worship in Calcutta, which dates its existence from the year 1724.

As we have pointed out in a previous chapter, (page 221) no one can lay sacrilegious hands on church property with impunity, for the over-zealous purchaser of the sacred vestments who had however bought them with the best of intentions, lest they should fall into the hands of Persian hawkers and Jewish curio merchants of Ispahan, met with a series of misfortunes, after his return from India, and underwent terrible sufferings in a foreign country, his present whereabouts being unknown. We must once more impress upon our readers that persons who wish to live peaceably and die peacefully should refrain from having anything to do with church property, whether belonging to a Christian place of worship, a Hindoo temple or a Mohammedan mosque as they are all places for the worship of God.

The good Agah Owenjohn Jacob Gerakh died in 1795 and was buried in the Armenian cemetery at Surat. There is a beautiful white marble tombstone over his grave, with an inscription in Armenian, which can be translated thus :—

"Lord | God
—— | ——
Jesus | Christ
Have mercy | on us.

This is the tomb of the charitable Agah Owenjohn the son of the late Agah Jacob of the Gherakheantz family of Julfa, departed from this world on Friday, the 10th day of Nirhan [7th March] 1795, at the city of Surat. Aged 77 years".

His wife, Goolistan, who had predeceased him, was a sister of the famous Agah Catchick Arrakiel of Calcutta. She is likewise buried in the Armenian cemetery at Surat, and the inscription on her beautiful marble tombstone can be translated thus :—

"Lord | God
—— | ——
Jesus | Christ
Have mercy | on us.

This is the tomb of the chaste lady Goolistan, the daughter of Arrakiel of the Gentloom family and the wife of Agah Owenjohn, the son of Jacob of the Gerakheantz family who departed from this world on Friday, the 16th day of Adam [17th May] in the year of our Saviour, 1788, and in the year 173 of the small era, aged 58 years."

The *Azdarar* (Intelligencer) of Madras, a monthly magazine and the *first* Armenian journal published in the world, from 1794—1797, has the following obituary notice in its issue for April 1795. "Not only it is sad to consider the present weak state of our nation, but we have to lament that the old amongst us, are decreasing, because Agah Owenjohn of the Gherakheantz family has died at Surat on the 9th day of the month of Nirhan. They write that his estate is worth 350,000 rupees, which he has, in his life time, bequeathed to cathedrals and others, according to his good wishes".

A brother of Agah Owenjohn Gerakh, named Gerakh, died at Madras in 1763 and is buried in the Armenian churchyard of that city. There are the graves of some members of the Gerakh family in the Armenian churchyard of Calcutta.

CHAPTER XXI

ARMENIAN JEWELLERS AT SURAT.

TRANSACTION OF A LARGE DIAMOND.

In the *Calcutta Review* for March 1848, there is an interesting article on 'Surat : Its Past and Present,' from which the following, connected with the history of Armenians there, is an extract :—

"Previous to the decline of the Mogul empire, the city was under a Governor, to whom the Cutwal was subordinate. There was also a Governor of the Castle, the two Governors being perfectly independent of each other, and solely responsible to the Emperor, who reserved to himself the power of life and death, and to whom reference was made before the infliction of capital punishment. There was a strict police surveillance, but the functionaries were, like other orientals, accessible to bribes. The Cutwal himself was obliged to parade the streets during the night, and persons found in them were ordinarily imprisoned. , Guards were placed at various stations, and at nine, twelve and three o'clock the Cutwal passed with tom-toms, horns, and the shouts of his attendants, who were answered by the detached police. An incident, however, which occurred during Thevenot's* stay, proves that all this was little more than an organized system of tyranny. A certain Armenian merchant had been robbed of two thousand four hundred sequins; at the same time two of his slaves disappeared and were suspected of the theft. After strict enquiry had been made, and neither money nor slaves discovered, a report gained ground that the slaves had committed the theft,

---

* Jean de Thevenot (1633—1667) was a native of Paris. He was an eminent oriental traveller and arrived at Surat from Basra in the ship "Hopewell" on the 10th January 1666. He was an accomplished linguist, skilled in Turkish, Arabic and Persian. On his way home to France, he died at Miyana in Persia on the 28th November 1667. He is the author of *Le voyage de M. Thevenot.*

that they had been drawn to the house of a certain Mussalman with whom they were in communication, and were murdered by him for the sake of the stolen property. The Governor urged upon the Cutwal the necessity of making good the Armenian's loss, for, if a report were sent to the Emperor, all blame would fall upon him. The Cutwal did not object, but simply demanded that they would wait a short time, until he might place the merchant and his servants under restraint and examine the latter by torture. The Governor consented; but, as soon as the Armenian was informed of the new turn which affairs had taken, he let the prosecution drop, and preferred losing the whole of his money to suffering the tortures which the Cutwal had in store for him."

The same article goes on to say :—

"There are about twenty Armenians with their priest [at Surat]. We know not how to account for the large proportion of women amongst them, but such there is; and when a report of the population of Surat was sent to England in 1824, the case was precisely the same, although in all other instances the numbers of males and females were about equal. The occupation of these once-active people is almost gone. No greater testimony could have been given to their industry, honesty, and ability, than the circumstance that they were employed by our factories to carry on their trade in the interior, the Company admitting that they could conduct it better than their own agents. In their altered position they still retain the respectability and love of order for which they are generally so distinguished."

By an arrangement made in 1799, the English were placed in possession of Surat city and the town of Rander. During the Mohammedan period, there seems to have been little security of life and property in that great city as the following incident clearly shows.

An Armenian jeweller arrived at Surat from Basra with a large stock of precious stones and hired a room in the immediate vicinity of the Armenian church. He had large dealings with Europeans, Armenians, Hindoos and Mohammedans buying and selling. One day the legal adviser to the Governor of Surat paid him a visit on the pretext of buying stones for the Governor. On finding the Armenian jeweller alone, his cupidity was aroused, and he stabbed him. After taking all his valuable goods, he took to his heels and made himself scarce. Two days after, which was a Sunday, and the Armenians not seeing him at church as usual, they became anxious about him. On going to his room, they found the body of the jeweller lying prostrate on the floor, stabbed in the region of the heart. After a careful search, the murderer was arrested with the stones in his possession. The Armenians of Surat demanded justice from the Governor for the atrocity perpetrated on their fellow-countryman, but were told by him that "for the life of an Armenian *even the point of the nail* of the legal adviser would not be cut."

Under such trying conditions the Armenians had to carry on their business at Surat and yet they prospered and amassed great wealth in that Mohammedan city by dint of perseverance and sheer industry. From a letter preserved in the archives of the All-Saviour's Cathedral at Julfa, and written from Surat in 1669, it appears that a large Indian diamond, weighing 159 ruttees, (about 140 carats) was purchased by two Armenian merchants of Surat for 11,000 thoomans, although we cannot say exactly what the Persian thooman was worth in those days, but it could not have been worth more than four Indian rupees.

The stone was bought jointly by two Armenians—Agah Johanness Akookhas and one Simon—but before the stone was taken delivery of, a dispute arose between them, as the former wished to admit one of his friends, one Sahak, as an equal partner by giving him a third share in the transaction. Simon naturally protested against the attempted violation of the contract, and seeing that, his tricky partner was trying to deceive him by leaving the city, he had him brought back and took the stone out of his hands by paying him a lump sum profit of 2500 thoomans. We give below a literal translation of the letter written in very poor colloquial Armenian by Simon to the leading Armenian merchants at Julfa which in those days was the tribunal and the Chamber of Commerce where the disputes of the Armenian merchants in India were settled by a body of veteran merchants.

"The reason of this letter is that on the 25th day of the month of Aram [21st January] in the year 1118 [1679], we arrived at the port of Surat. The broker had brought a diamond weighing 159 ruttees, and given to Johanness Akookhas. Johanness came to me and said, oh Simon, the broker has brought a stone, weighing 159 ruttees, come let us purchase it in partnership, I said very well, we will buy it jointly. He said let us buy it in equal shares. This arrangement was made between us. After five or six days, the broker came with the owner of the stone. Johanness sent for me to go and settle the price. I went to his house, we weighed the stone, which was 159 ruttees, and settled the price for 11,000 thoomans payable after 15 days. We gave a piece of brocade (zarbaff) as a present to the seller of the stone and another piece to the broker and came out. Johanness then said, oh Simon, since Sahak is with me, let one part be mine, one part Sahak's and one part yours, I said as we have already agreed, half is mine and the other half is yours, because there was no mention of Sahak's name before, you know best about your share and Sahak. Two days after I sent the broker to Johanness if I were to send him my share of the purchase money, but he sent word to say that he had returned the stone. I ascertained from the seller, as also from the broker that he had not returned the stone. I was afraid to have any words with Johanness because it is such a big stone and if the Governor came to hear about it, the stone would go out of our hands.

As the stone is going to Ispahan, I am writing to our Agahs there to appoint Messrs. Avietick and Minas both of Surat to arbitrate.

Johanness suddenly left Surat to go to Gujerat. Mr. Minas sent men and had him brought back and told him that he had purchased the stone in partnership with me and he was trying to go away with the stone. He (Mr. Minas) gave him a lump sum profit of 2500 thoomans and took the stone out of his hands."

The letter is witnessed by the following Armenian merchants of Surat:—

Agah Matthevosian, Gregore Agamalian, Catchick Avietickian, Malcom Dilakhian, Sarook and Michael Minasian.

We have not yet been able to trace the history of that large diamond, or of its shrewd purchaser, who, as we have seen proved more than a match for the unprincipled Armenian merchant of Surat, who, actuated by motives of greed and avarice, tried to secure the stone for himself and his friend, by a piece of sharp practice.

The stone purchased at Surat in 1679 cannot possibly be idenitfied with the famous Indian diamond, weighing about 195 carats which Khojah Johanness Rafael, an Armenian merchant from India, sold to Prince Orloff whom he met at Amsterdam in 1775, *en route* for Russia.

A short account of that historical diamond, may prove of interest to our readers.

The celebrated diamond once formed one of the eyes of the celebrated Hindu idol in Srirangum, a fortified island in Mysore. It was set in the Russian Imperial sceptre immediately beneath the Golden Eagle. It weighs 194¼ carats, has the underside flat, and is named after Prince Orloff, its purchaser, Mr. Edwin W. Streeter, in his *Great Diamonds of the World, says*:—"It was on his way from England to Russia that Khojeh [Rafael] met Prince Orloff in Amsterdam, and induced him to purchase the Indian gem for his mistress, the Czarina, Catherine II. Orloff was himself at the time also on his travels. Having fallen under the displeasure of Catherine, he had absented himself from Court until the storm should blow over. Khojeh's offer was now eagerly accepted, as affording an excellent opportunity for recovering the favour of the Empress, who is reported to have already declined the purchase as too cóstly, but who now accepted the jewel at the hands of her illustrious subject. Orloff paid the merchant £90,000 in cash, besides procuring him an annuity of £4,000. According to some accounts a patent of nobility was added." Mirza Abu Taleb Khan, the Persian traveller, who met Khojah Rafael at Leghorn, describes him as one "who had seen a great deal of the world, and undertsood a number of languages. He had left Persia when a young man, and had gone by sea to Surat; thence across the Peninsula to Bengal. After residing there some time, he made a voyage to England ; and after travelling over a great part of Europe, at length settled as a merchant in Leghorn".* (*Travels in Asia, Africa, and Europe* : London, 1814, vol. II., p. 301).

In all probability, Khojah Rafael secured the stone at Surat which has always been a great mart for precious stones and even to-day the leading pearl merchants of Bombay hail from that city.

---

* The Armenian colonists at Leghorn, in Italy, who were mostly from Julfa and India, were solely engaged in commerce. A press for printing books in the Armenian language was started there in 1643 by an Armenian monk named Johanness, a native of Julfa, the Armenian suburb of Ispahan. The first publication issued from that press was the Book of Psalms. Other important books, both sacred and secular, were subsequently published at that press in 1670, 1691, 1692, 1696, 1698 and 1701.

CHAPTER XXII

MRS. HRIPSIMAH LEEMBRUGGEN.

AN ARMENIAN LADY MERCHANT.

Another Armenian philanthropist of Surat whose liberal bequests to religious, educational and charitable institutions deserve to be recorded in the immortal pages of history, was Mrs. Hripsimah, or Coramseemee* Eleazar Leembruggen.

She was born at Surat in 1778 and was the only daughter of a wealthy Armenian merchant of that city, named Eleazar Woskan. When in her teens she was given in marriage to an old man, one Stephen Agabob,† a widower, who treated his girl wife so cruelly that she was compelled to run away from him and take refuge in the house of an English doctor who was an intimate friend of her family. In 1795, when her husband was still living, she married one Robert Henry Leembruggen, a Hollander who was in the Civil Service of the Dutch East India Company at Surat. From the Marriage Settlement, drawn up in Armenian and dated the 2nd day of June 1795, which is preserved with other documents in the archives of the Armenian church at Madras, it appears that at the time of her second marriage, Hripsimah Agabob, possessed Rs. 40,000 in hard cash, besides some valuable jewels

---

* Coramseemee or Khoromeseemee, is the corrupt form of Hripsimah (Ripsy) in Armenian.

†Stephen Agabob's first wife, Elizabeth, the daughter of one Nazar Milan, had died on the 24th March, 1784, at the age of 15, and is buried in the Armenian cemetery at Surat. Old Agabob, who evidently had a passion for girl wives, died in 1802, aged 60 years and lies buried in the Surat Armenian cemetery. Alas for posthumous vanity! for in the epitaph on his tombstone, he is called noble, (azniv), but we cannot understand how an old man, who treated his young wife ignobly, could be given that attribute after his death! Evidently the composer of the epitaph, a duty which in those days invariably devolved on the resident priests, was axious to flatter the rich man even after his exit from this world.

which she had inherited from her father, and it was stipulated that neither her second husband, nor her people, should have any control over her estate and she could do whatever she liked with her property. And it was further stipulated that she would be in no way or under any circumstances responsible for any debts which her second husband, Leembruggen, might have incurred before their marriage. They lived happily at Surat for sometime, although their presence must have been gall and wormwood to old Stephen Agabob, Hripsimah's first husband, who as we have seen, died in 1802, or seven years after his second wife's happy marriage with Leembruggen. From Surat, they were transferred to Colombo and afterwards to Negapatam. It appears from the letters of Mrs. Hripsimah Leembruggen that at the time of their marriage, her second husband, Leembruggen, was not only impecunious, but was at the same time heavily involved, which is very often the case when foreign husbands marry wealthy Armenian wives. With the money that Mrs. Leembruggen possessed, they started business at Negapatam which was carried on in the name of the wife. They seem to have been a loving couple for some years, as can be seen from a Will, dated, the 7th March 1806, which they had jointly made, when in Colombo, in the Dutch language by an eminent notary, but later on domestic troubles and dissensions arose owing to the dissolute habits of Leembruggen which compelled the wife to obtain 'judicial separation' from her husband, as can be seen from the Deed of Separation, dated Negapatam, the 4th day of August, 1817. Under the terms of that Deed, Hripsimah, the wife, as the sole owner of the business and her estate, gave her profligate husband a monthly allowance of 25 Porto-Novo, (pagodas) for life. Leembruggen* did not live long after the separation, for he died on the 6th November 1819, without a will, having nothing to bequeath, barring some dilapidated old furniture which the wife did not care to claim.

---

* He was buried in the Karicop Dutch cemetery at Negapatam and on his marble tombstone, erected by his widow, there is an inscription in English, which runs as follows :—

R. H. Leembruggen Esq., Civil Servant in the late Dutch East India Company's Service at Surat, who departed this life on the 6th November, 1819. Aged 60 years, 2, months 8 days.

Hripsimah continued her business singly, after the separation, and was in the habit of making out a Will every year, copies of which she used to deposit with the Trustees of the "Madras Armenian Orphans' Fund".

She died at Negapatam, after a lingering and painful illness, on the 21st May, 1833, and was buried in the Dutch cemetery of that city. On her beautiful marble tombstone, the following inscription is engraved in English :

> "Mrs. C. E. Leembruggen, widow of the late R. H. Leembruggen, Esq. formerly of the Dutch Civil Service at Surat. After a painful and lingering illness, she departed this life at Negapatam, May 21, 1833, aged 56 years. In her dealings, she was upright, in her religious principles, liberal, and in her charities, munificent."

Her last will and testament, which is in English, is dated the 25th day of January 1832, to which two codicils were added on the 29th August 1832 and the 25th January, 1833, with a Memorandum, dated the 29th January, 1833. Afted several bequests to Armenian religious, educational and charitable institutions, she left the residue of her large estate to the Armenian church at Madras for the benefit of the "Madras Armenian Orphans' Fund."

The Armenian community of Madras erected a beautiful cenotaph of pure marble in the Armenian church of that city, bearing inscriptions in Armenian and English. The English inscription is as follows: —

> "Sacred to the memory of Mrs. Córamsimee Leembruggen who departed this life at Negapatam on the 21st May, 1833. This cenotaph was erected at the expense of the Madras Armenian Orphans' Fund in gratitude of her unparalleled benevolence towards it.
>
> Madras, 1st July, 1836."

By her last will, Mrs. Leembruggen left the sum of Rs. 18,600 to the Armenian Philanthropic Academy, now the Armenian College of Calcutta and she left a similar bequest to the Armenian holy church of Nazareth, Calcutta, "for the sustenance and relief of the poor ladies, widows and orphans of the Armenian community at Calcutta."

There is inside the Armenian church at Calcutta a black marble mural tablet, fixed on the south wall, bearing inscriptions in Armenian and English. The English inscription is as follows :—

> " Sacred to the memory of Mrs. Hiripsimah Lembruggen, who, departed this life at Nagapatam on the 21st May, A.D. 1833. She was born at Surat in the year 1778. This tablet is erected as a mark of gratitude for her munificent bequest towards the relief of poor Armenians in Calcutta."

Mrs. Hripsimah Leembruggen was not, however, the *first* Armenian lady to marry a Dutchman at Surat, for we find that in 1623, a Hollander married an Armenian girl in the same city. Rev. Philip Anderson, M.A., one of the Honorable Company's chaplains in the diocese of Bombay, gives an account of this Armeno-Dutch wedding in his interesting work, *The English in Western India* (Bombay, 1854). He writes :—

> "Society was of the free and jovial kind. There were no English ladies, and if the Factors wished to enjoy the conversation of the gentler sex, they must resort to the Dutch Factory. We have an account of a wedding party there. The bride was an Armenian; the bridegroom a Dutchman. All the Europeans of the place were invited, and every lady came; so there were present one Portuguese and one Dutch matron, a young Maronite girl, and a native woman who was engaged to marry a Dutchman."

CHAPTER XXIII

THE LAST DAYS OF THE ARMENIANS AT SURAT.

The decline and the dispersion of the Armenians at Surat must have been very rapid, if not precipitate, for whereas during the last two decades of the 18th century (1780-1800) there were 33 merchants besides many others in humbler walks of life, in that city, their numbers had dwindled down to only 7 souls in 1820. Their names were : Mrs. Elizabeth Farbessian, Mrs. Maishkhanoom Avietian, Mrs. Mariam Vardanian, Stephen Petrus, Minas Margarian, Gregore Agahian and Arrathoon Balthazarian, the only well-to-do amongst them being the lady mentioned first.

And in January 1907, when we visited Surat, we were fortunate enough to find one Armenian, a venerable looking old gentleman who bore a purely Armenian name, *viz.* John Alexander Minas, a descendant of the famous Agah Minas family who lived and died at Surat during the 18th century and their graves can be seen in the Surat Armenian cemetery to this day. His reminiscences of the last days of the Armenian community at Surat were painfully interesting.

He remembered Rev. Gregory, the *last* priest who officiated, for a short time, in the Armenian church at Surat in 1861. When we asked him why he did not leave Surat in his younger days and go to Bombay or to some other important centre, like the other Armenian residents of Surat, he replied pathetically that he could not possibly think of deserting his ancestral house—a big and a beautiful two-storeyed building—in the immediate vicinity of the Armenian church. He wished to live and die in the place where his revered ancestors had resided in the good old days when Surat was "a no mean city." He was conservative and belonged to the old school and he seemed to be quite proud of his birthplace where he died shortly after our visit to that historic city, the glory of which had departed and ICHABOD was writ large on its portals.

Sic transit gloria mundi !

From the correspondence which passed between the Armenian priest at Bombay and the Bombay Government in 1825, the originals and copies of which we have in our possession, it appears that in view of the straitened circumstances of the Armenians at Surat, the Company's Government was graciously pleased to grant a monthly stipend of Rs. 60 for the maintenance of an Armenian priest at Surat for a period of 35 years. Here is the order of the Acting Secretary to Government on the Agent for the Governor at Surat for the payment of the stipend to the Armenian priest in that city.

No. 1707 of 1825.
General Department.

"To John Romer, Esq.,
Agent for the Governor at Surat.

Sir,

I have the honor to acknowledge the receipt of your letter of the 10th ultimo, and am directed to inform you that the Hon'ble the Governor in Council is pleased to allow a stipend of (60) Sixty Rupees per mensem for the maintenance of an Armenian Priest at Surat.

I have the honor to be
Sir,
Your most obedient Servant
(Signed) D. Greenhill,
Acting Secy. to Govt."

Bombay Castle,
1st November· 1825.

The Acting Secretary to Government simultaneously informs the Armenian priest at Bombay, as under :—

No. 1710 of 1825.
General Department.

"To,

THE REVEREND TER MARTYRUS TER CATCHATOOR,

SIR,

In reference to your letter of the 2nd of September to the address of the Venerable the Archdeacon, I am directed to inform you, that the Hon'ble the Governor in Council has been pleased to grant a stipend of (60) Sixty Rupees per mensem for the maintenance of an Armenian Priest at Surat.

I am,
Sir,
(Signed) D. GREENHILL,
Your obedt. Servt.
Acting Secy. to Govt."

Bombay Castle,
1st November· 1825.

The Agent for the Governor at Surat, duly informs the Armenian community of that city, of the monthly grant of Rs. 60 as a stipend for the Armenian priest. Here is his letter.

"The agent for the Governor has the pleasure to annex, for the information of the Community of Armenians at Surat, copy of a Letter from Mr. Acting Secretary Greenhill, showing that the Hon'ble the Governor in Council has been pleased to allow a stipend of (60) Sixty Rupees per mensem for the maintenance of an Armenian Priest at Surat.

Surat, 8th November, 1825."

The grant continued till the year 1859 when by an order of the "Principal Secretary of State for India',, it was discontinued. This unchristian fiat of the over-zealous Secretary of State for India, a post which came into existence after the passing of the Hon'ble East India Company's government to the Crown, after the Indian Mutiny of 1857, gave the death blow to the dying Armenian Church at Surat, which had to close its doors, as can be seen from the letters of Rev. Gregory Martyrose who had arrived from Julfa to succeed the deceased incumbent of the Surat church. ·Here is his letter.

"To

THE SECRETARY TO GOVERNMENT

in the Ecclesiastical Department.

SIR,

I have the honor to report for the information of His Excellency the Governor in Council that consequent on the demise of the Reverend Arratoon Jacob, I have been appointed by my Archbishop of the Convent [Cathedral] of Julpha and Primate of the Armenian churches of India to succeed the deceased and to continue for a period of six years as Minister of the Armenian church at Surat. From a letter from Government No. 168 of the 6th August, 1859 in the Ecclesiastical Department, communicated to the Armenian Minister at Bombay, it appears that H. M's Principal Secretary of State for India· has in a dispatch, dated 14th June, 1859 to this Government directed the discontinuance of the allowance hitherto granted to the Resident Armenian Priests at Bombay and Surat, "whenever a change may occur in the individuals officiating at these places respectively." Such being the case, and as a vacancy has now taken place at Surat, I regret to state that there will be no other alternative but to close the doors, for ever, of the once popular Armenian church at Surat, as the Armenians there now have not the means of maintaining a Priest to administer to them our religious rites and ceremonies and thereby will put the present remaining few, but very poor Armenians at that place, to serious inconvenience and great distress.

Under the circumstances I solicit that His Excellency the Governor in Council will be graciously pleased to recommend the continuance of the usual stipend allowed to the Armenian

Priest, since the last 35 years, until such time as there may be any Armenians resident in that city.

I have the honor to be,
Sir,
Your most obedt. Servant
(Signed) TER [REV.] GREGORY MARTYROUS,
Armenian Minister."

Bombay,
14th January, 1861.

The Acting Secretary to Government sent the following reply to Rev. Gregory's letter :—

No. 6 of 1861
Ecclesiastical Department.

From LIEUTENANT-COLONEL W. F. MARRIOTT,
Acting Secretary to Government

TO THE REVEREND GREGORY MARTYRIUS.

SIR,

I have the honour to acknowledge the receipt of your letter dated 14th instant and am directed in reply to inform you that His Excellency the Governor in Council is unable to recommend the continuance of the stipend hitherto allowed to the Priest of the Armenian church at Surat.

I have the honour to be
Sir,
Your most obedient Servant
(Signed) W. F. MARRIOTT.

Bombay Castle,
24th January· 1861.

Prior to the receipt of the above reply, Rev. Gregory goes to Surat and there addresses another letter to the Collector and Magistrate of Surat, as follows :—

"To

THE COLLECTOR & MAGISTRATE OF SURAT.

SIR,

Consequent on the demise of the Rev. Arratoon Jacob, the Armenian Minister of Surat, I have the honour to inform you that I have been directed to succeed him. I have this day arrived at Surat and received charge of the Armenian church of this place.

I have the honour also to enclose for your information copy of my letter addressed to Government in Bombay on the subject of the stipend allowed to the Resident Minister of the Armenian church at Surat and to solicit that you will have the goodness to recommend the continuance of the same, so long enjoyed by the Armenian Priest at Surat.

I remain,
Sir,
Your most obedt. Servant
(Signed) TER [REV.] GREGORY MARTYROUS."

Surat,
19th January, 1861.

The Acting Collector in charge at Surat, an uncouth official, did not condescend to write a letter to the Armenian Priest, but simply returned his letter with the following reply written at the back :

" No. 97 of 1861.
Ecclesiastical Department,
Surat, Collectors' Camp,
Rankooa, Chicklee Talooca.
28th January· 1861.

Returned to the Reverend Gregory Martyrous, Armenian Priest at Surat.

The allowance has been discontinued under orders conveyed in a Despatch from Her Majesty's Principal Secretary of State for India, No. 4 dated 14th June, 1859, and as an application for its continuance has been submitted to Govt. the undersigned declines to interfere in the matter.

(Signature illegible)

Acting 1st Asst. Collector in Charge."

In September 1861, a long letter was addressed to "The Honourable Lord Viscount Canning, Viceroy of India", by the Rev. Johanness Catchick of Calcutta, in his official capacity as the "Vicar-General of the Armenian churches of India and Vice-Archbishop of Persia," for the restoration of the stipend of the Armenian priest at Surat, but the appeal fell on deaf ears, for the fiat of the Principal Secretary of State for India was like "the law of the Medes and Persians which altereth not" (Daniel VI. 2).

After officiating in the Surat Armenian church for a short time, Rev. Gregory, the *last* minister of that ancient church, came down to Calcutta by the order of the Prelate of the diocese and was sent to Chinsurah as an incumbent of the Armenian church of that place. He died there on the 11th January, 1879, aged 55 years, and his body was brought down and buried in the Armenian churchyard of Calcutta on the following day.

His widow Thelthel· who died on the 6th December, 1891, aged 61 years and 6 months, is also interred there next to her husband.

Rev. Gregory had five sons and a daughter. One of the sons, Seth Gregory, was an eminent doctor and was for many years attached to St. Thomas' Hospital in London. The daughter had married one Aviet Thaddeus Christian, the grandson of a Polish Jew who had become a Christian in India and had adopted the name Christian as a surname.

They had an only daughter, a highly cultured and intellectual lady, who was a graduate of the Calcutta University having passed the B.A. Examination with distinction.

Miss Lily Mary Christian, the granddaughter of Rev. Gregory died on the 4th October, 1920, aged 44 years and was buried in the Armenian cemetery in Lower Circular Road where both her parents are buried. She was a devout lady and left all that she possessed—valuable books, jewellery and hard cash, amounting to Rs. 22,600—to the Armenian church at Calcutta, the annual income thereof (Rs. 880) to be applied for the relief of the poor of the local Armenian community.

The Armenian church committee, as a token of gratitude, erected in 1923, a marble mural tablet, which is fixed on the south wall of the south verandah of the church, with the following inscription in English only :—

"This tablet is erected to the memory of Miss Lily Mary Christian, B.A., the only daughter of Mr. and Mrs. Aviet Thaddeus Christian of Mozufferpore and the grand-daughter of Rev. Gregory of Julfa, who left all that she possessed at her death to this church for the benefit of the poor. 1923."

As the Surat church, with all its properties, movable and immovable, had come under the control of the wardens of the Armenian sister church at Bombay, when its doors were finally closed in 1861, we wrote, in 1924, to Mr. Henry Michael, the senior warden of the Bombay church, for some information about that ruined and deserted church which we had visited in January 1907. Mr. Michael, the doyen of the small Armenian community of Bombay, a charming and a most amiable person, religious and patriotic, with his characteristic kindness, replied to our enquiries, as follows :—

"The Surat church is no more, the whole structure fell down some years ago and the debris was sold off by the former wardens. I visited Surat some two years ago and found that everything had been removed except the altar with the dome on the top is still in existence. The open space was used as a public ground for squatters etc. I have let the place for a nominal rent to an old Parsi gentleman who has agreed to preserve the altar and to make the church grounds into a garden for the school children of an orphanage to play about. It is better to give it for this purpose than to allow it to go to wrack and ruin, as you say. I am enclosing a photo of the altar I took some years ago. If your wealthy friend would get the altar restored to its original state, it would be a great boon, to restore it properly and fence in the whole place will cost about 2 to 3 thousand rupees. It would have cost a mint of money to restore the whole church.

Some years ago when I took over the wardenship, I asked the Archæological Department to restore the church, but they refused to do it unless the whole property was made over to them and of couse I had no authority to do so and the matter remained as it stood. The old Armenian gentleman you refer to, died years ago."

Had the wardens of the Bombay Armenian church made over the Surat church to the Archæological Department, that ancient place of divine worship would have been standing to-day, not only as a "Protected Monument" but as a valuable landmark of the once prosperous Armenian community of good old Surat.

In 1861, when the Surat church was finally closed down, the then Wardens of the Armenian church of Bombay brought down all the sacred books, vessels and vestments of the Surat church and they are preserved in the Bombay church. Amongst these, there is a manuscript Bible in the Armenian language which was written at Surat in 1658, which is another proof of the existence of a national church in that city during the 17th century. There is also an old chasuble (shoorjar) belonging to the Surat church, on which the year 1782 is beautifully embroidered in gold thread. Apart from the manuscript Bible which was written at Surat in 1658, there is still another proof of the existence of an Armenian church in that city in the middle of the 17th century.

On page 297 of the *English Factories in India* (1661-1664) there is a rough map of Surat, showing the positions of the prominent buildings at the time of Sivaji's first raid on the city, early in January, 1664, in which the Armenian church is clearly shown.

They are marked from A to F, as under:—

A. The English Factory of that time which stood in the north-western part of the city, in what is now known as the Mullah's Ward.

B. The *Sarai* and mosque of Mirza Zahid still standing.

C. A building known as the Dadhimar or Racket Court. It was originally a *sarai* and may have been the one in which some Armenians and Turkish merchants secured themselves and their goods during the raid.

D. The Armenian church.

E. Shows the position of the French factory established a little later.

F. Is the site of the subsequent English factory, near the Mullas' Water Gate. Part of this building is still standing and has been erroneously labelled as the original factory.

During the sack of Surat by Sivaji, the Mahratta freebooter, an Englishman, Anthony Smith by name, falls into the hands of the bandit who threatens to cut off his head unless a ransom of Rs. 300,000 is paid for him, but through the kind intercession of an Armenian who was a friend of Sivaji, the rash Englishman was released on payment of Rs. 300 only.

In a long letter to the Court of Directors in London, dated the 28th January, 1664, the President and Council at Surat, after giving a detailed account of Sivaji's raid, they state that "wee had allmost forgott to tell you that Mr. Anthony Smith in the time of troubles was so inconsiderate as to come from Swally hither alone and was snapt comeing through the towne and carryed to the said Sevagy [Sivaji] ; who, after hee had threatened him with the losse of his head, caused him to bee bound with his armes behinde him amongst the rest of the prisoners, demanding 300,000 rupees for his ranssome, but by the friendship of an Armenian that was of his [Sivaji's] acquaintance, of whom Sevagy asked his quality and condition, who assured him that hee was a common man, the next day tooke 300 rupees and sett him free, sending him to us upon his peroul, with a message full of threats and menaces, but haveing him in our possession, wee were resolved not to sufferr him to returne, but sent our answere by those that came with him, that hee [Sivaji] was a rebell and a thiefe and therefore wee valued not his threats, and that Mr. Smith was our servant and wee would keepe him."

In view of the terror with which the English were struck during Sivaji's presence at Surat, it is not likely that they would have dared to send such an insolent message to the Mahratta brigand, calling him "a rebell and a thiefe." It is simply a bit of bravado on the part of the President and the Council at Surat to please their employers in London, who had no idea of Sivaji's power, rapacity and brutality.

Bernier relates that during the sack of the city, a Jew who had some valuable rubies, although thrice threatened with execution by the Mahratta bandit, still he would not give up his treasure. Here is the account:

"The pertinacity of a Jew, a native of Constantinople, astonished every body. Seva-Gi [Sivaji] knew that he was in possession of most valuable rubies, which he intended to sell to Aureng-Zebe; but he persevered in stoutly denying the fact, although three times placed on his knees to receive the stroke of a sword flourished over his head. This conduct is worthy of a Jew, whose love of money generally exceeds his love of life."

An event occurred at Surat in the year 1700, which should be rècorded here, as it shows the cordial relations that existed between the Armenians and their *confreres* in trade, the English.

When the new "English East India Company" started a Factory at Surat towards the end of the 17th century, to compete with the old East India Company known as the "Company of Merchants of London trading to the East Indies", the President of the new Company, Sir Nicholas Waite, was so hostile towards the President and the Factors of the old Company, both living and dead, that he would not allow, Mr. Edwards, the chaplain of the new Company, who died at Surat on the 25th March 1700, after an illness of thirty days, to be buried in the extensive cemetery of the old Company, and as there was no other English cemetery at Surat, the body of the deceased chaplain was interred in the beautiful Armenian cemetery of that place.

Rev. Philip Anderson, M.A., a chaplain of the Honorable East India Company in the diocese of Bombay and the well-informed author of *The English in Western India*, refers to this burial in the following caustic terms :—

> "Nothing can show more painfully the bitterness—we may say the ferocity—of the spirit with which the two companies were animated in their rivalry, than the fact that on this occasion Sir Nicholas Waite could not bury his dead in the ground where other bodies of his countrymen rested. There was the spacious cemetery of the old Company, with the grand mausolea of its Chiefs, and a few generations of Factors sleeping around them, but interlopers and competitors in trade might not sleep there. Persons professing not only to hold the same religion but also observing the same forms, had been driven by commercial antagonism to set up altar against altar, and to hinder their clergy from associating even in death. They initiated the odious jealousy of the blindest superstition.
>
> It must be recorded to their credit that the Armenians came forward and offered the use of their burial ground. Their liberal proposal was gratefully accepted, and the Chaplain's body found a resting place with strangers."

No tombstone could have been placed over the grave of the *first* chaplain of the new Company, by his callous employers, who were immersed in money-making, as there is no slab to mark his grave in that beautiful cemetery, where over two hundred Armenians of both sexes, sleep the eternal sleep in a strange land, far away from their homes.

It may not be out of place, before concluding this chapter, to say a few words about the origin of Surat which played such an important part in the history of the early British trade in India. Its origin appears to be comparatively modern, tradition assigning the foundation of the town to the beginning of the 16th century.

As early as 1514 A.D. it was described by the Portuguese traveller Barbosa as a "very important sea port." During the reigns of the Mogul Emperors, Akbar, Jehangeer and Shah Jehan, it rose to be the chief commercial city of India. From 1573—1612, before the appearance of the British on the scene, the Portuguese were the indisputed masters of the Surat seas, and as we have seen on page 98, a Portuguese naval officer, had the audacity to tell Captain William Hawkins in 1609 that "these seas belonged unto the King of Portugal and none ought to come here without his license." During the 18th century it probably ranked as the most populous city in India, its population being at one time estimated as high as 800,000, but with the transfer of its trade to Bombay, the numbers rapidly fell off until in 1847 its inhabitants numbered only 80,000.

It is distant from the sea 14 miles by water and 10 miles by land.

It is a purely Indian city, inhabited mostly by Hindoos, although there are a number of Parsis and Mohammedans.

The first and perhaps the last Indian Viceroy to visit Surat —the birthplace and the cradle of British power in India—was the late Lord Curzon, who according to an eye witness, paid also a visit to the Armenian church in that historic city.

Visitors to Surat are shown a quaint old building said to have been the old English Factory,* though this is not certain. It is still in an excellent state of preservation and is now used as a residence and an illustration of it can be seen in the *Indian State Railways Magazine* for January 1931. It is situated on the river Tapti which in the old days washed its base and sailing ships used to come right up to it to deliver and take away merchandise. Smuggling too, was carried on, it is said, by using the still present covered passage leading to the river, to evade the dues. In the verandah of the main building which used to be residence of the Governor in the early days of John Company, there is a tablet, with the following inscription, put up by the order of the late Lord Curzon, who did so much for the preservation of the antiquities of India :—

> "The English Factory originally built in A.D. 1618 under a treaty made with Prince Khurram (Shah Jehan) son of the Emperor Jehangir, through the Ambassador Sir Thomas Roe. It withstood a siege by the Mahrathas under Shivaji in A.D. 1664 and was again attacked

---

* An illustration of the old English Factory at Surat is given, as a frontispiece, in Sir William Foster's *The English Factories in India* (volume for the years 1634-1636).

> by the Mahrathas in A.D. 1703. It ceased to be used for its original purpose after Surat was annexed by the British in A.D. 1800."

The same inscription also appears in Gujerati. The word "Factory", in those days merely implied a receiving and a delivery house as nothing was manufactured in the "Factory". It may be mentioned that the original gate opening into the "Factory" is almost in its original state although more than 300 years have passed over it.

A few words about the beautiful mausoleums in the old English cemetery at Surat, may be interesting. The finest monumental structure in that cemetery is the tomb of Christopher Oxenden, the President of the Surat Factory, who died in 1659. There is a Latin inscription, in old English characters, carved on a small marble slab, written by his brother, Sir George Oxenden, who died in 1669, and is also buried in the same mausoleum. The bombastic epitaph can be translated thus :—

> "Here is laid Christopher Oxenden. In his life a pattern of fair dealing; in his death a proof of the frailty of Life. He comes and is gone. Here he ended his ventures and his life. Days only, not years, could he enter in his accounts; for, of a sudden death called him to a reckoning. Do you ask, my masters, what is your loss and what your gain? You have lost a servant, we a companion, he his life; but against this he can write 'Death to me is gain'."

In the same cemetery can be seen the magnificent mausoleum of Gerald Aungier, another President at Surat, a beautiful illustration of which appeared in the *Indian State Railways Magazine* for January 1931.

There is an equally imposing mausoleum in the adjoining Dutch cemetery, erected over the mortal remains of Van Reede, the Dutch Chief, who died a few years later than the Oxenden brothers. The Dutch, in a spirit of rivalry, tried to eclipse the noble mausoleum which was erected over the remains of the two Englishmen. Such was the jealousy that existed between the two rival companies even beyond the grave!

CHAPTER XXIV

ARMENIANS AND THE EAST INDIA COMPANY.

In Bruce's *Annals of the Honorable East India Company* for the years 1600—1708, published at London in 1810, in three quarto volumes, there are some references to the Armenians in India and Persia, and as they may prove of interest to our readers, we give extracts from them.

Unfortunately Bruce, who was the official historian or the historiographer, as he is called, to the Honorable East India Company, did not continue writing the history of the Company up to his own days, as he would then have supplied us with some more useful information about the cordial relations which existed between the Armenians and the Company during the 18th century.

We are however thankful to that eminent historian for the little he has said from which the readers will be able to form their opinion of the high esteem in which the Armenian merchants in India and Persia, were held by the Company, for their honesty, probity, integrity and commercial acumen of a very high order.

For the years 1637-38 :—

> "The state of the Company's affairs abroad in this season, can only be collected from the information which the Court [Court of Directors] received from Persia, and, indeed, from the circumstances under which Surat was placed, at the close of the last season, more particularly by the embarrassment from Captain Weddel's interferences, it was not possible to make up investments, in any degree proportioned to those of preceding years.
>
> The events in Persia unfold the reasons of the low state of this trade. Mr. Gibson, who had been Agent in Persia, died this season, and on examining his books, it was discovered, that instead of employing the Com-

pany's cash to the promotion of their trade, he had lent four thousand Tomands [Thoomans], or above £12,000 sterling, to the Dutch, which had enabled them to obtain silk, and to bear down the English purchases of that article. This fraud had disgusted the Persian government at his successor, who informed the President and Council of Surat, that unless a new Agent of character should be appointed, the trade must be ruined, and that the diminution of the Customs at Gombroon [Bandar Abhar] must be ascribed to this delinquency;—that, however, the accidental circumstance of the Dutch having borrowed money from the Armenian merchants, to the large amount of £100,000 and not having stock to discharge this debt, had roused this powerful class of people to make an application to the Court, [the Persian Court] to stop the export of silk by the Dutch, till the money due to them should be paid."

(Bruce's *Annals of the Honorable East-India Company,* vol. I, pp. 350-51).

For the years 1686-87 :

"The information from Persia affords a detail of the intrigues of the Dutch, to create a misunderstanding between that Court and the English; but, by the efforts of the Company's Armenian linquist at Ispahan, protection to trade, and a confirmation of the privileges, at Gombroon, had been obtained."

(Bruce's *Annals of the Honorable East-India Company,* vol. II, p. 578).

For the years 1688-89 :—

"As Bengal goods had lately been in great demand at the Company's sales, and as the imports of them, from Hughly, were uncertain, the General and Council of Bombay were to hold out every encouragement to the Armenian merchants, or, that they should receive not only protection, but a profitable market; any charges which might be incurred, in giving such encouragement, would be fully compensated, by the trade this people would introduce; the reasons assigned were that the Armenian merchants carried on trade, on their own funds and credit, and that they traversed all the provinces in India, and collected (though in small quantities and in a manner which had not excited the jealousy of the Natives), the most valuable commodities; if, therefore, they could be induced to make Bombay their principal market, the commercial effect would be incalculable; and farther, to induce them to accept of this offer, they were to be allowed to send their goods on the Company's shipping, to Europe, for sale.

As the Armenians were also the principal merchants in Persia, similar encouragements were to be held out to them, to bring silk and Caramania [Kerman] wool to Bombay, to be sent to Europe, as part of the Company's investment, by which means they would receive greater profits, than by sending Persian produce through Turkey, to Aleppo.

If this commercial system could be established, the Court concluded, that, with the large stock which would be annually sent, a valuable investment might be in store, ready to be shipped for Europe, and arrive to pre-occupy the market, before the Dutch imports could depress the prices."

(Bruce's *Annals of the Honorable East-India Company*, vol. II, pp. 617-18).

For the years 1688-89 :—

"The commercial orders recommended similar encouragement to be given to the Armenians, as authorized in the instructions to Sir John Child, at Bombay, but, more specifically, to offer them thirty per cent profit on the prime cost of such fine Bengal goods, as they might furnish for the investment, and to send as many taffaties as they could procure; but neither raw-silk, nor cotton-yarn, unless they could be purchased from twenty to thirty per cent cheaper than last season."

(Bruce's *Annals of the Honorable East-India Company*, vol. II, p. 621).

For the years 1691-92 :—

"The Court next approved the retaining the Gentoo soldiers in their service, and assigning them portions of lands for their maintenance :—they were also to be allowed half-pay, but, in this case, the Company were to receive half the produce of their lands; a regulation the more expedient, from the difficulty of finding a sufficient number of recruits in England to strengthen the garrison. To obviate the danger arising from entrusting the defence of the place to the Natives, the Court recommended to the Presidency, to engage (if *they could be obtained) about sixty Armenian* Christians, to serve as soldiers, and to offer them a bounty of forty shillings per man, and the same pay as the English soldiers, because, professing nearly the same religion, and being, in other respects, of good character, they might be deemed almost a regular part of the Company's military establishment."

(Bruce's *Annals of the Honorable East-India Company*, vol. III, p. 106).

For the years 1691-92 :—

"The encouragement given to the Armenians ought to be continued, and a duty of one per cent only, taken from them, for goods inported from Europe into India : —on the homeward-bound ships, a thousand tons of saltpetre, at least, were to be sent from Bengal, it being understood the French were sending ships to that country, this season, for this service only."

(Bruce's *Annals of the Honorable East-India Company*, vol. III, p. 107).

For the years 1691-92 :—

"After expressing their opinion of the integrity of the Armenians, the Court recommended, that if this people could engross the whole trade in Persian silks, this article might be allowed to be imported into Europe by them, on the Company's ships; and that, through them, the Agent should push the sale of English broad-cloths, of which a thousand pieces, of proper colours, had been shipped. On viewing all the circumstances of this trade, the Court were of opinion, that as three thousand pieces of broad-cloths were annually used in the kingdom of Persia, the sale of this staple might be extended, as a most profitable and popular measure; and founded this opinion on the fact, that as the Company paid no customs in Persia, and the freight from Bombay was small, they might sell cloth at cheaper rates, than the cloths which came from Aleppo, to the Persian market, without such advantages."

(Bruce's *Annals of the Honorable East-India Company*, vol. III, pp. 107-8).

For the years 1691-92 :—

"The new President and Council, in the meantime, (till the arrival of Sir John Goldesborough) were to direct their attention to the improvement of the revenue of Madras, which the Court held did not amount to one-fifth of what it might yield, under an efficient administration. This opinion they illustrated, by the analogy of the Dutch, who drew, at this time, a revenue from Batavia, estimated at £230,000 sterling, per annum; and were the Dutch in so strong a situation as Madras, which was as favourably situated for the Coromandel Trade, as Batavia was for the Southern Trade, they would soon realize a revenue, equal to that of Batavia :—it was, therefore, resolved, that the quit-rents should be increased, by a progressive duty on houses, taking a scale, from four to eighteen *fanams* each house;—and next, that a duty should be imposed on licenses for public-houses, kept by Europeans, in a scale from five to forty pagodas per annum, according to their magnitude or trade; and on the public-houses, kept by Natives, a similar duty of from one to four pagodas per annum;—the orders, therefore, for inclosing and raising fortifications round the Black Town, were to be carried into effect, which would facilitate the collection of the revenue;—the expenses of these fortifications were to be defrayed by the inhabitants, who derived protection from them, not by the Company;—the Christian part of the town was to be extended, and to form a quadrangle with handsome stone bridges over the river, and one quarter of it to be assigned to the Armenians, who might be able to induce skilful artificers to settle at a place, at which they would be under the protection of the Fort, without being exposed, as they had hitherto been, to depredations by the belligerent powers in the Carnatic:—in this quarter the Armenians were to be permitted to build a church, at their own charge, and houses for the merchants, on payment of ground rents to the Company. This order is accompanied with an interesting account of that distinguished class of merchants. The quarter set apart for the Armenians was to be called *Julfa* "that being the town from which Shah Abbas the Great had brought them, when he conquered Armenia, and settled them in a suburb of his new-made metropolitan city, Ispahan, and called the quarter he allotted there to the Armenians, Julfa, by the name of the city from whence he brought them, and they are increased there to be the richest people, and the most expert merchants we know of, in the universe."

These improvements at Madras, proceeding upon the plan of increasing the native inhabitants, explain the order given respecting the Corporation, into which, the Court were of opinion, too many Englishmen had been admitted, to the office of Aldermen, and therefore recommended "that, in future, the Aldermen should be different casts, *viz.* one Armenian, one or two Hebrews, one or two Portuguese, one or two Gentoos, and one Moor or Musselman."

(Bruce's *Annals of the Honorable East-India Company*, vol. III, pp. 109-11).

For the years 1692-93:—

"To promote the Company's trade on the Malabar Coast, the Armenians were to have the use of the

Company's Ware-houses at Carwar, to lodge their goods, on paying at the rate of four per cent per monsoon, for the accommodation.

The instructions to the Agent in Persia, corresponded with those detailed for Bombay:—he was directed to send the thousand pieces of cloth from Gombroon to Ispahan, by the first conveyance, and himself to proceed to that city, to concert with the chief of Armenians, respecting the measures to be adopted for promoting the Company's interests, and to get some young men, who had embarked from England, accommodated at Ispahan, to acquire a knowledge of the Persian and Armenian languages, to qualify them to conduct the Company's commercial concerns in that kingdom."*

(Bruce's *Annals of the Honorable East-India Company,* vol. III, p. 123).

For the years 1693-94:—

"The trade to Persia, during this season (as mentioned in the instructions to Surat and Bombay) had become, from the conditions under which the new grants were obtained, an important subject of consideration to the Court, because the sales of cloth, to the amount required, would be impracticable in India; unless a vent could be opened for them, in Persia. In the Courts' instructions to the Agent in Persia, to promote this sale, he was enjoined to collect as much Persian silk and Caramania wool, as could be procured by partial barter; and, to enable him to prosecute this plan effectually, the establishment in Persia was augmented, and was, in future to consist of a Chief, four Factors, and four writers; and the Factories at Gom-

---

* The valuable assistance which the Company received from the Armenian merchants at Ispahan in the disposal of their goods in Persia, was considered of such great moment, that they sent out young men from London to reside in the houses of the Armenians at Julfa (Ispahan) "to study their language and acquire their method of conducting business."

broon and Ispahan to be permanent :—the Chief was to reside at either place, as it might appear to him most advantageous for the promotion of this enlarged trade; —and, that the Company's servants might be qualified to take charge of the Subordinate duties, the writers of this season were to reside in the houses of the Armenians, to study their language and acquire their method of conducting business.

Under these general orders, as the King of Persia had offered the whole of the silk in Persia to the Armenians, for payments to be made within three years, the Agent was empowered to take one-third of the silk from the Armenians, on the Company's account, provided they would agree, that the remainder should be put on board the Company's ships for the Europe market, assigning as their reason for this expedient, that the French war had interrupted the Turkey merchants in their imports of silk, and that the article had risen, both in request and price. It was farther directed, that the English cloth should be consigned to the principal Armenian merchants, at Julfa, provided it could be bartered for silk, or ready money; or even for one-third in money, and two-thirds in silk :—the orders for Caramania wool were general, or to obtain as large a quantity as might be practicable, or, as much money and wool as the state of the trade would bear, to be forwarded to Surat, but with a prohibition to send any money to Bengal."

(Bruce's *Annals of the Honorable East-India Company,* vol. III, pp. 140-141).

For the years 1693-94 :—

"After repeating the information to the Presidency of Fort St. George, [Madras] that Sir John Goldesborough had been appointed General in India, and Sir John Gayer, Lieutenant General in the North of India, the separate instructions consisted in a repetition of the orders not to resettle Masulipatam, Madapollam, or Conimere, but to confine the Company's stations on the Coromandel Coast, to Fort St. George, Fort St. David and Vizagapatam, leaving Mr. Charnock with the sole authority in Bengal;—to invite the merchants at the Factories which were to be withdrawn, to settle at the Fort, and at Fort St. David;—to establish the mint, and to send such money as they could coin (particularly silver famains) to Bengal, which would pass current, both in that country, and at Bencoolen;—to adopt the same measures, respecting the Interlopers, which were prescribed to the Government of Surat and Bombay;—to have always two or three hundred tons of pepper in store at the Fort, and the like quantity at Fort St. David, to meet the shipping;—to sell all the Company's coasting ships, and to hire small vessels of the Armenians for that trade, for which, on no account, the Company's shipping were either to be detained, or employed."

(Bruce's *Annals of the Honorable East-India Company*, vol. III, pp. 142-43).

For the years 1694-95 :—

"After referring to the misfortune of the Company's ship, *Berkeley Castle*, having been sunk in the Channel by a French man-of-war, which had prevented the dispatching the first ships of the season, the Court ordered, that one of the ships, on its arrival, should be dispatched from Surat to Mocha, to take in coffee, olibanum, and myrrh :—the captain and an Armenian merchant, who was to assist him, were to be allowed as an encouragement, five per cent commission :—from Mocha he was to reteurn direct to England :—the Company's ships were not, in future, to touch at Cong, but to go direct to Gombroon, and all the lesser country vessels were to be sold, as they had been attended with an immense expense and risk :—though the insinuations against the Armenians had been received, the orders for fulfilling the contract with them, were continued, because the Court conceived that Armenian shipping, in India, would be of material advantage, as the duties which they paid at Fort St. George, amounted to a larger sum than what had been received from the Consulage at Gombroon :—if any interloping ship should arrive at Surat or Bombay, every expedient should be taken, to prevent her obtaining a profitable sale of her cargo, or an investment for Europe.

If the Court's instructions to Persia, in the preceding season, arose from the obligation into which the Company had entered, to export a large amount of British staple and other produce, and if, at that time, it was considered, that a small proportion of these goods could be disposed of in India, the event of the capture of the English and Dutch Turkey fleet by the French in 1693, became a new incentive to the encouragement of the Persian trade, and to the reliance of the Court on this market being rendered profitable by means of their contract with the Armenians at Ispahan."

(Bruce's *Annals of the Honorable East-India Company,* vol. III, pp. 159-160).

For the years 1694-95 :—

"The strength of the Arabs at Muscat, in shipping and forces, was, at this time, so great, as to excite an alarm, that they would obtain the command of the Persian Gulf. The Agent at Gombroon described the Arab fleet to consist of five large ships, on which they had embarked fifteen hundred men ;—that they had plundered Cong, to the amount of sixty thousand tomands, had captured a very valuable Armenian ship, and apprehensions were entertained they would attack Gombroon :—that it was supposed the King of Persia would march an army to resist them, and the Khan requested, on securing information that twelve Arab cruisers were in the Gulf, that the Company's ship *Nassau,* then at Gombroon, should be detained for twenty days, to assist in the defence of it, to which the Agent had consented :—farther from the Kings of England and Persia being in alliance, that the English would employ their fleet in repelling the attack, as it was supposed the Arab vessels would turn pirates. In answer, the Agent reminded the Khan, that three years' customs were due to the Company."

(Bruce's *Annals of the Honorable East-India Company*, vol. III, p. 169).

For the years 1695-96 :—

"When the Letters Patent were granted to the Company in 1694, it will be recollected, that a condition was annexed, of exporting to a large amount, the British staple of woollen-cloth, and it will, also, be recollected, that the Court had formed the opinion, not only that the greatest outlet would be found in the Persian market, but that it could be effected at less expence by the Armenian merchants, and in return, money, Caramania wool, and silk, obtained for it;—it was, also, conceived, that from this people [Armenians] finding their way, during the troubles in India, into the interior provinces, and bringing fine goods, in small quantities, that purchases from them would become a valuable resource for the Europe investment :—hence the Court embraced the opinion, that they were trust-worthy, and qualified to be their Agents, without reflecting that they were merchants, as well as themselves, who might have other mercantile connexions to prevent their executing the trust with probity and correctness :—and, the facts will verify these observations. When the large assortment of cloth arrived at Gombroon, and a proportion was forwarded to Ispahan, the Armenians, instead of receiving, with alacrity, so large a commission, and one for which they were to be so amply paid, or executing it with zeal, hesitated to take the charge upon them, till pushed by the Company's Agents at Ispahan and Gombroon, to bring the cloth to immediate sale, to prevent the article suffering in its qualities, by delay, and to afford the returns, either in Persian produce, or in money, anticipated by the Court, which had put such implicit confidence in their exertions.

In the course of this season (1695-96), it appeared that these Armenians were dealers in the cloth which had come from the Turkey Company, by Aleppo, and thence carried to Ispahan, to be sold in the Persian markets. The cloth, of course, remained unsold, and the Agents both at Gombroon and Ispahan, were obliged to make such exertions as they individually could, at reduced prices, to dispose of an article, on which the Court had expected an advance."

(Bruce's *Annals of the Honorable East-India Company*, vol. III, pp. 196-97).

For the years 1700-1 :—

"As neither the presence of Sir John Gayer at Surat, nor his, and President Colt's applications to the Governor, could relieve them from the demands for compensation, for damages done by the pirates, and as Sir William Norris, instead of abating the insinuations against the London Company, had brought accusations, not only before the Governor, but had forwarded them to the Mogul, the seizure of the Company's property, and the imprisonment of their servants, were again apprehended; it was, therefore, on consultation, resolved, to send an Armenian Vakeel [Agent or Envoy] to Court, to assist the Vakeel which President Pitt had dispatched from Madras, in frustrating Sir William Norris's plans, who was now preparing for his journey."

(Bruce's *Annals of the Honorable East-India Company*, vol. III, p. 376).

For the years 1700-1 :—

"Affairs were in this situation, when Sir William Norris was on his journey to Court, and when the Armenian Vakeel;* sent by the London Company to counteract his negotiations, reached Aurungabad, and received intelligence that the vakeel of President Pitt had arrived, and had been favourably received."

(Bruce's *Annals of the Honorable East-India Company*, vol. III, pp. 379-80).

---

* The name of the Armenian Vakeel sent by the old or the London Company from Surat to the Court of the Emperor Aurungzebe, was Khojah Avennees (Johanness). He was allowed by Sir John Gayer, the President at Surat, a credit of two lakhs of rupees to be spent in bribes at the Mogul Court to frustrate all the efforts of Sir William Norris.

ARMENIANS AT BOMBAY

CHAPTER XXV

ARMENIANS AT BOMBAY

It appears from the *Surat Factory Records* that when the island and port of Bombay was made over to the English in 1661, as a part of the dowry of the Infanta of Portugal who married King Charles II of England,* the English being aware of the important part played by the Armenians in the commercial world of India, invited them to come and settle in their new possession.

After Humphrey Cooke, had taken over the island from the Portuguese in January 1665, he asked Khojah Minas, the head of the Armenian community of Surat, to come and settle at Bombay promising them "land to build them houses and warehouses, also a church for the service of God". In appears from the records that Khojah Minas, with another notable Armenian merchant of Surat, Khojah Delaune, went and settled at Bombay in 1676.

Khojah Minas (Cojah Minaz) was, according to the Surat Factory Records "an able and a well reputed Armenian merchant" and in a letter, dated the 13th December 1665, from the President and his Council at Surat, to Bombay. Khojah Minas is styled "the President for the Armenians at Surat".

Thevenot, the traveller, says that the ship *Hopewell,* in which he had sailed from Basra to Surat in the beginning of 1660, was purchased by Khojah Minas for Rs. 16,000 from Oxenden, who had bought it from the Company for

---

* On the 23rd day of June, 1661, at the Palace of Whitehall, was signed the Marriage-Treaty between Charles II and the Infanta of Portugal, whereby the Port and Island of Bombay "with all the rights, profits, territories and appurtenances whatsoever thereunto belonging, were handed over to the King of Great Britain, his heirs and successors for ever."

Rs. 22,640. Khojah Minas had another ship, the *St. Michael* and in this ship, Rolt and Sainthill were to voyage to Mokha. According to the *Surat Factory Records* it was decided on the 29th July 1669 by the Council at Surat "to sell to Khojah Minaz all the ordinary broadcloth expected by the next fleet (except the portion required for the Malabar factories) at 4¾ rupees per yard, 100 pieces of fine broadcloth at 40 per cent. advance on the invoice prices and 250 pieces of damaged perpetuanos (remaining on hand) at 20 rupees each. As for the Phillippines, Khojah Minaz sent his ship *Hopewell* thither last year with a cargo of 15000 l [£15,000] in Calicoes etc."

The Records add :—

> "There is soe great hopes on this voyage that Cojah Meenas and the persons concerned have taken up money at avog (or bottomarie) thereon at 45, 50 and 60 per cent, and truly, were it not for the Dutch obstructing them at Malacca, most men here doe conclude it will turne well to accompt. Cojah Carricoos' [Khojah Kirakose] brother, who was with you in England, is gon supercargo on the ship, and hath neer one-third of the stock on his owne accompt."

As we have seen, the Armenians formed a commercial colony at Bombay during the second half of the 17th century. Their name will always be associated with the locality known as *Armenian Lane,* in the vicinity of the Armenian church, where the opulent Armenians resided in the good old days. Here they flourished for a considerable time as traders, but eventually dwindled away, only a few families now being left.

In 1796, through the munificence of Jacob Petrus, an opulent Armenian merchant of Bombay and a native of Hamadan in Persia, the indispensable national church was erected for divine worship in the Fort, a locality which has always been of great commercial importance owing to its favourable situation and the proximity to the harbour. It is situated in Medows Street, where an Armenian priest is maintained for the spiritual requirements of the few Armenian families.

At the foot of the altar of the church is a square tablet with an inscription in Armenian, of which the following is a *verbatim* translation :—

> "This holy church was erected in the name of the holy Apostle Peter, during the Patriarchate of His Holiness Lucas, the Catholicos of all the Armenians, by the munificence of Mr. Jacob of Hamadan, to the memory of his late parents, Mr. Petrus, his father, and Zanazan Khatoon, his mother, the foundation-stone of which was laid by Archbishop James, who was on an evangelical tour in India on behalf of the Holy See of Etchmiatzin in the year of our Lord 1796, on the 14th day of Thirah [12th October]".

Another tablet, over the door of the sacristy, bears the following inscription, here translated from the original Armenian :—

> "The outside parts of this holy church with the buildings attached thereto were repaired by the munificence of Agah Jacob, son of Arratoon Thageantz, to the memory of his late mother, the noble lady Thamar, and his sister [Miss] Anna, dead in Christ. The repairs were executed through the instrumentality of Archbishop James, on the 3rd day of Shams [4th April], in the year of our Lord 1801".

The inscriptions in the Bombay churchyard do not go beyond the 19th century, but there are five tombstones, bearing Armenian inscriptions, in the compound of a private dwelling-house at 9 Victoria Road, Byculla, a suburb of Bombay, the earliest being for 1767. The monolith tombstones of fine granite are all in a row in a separate enclosure, with a small door attached, and are fairly well preserved. These tombs are adjacent to an old building still standing, built in the original style, where the solitary Agazar family resided in the eighteenth century, when there was no Armenian church or a cemetery at Bombay. They were therefore obliged to bury their dead, without any religious ceremony, in their own compound, and their bones have since lain there undisturbed. We give below the translations of the five Armenian inscriptions which we copied in January 1895, with the kind permission of the European occupant of the house.

1. Under this tomb rests Gaspar, the son of Agazar, an Armenian by nationality and an eminent merchant. Born at New Julfa in Persia, he died in this city of Bombay on the 1st September 1767, aged 35 years.

There is also an inscription in Latin, as follows :—

> Sub hoc tumulo jacet corpus Gasparis mercat nationis Armenæ, filij Agazar obiit Bombay, ætatis 35, Annorum Die 10 Augusti Anno 1767.

There seems to be some discrepancy in the date of the Latin inscription, for according to the Armenian inscription, Gaspar Agazar died on the 1st day of September, but in the Latin epitaph the date of his death is given the 10th day of August 1767.

2. This is the tomb of Madlina, the wife of Phanoos and the daughter of Agazar of New Julfa. Owing to troublous times, she left her birthplace and sojourned at Bombay in India. Leaving this transient life in the world, she departed on the 28th day of Nirhan [25th March] in the year of our Lord 1777 and in the year 161 of Azaria. Now ye who read this epitaph, ask mercy for the soul of Madlina.

3. Qambarzipeh, the daughter of Johanness, descended from the Shkhoorian family was the wife of Agazar. To you readers she tells this: Born at New Julfa, I sojourned in India. In the mouth of [illegible] my body turned into dust and my remains were placed in this tomb. I repaired to the tribunal in the spirit trusting to your prayers for the remission of my sins. In the year of our Lord 1777 and in the year 162 of Azaria.

4. In this tomb lies interred the body of a pious person, Joseph the son of Agazar of the Gaspar family. An Armenian by nationality and a native of New Julfa. He was a believer in Christ and belonged to the orthodox Church of Armenia. He departed this transitory life on Thursday, the 27th day of Nakha [27th July] in the year of our Lord 1786, in this island which is called Bombay. Aged 47 years.

There is also an inscription in English, as under :—

This is the grave of Joseph Lazar,
Armenian, July 26, 1786.

5. In this tomb lies interred the body of a highly praiseworthy lady whose name was Hripsimah. She was the daughter of Gaspar of the Jrookentz family and the wife of Joseph Michael, the son of Agazar. She was an Armenian by nationality and a native of Julfa, being a descendant of the family of Budzeantz. She departed from this world to the Lord on Sunday, the 19th day of March, 1815, in her seventeenth year. Oh ye who meet at this tomb, pray for the soul of the deceased.

(Inscriptions Nos. 2-5 are in metrical verse in the original Armenian).

In Dr. J. Gerson da Cunhas' *Origin of Bombay,* published in 1900, we find the following account of the Armenians in Bombay :—

"The other class of merchants who were treated with remarkable civility and friendship in Bombay by the Government, were the Armenians, who in 1676 in an affair relating to the ship *S. Francisco* were afforded all the assistance they could desire.

These early Armenians, whose names official documents happily record, were Khoja Karakuz, Khoja Minaz and Khoja Delaune, and their number increased considerably within a short time. They resided mostly within the Fort enclosure where they have left the legacy of their name to the Armenian Lane. They dwindled down to a few families about the beginning of the present century. About fifty years since most of these scattered families were living at Byculla, their great Indian centre being then Calcutta.

More than a century ago, they had built a church, known as the Armenian church which was subject to the Patriarchate of Mesopotamia.* The church is still

* Dr. da Cunha is wrong, as the Armenian churches in India and the East owe their allegiance to the Catholicos of all the Armenians, who is the supreme head of the orthodox Church of Armenia, and

standing in Medows Street. It was built by Yakub Petrus when in affluent circumstances. Later on, when struggling with monetary difficulties, he sought to recover and convert it into a cotton screw. He naturally failed in his solicitation for assistance to the law, as the purpose to which the Armenian church was to be applied was both express and declared. The church is to the east of the Roman Catholic chapel of our Lady of Mount Carmel.* It is small and compact with a parsonage adjoining. A priest or a deacon or two are attached to it. At the time the Armenian community in Bombay was large and flourishing, the church was deemed to be wealthy. It is rich even now in the number of epitaphs in Armenian which it contains, and which adorn its floor making quite a unique pavement, a mosaic of inscriptions".†

---

resides at the ancient historic monastery of Etchimadzin, which was founded in the year 301 of the Christian era by St. Gregory the Illuminator who illuminated the dark land of heathen Armenia with the refulgent light of the holy Gospels and became the apostle of Armenia.

* This old Church in the Fort, is no more in existence, as it was sold by the Roman Catholics some thirty years ago and with the proceeds a much larger church was erected by them in Colaba Causeway. There was the grave of a Roman Catholic Armenian *inside* the old Chuch, with an inscription, in ancient Armenian, on a grey marble tombstone, of which the following is a translation :—

"This is the tomb of Johanness, the son of Catchick of the Qaramean family of Julfa, who departed from this world on the 23rd May, 1809, at Bombay, aged 84 years."

There was also an inscription in Portuguese, as follows :—

D.O.M.

O amor filial pozesta memoria de Joao da Cruz Armenio Catholico, falecido aos 23 do mez a Mayo 1809. R. I. P.

His widow, Catherine, who died at Bombay on the 15th August, 1836, aged 75 years, was buried in the Armenian churchyard of that city as she was not a Roman Catholic but belonged to the orthodox Church of Armenia.

† The old Armenian cemetery, situated in Kelewadi Lane, Girgaum, which was consecrated in 1812, and where many Bombay Armenians lie buried, was closed down in 1870 by the order of Government and a new one was started at Sewri.

In the old English cemetery in Bombay there are the graves of four Armenians who died between the years 1809 and 1812, before the

Mr. S. M. Edwardes of the Indian Civil Service, author of the *Rise of Bombay*, writes of the early Armenians in that city, as follows :—

> "The Armenians are wearing the Persian dress, and dyeing their hair and whiskers with henna. Armenian ladies pass their time either engaged in the care of their families, or in receiving and paying visits, drinking coffee or sherbet, embroidering and making delicious confections of *Hulwah* and various sweetmeats. They have very considerable influence in their families, understand business admirably, and are commonly entrusted with the full control of their property. Their condition is easy and agreeable, little restraint being placed upon their conduct, a slight degree of personal seclusion being considered honorable and dignified".

There must have been a fairly large number of Armenians in Bombay during the 18th century, for we find that in 1813, there were 105 Armenians living there, but their numbers dwindled down gradually, for when we first visited Bombay in January 1889, there were hardly thirty Armenians left in that prosperous city.

The only Armenian who rose to eminence, during the second half of the last century, was the late Dr. J. M. Joseph, M.D., who rose to the rank of Deputy Surgeon-General. He was the first Armenian who joined the Indian Medical Service as far back as 1852. After a useful career he retired on the 1st July 1885, but did not live long to enjoy his pension. The *Daily Post* of Bangalore had the following sketch of his career in its issue of 3rd July of that year :—

"Last Tuesday's *Fort St. George Gazette* notifies that Deputy Surgeon-General J. M. Joseph, M.D., has been permitted to retire from the public service from the 1st instant, on a well-earned pension of £950 per annum, supplemented by an annuity of £400, after having completed a very creditable career extending over well nigh thirty-three years of varied

---

cemetery at Girgaum was opened in 1812. An Armenian bishop, from Julfa, named Mackertich, who died in Bombay, on the 9th October, 1809, is buried in the old English cemetery.

professional experiences and good honest work. Looking back on his past official life, the worthy doctor has good reason to be proud of his career ; and the credit he has earned in the Department which he has served so well, as well as the general popularity he has secured outside the arena of his official duties, will lend additional lustre to the distinction he has so worthily attained.

"Dr. Joseph received his preliminary education under private tuition [at Bombay], and his entire medical training at St. George's Hospital, London, and in the St. George's School of Medicine adjoining that well-known institution. During the whole of his pupilage he was under the personal tuition of Dr. Samuel Armstrong Lane, the distinguished Anatomist and Surgeon of London, and the author of several scientific works. His earlier professional labours began at the Theatre of Anatomy attached to St. George's Hospital, where he for some time discharged the duties of a Demonstrator of Anatomy. In 1846 he obtained his diploma as a member of the Royal College of Surgeons, London, and six years later secured the degrees of Doctor of Medicine and Master of Surgery of the University of Glasgow. In 1858 he was elected a Fellow of the Royal College of Physicians of Edinburgh, and two years later became a Member of the Royal College of Physicians of London. The honorary degree of LL.D. was conferred upon him by his University in 1866, and in the same year he was, after a regular course of study, called to the Bar by the Honourable Society of the Inner Temple.

"His public career in connection with the Indian Medical Service began in November 1852, when he was nominated as an Assistant Surgeon on the Madras Establishment by Sir James Weir Hogg, the then Chairman of the E. I. Company's Board of Directors. Landing at Madras on the 1st of January 1853, Dr. Joseph was attached to the General Hospital there, but was soon after directed to do duty with the left wing of H. M.'s 94th Regiment, then stationed at the Bangalore Fort. Hundreds of his former patients here and elsewhere will bear grateful testimony to the fact that his genial manners and thorough-going character, no less than his professional skill, have earned for him a very large share of popularity and lasting esteem from every class of society with which he was come into contact during his long, active, and eminently useful public career".

The grades of his official career were as follows:—Assistant Surgeon, 20th November 1852; Surgeon, 14th December 1864; Surgeon-Major, 20th November 1872; Brigade-Surgeon, 27th November 1870; Deputy Surgeon-General, temporary rank, 25th April 1879; and Deputy Surgeon-General, permanent rank, 16th May 1880.

Descended from an old Armenian family of Surat, Dr. Joseph was born at Bombay* on 16th April 1826, and died at Madras in his sixty-first year, leaving a widow and five daughters. On the monument which covers his grave in the Armenian cemetery at Madras the following lines are inscribed:—

> "Sacred to the memory of Joseph Marcus Joseph, M.D., Surgeon-General (Retired), Madras Army, who died at Madras 17th October 1886, aged 60 years and 6 months. This monument is erected in loving remembrance by his sorrowing widow".

Some relations of Dr. Joseph are still to be found in Bombay, Mr. Henry Michael, the senior warden of the Armenian church, referred to on page 274, being one.

The late Mr. Arratoon Apcar, the founder of the well-known firm of Apcar & Co., merchants, shipowners and colliery proprietors of Calcutta, started business in Bombay in the beginning of the 1st century. In 1813, he married a Miss Catherine Thomas, an Armenian lady, born at Surat in 1800, who died in 1850, and is buried in the Armenian churchyard of Calcutta. Mr. Arratoon Apcar who traded with China and Manilla, transferred his business from Bombay to Calcutta towards the end of 1830.

---

* Where his father, Marcus Joseph, was a successful Armenian merchant during the first half of the 19th century. His elder brother also carried on, about the middle of the last century a Chemist's business there.

When the Armenian Philanthropic Academy, now known as the Armenian College, was founded in Calcutta in 1821, amongst the donations received in aid of that national institution, was one from Mrs. Catherine J. David of Bombay, who left a legacy of Rs. 18,500.

The last person to be buried in the Armenian churchyard at Bombay, as a mark of deep respect, was Mr. William Michael, the warden of the Bombay church for several years, who died on the 23rd July, 1886, aged 55 years.

He left three sons and two daughters. The eldest son, the late Mr. Charles Michael, was the secretary of the Bombay Chamber of Commerce for many years, highly respected by the commercial community of that great city. Like his father, he was, for several years, the warden of the Bombay Armenian church.

The second son of Mr. William Michael, named William, was for a number of years the popular secretary to the Bombay Corporation.

The youngest son, Mr. Henry Michael, a retired official of the G. I. P. Railway, is the senior warden of the Bombay Armenian church, referred to already. Their mother, the late Mrs. Susan Michael, (*née* Joseph) was a cousin of Dr. J. M. Joseph, M.D., the Deputy Surgeon-General.

ARMENIANS AT CHINSURAH

CHAPTER XXVI

ARMENIANS AT CHINSURAH.

THE SECOND OLDEST CHRISTIAN CHURCH IN BENGAL

The glamour of the East and the rich and highly lucrative trade of India in spices, precious stones, muslins, calico, indigo, and other equally valuable articles, which the country produced, attracted the principal maritime nations of Europe to come and exploit the wealth of the country from the 15th century onwards.

That heaven-born, but unfortunate Spanish mariner, Colombus, whilst trying to reach India, discovered America instead.

The Portuguese under the famous Vasco de Gama were more fortunate, as they succeeded to reach India in 1498. They were followed by the English, the Dutch, the French and the Danes who formed Settlements in India from the early part of the 17th Century.

The banks of the river Hughli in Bengal seem, however, to have had a special attraction for the early European traders, for we find important settlements were formed and trading Factories planted by the Portuguese at Bandel, the English at Calcutta, the French at Chandernagore, the Danes at Serampore and the Dutch at Chinsurah. The latter who had traded with India prior to the advent of the English traders and were their powerful rivals in those days, showing as much energy in war as in trade, had formed, in 1625, an important commercial Settlement at Chinsurah, a suburb two miles to the south of the old city of Hooghly. In 1767, the Dutch Governor, G. Vernet, built a church at Chinsurah entirely out of his own means. Prior to the erection of the church, another Dutch Governor, Schiterman, had already erected the Steeple in 1744. This old Dutch church is now being used by the English. It contains some interesting relics of the Dutch occupation in the shape of curious escutcheons of the early Dutch

Governors and funeral hatchments which are hung round the church.

Chinsurah was ceded to the English by the Dutch in 1826, in exchange for Sumatra, after they had held it for two centuries (1625-1826).

The Armenians who were great traders and influential politicians in the halcyon days of Mogul supremacy had attached themselves to their conferers in trade, the Dutch, at Chinsurah, in the year 1645, under the leadership of the famous Margar family.

The Armenian church at Chinsurah, which is the second *oldest* Christian church in Bengal was erected by the pious and opulent Margar family. In 1695, Khojah Johanness, the son of Khojah Margar, laid the foundation of the church which was completed, in 1697, by his brother Joseph, and dedicated to St. John the Baptist, in memory of his deceased brother. Khojah Johanness Margar died suddenly, on the 27th day of November, 1697, and his mortal remains were interred inside the church he had built. His revered grave can be seen to this day with a long inscription in classical Armenian verse, of which the following is a translation :—

"This is the tomb wherein lies interred the famous *qarib* (stranger) Khojah Johanness, the son of Margar of Julfa, in the city of Shosh. He was an eminent merchant, honoured by Kings and respected by Governors. He was handsome and amiable and had travelled south, north, west and all the four quarters of the world. He died suddenly, on the 27th day of November, 1697, in the eastern part of the country, at the city of Hooghly, and delivered his soul into the hands of the angel and rested here in a strange land in solicitude of a home.

The end of the world shall come, the cross of the East will dawn, the trumpet of Gabriel will be blown suddenly in the middle of the night, the judgment seat will be set up that the bridegroom may come and sit thereon and say, "come ye the blessed of the heavenly Father". And may He deem him [Khojah Johanness Margar] equally worthy, like the five wise virgins, to be in readiness to enter the sacred pavilion which only the righteous that are on the right, can inherit.

O ye who may come across this tomb pray for him earnestly and may God have mercy on your parents and on me, Reverend Gregory, who am a native of Erivan. Here endeth the inscription." Below the long Armenian inscription, there are four lines in Portuguese, as follows :—

AQVI IAZ JOAO
MARCOS AR
MENIO DA NAS
SAO ANO.
1697.

It can be translated thus :—

"Here lies Joao Marcos, an Armenian by nationality, 1697." There is however a glaring mistake in the Portuguese inscription, as the surname should have been "Margar" instead of "Marcos", which is also an Armenian name.

In all likelihood, the inscription was composed by Rev. Gregory, hence his craving for the Lord's mercy.

Khojah Johanness Margar had an elder brother, Khojah Joseph by name, who died in 1704, at Julfa (Isfahan) his birthplace, and according to the quaint inscription on his tombstone, he was as famous and illustrious as his younger brother, Khojah Johanness, having traded in India, in partnership with his said brother, for a period of fifty years. The interesting inscription further tells us that he (Khojah Joseph Margar) had been an eminent merchant in India, the favourite of Kings, the friend of noblemen and grandees, the captain of his own ship and the benefactor of many people. From his will, of which we have a copy in our possession, it appears that the two brothers entered into partnership at Hyderabad (Deccan) in 1666, and started business at Mylapore, with a joint capital of Rs. 27,550 only, the major portion of which (Rs. 18,550) was subscribed by Khojah Joseph Margar himself, whilst the younger brother, who lies buried at Chinsurah, laid out Rs. 9000/- only, as his share in the business.

After the sudden death of Khojah Johanness Margar in November, 1697, when the partnership ceased automatically and the accounts were finally made up, it was found that a nett profit of two million rupees had been made in 30 years on a capital of Rs. 27,550. Any wonder then that the two honest and industrious brothers were the favourites of Kings and of Governors all over India.

From the will of Khojah Joseph Margar, alluded to above, it appears that a sum of Rs. 20,000 was expended by his younger brother, Khojah Johanness, in building the Armenian church at Chinsurah* in 1695.

These two eminent Armenian merchants were the sons of the illustrious merchant-diplomat, Margar Avag Sheenentz, known as Marcara Avanchinz† who played an important part in the inauguration of the "French East India Company" in India in the second-half of the 17th century.

It is sad to reflect that the church built by the Margar family in 1695, is the only landmark left to-day of the once flourishing Armenian colony of Chinsurah. The place was deserted by the Armenians when it lost its commercial importance and they transferred their trade to Calcutta about the middle of the last century.

It is gratifying however to note that owing to its proximity to Calcutta, the historic church at Chinsurah is not likely to share the sad fate of the Armenian church at Saidabad (built in 1758) which is practically deserted and on the verge of ruin, for on the festival of St. John the Baptist, the patron saint of the church, which falls on the 14th day of January, divine service is held there annually, with celebration of the Holy Mass, and it is attended largely by the Armenian community

---

* When the church was built, it had no steeple. The present handsome spire, which serves as a belfry, was erected in 1822, through the munificence of Mrs. Sophia Bagram, a pious and a wealthy Armenian lady of Calcutta, in memory of her husband, Simon Phanoos Bagram. The foundation stone was laid by Daniel Anthony Overbeck the Dutch Governor of Chinsurah who died in 1840, and was buried in the Dutch cemetery at Chinsurah. On his tombstone there is an inscription in English as follows :—

> "Sacred to the memory of Daniel Anthony Overbeck, last Dutch Governor of Chinsurah, obiit 25 September 1840, aged 76 years. The memory of the just is blessed : and he shall be as the light of the morning when the sun riseth".

† For a fuller account of Marcara Avanchinz (Margar Avag Sheenentz) see pp. 318—320.

of Calcutta who make vows in that old church with the same zeal, devotion and religious fervour as the Roman Catholics at the Bandel church on the festival of the Novena which falls in November when hundreds of devout Catholics go there on a pilgrimage from Calcutta and elsewhere in Bengal.

The Roman Catholic church and convent at Bandel, a small village near Hooghly, is the *oldest* place of Christian worship in Bengal. The original church and the priory was built by the Augustinian Friars in 1599, but it was burnt down and entirely destroyed by the order of the Mogul Emperor Shah Jehan (who built the world-famed Taj at Agra) on the 24th day of June 1632.

The present church and the convent was re-built in 1640, by Joam Gomes de Soto, when the key-stone of the original church, with the date 1599, was placed over the eastern gate of the present church where it can be seen to this day. For a complete and an exhaustive account of the Roman Catholic church at Bandel, see the learned article by the late Father H. Hosten, S.J., in the pages of "Bengal—Past and Present" —the Journal of the Calcutta Historical Society—for January-March 1915, under the caption "A Week at the Bandel Convent, Hugli".

A few words about the graves in the church may be of interest to our readers. Although Armenians lived and died, in fairly large numbers, at Chinsurah, between the years 1695 and 1868, yet there are not more than a hundred graves, with tombstones, in the church, twenty eight of them being *inside* the sacred edifice. One of these old graves, is on the floor of the altar, with a small marble tombstone, bearing a short inscription, in Armenian, which can be translated thus:—

> "This is the tomb of Petrus, the son of Catchick, who died in the year 119, on the 5th Nakha."

that is on the 5th day of July, 1734.

There is at the foot of the altar a large brass tablet with a long inscription, in ancient Armenian verse from which it appears that the tablet was placed there as the entrance to the tomb of Petrus Catchick, for it is called *tapanadoor*, which means the door of a tomb. According to the inscription, the tablet was placed there by Mirzajan, the brother of the deceased, to commemorate the extensions which had been made to the church by Petrus Catchick, who had been an eminent merchant for twenty years, was very learned and incomparable, (khist gitoon yev an-nman) who departed this life, at the age of thirty eight years, on the 5th day of July, 1734, leaving his weeping and disconsolate brother, Mirzajan, to mourn his loss. There is an interesting grave, in the churchyard, where several old graves are still to be seen, in a fair state of preservation, with inscriptions which are quite legible, despite their exposure to the destructive elements for two centuries and more. We have seen, on page 148, that the body of an old Armenian priest, who died at Narwar, Gwalior State, on the 13th May, 1750, was disinterred after six months and brought down to Bengal to be interred in the Armenian church at Chinsurah.

In August 1894 when we were copying the old inscriptions in the Chinsurah Armenian church, for the *List of Tombs and Monuments in Bengal,* possessing historical and archæological interest which was being compiled by the late Professor C. R. Wilson, for the Bengal Government, we came across the grave and the last resting place of the priest from Narwar. The translation of the inscription on that grave, with several others from the same churchyard, can be seen in Professor Wilson's List, referred to above.

It was as under :—

> "This is the tomb of Rev. Arakiel, the son of Pogose of Julfa who rested in Christ in India. The 24th day of Aram [20th January], 1751."

As we have seen, he died and was buried at Narwar on the 13th May, 1750, but was buried a second time at Chinsurah on the 20th January, 1751. According to the inscription on his first grave at Narwar, his body was disinterred six months after the first burial, which must have been about the middle of November 1750, and in those days of slow transport, it must have taken two months to bring down the body all the way from Narwar to Chinsurah for its final burial. The slab covering his mortal remains is broken to pieces, being of sandstone which is soft and fragile and does not stand the ravages of the elements for any length of time, especially in a damp place like Bengal.

There is another interesting grave in the churchyard. It is the last resting place of David Freedone Melik Beglar, "the son of the *last* independent Prince of Karabagh in the province of Tiflis, Caucasus." We have referred to this descendant of one of the Armenian Meliks of Karabagh in Armenia, on page 178, who died at Chinsurah, on the 22nd September, 1884, at the patriarchal age of 89 years.

His eldest son, Joseph Beglar, the Executive Engineer and Archæological Surveyor in the Bengal Public Works Department, who died on the 24th April, 1907, aged 62 years, is also buried there.

The late Joseph David Freedone Melik Beglar, was born at Dacca in 1845. He received his primary education in Dacca and when his father went with his family to reside at Chinsurah, young Beglar attended the Hooghly College and then went to the Sibpur Engineering College, where he duly qualified himself as a Civil Engineer with distinction. His knowledge of Indian Archæology did not escape the attention of the Bengal Government, and he was placed on special duty to superintend the Archæological excavations at the far-famed Buddhist temple at Buddha-Gya, which, as everybody knows, was reclaimed from oblivion. He had the happiness of enjoying the friendship and the tuition of that eminent archæologist, the late talented General Sir Alexander Cunningham, Director-General, Archæological Survey of India.

He superintended the construction of the "Jubilee Bridge", near Naihati, which was opened in 1887, the year of the late queen Victoria's golden Jubilee, hence its name.

As an Archæologist of vast experience, he took part in the excavations at Gaur, Sarsaram and Malda. After his retirement from Government service, he resided at Chogdah, where he had built a beautiful house on a large plot of ground. He was of a literary turn of mind and a writer of merit.* In August

* Some years before his death, the late Mr. Beglar, who was always in his element when there was a talk about books and authors, told the writer of these lines that he once walked into the shop of a well-known

1892, he started publishing a monthly journal, in English, called ARA, devoted to Armenian politics, history and literature. All the articles, with a few exceptions, were written by the versatile editor. He wrote forcibly and with a patriotic zeal and fervour for his ill-fated fatherland and his oppressed nation groaning under Turkish tyranny, for he had inherited, in no small measure, the independent spirit and the fervid patriotism of his martial ancestors, the princes (Meliks) of the mountainous province of Karabagh in Armenia.

For want of sufficient support, which is the bane of Armenian journalism throughout the world, the publication of the only journal in India devoted to Armenian interests, came to an end early in 1895, the last number, which contained a full account of the indignation meeting which was held by the Armenian community of Calcutta at the old Theatre Royal, on the 21st January, 1895, to protest against the Turkish atrocities in Armenia, was published in February, 1895. Here we cannot but denounce the apathy and the callousness of the Armenians in Calcutta and elsewhere in India, for allowing that highly interesting and constructive publication to die an untimely death, considering that the subscription of the journal, replete with valuable and first-hand information relating to the history, literature and culture of the ancient race, was not more than three miserable rupees. During the last decade of the 19th century, there were a number of wealthy Armenians in Calcutta,—merchants, shipowners, jewellers, landowners, colliery proprietors and owners of race-horses—but none of them came forward to help the struggling editor-publisher of the *Ara,* in his self-imposed task, with the result that the national literature suffered a heavy loss.

In the history of oppressed and downtrodden nations we find that it is always the poor author and the struggling and starving editor who work zealously and with devotion for the regeneration of their race, since the rich have no time to waste

---

firm of publishers and booksellers in Calcutta and asked the assistant for the latest works on Archæology and Civil Engineering. When the book was produced, Mr. Beglar returned it to the assistant telling him that he wanted a later work, as he was the author of the book which was shown to him.

over national affairs, being engrossed in money-making and in pulling down their barns and building greater ones, like the man in the Parable, who would, after extending his barns, have told his soul "thou hast much goods laid up for many years; take thine ease, eat, drink and be merry, but God said unto him, thou fool! this night thy soul shall be required of thee; then whose shall those things be which thou hast provided. So is he that layeth up treasure for himself." (Luke XII, 16-21).

It may be mentioned, *en passant,* that during the past hundred years, when the Armenian merchants in India, Burma Java and elsewhere in the Dispersion, notably in the Caucasus, were piling up huge fortunes, which do not eixst to-day, a noble band of authors and journalists were labouring incessantly, and with a zeal and devotion that knew no bounds, for the regeneration and the emancipation of the race in the ill-fated Fatherland groaning under misrule, for as our Armenian readers know, what were Thaliadian, Abovian, Alishan, Nalbandian, Ardzrouni, Raffi, Portoukalian, Tcheraz and Arpiarian, but struggling authors and starving journalists, who by their pen, that "mightly instrument of little men", as Byron calls it, fought desparately, but successfully, against ignorance, illiteracy, superstition and bigotry in which the ancient race was groping after centuries of bondage and persecution.

But we have digressed.

There has been in the olden days an Armenian cemetery at Chinsurah in a place, not very far from the church, called Suripara. The only tombstone in that cemetery which is broken into three pieces, is to the memory of "Thang Khathoon, the adopted daughter of Gaspar, who died in 1747". All the other tombstones have disappeared long ago, washermen and others having removed them for their own use.

From the Register of Marriages, Baptisms and Burials of the Chinsurah church, preserved in the "Record Office" of the Calcutta Armenian church, we find that between the years 1826 and 1868, sixteen marriages were solemnized in the church at Chinsurah, the late Mr. Joseph Beglar being the last Armenian to get married there on the 5th August, 1868. Between the years 1817 and 1867, seventy two children were baptised in that church and between the years 1817 and 1881, fifty seven burials took place there. We find that thirteen priests officiated in that church during the period covered by the Register, which, it may be noted, is the only record left of that ancient place of worship, which, as we have seen, has been in existence since 1695.

Inside the Roman Catholic church built in 1740, now in ruins, in the immediate vicinity of the Armenian church, there is the grave of a Roman Catholic Armenian, with a marble tombstone, bearing inscriptions in Armenian and English. The latter is as follows :—

> "Sacred to the memory of Sarhad Leon Esq., who departed this life on the 4th September 1834. Aged 70 years".

In the Armenian inscription he is called "Agah Sarhad Leon".

His wife, Elizabeth, who belonged to the orthodox holy Church of Armenia, died in Calcutta on the 26th December 1852, aged 53 years, and was buried in the Armenian churchyard where her grave can be seen to this day. Agah Leon Sarhad's grave in the Roman Catholic church at Chinsuarh, which is on the verge of collapse, will soon disappear, but the grave of his widow in the Armenian church of Nazareth will remain undisturbed as long as Calcutta, the second city in the wide British Empire, exists, and it will exist for ages to be.

ARMENIANS

AT

CHANDERNAGORE

CHAPTER XXVII.

Armenians at Chandernagore*

Historic Chandernagore over which the French flag has flown since 1688, has witnessed the meteoric rise and fall of the Mohammedan power in Bengal, consequent on the decadence of the once-powerful Mogul Empire in India during the first-half of the 18th century.

It has seen the inauguration of British rule in Bengal after the famous and epoch-making battle of Plassey in 1757.

It has seen the gradual disappearance of the rival European traders—the Dutch and the Danes—the former from Chinsurah and the latter from Serampore.

It has seen the hordes of the Mahratta freebooters, under Raghowji Bhonsla, penetrating into Bengal from the West and threatening the safety of Calcutta, the "Mahratta Ditch" being a relic of their awe inspiring depredations.

It has sphinx-like, witnessed the formidable armies of Nawab (Viceroy) Murshid Kuli Khan (the founder of Murshidabad), Nawab Ali Verdi Khan, Nawab Suraj-ud-dowlah (the author of the Calcutta "Black Hole" tragedy) and Nawab Mir Kasim† pass and repass by its gates, and despite the memorable siege and sack of the place by the British under Colonel Clive and Admiral Watson in 1757, it is still standing as a glorius monument to the colonial and

---

*A paper read by the present writer before the "Chandernagore Historical Society" at *La Residence* (Government House) Chandernagore, under the Presidency of His Excellency Monsieur Valentin Champion, the *Administrateur* of the French Settlement, on Saturday, the 9th day of May, 1931. The Paper was published in the *Bengal: Past and Present,* the journal of the "Calcutta Historical Society" for July-September, 1931. It was afterwards translated into French and Armenian.

†Mir Kasim's Commander-in-Chief was an Armenian, Khojah Gregory Arathoon, better known by his orientalized name of Gorgin Khan. He commanded the Nawab's army from 1760-1763 when he was treacherously murdered by an unknown assassin. For a fuller account of this great Armenian soldier see the chapter on "Armenians at Monghyr."

commercial enterprise of France, though shorn of its pristine glory as an important centre and *entrepot* of French commerce in Bengal. And despite its many vicissitudes, Chandernagore stands to-day as a valuable landmark in the romantic annals of the Colonial Empire of France, and may it continue to exist, for ages to be, as a priceless relic of the French power in India—a silent but an eloquent monument to the genius of the great and immortal Joseph Francois Dupleix.

As the historian of the Armenians in India, I am deeply interested to see that the *oldest* tombstone in the Chandernagore cemetery covers the mortal remains of a countryman of mine, who died there in 1753. He was, according to the Armenian epitaph, the son of a military officer, (a commander) Lazar by name. I have not yet been able to trace the history of this soldier, but I am inclined to think that he was an officer in the military service of Nawab Ali Verdi Khan of Bengal, who, it may be mentioned, was very favourably disposed towards the Armenians residing in Bengal, one of his most intimate friends being an Armenian merchant of Murshidabad. This Armenian mechant-prince, was, by reason of his great piety, a *persona grata* with the Begum of the Nawab (Ali Verdi Khan) who used to address him by the endearing name of "brother". His name was Khojah Petrus Nicholas and he was the son of an Armenian priest.

There is still an *older* tombstone in the church, which at one time covered the grave of an aristocratic Armenian lady, Catherine Ovsky Erapiette (Hyrapiet) who had married M. Francis Daguin de la Blanchetiere, one of the oldest Governors, on the 4th June 1696. She died aged 49 years, on the 3rd February, 1729, having borne 11 children.

The inscription on her tombstone is as follows :—

> Cy git Catherine Ovsky, epouse de Mr. F. Dagvin de la Blanchetiere Directeur-General pour la Campagnie de France Royaume de Bengalle. Decedee le III Fevrier MDCCXXIX, agee de XLIX Ans. Priez Dieu pour elle.

It can be translated thus :—

> Here reposes Catherine Ovsky, spouse of Mr. F. Daguin de la Blanchetiere, Director-General for the

French Company in the Kingdom of Bengal. Died on the 3rd February, 1729, aged 49 years. Pray to God for her.

Of the eleven children, eight died in the lifetime of their parents. The death of the wife was too heavy a blow to the unfortunate Blanchetiere who died shortly after, and on his tombstone the following pathetic inscription, in Latin, can be seen to this day.

Juxta Dvlces Natos Vi Natas, II Spousam Quoqve Chariss Vir Vere Pivs Jacet Hic Franciscvs Dagvin De la Blanchetiere Pro. Gall. Ind. Societate in Reg. Beng. Director C. Nec Non et Cvriæ Praeses Obiit An R. S. MDCCXXIX die Augusti XXV. Ætatis Suae An 63 M.I. D 7. Sequiescat in pace.

It can be translated thus :—

Near his six sweet boys and two girls, and also his very dear wife, here lies that very pious man Francis Daguin de la Blanchetiere, on behalf of the French Indian Society, Director in the Kingdom of Bengal, and also President of the Court. He died in the year of his Redeemer 1729, on the 25th day of August, aged 63 years one month and seven days. May he rest in peace!

Joseph, the son of Catherine and Francis Daguin de la Blanchetiere, married Magdeleine Ycard, daughter of Matheu Ycard and Esperance, *nee* Lucas.

This is however not the *first* instance of an Armenian lady marrying a Frenchman of noble birth in India. In the days of Akbar the Great, an Armenian lady, Júliana by name, who was the lady doctor in the royal seraglio, was given by Akbar in marriage to Prince Jean Philipe de Bourbon of Navarre and of the royal house of France, when that royal adventurer appeared at the Court of Akbar, the Marcus Aurelius of India.

There is yet a third and an interesting tombstone in the church over the grave of an Armenian priest, Padre Joaó Armenio, who died at Chinsurah on the 1st February 1779, and his body was brought and buried at Chandernagore on the same day.

The following is a translation, by my learned friend Father H. Hosten, S.J. of St. Joseph's College, Darjeeling, of the entry of the burial of Father Joaó Armenio, in the church Registers :

> "On the first of February of the year one thousand, seven hundred and seventy nine, I, Priest Curé undersigned, certify having buried in the Chapel of the Cemetery of this parochial Church of Saint Louis of Chandernagore, the body of the late R. R. F. F. Dom Jouam, Armenian Priest of the Order of St. Anthony the first Hermit, Missionary Apostolic to the Armenians in India, "habitué" of this Church, commendable for his piety and charity and the great services he has rendered to the parish, aged about 77 or 78 years, who died to-day at Chinchurat [Chinsurah], whence he was brought and presented at the door of this Church by the Rev. Fr. Joseph of the Eleven Thousand Virgins, Prior and Curé of the Bandel and of Chinchurat. Assisted at his burial : the Rev. Fr. Abraham, Armenian Priest; the Rev. Fr. Jean Gualbert, Superior of the Hospice of the Italian Capuchins of this colony; Messieurs Nicolas, Labat, Bedon; the Rev. Fr. Ferdinand, Capuchin Vicaire of this parish, all of whom have signed the present deed with us on the aforesaid day and year.
>
> [Sd.] Fr. Joseph Francois,
> Capucin, Missionary Apostolic,
> Superior and Curé."

The said Padre Joaó Armenio, or the Armenian, celebrated several marriages at Chinsurah in 1771 and 1772 and baptized at Bandel on the 7th May and the 22nd October, 1776.

Father Abraham, who assisted at the burial of father Joaó Armenio, was also an Armenian. His full name was Abraham de S. Lourenco. He like Father Joaó, belonged to the Armenian monastic Order of St. Anthony, known as the "Antonians." He officiated for some time in the Murghihatta

Roman Catholic Cathedral at Calcutta and when he died on the 20th September 1782, he was buried, as a mark of great respect inside the old Murgihatta Church, but his grave cannot be traced now.

The Armenian inscription on the *oldest* tombstone in the Chandernagore cemetery, was first published in an Armenian periodical in Calcutta, known as the "Azgasare Araratean" (the Patriot of Ararat). The learned editor of the journal, Mesrovb David Thaliadian, who kept a private school in Calcutta for the education of Armenian boys and girls, took his pupils in February 1852, on a river excursion to Hooghly and back. At Chandernagore they were entertained by an Armenian resident of the place who afterwards conducted them, amongst other places of interest, to the cemetery, where they were shown the grave of an Armenian who had died there in 1753. And this is how, the Editor-educationist, writing in ancient Armenian, describes the cemetery as it was then :

"At Chandernagore, which belongs to the Red Republic of France or to the autocratic Empire of Louis Napoleon, a visit was paid to Mr. Arratoon Hyrapiet Arratoon, and under his guidance, to the cemetery of the place, where everybody, with every name, rested, without care and commotion, waiting for the advent of the Saviour to call them all to him by his grace and mercy.

Here amidst many beautiful and ornamental tombs, was to be seen an abandoned tombstone of black granite, with an inscription in Armenian, the following being a copy:

> "This is the tomb of Mathevos (Mathew) the son of Lazar, the Commander. Died on the 8th May, 1753".

In this connection I may mention that the friendly relations of the Armenians with the French in India date back to the year 1667, when on the inauguration of the "French East India Company," a well-appointed fleet was sent out to India, at the instance of M. Colbert, the famous minister of Louis XIV of France, known as *Le Grande Monarque*.

For an account of this important expedition, see *Histoire des Indes Orientales*, tom. III. p. 146, as also *Histoire de la Campagnie des Indes*, pp. 63-64.

It is stated in Dr. Nolan's "History of the British Empire in India and the East," that in the year 1667, it was resolved that some ships should proceed from Madagascar to the Indies with instructions for fixing an introductory establishment there.

The two gentlemen selected to superintend this expedition, were judiciously chosen, and possessed the requisite experience and judgment. The first of these was M. Caron, who had spent several years in the Dutch service and had risen to be the president of the Factory in Japan where he had suffered severely and having sought for an indemnification from the authority of the States-General in vain, retired in disgust and returned to France, at a crisis too, when such a man was badly wanted. He was soon introduced to the Minister, treated with distinction and favour and consulted on every subject in which the interests of the new Company were involved.

The other was M. Marcar Avanchinz, an Armenian, and a native of Ispahan, the capital of Persia, a man of high birth and great influence at home from whom the Company expected great things.

The Squadron arrived at Cochin on the 24th day of December 1667 and was courteously received by the Dutch governor, and thence proceeded to Surat* where it had been decided the *first* French Factory was to be erected.

In 1669, Marcar Avanchinz was despatched by the French as an envoy to the court of Abdulla Kutub Shah, the king of Golconda, where he had several powerful and personal friends, by whose favour and influence he expected to be able to secure for the French the privilege of trading through that kingdom, of purchasing whatever merchandise was required, of employing manufacturers and of obtaining licence to establish a Factory at Masulipatam on the Coromandel coast. This was a very delicate mission and the object difficult of acquisition.

---

*The *first* English Factory in India was opened at Surat, in 1612, by the permission of the Mogul Emperor Jahangeer, son of Akbar the Great. The Armenians, the pioneers of foreign trade in India, had established themselves at Surat long before the advent of the English, the Dutch and the French, being great favourites with the Mogul Emperors from Akbar downwards.

It was a well-known fact that the Dutch and the English, whose influence was very great at the Court of Golconda, had failed in obtaining concessions not merely so important, and that the representatives of the two nations referred to above, had instructions to use all their influence to frustrate the efforts of the French, and to crown all, Marcar Avanchinz, was scantily supplied with money, an article as indispensable to an Oriental, as to a European diplomatist.

Not disheartened by these untoward circumstances, he proceeded to Golconda where he successfully accomplished this important negotiation and on the 5th December 1669, Marcar obtained a Firman from His Majesty by which the "French East India Company" was privileged to trade to all parts of his territory, without paying any export or import duties —a favour the Dutch were never able to obtain and which the English had secured in 1665 at a very great expense.

The successful agent then proceeded to Masulipatam where he had his Firman registered. He also settled a Factory there of which he was appointed the President and in that capacity he conducted the trade of the French Company with zeal, honesty and diligence. These eminent services did not however shield the honest Armenian from envious aspersions and foul imputations. His colleague, M. Caron, had by his intrigues, ingratiated himself into the highest degree of favour with the Minister. M. Colbert, (a man of Scotch descent) from whom he obtained an order in 1671, by which he was raised to the second post in the "French East India Company's" service, with the result that all the friends of Marcar Avanchinz were removed from their employments and subjected to persecutions, although in the order there was not a single charge brought against him, not a word to incriminate him. He addressed a full and satisfactory justification of his conduct to M. Colbert, the Minister, who, after a minute and searching examination, made an impartial report to the king Louis XIV, who entirely approved of M. Marcar Avanchinz's conduct and testified to his innocence by a solemn *arret* (decree).

In a letter, dated the 15th April, 1668, from Sir Oxenden and his Council at Surat to the Court of Directors in London, they write concerning the new French Factory at Surat, as follows :—

> "The Dutch now, together with the French will be our competitours in all that wee shall enter uppon; which must certainly raise the price of commodityes. They [the Surat Factors] hope the Companyes shipps will arrive tymely and returne as soone or near the tyme for St. Laurenco [i.e., Madacascar] to winter, shall be able to gaine Europe &c. The French are fallen all to pieces amongst themselves, and little better than mutinyed against their great Directour, the Heer Charoon, the mounseers accounting it very dishonourable to be att the dispose and command of a Dutchman and an heretique (as they would have it) which hath raised their differences to that height that the Armenian* who was next in Councell to the Directour, was clapt up close prisoner, and since putt in irons and sent abroad their shipp &. The French credit is totally overthrowne in Surratt. The Dutch have but one shipp this year, come from Japan, which arrived here single. Her cargoe is the same they use to bring in the qualitye, but much short of the quantityes. Wee finde them droop in these parts, but they will soon gett upp again, now there is peace &c".

This Marcara Avanchinz is the famous Armenian merchant, Margar Avag Sheenentz, whose two sons, Johanness and Joseph Margar, were eminent merchants of Hooghly in the second-half of the 17th century. The beautiful Armenian church of St. John the Baptist, at Chinsurah, the *second* oldest†

---

* The Armenian referred to here was Marcara Avanchinz.

† The *oldest* Christian church in Bengal built by the Augustinian Friars in 1599, at Bandel, a village near Chinsurah, was destroyed by the order of the Mogul Emperor Shah Jahan, in 1632, but it was rebulit by Joan Gomas o Soto in 1640 when the keystone of the original church, with the date 1599, was placed over the eastern gate of the present church where it can be seen to this day. The old keystone is misleading however as many visitors go away with the erroneous idea that the *present* Bandel church was erected in 1599, whereas it dates its existence from the year 1640.

Christian church in Bengal, was built by these brothers in 1695. Johanness Margar died suddenly on the 27th November 1697 and was buried in the church which they had erected at Chinsurah where his grave, with a long inscription, in classical Armenian verse, can be seen to this day. The younger brother Joseph, died in 1704, at his birthplace, Julfa, the Armenian suburb of Ispahan, and on his tombstone it is recorded that he had been a very successful merchant in India for a period of 50 years and that he had been the captain of his own ships.

And as I am standing on French soil to-day, I must, before I sit down, express my deep gratitude to the noble and chivalrious French nation for their great hospitality by giving shelter to thousands, nay tens of thousands, of helpless and hapless Armenian refugees and emigrants from Turkey and Anatolia who have found a safe asylum in France and in the French mandatory Arab State of Syria, where they enjoy freedom of thought and speech and the free and undisturbed exercise of their own religion, under the ægis of the tri-colour—that glorious and inspiring emblem of liberty, fraternity, equality, chivalry and culture.

La Belle France has been the refuge and the safe haven of oppressed and persecuted Armenians since the last 650 years, for it may not be generally known, but it is nevertheless a historical fact, that the *last* Armenian king, Leo VI, of the house of Lusignan, died a refugee at Paris in 1393, having been driven out of his kingdom (Cilicia) by the terrible Mamelukes of Egypt in 1375. After his release from captivity in the land of the Pharaohs through the kind intercession of King John of Spain, Leo VI, visited Rome, Spain, France and England in the vain hope of enlisting the sympathy of Christian Europe with a view to regaining his lost throne, but evidently the spirit of chivalry, which was once the proud heritage of Christian Europe, had died with the Crusades and the appeal of the last Armenian king, an exile amongst mighty Christian kings, fell on deaf ears, and he died a broken-hearted man in Paris and was buried, amongst the kings of France, in the church of the Celestines, from which place his body was afterwards removed to St. Denis, where a beautiful black marble tombstone, with the king's effigy, bears the following inscription in French :—

> Cy gist le tres noble et tres excellent Prince, Lyon de Lusignan, quint Roi Latin du Royaulme d' Armenie, qui rendit l' ame a Dieu a Paris le XXIX jour de Novembre, l'an de grace MCCCXCIII.

It can be rendered into English thus :—

> Here lieth the noblest and the most excellent Prince, Lyon de Lusignan, the fifth Latin king of the royal house of Armenia, who delivered his soul to God in Paris on the 29th day of November, in the year of grace, 1393.

Shortly before his death, King Leo VI, rendered a very valuable service to the cause of humanity, which deserves to be recorded in letters of gold in the annals of France and England. By constant pleading and persuasion, he succeeded in bringing about a happy reconciliation between Charles VI of France and Richard II of England and thereby he put an end to the devastating war that had been going on between the two countries for nearly a hundred years.

It can be seen that the sympathy of chivalrous France with oppressed Armenians, under Mohammedan rule, dates back to the 14th century and it is to be earnestly hoped that it will continue, for ages to be, because French culture and sublime ideals have been the sources of inspiration of the *intelligentsia* of the Armenians in Turkey for the last hundred years. It may be mentioned that Armenians from Turkey fought in the "Foreign Legion" of France during the Great War, and it may be noted that in their loyalty to France, they yield to none.

And as a humble worker in the thorny field of historical research, where I have laboured incessantly for forty years, I have much pleasure in offering my sincere felicitations to the cultured citizens of Chandernagore on their success in founding a Historical Society with the praiseworthy object of studying and placing on record the interesting history of that small, but historic city, which like the famous "Rock of Gibraltar," has heroically stood the buffets of Time since the French flag—that emblem of liberty and culture—was first hoisted on the banks of the Hughli in 1688.

Long live the "Chandernagore Historical Society" which came into existence on the 29th November 1930, under the auspices and the immediate patronage of His Excellency Monsieur Valentin Champion, the Administrateur, and may it continue its useful work in rescuing from oblivion the valuable landmarks and the antiquities of that venerable French Settlement, which dates its existence from the year 1688, when by virtue of a *Firman*, granted by the Mogul Emperor Aurungzebe, a Factory was erected in this place, although there are records to prove the existence of a much earlier Factory, which, according to Strensham Masters. "Was in the occupations of the Dutch of the neighbouring city of Chinsurah in 1676."

ARMENIANS AT SAIDABAD

CHAPTER XXVIII

Armenians at Saidabad

Armenians formed their *first* settlement in Bengal in the year 1665 by virtue of a royal *Farman* issued by the Mogul Emperor Aurungzebe granting them a piece of land at Saidabad, a suburb of Murshidabad, with full permission to form a settlement there. Murshidabad was at that time the capital of Bengal, the richest province (*Subah*) of the Mogul Empire, justly styled by Aurungazebe, as the *paradise of nations*.

Bolts, in his *Considerations on India Affairs*, published in London in 1782, refers to the Armenian Settlement at Saidabad, as follows :—

"The Armenians, who have ever been a great commercial body in Hindustan, have also long had considerable settlements in Bengal, particularly at Syedabad. Their commerce was likewise established by the Mogul's *firman* whereby the duties on the two principal articles of their trade, piece-goods and raw silk, were fixed at three-and-a-half per cent."

For a period of about a hundred years since their settlement in that place, there is nothing on record of their activities—social, commercial or political. They were engaged in the peaceful pursuit of commerce, importing and selling piece-goods and exporting raw silk for which the Murshidabad district has always been famous.

By the middle of the 18th century, we find a large number of Armenians residing at Saidabad. The most notable Armenian merchant in the days of Nawab Ali Verdi Khan, the last of the great Nawabs of Bengal, who died in 1756, was Agah Petros, the son of Rev. Nicholas of Julfa. For his probity, urbanity, modesty and piety, he was a great favourite with Ali Verdi Khan, so much so that the *nawab's* wife used to call him *brother* and she would receive him and converse with him freely without observing *purdah*, (veil) contrary to the strict Mohammedan custom of those days. We are told by Thomas Khojamall that the grandees and the noblemen at the court of Nawab Ali Verdi Khan, paid great respect to the Armenian merchant and looked upon him, with great veneration, as a saint for his great piety. We shall have occasion to refer to this humane Armenian again when writing of the sufferings of the English prisoners who were taken to Murshidabad after the tragedy of the "Black Hole" of Calcutta in June 1756.

He died full of years and honours in 1767, and was buried in the Armenian churchyard at Saidabad where his revered grave, with a beautiful marble tombstone, can be seen to this day.

A few words about Ali Verdi Khan, the *last* of the great Nawabs of Bengal, may not be out of place. He was a stern but a just ruler, dreaded by the Mahratta freebooters, whom he turned out of Bengal. The English who were slowly capturing the trade of the country by peaceful penetration, dreaded him too as can be seen from the following episode. In 1749, an English man-of-war had seized some ships laden with the goods of various Hooghly merchants, Armenian and Mohammedan, and also containing valuable things belonging to the Nawab. Exasperated at the high-handed and unwarranted action of the English, Ali Verdi Khan immediately sent a *parwana* (order) to the Governor of Fort William, Calcutta, which concluded with the following menace, in which the terrible teeth of the fierce Bengal tiger were ominously visible. He wrote, "as you are not permitted to commit piracies, therefore I now write to you that, on receipt of this, you deliver up all the merchants' goods and effects to them, as also what appertains unto me, otherwise you may be assured a due chastisement in such manner as you least expect." The Council at Calcutta first attempted to pacify the infuriated Nawab by the present of a fine Arab horse, and at the same time contemplated measures of retaliation against the Armenian merchants of Calcutta, whose cause the Nawab had espoused. It soon appeared, however, that Ali Verdi Khan was in earnest and meant what he said, for he stopped the boats which were bringing down their goods, and cut off the supply of provisions at Dacca, reducing the Englishmen of that place to the greatest straits. He then surrounded the English Factory at Cossimbazar with troops, and finally compelled the English to accept the terms which he dictated. The English, the records say "got off after paying to the Nawab, through the Seths* twelve lakhs of rupees". On another occasion, Ali Verdi Khan demanded the estate of a rich Mohammedan who had died at Calcutta intestate and without any relatives. After his claim had been paltered with for many years, he again threatened to order an attack on the Factory at Cossimbazar, in 1751. The Calcutta Council knowing with whom they were dealing, immediately paid over the value of the deceased Mohammedan's estate, and were compelled to add a further sum on account of interest, lest they should rouse the ire of the Nawab and share the fate of the Mahrattas.

The next notable Armenian merchant at Saidabad was Khojah Petrus Arathoon, who achieved fame as a diplomat in the eventful days when Suraj-ud-dowlah, that monster of lust and cruelty, ascended the *masnad* (throne) of Murshidabad as the Nawab Nazim of Bengal, Behar and Orissa, as a successor to his grandfather, the great Nawab Ali Verdi Khan, referred to above, Khojah Petrus Arathoon, or the "Armenian Petrus", as Clive called him, played a very important part in the conspiracy which led to the overthrow of the young Nawab Suraj-ud-dowlah and the placing of a new Nawab on the tottering throne of Murshidabad.

The Armenian merchant-diplomat first appears on the scene, as a good Samaritan, immediately after the tragedy of the "Black Hole" when he spontaneously came to the assistance of the English in their hour of need, although he was afterwards misjudged by them and unjustly accused of having been a spy in the service of the Nawabs of Bengal from Suraj-ud-dowlah to Mir Kasim, as can be seen later on.

The humane Armenian hearing of the terrible sufferings of the English inhabitants of Calcutta, who with Drake, the Governor, had taken refuge in their ships at Fulta, after the fall of Fort William, he secretly supplied them with provisions

---

* The Seths, the Rothchilds of India, were rich Indian bankers at Murshidabad, who through their immense wealth, played a very important part in Bengal politics, as can be seen later on.

for a period of six months and but for the timely succour of Khojah Petrus, the unfortunate English refugees at Fulta might have been starved to surrender before the arrival of the Army of Retribution from Madras under Admiral Watson and Colonel Clive on the 20th December 1756. Khojah Petrus was afterwards employed by Clive as a confidential agent in negotiating with Mir Jaffier for the overthrow of Suraj-ud-dowlah, the author of the "Black Hole" tragedy. And in 1760, when it was found expedient to remove the imbecile Mir Jaffier and place his son-in-law, Mir Kasim, on the Masnad of Murshidabad, Khojah Petrus' services were again requisitioned as he was known to be very friendly with Mir Kasim. And for all the valuable services which Khojah Petrus had rendered to the English in Bengal, at the risk of his life, there is nothing in the records to show that he had been rewarded for his loyalty to the British cause. Being unable to get justice from Clive and his colleagues in Calcutta, for his loyalty, once the crisis was over and the tide had turned in favour of the English, he addressed a long letter to the Court of Directors in London on the 25th January 1759, enumerating the various services he had rendered to the British cause in Bengal since the capture and sack of Calcutta in June 1756. The following is a copy of the letter :—

Letter from Petrus Arratoon to the Court of Directors dated 25th January 1759.
"Honourable Sirs,

It is with the most humble submission I assume liberty to address the following narrative to your Honourable Board, to set in a true and faithful light—the indefatigable pains, charges, and imminent danger myself and the persons therein mentioned underwent to relieve the miseries of the English Gentry after they had been extirpated from Calcutta by the invasion of the Moor, and refuged on board their ships at Fulta and to be instrumental to bring matters to the happy state they are in at present.

The calamities and condition the English Familys were in on board their ships at Fulta, I need not describe, no doubt but the Honourable Company have had a very particular account of their dilemma and sufferings : I shall proceed to relate how far their deplorable state made impressions on one Abraham Jacobs (a Jew) and myself. The said Abraham Jacobs applyed himself to me with the prospect to join him to endeavour to contribute the English some relief. A proposition of that commiseration and humanity, I readily came into, solemnly plighted him my faith to yield them my utmost assistance with all imaginable alacrity, fervency and fidelity, even to the hazard of my life, upon this Abraham Jacobs remained in my house at Calcutta disguised in Moor's habit. We mutually consented and agreed the first step we were to take was to get the speech of Omichand* and to bring him over to be an instrument to promote our schemes who had great interest with the Moors and though Mr. Drake and Council addressed him twice before to no effect, he not so much as giving them an answer, yet we were so fortunate as to prevail with him to join our cause, and the first thing we effected was to obtain the country people to bring provisions to Fulta market which they were restrained from before—We likewise conveyed boats and *lascars* to attend the ships, and indeed we studied and laboured and left no stone unturned to yield them all the conveniences and necessarys we possibly could obtain either by interest or present out of our shipwrecked fortunes, for there were no favours, scare humanity to be expected from such mercenary wretches without the prevailance of presents. We then proceeded to advise Major Kilpatrick to send a letter to Monickchund, Governor of Calcutta, which he did and we delivered it to him and were so happy to have him receive it favourably and returned an answer. This success spirited us to advise the Major to write to Coja Wazeed and Jugut Seth and we carried these letters to Hughly and delivered them to the said Coja Wazeed and Jugut Seth's *gomastas* and returned with satisfactory answer to the Major. The good consequence of these correspondences was the obtaining of a cessation of hostility or disturbances of the Moors towards the English, which continued till the arrival of His Majesty's Squadron. The said Abraham Jacobs and myself were almost incessantly

* Omichand was a Punjabi Hindu merchant of Calcutta and had acted for many years as agent for the English in their purchases of saltpetre and other Indian goods in Bengal. His real name was Amir Chand but he is better known as Omichand.

employed in travelling up and down the river, carrying them all the assistance we could and giving them advices of all the occurrences we could learn, which brought on us great expenses by keeping a great number of servants, boats, small presents to the Moor's under-officers not to impede or molest us, as well as the inexpressible trouble and anxious fears lest we might be betrayed. As I hinted before, our fortunes were for the major part shipwrecked at the sacking of the town and our circumstances were at a very low ebb. All the money we received from Mr. Drake and Major Kilpatrick at Fulta amounted to no more than Rupees 150 and 380, which last sum was employed on this occasion. It was thought necessary towards accommodating matters with the Nabob we should have the King's *phirmaund* to produce if required, which was lost, but William Frankland Esquire accidently found among his papers the copy of the *phirmaund,* which we got fair translated, and paid that sum to an officer at Hughly who had the Mogul's *chap* [seal] to affix it to the same. In the beginnig of October 1756, Omichand went to Muxadavad [Murshidabad] in order to endeavour an accommodation when the said Abraham Jacobs wearied out with continual fatigue fell sick at Chinsurah so that the whole weight of affairs fell alone upon me, to be perpetually employed backwards and forwards to Fulta etc. as prementioned, till the arrival of His Majesty's Squadron, Admiral Watson of glorious memory and Colonel Clive, who finding nothing could be effected by fair means with Seraj-ud-dowla , he being a Prince whose word could in no wise be depended on, perfidious in his nature and a promise-breaker, which occasioned hostility to commence on the side of the English, and after retaking Calcutta* the Colonel and his army encamped to the northward of the town, and the Nabob soon marched his army from Muxadabad and encamped very near him. However a treaty was set on foot, and I was employed to negociate between both partys, but the brave Colonel Clive rightly conceivng the Nabob trifled and did not mean to come to any terms of accommodation, he judged it necessary to compel him by force of arms, accordingly he gave him battle,

* Calcutta was retaken by the British on the 2nd January 1757 and Drake, the former Governor, reinstated as President.

and God was pleased to crown him with victory which brought the Nabob to terms of peace which being settled and Articles confirmed he returned with his army to Muxadabad.

Afterwards William Watts Esquire and I were sent thither to receive what compensation was agreed on in the treaty of peace. A part thereof was received, the remainder withheld by the Nabob. Here words can't express what trouble Mr. Watts and self had in attendance and endeavouring to get from him the remainder. That gentleman perceived plainly the Nabob was dealing treacherously with the English, and had information he was privately perfidiously concerting measures with the French, and his behaviour confirmed Mr. Watts in the same, for which he sent me to demand from the Nabob the remaining money, he threatened if Mr. Watts presumed to make any further demand, to take his life away. Due advice of these particulars were remitted to Calcutta. In the interim, Mr. Watts, whose whole study was taken up for the good of the Company and publick cause, sent me to Jaffir Ally Cawn, one of the Nabob's noblemen, and who tacitly was disaffected with the Nabob's treacherous proceedings to him. I was to lay open a new scheme, which I did and had I been detected, nay even suspected herein, it would have cost Mr. Watts and me our lives, but to proceed. I brought Jaffir Ally Cawn to a concession to Mr. Watts' proposal, and to enter into the scheme, and appointed a day for Mr. Watts to have an interview with him in private, to accomplish which I provided in readiness a covered *palankeen* such as the Moor women are carryed in, which is inviolable, for without previous knowledge of the deceit no one dare look into it. At the appointed time Mr. Watts was carried to Jaffir Ally Cawn's house, and there concluded and confirmed the scheme until an answer of approbation could be had from the Select Committee at Calcutta. As soon as the same arrived, I requested leave of the Nabob for Mr. Watts and self to retire for three days to the Garden House without the city which being granted we lost no time to make our escape from thence to meet Colonel Clive who was on the march with the army for Muxadavad, and by the blessing of Providence got there safe, a narrow escape indeed, for had we deferred our flight three hours longer, though we acted with the greatest conduct and secresy till matters were ripe for action, we should have both been taken and put to the most miserable death. Your Honours may be pleased to observe here what risque Mr. Watts and self ran of our lives for your interest. I need not mention the wonderful effects and issue our labour has produced. What a happy change in the state of your affairs, to have a peaceable possession of Calcutta confirmed to you, etc. But I must beg leave to exhibit to Your Honours that though I have gone through such great travel, pain, anxiety, and dangers in assisting the English familys in the depth of their distress, being instrumental towards the happy Revolution, yet Your Honours have not taken the least notice or mention of me nor of Abraham Jacobs, my fellow labourer, until the fatigues, as prementioned, afflicted him with sickness, nor even the expenses we disbursed have not been repaid us, which incites me to believe that my services have not been represented to Your Honours. If they have, I have reason to believe not in a clear and genuine but very faint light, for had your Honours been made truely and particularly sensible of my vigor, fervency and fidelity in your service, I flatter myself, I should have been honoured with some instance of Your Honours' favour, therefore, I humbly refer this genuine, but short narrative in regard to the particulars, to your Honours' serious consideration, and hope you will consider me worthy of the gratuity to have some post in Your Honours' service conferred on me, and not forget the service of Abraham Jacobs, as in your wisdom you shall judge, I merit, or such reward as Your Honours shall deem fit. Permit me, Honourable Sirs, to tender my sincere wishes for prosperity and success to attend you in all your affairs, and most respectfully to subscribe, Hanourable Sirs, Your most obeidient and faithful humble servant,

PETROSS ARRATOON."

We have not however, been able to find out yet what reply the Court of Directors gave to the above letter, as the Records are silent on that point, but it is not likely that the Court of Directors would have ignored that valuable historical document entirely. And in order to prove by documentary evidence the important part played by Khojah Petrus in the negotiations which led to the establishment of British rule in Bengal, we shall now proceed to give some extracts from state letters and documents of the time which shed a flood of light on the history of the negotiations and the principal actor therein, as unfortunately very little is known of that great Armenian merchant-diplomat of Calcutta, who at the risk of his life, helped the English in their hour of need.

In a letter to Mr. Pigot, dated Camp, 25 January 1757, Colonel Clive writes :—

"Yesterday his (Nabob's) Prime Minister despatched one Coja Petrus, an Armenian, to me, desiring I would send a trusty person with our proposals, intimating that the Nabob was desirous of settling matters in a private manner without the mediation of the French. I have desired the gentlemen will send their proposals very fully explained that we may lay them before the Nabob as soon as possible."

On the 2nd February, 1757, we find Suraj-ud-dowlah again sending Coja Petrus to Clive asking for the despatch of envoys, but he did not wait for a reply.

On the following day, writing from Camp, Clive commences his letter to the Select Committee at Fort William, as follows :—

"Gentlemen—Coja Petruse is returned with a letter and present from the Nabob and I propose despatching the commissaries to him without delay, therefore request you will send me the proposals immediately."

On the 6th February 1757, we find Clive writing to the Nabob in the following terms :

"I sent two gentlemen to treat with you about a peace at Nabobgunge where, by your letter, and the promise from your own mouth to Coja Petruse, I expected they would have found you, instead of which they found you in Calcutta. This action sufficiently shows you meant only to amuse me."

In a letter from Mr. Watts to Colonel Clive, written 10 coss from Hooghly, and dated the 18th February 1757, we find the following :—

"I have certain advice from Coja Petrus and from two gentlemen I sent on purpose to Chinchura that the French are sending their effects there, they saw several boats loaded with chests, chairs, pepper, cotton etc., etc., some carrying on shore, so that you will find nothing but an empty shell. I am informed the Danes give the same protection, but of this you will be able to get better intelligence than I."

In a long letter to the Secret Committee at London, dated Camp opposite to Barnagul, Clive writes on the 22nd February 1757, as follows :—

"On the 3rd instant letters came in from the Nabob proposing to restore our settlement and make some reparation for the effects taken, and desiring proper persons to be sent to confer with him on the subject, at the same time the van of his army appeared in sight, and passed along towards Calcutta, just without reach of the cannon of our battery to the eastward.

Coja Petrus, an Armenian, who brought the Nabob's letters assured me that the Nabob had by his own mouth promised to wait at a place called Ganga where he then was till the conference was over and I directly wrote him testifying my satisfaction at his pacifick intentions and that two gentlemen would be deputed immediately to treat with him.

The next day, being the 6th, the Nabob decamped and removed to Dum Dumma, and the Armenian was again sent to me wth a letter from Rangeet Roy desiring if we meant peace to transmit our proposals to the Nabob who was inclined to comply with them."

In a letter from Mr. Watts to Colonel Clive, dated the 26th April 1757, we find the following :—

"Mir Jaffier two days ago sent for Petrus privately and told him the Nabob [Suraj-ud-dowlah] was greatly disliked, that he ill used and affronted everybody, that for his part whenever he went to visit him he expected assassination, therefore allways had his son and forces in readiness, that he was persuaded the Nabob would not keep to his Agreement and says he only waits till Monloll [Mohan Lall] is well and for some forces that are expected from Patna in eight or nine days to attack us. Mir Jaffieir therefore sent for Petrus and desired him to tell me that if you are content, he, Raheem Cawn, Roydoolab and Bahaudar Ally Cawn and others are ready and willing to join their forces, seize the Nabob and set up another person that may be approved of."

In a letter dated the 14th May, 1757, Mr. Watts writes to Colonel Clive as follows :—

"Mir Jaffier likewise having expressed an utter distrust and disgust at his being any ways concerned in the Treaty, and as delays are dangerous, I therefore with Petrus had a meeting with Mir Jaffier's confident [Omar Beg] who set out to-day with the accompanying Articles, which he says he is sure Mir Jaffier will comply with." In a letter to Colonel Clive, dated the 8th June 1757 Mr. Watts writes from French Gardens, Chandernagore :—"I have not been duped as you must know by this time and be convinced Omichand has been the occasion of the delay. As a further proof, I enclose you copy and translate of a letter from him to Petrus. Please send for Petrus' brother [Khojah Gregory, better known as Gorgin Khan] and ask him upon oath if Omichand did not dictate and he wrote such a letter to his brother [Coja Petrus]. If this will not satisfy you and Omichand's address has more weight than my proofs I will send you the original with his own signing. Let me beg of you to comply with this request not to divulge what I have inclosed or write you to Omichand till I am in place of security, as he is implacable in his resentments and may be induced to discover everything by writing up here [Chandernagore] in order to sacrifice Petrus and me to his resentment. The Nabob [Suraj-ud-dowlah] and Mir Jaffier are at open variance and it is apprehended troubles between them will soon ensue."

Omichand's letter to Coja Petrus, in the handwriting of Khojah Gregory [Gorgin Khan] was written in Armenian, the following being a free translation of a part of the letter which Mr. Watts sent to Clive with a copy of the original as stated above. The translation was no doubt made by Khojah Petrus himself for Mr. Watts.

"Omichand's compliments to Petrus.

There's letters gone for Mr. Watts to forbid his coming down till permission is given from hence. You and I are one : let us consider what is for our own interest and act so as to make it pass that we have had the whole management of this affair. If our friend [Mr. Watts] is not set out, keep him a few days : affairs are not settled here, hereafter I will write you the particulars. You have a good understanding, therefore there is no occasion to write you much. Our success depends upon each other. All my hopes are in you."

Facsimiles of Omichand's original letter with the rough copy of the same, were published by Sir Richard Carnac Temple, Baronet, in the *Indian Antiquary,* Vol. XLVII for November 1918. In the original copy, Omichand has signed his name in Hindi (Punjabi) as Amirchand. There is no signature on the copy and neither of them bears any date, but they must have been written on the 4th or 5th June 1757, as Mr. Watts refers to it in his letter of the 8th June which he wrote to Clive enclosing the letter in question. Needless to add that the clever plan of the wily Omichand miscarried because the Armenian Petrus remained true and loyal to the English, as in the past. Had Khojah Petrus complied with Omichand's request and kept back Mr. Watts, things would have taken a different turn and the British cause would have been endangered, since Omichand was no friend of the English and for his double dealings he got his desserts shortly after when the infamous forged treaty* was drawn up and shown to him as a reward for his treachery, villainy and chicanery.

---

*Clive, the heaven-born hero of Macaulay, played a shabby trick on Omichand which was quite unworthy of an Englishman of his position. For his participation, as an intermediary, in the conspiracy for the overthrow of Suraj-ud-dowlah, Omichand, claimed thirty *lakhs* of rupees as compensation for the heavy losses which he said he had sustained when Suraj-ud-dowlah had taken Calcutta in June 1756. He threatened to inform the Nawab of the plot unless his claim was satisfied. Clive, who was more than a match for the wily Punjabi, closed his mouth by means of a trick. He had two treaties drawn up, one on *white* paper and the other on *red.* The former, which was the *real* treaty, contained *no* stipulation as regards the compensation to Omichand and it was not shown to him The latter guaranteed Omichand's claim and was shown to him. It may be mentioned here that on the sham treaty Admiral Watson's signature was forged, by Clive without any compunction whatsoever, and when, some years after, he was arraigned before the House of Commons for the shameless forgery, he told his accusers nonchalantly, that he would do it again a hundred times! After the conspiracy had succeeded, *par excellence,* Omichand came to receive the promised amount, under the terms of the *red* treaty, but he was shockingly disillusioned when Clive showed him the *white* treaty by which he was to receive nothing. It was a case of "the biter bit".

As Omichand's letter to Khojah Petrus is rather an important document, from a historical point of view, inasmuch as it served to put Khojah Petrus on his guard to save Mr. Watts from falling into the hands of Nawab Suraj-ud-dowlah, as Omichand had cleverly planned, we shall therefore give a verbatim translation of the original Armenian letter, which, with the rough copy, were found among the Clive MSS. some years ago by Sir George Forrest.

Here is the translation :—

"To the most illustrious Sahib of Sahibs, Aga Petrus,

Be it known humbly in the service of him who is written above that up to the present time we have no favour from the Sahib. We are very anxious, and hearing of the arrival of Amirchand, I came to Gorothi and enquired about the real state of affairs about my Sahib.

He [Amirchand] told me to write these few words. Amirchand offers his devotions in the service of the Sahib. He says that they have written to Wach [Watts] from this place that no one is to come till we do not write. It remains that you and I are one. What will be good for us, do that. Be thoroughly manly till the end and everything is ours. And about your home, be of easy mind, I am here. And if the friend who is to come with you has arrived, it is good, if not, delay him for a few days, as there have been no deliberations here yet. I will write to you what is necessary to-morrow [when] the deliberations are over. It is not expedient to write details, because you are a wise man, moreover, my weal is yours and yours is mine. My entire affair I have left open to your wish. No more.

Amirchand."

Sir Richard Carnac Temple, in his interesting article on "Side-lights on Omichand" which appeared in the *Indian Antiquary* for November 1918, referring to the above letters says :

"Reviewing the conditions surrounding this remarkable letter, one cannot help considering what would have happened had Agah Petrus acted as Omichand desired and kept Watts in Murshiadabad until Surajuddaulla had him in his power. Clive's letter of 5th June 1757 to Watts shows that had Watts failed in his mission, as he would have done, if Omichand had had his way, Clive, for some months at any rate, would have dropped his scheme of deposing Surajuddaula and setting up Mir Jaffier as Nawab Nazim under British suzeranity, and the world-famous batttle of Plassey would not have been fought. No doubt so worthless a prince as Surajuddaula would not long have retained his power and no doubt Clive would in time have found means to obtain supreme authority in Bengal, but it would have had to be achieved in some other way. There was nothing then but the loyalty of Agha Petros to prevent the success of Omichand's proposal and a complete change in the story of British supremacy in India as we know it. The letter we have been discussing therefore just missed being of the first importance in history."

In a letter written by Colonel Clive to the Select Committee at Fort William, from Cutwa, on the 15th June, 1757, at noon, we find the following :—

"I arrived last night at Cutwa and as the *sepoys* who came by land are a good deal fatigued, I shall only proceed to Mirzajore to-day where I shall disembark the cannon etc., and I expect to reach Agra Diep in two days, to which place I shall order all the small boats. Mr. Watts with the gentlemen of Cossimbazar joined me yesterday afternoon, also Coja Petrus and a Moorman from Mir Jaffier. They left the city the 13th at night and acquaint us Mir Jaffier's party daily increases. The gunners and Laitee Cawn have joined him, so that there is the greatest probability of a happy issue to the expedition."

In a letter, without date, but received by Colonel Clive on the 23rd June 1757, Jafar Ali Khan [Mir Jaffeir] writes as follows :—

"Your note is arrived. Your trusty man is taken. I congratulate you on executing your design. Meirza Aumer [Omar Beg], or Mr. Watts or Coja Petrus, send one of them to me. I am here on the bank of the lake agreeable to your desire."

After such a brilliant record of valuable services, the loyal Armenian becomes the target of the attacks of the arrogant members of the Calcutta Council who forgetting the immediate past, falsely and unjustly accused him of treachery and disloyalty, as can be seen from the following extracts :

In their letter to the Honourable the Secret Committee for Affairs of the Honourable United Company of Merchants of England trading to the East Indies, the Council* at Bengal wrote under date, Fort William, the 11th March 1762, as follows :—

"The Armenian Ministers of the revolution Cojah Petruse and Khojah Gregory [Gorgin Khan] are in the highest degree of favour with the Nabob [Mir Kasim] and his adherents, the former resides in Calcutta, retained by Cossim Aly Chan [Nawab Mir Kasim], a known spy upon every transaction of the English of which he never fails to give his master the most regular intelligence, as was too apparent to Colonel Coote and Major Carnac, when they were at Patna. The latter of these Armenians has posts of the greatest trusts near the Nabob's person ; and through the means of these men the Armenians in general are setting up an independent footing in the country, are carrying on a trade greatly detrimental to our investments in all parts, and commit daily acts of violence, which reflect no small odium on the English, who are supposed to encourage their proceedings." The Court of Directors in their reply to the long letter of the Calcutta Council, said "this paragraph [36] requires no answer from us," which goes to show that the cool-headed English gentlemen who presided over the destinies of the Company's trade in India, attached no importance to the false and venomous accusations of their self-interested servants in Calcutta against the two Armenians whose friendship for the English and their loyalty to the British cause was above reproach, for in the Address to the Proprietors of East Indian Stock regarding the revolutions in Bengal, it is stated that "Mr. Holwell being well apprized that Coja Petruse (to whom the Company owed much in the last revolution, but much more in this) had the greatest weight with, and influence over Cossim Aly Khan [Nawab Mir Kasim],

* The Council at Fort William, Bengal, was then composed of the following members :—Eyre Coote, P. Amyatt, John Carnac, W. Ellis, S. Batson and H. Verelst.

had secured him on the side of the Company, and at a private interview with him, at Mr. Holwell's garden, on the same day of the conference between the Governor and Cossim Aly Khan, Mr. Holwell framed a rough plan of the terms which must be insisted on for the Company, in lieu of the protection and support to Cossim Aly Khan, which Coja Petruse engaged he would promote, to the utmost of his power and influence. The next morning, the 24th September, Mr. Holwell communicated his conference with Petruse and laid the rough plan before the Governor and the Select Committee, who approved of it, with little variation, and the 25th was appointed for the conference between him and Cossim Aly Khan."

After such valuable services to the British cause in Bengal, the loyal Armenian was painted black by the Calcutta Council who stigmatized him as a "spy" in the service of the Nawab.

In the proceedings of the Calcutta Council for 24th March 1763, Mr. Batson laid before the Board the following minute :—

"The evil designs of the Nawab [Mir Kasim] against us appearing now in a glaring light, and it being wellknown through the whole country that Coja Petruse, the Armenian, acts as the Nawab's spy in this place, Mr. Batson proposed that he and his family be turned out of Calcutta immediately and desires it may be put to the vote."

The motion contained therein being put to the vote, agreeably to Mr. Batson's desire, the Members delivered their opinions, but Mr. Watts who knew Coja Petrus intimately since the dark days of the fall of Calcutta and the tragedy of the "Black Hole" in June 1756, and had always spoken highly of his loyalty, because he had saved his life, as we have seen, yet he did not hesitate to echo the sentiments of some of the members and stated that :—

"Petruse is wellknown to be an intriguing person and to have raised himself, I believe, being a spy betwixt us and Seraja Dowla. During Clive's Government he was ordered to quit this Settlement (Calcutta) and not to have any connections at the Durbar, for having spread and told the Chutta Nawab Meeran (Meir Jaffeir's son) that Colonel Clive intended to take away his life, I therefore think he ought to be ordered to quit this

Settlement, that his constituents cannot suffer any losses by our taking such a step, as his business can be carried on equally the same as when he was absent in a late visit to the Nawab." But fortunately for Khojah Petrus, who had evidently become the victim of the hatred and malice of the Calcutta Council, the President pointed out that ordering a merchant of long standing out of the Settlement would be arbitrary, and would shake all confidence, but he was forbidden to act for the future as Vakil to the Nawab (Mir Kasim) and to the chagrin of his crestfallen enemies, Khojah Petrus was honourably acquitted by the Government. A glorious instance of British fairplay and justice indeed. Later on, the much harassed but loyal Armenian was suspected by Major Adams to have been a spy for the Nawab Mir Kasim during the memorable campaign of October 1763, and was seized as such and ill-treated, but he finally convinced the Government of his innocence and unshaken loyalty to the British cause by writing to them on the 21st November 1763 as follows :—

"Your petitioner begs leave to observe to this Hon'ble Board at Ouda Nulla, a place where the enemy had strong works and great forces, your petitioner by direction from Major Adams wrote two letters to Marcar and Arratoon, two Armenian officers, who amongst others commanded the enemy's forces, and intimated to them that as the English always favoured and protected the Armenian nation, so the Armenians in justice ought to direct their steps towards the good of the English.

That he is now about 14 or 15 years or thereabouts an inhabitant of this Settlement, and took up arms in the Factory when Seraju Dowla came down against Calcutta, when the English abandoned this place and retired to Fulta, and were in great distress there for provisions, your petitioner by carrying and bringing letters found means to introduce a correspondence between Raja Manukchand and Major Kilpatrick, which opened a passage for provisions to the English at Fulta. The King's Firman being lost in the capture of the place [Calcutta] Your petitioner with a copy of it that was saved by Mr. Frankland, ventured up to Hooghly and got two attested copies of it drawn out with the Cazie's seal fixed to them, and brought and delivered them to Mr. Drake at Fulta. In short, your petitioner was as useful and serviceable to the English at Fulta as he could, until the arrival of their forces and the retaking of Calcutta, and your Petitioner was no less serviceable to the English when Seraju Dowla came to attack Calcutta the second time, as he was the person by whose means in carrying and bringing letters between Colonel Clive and Seraju Dowla, a general accommodation and peace was brought about, your petitioner afterwards went up with Mr. Watts to Cossimbazar where he did render all the services that he was ordered very zealously, and the same zeal animating him in sipte of the numberless dangers to which he was exposed, he went between the English and Jaffir Ally Khan till the treaty was formed between them, and even to this day whatever the Hon'ble the President and Council have been pleased to order, your petitioner has always faithfully executed."

For his loyalty to the British in Bengal, Khojah Petrus suffered much. Here is another instance. During the campaign in the second half of the year 1763, when the British were fighting against Mir Kasim, the last independent Nawab Nazim of Bengal, Behar and Orissa, whose formidable army was under the command of Gorgin Khan, the youngest brother of Khojah Petrus, Major Adams, who commanded the British troops fearing lest Gorgin Khan or the other Armenian commanders of the Nawab might harm the British prisoners in the hands of the Nawab, kept (as a precautionary measure) Khojah Petrus as a hostage in his camp, as can be seen from the letter which the Major wrote to Governor Vanisttart on the 3rd October 1763.

"We had a report yesterday that Coja Gregore [Gorgin Khan] had been wounded some days ago by a party of his Mogul cavalry who mutinied for want of their pay between Sonage Gurree and Nabob Gunge. It is just now confirmed by a Hircarra arrived from the enemy with this addition that he died the next day and that forty principal people concerned were put to death upon the occasion, though it was imagined that the Moguls were induced to affront and assault Coja Gregore by Cassim Ali Cawn who began to be very jealous of him on account of his good behaviour to the English. If this should prove true, Coja Petruce can be of no further service to us. I, therefore, would recommend sending him down to Calcutta, but shall wait the directions of the Board on that head.

I must confess this piece of news gives me some concern as by all accounts he behaved very well to our gentlemen. And it was that only that occasioned him to fall under Cassim Ali Cawn's displeasure. Had he lived, he might probably have assisted in effecting their escape, as we hear he frequently was the means of saving their lives as well as the Setts and other prisoners."

And for trying to save the lives of the British prisoners, out of love and affection for his brother Khojah Petrus, who was a staunch friend of the English, Gorgin Khan, "one of the greatest men of the age," according to Marshman, lost his precious life by falling a victim to the rage of the Anglophobe Nawab Mir Kasim of Bengal. Had he lived the blood-curdling massacre of Patna would have been prevented through his influence and the Juggut Seths would not have been cruelly murdered by the Nawab Mir Kasim.

That well-informed researcher and learned antiquarian Sir Richard Carnac Temple, in his illuminating article on "Side-lights on Omichand" in the *Indian Antiquary* for November 1918, writes of Khojah Petrus in the following terms :—

"Petros Arratoon, usually known as Coja (Khwaja) Petrus (Petrose), was an important Armenian merchant, whose brother Grigor Arratoon (Gorgin Khan) was a general of Mir Kasim. He had resided in Calcutta since 1748 and had rendered valuable service to the English at the time of its capture and in the negotiations following its recapture. He seems to have accompanied Watts and Omichand to Murshidabad, as he is mentioned in a letter of the 18th February [1757], immediately after their arrival, and subsequent letters show him to have been employed as an emissary by both Watts and the Nawab. On the 24th April 1757, Mir Jaffir, Surajuddaula's *Bakhshi* or Paymaster General, who had previously agreed to countenance Yar Lutf Khan's pretensions, but had since been approached by the Seths as a more suitable candidate, sent for Petros and desired him to tell Watts that he could secure the adhesion of the Nawab's chief officers in support of his own claims it these were put forward : "This scheme" Watts considered "more feasible than the other" and he urged its adoption by Clive, who readily acquiesced, since he was doubtful of the wisdom of setting up so comparatively an unimportant a man as Yar Lutf Khan, while Mir Jafir, brother-in-law of the late Nawab Governor, Alivardi Khan, was a personage of weight and influence."

Khojah Petrus or Petros—the Armenian name for Peter—had two younger brothers in Bengal, one of them was the famous Khojah Gregory or Gorgin Khan—the Commander-in-Chief of Nawab Mir Kasim of Bengal—and the other, an eminent merchant, Barsegh (Basil) Arratoon by name, who suffered much at the hands of Governor Harry Verelst and Francis Sykes in 1767, as can be seen later on.

Bolts, the well-known author of *Considerations on India Affairs,* who espoused the cause of the much-harassed Armenian merchant, calls him Parseek Arratoon.

It is sad however to reflect that all the three brothers suffered in some way or other for their loyalty and devotion to the English in Bengal. The first, Khojah Petrus, after a brilliant record of valuable services to the British, as we have seen already, was pilloried and accused afterwards of disloyalty, intrigue and espionage, and was even threatened with expulsion from Calcutta with his family. The second, Khojah Gregory, or Gorgin Khan—Nawab Mir Kasim's Minister and Commander-in-Chief—and one of the greatest men of the age, lost his precious life for being kindly disposed towards the English during the latter end of the regime of the Anglophobe Nawab Mir Kasim of Bengal, whilst the third, Barsegh (Parseek) Arratoon, incurred the displeasure of Governor Harry Verelst for being a successful and an independent merchant and therefore a thorn on the side of the self-interested Governor and his clique in the glorious days of the memorable but infamous "Monopoly of Salt, Betel-nut and tobacco," when the servants of the Company were reaping a fair harvest from trading privately to the detriment of the Company's trade.

Hitherto we have seen Khojah Petrus in the light of a clever diplomat. Let us now see him as a private individual and a successful merchant of Calcutta. He was the head of the Armenian community in Calcutta and was held in high esteem by his compatriots for his benevolence and his charities. He built the beautiful Armenian church at Saidabad* near Murshidabad, in 1758, entirely at his own expense, in memory of his parents. He repaired and embellished the Armenian church of Calcutta in 1763 and built two additional altars inside the church, one on the right side of the main altar, in memory of his brother Gorgin Khan, who was assassinated near Monghyr, and the other on the left side to commemorate his memory. Joseph Emin, an Armenian of Calcutta, in his "Life and Adventures" printed in 1792 in London, calls Khojah Petrus "the earthly God of the Calcutta Armenians" which clearly shows the high esteem in which he was held by his countrymen.

It may be mentioned, *en passant*, that Khojah Petrus was a personal friend of Warren Hastings and when that much maligned statesman was badly in need of funds for his subsistence in England after his successful administration in Bengal, he obtained an accommodation of Rs. 12,000 from his Armenian friend in Calcutta after vainly trying to get it from his own Indian Diwan. And this loan, it may be added, was not repaid by Warren Hastings till 10 years after when he came out to Madras.

His son, Agah Arathoon Petrus, founded in 1820 the Armenian Alms House in Calcutta where thousands, nay tens of thousands of itinerant and poor Armenians from all parts of the world, have found shelter all these years and blessed the memory of the devout Founder, who according to the Armenian inscrption on the black marble tablet which can be seen to this day over the gate of the building "was zealous of the glorious deeds of his illustrious and hospitable ancestors."

---

* There was a brass tablet on the north wall of the Armenian Church at Saidabad—dedicated to the Virgin Mary—with an inscription in Armenian, from which it appears that the church was built by Khojah Petrus to the memory of his revered parents, Arathoon his father and Hosannah his mother, Dastagool his wife, Khojah Grégory [Gorgin Khan] and Agah Barsegh his brothers and all his blood relations, whether dead or alive. This tablet is now in the picture gallery of the Armenian church at Calcutta.

Khojah Petrus, the diplomat, the merchant prince and the respected head of the Armenians in Calcutta, died in 1778, aged fifty-three years, and his revered grave can be seen in the chancel of the Armenian church of Nazareth, Calcutta, with a long inscription, on a white marble stone, in classical Armenian verse, of which the following is a translation :—

"The eminent princely chief Agah Petrus Arathoon of Erivan, New Julfa, [Ispahan] of the family of Abraham, was a lustrous hyacinthine crown of the entire Armenian nation. He worked assiduously and expended lavishly. His generosity towards the destitute orphans and widows was without parallel. By his frequent munificent gifts he erected handsome and well-embellished churches. He departed in the hope of salvation at the age of fifty-three, and was placed in this tomb with pomp, in the year of our Lord 1778, the 29th of August, and in the year 163 of the era of Azaria, the 12th day of the month of Nadar."

His widow, who survived him by 27 years, died in 1805 and lies buried beside her husband under a black marble tombstone with an inscription in classical Armenian of which the following is a translation :—

"This is the tomb of Dastagool, the daughter of Agah Minas of the family of Khojah Minas of Erivan [a parish of Julfa] and wife of Agah Petrus. She departed this life on the 3rd of June 1805."

It is to be hoped that when the history of those eventful years, which saw the dawn of a new era in Bengal, comes to be fully written, the deeds of the Armenian Khojah Petrus will not be forgotten and his valuable services to the British in Bengal will not be ignored, as in the past.

The Armenian inhabitants of Saidabad and Agah Manuel Satoor in particular, rendered valuable assistance to the English when Holwell and his fellow-captives, the survivors of the "Black Hole" tragedy, were taken as prisoners to Murshidabad by the order of Suraj-ud-dowlah.

According to Thomas Khojamall, a contemporary, Agah Petrus, the son of Rev. Nicholas, referred to on page 325, being a man of great influence at the court of Murshidabad at that time, succeeded in releasing the women prisoners by making valuable presents to the high officials. Having brought them to his house, he kept them for some days before sending them to the Dutch Settlement at Chinsurah and from thence to Calcutta, supplying all their needs and requirements.

One of these English women was Mrs. Frances Watts, the wife of William Watts, Senior Member of the Supreme Council of Calcutta and Chief at Murshidabad, who but for Khojah Petrus Arathoon's protection would have fallen into the hands of the infuriated Suraj-ud-dowlah as we have seen already on pages 331-332. After Watts' death in England, his widow returned to Calcutta and on the 1st June, 1774, she married the Rev. William Johnson, a chaplain in the Presidency of Fort William. She was known thenceforth as the "Begum Johnson." Her end came in 1812, at the ripe old age of eighty seven and her funeral was attended by the Governor-General and all the high officials. She was buried in St. John's churchyard where her grave, known as the "tomb of Begam Johnson," an imposing massive old structure, can be seen to this day . She had married four times and on her tombstone the names of the four husbands, with the dates of their marriages, are faithfully recorded. According to the interesting epitaph, she was "the oldest British resident in Bengal, universally beloved, respected and revered." She was born on the 10th April, 1725, at Fort St. David, on the Coromandel coast, where her father, Edward Crook, was the Governor.

And but for the chivalry of the Armenian Agah Petrus Nicholas, (not to be confounded with Khojah Petrus Arathoon) this remarkable English lady might have fallen a victim to the bestiality and the savagery of Suraj-ud-dowlah—the monster in human form.

There are no Armenians at Saidabad to-day, for like Chinsurah, it was deserted when it lost its commercial importance, by the middle of the last century, and the only vestiges of the once prosperous Armenian colony in that place are the Armenian church which is crumbling very fast and a large number of graves in the churchyard, with beautiful tombstones, most of which are broken and damaged and need repairs very badly, otherwise they will disappear in the course of a decade or two.

In the Library of the Armenian church at Calcutta, founded by the late Mr. A. G. Apcar in 1896, in memory of his daughter, Mary Araatoon Gregory Apcar, who died in London in 1895, there is a beautiful and a well preserved manuscript copy of a collection of 306 hymns, canticles and melodies composed in ancient Armenian, by the Fathers of the Armenian Church from time to time.

The work, as can be seen from the title-page, was compiled by Petrus Amirjan, a chorister, but the date and the place of the compilation is not given. It appears from the colophon (*hishatakaran*) that the copy which is now in the Calcutta church Library was made at Saidabad from the original of Petrus Amirjan, by a young Armenian, named Arakiel, the son of Mahtesy Johanness, who laboured for four months, with great zeal and devotion, and completed his self-imposed task on the 17th August, 1757.

The colophon tells us that the paper was supplied by Martyrose, the son of Arathoon and the cost of the binding was borne by Petrus, the son of Rev. Nicholas, the pious and the zealous warden of the Saidabad Armenian church. We are further told that Carapiet, the son of Mathew, helped the copyist by reading the original, thereby enabling him to revise the copy. The volume, according to the interesting colophon, was presented by the scribe, Arakiel Mahtesy Johaness, to the Armenian church at Saidabad, on the 3rd August, 1759, in memory of the persons enumerated above, who had participated in its production. The devout copyist entreats all those who may see or use the book to pray for the repose of their souls, and God shall have mercy on them "on the day that has no night" (*havoorun anerekee*).

The manuscript is composed of 320 quarto pages, measuring 10″ × 7½″. It is beautifully written, like print, with a reed pen on thick hand-made glazed paper, in jet black Indian ink, with the headings and the first letters of the lines in red ink. Although written 180 years ago, it is in a very fair state of preservation, despite the damp climate of Bengal.

But it was for his loyalty to the British that brought him into prominence as one of the foremost citizens of Calcutta shortly before his untimely death, which occurred in 1790 at the early age of forty-eight years.

In the Second Volume of *Selections from the Calcutta Gazettes of the years 1789-1797*, published in 1865, under the sanction of the Government of India, there is, at page 220, an account of the great rejoicings and the festivities which took place in Calcutta in the month of July 1789, on receipt of the happy news of the recovery of King George III of England from his unfortunate malady which, as every student of history knows, was madness.

The writer of the article, after giving a full and vivid account of the proceeedings on that festive occasion on the part of the Government and the citizens of Calcutta, of all classes and denominations, concludes thus :—

"We cannot pass over in the occurrences of Tuesday, the liberality of a Lady of the Settlement who presented a thousand Rupees to be distributed by the Committee for the relief of debtors in such manner as they judged most beneficial.

Another instance of liberality was also exhibited by Mr. Catchick Arrakiel, a wealthy Armenian merchant and an old inhabitant of this Settlement, who liberated, at his own expense, *all* the debtors confined by the Courts of Requests, to the number of one hundred and thirty eight. This act of generosity cost Mr. Catchick Arrakiel, as we understood, three thousand Rupees. This gentleman and many other Armenians, illuminated their houses and their church in the most splendid manner."

The Commissioners of the "Court of Requests" lost no time in informing the Governor-General of the release of all

---

Armenian, Samuel Johnson's *Rasselas,* which was printed at the Press of Academy. He translated Father Michael Chamchian's *History of Armenia,* known as *Khrakhchan,* into English, in 1827. For nearly fifty years, he was a Member of the "Asiatic Society of Bengal." He died on the 11th July 1870, aged 67 years and was buried in the Armenian churchyard of Calcutta. It is sad to remark bowever, that none of his four sons walked in his foot-steps, as men of letters.

We reproduce that article, *in entenso*, as it confirms all that we have said in the past thirty years, after our several visits to that historic ancient church, that the present caretaker is not a fit person to be in charge of that place.

Let the *Gazetteer speak*:—

"Times have changed in Berhampore as well as everywhere else, and the Armenians have given place to others in the local commercial world. The places where they lived are levelled to the ground, and down in Saidabad, where their residences were, one only finds grass and moss-grown ruins. The very roads over which they walked have disappeared, and all that remains of this ancient colony is an occasional walled-in plot of land. To the question 'what place was this?' the guide invariably replies—'A rich Armenian merchant lived here. He was ruined, and the house fell'. The crumbling decay of ages, however, has spared to some extent the old church. Time has dealt more gently with it than with the old town, [Saidabad] and it stands a grim and time-stained monument of an almost forgotten prosperous community of merchants. The sacred building is now only a dilapidated barn. Its walls are bare and crumbling. The inscriptions, mostly in the Armenian tongue, on the upperstones of flat graves are slowly being obliterated, and the little niches and stoups that once marked the spots where the faithful were wont to bless and sprinkle themselves are almost invisible by the accumulation of the dust and the dirt of fifty years of cruel neglect. The font, in the sacristy, where the ancestors of many of Calcutta's prominent Armenian citizens of to-day were admitted into Holy Church, is now a receptacle for rags, whilst on the other side of the building, in another vestry, wherein the registers and vessels of the altar were once carefully guarded, was found a specimen of faded millinery probably cast on one side as useless by one of the caretaker's children. The main body of the church is absolutely a dreary waste; a place of desolation, the evidences of a former grandeur on the inner roof and walls but accentuating the impression of that condition.

But this is not all. For in the east end of the building towers a tall structure that was once the centre of devotion and worship [the altar] of the old-time Armenian community of the district. Aloft, stands a huge picture frame [the altar piece] from which the ragged edges of canvas still flutter, and one is told that from here at one time looked down on the worshippers a beautiful picture of Christ. It is satisfactory to know that this beautiful work has been removed to Calcutta and duly preserved. Underneath this great frame-reredos are three rows, one on the top of the other, of quaintly painted panels, all in a fair state of preservation, representing incidents in the life of Christ and the ministry of his apostles. From the point of view of artistic merit, these are perhaps unimportant, but they have a history contemporary with that of the church itself, and are or should be of far too great interest to those who love the memories of the time when their ancestors knelt beneath them, to be allowed to be the perching places of the caretaker's poultry which alas, appears to be their only present use. Little or none of the altar furniture has been left in the church. In one of the vestries is a tangled mass of lampware and old chains, and on the masonry altar-table were seen two old candle-sticks and an ancient wooden book-rest. The verandah surrounding the building, and the tiny compound in which it stands, are covered with grave-stones of Armenians, who lived and flourished in the district between the years 1758, when the church was built, and 1858, when the last burial is believed to have taken place. The last date appears to be the 17th December, 1858, the grave, inscribed in English, being that of S. M. Vardon Esquire.

The church is now rarely visited save by the curious and according to the caretaker, himself an Armenian, with an imperfect knowledge of English, each year produces two or, at the most, three faithful persons who linger within the once sacred precincts to offer a prayer for the souls of the faithful departed whose last resting-places are within the shadow of the historic old bulding."

The above unbiased account of the deplorable state of the Saidabad church, by an independent eye-witness, should serve as an incentive to those who, as custodians of the ancient church and its lands, are responsible for their preservation. It is to be hoped that when these lines meet their eyes, they will be up and doing before it is too late, for if there is a violent storm or an earthquake, the tottering edifice will collapse, smashing to pieces the large number of beautiful marble tombstones in the three verandahs round the church, and then, woe to those through whose negligence and apathy, the sacred edifice will be no more, for the troubled spirits of all those who lie buried there, will, under the leadership of the good and Godly Khojah Petrus, builder of the church, enter a strong protest before the throne of the Almighty for the destruction and the desecration of their hallowed graves.

In this connection we may mention that for the desecration of a few graves in the old Armenian cemetery in Colootollah Street, Calcutta, by converting a portion of the consecrated ground, on the west side, into a stable, in 1888, a God-fearing member of the Armenian community of Calcutta, the late Mr. A. G. Apcar filed a suit in the Calcutta High Court against the then warden of the Armenian church of Calcutta and had him removed from office, and as a result of that suit, the present Scheme for the Management of the properties and the funds of that rich church came into existence.

In August 1894, when we paid our first visit to the Saidabad church the then caretaker of the church, a good and a Godly old gentleman, named Mackertich Lucas Khojamall, told us that when he was placed in charge of the church by the late Mr. A. G. Apcar, in January 1890, he found that a large portion of the ground on which the priest's quarters were originally standing, with a number of graves adjoining it, had been let out by his predecessor, to local farmers for sowing mustard seed !

Shade of Khojah Petrus Arathoon !

In striking contrast to the Saidabad church, the sister church at Chinsurah (which as we have seen in a previous chapter, is likewise deserted) is kept fairly clean by the present caretaker, at a very heavy cost however, but then that man does not desecrate the place by rearing cattle and poultry, like the illiterate, uncouth, unkempt and unwashed vandal at Saidabad, who like Alexander Selkirk, is "the lord of the fowl and the brute." His employers should, if they wish to save the church from further desecration, replace him by a God-fearing Hindoo durwan, who will, we are sure, have more respect for the sacred edifice than the ungodly villager from Charmahal, who has been a heavy burden on his employers, as they have had to support not only him and his Indian wife, but have spent thousands of rupees for the education of his children during the past thirty years.

In his diary for the 29th December, 1816, the late Agah Owenjohn Elias of Calcutta, who was a native of Saidabad, where he was born in 1786, gives the names of all his ancestors and relations who lie buried in the Armenian churches at Saidabad, Chinsurah and Calcutta. The graves of seven of his relatives, who were buried in the Saidabad church, cannot be traced to-day. The tombstones on their graves, which must have been grand, as they were all wealthy people, have disappeared. Where have they gone? The present caretaker, who as we have said, is "the monarch of all he surveys", may perhaps be able to explain. It may be noted that large marble tombstones have a special fascination for washermen all over India who pay good prices for thick slabs.

In this connection we may mention that some of the tombstones which were there when we *first* copied the inscriptions in August 1894, have also disappeared. It may interest our readers to know that one of them bore the date 1726 and it was to the memory of Mackertoom, son of Agajan, another marked the last resting place of Ogostos of the family of Chugnaz, who died in 1750, whilst a third bore the date 1763 and it covered the mortal remains of Pogose, the son of Hyrapiet of Kars, who was known by the nickname of "Khalash".

It appears that the ground on which the Saidabad church was erected, was the old Armenian cemetery, as there are a few tombstones still *in situ*, which bear dates anterior to the erection of the church in 1758. This was nothing unusual in those olden days, as the Calcutta Armenian church of Nazareth was also erected on the old cemetery, so were the churches at Dacca and Madras.

Khojah Petrus Woskan, a wealthy and a public-spirited Armenian merchant of Madras, constructed in 1726, as we shall see in a succeeding chapter, a beautiful stone bridge of many arches, over the river Adyar in Madras, on which he spent the large sum of 30,000 *hoons*, or pagodas, the pagoda being then worth Rs. 3/8, and he had the foresight to place a fairly large sum in the Company's treasury, the annual income accruing therefrom to meet the necessary repairs.

The Armenian merchants of the olden days who erected churches in India, lacked the foresight of Khojah Petrus Woskan, as they made no provisions for the upkeep of the sacred edifices, with the result that when the Armenians deserted Agra, Delhi, Gwalior, Surat, Patna, Saidabad and Masulipatam, their churches fell into decay and dilapidation, some of them having disappeared already, as has been pointed out in these pages. One of the Armenian merchants of Saidabad, Petrus Stephen by name, left in 1801, the handsome bequest of Rs. 31,700, the annual income to be distributed amongst the officiating priests of the Armenian churches at Saidabad and Calcutta and the poor Armenians of Saidabad, Calcutta and Julfa. The annual income of the Trust in 1801 was Rs. 1305, but owing to the reduction in the rate of interest on Government Securities, the Trust now yields an income of Rs. 970 only per annum. This sum is distributed, in terms of the will of the testator, as under :—

1.	To the officiating priest of the Saidabad church	Rs. 320
2.	To the officiating priests of the Calcutta church	,, 320
3.	To the poor Armenians of Saidabad	,, 110
4.	To the poor Armenians of Calcutta	,, 110
5.	To the poor Armenians of Julfa	,, 110

The devout testator stipulated in his will that once a week the officiating priests of the Armenian churches at Saidabad and Calcutta, were to offer prayers and celebrate the holy Mass for the repose of the souls of the testator (after he was dead) and of his deceased wife Ooroogloo*, as also of his brothers who had predeceased him.

* Oroogloo, the wife of Petrus Stephen, died on the 2nd February, 1801, aged 41 years, and was buried in the Armenian churchyard at Saidabad, where her grave, with a beautiful black tombstone can still bs seen, with a long inscription in old Armenian. The graves of Petrus Stephen and one of his brothers cannot be traced. The grave of his brother David who died on the 31st May, 1800, is in the Calcutta Armenian churchyard. He left a bequest of Rs. 5500 to the Armenian church of Calcutta, the annual income, amounting to Rs. 275, to be equally divided between the church and the local poor.

But as there have been no officiating priests at Saidabad since 1860, the annual income left for that incumbent, as per item 1, has been paid, all these years, to the officiating priests of the Armenian church at Calcutta, which is not in accordance with the provisions of the will of the devout testator.

Similarty, the amount left for the Armenian poor of Saidabad, as per item 3, has been paid to the Armenian poor of Calcutta, which is also contrary to the wishes of the testator.

Since the devout testator has already provided for the priests and the poor of Calcutta, as per items 2 and 3, the annual income left for the priests and the poor of Saidabad, which by an irony of Fate have ceased to exist, should have been spent on the repairs of the Saidabad church, and not allowed that sacred edifice to fall into dilapidation and to complete the destruction of the deserted church, the present caretaker has, with impunity, converted the place into a barn where his cattle and poultry desecrate the sacred edifice and the consecreted grounds daily!

Should these lines meet the eyes of the Official Trustee of Bengal, in whose able hands the Trust is placed, or those who are directly responsible for the administration and the distribution of the income, we hope they will see that the annual income of Rs. 430 is not diverted into other channels, as in the past, for we feel certain that the soul of the devout testator must be revolting against the misfeasance of his Trust.

The Armenian church at Saidabad, dedicated to the blessed Virgin Mary, closed its doors in 1860, and for 75 years no prayers have been said or Masses celebrated in that church "for the repose of the souls of the devout Petrus Stephen, his wife and brothers," yet a sum of Rs. 24,000 has been paid to the officiating priests of the Calcutta Armenian church for services which they have not performed. Had this large sum been expended on the repairs of the Saidabad church, it would have given the sacred edifice a fresh lease of life for another hundred years.

We venture to hope that this humble appeal for the preservation of that ancient church will not fall on deaf years, as it is the only memorial left of the once prosperous Armenian colony at Saidabad. We feel certain that the officiating priests of the Calcutta Armenian church, will, gladly forego that annual income when it is proposed to devote the same for the preservation of the house of God, where, for a hundred years, (1758-1860) their predecessors have invoked the blessings of Heaven on their devout congregation through the celebration of Holy Mass every Sunday morning.

Deserted Saidabad, on the portals of which the ominous word ICHABOD* is writ large, can be proud of another eminent Armenian merchant who flourished there in the early part of the last century. Though he did not possess great wealth like the famous Khojah Petrus Arathoon, the merchant-diplomat, yet he was a great and an equally illustrious member of the Armenian community of Saidabad, whose name and deeds deserve to be recorded in letters of gold for the valuable services which he rendered to the cause of national education in India and the East. Whilst the Armenian merchants of his day were piling up huge fortunes at Calcutta and elsewhere in India and the East, Manatsakan Sumbat Vardon, a merchant of Saidabad, saw the urgent need of national education in India and with a praiseworthy zeal, he founded after strenuous efforts, the "Armenian Philanthropic Academy" in Calcutta. The Academy, which opened its doors on the 2nd April, 1821, still continues its useful work in educating poor boys, mostly from the Armenian villages of Charmahal in Persia.

We shall refer to this venerable institution when writing of the educational activities of the Armenians of Calcutta during the first-half of the 19th century when the community could be justly proud of men like the Rev. Joseph Stephen, Aviet Gentloom, Arratoon Kaloos, Johanness Arathoon Isahak Aganoor, Martyrose Mackertich David, Mesrovb David Thaliadian, Johanness Avdall, Thaddeus Catchick Avetoom. Pogose Vejinian and several others, who by their literary efforts gave an impetus to the spread of national literature in India, by founding printing presses, publishing journals and works of literary merit in the ancient language of Armenia, a language which has always had the Armenians in India and the East amongst its most ardent and enthusiastic admirers.

---

*Ichabod is a Habrew word which means "the glory is departed."

Although the times have changed and the printing establishments, with the authors and the journalists, who kept them going, have disappeared long ago, still it is gratifying to note that there is one solitary literary worker to-day, who walking in the footsteps of the immortal Mesrovb David Thaliadian, the patriotic poet, author, journalist and educationist of India, keeps the glimmering torch of the classical Armenian burning by writing books and articles in that charming, but neglected language, a language which can vie with Latin, Sanscrit and ancient Greek, in beauty, elegance and richness. But we have digressed.

Manatsakan Vardon, the great benefactor of Armenian youth thirsting for knowledge, departed this life at Saidabad on the 13th day of October, 1827, aged fifty five years, and his revered grave can be seen in the now deserted Armenian church of that place, with a beautiful white marble tombstone, on which are inscribed twenty eight lines in ancient Armenian verse.

Should these lines meet the eyes of the present Managers of the "Armenian Philanthropic Academy", now known as the "Armenian College", we would suggest that on the anniversary of his death, which falls on the 13th October, some ten boys be sent up to Saidabad, annually, to pay homage to the revered memory of the FOUNDER, by placing flowers and burning candles and incense over his forgotten grave, so that they may, from their youth, learn to honour and respect the memory of national benefactors, since it is said that "sweet is the memory of departed worth".

They should be taught to learn by heart Long-fellow's beautiful *Psalm of Life*, in which the poet has said that :—

"Lives of great men all remind us
We can make our lives sublime,
And, departing, leave behind us
Foot-prints on the sands of Time".

The deserted Armenian church at Saidabad, should in future, become a place of pilgrimage for the boys in the College founded by Manatsakan Vardon, and for that reason alone, if for nothing else, the church should be kept standing and in good repair as an ancient monument and a landmark of the once prosperous community whose bones rest under the shadow of that sacred edifice, erected by Khojah Petrus Arathoon to the glory of God and for the preservation of the Christian religion in a purely Mohammedan province ruled by bigoted Moslems of Suraj-ud-dowlah type.

As an alumnus of the Armenian College, where we studied, as a day scholar, for six months only, in 1890, we have during the past forty five years, paid several visits to the shrine of the Founder, as a humble pilgrim, praying over his grave and seeking inspiration for our labours in the thorny fields of national service.

It appears that the Armenian community of Calcutta during the first half of the 19th century, being deeply immersed in money-making, were rather slow in appreciating departed worth, for whereas the great philanthropist Agah Catchick Arakiel died in 1790, yet no tribute was paid to his memory till 1837 when a memorial tablet was placed in the church which he had endowed with a valuable English tower-clock and a handsome two-storeyed Parochial House, both of which are still serving the purposes for which they were put up. In the same way nothing was done to perpetuate the memory of Manatsakan Vardon, the Founder of the "Armenian Philanthropic Academy", till the year 1846, when a marble tablet was put up on the walls of the institution, with appropriate inscriptions in Armenian and English, the following being a copy of the latter.

"Sacred to the memory of MANATSAKAN VARDEN, Esquire. This tablet is erected by the members of the Armenian Philanthropic Academy at Calcutta, in acknowledgment of the high esteem and veneration in which he was held by their community, for his virtues in social life and zeal in behalf of the education and welfare of his countrymen, and in which he was at all times ready, equally with his purse and heart, and by his means, as well as the donations of other benevolent Armenians, *founded this Philanthropic Academy*, which dates its existence from the 2nd April 1821. Born at Julfa in Ispahan, on the 6th September 1772, died at Syedabad in Moorshidabad, on the 14th October 1823."

We must point out, however, that the members have made a serious blunder in recording the date of the demise of the Founder, who died at Saidabad in 1827, and not in 1823, as inscribed in the bilingual inscriptions which can be seen in the institution to this day. Had the zealous members of the Academy, with the Rector, Johanness Avdall, as their Nestor, consulted the records of the Academy or the registers of the Saidabad church, the glaring error would have been obviated and the Founder's soul would have rested in peace, instead of being troubled, over the shortening of his already short life by four years! This is how history is often distorted through wrongly-dated memorials.

It may be argued, however, that the date of the death of Manatsakan Vardon, as inscribed on his tombstone in the Saidabad Armenian church, may not be correct, but fortunately we have the unassailable evidence of the late Agah Owenjohn Elias, a resident of Saidabad, who gives the 13th day of October, 1827, as the date of the demise of the Founder of the "Armenian Philanthropic Academy."

And were the perishable memorials erected at Saidabad and Calcutta, to disappear some day, in the natural order of things, the revered name of MANATSAKAN VARDON will remain indelibly inscribed, forages to be, on the roll of the immortals.

CHAPTER XXIX.

AGAH BARSICK ARATHOON.

THE VICTIM OF GOVERNOR HARRY VERELST'S TYRANNY.

As we have seen in the preceding chapter (p. 344) Khojah Petrus Arrathoon, the merchant-diplomat, had two younger brothers—Khojah Gregory and Agah Barsick—both of whom were engaged in trade. The former, through sheer merit and native genius, had risen from the humble position of a cloth-seller at Hooghly to be the Minister and the Commander-in-Chief of Nawab Mir Kasim of Bengal, whilst the latter carried on business, peaceably, as a merchant, at Saidabad. During the troublous days of the infamous monopoly of salt, betel-nut and tobacco, in Bengal, Agah Barsick Arathoon was greatly harassed by Harry Verelst, who had succeeded Clive as Governor, in 1767, after Clive's second able Governorship, which lasted for two years only (1765-1767). It will be interesting to follow the history of that monopoly and the events connected therewith, as the trade of the Armenian merchants suffered considerably during that period, through the high-handed policy of the English who had now become the virtual rulers of Bengal after the battle of Plassey in 1757.

During the eventful years 1760-64, which saw the fall of the Nawab Meer Jafir, and the rise, revolt, and rout of his substitute, the formidable Nawab Mir Kasim, the affairs of the Company were in a chaotic state of disorder and mismanagement. The Company were the actual rulers and Nawab-makers of Bengal; and Clive who was a great soldier but not an able administrator, had during his first Governorship (1758-60) indicated no proper system of Government in Bengal, but merely, as Hunter remarks, "the tradition that unlimited sums of money might be extracted from the natives by the terror of the English name," a policy which was followed many a time and oft.

Clive was absent in England from 1760 to 1765. In a long and important letter to the Hon'ble the Court of East India Directors, dated "Berkeley Square, the 27th April 1764," proposing to return to Bengal as Governor of the Company's Settlements, he, after mature deliberation, gave them, among other things, his opinion with reference to the troubles in connection with the revolt of Nawab Mir Kasim, to the following effect :—

"That it was the encroachments made upon the *Nabob's prescriptive rights,* by the Governor and Council, and the rest of the servants in Bengal trading in the articles of salt, beetle-nut and tobacco, which had greatly contributed to hasten and bring on the troubles with Nabob Cossim Ally Khawn. That, therefore, as the trading in salt, beetle-nut and tobacco had been one cause of the disputes which then had subsisted, his Lordship hoped those articles would be restored to the Nabob, and the Company's servants absolutely forbid to trade in them. This would be striking at the root of the evil, tend to restore that economy which was so necessary in the service of the Company, and serve to prevent the sudden acquisition of fortunes that had of late taken place, and which, if not put a stop to, the Company's affairs must greatly suffer. And his Lordship promised, as a means to alleviate in some measure the dissatisfaction that such restrictions upon the commercial advantages of the Company's servants might occasion in them, *that he would not engage in any kind of trade himself,* but leave all commercial advantages (the Governor's portion of which used to be always very considerable) to the servants to be divided amongst themselves."

Lord Clive's favourable representations to the East India Directors, and his professions of disinterestedness, although feigned, produced the desired effect, and his Lordship was accordingly nominated a second time by the Court of Directors to the Government of Bengal.

Clive, now Baron Clive of Plassey in the peerage of Ireland, arrived at Calcutta, on 23rd June 1765, as Governor of Bengal. He held that high appointment until 1767, and discharged his onerous duties in such an able and statesmanlike manner that he succeeded in placing the Indian administration on what was then considered to be a sound and firmer basis—a task of considerable magnitude, viewed from a diplomatic standpoint.

Among the many reforms which Clive introduced and successfully carried through during his second Governorship, the re-organization of the Company's Service deserves more than a passing notice. By way of encouragement, the Company's servants had been allowed the lucrative privilege of trading privately on their own account, in order to add to their legal salaries, which were rather paltry. Clive, in his zeal to purify the Service from the common corruption which was rather prejudicial to the interests of the Company, strictly prohibited them from continuing private trade, and endeavoured to stamp out their illicit gains in the shape of gifts and presents to them from native chiefs and rulers; but as a recompense, their salaries were largely augmented, the increase being provided out of the *monopoly of salt*. By this monopoly the trade of the Armenian merchants in that commodity was seriously affected, and they were subjected at times to acts of violence and oppression at the hands of the monopolists. Clive is said to have been mainly actuated by considerations of private interest and gain in promoting the monopoly, in which he held a large share : the provision for the Company's servants out of it was merely a subterfuge.

Bolts with his impartial criticism "On the late Monopoly of Salt, Beetle-nut and Tobacco," strongly comments upon it :—

"We come now to consider a monopoly the most cruel in its nature, and most destructive in its consequences, to the Company's affairs in Bengal, of all that have of late been established there. Perhaps it stands unparalleled in the history of any government that ever existed on earth, considered as a public act ; and we shall be not less astonished when we consider the men who promoted it, and the reasons given by them for the establishment of such exclusive dealings in what may there be considered as necessaries of life."

On Clive's representations, the Court of Directors were pleased to sanction the restoration of the trade in salt, beetle-nut and tobacco to the Nawab, and accordingly they appointed a Select Committee, "consisting of his Lordship, Mr. William

Brightwell Sumner, Brigadier-General Carnac, also Messrs. Harry Verelst and Francis Sykes, with full powers to pursue whatever means they should judge most proper, to attain the desirable ends of restoring and establishing peace and tranquillity in Bengal." But Bolts tells us that "the Committee soon lost sight of the orders and intentions of the Court of Directors, and, in contradiction to his Lordship's most solemn declarations, a universal public monopoly of those three articles was determined on : the profits of which were to be divided among themselves, and such others of the Company's servants as they thought proper."

At a meeting of the Select Committee, held on the 10th August 1765 at Fort William, "to take under their consideration the subject of the inland trade in the articles of salt, beetle-nut and tobacco," several resolutions were passed, and a notification, which shows the mode adopted for carrying them into execution, was published in different languages and posted up in several parts of the town, of which the following is a true copy :—

ADVERTISEMENT.

> "The Honourable the Court of Directors having thought proper to send out particular orders for *limiting* the inland trade, in the articles of salt, beetle-nut and tobacco, the same is now to be carried on *in conformity to those orders*, by a public society of proprietors, to be formed for that purpose ; and an exclusive right to the trade of those articles will be vested *in this society, by an authority derived from the Company and from* THE NABOB*;* all manner of persons dependent upon the Honourable Company's Government are hereby strictly prohibited from dealing in any respect, directly or indirectly, in the articles of salt, beetle-nut or tobacco, from the date hereof ; that is to say, that they shall not enter into any new engagements, unless as contractors, either for the purchase or sale of those articles, with the society of trade".

With reference to this odious monopoly, Bolts acquaints us with the fact that

"The Court of East India Directors repeatedly, and in the strongest terms, forbade this monopoly in salt, beetle-nut and tobacco; and particularly in their General Letter to Bengal per the *Lord Camden*, dated the 19th February 1766, wherein they positively directed their Governor and Council to make a formal renunciation by some solemn act to be entered on their records, of all right to trade in those articles; directing their said Presidency to transmit such renunciation in form *to the Nabob*, in the Persian language, with adding these express words:

" 'Whatever Government may be established, or whatever unforseen occurrences may arise, it is our resolution to prohibit, and we do absolutely forbid this trade in salt, beetle-nut and tobacco.' "

And in all their subsequent letters they continued to repeat this prohibition, giving as their sentiments, that "such innovations and illegal traffic had laid the foundation of all the bloodshed, massacres and confusion which had happened in Bengal."

In one of his letters to the Court of East India Directors, Clive, who was the moving spirit in the establishment of the monopoly, said that it was not an *unprecedented thing*, in proof whereof he mentioned that:—

"It is an erroneous opinion, that salt was formerly an open trade; it ever was, *and ever must be*, a monopoly. Some great favourite, or favourites, always had the whole in their own hands, for which he not only paid an annual *Peshcush*, or acknowledgment in money to the Subah, but likewise gave considerable presents both in money and curiosities to him and to his ministers."

The "great favourite" referred to by Clive was the Armenian Khojah Wazeed, concerning whom Bolts gives the following information:

"In the time of the Nabob *Allaverdy Khawn*, his favourite, Cogee [Khojah] Wazeed, was irregularly allowed to farm the trade in salt: but that merchant sold his salt then *five hundred per cent. cheaper* than it was sold after the establishment by this Committee of the monopoly now under consideration. In many parts of Bengal, Cogee [Khojah] Wazeed used to sell his salt for *forty, fifty, or sixty* Rupees *per hundred Maunds;* and at Patna, before this monopoly took place, at one time the market price of salt was so low as *one hundred and fifty* Rupees *per hundred Maunds.* After this monopoly was established, salt was sold in many parts of Bengal for upwards of *three hundred* Rupees *per hundred Maunds,* and in some parts of the Patna province it was raised to upwards of *eight hundred and fifty* Rupees *per hundred Maunds.*"

Marshman, in his *History of Bengal,* writes regarding this monopoly and Khojah Wazeed's perfidy to the Nawab :—

"Khojah Wajeed was a great favourite of Alivardi Khan and had possessed a monopoly of the trade in salt. He had become so exceedingly wealthy, that his daily expenditure was a thousand rupees, and he on one occasion presented fifteen lakhs of rupees to the Nawab. He had formerly been the Agent of the French at Moorshedabad, but when their power was destroyed by the fall of Chandernagore, he came over to the English. Sirajooddowlah placed great confidence in him; yet he was the principal actor in inviting the English to depose that Nawab."

This odious monopoly, at its initiation, was conducted in a violently oppressive and highly arbitrary manner :—

Bolts writes :—

"Upon the establishment of the private copartnership, or society, of the gentlemen of the Committee among themselves, there was an Armenian merchant, named Parseek Arratoon, who had about 20,000 maunds of salt lying in warehouses upon the borders of the Rungpore and Dinagepore provinces. The Armenian, sensible, as well as the gentlemen of the Committee, that the price of salt would rise, ordered his *gomastah to* fasten up his warehouses, and not to sell. As the retailing of this salt in those parts might hurt the partnership's sales, it was thought expedient, at any rate, if possible, to get possession of it. Upon failure of the artifices which were practised to induce the *gomastah* to sell it, the Armenian merchant's warehouses were broke open, the salt forcibly taken out and weighed off, and a sum of money, estimated to be the price of it, was forced upon the Armenian's *gomastah,* on his refusing to receive it. Such are the facts sworn to in the depositions of several witnesses, upon an action, or bill of complaint filed in the Mayor's Court of Calcutta, the 15th September 1767, by Parseek Arratoon, plaintiff, against the *gomastahs* or agents of Messrs. Verelst and Sykes, for current rupees 60,432, and if the proceedings of the Mayor's Court have been transmitted home with the same punctual regularity as formerly, there must be sufficient proof of these facts among the records now in Leaden Hall Street."

Parseek Arratoon appealed to the equity of the Honourable Company's Courts, by filing a suit in the Mayor's Court against the unwarrantable conduct of the agents of the Governor Harry Verelst and Francis Sykes. Justice would have been administered in his case, had the said Governor, whose interests were at stake and at whose instance the oppression was committed, not arbitrarily put a stop to the proceedings in a most unjustifiable manner. Bolts, however, took up the matter. He writes concerning it :—

"We now come to the exemplification of what we have advanced, by real facts, in which the writer will either confine himself to matters of which he himself hath perfect knowledge, and can even produce proof, or to such others as appear well vouched by authentic documents exhibited in different parts of this work; and we will begin with the Mayor's Court.

"In consequence of a most extraordinary oppression in the inland parts of the country, of which particular notice is taken in our 13th chapter, an Armenian merchant, named Parseek Arratoon, on the 15th September 1767, filed a bill in the Mayor's Court against the *gomastahs* or agents of Governor Harry Verelst and Francis Sykes, Esquires, for 60,432 current rupees or about 7,500 pounds sterling, principal amount of salt, said to have been forcibly taken out of the plaintiff's warehouses. The cause was brought to an issue; and in the month of August 1768, on a day appointed for the hearing, all the proceedings and depositions were read and fully considered; the demand of the plaintiff established to all appearance, and judgment upon the point of being pronounced, when the Mayor, while sitting in judgment, received a private letter* or note,

*The writer of these sheets being an Alderman of the Court, and having been absent when this extraordinary transaction happened, as

sent from the Governor, to put a stop to the proceedings, because, as alledged, he, the said Governor, was a party concerned in the cause, and was in expectation of settling matters by a private compromise. To the astonishment of the plantiff's solicitor, who declared he knew of no compromise, and had received no instructions from his client upon this matter, the request contained in the letter or note was complied with, and a stop was at once put to the proceedings; the plaintiff being left without any satisfaction.

"After an instance of this sort, it may be thought needless to produce others of a less criminal nature. But it is notorious in Calcutta, that in cases wherein the said Governor and Council, or those of their connections, have been any wise interested, private applications, by letter or otherwise, have been frequently received by the Court; who, setting aside the formalities of process as directed by the Charter, have actually proceeded to hear and determine upon such private applications, particularly against the attorneys or solicitors of the Court, who have found it a hazardous matter to undertake any suit in matters of arbitrary proceedings, wherein the Governor and Council have been in the least degree interested separately or collectively."

We have already seen that the Court of Directors strictly prohibited, since its commencement, the monopoly in salt, betel-nut and tobacco; but, as communication with England was very slow in those days, the monopoly continued for two years before

---

soon as he heard of it, wrote to the Mayor upon the subject, desiring to have a sight of the letter sent by, or by the order of, the Governor, then Harry Verelst, Esquire, in consequence of which the proceedings had been stopped. After some days' consideration, the Mayor wrote the following excuse, the original of which is now in the writer's possession:—

" 'To William Bolts Esquire.

" 'Dear Sir,—I should have sent you the note as I promised, if I had found it; but having not met with it among my papers, convinces me that I must have destroyed it, with other papers that I *deemed useless*.

I am, Sir, Your most obedient servant,
Cornelius Goodwin.

" 'Calcutta, the 11th August 1768.' "—*Bolts*.

it was finally put a stop to by the Directors at home. There were sixty shares in the concern, and the shareholders, who were the rulers of the country, had during that short period made a profit of Rs. 1,074,002 ! That the monopoly was highly profitable, may also be inferred from the fact that on one occasion two wealthy native merchants of Calcutta, who were accused of having sold salt at other prices than that fixed by the monopolists, were fined to the amount of Rs. 40,000.

In a subsequent chapter, "On the General Modern Trade of the English in Bengal; on the Oppressions and Monopolies which have been the causes of the decline of Trade, the Decrease of the Revenues, and the Present Ruinous Condition of Affairs in Bengal," the same author, writing of the oppressions consequent on the enforcement of other monopolies, mentions, among others, the following instances, in which the peaceable Armenians were the injured parties and sufferers, in defiance of treaty obligations and solemn stipulations on the part of the Honourable Company :—

"With every species of monopoly, therefore, every kind of oppression to manufacturers, of all denominations throughout the whole country, has daily increased; insomuch that weavers, for daring to sell their goods, and *dallals* and *pykars,* for having contributed to or connived at such sales, have, by the Company's agents, been frequently seized and imprisoned, confined in irons, fined considerable sums of money, flogged, and deprived, in the most ignominious manner, of what they esteem most valuable, their castes. Weavers also, upon their inability to perform such agreements as have been forced from them by the Company's agents, universally known in Bengal by the name of *Mutchulcahs,* have had their goods seized, and sold on the spot, to make good the deficiency : and the winders of raw silk, called *Nagaads,* have been treated also with such injustice, that instances have been known of their cutting off their thumbs, to prevent their being forced to wind silk. This last kind of workmen were pursued with such rigour during Lord Clive's late government in Bengal, from a zeal for increasing the Company's investment of raw silk, that the most sacred laws of society were atrociously, violated; for it was a common thing for the Company's seapoys to be sent by force of arms to break open the houses of the Armenian merchants established at Sydabad (who have, from time immemorial, been largely concerned in the silk trade) and forcibly take the *Nagaads* from their work, and carry them away to the English factory."

In the same chapter the author observes :—

"The public monopoly next in consequence, as of late practised, has been that of piece-goods fit for the markets of Bussorah, Jedda, Mocha, Bombay, Surat and Madras. Of those goods there are many sorts which the English Company do not deal in, such as, at Dacca, the coarser kinds of Mulmuls, called Anundy, Hyaty, Sonargoung and Sherbetty; and at Cossimbazar and Radnagore several sorts of Sarries, called Chappa, Mugga, Tempy, Tarachaundy and Mucta; also Soocies and Soocy-Sarries, Cuttanees and Tasseties, &c., in the provision of which nevertheless, under the same influence, like oppressions are practised as for the Company's investment.

"For the disposal of the goods of this joint concern, another monopoly is established of the exclusive right of exportation, particularly to Bussorah, Jedda and Mocha, which used to be the most profitable voyages. For this purpose, the Governor and Council of Calcutta fit out ships, generally known by the denomination of the Freight Ships, on which the goods of this joint concern are first shipped, and the remainder of the tonnage is fitted up on freight. The management of this concern is under the direction of a member of the Council, who is acting-owner, and keeps a warehouse for this purpose, generally known in Calcutta by the name of the Freight Warehouse. When one of these freight-ships is set up, no other persons among the few that can provide goods dare attempt to set up another on the same voyage, without the permission of the Governor and Council; nor is any person suffered to load their goods on any other ship for those markets, if such should be permitted to be set up, until the loading of the freight-ship of the Governor and Council be completed. Frequent instances have been known of the goods of private merchants, even Europeans, but particularly of those belonging to Armenians, Moguls and Gentoos,*

---

* *Gentoo* is a Portuguese word, meaning *Gentiles* in the Biblical parlance. By this general appellation they at first called all the natives

being, in consequence of this monopoly, stopped on the public road, and by force carried to the freight-warehouse; and the proprietors of such goods have been obliged, contrary to their wills, to see their goods shipped on vessels they had not a good opinion of, and going on voyages whose destination and management were often contrary to their own private schemes of trade: in consequence of which unwarrantable proceedings, those merchants have frequently lost their sales, have had their goods damaged, left at ports they never designed they should touch at, and have sometimes lost even the goods themselves. By all which cruel circumstances there have been in Bengal many instances of families of Armenians, principal traders in this branch to Persia and Arabia, the former of which may properly be called their own country, who have been *totally ruined*."

Agah Barsick Arathoon, the victim of Governor Harry Verelst's tyranny and oppression, died on the 21st August, 1769, and was buried in the Armenian churchyard at Saidabad, where his grave, with a beautiful granite tombstone, can be seen to this day.

---

of India, whether Hindoos or Muhammadans, and from them the English adopted the term *Gentoo*—an appellation by which they distinguished the Hindoos, as followers of Brahma, from the Muhammadans or Musalmans, whom they commonly, though improperly, called *Moors*, or *Moormen*.

CHAPTER XXX.

Gregore Khojamall and Johanness Rafael

Some more victims of Verelst's Tyranny.

Governor Verelst not contented with the tyranny he exercised over the Armenian merchants in Bengal, had two highly respectable merchants of that nation, Gregore Khojamall and Johanness Rafael, brought down from the dominions of Nawab Sujah-ud-dowlah of Oudh and had them imprisoned for some months, because the business they carried on greatly interfered with the private views of the Governor and some members of the Council at Calcutta.

The Governor and Council at Calcutta had now assumed the powers of an autocrat and carried on the Company's government with despotism and corruption, once Clive had left Bengal for good.

The years 1767-69, as regards the commercial affairs of the Armenian merchants in Bengal, were rather eventful, and we cannot refrain from dwelling upon them at considerable length. We have already seen that, by virtue of a certain Charter, the Armenians were placed in 1688 on an equal footing with the English in India. So long as the East India Company was a purely commercial concern, they enjoyed all its chartered rights and privileges. The Directors had even declared and stipulated.

"That we will not continue any Governor in our service that shall in any kind disturb or discountenance them [the Armenians] in the full enjoyment of all the privileges hereby granted to them, neither shall they pay any other or greater duty in India than the Company's Factors, or any other Englishmen born, do, or ought to do."

Matters took quite a different turn, however, when the Company embarked on territorial power, so as to consolidate its position in India, and was apparently guided by a resolution passed to that effect, which ran as follows:—

"The increase of our revenue is the subject of our care, as much as our trade; 'tis that must maintain our force when twenty accidents may interrupt our trade, 'tis that must make us a nation in India."

Bolts, who was singularly well informed on Indian affairs, writes :—

"The Armenians, who have ever been a great commercial body in Hindostan, have also long had considerable settlements in Bengal, particularly at Sydabad. Their commerce was likewise established by the Mogul's *firmaun,* whereby the duties on the two principal articles of their trade, piece-goods and raw silk, were fixed at three and one half per cent. But after the subversion of the Mogul empire, and during the reigns of the independent Nabob-usurpers, they, as well as the Europeans, were at times exposed to great impositions, and interruptions of their trade. At present, since the English Company have taken the sovereignty of the country into their own hands, they all trade under the appearance of the old forms, subject in all places within the Bengal provinces, out of the jurisdiction of their respective settlements, to such regulations as the English are pleased to impose on them,* through the nominal Nabobs; which regulations on many occasions amount to a total prohibition of their trade, being in general temporary, contradictory, and wholly calculated for obstruction.

"The difference also between the lawful trade of the Company's servants and that of English free merchants and other persons residing under the Company's protection was, that the covenanted servants of the Company, as hath been observed in another place, were, by connivance of the country Government, and long established usage, indulged with *dustucks*† for the carrying on of their trade duty-free; while the others, for want of that *dustuck,* were subjected to the payment of the Government duties. It is true, the inconveniences and impositions, which the want of this *dustuck* exposed the European free-traders to, were such as generally induced them to prefer contracting with the Company's servants for the delivery of such goods as they wanted in Calcutta; and it, in fact,

*When the foreigners prove refractory, the Fowzdar of Hooghly is made to surround their settlemtnts with troops, in the name of *the Nabob* to stop their provisions, and obstruct their business. This has actually been frequently practised.—*Bolts.*

†An order or passport.

amounted to an almost total exclusion of them from the inland trade, from one place to another, which, when Bengal flourished, was generally very beneficial. With respect to the trade that was actually carried on within the Company's principal settlements of Calcutta, Madras and Bombay, all were, or ought to have been, upon an equal footing.

"Such was the situation of trade before the English Company made themselves the Sovereigns of Bengal; and this representation is agreeable to the ideas of the former Courts of Directors in England, who, in their general letters to India down to the year 1757, and particularly in that year, gave their express sentiments and directions upon this subject to their different presidencies in this manner :—

" 'That all persons under the protection of the Company should have the liberty of resorting to and trading at all and any of the Company's settlements in the East Indies, and at all other places within the Company's limits, in as full, true and extensive a manner as the rest of the Company's servants; they paying the duties, according to the usual and customary methods and rates established at such places.'

"And about the same time, in order to ascertain the rights of persons residing upon the western coast of Sumatra, the Court of Directors were also pleased to give their sentiments to their President and Council at Bombay in the following words :—

"All persons residing upon the west coast of Sumatra, who shall resort to, or trade either by themselves or their agents, at Fort St. George, Fort William, or Bombay, and their respective dependencies, are to buy and sell publicly or privately, as they themselves shall choose; dealing freely, and without restraint, with whomsoever they shall think proper; and if, contrary to this article, they shall be oppressed or injured by any person whatsoever, such person, or persons, let their rank be what it may, will incur our highest displeasure, and shall certainly feel the weight of our resentment.'

"Those were the judicious orders given for the protection of trade by former Courts of Directors: and by the representation which has just been given to the nature of the English Company's trade in India, the reader, who is a merchant, will easily see that upon a footing of fair trade, it must be ever for the interest of the Company, though not for that of their servants, to encourage private traders of all nations, in India, for these obvious reasons; that the more traders, the more purchasers of the Company's staple imports, the sales of which would be the more industriously pushed in every corner of India; and the more providers of goods at the manufacturing towns, the more the manufacturers would be encouraged, and upon a free inland trade, the more goods would come to market. But since the English East India Company have become the Sovereigns, they and their substitutes have been exclusively the sole merchants of Bengal, and seem to have adopted sentiments as repugnant to the true spirit of mercantile affairs, as could possibly be conceived: nay they have of late even ventured to assert, that they *alone* have a right *to trade in India;* and in consequence of that absurd opinion, they have directed certain merchants, inhabitants of Calcutta, not to trade; alleging, very nicely, that though they may have a legal right to reside at their settlements, they could have no right to trade there; which is the same thing as telling a man he may have a right to live, but no right to use the means of his profession for acquiring the wherewithal to support life.

"It is true that such restrictions have never been laid but upon particular persons whom the Company designed to oppress and crush. But how miserable and despicable must that state of the government of the Company's affairs be, wherein the general system of justice is stopped or perverted, for the sake of oppressing an individual!"

Bolts was perhaps the best authority on the subject, and, in writing "Of the Courts of Law established by the Charter granted to the Company, and of the Government, Police, and Administration of Justice in Bengal," he criticises the policy adopted by the Company's Governors and Council and their utter disregard of treaty stipulations after the battle of Plassey, when they assumed sovereignty over Bengal. In support of his arguments and criticisms, Bolts cites cases of oppression, violence and miscarriage of justice. For example :—

"One more extraordinary instance we will give of the convenient uses which are made of the Nabobs by the Governor and Council in Calcutta, under whose direction alone they act, whenever it is necessary for any private purpose to oppress individual; and this is of certain *Armenian merchants* of established credit and reputation, who, like many hundreds of others, had been long established in India, and were at this time peaceably engaged in carrying on their own mercantile business in the dominions bordering on Bengal, which the Campany had taken from, and afterwards restored to, the Nabob Sujah-al-Dowlah. The business they carried on greatly interfering with the private views of the Governor and some of the Council at Calcutta and their connections, it was thought necessary to have them removed. Not contented with their being suddenly seized by the Company's troops and confined, without ever being accused, confronted, or heard upon any pretended crime or misbehaviour whatever in the dominions of Sujah-al-Dowlah, the Governor and Council had them brought down into their own provinces, where they could more conveniently manage them, and where they were kept imprisoned for some months, to the utter ruin of themselves and families. After they had been long enough imprisoned to serve the purposes intended, they were set at liberty, but without being acquainted with any reason for such imprisonment: and, despairing of ever obtaining justice in Bengal, two of them came over in quest of it to England; where, flattering themselves that the Court of Directors would naturally discountenance such oppression, they presented a very respectful petition to the Court; which, as it will give the best state of their case, we will present the reader with a copy of, as follows :—

" '*To the* HONOURABLE THE COURT OF DIRECTORS *for the affairs of the Honourable the United Company of Merchants of England, trading to the Indies,*

" '*The Petition of* GREGORE COJAMAUL *and* JOHANNES PADRE RAFAEL, *Armenian Merchants, late of Bengal,*

" 'Humbly Sheweth,

" 'That your petitioners, who are natives of Ispahan in Persia, have for many years resided in India, particularly in the provinces annexed to Bengal, and in the dominions of the different princes bordering upon those provinces, where they have carried on for themselves and others, a very extensive trade, always with the permission and approbation of the different princes, in whose dominions your petitioners resided; always paying the duties exacted by such princes, and always cheerfully submitting themselves to the laws of such countries.

" 'That it has ever been the custom, from time immemorial, for Greeks, Georgians, Turks, Persians, Tartars, Cashmeerians, Armenians, and other nations, to resort to and traffic in India, where the country Nabobs, sensible of the benefits arising from the resort of foreign merchants and the increase of trade, have at all times encouraged such persons to the utmost of their power.

" 'That besides their own traffic, your petitioners likewise, for about seven years last past, have been honoured with business upon commission from sundry English gentlemen, several of whom are now in England.

" 'That your petitioners in such transactions have ever acted to the satisfaction of their constituents, and with credit to themselves; having ever studiously avoided interfering in any other than their own mercantile affairs; and they have ever been well-wishers to the Honourable English East India Company, having never, in the most distant manner, acted contrary to the interests of that Company.

" 'That your petitioners were lately resident in the dominions of the Nabob Sujah-al-Dowlah,* and the Rajah Bulwant Sing, who, to the great surprize of your petitioners,

*Sujah-al-Dowlah was the Nawab Wazir of Oudh, and according to Marshman, "the only chief of importance in the north" In November 1763 he had afforded an asylum to the notorious Sumru. Actuated by motives of avarice and ambition, he adopted a policy of aggression, marched down at the head of an army of 50,000 men, and on the 3rd of May 1764 laid siege to Patna, where the English army had retired from the field for want of provisions. With great difficulty he was repulsed, and was obliged to retire to Buxar to encamp for the rains. Here on the 23rd October the celebrated victory was gained by Major (afterwards Sir Hector) Munro over the allied forces of Sujah-al-Dowlah and Mir Kasim, who had joined the Nawab Wazir's camp. The battle of Buxar made the English masters of the entire Gangetic valley, and placed the *subah* of Oudh at the feet of the conquerors.

received orders from your Presidency of Calcutta, or Fort William, to banish your petitioners out of their countries.

" 'That those princes communicated the orders which they had received from your said Presidency to your petitioners, who had the honour to be favoured with the friendship of the said princes; who proposed various expedients to screen your peititoners from violence, as your petitioners can shew by authentic documents in their hands, to the satisfaction of this Honourable Court.

" 'That the friendship of those princes having induced them to evade the immediate execution of such tyrannical orders, for which they knew no cause, your President Mr. Verelst wrote again in repeated letters, and in most peremptory terms, to have your petitioners seized, imprisoned and sent down into the Company's provinces to Patna and Murshidabad; and for feat of further delays or evasicns, orders were given to the immediate servants of the English Company, who were employed to seize and imprison your petietioners, as they are likewise ready to prove to the satisfaction of this Honourable Court, by authentic documents and writings under the hands and seals of the said Company's servants.

" 'That accordingly your petitioners were seized in the most sudden, cruel and inhuman manner, and brought down to the Company's factories at Patna and Murshidabad, being obliged to quit instantly all they were possessed of in that country, to a very considerable amount, together with their books and papers, and the effects of many other persons with which they were intrusted, and for which they are accountable.

" 'That during the confinement of your petitioners, their relations did deliver to your President, Mr. Harry Verelst, sundry petitions, particularly one of the 15th May 1768, and one of the 13th June 1768 (which your petitioners imagine stand recorded upon your Calcutta consultations), requesting the releasement of your petitioners, and offering to give any such security for money, or the appearance of your petitioners, as might appear reasonable to your said President and Council.

" 'That the said petitions were paid no regard to, but your petitioners were continued under confinement; your petitioner *Gregore Cojamaul* having been confined from the

14th March 1768 to the 23rd May 1768, being two months and nine days; and your petitioner *Johannes Padre Rafael*, from the 27th March 1768 to the 28th August 1768, being five months; during which time they wer treated worse than convincted felons: Cogee [Khojah] Rafael being first imprisoned in a horse-stable, and afterwards both kept in close confinement under a strong guard of the Company's seapoys, with fixed bayonets, who never suffered your petitioners to stir out of their sight.

" 'That being at last released from confinement, your petitioners and their friends waited upon your President, Mr. Harry Verelst, not only to be acquainted what were the causes of his displeasure, and why they had been confined, but requesting leave to return up the country to secure their effects and outstanding concerns, thereby to preserve themselves and families from ruin; but, to the misfortune of your petitioners, all their applications were paid no regard to, nor could they ever obtain any satisfaction, or be acquainted why they had been thus conspicuously imprisoned for so long a time, and then set at liberty, without being accused of even a fictitious misdemeanor?

" 'That, to the great astonishment of your petitioners, upon their arrival in Calcutta, they were informed, that your Governor, Mr. Harry Verelst, and his Council had been pleased to publish an edict, under date of the 18th May 1768, prohibiting all Armenians, Portuguese and their descendants, *from residing or trading in any part* OUT *of the provinces of Bengal, Behar and Orissa, or attempting to transport any merchandise beyond those provinces, under penalty of the utmost severe corporal punishment, and the confiscation of such merchandize*; an attested notorial copy of which most extraordinary public edict [*see* p. 90] is in the hands of your petitioners, for the inspection of this Honourable Court.

" 'That your petitioners were hereby not only deprived, among others, of those rights which were due to them, as men, by the law of nations, but were deprived of that freedom of trade which their nation had always enjoyed in the times of the worst of the ancient BLACK NABOBS, and in particular were also deprived of all hopes of ever recovering those effects from which they had been thus forcibly and capriciously taken.

" 'That your petitioners, who have been therefore necessitated at a great expense to come to England for justice, now appeal to the equity of this Honourable Court; requesting, that they will either indemnify your petitioners from the great losses they sustain, or that they will be pleased to order home, to answer for themselves, the President Mr. Verelst, and such of the Company's servants as to this Honourable Court may appear to have been the acting persons in the oppressions complained of.

" 'And your petitioners, as in duty bound, shall ever pray.

(Sd.) " 'GREGORE COJAMAUL*
(,,) " 'JOHANNES PADRE RAFAEL.†

" 'London, the 12th September 1769.' "

Bolts, who, in his official capacity as an "Alderman or Judge of the Honourable the Mayor's Court of Calcutta," knew but too well of the high-handed policy of the Governor and Council of Calcutta, and of the want of equity of the Honourable the Court of Directors, makes the following observation regarding the above petition:—

" 'It was natural for these injured Armenian merchants, who then knew but little of the state of the Company and the party views of its Directors, to imagine that the Court would have shewn some readiness, if not a serious disposition, to redress their wrongs. But, to their [the Court of Directors'] shame be it spoken! the petition is said to have been thrown

*We find in an Armenian book, printed in 1788, at St. Petersburg, that Gregore Cojamall had, after a stay of ten years in London, gone over to St. Petersburg and started an Armenian press there, the *first* in that metropolis. He had the type cast for the same while at London, "and that at a great cost," it having been his cherished desire from his youth upwards to start a new press. His death at the Russian capital must have occurred before 1788, the year in which the book was printed "at the press of the late Mr. Gregore, son of Cojamaul, of the family of Khaldareantz."

†It was this Khojah Rafael who in 1755 sold the celebrated Indian diamond to Prince Orloff, whom he met at Amsterdam, *en route* for Russia. For a fuller account of this historical Indian diamond, see pp. 261-62.

aside, and to have lain by, unanswered and disregarded to this day;* while these *foreign gentlemen*, as is said, have been left to seek redress at law, exactly in the distressful situation already described; exposed to the necessity of sending commissions to India for evidence, and of waiting for the precarious arrival of their oppressors from India ; some of whom may perhaps shamelessly attempt to screen themselves by the practised and now usual subterfuge, of pretending the matter complained of was transacted by THE NABOB, in the extra-judicial districts of the Charter.

"Many other instances might be given to prove the badness of the Government, Police, and administration of justice in those distant dominions; some of which, though these looked upon as trifles, would in this country be considered as matters of the most serious consequence. Indeed, to enumerate all the facts of that nature which have come within the writer's knowledge would be to fill a large folio volume. It would, moreover, be a task shocking to humanity; and as it is presumed sufficient have already been produced to convince the reader of the truth of our assertions upon the subject-matter of this chapter, we shall hasten to a conclusion of it."

The edict referred to in the petition of the two injured Armenian merchants, issued at Calcutta by the Governor and Council, ran thus :—

" 'Fort William, 18th May 1768.

" 'Notice is hereby given that, after the expiration of Two Months, from the 27th April, no *gomastahs* employed by English shall be permitted to remain in any part *out* of the provinces of Bengal, Bahar, and Orissa; and after that period, that no Company's servant, free merchant, or other European residing under the Company's protection, shall be suffered to carry on any inland trade, directly or indirectly, *beyond* those limits, under penalty, if a Company's servant, of being immediately dismissed the service; if a free merchant, or other European, of forfeiting the Company's protection : and that, if

*That is, the year 1772, when he published in London his *Considèrations on India Affairs*, from which the above is an extract.

any Europeans whatsoever shall attempt to transport any merchandize *beyond* the provinces, all such merchandize shall be seized and confiscated and the *gomastahs*, having charge of such contraband trade, shall be punished with the utmost severity.

" 'All Armenians, Portuguese, or the descendants of Armenians and Portuguese, living under the Company's protection, are included in the above destrictions. It being intended that none but *the natives* of the country (Mussulmen and Hindoos) shall in future enjoy this privilege.

" 'SIMEON DROZ, *Secretary.*'

" 'I, John Holme, Notary Public, dwelling and practising at Calcutta at Fort William in Bengal, do hereby certify and attest, that the within writing is a true copy of a paper affixed to the door of the Town-Hall of Calcutta aforesaid, carefully collated by me with the original, exhibited to me for that purpose.

" 'In faith and testimony whereof, I have hereunto set my hand and seal, at Calcutta, the first day of July, in the year of our Lord one thousand seven hundred and sixty eight.

(Sd.) ' 'JOHN HOLME, Notary Publick.' "

Bolts makes the following comments on the edict:—

"To particularize, in a mercantile community, all the gross absurdities and the injustice of such an order, would be to offer an insult to every man of understanding; we will therefore only remark, that this order principally contributed to the producing of two ruinous effects; one, the prevention of extending the Company's sales of British woollens and other staple commodities of this kingdom, and the other, adding to the discouragement of the inland importation of bullion, by lessening all mercantile connections with the merchants of the interior parts of Hindoostan. From whence the Company, or their Governor and Council, could derive these powers of confiscation and punishment, or by what authority they could deprive of their natural rights, the Armenians and Portugueze established in Bengal, who, as well as their forefathers, were natives of that country equally with the *Mussulmen* and

Hindoos; or with what view they wanted to prevent all trade in the dominions bordering upon Bengal, notwithstanding the Princes of such adjacent countries permitted, encouraged, and according to *the usages of the empire,* could not prevent such trade, it must be hard to account for, unless from *private selfish motives;* which latter we are the more inclined to believe must have been the case, as the gentlemen who made this restrictive order also continued their own agents and *gomastahs* in the interdicted districts."

A few words of comment on the scurvy treatment meted out to the Armenian merchants in Bengal by their new masters, the English, may not be out of place. Apart from treaty obligations which had placed the Armenians in India on an equal footing with the English in 1688, (see pp. 233-239) when it was solemnly declared and stipulated by the "Governor and Company of Merchants of London Trading to the East Indies," that "they will not continue any Governor in their service that shall in any kind disturb or discountenance them in the full enjoyment of all the privileges granted to them, neither shall they pay any other or greater duty in India than the Company's factors, or any other Englishmen born, do, or ought to do," (p. 234) the English in Bengal who harassed the Armenians after the battle of Plassey, owed them a deep debt of gratitude, for it was an Armenian, Khojah Israel Sarhad, who according to the Company's records "had managed our affairs in Mahomed Azeem's Durbar and by his prudent conduct and winning address insinuated himself into favour and procured for us the Grant of this place [Calcutta] and the dependant Towns which we now enjoy, and that for a small expence in comparison of the benefit." But then human memory is miserably short and the English seem to have totally forgotten the valuable services of another Armenian, Khojah Petrus Arathoon, who had saved the English fugitives at Fulta from starvation, after the "Black Hole" tragedy of 1756, as shown in a previous chapter. And for all these valuable services to the British cause in Bengal, respectable and peace-loving Armenian merchants were harassed, arrested and imprisoned in dirty stables as if they were felons and murderers, but then where rank materialism reigns supreme, that extremely rare virtue, called *gratitude*, is *non est.*

O tempora ! O mores !

ARMENIANS AT MONGHYR

CHAPTER XXXI.

KHOJAH GREGORY, *ALIAS* GORGIN KHAN.

THE ARMENIAN COMMANDER-IN-CHIEF AND MINISTER OF NAWAB MIR KASIM OF BENGAL,

FROM

1760-1763.

In the Paper which we read at the Lucknow Session of the "Indian Historical Records Commission", in December 1926, on "Hindoos in Armenia 150 years before Christ," we stated that Armenians had been connected with India from the days of remote antiquity. We narrated in that Paper the history of two fugitive Hindoo princes from Kanauj who found an asylum in far-off Armenia in the year 149 B.C. from which it is evident that there was a friendly intercourse between Hindoos and Armenians 2,000 years ago, hence the flight of the two Indian princes to Armenia and not to any of the neighbouring countries, such as Ceylon, Burmah or Siam.

For twenty centuries and more Armenians have been connected with India as a commercial people and have, through their integrity, achieved success in the domain of trade and commerce during the Hindoo, the Mohammedan and the British periods. Although a purely commercial community, yet when an opportunity presented itself, they showed themselves to be more than ordinary merchants and traders.

We have seen in the early part of this work, how the son of an Armenian merchant of Cashmere, Mirza Zul-Qarnain, or Alexander by name, rose to be a grandee of the Mogul Court during the reign of Akbar, through sheer merit, and continued to enjoy that high privilege and distinction during the reigns of Jehangeer and Shah Jehan, and despite the blandishments and the persuasions of Jehangeer and the persecutions of Shah Jehan, the Armenian grandee remained firm and steadfast in the faith of his forefathers and lived and died a good

Christian, a staunch friend and a patron of the good Jesuit Fathers at Akbar's Court who wrote of him as "the pillar of Christanity in India." The Chief Justice-Mir Adl-of Akbar's Court was likewise an Armenian, Abdool Hai by name.

An eminent Armenian merchant of Bengal, Khojah Israel Sarhad, rose to be a diplomat and an envoy and was instrumental in securing the "Grand Farman" for the English East India Company from the Mogul Emperor Farrokhsiyar in 1715. And as we have seen, another well-known Armenian merchant of Calcutta, Khojah Petrus Arathoon, better known as the "Armenian Petrus," rendered yeoman services to the British cause in Bengal after the tragedy of the "Black Hole" and acted as an envoy between the English and Mir Jaffir for the overthrow of Nawab Siraj-ud-dowlah and was equally successful afterwards in the removal of the imbecile Nawab Mir Jaffir from the *Masnad* of Murshidabad and in the appointment of Mir Kasim, in 1760, as the Nawab Nazim of Bengal, Behar and Orissa.

Since the days of Akbar, a great patron of the Armenians, who reigned from 1556-1605, up to the middle of the 18th century, or a period of 200 years, the Armenians in India, apart from being eminent merchants, had given a Chief Justice, and a grandee to the Mogul Court, an envoy to the British, but they had not yet distinguished themselves in the military service of the country of their adoption. Yet when the psychological moment arrived, a humble Armenian cloth-seller of Hooghly, Khojah Gregory by name, and a younger brother of the "Armenian Petrus" referred to above, laid down the iron yard measure and took up a gun in the same way that Clive, a humble writer on the Madras Establishment, had exchanged his quill for a sword and with what wonderful results!

Khojah Gregory, better known by his orientalized name of "Gorgin Khan," was a cloth-merchant at Hooghly and for championing the cause of Mir Kasim, he became his confidant and when Mir Kasim ascended the *Masnad* of Murshidabad in the place of his father-in-law, Nawab Mir Jaffir, in 1760, he immediately appointed Gorgin Khan as the Commander-in-Chief of the Bengal Army.

Unfortunately very little is known of this remarkable military genius—the erstwhile cloth-seller of Hooghly—for the Mohammedan historians of the time, have, through racial jealousy and religious antipathy, painted him black by calling him a "traitor" and "the evil genius of Mir Kasim."

Had he not fallen a victim to the sword of an unknown assassin as we shall see later on, that great Armenian soldier, who for three years (1760-1763) was the virtual ruler of Bengal, Behar and Orissa, would, in time, have become the Nawab of Bengal with the help of the well-disciplined and powerful Army at his command, and he would have done exactly what those two soldiers of fortune,—Mustapha Kemal Pasha and Reza Khan—did in Turkey and in Persia in our own days.

Amongst the English historians, Marshman, who is regarded as the best authority on Indian History of that period, writes of Gorgin Khan, as follows :—

"Meer Caseem met the difficulties of his position with great energy. He curtailed the extravagance of the Court establishments. He abolished the "Ram Office", the "Antelope Office", the "Nightingale Office", and many other useless and costly appendages of the menagerie department. He subjected the public accounts to a severe scrutiny, and obliged the officers to disgorge the plunder they had acquired. He exacted all arrears of rent with unexampled rigour, revised the assessment of the land, and made an addition of a crore of rupees to the annual revenue of the three provinces. These measures gave him the means of discharging all the obligations he had contracted to the English, after which he gave his entire attention to the great object of emancipating himself from the pressure of their authority, and restoring freedom to the Soobah. He removed the seat of Government to Monghir,*

*Monghyr came into province in 1761 when Mir Kasim made it his capital, instead of Murshidabad, from which place he removed all his treasure, his horses and elephants, and even the gold and silver decorations of the Imambara. He built himself a beautiful palace inside the Fort, with a breast-work before it for 30 guns and had the fortifications strengthened. Gorgin Khan established an arsenal there and the manufacture of fire-arms, which is still carried on at Monghyr dates back a distance of 320 miles from Calcutta, where, free from observations, he prosecuted his plans of independence with such earnestness that, in less than three years, he considered himself in a position to set their power at defiance. For this rapid progress he was mainly indebted to the exertions of an Armenian, born at Ispahan, generally known by his orientalized name of Gurghin Khan. He was originally a cloth-seller at Hooghly but when entrusted with the responsibilities of office, turned out to be a man of original genius and vast resources. In less than three years he created a force of 15,000 cavalry and 25,000 infantry, disciplined on the modes of the company's army, he manufactured firelocks, which were superior to the Towerproof muskets, he established a foundry for casting cannon, and trained up a corps, of artillerymen who would have done credit to the Company's Service. Nothing was wanting to render Meer Cassim more powerful than Ali Verdy Khan had ever been, but a few years of undisturbed leisure."

Holwell of the Calcutta "Black Hole" fame, writes of Gorgin Khan as follows :—

"Khojah Gregory is in the highest degree of favour with the Nawab [Mir Kassim] and his adherents, and has posts of the greatest trust near the Nawab's person, and through him the Armenians in general are setting up an independent footing in this country and carrying on a trade greatly detrimental to our investments in all parts."

---

to that period. On the top of the hill called Pirpahar at Monghyr, Gorgin Khan built a fine house for his residence and it was here that Vansittart, the Governor of the East India Company, was entertained when he visited Monghyr in 1762. The house is still standing on the hill, which is also called the hill of Sitakund in the *Seir-Mutaqherin*. Both the hill and the house are now owned by the princely Tagore family of Calcutta. In this connection we beg to humbly suggest that the present owner, the enlightened Maharaja Sir Prodyot Kumar Tagore Bahadur, K.C.I.E. the premier nobleman in Bengal, be graciously pleased to place a memorial tablet in that historical house, with the following inscription.

> "In this house, Gorgin Khan, the Armenian Minister and Commander-in-Chief of Mir Kasim, the last of the great Nawab Nazims of Bengal, Behar and Orissa, lived from 1760-1763, and it was here that Vansittart, the Governor of the East India Company, was entertained when he paid a visit to Nawab Mir Kasim in 1762.

Complaints of a similar nature were received from the Chief at Patna, as can be seen from the following copy of a letter, written by Mr. Ellis to the Governor and Council at Calcutta, on the 26th January, 1762.

"From the late frequent interruptions given to our business, I am necessitated to acquaint you of the general disregard shewn to the English *dustucks* throughout the country, but more particularly so in those parts where the Armenians have any influence.

In pursuance of our Honourable masters orders, per *Lord Mansfield*, a quantity of turmerick was purchased near Mow, which when ready I sent a *dustuck* for, but to little purpose; for Coja Antoon (the prisoner sent to Calcutta) declared it of no effect; and had the insolence to give one himself under the seal of Coja Gregory, alias Goorgheen Cawn, an Armenian, which I have now the honor to inclose you. Upon my asking him, how he dared presume to give a dustuck for the Company's goods? He replied, "to prevent their being stopped, which mine would not have done, because we are not sufficiently known."

I have frequently complained to the Nabob of these insolences, and have constantly received evasive and dissatisfactory anwers; once, indeed, on a representation made him at the instance of Mr. George Gray, he sent me a letter for Meer Sheer Allee, the Purnea Naib, which he informed me, was an order to give every assistance to the gentleman residing at Malda; but I find it proved of no effect, as I suppose Mr. Gray has already acquainted you.

Mr. Howit has had boats; with a *dustuck*, stopped in the Purnea country, for near three months; and there are many more, on different parts of the river, in the same situation. This disregard of the *dustuck*, may be attended with the worst consequences to the Company's business, as well as private merchants; I therefore submit it to your determination, whether (since the Nabob seems to allow of it) it would be most eligible for us to punish severely any who may impede the carriage of merchandize, having an English *dustuck*."

Extract of a letter from the Chief and Council at Patna (Ellis, Lushington, and Howit) to the Governor and Council at Calcutta, dated January 28, 1762.

"Some days ago Mr. Smith, being at Mow, informed the Chief from thence of one Coja Antoon, an Armenian, having seized five maunds of salt-petre, and sent it to Mongheer; in consequence of which, a party of seepoys was detached to bring the Armenian prisoner to this factory. On being examined, he acknowledged the fact, as likewise the inclosed letter, in answer to one which our *gomastah* wrote to him on the subject.

Having not the least prospect of any redress from the Nabob for this contempt of the perwannah, we have thought proper to send the Armenian under a guard to Calcutta; not doubting, but that you will cause such a punishment to be inflicted on him, as may deter others from the like practices in future."

Extract of a consultation, held at Calcutta, on the 11th of February, 1762 (present: Vansittart, Amyatt, Johnstone and Hay).

"Coja Antoon an Armenian, born at Delly, residing at Mulky, on behalf of Sedderam, the Naib of Coja Gregory (who rents eight gauts in that part the country) having been seized and sent down by the Chief and Council at Patna, for having presumed to give a *dustuck* for goods belonging to the Company, which had before their own proper *dustuck;* likewise for taking from the Company's Nunneas* five maunds of petre; being brought before the Board, was shewn the *dustuck* which he gave with the goods, and the letter he wrote to our *gomastah,* regarding the five maunds of salt-petre, and asked, whether he wrote them, and what were his reasons for so doing?

Coja Antoon acknowledges the *dustuck* and letter to have been wrote by him; and declares, that he did not tear or take away the company's *dustuck,* but only took a copy of it, and returned it with a *dustuck,* under the seal of Sedderam, to enable the goods to pass the gauts belonging to Sedderam; that

*Nunneas were the people who worked the salt-petre.

it was always the custom to do so, and that he did the same with the Nabob's. With regard to the salt-petre, he says, a Nunnea, belonging to the Sircar, came from the opposite side of the river, in order to purchase ten rupees worth of salt-petre; that he thereupon sent for one of the Coupany's Nunneas, and desired him to let the other have the salt-petre; to which he readily consented; that as soon as the salt-petre was obtained, he sent the Nunnea, belonging to the Sircar, with the salt-petre across the river, accompanied by one of his own servants, to prevent his being stopped.

The Board being of opinion, that upon the whole, Coja Antoon has taken upon himself an authority which he has no right to; and it being requisite, that he be made an example of, to prevent others from the like practices in future; but as he is a servant of the government's, it properly belonging to the Nabob to chastise him :

Agreed he be sent to Patna under a guard, and that the gentlemen there deliver him to the Nabob with a letter, which the President is desired to write to him, insisting upon his punishing Coja Antoon in a public manner, to prevent others from carrying the salt-petre out of the country, and calling our *dustucks* in question; and we desire the gentlemen at Patna, to inform us particularly what punishment he inflicts upon him."

Extract of a letter from Mr. Ellis, Patna, to the Governor and Council, at Calcutta, dated February 13, 1762.

"A Company of seepoys was detached down the river, in quest of deserters; of which I apprized Rajebullub, and desired an order for the serjeant of the party to be admitted to search the fort of Mongheer. This he assured me was sent down; but the serjeant, on his arrival near Mongheer, having dispatched a messenger to desire admittance, received an answer from one Siujan Sing (Coja Gregory's deputy) that if he did not keep out of the reach of his guns, he would fire on him; and, at the same time, he posted all his people round the walls; upon which the serjeant, who had positive orders to give no offence to any person whatever, went about two coss off, where he remains, with his party, in the utmost distress for provision, Shujan Sing having forbid any to be sold them. I have not yet ordered them back, because there is certain advice of four of our deserters being concealed in Mongheer fort. This, gentlemen, is another instance of Armenian insolence."

Translation of a letter from the Nabob (Mir Kasim) to the Governor, Consultations, February 22, 1762.

"This day, which is the 19th of the month Rejub, I have heard by a letter from Shujan Sing, Naib of the fort of Mongheer, and from the advices of my Hircarras, that two or three companies of seepoys were sent out by Mr. Ellis, the Chief of the factory at Patna, on the report of some soldiers who had deserted from the factory, to the east of Patna; who accordngly arrived on a sudden, near the fort of Mongheer, and marched against it, but finding the gates shut, they surrounded the fort. The Naib of the place fastened all the gates, and sat within in fear of his life and honor. I am ignorant what provocation has induced the gentleman to send seepoys to attack the fort of Mongheer. I have ever regarded the solemn and sacred obligations of the treaty, which subsists between us; and have, in no instance, failed in any of the duties of friendship. But why you, gentlemen, in defiance of the treaty, should thus commit hostilities against my fort, and my servants, I cannot conceive. Depending on your justice, and the inclination which you have shewn to befriend me, in all my affairs, in conformity with the treaty, I have wrote you of the affair, and send you the advices above-mentioned for your information. I am here taking such measures for regulating the concerns of this quarter, as you might approve of, and have stationed men in the forts and tannahs, If this is contrary to your inclination, intimate it to me, that they may be recalled. What necessity was there to send an armed force against my people? Whatever you judge advisable and proper on this occasion, do you determine, and inform me, that I, who regard your satisfaction, beyond every other consideration, may act agreeably thereto. The disgrace which my authority has suffered, is beyond description.

P. S. Mr. Ellis having wrote to me, and requested a *perwannah* to Sheer Allee Cawn, not to stop any goods; I have at this time received advice, that for a trifling cause, that gentleman has disgraced and carried away Coja Antoon, the Aumil to Punchmla Perganah, in the jurisdiction of Mongheer, a prisoner to the factory. The answer, which on this occasion I wrote to him, I send you inclosed, and desire you will read it."

Translation of a letter from Rajebullub to the Nabob.

"This day being Sunday, the 27th of the month Jemmady-ul-sany, at noon, Bya Sedderam, the Peshkar of Coja Goorgheen Cawn, came and acquainted me, that Coja Antoon, an Armenian, who is one of his (Goorgheen Cawn's) kinsmen, and appointed by him to the charge of the affairs of Punchmala, etc. in the districts of Mongheer, was seized and carried away by about four hundred Europeans and seepoys in the English service, who were dispatched to that place. The affair is this. It was reported, that he had bought a small quantity of salt-petre, which he was accused of having plundered from the factory. I was going to send Golaum Mohomed Cawn to enquire into this affair; when Bya Sedderam again sent me word, that they had brought Coja Antoon to the factory. Accordingly, I sent Golaum Mahomed Cawn to Mr. Ellis, the Chief of the factory, to represent to him, that Coja Antoon was a man of credit, and entrusted with affairs of great consequence under the Government; and that to treat him in so violent a manner was improper; that if he would send him to me (which was proper) I would examine him. But this he would by no means consent to; but replied, that the man had done great prejudice to the business of the factory, and that he would put him in irons, and send him to Calcutta. I again sent word, that he ought to send the said Coja to me; and if Mr. Ellis had any claim upon him, it should be debated before him. He answered, "I will neither release him, nor send him to you, but he shall not be ill treated". I have wrote this for your information, and wait your orders regarding this affair."*

---

*The above extracts are taken from Volume I of the *Narrative of the Transactions in Bengal from the year 1760 to the year 1764,* during the Government of Henry Vansittart, published by himself, in 3 volumes. London, 1796.

An Armenian contemporary writer, Thomas Khojamall, who died at Delhi in 1780 and lies buried in the old Armenian cemetery at Agra, speaks of Gorgin Khan in terms of the highest praise, but as the encomiums bestowed upon our hero come from an Armenian, we shall, for obvious reasons, refrain from quoting from Khojamall's writings lest it be said that we have got an Armenian to sing the praises of another Armenian. We intend however to incorporate Khojamall's account of Gorgin Khan and his Armenian generals in our *Life of Gorgin Khan* which will be a valuable contribution to the history of Bengal from 1760-1763.

We must not however omit to mention the interesting account given by the well-known Bengalee novelist, Bunkim Chandra Chatterjee, in his historical romance called *Chandrashekhar,* of which an English translation was published by Messrs. Thacker, Spink & Co., in 1905. In the second chapter (pp. 37-42) the immortal author of "Bande Mataram," speaks of Gorgin Khan as follows :—

"The name of the addressee of Dalani's* letter was Gurgan Khan."

Of all the state-officers who were employed in Bengal at that time, Gurgan Khan was one of the highest and best. By nationality he was an Armenian; Ispahan was his birth-place. A report is current that in early-life he was a clothier, but he was a man of great genius and extraordinary talents. Within a short time of his service, he rose to the rank of Commander-in-Chief of the Army. Not only that, soon after he came to his new position, he formed an artillery force. He had it properly trained and equiped after European methods; the guns and muskets he manufactured turned out to be even superior to those manufactured in Europe. His artillery force became in every respect equal to the European artillery soldiers. Mir Kasim too, had his hopes that with Gurgan Khan to help him, he would be able to defeat the English. With his rise, Gurgan Khan's influence increased apace. Mir Kasim would not engage in any undertaking without his

---

* Dalani, according to "Chandrashekhar," was the Begum of Nawab Mir Kasim of Bengal.

advice. He would not listen to anybody who spoke contrary to it. In a word Gurgan Khan grew up to be a little Nawab himself; naturally the Mahommedan officials became jealous.

It was midnight; but Gurgan Khan had not yet retired. Alone in lamplight he was reading some letters. They were from certain Armenians at Calcutta. After finishing the letters he called to a servant. A footman came and awaited orders. Gurgan Khan asked:

"Have all the doors been kept open?"

"Yes," answered the footman.

"If any one should like to see me, he must not be obstructed or asked who he was. Have you explained this?"

"Your Excellency's order has been carried out," replied the footman.

"Very well, you can go."

After the footman had gone Gurgan Khan tied up the letters and secreted them in a fitting place. Then he began to meditate. "Now which path to follow? This Hindusthan is now like a sea, whoever dives most, will pick up the largest number of gems. What is the good of counting the waves from the shore? Take my case: I used to measure out cloth with the yard-stick and sell it. Now all India is trembling at my name. I am the master of Bengal. Am I really the master of Bengal? Then who if not I? No, the English merchants are the master, and Mir Kasim is their slave. I am the slave of Mir Kasim, therefore, I am the slave of the master's slave. A very high position indeed! Why shouldn't I be the master of Bengal? Who can stand before my guns? The English? Let me once catch them. But unless I cast them out of this country I cannot be the master. I want to be the ruler of Bengal. I don't mind Mir Kasim; I will tear him away from the throne the very day I shall wish it. He is merely my ladder to mount up to my exalted position. Now that I have got up to the terrace, I can safely kick it. The rascally English are the only thorn. They want to have me under their thumb, I want to have them under mine. But they will never come under my thumb; therefore, I must drive them away. Let Mir Kasim continue on the throne for the present; I will co-operate with him and obliterate the British name from Bengal. With that object I am contriving to bring about this war; all this done, I will bid adieu to Mir Kasim. This is the right path. But why do I get this letter so unexpectedly to-day? Why has this girl launched in this reckless adventure?"

Just then the person who occupied his mind entered appearance and stood before him. Gurgan Khan conducted her to a separate seat. She was Dalani Begum.

"I am very glad," said Gurgan Khan, "to see you after such a length of time. I have not had the pleasure of seeing you since you entered the Nawab's seraglio. But why have you embarked in this mad adventure?"

"How mad?" asked Dalani.

"You, the Nawab's Begum," replied Gurgan Khan, "have secretly stolen out at night to my place; if the Nawab should come to know of it, he would kill us both you and me."

"If he at all comes to know of it, I will disclose our relationship. After that there will be no further cause for his displeasure."

"You are a mere girl, therefore you expect such a thing. We have not disclosed our relationship to any one up to this time. That you know me, or that I know you, none of us have yet revealed; and if at the time of danger it is made public, who will believe it? People will call it a subterfuge for escape. You have not done well to come here."

"What is the chance of the Nawab's knowing of it? The sentries are all under your control, and they have let me pass on seeing your token. I have come to ask one word only. Is it a fact there will be war with the English?"

"Don't you hear it talked about in the fort?"

"Yes I do. It is current there that war with the English is inevitable, and you have brought it about, why?"

"You are a mere girl, how shall you understand it?"

"Am I talking like a girl, or am I in the habit of acting as such? When you yourself have planted me in the seraglio as an instrument of your self-advancement, then what is the good of ignoring me as a girl?"

"Let there be war. This war with the English can neither harm you nor me. If it should be war, let it be."

"Do you expect to be victorious?"

"Our victory is most likely."

"Who has been able to defeat the English up to the present moment?"

"How many Gurgan Khans have they fought?"

"Serajuddowla also thought in a similar strain. However, let that go. I am a woman, I believe in what my mind prompts me to. To my mind it seems, that in our war with the English we shall never come off victorious. This war will be our ruin. Therefore, I have come to beseech you—do not advise this war."

"In matters like this a woman's advice is not to be accepted."

"Oh, do listen to me! Be my saviour, I see darkness all around!" and Dalani began to weep.

Gurgan Khan was astonished. "Why do you weep?" he asked. "Suppose Mir Kasim should lose his throne, I would take you back to our native country."

Dalani's eyes flashed fire. In a paroxysm of rage she cried, "Dost thou forget that Mir Kasim is my husband?"

A trifle taken aback and confused, Gurgan Khan replied, "No, I do not. But no one's husband lives for ever. After the first, one can take a second husband. I entertain hopes that one day you will be another Nurjehan of India."

Trembling with passion Dalani stood up. She stifled her tears and with dilated eyes and trembling limbs, she began to pour forth :—

"Perdition take you! In an evil moment was I born your sister; in an evil moment did I pledge myself to help you. That a woman is capable of charity, affection, and virtue, does not enter your head. If you desist from instigating this war, well and good; if not, from this day forth, I will disclaim you; or why disclaim only, henceforth I will look upon you as my enemy. I will consider you as my 'dearest foe,' and I wish you also, to know me as such. I will remain your mortal enemy in the palace."

With these words Dalani flung out of the room and went away.

When Dalani had gone away Gurgan Khan began to reflect. He knew that Dalani was no longer his, she was Mir Kasim's. She might have a sister's affection for him but her love for Mir Kasim was far stronger. When she has known, or will know, that the brother is no well-wisher of the husband, she might do the brother an ill-turn for the good of the husband. Therefore, she must not be allowed to enter the fort again. With this decision Gurgan Khan called to a servant.

One of the armed attendants appeared. Gurgan Khan sent orders through him that the sentries must not allow Dalani to enter the fort.

On horseback the courier reached the gate of the fort in advance. Dalani duly arrived there, and was told that her admittance had been forbidden.

At this, she slowly sank on the ground like a torn creeper. Torrents of tears flowed from her eyes, and she exclaimed. "Alas, my brother ! you have made me completely desolate."

"Come," suggested Kulsam, "let us go back to the Commander-in-Chief's house."

"You can go if you like," said Dalani, "I will take shelter within the billows of the Ganges."

"In that dark night Dalani stood on the public high-way and wept. The stars were shimmering overhead; the scent of new-blown flowers came floating from the trees; the leaves, mantled in darkness were rustling in a current of gentle breeze; and Dalani,* through her tears muttered 'Kulsam.' "

Alas for human greatness and ambition ! The phenomenal administrative success and advancement of Nawab Mir Kasim and the meteoric rise of his Chief Minister and Commander-in-Chief to power and prominence did not last long, since every rapid success is invariably followed by a rapid fall. The

*Dalani Begum, the heroine of *Chandrashekhar,* was not however a historical figure, as Gorgin Khan had *no* sister in the Nawab's seraglio. He had only two brothers in India both of whom were well-known merchants at Saidabad. He had also a nephew Hakobjan by name, who was an officer in the Army which he had raised for the Nawab.

fall was however, precipitated by the English, for according to Marshman, "the unprincipled conduct of the Council Board in Calcutta," which eventually deprived Mir Kasim of his throne, brought on a rupture between him and the English, which resulted in several battles that were fought between the two armies. The last of these well-contested battles was fought at a place called Gheriah, on the 2nd day of August, 1763, regarding which Marshman writes :—

"The battle lasted four hours, and in the opinion of Clive, never did troops fight better than those of the Nabob. At one period of the action, indeed, they penetrated the English lines and captured two guns, and victory appeared for a time likely to them, but the gallantry of the Europeans and the steadiness of the sepoys bore down all opposition, and the Nabob's troops were constrained to abandon all their guns and stores and retreat to Oodwanulla."

A week after the memorable battle of Gheriah, Gorgin Khan met his death at the hands of an unknown assassin, who it is said had been instigated by the Nawab Mir Kasim. Marshman in his "History of Bengal" gives the following version of the tragic event. "It came out that in the evening three or four Moguls had entered his tent and slain him. It was given out that they had gone to the Commander to ask for their arrears of pay, but he had ordered them to be driven away, on which they drew their swords and murdered him. The fact was that no pay was then due to them, they had been paid nine days previously. At all events, this seems in a manner certain that Kasim Ali [Mir Kasim] had treacherously sent them to kill his Commander-in-Chief Gurgin Khan. A brother of the latter, named Ḳhojah Petrus [Clive's Armenian Petrus], resided in Calcutta and was on terms of great friendship with Messrs. Vansittart and Hastings. He had secretly written a letter to Gurghin Khan, urging him to quit the Nawab's service, and if he had a good opportunity to make him a prisoner. The Nawab's chief spy got intimation of this, and went at one clock at night to his master, and put him on his guard, by informing him that his Commander-in-Chief was a traitor. Within twenty-four hours of that time the Armenian General, Gurgin Khan, one of the greatest men of the age, was a corpse."

There is no evidence that Gorgin Khan had ever intrigued with his brother in Calcutta; on the contrary, his extraordinary talents in military matters had been wholly devoted to Nawab Mir Kasim's cause, and not even the fraternal affection that he had for his brother Petrus, who was in such high favour with the opposing forces, could have seduced him from his unswerving loyalty to the Nawab. Thomas Khojamall, the Armenian contemporary writer, already referred to, says that when the English secretly wrote and asked him to make a prisoner of the Nawab, for which he would be handsomely rewarded, he replied :—

"I was a humble individual, Kasim Ali Khan trusted and raised me to this high post of honour, I cannot therefore comply with your request. Far from it, that I should betray my master, particularly as it is a distinct national characteristic of the Armenians never to betray their masters, but serve them faithfully and remain loyal to them always."

A man remarkable for his genius and foresight Gorgin Khan played a prominent part in the history of those times and would probably have distinguished himself more in the early days of the British conquest of Bengal, had he not fallen a prey to the sword of an assassin which sad event prematurely closed his illustrious career on Monday, the 11th day of August, 1763.

He was a pious Christian and sent for an Armenian priest to whom he humbly confessed his sins and received the Blessed Sacrament at his hands with great faith and devotion before he expired. His body was removed from the camp with great solemnity and honour and was buried in the village of Barh, where the renegade Sumru,* one of the Commanders of Gorgin Khan, had encamped with his regiment.

*He was born of obscure parents at Treves, on the Moselle in the duchy of Luxemburg, Germany, and was either a Swiss or a German by birth. He found his way out to India as a sailor in the French navy. Shortly after his arrival in India, he deserted and joined the British in Bengal, where he bore the name of Walter Summers, of which Samru or Sombre was the corrupted form. His real name, however, was Walter Reinhardt. He in turn deserted the English and took service again under the French at Chandernagore as a serjeant. He next deserted the French a

Major Adams who defeated the Nawab's troops at the memorable battle of Oodwanulla, writing to Governor Vansittart on the 3rd October, 1763, says :—

"We had a report yesterday that Coja Gregore [Gorgin Khan] had been wounded some days ago by a party of his Mogul cavalry who mutinied for want of their pay between Sooage Gurree and Nabob Gunge. It is just now confirmed by a Hircarra arrived from the enemy with this addition that he died the next day and that forty principal people concerned were put to death upon the occasion, though it was imagined that the Mogals were induced to affront and assault Coja Gregore by Cassim Ali Cawn who began to be very jealous of him on account of his good behaviour to the English. If this should prove true, Coja Petruce can be no further service to us. I therefore would recommend sending him down to Calcutta, but shall wait the directions of the Board on that head.

---

second time, and entered the service of Mir Kasim, the Nawab of Bengal. After the tragic death of Gorgin Khan, the Commander-in-Chief, who had refused to comply with the Nawab's desire to put to death the English that were at the Factory in Patna, the hideous task was undertaken by this inhumane, unprincipled desperado. About 200 of the Nawab's prisoners at Patna, amongst whom were three Members of Council, *viz.*, Ellis, Hay, and Lushington, fell by his hand on the night of the 5th October 1763. The English Government had offered a reward of Rs. 40,000 for his capture, but he made good his escape. After serving different native chiefs, he finally entered the service of Mirza Najif Khan, Minister of the Emperor Shah Alum II., from whom he received the village of Sirdhana, near Meerut, as a jagir. He died in 1778 at Agra, and, with shame be it said, lies buried in a handsome mausoleum at the old Christian cemetery of that place, called 'Padre Santo' by the natives, where, according to Keene, in his interesting *Handbook to Agra,* "the older inscriptions are all in the Armenian character." Sumru was succeeded in his *jagir* by his supposed widow, the notorious Begum Sumrú, originally a Muhammadan dancing girl and a native of Cashmere. According to Bishop Heber, she was, in 1823, a "a little queer-looking old woman, with brilliant but wicked eyes, and the remains of beauty in her features." She embraced in 1781 the Christian faith, was baptised into the Roman Catholic Church, and christened Johanna Nobilis. This Indian Cleopatra, the Zeb-ul-Nisa, or the ornament of the sex, as designated by her suzerain the Mogul Emperor, died in extreme old age in 1836, and was buried in the beautiful church which she had erected at her capital of Sirdhana. After her death the principality lapsed to the English.

I must confess this piece of news gives me some concern as by all accounts he behaved very well to our gentlemen. And it was that only that occasioned him to fall under Cassim Aly Cawn's displeasure. Had he lived, he might probably have assisted in effecting their escape, as we hear he frequently was the means of saving their lives as well as the Setts and other prisoners."

There seems to be some discrepancy in the above account about the date of Gorgin Khan's assassination. Marshman says the tragedy was enacted a week after the battle of Gheriah, which was fought on the 2nd day of August, 1763, and it coincides with the date given by Thomas Khojamall, who says that the Commander-in-Chief was murdered on Monday, the 11th day of August, 1763. It is very strange that Major Adams who should have known better, only heard about it on the 2nd October, or about two months after Gorgin Khan had breathed his last!

The following account of the assassination of Gorgin Khan is from the pages of *Tarikh-i-Muzaffari,* a Persian manuscript, in the Library of the "Royal Asiatic Society of Bengal." (page 576 of Ms. No. 182). The author of the above history is one Muhammad Hidayatullah.

"When Kasim Ali Khan [Mir Kasim] heard the news of the defeat of Adhwa [Oodwanalla] he rolled himself in the bed of sorrows and lamentations, and, having left taking counsels from Gorgin Khan, returned to Monghyr. Having left Irrat Ali Khan, who was one of the officers of Gorgin Khan, in charge of Monghyr, he marched, with 200 soldiers, towards Patna. He also took Mr. Ellis, Mr. Hay and Mr. Lushington, with him. Having crossed the river Adhwa, near Tarhia, in the *pargana* of Salaiman Abad, pitched his camps there. Gorgin Khan, also, as usual, came from behind the army and entered the camp. In the meanwhile certain Turkish cavaliers, who were in his service, came and demanded their salary. He gave them a harsh reply but they persisted still more in their demand. Gorgin Khan in his extreme wrath ordered that they may be arrested and imprisoned, but before they could be arrested they killed him and fled away on horses.

On this occasion there was great confusion in the army for knowing the real cause of his death. Kasim Ali Khan, having marched from there encamped at Rahmadar, or Barh, and passed orders for the execution of Jagat Seth, Raja Mahtab Roy and Rajah Surup Chand, and his orders were carried out immediately."

The cause of the assassination of Gorgin Khan is shrouded in mystery and we have our doubts about the plausible reasons, put forward by a certain school of interested historians, for the dastardly act, but as we shall deal fully with the subject in our *Life of Gorgin Khan*, we shall at present, "let it went", as a school boy in an old-established institution in Calcutta was once heard to say, when he wanted to say "let it go" !

As there are various accounts of the murder of Gorgin Khan, we shall now give a detailed account of the assassination, by a Frenchman, Monsieur John Baptiste Joseph Gentil, a personal friend of the Armenian General and an eye witness of the tragedy. The account is to be found on pp. 217-235 of Gentil's "Memoires sur l' Indoustan, ou Empire Mogol" published at Paris in 1822. For the English translation of the extract we are indebted to our esteemed friend, the late Father H. Hosten, S.J.

Mr. Gentil* who was an officer under Gorgin Khan pays the highest tribute to the memory of his friend and expresses the highest admiration of the character of his master and it is the best account we have yet seen coming from a non-Armenian —after what the Mohammedan, Indian and English historians have said of our hero.

---

*Jean Baptiste Joseph Gentil, Colonel of Infantry and Chevalier of the Royal and Military Order of Saint-Louis, was born in 1726. He went out to India in 1752 with his regiment, and served with distinction under Dupleix, de Bussy, Lay of Lauriston, de Conflans and de Lally. After the capitulation of Chandernagore to the English, he entered the service of Mir Kasim, (Qasim Ali Khan,) being a personal friend of Khwaja Gregory, better known by his Persian name, Gurgin Khan, the Nawaḅ's Armenian general. After Qasim 'Ali's defeat and expulsion across the Karamnasa, Gentil joined Shujah-ud-daulla, the Nawab of Oudh and Wazir-ul-mulk, and was present with him at the battle of Buxar. He retired to his own country in 1778, and died in 1799, at the age of 73, at Bagnols, where he had been born.

Here is Monsieur Gentil's unbiased account of Gorgin Khan translated from the original French :

"After the capture of Rajmahal, Qasim Ali Khan wrote from his camp to the English general, i.e. Major Thomas Adams, to the effect that if he {Adams] advanced any further, he would swear upon the Quran that he would have all the English prisoners in his control killed.

Major Adams, regarding this threat as merely a scheme conceived in his weakness by the Nawab to prevent him advancing, continued his march. The Nawab turned back to Monghyr, had all his treasure and baggage sent off to Patna, and started for that city himself.

On the Road to Patna the Jagat Seth brothers sent word *begging of me to intercede for them with Gurgin Khan. But* this latter Officer made me promise not to persist in pleading for them, not only because I could never be successful, but also because by such a step I would find myself involved in their disgrace, there being no possibility of getting them pardoned.

On the way the enemies of the Nawab persuaded him that Gurgin Khan was betraying him. From that moment the Prince vowed he would put an end to that faithful minister, whom calumny had painted as a traitor. Gurgin Khan was not unaware of this detestable design. I was always encamped close to this Minister,* and used to have my meals with him. One day when he was late in coming to dinner, the various dishes that used to be brought each day from the Nawab's camp had been laid out in front of me, and I had commenced to partake of them. Just then the Minister arrived and forbade me to eat any more, saying :—"What are you doing? What ! do you not know that you might be poisoned ! How imprudent you are, after you have learnt what has been said about me and my brother ! I have enemies. Be suspicious of everything." He had the dishes removed forthwith, and had others served up, prepared by hands he did not distrust.

Half way between Monghyr and Patna, an attempt was made to assassinate him; but as I had had my bed placed in

---

*Gorgin Khan is always described by Gentil as the Minister (*ministre*) indicating how largely administrative were his functions.

front of his tent and by the side of the sentinel, in the open air, solely on occount of the great heat, the assassins, thinking their design had been discovered, postponed its execution till the following day.

Next day—a day on which the army had marched—arriving later than usual in consequence of the bad roads, the Minister had dinner served up immediately. After our meal, the heat being excessive, he said to me:—"Let us go over to my Bakhshi's* tent; perhaps it will be cooler there." When he arrived there, not finding it any more comfortable, he decided to go back again to his own quarters. As he was passing through the camp of his Mughal cavalry, when he was in the midst of the horses, a trooper approached and asked him for some money, complaning that, inspite of his pay which he had just received, he had not enough to live upon, having regard to the dearness of provisions. Gurgin Khan, incensed at the demand, called one of his attendants in a loud voice. The trooper withdrew. When he had been talking of other matters, overcome by the heat and anxious to get under shelter, I left him. I had hardly gone thirty steps when I heard shouts for help from three men who had remained with the Minister. Turning round at once I saw the same trooper striking Gurgin Khan with his sword. The men with him were without arms, and dressed in muslin, as was the Minister himself. No assistance could be rendered as three strokes had been inflicted as quick as lightning; the first cut nearly half way through his neck, the second cleft his shoulderbone, and the third cut open his loins The assassin struck him again in the face when he fell down, tripped up by the long tethering ropes of the horses, over which he had sought to pass to reach his tent, fifty paces away. As he was dressed in muslin, the force with which the sword cut can be imagined. The trooper had scarcely struck him when he disappeared. Running up I helped to place the Minister in his palanquin, and had him carried to his tent. As he made a sign that he wanted a drink, he was given some water, but it came out again through the wound in his neck.

Seeing me by his side, Gurgin Khan fixed his gaze upon me, and made a sign with his hand, being no longer able to

*The Bakhshi was the Paymaster-General in the army.

speak, striking his thigh with it three times, giving me to understand that he had been the victim of calumny, and that I should be very careful about myself.

While the friends and servants of the Minister were tending him with all care, the Mughal trooper, joined by his comrades, threatened to come and massacre the Armenians who were attached to Gurgin Khan's service. Warned by his secretary (who came and snatched me from the arms of my dying friend) of the danger we were exposed to, I insisted on the Armenian commanders, who ran the same risks, placing strong guards at the four corners of the tent in which the Minister was being tended. They had scarcely followed my advice when the Mughals trained a piece of cannon upon the tent where all were mourning the deplorable end of Gorgin Khan. The Armenians having discovered this, I made them forestall the gunner, who was on the point of putting a light to the gun, by shooting him. This they did, the gunner was killed, and the terrified Mughals dispersed and did not show themselves again. Mounting a horse as soon as ever my unfortunate friend had breathed his last, I rode straight to the Nawab's camp, where all were under arms. Each of the commanders was coming up with his troop from the direction of Gurgin's Camp, which was beyond the Nawab's rear-guard. A report was being spread at this time that the English had just attacked the Minister's camp. At this rumour the troops were assembling without any proper order between the two camps, when Qasim 'Ali Khan* came up seated on his elephant, just as I arrived from my side. As soon as the Nawab saw me, he called me up and asked me what had happened. I related briefly the sad and painful spectacle I had just witnessed. The prince appeared affected thereat, and said :—"I had particularly told him never to go about by himself." Then turning round towards some commanders who accompanied him, he said; "You have just heard what has happened; go back to your tents, "kaire salla" (all goes well)." These last words, uttered in a tone of satisfaction, recalled to my mind

*Gentil refers to Qasim Ali Khan (Mir Kasim) sometimes as the Prince and sometimes as the Nawab, although the latter was the correct appellation used to designate the Mohammedan rulers of Bengal.

the just apprehensions of the Minister as to the fate that was being prepared for him by jealousy and slander. Overcome by the horrible blow that had deprived me of a friend and of all my hopes, I returned to the Nawab's camp.

My situation was critical. A friend—a bosom friend of Gurgin Khan whom I had never left since I had first come to know him, I had just seen him perish under my very eyes without being able to save him. I had escaped myself, I know not how, from the hands of the assassins. In a state of painful uncertainty of mind I went straight to the tent of a Mughal friend of mine, Said-ullah Khan, brother of Mehdi 'Ali Khan, the governor of Patna already mentioned. He received me with all courtesy. It was then 6 p.m. I told him, what had just taken place in a manner that showed my indignation and sympathy with the deceased. The Mughal replied: "Our friend Gurgin Khan had enemies who had defamed him to such an extent that the prince, convinced by all that was told him, may have been incited to this extreme course. I would not like however, to be certain as to this, but all that I have heard said make me think that it is quite possible. It is pretended that he was a traitor to the Nawab, that the English were in league with him, and this was why they kept his brother Khwaja Petrus in their camp." "What a shocking calumny!", I replied, "I have been privy to the most secret acts of Gurgin Khan, and I never observed the slightest infidelity on his part. The English had proposals made to him to leave the Nawab, assuring him that by this step he could save the life of his brother, whom they were carrying as a prisoner in their camp. What was his answer? It was this: I have pledged my faith to Quasim 'Ali Khan; I shall not abandon him while life is in me. I grieve at the lot of my brother: but I could not stoop to better it by a base act. I can make no proposal that would be contrary to the interests of the prince, the master of my destiny, as the English are of that of my brother. I leave all in the hands of Providence. Never was calumny so horribly concocted. How pitiable are human beings when their passions are so inflamed by venom as to blind them!

Gurgin Khan was far from deserving such a dreadful fate. Not only did Qasim 'Ali Khan owe in part to him the great fortune he had attained, but also the general order that had been introduced in the system of government. Nothing escaped his unremitting vigilance over all branches of the administration. Just, generous, prudent, energetic, of unassailable integrity, he was incessantly busied with everything that could benefit his master or his subjects. The greatest simplicity reigned in his habits, in his equipage, his table and all that pertained to his home. Everything about him disclosed the merits, the goodness and the disinterestedness of the man. In justice I owe him this, and I render it him with the profoundest satisfaction, as a substitute for the flowers that I would like to have been able to lay every day upon his grave.

The illustrations of justice, of generosity and of strict integrity that I could relate of this minister would help to make his character better known. But, however strong be my feelings of affections and gratitude towards him, any description that I might give would be inadequate."

That well-known Mohammedan historian of the period, Seyed Gholam Hossain Khan, the author of the *Seir Mutaquherin,** or "Review of Modern Times," who wrote both as an actor and a spectator, gives the following accounts of the murder of Gorgin Khan and of the events which led to the rout of Mir Kasim's formidable army after the guiding and the master mind had been removed. For obvious reasons, Gholam Hossain Khan, like all the Mohammedan historians of the period, paints Gorgin Khan black, and the reason is not far to seek, for it was gall and wormwood to the orthodox Mohammedan "nobleman of high rank," as Monsieur Raymond calls him, to see a foreigner, an Armenian and a Christian at the same time, at the helm of the military affairs of Bengal, Behar and Orissa, enjoying the full confidence of

---

*The *Seir-Mutaquherin* or *Suyar-ui-Mutakherin,* that is a "Review of Modern Times" (or more correctly "The Manners of the Moderns") is the chronicle of the decay of the Mogul Empire and the Mohammedan domination of India during the reigns of the seven last Emperors of Hindoosthan. It was written in Persian in 1780 A.D. (1194 A.H.) by Syed Gholam Hossian Khan, a Moslem nobleman, who used to reside, with his father, at the courts of the Nawabs of Bengal, Behar and Orissa, prior to the days of British supremacy.

Nawab Mir Kasim, who according to Marshman, "was mainly indebted to the exertions of an Armenian for his rapid rise." Is it any wonder then that the Mohammedan chronicler, biassed and prejudiced to a degree, gloats over the assassination of the Armenian Commander-in-Chief and consoles himself with the thought that "that ill-fated man, in retribution for his malicious turn of mind, was hastily sent over the stream that divides the world from the other." Could such malice, vituperation, racial hatred and religious antipathy in a historian be surpassed?

As a matter of fact, when he introduces Gorgin Khan to his readers for the first time, he speaks of him with an animus begotten of spite, hatred and jealousy as will be seen from the following introduction.

"But a man who now appeared for the first time upon the horizon, and soon rose to engross the Navvab's unbounded confidence, was an Armenian called Qhadja-Gurgin brother to Qhadja-Bedross. He was put at the head of the artilllery, with orders to new-model it after the European fashion, and likewise to discipline the musketeers in his service after the English manner; troops, which to this day have retained the name of Telingas, in imitation of their patterns and models. To raise his character, he was henceforward called Gurghin-Khan, and distinguished by many favours, and he soon became the principal man in the Navvab's service. There was no man equal to him in that prince's employment : none had so much credit upon his mind; and to this day, no General ever had the art of governing his master in so complete a manner; he, like the devil, was endlessly running after Mir-Cassim-qhan, and having once laid hold of him, he mastered him, and kept him under at pleasure."

Throughout his account of the events which occurred in Bengal during the rule of Nawab Mir Kasim, from 1760-1763, he never misses an opportunity to disparage, vilify and calumniate Gorgin Khan, who by sheer merit had risen to the highest post in the government of the province, for he was not only the Commander-in-Chief of Nawab Mir Kasim, but his Minister. and adviser as well.

And this is how Gholam Hossain Khan narrates the events of that memorable campaign of 1763 in which Gurgin

Khan lost his life, Mir Kasim his throne and the *Subah* its independence.

"The second night, the date of which I cannot remember, a mighty revolution happened suddenly, and an important event took place unexpectedly. Gurghin-Khan was killed; and that ill-fated man, in retribution for his malicious turn of mind, was hastily sent over the stream that divides the world from the other. This strange event happened in the following manner: Gurghin-qhan, who was upon ill terms with all the world, but who studied the English in every thing, wanted to carry a high hand over the soldiery; and in a time of confusion and misfortune, he strove to keep them under that strictness of discipline, which he had seen practised amongst those of that nation; he was not aware that this power of the English over their soldiers, was a gift of Providence; and that that nation had found the art of turning the particular customs of their country into a second nature in their troops.

'Great will ever be the distance between the pattern and the copy.'

How could the poor Armenian, after having sold cloth by the yard throughout his whole life, pretend, that with an authority of only two days standing, he would be able to pass rules of strict obedience and discipline over a nation, not his own, and which was not yet accustomed to so much regularity and strictness?

"The crow, wholly intent on learning the linnet's note,
Forgot to look at it's own black coat first of all."

The Navvab having taken post on the banks of the Rahva, where he tarried two or three days, Gurghin-qhan, who conformably to his custom, always came the last of all, and always encamped by himself was actually in his tent when two or three Mogul troopers from amongst those he had disciplined and trained himself, came and asked something about their pay. The General answered in an angry peevish manner; but the two men, availing themselves of the unprosperous state of affairs, and of the revolution that had taken place, had the daringness to speak with violence. Gurghin-qhan, without attending to the difference of times, screamed out, *what? is there no one there to take these men into confinement?* He had hardly uttered these four words, when those men finding themselves alone with him, drew their sabres, and in three or four strokes, stretched him on the ground; and their horses being just at the door, they got upon them in an instant, and fled through the fields. The servants having immediately raised an outcry, which brought General Marcar, another Armenian; the latter, on descrying the troopers beyond the reach of a musket-ball, fired at them with two or three pieces of cannon that were at hand, loaded with grape; and the report being heard by Mir Cassim's army, which was at a small distance, every one concluded that the English were arrived, and had already engaged Gurghin-qhan. Instantly Mir-Cassim had the same thought; instantly he got upon his elephant, and took to the fields. At the same time, a general scream, and now and then some confused cries, coming from Gurghin-qhan's quarters, struck such a terror into Mir-Cassim's camp, and especially amongst the sutlers and other market-men, that the whole of them, without making the least inquiry, fled on all sides, most of them towards the bridge on the Rahva. The multitude, which was encamped with me on the other side of the river, surprised to see crowds of runaways endlessly pouring upon them, catched their fears and trepidation; and night coming on, nothing was heard but cries and screams. But, as every one was involved in the general confusion and saw the mob running to and fro. like so many mad men, whilst the great ones were advancing in haste with burning tapers, such a sight thunderstruck Yosofaaly-qhan, one of our company, who being as well as Mirza-bakyr, full as much frightened as any other resolved at any rate to inquire into the cause; and then sent people to take some information from the runaways. But, every one of these giving a different answer, served only to perplex. This diversity augmented our consternation, as there was no getting certain information, about the tumult, and some people conceived causes, which they did not dare to mention, for fear of Mir-Cassim's resentment. All these discordant reports, however, agreed in one point, and this was, in producing some piece of extravagant news, which being spread in a twinkle amongst the runaways, increased thoir fears and added to the confusion. Meanwhile the throng became innumerable at the bridge, and the passage being now dangerous, seemed to retrace an idea of the bridge of *Seratt,* at the day of judgment, for the crowds were now pouring in such numbers on both sides, that the passage became impracticable for people on foot.

Elephants and carts cut their way through the multitudes, and, as their treading over the boards of the flooring forced the boats to strike against each other the noise bore a likeness to a report of distant firing of cannon : news then came that the English had gained the victory, and as it was thought that the little river only divided the combatants, people prepared their cannon also on this side, and Yosofaaly-qhan resolved either to pack up his baggage, and get ready at all events, or to run away to some place of shelter. But, he was prevented by Mir-Shetari and myself, who insisted on some information. At about midnight the uproar commenced subsiding, and I sent a trusty servant, with orders to stop on this side of the bridge, and as soon as he should discover any person of some consequence, to let him pass first, and then only to ask what was the matter? The man did as he was bid, and stopping at the bridge, he saw a close paleky making towards it with three or four horsemen attending, the man walked a while with them, and then asked whose lady was in the close paleky? One of the horsemen answered. It is not a lady, it is Gurghin-qhan's corpse : we carry it to the fields for burial. It is the Nawab's order.

On this answer, the man returned with this intelligence, and made us all easy, so that we passed the remainder of the night quietly enough. On the morning, Mir-Cassim himself passed the river and encamped on the spot where we were. The next day he advanced to the town of Bar, where he ordered Djagat Sett Mahtab-Roy and Radja Seropchund, his brother, to be hacked to pieces."

Monsieur Raymond,* the translator of the *Seir Mutaqhein,* in a long foot-note on page 279 of the second

---

*Monsieur Raymond was a French Creole born in Constantinople. He went to France in 1741 and was educated at Paris. In 1751 he came out to India and was employed as a writer in the French Service on the Coromandel Coast till 1756. He then joined the English Service in Bengal as interpreter to Clive but was dismissed by him in 1758. He

volume of the *Seir,* printed at Calcutta in 1789, speaks of the causes which led to the murder of Gorgin Khan as follows :—

"The causes, which no one dared to mention, are a conspiracy said to be brewing by Gurghin-qhan, incited under-hand by the English. His brother, Aga Bedross, alias Codja Petruss, then residing at Calcutta, and an acquaintance of Governor Vansittart's, as well as of Mr. Warren Hastings, had, on their joint request, wrote pressigly to his brother, to engage him by all the motives which religion and a regard for his own safety could suggest, to lay hold of the person of Mir-Cassim qhan, or at least, to come himself to the English camp with his own troops and friends. But, this negotiation having been somehow smelt out by Mir-Cassim's head-spy, he came at one clock in the morning, ordered him to be waked, and laying hold of him by the arm, *what are you doing in your bed,* said he, *whilst your General, Gurghin-qhan, is actually selling you to the Frenghis? He is of intelligence with those without, and possibly with those within, with your prisoners.*

Such was then the general report at that time, and I remember that the very purport of the letter was handed about by the Armenians of Calcutta. As to the Moguls murmuring for their pay, as pretends our author, their plea must have been mustered and paid a week before. It is also certain, that there never was the least murmuring amongst the troops, as they were regularly paid as late as the passage over the

---

tried to reach Pondicherry but was stopped on his journey at Masulipattam and sent with his Papers to Bengal to be tried as a spy. He was imprisoned for some months but was released in March, 1761. He then went to Manilla in 1761 but returned once more to Bengal when he was employed by Governor Vanisttart in the inland trade. In 1770 he went on a pilgrimage to Mecca and assumed the name of Hajee Mustapha from which it is quite evident that he had embraced the faith of Islam. He was an accomplished linguist and at the request of his English friends, translated from the original Persian the "Seir" of Gholam Hossain Khan and published it at Calcutta in 1789. It was dedicated to Warren Hastings who was a great patron of oriental learning. The whole edition of the translation was however lost on the voyage to England except a few copies that were circulated by the translator. And it is from one of these rare copies, in the Library of the "Royal Asiatic Society of Bengal," that the extracts about Gorgin Khan, have been taken. Monsieur Raymond, *alias* Hajee Mustapha, died as a Mohammedan, in 1791.

Ceremnassa. This much is certain, that it was this rumour of a conspiracy that put Mir-Cassem on one hand upon dispatching his General, and on the other, upon riding himself of his prisoners of all sorts, and some such things appear, not only in the Prince's speech to Ferhat-Aaly, but also in our author's narrative, who positively says, that the English prisoners had found means to provide a quantity of money, with a sufficiency of ammunition and arms. As to that Gurghin-qhan, upon whom our author, out of natural antipathy, or for some other cause, is endlessly pouring a deal of abuse, it appears evidently, that he was a man of superior talents and a soaring genius. What are we to think of a seller of cloth by the yard, who conceives and executes the scheme of discilpining troops in the European manner, or making better cannon and better muskets than the English themselves, of casting, mounting and training an artillery, nearly equal to theirs, of introducing order, subordination and discipline, amongst people totally strangers to them? Had Mir-Cassem-qhan possessed three more such geniuses as Gurghin-qhan, Manhomed-taky-qhan and Nedjef-qhan, it is highly probable that the author of these remarks would never have worn an embroidered *malmal* worth fifty rupees on his back, nor stuck a poniard of jewel-work in his sash."

In another Foot-note in the *Seir,* Monsieur Raymond speaks of Gorgin Khan as follows :—

> "It was he who trained and disciplined the Navvab's cavalry, infantry and artillery, in the English manner, and if half trained, as were those troops, a simple detachment of them fought and defeated the troops of Major Castairs, which were full as numerous as those that won the battle of Plassy, what would he have not done had he had a delay of two years more, to train them thoroughly. It is probably that he would have ruined the English in time; for he has taking every measure which could render the Navvab independent. But so far was he from precipitating his master into a war with the English, that whenever he saw him impatiented at the haughtiness and pride of these strangers, he used to say: "bear and forbear;

you are not fledged, reserve that anger, till the time when you shall have feathers to your wings."

Would such a loyal and faithful servant have conspired against his master? But then the Mohammedan historians in general, and Gholam Hossain Khan in particular, say that he was a traitor and in league with the English, and in the words of Marc Antony, "they are all honourable men"! Let history pass its verdict after hearing the testimony of the two unbiassed Frenchmen, Messieurs Gentil and Raymond, both of whom knew Gorgin Khan personally and were well aware of his innocence.

Gorgin Khan had gathered round him about one hundred brave Armenians from various places, some of whom he appointed as generals, colonels and captains in the army which he had raised and equipped for Mir Kasim, on the modes of the Companys army. Their names, as given by Thomas Khojamall, a contemporary, are as follows :—

1. Margar Johanness Khalanthar, a native of Julfa.
2. Arathoon Margar, a native of Julfa.
3. Gregory Nahapiet Aivaz, a native of Julfa.
4. Petrus Astwatsatoor, from the village of Aneas, in the district of Ardzakheek in Armenia.
5. Lazar Jacob, from the village of Qora in the district of Maragah, in Azarbaijan, Persia.
6. Martyrose Gregory from the dictrict of Maragah, Persia.
7. Sookias Avietick, a native of Tabriz, in Persia.
8. Johanness Nazareth, a native of Tabriz, in Persia.

Margar Johanness Khalanthar, the first in the list, was a famous general in Gorgin Khan's army, who distinguished himself in the capture of Patna. Monsieur Raymond, the well-informed translator of the *Seir-Mutaqherin,* speaks of general Margar as follows :—

"This Armenian had served in Holland and on more than one occasion proved himself possessed of a very eminent qualification in a General, taking his party suddenly, in sudden emergencies. He is now in Calcutta, subsisting upon the benevolence of his countrymen. He is a well-looking, square-set man, very strong".

The remaining seven were colonels in the army. The names of some of the leading captains are also recorded by Khojamall and they are as follows :—

1. Mackertich Zacharia from the parish of Charsoo in Julfa.
2. Malcom from Astrakhan.
3. Nicholas from the parish of Erivan in Julfa.
4. Jacob Gregory, a native of Julfa.

After the defeat of Nawab Mir Kasim, consequent on the treacherous assassination of Gorgin Khan, two of his Armenian officers, Colonels Gregory Nahapiet Aivaz and Sookias Avietick, entered the miliary service of the Nawab Sujah-ud-dowlah of Oudh, whilst the remaining five came down to Calcutta. Descendants of Colonel Gregory Nahapiet Aivaz, are living in Calcutta to-day. His grandson, Gabriel Aivaz Gregory, had two sons, Gasper and Chater, and two daughters, Mrs. Seth and Mrs. Moses, known as Mrs. Moss, Gasper Gregory, who was an advocate of the Calcutta High Court, (enrolled in 1868) had a son, Mr. Walter Gregory, who is one of the oldest and leading barristers of the Calcutta Bar having been enrolled as far back as 1889. Chater Gregory, the younger son of Gabriel Aivaz Gregory, was a Pleader, enrolled in 1860, practicing in the Appellate side of the Calcutta High Court. He had two sons, Gasper Ivaz M. Gregroy and Charles Olynthus Gregory, both of whom were enrolled as advocates of the Calcutta High Court, the former in 1890 and the latter in 1891. Mr. G. I. M. Gregory, the elder of the two brothers, who had taken to trade and was a successful jute merchant for many years, has retired from active life, but his younger brother, Mr. C. O. Gregory is still engaged in business. He is the author of *The Sultan's Mandate*, an interesting Armenian romance, published in London, in 1898.

The late Mr. Joseph Beglar, a retired Executive Engineer in the P. W. D. (Bengal) and an archæologist of repute, told the writer of these lines in 1896, after the publication of our first historical work on the Armenians in India, that he had seen in Monghyr, when carrying on some archæological excavations in the Monghyr district, a beautiful sword of Gorgin Khan, with his name, artistically inlaid with gold on the scabbard, in Persian characters. The historical sword was then in the possession of an old respectable Mohammedan family who greatly treasured it as valuable relic, if not a talisman, and could not think of parting with it at any price. They told Mr. Beglar that their remote ancestor had been in the service of Gorgin Khan as an officer in his grand army. The officer must have secured the sword in the great confusion which took place in the Nawab's camp after the cruel assassination of the Commander-in-Chief (Gorgin Khan) which tragic event, as has been stated above, occurred on the 11th day of August, 1763.

In November 1927, when we were writing a Paper on Gorgin Khan, which was read at the Annual Meeting of the "Indian Historical Records Commission", held at Rangoon, in December 1927, we paid a visit to Monghyr to see if we could possibly secure the sword, referred to above, but we were informed by the old Mohammedan residents of the place that it was sold, some years ago, to some rich European at a fancy price of course, but our informants could not say whether the lucky purchaser was an Englishman or a foreigner, collecting curios or historical relics in India. We then visited the workshops of the local gun-makers with the object of collecting some information, from traditions which may have been handed down from generation to generation in that fraternity, who owe their existence to Gorgin Khan, who had made Monghyr the Birmingham of India, by starting an arsenal and a gun-foundry there. That well-informed Frenchman, Mousieur Raymond, (alias Hadji Mustapha or Mustapha Khan) the translator of the *Seir-Mutaqharin,* writes of the Monghyr made rifles as follows :—

"The European reader may possibly hear with surprise that the fire-locks manufactured at Monghyr proved better than the best Tower-proofs sent to India for the Company's use; and such was the opinion which the English officers gave when they made the comparison by order of the Council of Calcutta. The flints were all Rajmahal agates, and their metal more mellow".

This was written, shortly, before the year 1789. And in the Preface to Khojamall's short history of India, in ancient Armenian, written at Allahabad in 1768, and edited and published by Mesrovb David Thaliadian, at Calcutta, in 1849, the publisher says that when he was returning to Armenia, in 1831 after completing his education in the "Bishop's College" of Calcutta, he took with him a gun manufactured at Monghyr and when it was shown to expert gun-makers and Russian military officers at Erivan, the capital of Armenia, they could not say whether it was English-made or manufactured in India.

But to return to the gun-makers at Monghyr. We found them busy, manufacturing, with crude and antediluvian implements, beauiful and well-finished rifles for some well-known European firms of gun-makers in Calcutta. They can make very good imitations of any guns that may be given to them, single or double-barrelled breechloaders. The former is sold at Rs. 8 to Rs. 10 and the latter at Rs. 15 to Rs. 20. The guns made to order fetch higher values, according to quality. A single-barrel breech-loader costs Rs. 30 and a double-barrel breech-loader, Rs. 50. Not only guns, but also pistols and sword-sticks are turned out by the skilled artisans of Monghyr.

The busy artisans were at first loquacious as they expected to sell a gun or a sword-stick to us, but when they found we were not a prospective purchaser, they were visibly disappointed and became reticent. They continued silently to file, polish and burnish their rifles which were nearing completion and whilst we were watching the dexterity of the artisans with great interest, not daring to disturb them with further questions regarding the gun-trade, a venerable looking old man, who seemed to be the Nestor of the gun-makers' guild or fraternity, broke the silence by asking us if we were a government official, or an officer of the Arms Department, but we set their minds at rest by telling them we were neither, but had only come to Monghyr on a pilgrimage to visit the house on Pirpahar hill where our great compatriot, Gorgin Khan, had lived when he was the Commander-in-Chief of the grand army of Mir Kasim, the last of the great Nawabs of Bengal, Behar and

Orissa, 167 years ago. The magic name of Gorgin Khan simply electrified the unsophisticated artisans and they all commenced, with great veneration, to bless the pious memory of the military genius, praying to the Almighty to rest his soul in peace, because he had, they said, brought fame to their old city by starting an iron foundry and an arsenal (Selakhaneh) at Monghyr and they added that they owed their present existence to that great "General Sahib", whose name they said, is a household word in Monghyr to this day.

When bidding good-bye to the descendants of the clever artisans whom Gorgin Khan had taught the art of manufacturing guns, pistols and swords 167 years ago, we were requested to accept a sword-stick as a small souvenir of our visit to their humble workshops, where, for one whole hour, we had enthused and kept them spell-bound by narrating the history of the glorious achievements of Gorgin Khan, their remote benefactor. For obvious reasons, we had to decline their kind offer with many thanks, as we did not wish to get into trouble for possessing a sword without a license, the Arms Act being very strict in India. With the disappearance of Gorgin Khan's beautiful sword, there are *no* other relics of that great soldier left in India and his very grave, where his mortal remains were laid to rest on the 12th day of August, 1763, at a place called Brae or Barh cannot be traced, despite our careful searches during the past ten years.

There are among the Clive Mss. in London, two letters, in Armenian, which are in the handwriting of Gorgin Khan. These letters, of which one is an unsigned copy, were writtten to Khojah Petrus Arathoon by his brother Gorgin Khan, then Khojah Gregory, for Omichand, by whom the original is signed in Punjabi characters as Amirchand.

Facsimiles of these letters were published by Sir Richard Carnac Temple, Bt. in the *Indian Antiquary* for November 1918, in connection with an interesting article entitled *Side-lights on Omichand*, from which we have given some extracts on pages 337, 338, and 343.

After the tragic death of Gorgin Khan, his afflicted brother, Khojah Petrus of Calcutta, in order to commemorate his memory, had an additional altar erected in the Armenian church of Calcutta and had it dedicated to his memory and that sacred edifice, it is sad to reflect, is the only vestige that is left of that remarkable man.

Before concluding we may mention that there exists somewhere in Bengal a portrait of Gorgin Khan, in oriental costume, with a peculiar head-gear, and our friend, Mr. A. F. M. Abdul Ali, the well-informed "Keeper of the Government of India Records", tells us that he has seen it some years ago, but cannot now remember where. We have, despite our strenuous efforts, not succeeded yet in tracing the same, and shall be glad if any of our readers will let us know where it can be seen.

There is however a beautiful pen-portrait of the remarkable military genius by Monsieur Raymond, the translator of the *Seir Mutaqherin,* who describes Gorgin Khan in the following terms :

"Gurgin-qhan was a man born at Ispahan, the capital of Persia, and had very remarkble physiognomy. He was above the ordinary size, strong built, with a very fair complexion, large black eyes, full of fire, an aquiline nose, forming a ridge in the middle of its length, and eyebrows very arched, that joined together, so as to form a point going downwards towards the nose. He was then aged about thirty-six and I have spoke twice to him. Nothing was wanting to that man to render him capable of shining, even in Europe, but education. He owed everything to his own genius, and nothing to art or cultivation."

Monsieur Raymond has however overstated the age of Gorgin Khan, for he was only thirty when he took service under Nawab Mir Kasim in 1760, and was therefore in his thirty-third year when he fell a victim to the sword of an unknown assassin on the 11th August 1763.

Peace to his soul rest to his ashes, and may his revered memory be cherished and kept green at all times by his countrymen, from the banks of the Ganges to the Aras, the sacred river of Armenia.

ARMENIANS AT CALCUTTA

CHAPTER XXXII.

ARMENIANS AS POLITICAL STEPPING-STONES IN INDIA.

KHOJAH ISRAEL SARHAD.

In an illuminating article which the late Professor C. R. Wilson, published in the now defunct *Englishman* (Calcutta), on the 31st January 1895, under the caption ARMENIAN FOUNDERS OF CALCUTTA, the learned author of the *Early Annals of the English in Bengal,* referring to the *oldest* Christian tomb in Calcutta, bearing the date 1630, discovered by the writer of these lines in the Calcutta Armenian churchyard, in August 1894, wrote as follows :—

"It is gratifying to learn that the efforts which have recently been made by various enquirers and in various ways to push back the history of Calcutta to the remoter past, before the formation of the English Settlement under Job Charnock, have not been altogether without fruit. By slow degrees evidences are being accumulated which tend to connect Calcutta with earlier traders and prove that even before the building of Fort William the place was not without importance. Among such evidences one of the most striking is the discovery which has recently been made by Mr. M. J. Seth, an enthusiastic Armenian scholar, who at the instance of Government has translated a large number of the classical Armenian inscriptions in the churchyard of St. Nazareth, Calcutta. The earliest inscription runs as follows :—'

> This is the tomb of Rezabeebeh, the wife of the late charitable Sookias, who departed from this world to life eternal on the 21st day of Nakha in the year 15 *i.e.,* on the 21st July, 1630.

What a world of questions is suggested by this newly-found record? Why was this source of information never utilized before, who was the 'charitable Sookias' and how did his family come to be living in Calcutta sixty years before the advent of the English? Was there already an Armenian Settlement here? Are the Armenians after all the Founders of the city?

Upon these considerations our early records do not cast much light, but they supply other equally important information about the Armenians in Calcutta. If they do not enable us to decide whether there was an Armenian colony settled here before 1630, they show that it was through the Armenians that the English Colony secured a footing in the country. If Job Charnock be the founder of Calcutta, the author of its privileges and early security is the great Armenian merchant, Khojah Israel Sarhad. In a recent article we mentioned this remarkable man as one of the Embassy sent to Delhi in 1715; such a bare notice does but scanty justice to the services which he rendered on that occasion, and not on that occasion only, but at a still earlier period, when the English were even more in need of help. It was at the time of the rebellion of Subha Sing when the English were just begining to build their Fort, that 'Cojah Surhaud', as he was called, first appears in the records. In June 1697, he was sent as Political Agent to the camp of Zabardasth Khan, the Mogul General engaged in suppressing the revolt. Here, however, he met with no success till at the end of the year when Azim-ush-Shan arrived in Bengal and assumed command. At the court of this easy-going Prince, Sarhad succeeded in ingratiating himself by his prudent conduct and winning address and in particular in becoming a prime favourite with Azim-ush-Shan's young son, Farrukh Siyar, then about fourteen years old. The friendship of the future Emperor was won by presents of toys, at that time very acceptable, for which he expressed a great deal of satisfaction, often sending for Khojah Sarhad and making him sit by him many hours to show what uses they were for. The result of this judicious management was that in July 1698, for the sum of sixteen thousand rupees, the English acquired letters-patent from the Prince, allowing them to purchase from the existing holders the right of renting the three villages of Calcutta, Sutanati and Govindpur. After this remarkable achievement, Khojah Sarhad drops out of sight for some time. He was apparently more successful as a Political Agent than as a merchant.

In 1713, Sarhad comes to notice again as a negotiator. The English were now bent on sending off their embassy to

Furrukh Siyar, now Emperor at Delhi, and his quondam play-fellow was of the greatest use in arranging the preliminaries Through another Armenian, Khojah Manur, who was then in attendance on the Badishah Begum, the daughter of Aurungzebe, he prevailed with the king to order a *hasb-ul-hukum** to be given, ordering all *subahs*, governors, and officers whatsoever to guard our present for the King through their several Governments till it shall arrive, with the English that shall accompany it and Cojah Surhaud at Court'.

It is not surprising, therefore, that when the present was at length sent off, Sarhad was made second in the management of the embassy.

On the 5th of June, 1714, 'it was unanimously agreed that Cojah Surhaud, whose interest at Court has already had the good effect of procuring us the *hasb-ul-hukum* and several other useful orders from Court, be sent to assist in suing for the King's *firman*, and that he sit and vote in the Council along with the three English gentlemen.' 'It is absolutely necessary', adds the record book, 'that some person who is perfect master of the Persian language and understands our affairs very well, and what may be useful for us, be sent, and we know no man so qualified in both these respects as Cojah Surhaud. He is therefore, the fittest man to send'. The event, as is well known, justified this selection. The English embassy, aided partly by the favourable impression produced by the skill of Dr. Hamilton† and still more by the diplomatic talents of

---

*The *hasb-ul-hukum* was an official confirmation, under the seal of the *vazir*, enforcing obedience to the Emperor's *farman*.

†Surgeon William Hamilton died at Calcutta in 1717. There is a slab in the Charnock Mausoleum in St. John's churchyard with inscriptions in English and Persian. The interesting epitaph in English is as follows :—

> "Under this stone lyes interred the body of William Hamilton, Surgeon, who departed this life the 4th December, 1717. His memory ought to be dear to this Nation, for the credit he gained the English in curing Ferrakser the present King of Indostan of a malignant distemper, by which he made his own name famous at the court of that Great Monarch ; and without doubt will perpetuate his memory, as well in Great Britain as all other nations in Europe."

Khojah Sarhad, procured from Furrukh Siyar a number of privileges which, though never realised to their full extent, were yet sufficient to keep Calcutta and its trade safe from molestation till the days of Suraj-ud-Dowlah."

We have in the course of our researches into the dim past, come upon certain data which go to prove the truth of the learned antiquarian's dictum that "if Job Charnock be the founder of Calcutta, the author of its privileges and early security is the great Armenian merchant, Khojah Israel Sarhad."

We find that after Job Charnock had settled in Calcutta in 1690, it was deemed necessary to build a Factory with its usual adjunct-a Fort-for the protection of their emporium and the valuable goods to be stored therein, and for such extensive buildings, large tracts of lands were necessary, but how were they to acquire the lands without the permission of the hostile Mogul Government which viewed the growth and the expansion of the Company's trade with suspicion. It may be mentioned that the Armenians were the most favoured subjects of the Delhi government at that time and had been held in high esteem by the Mogul Emperors from the days of Akbar downwards for their loyalty and integrity. The English were not slow in recognising the worth of the Armenians in Bengal, whose valued friendship they eagerly sought for the furtherance of their cause in the country. There resided at that time an eminent Armenian merchant at Hooghly, Khojah Israel Sarhad by name, a nephew of the illustrious Khojah Phanoos Kalandar of Surat with whom he had been to England in 1688.

The Persian inscription beautifully carved is equally interesting. It can be translated thus :—

"William Hamilton, Surgeon, Servant of the English Company who had accompanied the English Ambassador to the splendid court, and had raised his name in the four quarters of the country by curing the King of Kings, the protection of the world, Muhammad Farrukh Siyar Ghazi, having with a thousand difficulties, obtained from the Court, the asylum of the world, permission to go home, died, as decreed by God, in Calcutta, on the 4th of December, one thousand seven hundred and seventeen. He lies buried in this place."

The English being aware of the abilities of the Armenian merchant, approached Khojah Israel Sarhad and requested him to proceed to the Camp of the Mogul Emperor, Azim-ush-Shan, the grandson of the Emperor Aurungzebe, who had come down from Delhi to quell the rebellion of Subah Singh of Bengal towards the end of the year 1697.

Let the age-worn and musty records speak :—

In the *Chutanuttee Diary and Consultations* for June, July and August, 1697, we find the following entry under date the 24th June, 1697 :

> "Cojah Surhaud having offer'd his servis to goe to the Nabob's son Zubberdast Cawn, General of the Mogull's forces against the Rebell, and Governor of all these parts at present to make Application in behalf of the Right Honourable Company against the interlopers, it's resolved and agreede to and by us, that he proceede accordingly and because persons who have business are not acceptable and welcome to these great persons, empty handed, for the more effectual and Speedy procuring redress and getting out *Perwannas* to prevent the interlopers from trade. It's Agreede and resolved that an Arrazdaast or Letters be sent to Nabob's Son to the same effect : Also a Present to the value of a thousand Rupees, in broad cloth, flint ware &s. as under specified, and that verball directions be given. Cojah Surhaud to countenance and forward his proceedings against the Interlopers, and more especially to insist upon the late servises we have done the King."

In the same *Diary and Consultations* for the 8th day of July, 1697, it is recorded.

> "Cojah Surhaud being returned to us from Zubberdast Caun with his *Perwanna* on the Governors of Hughly and Ballasore to hinder the Interlopers from trade, it's Ordered that the *Perwannas* be dispeeded forthwith to said Governor."

The following entry appears in the *Chutanuttee Diary and Consultations* for 22nd September 1698.

> "Mr. Walsh and Cojah Surhaud being arrived with us from the Embassage to the young Prince,

having finished all business to our great satisfaction and the honour and credit of our Right Honourable Masters and intimating us that they promised the Prince three Brass small pieces of cannon, his curiosity or rather warlike disposition hankering after a handsome and decent Artillery. In consideration whereof and that they would be very acceptable to him.

It's Agreede and Ordered that they be forthwith dispeeded to him. And because very suddenly we may have further occasion to make use of his favours in matter wherewith the Right Honourable Company's affairs may receive great prejudice without his countenance and protection.

It's further resolved that a present of the New Flint ware that came by the *Anna* (being the best and the greatest curiosities that has come out of England these many years) be tendered him to preserve the friendship and affection he hath in a more special manner demonstrated to the English above other nations".

And it was the same Khojah Sarhad who, in 1715, accompanied the Surman Embassy to Delhi and succeeded in obtaining from the Mogul Emperor Farrukh Siyar, the historic "GRAND FARMAN" for the English, which laid the foundations of British rule in India. In the several reasons given by the Calcutta Council at the meeting held on the 27th day of January 1714, for appointing Khojah Sarhad in the negotiations at the Court of the Great Mogul, they state, among others that :—

"1st. He managed our affairs in Mohamed Azeem's Darbar and by his prudent conduct and winning address insinuated himself into favour and procured for us the Grant of this place [Calcutta] and the dependent towns which we now enjoy and that for small expence in comparison of the benefit.

2nd. He was personally known to Prince Feruckseer [Farrukh Siyar] the present King, then about fourteen years old and made him presents of toyes at that time very acceptable, for which he exprest a great deal of satisfaction often sending for Cojah Serhaud and making him sit by him many hours to show· what uses they were for. This we believe the King remembers and is probably one cause of his readily ordering a *Husbull Hookum* for us at the request of Cojah Serhauds' friends and agents at Court and appointing him to be particularly named in that, and all the *Perwannas* we lately received, commanding safe conduct for him also for our Present and English Gentlemen that shall accompany it.

3rd. It is absolutely necessary that some person who is perfect master of the Persian language and understands our affairs very well and what may be useful for us be sent and we know no man so qualified in both these respects as Cojah Serhaud is. He is therefore the fittest man we can send.

4th. If we should send him as *Vacqueel* only and inferior to all the English Gentlemen, we may reasonably suppose the King would in that case regard him most, which would be an affront to our nation. But that is not now likely to happen because he is joined in commission and second in negotiation and it will be his interest to get favour and respect for the whole."

And on the 5th June, 1714, adds the record book.

"It was also unanimously agreed that Cojah Serhaud whose interest &c. at Court has already had the good effect of procuring as the *Hasbull Hukum* and several other useful orders from Court be sent to assist in suing for the Kings' *Phirmaud* [Farman] and that he sit and vote in Council along with the three English Gentlemen. All which considerations being unanimously agreed to. We do appoint that Mr. John Surman be first, Cojah Surhaud second and Mr. John Pratt, third in this negotiation and that they consult together upon all occasions and according to the result of their consultations And that they may not want sufficient help nor have any reasonable cause to keep the accounts of their Transactions or of expences behind hand, we do appoint Mr. Edward Stephenson, Secretary and accomptant to the negotiation and [take down] the minutes when they sit in consultation. Cojah Surhaud being thus elected second in this negotation, the Terms agreed to with him are next to be explained, and those are :—

First. If all the privileges the Company have at any time heretofore enjoyed in the Mogull's dominions be confirmed in the new *Philrmanand* and he gets our bounds enlarged as far as we desire southward and to near Kidderpoor and that the shore on the side of the river [Howrah] opposite to this place [Calcutta] be also granted us. Also if he endeavour earnestly to get the grant of the Dew [Diu] Island near Metchlepatam [Masulipatam] which the President and Council at Madras desire may be obtained for that Presidency. His reward is then to be fifty-thousand Rupees but he is to have nothing if the fails in those points.

Secondly—If he procures the privilege of our nation to trade custom free at Suratt which he will attempt, he is to have fifty-thousand Rupees more for that service, but if he fails in that he is not to have the reward. He is nevertheless to endeavour to get the custom we pay at that port reduced to 2½ per cent".

The history of this all-important, if not epoch-making, Embassy to Delhi in 1715, is faithfully chronicled by the late Professor C. R. Wilson in his learned work—the *Early Annals of the English in Bengal*—published in London in 1895, we need not therefore dilate on the many advantages derived therefrom by the Company.

Stewart, in his *History of Bengal,* states that "the inhabitants of Calcutta enjoyed, after the return of the Embassy, a degree of freedom and security unknown to the other subjects of the Mogul Empire, and that city increased yearly in wealth, beauty and riches."

That well-informed critic and shrewd observer, William Bolts, in his *Considerations on India Affairs,* published in London, in 1782, referring to this important deputation, says :—

> "The trade of the English Company in Bengal had, from the period of their submission to Aurungzebe, continued to grow daily more important, but it was not carried on without frequent interruptions from the officers of the Mogul government, which it was hardly possible to avoid with a colony so situated. Being sensible likewise of the precarious tenures of their establishments in Bengal and elsewhere, in the year 1715 the Company sent a deputation of two gentlemen, named John Surman, and the other a very considerable Armenian merchant, named Coge [Khojah] Serhaud, to solicit redress for past, and security against future, oppressions ; for an extension of their old, and for many new privileges; and particularly for a small spot of ground to be allowed them wherever they settled a Factory.

Such was the language used by the English only forty years before the memorable battle of Plassey, the successful termination of which made the English the absolute masters of Bengal. It was upon this deputation that the Company obtained their GRAND FARMAN*; exempting them from paying any duties upon their trade within the Mogul's dominions, on payment of a *pheshkhash,* or present, of ten-thousand rupees per annum.

There are no references to Khojah Sarhad in the records after the return of the Embassy and we have not been able to find the date of his death or the place where he died . He is not buried at Calcutta, Chinsurah, Saidabad, Hooghly or Dacca where Armenians lived and died in the first-half of the 18th century. He may have returned to his birthplace (Julfa) and died there.

---

*A translation of the *Grand Farman* was made by Mr. James Fraser, (a gentleman well acquainted with the Persian language) and inserted in his *History of Nadir Shah.*

There is, *inside* the Armenian church at Madras, the grave of a Sarhad who died there in 1701. He may have been the father of Khojah Israel Sarhad, the diplomat.

It may be mentioned that only eminent persons are buried *inside* Armenian churches.

CHAPTER XXXIII.

THE ARMENIAN CHURCH OF NAZARETH

THE OLDEST PLACE OF CHRISTIAN WORSHIP IN CALCUTTA

We have seen in the preceding chapter that the Armenians had formed a Settlement at Calcutta during the first half of the 17th century, before the arrival of the English under Job Charnock, and a valuable relic of the early Armenian Settlement, in the form of a tombstone, is happily preserved to this day.

The present church, the *oldest* in Calcutta, was erected in 1724 on the burial ground of the community by one Agah Nazar, hence its name, Nazareth's church. The beautiful belfry which acts as a clock-tower, was built in 1734 by the opulent Hazarmall family, some members of which lie buried there. According to the *Bengal Obituary*, published in 1848 by Holmes & Co. a firm of Calcutta undertakers, the ground was purchased by one Kenanentch Phanoos and it was used as a cemetery until 1724 when the church was erected there, by national contributions under the auspices of Agah Nazar, Prior to the erection of the church, the Armenians worshipped in a small church in the immediate vicinity of their burial ground, as can' be seen from a letter which Agah Moses Catchick Arrakiel wrote to one Mr. Hawksworth who published the same in 1801 in his *East Indian Chronologist*. It contains a summary of the early history of the Armenians in Calcutta and we reproduce the same for the information of our readers.

It is as follows :

"Sir,—I have the pleasure to give you such an account of the Armenian inhabitants of Calcutta as I can confidently assert to be exact. I myself was born in that metropolis, and what I am about to write is the collective information from the oldest Armenians now living there. The Armenians settled in this country upwards of 150 years ago, and I feel a pride in adding they have been always faithful subjects to the English Government; by referring to Bolts you will find that my great-great-grandfather, Phanoos Calender, was, in consequence of his confidential services to the English, honoured with several privileges and public rights from Government.

"Shortly after the establishment of Calcutta by the English, the Armenians settled among them and erected a small chapel in China Bazar, where Mr. Joseph Emin's house now stands. The site of the present Armenian church was at that time their burying-ground, in which there are tombstones dated 80 years back, and consequently older than the present church. The Armenian church was built in the year 1724 by one Aga Nazar, and the steeple was added in 1734 by one Manuel Hazarmall, the expenses attending which were defrayed with a sum appropriated for that purpose by his father, Hazarmall Satoor. The architect, Gavond, was an Armenian from Persia. No material alteration was made at the Armenian church from the above period until the year 1790, when my deceased father, Catchick Arrakiel, embellished the church inside, presented the clock, added the houses for the clergy, and built the surrounding walls. The church now goes by the name of Nazareth's church, in honour of the founder. The church at Chinsura is the oldest that the Armenians have in this country. It was erected in 1695, and dedicated to St. John".

There have been, after Agah Catchick Arrakiel, many others who have endowed the Calcutta Armenian church with liberal benefactions which have made the church the richest in Calcutta, its present monthly income being over Rs. 12,500 derived from landed properties, investments and various trusts.

There are several mural tablets and memorials, erected, inside and outside the church, by the grateful Armenian community of Calcutta, to the memory of the pious benefactors, and as these may serve as an incentive to the present and future generations of Armenians to emulate the noble deeds of their revered ancestors, we give copies of the inscriptions engraved on the tablets, commemorating the princely donations of former benefactors, whose names deserve to be inscribed in letters of gold for their solicitude for the poor, as the church exists for the relief of the poor and the needy members of the community.*

The inscriptions referred to above are as follows:

On a long narrow copper tablet, fixed over the main entrance to the church, there is an inscription of two lines in ancient Armenian, which can be translated thus:

1. "Holy Nazareth, our mother kind, with outstretched arms, wide openeth, her holy bosom for her sons, to nourish them with the milk of grace".

This tablet was originally placed over the west gate of the church, facing Bonfield's Lane. It unfortunately bears no date, but in all probability it was put up there in 1724 on the completion of the church.

Translation of the Armenian inscription on a wooden tablet fixed over the door of the right sacristy.

2. "This holy altar, dedicated to the Illuminator [St. Gregory] is in memory of his namesake, Mr. Gregory, the son of Arathoon of old Erivan, dated the 25th Hamirah, (22nd December) 1763".

Translation of the Armenian inscription, on a wooden tablet, fixed over the door of the left sacristy.

3. "This holy altar, dedicated to the holy apostles Petrus and Paul, is in memory of his namesake, Agah Petrus, the son of Arathoon of old Erivan, dated the 25th Hamirah, (22nd December) 1763".

---

*The late Rev. Graham Sandberg, in an article in the *Calcutta Review*, for July 1891 writes:

> "Everywhere, it would seem except in their native land, they are notably prosperous; the richest merchants and bankers in Eastern towns belonging to this nationality. Confirmed money-makers, they are lavishly charitable to their own people; and in a philanthropic investigation in Calcutta, concerning the distributing of charitable relief to the poor of all nations in that city, only one Armenian was reported to be in want—a man who had offended the community by leaving their church"

The two extra altars over the sacristies, a strange innovation in an Armenian church, were erected in 1763 by Agah Petrus Arathoon, "the earthly god of the Armenians in Calcutta," as Joseph Emin calls him, one in memory of himself and the other to the memory of his younger brother, Khojah Gregory, better known by his orientalised name, as Gorgin Khan, the Minister and the Commander-in-chief of Nawab Mir Kasim of Bengal, from 1760-1763, who was treacherously murdered by an unknown assassin on the 11th August 1763, near Monghyr, after the battle of Oodwanalla.

On a black marble tablet fixed on the right wall of the belfry.

4. "In memoriam of Arrathoon Kaloos, Esquire, who endowed the Church with thirtyfour thousand rupees for the relief of the poor."

Arrathoon Kaloos, the Rector of the "Armenian Philanthrophic Academy" and a teacher for 35 years, died in Calcutta, on the 10th November 1833, aged 56 years, and was buried in the Armenian churchyard.

On a marble tablet on the south wall of the church.

5. "Sacred to the memory of Mrs. Hiripsimah Limbruggen* who departed this life at Negapatam on the 21st May, A.D. 1833. She was born at Surat in the year 1778. This tablet is erected as a mark of gratitude for her munificent bequest towards the relief of poor Armenians in Calcutta".

On a black marble slab on the north wall of the church.

6. "Sacred to the memory of the late Catchick Arakiel Esqr., whose patriotism endowed this church with a splendid clock, parochial building, and the surrounding walls. Gratefully inscribed by the Armenian community of Calcutta. Anno Domini 1837. Exegi monumentum œre perennius".

---

*For fuller information about Mrs. Hripsimah Limbruggen, see chapter XXI.

Agah Catchick Arakiel died on the 25th July 1790, and as a mark of great respect, was buried inside the church, but no tribute was paid to his revered memory till 47 years after his demise, when the above tablet was placed in the church. Very quick appreciation of departed worth indeed! For fuller information about Agah Catchick Arrakiel, see chapter XXXIV.

On a brass tablet fixed on the right hand pillar of the shade leading from the main gate of the church to the belfry.

7. "This roof and the shade over the gate were erected to the memory of the late Sarkies Ter Johannes Esquire by his grandson, Johannes C. Sarkies Esqre. during the wardenship of Zorab M. Manuk Esqre.

Calcutta 1st August 1854".

Agah Sarkies, the son of Rev. Johannes, an illustrious member of the Armenian community of Calcutta died in 1812, and was buried in the Armenian churchyard of Calcutta where his revered grave, with a beautiful white marble tombstone and a long inscription,* in ancient Armenian, can be seen to this day.

On a marble tablet on the south wall of the church.

8. "Sacred to the memory of the late Owen John Elias Esquire, born 1st November, 1786, died 12th March 1860.

*The inscription, which is a panegyric in metre, can be translated thus:

"The cruel bitter wind of death has flown out the light of the Armenian nation, the Armenian chief [leader] Agah Sarkies, the son of Rev. Johanness. The sword of death has cut down and destroyed the crown of the Armenian community. He was an eloquent and an honest man. His manners were amiable to all. Like Tobit he was charitable to the homeless and distributed money bountifully. He was put in this dark narrow cell at the age of 73 years. Now, O Ye people, follow this suitable advice. Put not your trust in vain in life which is pleasant but not real, but follow good meditations and lay up treasure which is incorruptible.

The date of this man's departure to the Creator of all, was the year one thousand, eight hundred and twelve, on the eighteenth day of the month of Qamar [17th August]."

This tablet is erected by the Armenian community of this place as a mark of their appreciaton of his private and public virtues. His charities to widows and orphans and the poor will not remain unrewarded in heaven. His gifts to churches, schools, asylums and hospitals, which have made his name to be generally respected have specially endeared it to his own countrymen."

Agah Owen John Elias died in Calcutta aged 74 years, and was buried on the right side of the entrance to the church under the belfry. He was born at Saidabad. He had two daughters, one of whom married Gregory Paul Melitus of Madras, and the other married Simon Bagram of Calcutta. Mr. P. G. Melitus C.I.E., late of the Indian Civil Service, was the son of the former.

On a black marble tablet fixed on the right side of the chancel.

9. "In memoriam of Stephen G. Bagram Esqurie, who endowed the church with thirtyfour thousand rupees for the relief of the poor."

Stephen George Bagram died at Chandernagore on the 21st November 1863 and his body was brought down and buried in the south covered verandah of the Armenian church near the south gate. He was 38 years old.

On a black marble tablet on the left wall of the belfry.

10. "In memoriam of P. J. Paul Esquire, who served the Armenian church gratis for 26 years, as a legal adviser".

P. J. Paul attorney-at-law of the Calcutta High Court and the father of the late Sir Gregory Charles Paul, Advocate-General of Bengal, died in Calcutta on the 29th September, 1862, aged 58 years, and was buried in the Armenian churchyard.

On a black marble tablet fixed on the north wall outside the church.

11. "George Joseph* Esqre. Born in Julfa. By whose munificence a school is established in the land of his birth for

*As stated on page 206, the school founded at Julfa, through the munificence of George Joseph of Jullunder, was amalgamated, with the

the instruction of Armenian youths, in the Armenian, English and Persian languages and by whose liberality a fund is also provided for the relief of the poor. He departed this life in Jullunder on the 6th December 1864".

Translation of an Armenian inscription on a brass tablet fixed on the big almirah in the church Library.

12. "This library was made over to the wardens and the commissaries of the Holy church of Nazareth for the perusal of our Reverend Priests, Calcutta, May 1896.

In memory of Miss Mary, the daughter of Arratoon Gregory Apcar. Born at Calcutta on the 21st July 1856, departed this life in London on the 22nd February 1895".

Translation of the Armenian inscription on a black marble slab fixed on the south wall of the Reception Hall on the first floor of the Parochial building.

13. "This marble floor was laid at the expense of Mr. Arrathoon Stephen of New Julfa, in memory of his deceased parents, Stephen and Hannan, and his brother Martyrose. In the year of our Lord 1900".

Mr. Arathoon Stephen died on the 14th May 1927, aged 66 years, and was buried in the Armenian churchyard of Calcutta on the following day, in the presence of a large gathering-Armenians, Europeans and Indians,-but for reasons unknown to us, there is *no* inscription on the beautiful white marble tombstone with a massive cross on it, in black marble, which cover his mortal remains. Should any future enquirers wish to know where the nameless grave is situated, they can find it on the east of the grave of Mrs. Lizzie T. M. Thaddeus.

On a black marble tablet fixed on the south-west wall of the belfry, facing the tablet to the memory of Arratoon Kalooss.

---

consent of his widow, with the Church Missionary Society's School in 1870.

14. "In memory of Martin J. Camell Esqre. died 15th January 1898, who served the Armenian church gratis as legal adviser for a period of 18 years".

The late Mr. Martin Joseph Camell, a well-known solicitor of Calcutta, during the second-half of the 19th century, was the eldest son of Joseph Arrathoon Camell, also a solicitor, who in April 1849, seceded from the holy Apostolic Church of Armenia and joined the Anabaptists, by which name the present-day Baptists were known in those days. He was a good Armenian scholar, gifted with a good voice, and had served the Calcutta Armenian church as an honorary chorister (duprapiet) since his youth. The unexpected secession caused a great stir amongst the Armenian community of Calcutta, as he was liked and respected by everybody for his great piety and sterling qualities of the head and heart, and in the leading articles which appeared in the *Azgasare Araratian,** for the 25th April and the 5th May 1849, the editor, Mesrovb David Thaliadian, discusses at great length the causes which led to that unhappy event. And when he died on the 21st October, 1851, aged 45 years, 3 months and a few days, the same journal, in its issue of the 15th November, 1851, wrote a most touching obituary, extolling the virtues and the high attainments of the deceased, whose untimely death was considered as a national loss. It is gratifying, however, to note that after his death, all his children (three sons and five daughters) returned to the bosom of the mother Church. The late Mr. Martin Camell, who like his father, was gifted with a good voice, used to sing, in the Armenian church of Nazareth even in his old age, during the Passion week solemn services. His younger son, Mr. John Camell, an advocate of the Calcutta High Court, is the present chairman of the Armenian church Committee.

On a brass tablet, fixed on the east wall, next to the left sacristy.

15. "In loving memory of Carapiet Balthazar and Hosanah Balthazar. The altar-piece consisting of three

*The *Azgasare Araratian*—the Patriot of Ararat—was an independent journal, published in classical Armenian, under the able editorship of that great scholar and poet, Mesrovb Thaliadian, from 1845—1852.

paintings, representing "The holy Trinity", "The Lord's Supper" and, "The enshrouding of our Lord", painted by Mr. A. E. Harris, an English artist, was presented to the Holy church of Nazareth, Calcutta, in July 1901, by their children.

1. Mrs. Annie A. T. Apcar.
2. Mrs. Rosie A. M. Sarkies.
3. Mr. Gregory Balthazar.
4. Mrs. Elizaberth M. J. Joakim.
5. Miss Mary Balthazar.
6. Miss Aileen Balthazar.
7. Mr. Balthazar Carapiet Balthazar.
8. Miss Edith Balthazar.

The altar-piece was, with the sanction of His Eminence Bishop Malachi, the Prelate of Persia, India and the East, consecrated on the 21st July, 1901, by the Revd. Mackertich Peters, assisted by Revds. Mesrope C. David and Basil P. Alexy, during the wardenship of Mr. Arratoon Thomas Apcar and Mr. Marcar Chater.

This tablet was placed by the Church Committee."

Mr. Carapiet Balthazar died in Calcutta on the 4th February 1901, aged 62 years, and was buried in the Armenian churchyard, in the covered verandah, behind the altar, where his wife, Hosanah, who died at Colombo, on the 22nd March 1895, aged 42 years and 7 months, was also buried.

On a black marble tablet fixed on the outside south wall of the church.

16. "This tablet is erected as a mark of rememberance of the kindness of Mr. John Boisogomoff of Tiflis in furnishing the church and the 1st and 2nd flats of the Parochial buildings with 39 electric fans and wiring for installation on the 27th of January 1902."

Mr. John Boisogomoff, an Armenian from Russia, was in the first decade of the present century, a successful jute merchant and a colliery owner afterwards. He is now living in retirement in Calcutta. He came out to Calcutta some fifty years ago, in company with another Armenian from Russia, a claimant and an heir to a big estate in Calcutta, but before he could establish his claim, he became an inmate of the Lunatic Asylum, unfortunately, where he died some years after, and his companion, Mr. John Boisogomoff, entered the jute trade at Narainganj and was in the service of Messrs. M. David & Co., for some years, before starting on his own.

Translation of the Armenian inscription on a brass tablet fixed on the right wall, above the steps, leading to the top flat of the Parochial House.

17. "This newly-erected third flat was constructed completely in the year of our Lord 1906 on the original building (constructed by Agah Catchick Arakiel in 1790) for the residence and dormitory of the officiating clergymen of the holy church of Nazareth of this city and for their exclusive use only, for the glory of the all-bountiful God, for the splendour of the Church, for the honour of this Holy house and for the pride of the Armenian nation.

This memorial, inscribed in Armenian characters, must remain always immovable and unalterable, fixed on the walls of this newly-constructed building, under the care of the wardens, in everlasting memory of the pious dead whose names are recorded in the Book of Life, in the following order :

In memory of :—

	Born	Died
Mr. Arratoon Apcar of New Julfa ...	1779	1863
Mrs. Catherine Arratoon Apcar ...	1800	1850
Mr. Gregory Apcar of New Julfa ...	1795	1847
Mr. Katchkhathoon Gregory Apcar ...	1811	1863
Mr. Emin Joseph Emin of Calcutta ...	1807	1868
Mrs. Mariam Joseph Emin	1813	1839
Mr. Michael Joseph Emin of Calcutta ...	1809	1846
Mrs. Catherine Michael Emin of Madras	1808	1864
Mrs. Merine Arratoon Gregory Apcar ...	1833	1905
Miss Mary, the second daughter of Arratoon Gregory Apcar	1856	1895
Mr. Joseph Chater of New Julfa ...	—	1899

This tablet is also to the memory of the dead and the living children of the above-menoitned deceased in peace.

Armenian Holy church of Nazareth, Calcutta.
1906."

The third flat of the Parochial House was erected, by the late Mr. A. G. Apcar, entirely at his own expense, but with his usual modesty, he did not have his name inscribed on the tablet.

On a white marble tablet, fixed on the south wall of the nave.

18. "Sacred to the memory of John Michael, merchant of this city, the only child of Haik and Ripsima Michael, died at Calcutta on 4th February 1909, aged 75 years. Interred at the Tangra cemetery.

This tablet was erected by the Church Committee in *appreciation of the charities endowed by him for the relief* and education of the Armenian poor in Calcutta."

Mr. John Haik Michael, the son of humble parents, rose through sheer merit, to be a leading merchant and land owner in Calcutta, during the last decades of the 19th century. He left large bequests for the poor Armenians of Calcutta* and for the education of poor Armenian girls and boys in the La Martiniere (for girls) and in the local Armenian College.

On a black marble slab, with white border, fixed on the north wall of the nave.

19. "Sacred to the memory of the late Rose Catherine Galstaun, the beloved wife of Johannes Carapiet Galstaun, and the eldest daughter of Mr. and Mrs. Johannes Shahnazar Sarkies† Born in Batavia on the 26th November 1866, died

---

*Mr. John Haik Michael left a bequest of Rs. 102,600 to the Armenian church of Calcutta for the benefit of the poor.

† The late Johanness Shahnazar Sarkies, a nephew of the present writer's father, was an eminent merchant of Batavia and the senior partner in the firm of Sarkies, Edgar & Co. of Batavia, Sourabaya and Singapore for a period of thirty years (1855-1885).

in Calcutta on the 14th August 1910, and buried at the Armenian cemetery in Lower Circular Road. This tablet is erected by the Church Committee, A.D. 1911, in recognition of Mr. Galstaun's many acts of kindness to his community and great and continuing services to this Holy church."

Mr. J. C. Galstaun, O.B.E., the doyen of the Armenian community of Calcutta, has, amongst other commercial activities, beautified Calcutta and added to the many architectural beauties of the city considerably, by erecting majestic buildings, such as the "Galstaun Park," the "Galstaun Mansions," the "Harrington Mansions" and others. He has for several years, acted as the Manager of the "Armenian College," the Warden of the Armenian church, and the Chairman of the Armenian Church Committee, with great zeal and devotion. Although in his 77th year, he is still very active and energetic. May Heaven prolong his useful life for many more years for the benefit of his nation, whom he has served loyally for the last forty five years. We must not however forget to mention that our worthy and *debonair* compatriot was the *only* person who was honoured by a private visit from His Royal Highness, the Prince of Wales, now King Edward VIII, when he visited Calcutta fifteen years ago. It was at his palatial residence, known as "Galstaun Park" that Mr. Galstaun received the august guest in December 1921. The palatial house in Lower Circular Road thus becomes one of the several places of historical interest in Calcutta and had Lord Curzon been living to-day, he would, no doubt, have ordered a tablet to be

---

He was a good Armenian and English scholar having received his education at the feet of that well-known Gamaliel, the immortal Mesrovb David Thaliadian in "St. Sandukth's school" in Calcutta, from 1848-1852. He had been a teacher of the English language, for a couple of years, at Melbourne, during the gold boom of 1850-1855. He died full of years and honours at Singapore in February 1904, leaving two daughters, one of whom was the late Mrs. Rose Galstaun and the other, Mrs. Mary Michael Martin who is living with her children at Singapore, where her late husband, Mr. Michael S. Martin was a merchant for many years. Nanajan Sarkies, the widow of Johanness Shahnazar Sarkies who died on the 1st day of March, 1936, aged 90 years, erected, some twenty five years ago, the handsome two storeyed Parochial House in the Singapore Armenian church, in memory of her deceased husband.

fixed at the gate, as he did with other buildings, when alive. During his visit to Calcutta, the Prince presented a cup for the Calcutta Races and this much-coveted trophy was won by Mr. Galstaun, whose famous horses had carried off several such trophies—cups presented by the King Emperor and the Viceroy —before. Mr. Galstaun, a public-spirited citizen, with his usual generosity and *bonhomie*, presented the Stakes, amounting to Rupees fifteen thousand, to the Prince, as can be seen from the following letter which His Royal Highness addressed to the charitably-disposed and magnanimous citizen of a "no mean city".

"Government House,
Calcutta, 30-12-21.

DEAR MR. GALSTAUN,

I want first of all to thank you very much for handing over the stakes of my cup to me for charitable purposes.

I shall consult with Lord Ronaldshay as to the exact object to which to devote this handsome sum. I must also thank you for so kindly mounting me in the paperchase; I enjoyed my ride on your big chestnut horse very much indeed. I was also interested to see over your stables.

Wishing you a successful season on the turf and thanking you again for your generosity.

I remain,
Yours truly
EDWARD P."

This is not, however, the only instance of Mr. Galstaun's liberality, for he gave the handsome donation of Rupees twenty-five thousand towards the cost of the erection of that noble monument—a dream in marble, and a replica of the world-famous Agra Taj—known as the "Victoria Memorial". And during the Great War, Mr. Galstaun, as a loyal citizen, placed his palatial residence-"Galstaun Park"-at the disposal of the Military authorities, for the sick and the invalid British soldiers, and in an appreciation of that noble act, the Indian government were graciously pleased to confer on him the title of O.B.E. (Order of the British Empire) although he merited a much higher recognition for the great sacrifices he had made on that and on other occasions.

On a white marble tablet, with black border, fixed on the north wall of the sacristy.

20. "In memory of Mrs. Helen Moses, widow of the late M. J. Moses, Esq., of Singapore, born in Calcutta on the 4th March 1843, died in Calcutta on 2nd May 1917, and of her brothers Carapiet Thaddeus Avetoom, born in Calcutta on 16th February 1847, died in Calcutta on 2nd September 1915, and Avetoom Thaddeus Avetoom, born in Calcutta on 23rd January 1853, died in Calcutta on 20th June 1914.

Mrs. Moses left charities for the relief of the poor Armenians of Calcutta and for the benefit of this church."*

The late Mrs. Helen Moses was one of the daughters of Thaddeus Catchick Avetoom, an eminent Armenian merchant of Calcutta and a man of letters, being a good classical Armenian scholar. He translated Oliver Goldsmith's *Vicar of Wakefield* into classical Armenian and it was printed at the press of the "Araratian Society" of Calcutta in 1848. He was also the author of an interesting historical novel, in modern Armenian, called *Aramais,* which was likewise printed in the "Araratian Society's" press in 1846. He died on the 12th February, 1863, aged 52 years, and was buried in the Armenian churchyard of Calcutta. His widow, Mariam, who was born at Shiraz in 1813, died at Calcutta on the 23rd December 1896 and was buried in the Armenian churchyard next to her husband. He had five sons and three daughters. Four of his sons, Catchick, Carapiet, Zorab and Avetoom were merchants, whilst the youngest, Sarkies, a retired I.M.S. officer is living in London. Lt.-Col. Sarkies Avetoom, although an octagenarian, is still active and in full possession of his faculties and physical powers. May he complete the century and continue to enjoy his well-earned pension for many

*Mrs. Helen Moses left a bequest of Rs. 32,000 for the poor Armenians of Calcutta.

years to come. His late brother Avetoom Thaddeus Avetoom, commemmorated in the tablet to the memory of Mrs. Helen Moses, was the Chairman of the Armenian Church Committee of Calcutta for several years.

One of the daughters of Thaddeus Catchick Avetoom, Mrs. Zumrood Johanness Agabeg, was the mother of Mrs. Diana Agabeg Apcar, an authoress and a writer of distinction, who is living at Yokohama with her children. The other daughter of Thaddeus Catchick Avetoom Mrs. Hosannah Mesrope Thaddeus of Calcutta, was the mother of that great national benefactor, the late Mr. T. M. Thaddeus, whose liberal bequests for the Armenian poor of Calcutta and for the education of poor Armenian boys and girls in Calcutta deserve to be recorded in letters of gold. (See inscription No. 27).

Inscription on the four silver plates covering the steps of the altar :

21. "The silver plates covering the Holy altar were presented by Mrs. Mary Abraham in loving memory of her husband, Johannes Abraham, who departed this life at Calcutta, on the 24th November 1922, aged 60 years."

The donor, Mrs. Mary Abraham, died on the 4th August 1927, aged 74 years and was interred in the Armenian churchyard of Calcutta.

On a white marble slab, with black border, on the north wall of the nave of the church.

22. "This tablet is erected by the Armenian community of Calcutta to the revered memory of the parents of the Hon'ble Sir Catchick Paul Chater, Kt., C.M.G., of Hongkong, in grateful recognition of his munificent gift of Rupees Fifty thousand to this church.

1922."

On a white marble tablet, with black border, fixed on the right side of the altar.

23. "This tablet is erected as a tribute of profound esteem and gratitude to that most noble philanthropist, the Hon'ble Sir Catchick Paul Chater, Kt., C.M.G., of Hongkong who endowed the church with Rupees two lakhs and a

half by founding the "Sarah Chater Endowment Fund," for the relief of the local poor of the Armenian community, in memory of his deceased sisters, Sarah and Eliza.

1923."

Sir Catchick Paul Chater, the. "Grand Old Man" of Hongkong, died on the 27th May, 1926, at his palatial residence, known as "Marble Hall," in his 80th year, and was buried in the Protestant cemetery at Happy Valley, after an impressive service in St. John's Cathedral, Hongkong. We shall refer to the achievements of this great philanthopist again.

On a white marble tablet, with a black border, fixed on the south wall of the south verandah of the church.

24. "This tablet is erected to the memory of Miss Lily Mary Christian, B.A., the only daughter of the late Mr. and Mrs. Aviet Thaddeus Christian of Mozufferpore and granddaughter of Rev. Gregory of Julfa, who left all that she possessed at her death to this church for the benefit of the poor.

1923."

Miss Lily Mary Christian died in Calcutta on the 4th October 1920, aged 44 years, and was buried in the Armenian cemetery in Lower Circular Road.

On a white marble tablet, with black border, fixed on the south wall of the south verandah of the church.

25. "This tablet is erected as a tribute of esteem and gratitude to the memory of Mr. Thomas Malcolm for his valuable services to the church as a Warden and Chairman of the Church Committee for a period of 50 years.

1923."

Mr. Thomas Malcolm, the Nestor of the Armenians of Calcutta died on the 6th March, 1918, aged 81 years, and was buried in the Armenian cemetery in Lower Circular Road. He was born at Bushire in 1837, and was a grandson of Arathoon Malcolm, the ancestor of the aristocratic Malcolm family of that place. One of the nephews of the late Mr. Thomas Malcolm, is Mr. James Malcolm, a well-known figure in commercial circles in London, whilst another, Mr.

Leo Malcolm, is an eminent merchant at Bushire, being the sole proprietor of the century-old and reputable mercantile firm of Messrs. A. & T. J. Malcolm of Bushire—that great and important port on the Persian Gulf.

On a white marble tablet, with black border, fixed on the left side of the left sacristy.

26. "The marble tablets with carved sacred pictures which are erected on both sides of the Holy altar were presented by Mr. Mackertich Aram Manuk in loving memory of his parents, Manuk Thorose Manuk, and Regina Manuk both of Calcutta."

1924."

Mr. Mackertich Aram Manuk is the youngest son of the late Mr. Manuk Thorose Manuk, who served the Armenian church of Calcutta, faithfully, as a vestry clerk, for a period of 40 years. He died on Sunday, the 22nd day of June, 1913, aged 84 years, and was buried in the Armenian cemetery in Lower Circular Road. Mr. Mackertich Aram Manuk, has acted, since his youth, as an honorary chorister and deacon of the Calcutta Armenian church, being gifted with a good voice like his revered father, who was likewise a chorister of the church for over sixty years, having been a permanent resident of Calcutta since 1851. His father, Thorose Manuk Thorose, known as "Thorose varjapiet" (teacher), died in Calcutta on the 20th July 1858, aged 49 years and was buried in the old Armenian cemetery in Coolootollah Street, on the east side near the gate. He was the maternal grandfather of the writer of these lines.

On a white marble tablet, with black border, fixed on the left side of the altar.

27. "Sacred to the memory of Thaddeus Mesrope Thaddeus, merchant, born in Calcutta on the 17th January 1856, died in Calcutta on the 28th October 1927.

This tablet has been erected by the Church Committee in appreciation of his munificent donations for the establishment of a fund for the education of poor Armenians in Calcutta, and also to this Church for the relief of the poor."

Mr. Thaddeus Mesrope Thaddeus was a successful jute merchant in Calcutta for many years. He built the beautiful "Park Mansions" on the site of the old "Doveton College" in Free School Street. He owned first-class race horses, which won for him several important trophies in the Calcutta Races. He left a bequest of Rs. 567,500 for the poor Armenians and for the education of poor girls and boys of Calcutta. He left a son and three daughters.

Although no tablet has been put up in the Armenian church of Calcutta to the memory of the late Mr. Joseph Paul, commemorating his munificent bequests to the poor of Calcutta and Julfa, yet the inscription on his marble tombstone, surmounted by a rustic cross, in the covered verandah at the back of the altar, in the Armenian church of Calcutta, is eloquent proof of his benevolence. It is as follows :—

> " Sacred to the memory of JOSEPH PAUL Esqre., of Julfa, a benefactor of great zeal, who left by a deed the greater part of the fruits of his arduous labour for establishing in New Julfa a free national dispensary, for helping the orphans and the poor of New Julfa, and for repairing the Holy churches of New Julfa, Shiraz and Bushire, in Persia.
>
> Died at the age of 64 years on the 4th November, 1905, in Calcutta.
>
> In the world of sorrow he lived and laboured to comfort the poor."

The late Mr. Joseph Paul left a bequest, the annual income of which, amounting to Rs. 600, to be distributed amongst the poor Armenians of Calcutta during Holy week every year and a similar sum amongst the poor of Julfa during Passion week, in addition to other charities for the benefit of the poor of his birthplace.

We find that there is no tablet either to the memory of the late Mr. A. S. Mackertich, who left by his will an annual donation of Rs. 1000 to be distributed amongst the poor Armenians of Calcutta for X'mas, and a similar donation for the poor Armenians of Julfa for the same festive occasion.

Mr. A. S. Mackertich, a successful jute merchant of Calcutta, died in London some fourteen years ago. His last will is dated the 31st January, 1921.

Before concluding this chapter, it may be noted that there is *no* tablet, either inside or outside the church, to the memory of that truly great man, the late Mr. A. G. Apcar, who in 1891 gave the Calcutta Armenian Church its present Constitution—the scheme for the management of the properties and affairs of the Armenian churches at Calcutta and Chinsurah—which was sanctioned by the Calcutta High Court. It was he who during his able Receivership (1889-1891) raised the miserable salaries of the officiating priests and provided them with a carriage and a horse. It was he who in 1896 presented a well-stocked Library to the church for the benefit of the clergymen and it was he again who in 1906 built a new flat of four rooms, over the old two-storeyed Parochial House, for the exclusive use of the clergymen. And yet there exists *no* memorial, commemorating the valuable services and the gifts of that pious benefactor who has left handsome bequests to the church for the benefit of the clergymen and the poor, to say nothing of the princely benefactions left by him for the poor of his revered fathers' birthplace, namely Julfa, the ancestral home of the Armenian merchant-princes of India, Burma, the Straits Settlements, Java and the Far East.

Mr. Arratoon Gregory Apcar, the "Grand Old Man" of the Armenian Community of Calcutta, died on the 1st February, 1916, aged 88 years, and was buried in the Armenian churchyard, in the portion reserved for the members of the Apcar family. His wife, Merine (*neé* Emin) who died on the 17th January 1905, is also buried there. Of their two sons and three daughters, the only surviving one is Miss Amy Apcar of No. 44, Chowrighee Road, referred to on page 468.

CHAPTER XXXIV

AGAH CATCHICK ARRAKIEL

A loyal and an eminent Armenian merchant of Calcutta in the second-half of the 18th century.

An illustrious member of the aristocratic Gentloom family, Agah Catchick Arrakiel, was the head and the most respected member of the Armenian community of Calcutta in the second-half of the 18th century, and his liberal gifts to the Armenian holy church of Nazareth, (Calcutta) speak eloquently of his great piety. He had the church compound surrounded by a substantial wall, greatly embellished the sacred edifice inside and built the present beautiful parsonage within the church enclosure in 1790, to which a third storey was added, in 1906, by his great-grandson, the late Mr. Arratoon Gregory Apcar of the well-known firm of Apcar & Co. of Calcutta. Agah Catchick Arrakiel presented the church also with a valuable English clock, which after having measured time for about a century and a half, on the belfry attached to the church, is still considered to be the best of its kind in Calcutta. The clock was ordered from England in 1789, the year before his death, but it arrived in Calcutta two years after he had been laid to rest, as can be seen from the following inscription which is engraved on the works inside the clock tower :—

> "Ordered from England and fixed at the expense of the late Catchick Arrakiel Esquire, in the year 1792.
>
> Alexander Hare, Maker, London.
>
> Repaired and two more dials added during the wardenship of Johannes Avdall* in the year 1838, by E. Gray, Calcutta."

---

*Johanness Avdall, a native of Shiraz in Persia, was for a period of 45 years, the Armenian Head Master and Rector of the "Armenian Philantnropic Academy" of Calcutta. He was a good classical Armenian scholar and knew English fairly well. In 1826 he translated into classical

But it was for his loyalty to the British that brought him into prominence as one of the foremost citizens of Calcutta shortly before his untimely death, which occurred in 1790 at the early age of forty-eight years.

In the Second Volume of *Selections from the Calcutta Gazettes of the years 1789-1797*, published in 1865, under the sanction of the Government of India, there is, at page 220, an account of the great rejoicings and the festivities which took place in Calcutta in the month of July 1789, on receipt of the happy news of the recovery of King George III of England from his unfortunate malady which, as every student of history knows, was madness.

The writer of the article, after giving a full and vivid account of the proceeedings on that festive occasion on the part of the Government and the citizens of Calcutta, of all classes and denominations, concludes thus :—

"We cannot pass over in the occurrences of Tuesday, the liberality of a Lady of the Settlement who presented a thousand Rupees to be distributed by the Committee for the relief of debtors in such manner as they judged most beneficial.

Another instance of liberality was also exhibited by Mr. Catchick Arrakiel, a wealthy Armenian merchant and an old inhabitant of this Settlement, who liberated, at his own expense, *all* the debtors confined by the Courts of Requests, to the number of one hundred and thirty eight. This act of generosity cost Mr. Catchick Arrakiel, as we understood, three thousand Rupees. This gentleman and many other Armenians, illuminated their houses and their church in the most splendid manner."

The Commissioners of the "Court of Requests" lost no time in informing the Governor-General of the release of all

---

Armenian, Samuel Johnson's *Rasselas*, which was printed at the Press of Academy. He translated Father Michael Chamchian's *History of Armenia*, known as *Khrakhchan*, into English, in 1827. For nearly fifty years, he was a Member of the "Asiatic Society of Bengal." He died on the 11th July 1870, aged 67 years and was buried in the Armenian churchyard of Calcutta. It is sad to remark however, that *none* of his four sons walked in his foot-steps, as men of letters.

the debtors, confined in the prison of the Court. Here is their letter:

"TO EARL CORNWALLIS, K. G.,
Governor-General, &c., &c., &c.

My Lord.

A sense of duty and the pleasure we derive from communicating to your Lordship an act of Benevolence, which has been particularly directed into a mark of Loyal attention to the day you have appointed for the celebration of His Majesty's late recovery induce us to acquaint your Lordship that Coja Cacheek Arakell in Testimony of the Satisfaction he feels on the Joyfull Event, has this morning released all the Debtors confined in the Prison of this Court to the Number of 138 Persons whose Debts he has paid, and humanely distributed 2 Rs. to each for his immediate subsistence.

We have the Honor to be
My Lord
Yours Lordships Most Faithfull
& Obedient Humble Servants
F. PIERARD
JOHN DURHAM
RD. CS. BIRCH
Sitting Commrs. of the Court of Requests."

Court of Requests
Calcutta
the 28th July 1789.

The Court of Directors of the "East India Company" in London, brought this noble act of the magnanimous Armenian merchant to the notice of the King, and as a mark of royal approbation, His Majesty King George III, was graciously pleased to present Agah Catchick Arrakiel with his miniature portrait and a valuable sword. Perhaps no higher honour would be conferred by a British king on a humble subject. But unfortunately Agah Catchick Arrakiel had departed this life on the 25th day of July 1790, before the royal gifts reached Calcutta, and they were therefore presented to his eldest son, Agah Moses Catchick Arrakiel, by the Governor-General, the most Noble Marquis Cornwallis, at a public levee in Government House with the request that he should always appear at levees and public entertainments decorated with those interesting souvenirs of his sovereign's signal favour. The writer of these lines has had the pleasure of handling that valuable miniature portrait in 1891 when it was offered for sale to an Armenian jeweller of Calcutta, by a distant member of the Arrakiel family, then resident in Calcutta.* It was a bust in miniature, of the august sovereign, King George III, neatly painted on a plate of ivory, and mounted in a substantial gold frame of the finest workmanship. The whole was surmounted by a miniature gold crown and was suspended by a solid gold chain long enough to go round the neck, as is customary with medallions and pendants of that nature.

That he was a very prominent citizen of Calcutta is evident from the following interesting obituary notice which appeared in the *Calcutta Gazette* on the 29th July 1790, and which clearly portrays the character of Aagah Catchick Arrakiel and depicts the great esteem in which he was held not only by his own countrymen, the Armenians, but other nationalities, especially the Greek residents of Calcutta :

There is the tribute paid by an English journal to the memory of an Armenian Phlianthropist of Calcutta.

The 29th July, 1790.

> "On Saturday last, in the morning of the 25th instant, departed this life that truly respectable and worthy character, Mr. Catchick Arrakiel, an Armenian merchant of the first rank and eminence in Calcutta and

---

*In 1925, we were requested by the late Sir Catchick Paul Chater, the Armenian multi-millionaire of Hongkong, to try and secure that interesting family relic for him, as he was a descendant of Agah Catchick Arrakiel, through his mother. We succeeded, after repeated advertisements in the local papers, in tracing the historic relic, but while the negotiations for its purchase were going on, Sir Paul Chater breathed his last at Hongkong on the 27th May 1926, and there were no other patriotic Armenians amongst the wealthy Armenian community of Calcutta to come forward and secure that historic and priceless relic for the nation. Alas for the callousness of the Indo-Armenians of the present day, who seem to be utterly indifferent to all noble sentiments and ideals in this materialistic age. Shades of Khojah Petrus Arratoon and Agah Catchick Arrakiel !

the head and principal of the Armenian nation in Bengal.

The goodness, humanity and benevolence of this man towards all mankind, his liberal spirit in contributing to the public welfare on every occasion, the affability of his deportment and friendly disposition to all, were distinguished traits of his character, he was so warmly and gratefully attached to the English nation, that he was continually heard to express his happiness and a sense of his fortunate lot in being under their Government. He possessed the regard of the whole Settlement, unsullied by the enmity of a single individual. Among his own beloved nation, the Armenians, he was looked up to as a guide and director in all their difficulties and disputes which he was ever studious to settle with paternal affection.

The inward satisfaction of doing good and love to God were the sole motives which governed this virtuous man in the exercise of his charity and benevolence, without any mixture of vanity or ostentation. He has left a disconsolate widow and a numerous family of seven children, whom he most tenderly loved. He died lamented, not only by his own nation, but by all the different sects in Bengal, and especially by the Greeks, to whom he rendered the most essential service.*

---

*The Greek traders in Calcutta, who relied upon the patronage of the influential Armenian merchants, had entered into an agreement with them in terms of which they paid into the Armenian church of Nazareth, the sum of one Arcot rupee on every pale of merchandise that they brought down to Calcutta from Murshidabad, Patna, Bandana, Dacca, Sylhet and Assam.

This fact affords the strongest proof of their being under a deep debt of gratitude to the Armenians.

Alas for the vicissitudes of Time, for the Greeks who were under an obligation to the Armenians in the days of Agah Catchick Arrakiel, 150 years ago, have surpassed their patrons in the commercial world of Calcutta, one of the leading mercantile firms in that city, with a world-wide reputation, being owned by Greeks. Where are the Armenian merchant-princes—the Sarhads, the Nazars, the Hazarmalls, the Arathoons, the Arrakiels, the Owens, the Agabegs, the Apcars, the Mooradkhans,

In short, no individual ever died more universally regretted, or whose loss will be longer and more sincerely felt.

To this good man, without the smallest deviation from the truth, may be applied the scriptural character given to Job. (Chap. xxix).

"I was a father to the poor, and the cause which I knew not, I searched out, I was eyes to the blind and feet to the lame, I put on righteousness, and it clothed me. My judgment was a robe and a diadem, then I said I shall die in my rest and I shall multiply my days as the stars of the firmament."

Mr. Catchick Arrakiel was born in Upper Armenian* and died in the forty-eighth year of his age; he was descended from a very respectable family, one of his immediate ancestors† was Cazee (Khojah) Phanoos Calandar (Kalandar) who was greatly distinguished about a century ago for his zeal and attachment to the English, and by whose conduct and management the "English East India Company" was induced‡ to grant certain beneficial commercial privileges to the Armenians either trading in or to India.

His remains were interred on Sunday morning, between ten and eleven o'clock, in the Armenian

---

the Babajohns and a host of others, who by their enterprise and commercial activities made the Armenian name lustrous during the 18th and 19th centuries? Where are the great merchants whose extensive shipping gave the name to the *Armenian Ghat* near the present Howrah Bridge in Strand Road?

*This is not correct, Agah Catchick Arrakiel was *not* born in Upper Armenia. His father, who died at Dacca in 1742, was a native of Julfa, the Armenian suburb of Ispahan, in Persia.

†This is not correct either. Khojah Phanoos Kalandar was not the immediate ancestor of Agah Catchick Arrakiel, but the great grand-father of his wife Begoom, who was the daughter of Satoor Tharkhan of Surat. Satoor Tharkhan's wife was the grand-daughter of Khojah Phanoos Kalandar.

‡The Armenians and not the "English East India Company" were *induced* to enter into a commercial Treaty with the English, in 1688, through their respected representative, Khojah Phanoos Kalandar, as shown in Chapter XVIII.

> church after the celebration of High Mass. The funeral was attended by a very numerous and respectable company, the Armenian bishops with all the clergy of the same Church, Colonel Fullarton and two Aides-de-Camp of the Right Honourable the Governor-General with many other gentlemen, Civil and Military."

In him the Armenian community of Calcutta lost their head and respected leader. His remains were greatly honoured by being buried *inside* their church, where his grave, with a white marble tombstone, may be seen to this day, bearing an inscription in classical Armenian, surmounted by the figure of a rider on a fiery steed in bold relief, holding in his right-hand a spear and in the left a pair of scales, symbolic of righteousness. The inscription on his tombstone can be translated thus :

> This is the tomb of Agah Catchick, the son of Arrakiel of the Gentloom family, who was forty-eight years old when he died on the 25th July 1790, at Calcutta.

His widow Begum, who survived him thirty-five years, died on the last day of November 1825* and her remains were placed next to those of her husband. A black marble slab, with an inscription in ancient Armenian, marks her grave *inside* the Armenian church of Nazareth.

The inscription on her tombstone, can be translated thus :

> This is the tomb of Begoom, the daughter of Satoor Tharkhan, and the wife of Agah Catchick Arrakiel of the Gentloom family, who died on the 30th November 1825 aged 70 years.

In 1837, the Armenian community of Calcutta awoke at last from their lethargy, and remembering the worth of that

---

*At the funeral of Mrs. Begoom Catchick Arrakiel, which was very largerly attended, the immortal Mesrovb David Thaliadian, the future poet, author, educationist and journalist of the Armenians in Calcutta—then a humble student in "Bishop's College,"—delivered a most impressive funeral oration in classical Armenian, extolling the virtues of the deceased, who like her lamented husband, was held in great esteem by the Armenian community of Calcutta for her piety, philanthrophy and noble qualities of the head and the heart.

truly great man, erected, 47 years after his death, a black marble mural tablet in their church, near his grave, as a tribute to his memory, with appropriate inscriptions in Armenian and English, the following being a copy of the latter :—

Sacred to the memory of the late CATCHICK ARRAKIEL ESQ., whose patriotism endowed this church with a splendid clock, the Parochial Buildings and the surrounding walls. Gratefully inscribed by the Armenian community of Calcutta. Anno Domini 1837. Exegi monumentum œre perennius.*

Agah Catchick Arrakiel had seven children—two sons† and five daughters‡ Their descendants in the female line are living in Calcutta, Bankipore and London. There are no descendants in the male line. *Sic transit gloria mundi* !

The following account of the Armenians in Calcutta, in which there is an allusion to Agah Catchick Arrakiel, appeared in the *Indian Recreations* published in Edinburgh in 1803 :—

"The Armenians are the most respectable and perhaps the most numerous body of foreign merchants in this Capital.

---

* This can be translated thus :

"He wrought out a monument more lasting than bronze."

† Agah Catchick Arrakiel's younger son, Rev. Johanness Catchick Arrakiel who had been ordained a priest for the service of the Armenian church of St. John the Baptist, at Chinsurah, at the special desire of his pious mother, died at Calcutta on the 29th October 1832, aged 52 years, and was buried *inside* the church of Nazareth, where both his parents and elder brother are interred, in the north aisle.

‡ One of the five daughters of Agah Catchick Arrakiel, Elizabeth, married in 1796, Johanness Sarkies, son of the illustrious Agah Sarkies Johanness of Calcutta. They had eight daughters, one of whom, Khatchkhathoon, married in 1827, Gregory Apcar, a younger brother of Arratoon Apcar, the founder of the well-known firm of Apcar & Co. of Calcutta. Gregory Apcar was the father of the late Arratoon Gregory Apcar referred to in the beginning of this chapter. His eldest son, John Gregory Apcar, an advocate of the Calcutta High Court and the Clerk of the Crown for many years, who died in London a few years ago, left by his will, a bequest £10,000 to the Armenian Holy Seė of Echmiadzin (the Vatican of Armenia) and the residue of his estate, amounting to £58,000, for the relief of Armenian orphans and widows in Armenia. The amount is held in trust in London and the annual income is remitted to Armenia by the Trustees.

They carry on an extensive trade from China and most of the Sea ports to the Eastward and to the West, as far as the Persian gulph. Their information from all these different quarters is deemed the most accurate and minute of anybody of men in their profession. They are attentive, regular and diligent in business; and never think of departing from their lives and indulging in dissipation, even after a competency has been acquired. Their houses are therefore of old standing, and many of them are possessed of large Capitals, as subjects they are perhaps the most peacable and loyal to be found in any country, as members of Society, they are polite and inoffensive.

When the convalescence of His Majesty,* after a severe indisposition, was publicly notified in Calcutta, a general expression of joy was made by all the inhabitants. But the most conspicuous and brilliant illuminations were displayed by an Armenian merchant by the name of Catchick Arrakiel, because accompanied by an act of charity. His loyalty did not escape the notice of Lord Cornwallis who on interrogating him what particular interest he felt in the life of His Britannic Majesty, received this reply, "I have, my lord, lived under his Government for near thirty years, it has never injured me, but on the contrary always afforded its protection, and this, with industry has enabled me to accumulate a very plentiful fortune." This speech is not perhaps the most eloquent, but I confess that to me it has conveyed a more advantageous idea of his understanding than if he had composed volumes of our political Sophistry.

When these circumstances were reported to His Majesty, by the Governor General, Mr. Cachick Arakel was presented with the miniature of his sovereign which he continued to wear till his death† and his son now wears it in honour of his family.

Some of the more respectable Armenians are commonly invited to public balls and entertainments given in Calcutta

---

*King George III of England, who recovered from his unfortunate malady (madness) in 1789.

†This is not correct, for when the medallion portrait of King George III reached Calcutta, Agah Catchick Arrakiel had departed this life, and it was presented to his eldest son, Agah Moses Catchick Arakiel, as stated on p. 460.

where they invariably behave with all that decorum and correctness which a knowledge of mankind generally produces. A few priests of their persuasion are maintained by them, not only in affluence but in some degree of splendour. In their fondness for show and elegance, the Armenians approach nearer the English than any merchants here, they are, however, more guarded in their expense, for they are seldom seen displaying their equipage till they are fully able to defray its charge"

CHAPTER XXXV

AGAH MOSES CATCHICK ARRAKIEL.

A WORTHY SON OF A WORTHY FATHER.

Agah Moses Catchick Arrakiel, the elder son of Agah Catchick Arrakiel, who had inherited the loyalty of his noble father, rendered valuable services to the British Government in 1801 by raising in Calcutta and keeping up at his own expense, a Company of 100 Armenian volunteers, over whom he was appointed Captain Commandant, when the greater part of the regular Army was required for active service in the Deccan against the French. For this act of loyalty, the Governor-General, the Marquis of Wellesley, was pleased to present him with a valuable sword at a full levee at Government House in Calcutta.

For some time, Agah Moses Arrakiel carried on successfully the extensive business left him by his father, but he suffered heavy financial losses during the war between England and France, when his two ships, with much valuable cargo on board, were captured by French privateers in the Indian Seas, and as no insurance could be effected in Calcutta at that time, for obvious reasons, he could not therefore recover his losses which must have been very heavy. Added to this great, if not crushing, misfortune, he sustained heavy losses on his large shipments to England which practically completed his ruin.

Alas for fallen greatness! for in August 1833, we find him bringing his distressed circumstances to the kind notice and consideration of the Governor-General, Lord William Bentinck, with a view to obtaining some employment under the benign Government, to whom, in his palmy days, he had rendered devoted and yeoman services. But as gratitude has always been a rare virtue, the paternal Government, after a protracted correspondence, in which great and profound sympathy was expressed for the erstwhile merchant prince of Calcutta, condescended to grant him "an allowance of Sicca Rupees 100 per mensem" with effect from the 1st December 1834.

It was most noble of the highly magnanimous Government of the day to grant such a handsome allowance to a person who in his prosperous days had cheerfully sacrificed his valuable time and lavishly spent his thousands for the sole benefit of a paternal Government in their dark hour of need. Perhaps that was how loyalty and patriotism were rewarded in those days by a highly materialistic Government which in a fit of generosity, offered the proud and the erstwhile affluent Armenian the paltry sum of one hundred rupees as a recompense for the valuable services and the monetary help he had rendered to Government in 1801 at the time of the Calcutta Militia. As the correspondence which passed between him and the Government is interesting from many points of view, it is therefore given *in extenso* :

"To the Right Honourable Lord W. C. Bentinck,
G.C.B. & G.C.L.H.,
Governor-General and Council.

My Lord,

Your Lordship having pleased to open the public service to all classes of Indian British subjects, and His British Majesty's Ministers having manifested their intention to act on the same just and benevolent principles, I beg leave to offer myself to your Lordship's notice and to solicit such favourable consideration as the particulars of my case shall, in Your Lordship's judgment, render me worthy. Your Lordship must be too well acquainted with the History of British India to need being informed that the "British East India Company" in first forming a Settlement in this part of India received great assistance from my countrymen and especially from one Cojah Phanoos Calandar. The high estimation in which the said services were regarded by the British Rulers of those days is abundantly recorded in historical works and other Public Documents and it in part appears from the Agreement* between the Governor of the "East India Company" and members of our nation dated the 22nd June 1688, and from two other docu-

*For copies of the Chaters or Agreements see the Chapter XVIII.

ments dated on the same day, one being a personal favour granted to the said Cojah Phanoos Calandar. The titles of the said three documents are given below* and a copy of the whole annexed severally marked A. B. C.

The said Cojah Phanoos Calandar in rendering assistance to the English merchants trading to India, may be said to have been the most distinguished of all the Armenians residing in India, and I trust that branch of his family, whereof I am a humble individual, have not failed, as occasions offered, duly to manifest their attachment to the British nation. Accordingly in the year 1789, on the recovery of His Majesty King George the III, from a grievous indisposition being known in India, Aga Catchick Arrakel (Coja Phanoos Calandar's grand-daughter's husband and my revered father), in expression of the lively gratification which he felt on the occasion, liberated all the prisoners confined for debt in the Calcutta Jail, which act it appears was viewed in so favourable a light by His Majesty and the British Government that a miniature of the King attached to a gold chain was sent out from England to be conferred on the said Aga Catchick Arrakel. When this mark of Royal approbation reached Calcutta, my worthy and much esteemed parent having ceased to exist, it was publicly conferred on me, his eldest son, at a Levee by the Most Noble Marquis Cornwallis, who, as also the Most Noble Marquis Wellesley desired me always to appear at their Levees and Public entertainments decorated with the said signal mark of their sovereign's favour, a favour which I am informed is seldom conferred on a British subject.

In the year 1801, when the British nation was at war with France and the greater part of the army of the Presidency [Bengal] was required to act at a distance against Tippoo Sultan.† the local British Government considered it expedient

* "An agreement made between the Governor and Company of Merchants of London trading to the East Indies and the Armenian nation, dated 22nd June, 1688, marked A. Two documents, each headed Governor and Company of Merchants of London trading to the East Indes, to all whom it may concern, send greeting, dated as above, marked B and C."

† This is clearly a chronological error, for the war against Tippoo Sultan was terminated by the capture of Seringapatam on the 4th day of May 1799.

to raise a Militia at Calcutta and accordingly the Christian inhabitants in general were desired to enroll themselves on this occasion, I, at the desire of His Lordship the Governor-General, raised one hundred of my countrymen, and such of them as were not in affluent circumstances, I clothed and occasionally armed at my own expense. I was appointed Capt. Commandant of this Company and continued to command it as long as the Calcutta Militia was required by Government, also while holding this Command the Governor-General, the Most Noble Marquis Wellesley was pleased in a full Levee to confer on me with his own hands a sword to be worn whenever I was not on duty with my Company, neither was this the only kind attention which I received from His Lordship. Thus favoured by my Sovereign and his representative in India, I cheerfully bore the expenses of clothing and occasionally arming my countrymen for the service of Government nor did I repine when our connection with the British nation much more seriously affected my fortune and eventually produced my ruin.

My father Aga Catchick Arakel was an eminent merchant in this Presidency. I was brought up and educated to carry on his business to which I succeeded on his demise. After having for sometime successfully prosecuted my mercantile concerns in the late war between England and France, my two ships with much valuable cargo on board were captured by French Privateers in the Indian Seas. No Insurance could be effected in Calcutta. This serious misfortune together with heavy losses on my shipments to England obliged me to break up my commercial establishment in Calcutta. No longer able to carry on the business entrusted from my father, I engaged myself in manufacturing indigo and for many years I laboured industriously in this my new vocation with various success. Eventually I might have succeeded but the late almost general failures of Calcutta agents depriving me in common with many others of the requisite pecuniary accommodation, I was compelled to retire from my Factory and to make over to my agents.

Thus when too far advanced in life to enter on uncertain or hazardous undertakings, I anxiously desired to obtain such employment under Government as will enable me creditably to support myself and family. Hoping I have ever acted as a faithful British Subject, also hoping I have never done any discredit to the reputation of my revered parent Aga Catchick Arakel and my ancestor, the much esteemed Coja Phanoos Calandar, I respectfully solicit from Your Lordship any such situation as I may be considered qualified to hold and I shall desire to enjoy public employment only so long as I faithfully perform the duties imposed on me.

I am, Lord, with the greatest respect,

Your Lordship's
Most Obedient Humble Servant,
M. C. ARAKEL.

Calcutta,
16th August 1833."

The following is a copy of the letter which the Governor-General, Lord William Bentinck, wrote to the Court of Directors, recommending some relief for the impoverished but the noble Armenian.

"General Department.

To

The Honourable the Court of Directors for the affairs of the Honourable the United Company of Merchants of England Trading to East India.

Honourable Sirs,

We have the honour to submit for the consideration and orders of your Honourable Court the accompanying copy of a communication dated 16th of August last, from Mr. M. C. Arakel, an Armenian Gentleman, with copies of its enclosures.

2. It appears that Mr. M. C. Arakel, who thus brings his altered and distressed circumstances to the notice of the Government, is the eldest son of Aga Catchick Arakel, an Armenian who displayed such generosity and benevolence at Calcutta in the year 1789 on the celebrations of rejoicing after the recovery of His Majesty George the III by liberating all the debtors confined in the prison of the Court, which was considered by Your Honourable Court so extraordinary an act

of humanity and munificence that to testify your sense of such conduct Your Honourable Court was pleased to forward a portrait of His Majesty to be presented to Aga Catchick Arakel, and having heard of his decease Your Honourable Court directed in a despatch dated 16th of May 1792 that the portrait might be presented to his representative. This honour it would appear was conferred on Mr. M. C. Arakiel, the present appellant.

3. It would further seem that Mr. M. C. Arakel evinced his attachment to the British Government in the year 1801, at the time that a Militia was formed in Calcutta, on which occasion the Marquis of Wellesley presented him with a sword as a mark of his approbation and esteem.

4. Mr. M. C. Arakel details the circumstances under which he has fallen into distress, and petitions the Government for relief by giving him some public employment.

5. We have no employment in which we can make use of Mr. M. C. Arakel's service, and we do not feel ourselves competent to grant him a pension, but it is painful to associate his present straitened circumstances at an advanced period of life with the conduct which brought his father to the notice of the Honourable Court in 1789, and we therefore submit his case that Your Honourable Court may if you think proper order some relief to be bestowed upon him.

We have the honour etc.,
W. C. BENTINCK,
C. T. METCALFE.

Fort William,
30th September 1833."

On the same date, a letter was forwarded to Agah Moses Catchick Arakiel, of which the following is a copy.

"General Department.

To
Mr. M. C. Arakel.

Sir,

I am directed by the Right Honourable the Governor in Council to acknowledge the receipt of your letter dated the

16th of August last, applying for employment in some situation in the Public Service.

In reply I am instructed to inform you that His Lordship in Council is much concerned to hear of the adversity of your fortune, and proposes to bring your altered circumstances to the notice of the Honourable the Court of Directors, that they if they think proper may order the Government to make a provision for your declining years. I am directed to express the regret of His Lordship in Council that there is no situation at his disposal in the Public Service to which you are eligible.

I am, Sir,
Your most obedient Servant,
G. A. BUSHBY,
Offg. Secy. to the Government.

Council Chamber,
30th September 1833."

As communication was very slow in those days, Mr. M. C. Arakiel was informed, 14 months after, that his application had received the favourable consideration of the Court of Directors in London.

"Barrackpore, November 27th, 1834.

To
Mr. M. C. Arakel.

Dear Sir,

I have the honour to inform you that the orders of the Honourable the Court of Directors authorizing this Government to confer upon you such moderate pension for life as your situation and circumstances may appear justified by the Government upon public grounds, the subject, I am directed to add, will receive the attention of His Lordship in Council as soon as the weighty matters, now pressing for decision, are disposed of.

I remain, Dear Sir,
THOMAS PACKENHAM,
Private Secretary.

At long last, Mr. M. C. Arakel was informed that the Court of Directors had been pleased to grant him a pension for life. Here is the letter.

"General Department,

To

Mr. M. C. Arakel.

Sir,

With reference to your letter to the address of the Right Honourable the Governor-General in Council, under date the 16th August 1833, I am directed by the Right Honourable the Governor of Bengal to state that His Lordship has received the authority of the Honourable Court of Directors, to whom a reference was made on the subject, as intimated in the letter of this Department to you dated the 30th September 1833, to assign a moderate stipend for life in aid of your reduced circumstances. An allowance of Sicca Rupees 100 per mensem has accordingly been made payable to your receipt from the General Treasury of this Presidency to commence from the 1st instant.

I am, Sir, Your most obedient servant,

H. T. PRINSEP,

Secretary to the Government.

Council Chamber,

19th December, 1834."

Alas for relentless Fate, and the vicissitudes of Time, for Agah Moses Arrakiel, who was born in the lap of luxury and had never known want, was, through adverse circumstances, over which he had no control, reduced to such a state of penury that he was obliged to accept the petty allowance of one hundred rupees in the vain hope of receiving a much larger sum afterwards, as can be seen from the following letter, full of pathetic reflections, which he addressed to the Government, for the last time, on the 30th October, 1836.

"To the Right Honourable George Lord Auckland, G.C.B.,
Governor-General of India in Council.

My Lord,

When under the sanction of the Honourable the Court of Directors the allowance of a hundred rupees per month was given to me by Government, although understanding that His Lordship the Governor-General kindly wished to give a larger sum, I did not think it right to solicit an increase, because it was said that the Revenues of Government were not sufficient to meet the current expenditure here and in England, moreover, at the time in question, I hoped, that arrangements would be made respecting a large estate at Dacca which would prove beneficial to me, also other expectations existed, but I have been disappointed in all.

During the intervening time I have been obliged to live on the allowance accorded to me and it hardly can be requisite to state that even with the assistance of the extra 1450 rupees kindly given to me by His Lordship in Council, I have experienced very great difficulties in procuring the necessaries of life with the sum in question, and unless the Government please to augment my present allowance, my difficulties of course will increase. Now I understand that the revenues of the country are more than sufficient to meet all demands, both here and in England, I therefore presume that such increased allowance will be conferred on me as His Lordship the late Governor-General would have granted even under less favourable circumstances. His Lordship, before recommending my case to the consideration of the Court of Directors, satisfied himself through enquiries made to the Secretary, Mr. Bushby, that the representation contained in my address of August 16th, 1833, respecting the expense incurred by me in the Calcutta Militia, was correct, but as the expense was incurred voluntarily, consequently I have no legal claim for remuneration. But as the amount expended by me in the service of Government (which amount Government would have paid) with accumulation of interest, would, at the present day, procure for me a very considerable annuity, I hope therefore that this fact will be favourably considered on my applying for an increase of allowance. Being so reduced by my misfortunes as to need not only the comforts, but it may be said, even the common necessaries of life, I wished as long as Heaven blessed me with the ability to labour to have earned my bread by serving Government in such capacity as my humble services might be considered available, but His Lordship the Governor-General's kind consideration of my former condition in life caused him to decline offering me any situation which then could be held by any person not a covenanted servant of the Honourable Company. The correctness of what is here stated will appear from my address of August 1833 and upon Mr. Bushby's letter to me dated September 30th, 1833. I now most respectfully solicit that Your Lordship will please to make such addition to my present allowance as will enable me to pass the few remaining years of my life with some degree of comfort.

Your Lordship's most obedient servant,
M. C. ARAKEL.

Needless to add that this final appeal of the loyal citizen, whose strong attachment to the British had produced his utter ruin, simply fell on deaf ears, as was to be expected.

O tempora ! O mores !

Agah Moses Catchick Arrakiel, the last worthy representative of the noble Gentloom family* died at Calcutta, a poor Government pensioner, on the 15th October 1843, aged 71 years, and his mortal remains were honoured by being

---

*We have not yet been able to trace the origin of this old and aristocratic family, as the name Gentloom is a queer nomenclature and we have not yet seen it borne by any other Armenians outside India.

We are however inclined to think that the ancestor of the family got the *sobriquet* of "gentilhomme" from the French with whom he may have come in contact, either commercially or diplomatically, either in France or in India, as it is a historical fact that French trade in India was established in 1667 through the efforts of an eminent Armenian merchant, Khojah Margar Avagsheenentz or "Marcara Avanchinz," according to the records of the "French East India Company". As every body, who is conversant with the French language, knows, the word *gentilhomme* means a gentleman, a nobleman, and it is quite possible that the French, who are noted for their suavity and can appreciate gentility, gave that nickname to the genteel Armenian.

buried near his parents, *inside* the Armenian church of Calcutta, poor as he was at the time of his death.

His mother, Begoom, was a great-grand daughter of the renowned Khojah Phanoos Kalandar,* who, in 1688 entered into a commercial Treaty with the English on behalf of the Armenian nation, whereby the Armenians trading in India were placed on an equal footing with the British merchants.

One of the daughters of Agah Moses Arrakiel, Anna Maria, married Gregory, the son of Astwasatoor Mooradkhan, the Founder of the "Armenian Philanthropic Academy" of Calcutta, now known as the "Armenian College," located at No. 39 Free School Street.

Anna Maria Mooradkhan died on the 19th August 1815, aged 21 years, "deeply regretted by all those who knew her," Her husband, Gregory Astwasatoor Mooradkhan, died on the 11th June 1826 and they both lie buried in the Armenian churchyard of Calcutta. Their descendants, by an irony of Fate, are in straitened circumstances to-day.

One of the great-grandsons of Agah Catchick Arrakiel, in the female line, was the late Sir Catchick Arrakiel Paul Chater, the multi-millionaire of Hong Kong, who prior to his death, in 1926, endowed his Alma Mater, the La Martiniere College of Calcutta, with the princely donation of eleven lakhs of rupees and left the residue of his large estate, amounting to about 75 lakhs of Rupees, to the Armenian church of Calcutta —where he had been christened on the 3rd day of October 1846, and where most of his illustrious ancestors sleep.

Mr. P. C. Manuk, the popular and eminent advocate of the Patna High Court, who is a grand nephew of the late Sir Catchick Paul Chater, is also a descendant, in the female line, of the illustrious Agah Catchick Arrakiel of Calcutta.

Miss Amy Apcar† of No. 44 Chowringhee Road, Calcutta—that staunch advocate of the preservation of the

---

* For fuller information regarding Khojah Phanoos Kalândar, see Chapter XVIII.

† Miss Amy Apcar, is the authoress of the *Melodies of the Holy Apostolic Church of Armenia,* (Calcutta 1897) and of the *Melodies of Five Offices in Holy Week, according to the Holy Apostolic Church of*

beautiful ancient hymns and melodies of the holy Apostolic Church of Armenia—is also a descendant, through her father, of the renowned Agah Catchick Arrakiel.

Armenia, (Calcutta 1902). Both the above works have been written down in modern musical notation by the authoress, who is a great scholar of ancient and modern music, and an authority on Armenian sacred music. A choir, consisting of some twenty boys recruited from the local Armenian College, and trained by her, join in the services held in the Armenian church of Calcutta on Sundays and on great festivals, to the accompaniment of an organ, by a specially trained organist.

In 1918, Miss Apcar edited and re-published the autobiography of her ancestor, Joseph Emin, which was published originally in London in the year 1792, under the title of *The Life and Adventures of Joseph Emin, an Armenian, written in English by himself.* (1726-1809).

CHAPTER XXXVI

ARMENIANS AND THE BLACK HOLE OF CALCUTTA.*

Every school boy and many grown-ups too, in India and elsewhere, know the history of the "Black Hole" of Calcutta and the tragedy that was enacted in that dungeon on the night of the 20th June 1756—a tragedy which, in the words of Macaulay, was "memorable for its singular atrocity, memorable for the tremendous retribution by which it was followed."

But as Thomas refused to believe that Christ had risen from the dead and appeared to his disciples in the flesh, there are in the same way sceptics and doubters in the present day who cannot believe that there has ever been a "Black Hole" tragedy in Calcutta.

In the journal of the "Calcutta Historical Society" called *Bengal : Past and Present,* for July-September, 1915, the late Mr. J. H. Little, a historian of repute, published an article, in which he made the astounding comment that Holwell's story of the Calcutta "Black Hole" was a "gigantic hoax," since none of the contemporary Mahomedan historians of Bengal had made any reference to such an important event in their works.

Later on, at a special meeting of the "Calcutta Historical Society", held in the hall of the Asiatic Society of Bengal, on the 24th March, 1916, under the chairmanship of the Venerable Archdeacon W. K. Firminger, M.A., B.D., a very interesting debate took place on the subject, in which the following gentlemen, all well-known historical and research scholars, took part :—Mr. J. H. Little, who opened the debate, was followed by Professor E. A. Oaton, the Hon ble Mr. E. J. Monahan and Mr. Akshaya Kumar Mitra, B.L.,

---

* We have, in the past, appealed, in the public press, to the citizens of Calcutta, to honour the memory of the victims of the "Black Hole," by placing wreaths on the Holwell Monument on the anniversary of the tragedy, but our humble appeal has fallen on deaf ears.

all of whom expressed their views, pro and con, in a scholarly manner, which displayed deep erudition and historical acumen of a very high order. Full proceedings of the debate can be had from the Honorary Secretary of the "Calcutta Historical Society," Imperial Records Office, Calcutta.

The traducers of old John Zephaniah Holwell are perhaps not aware of the fact that there can be no smoke without fire and in the words of Christ, "a city that is set on an hill cannot be hid."

If the Mohammedan historians of that period have not referred to that great crime, which as every student of history knows, formed the *casus belli* between the English and the Nawab Suraj-ud-dowlah, it was perhaps from motives of prudence, as they did not wish to record an event which had led to the downfall of the Mohammedan power in Bengal through the insensate act of the unpolitic and haughty young Nawab.

Had there been no holocaust in the old Fort on that memorable night, Holwell would not have erected, at his own expense, an obelisk, fifty feet high, on the site of the "Black Hole" and he would not have raised a monument over the mortal remains of his dead fellow-captives whose bodies were thrown promiscuously into a pit that was dug in the immediate vicinity of the old Fort on the morning of the 21st June 1756. He could not have carried the deception so far, had there been no victims of Suraj-ud-dowlah's wrath, but then the doubting Thomass say that there was no "Black Hole" and no tragedy, and that the whole story was invented and concocted by Holwell for self glorification so that he may find a niche in the history of India as a brave Englishman and a national hero.

Let us now remove the curtain which has been hanging so long over this vexed question and show to the sceptics that the dreadful tragedy did take place, but not with that violence and severity as related by Holwell, one of the survivors. Holwell's narrative, we are sorry to say, is greatly exaggerated and his picture highly coloured, as can be seen presently.

An eminent Armenian merchant of Calcutta, Joseph Emin by name, writing to his son, Emin Joseph Emin in London, in

1757, refers to the sack of Calcutta by Suraj-ud-dowlah in the following pathetic terms :

"The wicked Suraj-ud-dowlah came with a vast army, destroyed almost 40 innocent English gentlemen in one night in the Black Hole. Calcutta was overset by him. For my share, I have lost 16,000 rupees, and all the Armenians in proportion. We are all become as poor as you were when you went from this place. I have written to Mr. Davis to pay you the 500 rupees deposited in his hands. The glorious English army came with the fleet, re-took Calcutta,* destroyed Chandernagore, and drove the Mussulman army to the bosom of their Prophet Mahomed, and I am in hopes that the whole kingdom, in a dozen years' time, will be subdued under the blessed mild government of the English, which you used to prophesy when you were here. Walk in the way of God and be happy, without fear, put your trust in Him, who knows but He may one day or other, set your countrymen free from the slavery of the unmerciful Mahomedans".†

Another Armenian merchant, Thomas Khojamall, who wrote a short history of India in ancient Armenian, at Allahabad, in 1768, and which was edited and published by Mosrovb Thaliadian in 1849, at Calcutta, referring to the events in Bengal and to the sack of Calcutta, writes as follows :

"After this, the army of Suraj-ud-dowlah suddenly attacked the city of Calcutta, and as there was no military fortress there but only a small Fort, which was surrounded by a wall, and in that were the house of the governor and all the goods of the merchants, which the troops of Suraj-ud-dowlah surrounded, there being not sufficient Christian soldiers there, not more than four hundred in all. And all the Christian merchants, of whom one hundred and fifty were of our Arme-

---

*Calcutta was re-taken by the English on the 2nd January 1757 and Drake, the former Governor, reinstated as President.

† At that time, Armenia, was groaning under the iron yoke of the Persians, and Mr. Emin Joseph Emin, an emotional youngman of thirty, imbued with strong patriotic sentiments, was dreaming of being able some day to deliver his ill-fated and unhappy Fatherland from the thraldom of the Mohammedans, who in the words of Byron, "had desolated the region where God created man in His own image."

nian nation, all great and wealthy merchants, together with many others, that is Greeks, Syrians and Portuguese, who being unable to hide their goods, owing to the sudden arrival of Suraj-ud-dowlah, left their houses full of merchandise and fleeing entered the Fort. The army of the enemy then began to pillage the city of Calcutta. The English inside the Fort seeing there was no chance of escape, became hopeless and having opened the small gate that was on the river Ganges, [Hoogly] they all fled tô the ships and having cut the ropes of the anchors, went southwards. Suraj-ud-dowlah then looted the Fort, which was full of goods and treasure, and having caught many of the English soldiers, who were unable to escape, threw them into a small prison, where for want of sufficient space, they were heaped one over the other, by the cruel soldiers of Suraj-ud-dowlah, acting on his orders. Of these, more than fifteen soldiers died in one night.

After taking the city and plundering all the wealth that was there, he remained there for twenty five days and re-named the city [Calcutta] Alinagar.

Although, as stated by Khojamall, one hundred and fifty of the Armenian inhabitants of Calcutta had taken refuge in the old Fort, when Suraj-ud-dowlah pounced upon the city, like the Assyrian "who came like a wolf on the fold," as immortalized by Byron, yet none of them were thrust into the "Black Hole" prison, because the peaceful Armenians of Calcutta were not considered as *enemies*, like the English, in the eyes of the Nawab, who evidently was quite satisfied with the rich booty he had robbed from these harmless merchants, when he sacked Calcutta, and for which, it may be mentioned *en passant*, his successor, Nawab Mir Jaffir had to pay a compensation of Rs. 700,000, in terms of the treaty which was drawn up, between the new Nawab and the English, before the former was placed on the *masnad* (throne) of Murshidabad. Clause 7 of that treaty is as follows :

"For the effects plundered from the Armenian inhabitants of Calcutta, I will give the sum of seven lacs of rupees."

We mention this inportant fact, because a certain Eurasian, who was in the service of the local Armenian College, as a teacher, 47 years ago, with the object of pleasing his employers in particular and the Armenian community in general, published a letter in the pages of the *Statesman*, in June 1889, under the caption *Armenians in Calcutta,* in which, pedant-like he authoritatively stated that "the Armenians shared the fate of the English in the Black Hole."

Persons with a superficial knowledge of matters historical, should not rush into print and make bold statements in the public press, which are not only misleading, but are fraught with mischief. This would-be historian is still posing as a historical scholar, and we had to curb his ardour by exposing his lack of historical knowledge in the pages of a well-known local English daily in May 1933. See pp. 100-101.

From the writings of the two Armenian merchants, the former, Mr. Emin being an eye-witness of the sack of Calcutta the "gigantic hoax" of Holwell, as the late Mr. Little called it ironically, is once more proved to be a solid historical fact, despite the laborious researches of would-be historians of the late Mr. Little's school. There is a good deal of exaggeration however in Holwell's narrative, for whereas he gives the number of the victims who perished in the "Black Hole" as one hundred and twenty three, Mr. Emin, in his letter to his son says that "the wicked Suraj-ud-dowlah destroyed almost 40 innocent English gentlemen in one night in the Black Hole", and the Armenian historian, Thomas Khojamall, gives the number of the victim's of the tragedy "more than fifteen soldiers who died in one night".

British Indian historians, including that critical writer, Macaulay, have one and all followed blindly Holwell's garbled and greatly exaggerated narrative of the "Black Hole" tragedy, accepting, as gospel truth, that 146 persons, men and women, were thrown into the small prison of the Fort, measuring only 18 feet by 15 feet.

Old John Zephaniah Holwell must have been gifted with a very vivid imagination, otherwise how could he have thought it at all possible for that large number of people to be huddled into a small place, unless by a wonderful stretch of imagination the massive walls of the small dungeon were stretched out like rubber to hold that large number of prisoners. Truly what wonders and hallucinations human imagination cannot create! It was the fertile imagination of Jules Verne (1828-1905) that led to the invention of the aeroplane, the submarine, the wireless and television.

A few words about the old Fort and the "Black Hole" will not be out of place.

The old Fort, with its adjoining warehouses, covered the site of the present General Post Office, the Collectorate, the Custom House, Fairlie Place, where the East Indian Railway Offices are located, and the adjoining Koila Ghat Street. It was erected in 1698 and named Fort William, after Edward III of England. In 1819, a portion was pulled down to make room for the Custom House, and the remainder was removed in 1856, when the present General Post Office was built.

The historical "Black Hole" of Calcutta, a small dungeon, 18 feet by 14 feet and 10 inches, with only two small barred windows, was the military jail of old Fort William. This site was commemorated by an obelisk, fifty feet high. This monument, erected at the expense of Holwell, one of the survivors, was once struck by lightning in 1819. It was pulled down by the order of the Governor General of that time, the Earl of Moira and the Marquis of Hastings on the ground that "it served to remind the natives of the country of the former humiliation of the English".

With greater reason, it might be said to have reminded the natives of the determination and the prowess of the British who stimulated by the cowardly tragedy of the "Black Hole", had avenged its atrocities, as was meet and just, and asserted their power and supremacy over Bengal at the epoch-making battle of Plassey. The site of the "Black Hole" is on the right side of the gate, dividing the General Post Office from the Calcutta Collectorate. A black marble tablet fixed on the north wall of the site of the "Black Hole", bears the following inscriptions, in letters of gold.

"The marble pavement below this spot was placed here by Lord Curzon, Viceroy and Governor-General of India in 1901, to mark the site of the prison in old Fort William, known as the Black Hole, in which 146 British inhabitants of Calcutta were confined on the night of the 20th June, 1756, and from which only 23 came out alive. The pavement marks the exact breadth of the prison, 14 feet, 10 inches, but not its full length, 18 feet, about one third of the area at the north end being covered by the building on which this tablet is fixed".

Hitherto we have followed the history of the terrible tragedy that was enacted in Calcutta on the night of the 20th June 1756, a thrilling and a graphic account of which is given by Macaulay in his critical essay on Lord Clive. We have also seen what happened to those Englishmen, who acting on the principle that discretion is the best part of valour, sought refuge in flight by getting on board their ships, which were lying alongside, sailed down the river and anchored at a place known to this day as Fulta. Amongst these were the timid Governor (Drake) and the equally timid and timorous military commandant of the Fort. At Fulta the fugitives were suffering great hardships and privations for want of provisions, who, with Drake, the Governor, had taken refuge in their ships at Fulta, after the fall of Fort William, supplied the fugitives with provisions, secretly, for a period of six months, but God raised a good Samaritan to come to their rescue and save them from starvation. Our readers will, no doubt, be curious to know who this humane person was, since the British Indian historians of the period are silent about it, but the spade of the researcher can delve very deep and bring to light many a hidden fact.

There resided at Calcutta at that times an eminent Armenian merchant, Khojah Petrus Arathoon by name, who actuated by humanitarian motives, came spontaneously to the assistance of the hapless Britishers in their hour of need, although he was afterwards misjudged and maligned by them, and unjustly accused of having been a spy in the service of the Nawabs of Bengal from Suraj-ud-dowlah to Mir Kasim and that by one (Watts) whose life he had saved, as stated on page 340.

Khojah Petrus, or as he was afterwards called the "Armenian Petrus", a name given him by Clive, hearing of the terrible sufferings of the English inhabitants of Calcutta, who, with Drake, the Governor, had taken refuge in their ships at Fulta, after the fall of Fort William, supplied the fugitives with provisions, secretly, for a period of six months, before the arrival of the Army of Retribution from Madras on the 20th December 1756, under Admiral Watson and Colonel Clive, and but for the timely succour of the humane Armenian the British fugitives at Fulta might have been starved to surrender.

Khojah Petrus was, for his loyalty and integrity, employed afterwards by Clive as a confidential Agent in negotiating with Mir Jaffir for the overthrow of Suraj-ud-dowlah, the author of the "Black Hole" tragedy, and in 1760 when it was deemed expedient to remove the imbecile Mir Jaffir and place his son-in-law, Mir Kasim, on the *Masnad* (throne) of Murshidabad, the valuable services of Khojah Petrus were again requisitioned, as he was known to be very friendly with Mir Kasim. And for all the valuable services which this great Armenian had rendered to the English in Bengal, at the risk of his life, there is nothing in the Company's records to show that he was rewarded for his loyalty to the British cause in Bengal. Being unable to get justice from Clive and his avaricious colleagues in Calcutta, for his loyalty and devotion, once the crisis was over and the tide had turned in favour of the English, he addressed a long letter to the Hon'ble Court of Directors of the East India Company in London, enumerating the various services he had rendered to the British cause in Bengal since the capture and sack of Calcutta in June 1750.

A copy of this letter dated the 25th January, 1759, is given on pp. 328-332.

And when the survivors of the "Black Hole" tragedy, men and women including Holwell, were taken to Murshidabad as prisoners, by the order of Suraj-ud-dowlah, the Armenian residents of Saidabad as fellow Christians, greatly ameliorated their sufferings, as has been shown on pp. 346-347.

A few words about the "Holwell Monument"—that beautiful octagonal white marble obelisk on the north-west corner of Dalhousie Square—may prove of interest to our readers.

The original monument, constructed of brick and mortar, was erected by Holwell, at his own expense, over the mortal remains of the unfortunate sufferers in the "Black Hole" prison. This was pulled down in 1821 by the vandals of the 19th century on sentimental grounds, and but for the solicitude of the late Lord Curzon there would have been no "Holwell Monument" to-day to remind the citizens of Calcutta of the terrible tragedy which led to the establishment of British rule in India. Verily out of evil cometh good, for had there been no "Black Hole", there would have been no retribution and the epoch-making battle of Plassey would not have been fought and the British merchants in Bengal would have continued to be the victims of the rapacity of the avaricious and capricious Nawabs of Bengal.

But to return to the "Holwell Monument". The late Lord Curzon, the only Indian Viceroy who manifested an active interest in the preservation of ancient monuments, whether of the Hindoo or of the Mohammedan and British periods, erected in 1902, at his own expense, a beautiful monument, an exact replica of the original, in pure white marble, with six inscribed tablets fixed on it. On one of these tablets, the names of the sufferers in the "Black Hole" dungeon, as recorded by Holwell on the original monument, are inscribed, but then there are the names of only 27 persons "who perished in the Black Hole prison."

This clearly shows that the number of the dead in the "Black Hole" was not one hundred and twenty three, as stated by Holwell, but somewhere near thirty. And in an additional list, inscribed on another tablet, there are the names of 33 persons who are supposed to have also died in the dungeon which Lord Curzon states "have been recovered from oblivion by reference to contemporary documents."

Assuming that the additional list, as prepared by Lord Curzon, is reliable and correct, it just brings up the total number of the dead, in the den of horrors, to sixty only—27 in the original and 33 in the additional list.

If, as Holwell would have us believe, 123 persons had perished in the "Black Hole" prison, how is it that he did not state, after recording the names of the 27 persons, that another 96 unfortunate men had shared the sad fate of those whose names he had inscribed on the tablet, fixed on the monument he had erected to the memory of his fellow sufferers? After such glaring discrepancies and palpable incongruities, which the credulous, have, for 180 years, accepted as gospel truth, history can safely dub good old John Zephaniah Holwell as a hopeless exaggerator, gifted with a vivid and a fertile imagination. We are now fully convinced that the number of the victims of the tragedy, as given by Joseph Emin of Calcutta and Thomas Khojamall of Allahabad, are quite reliable and may be accepted as correct, as those two disinterested and independent Armenian chroniclers had no reason to give a garbled or a distorted account of the tragedy.

As has been stated on page 478, the present "Holwell Monument" dates its existence from 1902, and for some years before that, the marble statue of a former Lieut.-Governor of Bengal, seated on a chair, marked the spot of the original monument, which, as we have said, was pulled down in 1821. In March 1889, when we first came to Calcutta, we went to see, amongst other places of historical interest, the "Holwell Monument", an account of which we had read in some old work on Calcutta, but no such monument was visible in Dalhousie Square, the old "Tank Square" of the Company's days. We enquired from an elderly Eurasian gentleman who was passing by where the monument had gone and we were informed by that well-informed East Indian, (by which name they were called in those days) that the "Holwell Monument" once stood where Sir Ashley Eden's marble statue was adorning the north-west corner of Dalhousie Square, facing Clive Street.

What a sacrilege, we said! What a wanton desecration of hallowed ground by placing the statue of a bureaucratic Lieutenant-Governor of Bengal on the sacred bones of the unhappy sufferers in the "Black Hole" dungeon! What a bankruptcy of British sentiment, chivalry and good taste! Was there such a lamentable dearth of public opinion in Calcutta, in the eighties of the last century, that nobody raised a voice of protest and just indignation against the vandalism of the bureaucrats who were placing that statue on the site of the historic "Holwell Monument"? Would the citizens of

Patna have tolerated the removal of the Monument,* commemorating the last resting place of the unfortunate victims of Nawab Mir Kasim's wrath, and the placing of a Lieutenant-Governor's or any other person's statue on the site?

It seems Calcutta, the proud metropolis of the Indian Empire, with a large European population, had eyes in those days, but could not see, when the vandals were busy erecting the statue of Sir Ashley Eden on the site of the historic "Holwell Monument".

---

* At Mahalla Gorhatta, Patna City, just on the southern side of the main road, running from Bankipore to Patna City, there is a marble pillar, erected over the remains of the English prisoners who were brutally massacred by the order of Nawab Mir Kasim, on the night of the 11th October 1763, at the hands of that notorious renegade, known as Sumroo, alias Walter Reinhardt, the future husband of the famous Begum Sumroo of Sirdhana (see page 398 foot-note). Nawab Mir Kasim, whose formidable army had been defeated by the English at the battle of Oodnallah, fled in haste from Monghyr, his capital, to Patna, and Monghyr fell into the hands of the English. There were no bounds to his rage against the English. He ordered his military officers to go to the prison and put them to death, but the humane officers replied they were not executioners that they should kill the Englishmen without fighting, but if he would put arms into their hands, they were ready to fight them. The enraged and demoralised Nawab then gave these sanguinary orders to Sumroo, that monster in human form, who accompanied by some soldiers, proceeded to the prison and put them all to death, with the exception of Doctor Fullarton. Forty eight English gentlemen and officers, with one hundred and fifty English soldiers were thus slain. Among the unfortunate English gentlemen who were brutally murdered in that terrible massacre, were three Members of Council, namely, Ellis, Hay and Lushington. It may be mentioned that Lushington was one of the survivors of the Calcutta "Black Hole" tragedy, and it was he who at the instance of Clive, had forged the signature of Admiral Watson on the sham, or red, treaty that was given to Omichand to keep his mouth shut about the conspiracy which was hatched for the overthrow of Nawab Suraj-ud-dowlah.

CHAPTER XXXVII.

THE ARMENIAN PHILANTHROPIC ACADEMY.

It is a noteworthy fact that the Armenian colonists in India, amid their multifarious commercial pursuits, have neither been backward in the matter of education nor indifferent to the advancement of their national literature. This fact is evidenced by their efforts in establishing schools to train up and educate their children in the language and faith of their forefathers, without which their nationality could not have been so faithfully preserved in the land of their adoption.

One, named Margar, a *Commandant,** used to instruct Armenian youths at his house in Calcutta ; but the first regular Armenian school here was started in the year 1798 and conducted by Arratoon Kaloos, a native of Tokat† in Armenia. For twenty-five years he instructed Armenian youths in that language, and stimulated the Armenian community to further exertions in the cause of education. Among many others, the late Johanness Avdall received his education at the feet of this Gamaliel, whose memory he worshipped throughout his life, so much so that he had named one of his sons after his mentor, Arratoon Kaloos. The course of instruction at Arratoon Kaloos' school having been found insufficient for the progressive requirements of the period, the Armenian

---

* In all probability this *Commandant* was the same "Margar Johanness Khalanthar of Julfa" (see p. 413) who served under Gorgin Khan in the Army he had raised and disciplined for the Nawab Meer Kasim Ali Khan.

† Tokat, the Armenion Evdokia, is a town of some importance in the *vilayet* of Sivas, a province of Turkish Armenia, now known as Anatolia. In the Armenian cemetery of that place may be seen the humble and sequestered grave of the Rev. Henry Martyn, B.D., chaplain to the Honourable East India Company and the pioneer of missionary enterprise in the East, who breathed his last at Tokat, on the 16th of October 1812, on his way to England, from India, *viâ* Persia. While in India, he translated into Hindustani the Parables and the New Testament; and he rendered during his prolonged stay at Shiraz, the farfamed seat of Persian literature, into Persian, the Psalms of David and the New Testament.

Philanthropic Academy was inaugurated, in 1821, at 358 Old China Bazar Street, Calcutta, in the immediate vicinity of the Armenian Church of Nazareth. There was a Girl's Department in the Philanthropic Academy when it was founded but it was abandoned in 1842.

The idea of a national academy was first conceived by one Astwasatoor Mooradkhan,* who by his will, dated the 30th July 1797 (of which we have a copy in our possession), left sicca Rs. 8,000 towards the establishment of an Armenian school in Calcutta "for the education of the Armenian youth." To this nucleus were subsequently added further sums of money raised by subscription among the Armenian community, through the strenuous exertions of the late Manatsakan Varden, who was greatly instrumental in collecting the subscriptions, as testified by the tablet erected to his memory.

The Armenian Philanthropic Academy was finally opened on the 2nd April† 1821, and with it was amalgamated Arratoon Kaloos' school in 1825 at the express desire of the Armenian community Arratoon Kaloos‡ who had devoted his life to the instruction of Armenian youth, died on the 10th November 1833, aged 56 years, and was buried in the Armenians churchyard of Calcutta, where his grave can be seen to this day. Being of a charitable disposition, and having no issue, he endowed the church of Nazareth with Rs. 10,000 for the relief of the poor attached thereto. A black marble slab

---

* Astwasatoor Mooradkhan died on the 30th day of the month of Nadar (28th September) 1799 and was interred inside the Armenian Church of Calcutta.

† The Armenian New Year, according to the Era of Azariah, started on the 1st day of the month of Shams, which corresponded with the 2nd day of April, hence the opening of the Academy on that auspicious day.

‡Arratoon Kaloos did not know either Armenian or English when he arrived in Calcutta in the last decade of the 18th century, but being an intelligent young man, he learnt the classical Armenian from Agah Joseph Emin of Calcutta. He then managed to get admitted into the Calcutta Free School where he gained a fair knowledge of the English language which enabled him to open a private school in Amratolla Street in 1798.

was placed on the outside wall of the church to the west, with the following inscription :—

"In memoriam of Arratoon Kaloos, Esquire, who endowed the church with ten thousand rupees for the relief of the poor."

He also left bequests for the Armenian churches at Shiraz and Bagdad.

In 1846 the members of the Armenian Philanthropic Academy paid tributes to the memory of the two patriotic founders of the institution by erecting within that institution two marble tablets. That to the memory of Astwasatoor Mooradkhan has the following inscription.

"Sacred to the memory of Astwasatoor Mooradkhan, Esquire. This tablet is erected by the members of the Armenian Philanthropic Academy at Calcutta, to preserve the name and virtues of the abovementioned philanthropist, who, at his death, left a donation of eight thousand rupees by will, dated 30th July 1797, for aiding the establishment of such an institution. Died at Calcutta, 29th September 1799."

The other, to the memory of Manatsakan Varden, runs :—

"Sacred to the memory of Manatsakan Varden, Esquire. This tablet is erected by the members of the Armenian Philanthropic Academy at Calcutta, in acknoweldgement of the high esteem and veneration in which he was held by their community, for his virtues in social life and zeal in behalf of the education and welfare of his countrymen, and in which he was at all times ready, equally with his purse and heart, and by his means, as well as the donations of other benevolent Armenians, founded this Philanthropic Academy, which dates its existence from the 2nd April 1821. Born at Julfa in Ispahan on the 6th September, 1772, died at Syedabad in Moorshidabad, on the 14th October, 1823."

As has been pointed out on page 358, the date of the death of Manatsakan Varden is 1827 and not 1823, as wrongly inscribed on the above tablet. The correct date of his demise is inscribed on his marble tombstone (one corner of which is broken) in the south verandah of the Armenian church at Saidabad.

With a view to preserve the names of those patriotic and opulent Armenians in India who have, from time to time, made handsome donations and left liberal bequests in aid of the Armenian Philanthropic Academy, the following list, which embraces a period of fully fiftyyears, from 1797 to 1850, has been carefully prepared :—

Astwasatoor Mooradkhan	8,000	0
Manatsakan Varden	3,000	0
Yearly contribution of Rs. 1,560 from the church of Nazareth, Calcutta, from 1820-1840 ...	32,760	0
Elias Minas and Owenjohn Elias Minas, to 1848	38,920	0
Joseph Johanness Amirean of Samarang ...	5,500	0
George Manook*	30,000	0
Malcom Manook	2,000	0
Stephen Mackertich	250	0

* George Manook was the greatest Armenian merchant of Java in the early part of the nineteenth century. He enjoyed the friendship of the Viceroy of the island, and on several occasions lent large sums to the local Dutch Government. Born of poor parents at Julfa, Ispahan, he died a millionaire at Batavia on the 24th October 1827, aged 46 years. He lived and died a bachelor. In making out his last will and testament in 1820, he left the greater portion of his fortune of five million Dutch guilders to his two sisters at Batavia and the children of his brother, Malcom, who died at Calcutta in 1826. The following liberal bequests, amounting to Sicca Rs. 1,10,000 were left by him in aid of Armenian charities and literary institutions :—

	Sicca Rs.
The Armenian Philanthropic Academy of Calcutta ...	30,000
The Armenian School of Madras	30,000
The Holy See of Etchmiatzin in Armenia	25,000
The Armenian Monastery of St. James at Jerusalem ...	10,000
The Cathedral of All Saviour at Julfa in Ispahan ...	10,000
The Nunnery of St. Catherine at Julfa in Ispahan ...	5,000

The Armenian School at Madras having ceased to exist, owing to paucity of pupils, the bequest left by George Manook for that institution, amounting to Sicca rupees 30,000, was through the efforts of the late Mr. Gregory Sam of Madras, transferred, by the sanction of the Madras High Court, to the Armenian Philanthropic Academy at Calcutta, some twenty years ago, and with the income from that bequest some boys are being educated in the school as the "Madras School" foundationers.

Aviet Agabeg	2,000	0
Martyrose Ter Stephen	1,000	0
P. Bagram and S. P. Bagram	2,000	0
George Phanoos Bagram	1,000	0
Sarkies Owen	500	0
Arratoon Petrus	1,000	0
Fatholah Hannah and Jubrah Usoff Asfars ...	1,000	0
Manuel Peter	100	0
Malcolm Gasper	100	0
Nazar Shahnazar	1,000	0
Johanness Hyrapiet	1,500	0
Thaddeus Satoor	1,000	0
Woskan Jacob	200	0
Adam George	20	0
Colonel Jacob Petrus of Gwalior* ...	2,000	0
Simeon Gregory	200	0
Carapiet Arakiel of Penang†	7,394	0
Agah Usoff Jevany	500	0
John Lucas	500	0
Hyrapiet Ter Gabriel	52	0
Aviet Philip Ptoom	100	0
Lazar Jacob	1,000	0
Sarkies Manook of Rangoon	1,000	0
Anthony Johanness Oozoom	200	0
Catchatoor Galustaun‡ and Nierses		

* For an account of Colonel Jacob Petrus of Gwalior, see chapter X.

† There is a tablet, to the memory of Carrapiet Arrakiel, fixed on the outside wall of the Calcutta Armenian church, near the belfry, bearing the following inscription :—

"Sacred to the memory of Carrapiet Arrakiel Esq., formerly of Calcutta, and late of Penang. Eminently distinguished for his philanthropy and benevolence, who departed this life on his passage from Penang to Calcutta, Anno Domini 1819."

‡ Catchatoor Galustaun, or, as he was otherwise called, Agah Catchatoor, was a prominent Armenian merchant of Penang. There, in 1822, he erected the Armenian church of St. Gregory the Illuminator at a cost of over $20,000. He died while on a visit to Calcutta in 1841, and on his tombstone, in Nazareth's churchyard, the following lines are inscribed :—

"Sacred to the memory of CATCHATOOR GALUSTAUN, Esq., an Armenian gentleman, who for upwards of thirty years, was an eminent and respectable merchant in the Prince of Wales Island [Penang] where

Ter Mackertich of Penang	208	0
Arratoon Anthony	10	0
Johanness Simon	228	0
Kirakose Arratoon	400	0
Seth and Gregory Sam of Madras ...	300	0
Carapiet Jacob	300	0
Pogose Jordan	300	0
Lazar Agabeg	374	0
Arratoon Kaloos	150	0
Manook Nicholas	500	0
Juntloom Aviet	2,000	0
The members' subscription in 1825 ...	5,791	0
Carapiet Johanness Petrus	200	0
Thorose Gregory	1,000	0
Catchick Astwasatoor George	250	0
Rev. Joseph Stephen	250	0
Sarkies J. Sarkies	500	0
Arratoon M. David	500	0
Philip Astwasatoor George	100	0
Malchus Isaac Malchus	200	0
Vertanness Zachariah	50	0
David Barsick	100	0
Aviet J. Aviet	50	0
Gregory Astwasatoor Peter	16	0
Carapiet Arratoon Vertanness	125	0
George Gregory, surnamed Bonaparte ...	3,917	14
Reginald Heber, Bishop of Calcutta ...	100	0
The Armenian Community of Calcutta in 1828 ...	783	0
Contribution in aid of Orphan's education ...	1,000	0

---

he erected a magnificent Armenian church entirely out of his own means; whose piety was without ostentation, and whose heart burned with true patriotism; whose happiness consisted in alleviating the wants of his distressed and itinerant countrymen; the charities and gifts of whose right hand were unknown to his left; who departed this transitory life at the age of 60 years on 26th January 1841 at Calcutta."

The "magnificent Armenian church" erected at Penang by Agah Catchatoor Galustaun in 1822, is alas no more, as it was pulled down by a vandal, the unworthy and irreligious grandson of an Armenian priest some twenty years ago, as stated on page 221.

Contribution from the Armenian Community of Singapore	500	0
Arratoon Apcar	1,000	0
Vardon M. Vardon & Bros.	250	0
Mesrovb David Thaliadian	25	0
J. G. Lucas' bequest	1,666	0
Gregory Mooradkhan	20	0
Philip Catchick's bequest ...	2,625	0
Peter J. Sarkies	250	0
Mackertich S. Owen	250	0
Martyrose S. Owen	250	0
Johanness Avdall	200	0
Gregory Apcar	60	0
Manook M. Manook	250	0
Peter J. Paul	600	0
Joseph Agabeg	250	0
Johanness Agabeg	250	0
Aviet Galustaun	250	0
Apcar A. Apcar	250	0
Zorab M. Manook	250	0
Gasper M. Gasper	250	0
Johanness G. Bagram	250	0
Mrs. Hossanna M. S. Shookoor's bequest ...	1,000	0
,, Mariamjan Sarkies' bequest ...	5,000	0
,, Hripsimah Eleazar Leembruggen ...	18,600	0

The Academy, during its existence of a hundred and fifteen years* has afforded shelter and education to thousands of Armenian youths from Julfa, Ispahan, and elsewhere.

Johanness Avdall, who was connected with it for about forty years, first as a teacher and afterwards as a rector, was a native of Shiraz in Persia—the birthplace of the two famous Persian poets, Saadi and Hafez,—and the last resting-place of that immortal Armenian poet, Mesrovb David Thaliadian of whom more hereafter.

* The Armenian Philanthropic Academy, now known as the Armenian College, is the second oldest educational institution in Calcutta, the *oldest* being the Calcutta Free School, which was founded in 1789.

Johanness Avdall came to India when quite a youth, early in the last century. Being of a studious and retiring disposition, and having an insatiable thirst for knowledge, he devoted his days and nights to the study of the Armenian and English languages, and soon distinguished himself as a scholar. He left no original works, with the exception of an essay of self glorification, in classical Armenian, which was published, with his portrait, at the Mechitharist press, Venice, in 1858. He has left some translations in Armenian and English, as stated in the foot-note on page 448.

His literary fame was surpassed, however, by that of his contemporary, the immortal Mesrovb David Thaliadian, whose standard works, in the beautiful language of ancient Armenia, bear ample testimony to his literary attainments and scholarship of a very high order. We shall refer to him in the next chapter as very little is known about that great scholar, poet, journalist and educationist.

After long peregrinations, extending over sixty years, the Academy, found its haven of peace at No. 39, Free School Street, in 1883, when the present three-storeyed house,* with its large compound, was purchased, for Rs. 48,000, by the then Manager, the late Mr. M. J. Galstaun, the uncle of our worthy compatriot, Mr. J. C. Galstaun, O.B.E. It may not be generally known that it was in that ancient house that the famous novelist, William Makepeace

---

* In 1930, the adjoining premises, No. 4, Kyd Street, known as the "Delta Club", was purchased at a cost of Rs. 2,00,000, to provide accommodation for the increasing number of boys in the institution, and shortly after, a plot of land, lying on the south was purchased at a cost of a lakh of rupees and thrown into the compound, making the school play-ground an ideal one, as regards size.

And in the same year, Mr. P. H. Crete, an ex-pupil and a former Manager of the College, presented the institution with a handsome Swimming Bath, constructed in the south compound for the use of the boys. The water in the Bath is supplied from a tube-well, so that its purity is guaranteed. A white marble tablet with bilingual inscriptions, is placed on the north-east wall of the Bath. The opening ceremony was performed in April 1931 when an address was read by the writer of these lines in classical Armenian thanking the donor for his benevolence to his Alma Mater.

Thackeray, was born on the 18th July 1811, as indicated by a black marble slab fixed on the right side of the main entrance to the house.

Amongst those who studied in the Armenian Philanthropic Academy during the Rectorship of Arratoon Kaloos and his worthy pupil, Johanness Avdall, we may mention the names of Mackertich Emin, Thaddeus Catchick Avetoom, Arathoon Thaddeus Owen, Catchick Abraham Thomas, Thomas Malcolm and several others. The first, Mackertich Emin, distinguished himself as a scholar of great repute in the Lazareff College at Moscow, founded by the opulent Lazars of Julfa in 1815.

The second, Thaddeus Catchick Avetoom, was a good classical Armenian scholar and an able translator, as stated on page 442.

The third, Arathoon Thaddeus Owen, the author of the *History of New Julfa,* in 3 volumes, printed at the press of the All-Saviour's Cathedral at New Julfa, in 1880, was for several years the Secretary of the Cathedral at Julfa, known familiarly as "Mirza Arathoon". He died suddenly on the 26th May 1871, aged 43 years, leaving two sons and five daughters. His father, an eminent merchant, died on the 18th April 1849 at Penang, aged 52 years and lies buried in the churchyard of the demolished Armenian church of that place. The elder son of the historian, the late Mr. Thaddeus Arathoon, who died at Monte Carlo a few years ago, was a successful jute merchant in Calcutta some forty years ago. He founded, entirely at his own expense, the "Arathoon Jute Mills", now a Limited Liability Company, under the name of "Lansdowne Jute Mills." He retired from India, before the Great War, and settled at Monte Carlo, where he erected some palatial buildings adding to the many architectural beauties of that renowned city of Casinos. He had received his early education in the Armenian Philanthropic Academy during the Rectorship of the late Mr. Thaddeus Stephen.

He left one son and three daughters, all of whom were educated in England.

One of the daughters, Miss May Arathoon, a highly cultured and an accomplished young lady, residing at Monte

Carlo, has inherited, in no small measure, the urbanity and the suavity of her noble father and the patriotism and the intellectualism of her revered grandfather, the immortal historian of Julfa. She is deeply interested in everything appertaining to national history and culture, and follows the regeneration of the nation in the Fatherland with breathless interest.

Would that every Armenian lady, young and old, did her little bit for the benefit of the Fatherland, which like the proverbial Phœnix, has risen from its ashes after a terrible bondage and thraldom of 500 years, so that Mother Armenia, born anew, may justly he proud of her *tiknaikh phaphkasoonkh* (ladies brought up delicately), as she was in the days of the memorable Wars of the Vardanians* in the fifth century, when the mighty Sassanians of Persia tried to introduce the religion of Zoroaster and the worship of fire in Christian Armenia during the reign of Yezdigerd, as faithfully chronicled by Egishe Vardapiet, justly styled the historian of a golden pen (voskegritch).

But we have digressed.

The late Catchick Abraham Thomas, a native of Bushire, was one of the foremost pupils of Johanness Avdall. He had gained a complete mastery over the classical Armenian as can be seen from his elegant translation of the *Life of Clive* which was published by the Mechitharist Society of Venice.

The late Mr. A. G. Apcar† referred to on page 447, was one of the many pupils who studied with success at the feet of Johanness Avdall, so was the late Mr. Thomas

---

* The *History of Vartan, and of the battle of the Armenians, containing an account of the religious wars between the Persians and Armenians, by Elisæus,* was translated into English from the original Armenian, by that great orientalist, C. F. Neumann, and published in London by the "Oriental Translation Fund" in 1830.

† In 1896, the late Mr. A. G. Apcar, erected at his own expense, the two-storied building in the Armenian College compound, on the east of the old three-storied house, near the gate in Free School Street, in memory of his second daughter, Mary Apcar, who died in London in 1895. The upper floor serves as an additional dormitory, whilst the ground floor is let out as shops, and with the income derived from the shops, a couple of boys are educated in the college as "Mary Apcar Trust" foundationers.

Malcolm, referred to on page 444, both of whom were good Armenian scholars.

It is pleasant to note that after the death of Johanness Avdall, his mantle fell on the late Mr. Thaddeus Stephen, who proved a worthy successor, for during his Rectorship for a period of twenty years, (1863-1883) he kept the torch of classical Armenian burning luminously in the Academy and among the foremost pupils of that period may be mentioned the honoured names of the late Mr. C. J. Zeytoon, Drs. M. M. Basil, M. S. Aganoor and Seth Gregory, Messrs. G. G. Gasper, Leon Mackertich, Nicholas G. Arratoon, A. G. Arratoon, G. L. Apcar, S. L. Apcar, Marcus Galstaun, George M. Johanness, J. N. Galestin, Thaddeus Arathoon, S. T. Creet, Thaddeus Paul, Tigran R. David, Arathoon Stephen, Michael S. Martin, P. Z. Martin, Rev. Isaiah S. Johanness, Messrs. A. S. Mackertich, John Seth, Manatsakan Stephen, Seth Paul, Carapiet Malcolm, and Tigran Sarkies, and amongst those still living, and may they live long, we may mention the names of Messrs. C. L. Phillipps, J. C. Galstaun, Peter H. Crete, J. C. Jordan, S. M. Gregory, George Michael, G. M. Gregory, A. C. Martin, David Alexander, M. J. Michael, G. M. Apcar, Dr. M. M. Apcar and many others, who by their activities in the different walks of life, have shed lustre on their Alma Mater, the good old MARDASIRAKAN.

It may interest our Armenian readers to know the reasons which compelled the late Mr. Thaddeus Stephen, to sever his connection with the Academy, after serving it meritoriously for an uninterrupted period of twenty years, during which time the national institution had risen to the pinnacle of its glory as a beacon of light and a centre of Armenian learning and culture in India and the East. Although we were not in Calcutta then, (1883) but being interested in the past history of the venerable institution, we investigated, from reliable sources, the causes which led to the rupture between the veteran Rector and the then Managers of the Academy, and were fully satisfied that the Managers were to be blamed, for having driven him to take that course, by lending a willing ear to the calumny, slander and vilification of a low-born adventurer from Turkey, an adept in the nefarious art of intrigue. That hydra-headed monster with fangs full of deadly venom, has alas ! been the bane of the human race since the creation of the world, for did not our first parents fall an easy prey to the intrigues of Satan, in the Garden of Eden?

In 1882, an adventurer from Constantinople, Carapiet Petrus Moorat by name, hearing of the fabulous wealth of India, takes a passage at Alexandria for Hong Kong, thinking he was going to India to shake the proverbial "Pagoda Tree". Arriving at Hong Kong he goes to an Armenian resident of the island and asks him to secure a job for him as a teacher of Armenian. He is told that he had gone to the wrong place and that he should have gone to Calcutta instead. The kind-hearted gentleman secures a free passage for the would-be Armenian teacher, in one of Apcar & Co's steamers, and he is sent to Calcutta. On his arrival here he has an interview with the Managers of the Academy and tells them that he is a great French scholar. The Managers, without making any enquiries about his knowledge of the French language, appoint him as a French master in the institution, although he knew as much French as we know Sanskrit or German.

Mr. A. C. Martin of Rangoon, an ex-pupil of the Academy, has related to us the following amusing story which shows how deception can be exposed, sooner or later. In 1882 a powerful telescope was installed in the famous observatory of St. Xaviers College, and Mr. Arakiel Martin who was then studying there, for higher education, as a day scholar, but staying at the Academy, tells Mr. Thaddeus Stephen about the telescope. Mr. Stephen being a cultured person, expresses a desire to see the same. Mr. Martin makes an appointment and takes the Rector there one evening. The so-called French master of the Academy requests the Rector to be allowed to accompany him. When they arrive at the College of the Jesuit Fathers, Mr. Martin introduces Mr. Stephen as the Rector of the Armenian Academy, and the adventurer is introduced as their "French Master", whereupon the Rector of St. Xaviers College who happened to be a Frenchman, starts speaking to the "French Master" of the Armenian Academy in French. The bubble bursts and the fraud was exposed, for the so-called French Master was so non-plussed that with the exception of the word *oui* (yes) he could not utter another word in French.

After seeing the moon, the stars and the other heavenly bodies, the trio return to the Academy after profusely thanking the good Jesuit Father for the intellectual treat they had enjoyed, through his kind courtesy.

On the way home, the Rector asks the "French Master" why he was unable to carry on the conversation with the Rector of St. Xavier's College in the French language, since he professed to be a great French scholar. The crest-fallen imposter nonchalantly replies that the Frenchman spoke to him in *old* French whereas he knew *modern* French. What a silly excuse, what an asinine plea, as if there is such a thing as ancient and modern French, like we have ancient and modern Armenian or Greek. The impostor seeing that his days, as the "French Master" in the national institution, were numbered, started from that day intriguing against the Rector and he succeeded *par excellence,* as all intriguers invariably do, especially if they are graduates of the "College of Sycophants", founded by the Pharisees of Judea 2000 years ago.

The Managers of the Armenian Philanthropic Academy in 1883, although successful businessmen, were ignorant of matters educational and could not therefore appraise the value or appreciate the sterling worth of an able teacher like the late Mr. Thaddeus Stephen, with the result that they became an easy prey to the machinations of the adventurer from Constantinople, who had, as we have said, crept into the national institution by fawning and adulation, the stock-in-trade of all adventurers and intriguers.

After the departure of the veteran Rector, in July 1883, the adventurer was appointed the Armenian Head Master and from that day, it may safely be said, the glory departed from the Armenian Philanthropic Academy, as the seat of Armenian learning in India, for the newly-appointed Head Master knew as much classical Armenian as the present incumbent knows English, although he has been in an educational institution for 24 years!

In an article on *The language and literature of Armenia*, published in the *Indian Empire* for April 1890, we find that the adventurer is called the "Professor of Armenian in the Armenian College, Calcutta", by his Eurasian brother-in-law who was the Principal of the College at that time.

The adventurer, who in 1882, had duped the then Managers by making them believe that he was a French scholar, had in the same may duped the non-Armenian Principal of the College and made him believe that he was a Professor of the Armenian language, when he was an ignoramus, as far as his knowledge of the classical Armenian was concerned.

In 1892, the Managers of the College, all of whom were graduates of English Universities, saw that their Armenian Head Master was a worthless person, fond of intrigues, as he had intrigued even against his own brother-in-law, the then Principal of the institution. They decided to replace him by a competent teacher and as they did not know of any Armenian teachers in Calcutta, they approached the late Mr. John S. Sarkies, one of the Members of the institution, and requested him to recommend a teacher, well versed in Armenian and English, to succeed the adventurer from Turkey.

Mr. Sarkies, who was a very good Armenian scholar, (see. p. 439) sought our advice in the matter and we strongly recommended Mr. Thedore Isaac, who was then a teacher in the Theological Seminary at the Armenian monastery of St. James, in Jerusalem. Mr. Sarkies communicated with him and he accepted the terms offered by the Managers of the College. He arrived in Calcutta in October 1892 and was placed on the chair which had been worthily occupied in the past by such eminent Armenian scholars like Arratoon Kaloos, Mesrovb Thaliadian, Johanness Avdall, David Melik Beglar, Thaddeus Stephen and Mackertich Agabeg, but whereas most of the pupils who studied at the feet of those Gamaliels rose to eminence in the literary, commercial and industrial world, none of the pupils of the teacher from Jerusalem, some of whom are living in Calcutta at the present day, distinguished themselves "in the world's broad field of battle."

Early in 1895, we were asked by the Managers, to find a suitable Armenian teacher to succeed Mr. Theodore Isaac, who was constantly quarrelling with the English teachers in the institution, and we immediately wrote to the late Mr. Thaddeus Stephen, requesting him to come back to his old school, the scene of his early labours. We were glad when he cheerfully complied with our request and joined the national institution, a second time, in March 1895. All the well-wishers of the good old MARDASIRAKAN were very pleased that the study of the classical Armenian, which had been neglected for twelve years, would be revived once more under the fostering care of the good old "Varjapiet" (teacher) who was deservedly loved and respected by one and all for his paternal solicitude for the boys in the national institution. He continued, old as he was, to teach the mother language, as it should be taught, till the year 1904, when owing to old age and declining health, he retired from India and went to live in London, with his nephew, the late Mr. S. T. Creet. He died some fifteen years ago in Canada where his nephew had finally settled with his family. Peace to his soul, rest to his ashes and may his revered memory be ever kept green in the national institution where he laboured with unbounded zeal and devotion for thirty years. After the late Mr. Stephen had finally severed his connection with the institution, we were again asked to find a suitable substitute and we recommended Mr. V. M. Galoostian, one of the pupils of the retiring master, to succeed him, and we were glad that he fully justified the confidence we had placed in him. With a break of a few years, when he went to Julfa to get married, Mr. Galoostian taught the boys till the year 1919, when he suddenly resigned his post in the College and proceeded to California with his family. He was, in the absence of a competent teacher, succeeded by the present incumbent, another Armenian from Turkey, as the Head Master in Armenian, although he knows as much classical Armenian as the adventurer from Constantinople, who was however honest enough to confess to us, in 1890, that he did not know the ancient Armenian (grabar), as that difficult language was not taught, he said, in the school where he had received his early education in his native town. And before concluding our account of that impostor, we have to expose another hoax which shows the utter lack of veracity in the man.

It appears he had beguiled his Eurasian wife even by telling her a number of yarns about his past career before coming to Calcutta in 1882. The gullible wife must have accepted the fibs of her garrulous husband, as gospel truth, as can be seen from the following inscription, on a marble cross, placed horizontally, over the grave of the "surgeon," by his "sorrowing widow", in the Armenian cemetery, Lower Circular Road.

Here is the misleading inscription :—

"In loving memory of Carapiet Petrus Moorat. Born at Constantinople, 26th July 1852, died at Liluah, 18th October 1906.

Late Secretary, Khedive's architect, Egypt, 1874. Surgeon, Turkish Army during Russo-Turkish war. Surgeon, Singapore Hospital. For eight years Head Master, Armenian College. The benefactor of many Armenian boys for whose education he paid.

This memorial has been erected by his sorrowing widow and from a scholarship earned by his son.

Mark the perfect man, for the end of that man is peace.' Ps. 37—37."

In the above panegyric, the imbecile adventurer is called a "surgeon", when he had no knowledge of medicine or surgery and we doubt if he knew the difference between Iodoform and chloroform. Then again, we are to bělieve that he had acted as the "Secretary" to the Khedive's architect in Egypt, when he did not know any European language, and to crown the deception, we are told that he was "the benefactor of many Armenian boys for whose education he paid," when we know that his maximum salary did not exceed Rs. 120 a month, and with that miserable income he had to support himself, his wife and a child in an expensive place like Calcutta. In this connection it may be mentioned that all the boys of that period, numbering about fifty, were educated in the College either at the expense of the Calcutta Armenian church or the Batavia Armenian Association and others. There could therefore have been no necessity for the impecunious Head Master to pay for the education of any of the boys in that wealthy institution.

A few words about the present Armenian Head Master may not be out of place. He, like the "surgeon in the Turkish Army", hails from Turkish Armenia, now called Anatolia. He has been heard to tell his credulous admirers that before coming out to India, he held the post of Principal in the Armeno-German College at Van, but we who have received our early education in a Mission school, under a strict German Principal, the late Dr. Hoernle of blessed memory, cannot believe that the shrewd German missionaries at Van could have appointed one who did not know German, English or any other European language as the head of that educational institution. Unfortunately the college of the German missionaries has ceased to exist at Van owing to the wholesale deportations of the Armenian population from Anatolia during and after the Great War, otherwise we could have obtained reliable information about the position he held in that institution.

This man, like "the secretary of the Khedive's architect," hearing of the glamour of the gorgeous East, goes from Van to Egypt and there he secures a passage on a steamer bound for Singapore, thinking, no doubt, that he was going to India. On his arrival at that great port, the Gibraltar of the East, he is told by the Armenians there that he had gone to the wrong place in search of an employment as a teacher of Armenian, and is sent to Calcutta. This was in 1913 when we were one of the Managers of the Armenian College. He came to us for a post in the national institution, but we told him that we had two Armenian teachers already and there was no room for a third. He wrote to us saying he was a native of Van, "the heart of Armenia," but that bombastic appeal to our national sentiments did not have the desired effect. Seeing that we were adamant, he went to the late Mr. Thomas Malcolm, and begged of him to induce us to have him admitted into the College, as an additional teacher in Armenian and it is very strange that he did not ask to be placed on the Principal's chair.

Mr. Thomas Malcolm, the Nestor of the Armenians in Calcutta, for whom we had the highest respect, called on us and wished to know why we had refused to engage the services of the erstwhile Principal from Van. We told him that we had no place for an extra teacher and if he wished that we should employ him, we had to dispense with the services of one of the teachers in the College. He then asked us to engage him as a "Sergeant" in the school, but we told him that the College was not in a position to employ a sergeant, whereupon he said that if we admitted him, he would get the Armenian church to pay his salary so that the school may be spared the additional expense. After that assurance, we could not possibly refuse to admit him and for three years, the Armenian church paid his salary, which was only Rs. 30 per month, till the wheel of his fortune turned and he was appointed a teacher in Armenian, in the absence of a competent teacher.

In 1926, on the advice of a compatriot, another Armenian from Turkey, he resigned his post and went to Assam to cut down trees, and flood the Calcutta market with timber, but he failed to achieve success as a timber merchant, for a person who is used to a life of ease and comfort, in an educational institution cannot stand the hardships of life in snake infested jungles. After losing his money and his health, he came down to Calcutta, and the Managers seeing his straitened circumstances, took him back into the national institution, out of sheer pity, in September 1931. He is still there and from what we can see, he shall remain in that abode of peace and plenty till the Hooghly dries up!

In the Annual Reports of the College, we find in the list of teachers, the mysterious initials, C. T. Sc. placed after the Head Master's name, but as he does not possess any College or University degrees and no academical qualifications, we infer that the initials indicate *Care taker of School*. We shall be glad to know if they mean something else.

With a view to raise the standard of the Academy, the Managers started, in 1888, College classes for preparing boys for the First Arts and the higher examinations of the Calcutta Universtiy, with classical Armenian as the second-language, and it was then that the Acadamy came to be known as the "Armenian College". The College classes were discontinued in 1891, owing to the paucity of students willing to continue their studies for higher examinations. The Academy was affiliated to the Calcutta University in 1871 when the first batch of students were sent up for the then Entrance, now Matriculation Examination, with classical Armenian as their second-language. Among the successful candidates who appeared at the *first* Examination of the foremost University in India, may be mentioned the names of the late Messrs. C. J. Zeytoon, Nicholas G. Arratoon, Leon Mackertich, Carapiet Malcolm, Basil Ter Minas, Manatsakan Stephen and G. G. Gasper, all of whom distinguished themselves, as eminent merchants in India, Java and elsewhere.

The Academy possessed a Library, founded on the 7th April 1828 and known as the "Araratian Library," and in the "New Rules and Regulations" of the institution, printed in 1843, at the press of the Academy, in Armenian and English, we find that there were at that time about a thousand volumes, mostly rare manuscript works, on its shelves.

The late Mr. Thadduns Stephen told us in 1891, that when he left the Academy in 1883, the "Araratian Library" was quite intact, and we have heard from one of the foremost pupils of the institution, the late Mr. C. J. Zeytoon, that the Library used to be looked after with great care and the books dusted every Saturday by the Rectors' orders.

When we were attending the College as a day-scholar in 1890, we asked one of the senior boys, now in holy orders, to show us the College Library and he very kindly took us to a room on the ground floor where we were shown a dilapidated wooden almirah, filled with torn Armenian printed books, but no manuscripts. These were the remnants of the once famous "Araratian Library". Where had the numerous manuscripts gone? We were informed that they had mysteriously disappeared after the departure of the former Rector.

The fame of the "Araratian Library" had spread far and wide, as can be seen from the following incident. In January 1890, the late Professor Frederick Conybeare, a distinguished Armenist of international reputation, paid a visit to the College, accompanied by his accomplished wife, who was a daughter of the world-renowned Orientalist, Max Muller. He wished to see the College Library, expecting to find some rare

Armenian manuscripts, as he had found in Armenia during a tour in 1888. We happened to be present in the College at that time, and acted as the cicerone, not knowing who the strange visitor, with long hair, was. We showed him the remnants of the once famous Library and placed in his hands an Armenian work, printed at Madras by Jacob Shameer, in 1772, thinking we were showing him a rare publication, but he said that he had seen it already in the Madras Armenian church Library. He then desired to see the Manuscripts, and was visibly disappointed on learning that they had disappeared long ago, no one knew wither.

In this connection it may be mentioned that the "sorrowing widow" of the Armenian Head Master from Constantinople had sold, some years ago, a manuscript translation of the Koran, in classical Armenian, to the Begum of Bhopal, for Rs. 500. The gentle reader can easily, and without any stretch of imagination, guess where that rare manuscript came from. A few words about that work may be of interest to our Armenian readers. At the suggestion of the late Father H. Hosten. S. J. who had paid a visit to Bhopal 1922 in search of the Bourbon relics and records, the Koran was sent to us by the Librarian of the Bhopal State Library for information concerning the translator and the place and the date of the translation into Armenian. We prepared a Paper, which was read before the "Royal Asiatic Society of Bengal" and subsequently published in the journal of the Society. We exhibited on that occasion the rare manuscript and it was greatly admired for its beautiful caligraphy and marginal decorations.

From the colophon (hishtakaran) at the end of the manuscript, it appears that the Koran was translated into classical Armenian from the Latin version, by one Stephanos of Ilou, "a profound scholar and an erudite doctor," who had entered the Armenian monastery at Etchmiadzin—the Vatican of Armenia—as an inmate, in 1635, during the pontificate of Phillipos, the Catholicos of all the Armenians, who was ordained on the 13th January 1633 and died in 1655.

The "Araratian Library" having ceased to exist with the mysterious disappearance of the numerous books in the Armenian, English, Latin, Greek, French, Dutch, Persian,

Chinese and other languages, as stated in the "New Rules and Regulations of the Armenian Philanthropic Academy," referred to above, the necessity of a school Library was keenly felt and this want was supplied by the late Mr. A. S. Mackertich, an ex-student of the College, who in 1909, laid the foundations of a new Library in the college by presenting some large strongly-made teak-wood almirahs, with a large number of English books, including some rare historical works. At the request of the donor, we compiled the Library Catalogue which was printed and circulated with an appeal for further presentations and we are glad to say that the College possesses to-day a well-equipped Library of Armenian and English books. Further presentations will be gratefully accepted by the Managers of the College from the members of the Armenian community of Calcutta and elsewhere especially from such ex-pupils, and their name is legion, who have had the benefit of *free* education in the institution. The former ex-students who studied in the Academy during the Rectorship of the late Mr. Thaddeus Stephen, have, with commendable zeal, paid their debt of gratitude to their Alma Mater by founding Trusts for the benefit of the national institution. Foremost amongst them were the late Messrs. Manatsakan Stephens and Seth Paul, who not only donated large sums themselves but were instrumental in raising substantial subscriptions amongst the ex-pupils and others in Java, Burma and Calcutta, for the laudable purpose. And with the princely donations, running into six figures in Indian rupees, two distinct Trusts were created in London, in January 1917, one in the name of the "Armenian College, Calcutta," with a capital, at the time of its formulation, of £9000, the income from which is devoted entirely towards the salaries of the teachers of the said College. The other Trust or Deed is "for the advancement of education amongst Armenian Communities," with a capital, at its formulation, of £12960-12-2. The income from this Trust must be devoted to the "Armenian National Central School" at Julfa, now known as the "Shah Abbas School," and a small percentage from the residue thereof to the Armenian College at Calcutta. The Trust, with a capital of £9000, is styled, in the Report of "the Armenian Education Trust Funds, London," as "The Armenian

College Fund", whilst the one, with a capital of £12,960, is called "the Armenian Education Fund". It may be mentioned however that both the above Trusts have been amalgamated and are now known under the name of "The Armenian Education Trust Funds, London".

The Armenian College at Calcutta receives annually a sum of Rs. 6000 from the above Trust Funds and a sum of £600 is remitted annually to the "Armenian National Central School at Julfa" from the same Trust Funds in London. The present Trustees of the Funds are Messrs. S. M. Gregory, A. P. Hacobian, John & George Stephens, all of London. The Bankers, or the Custodian Trustees, as they are called, being the London County, Westminister, and Parr's Bank, Ltd.

The first General Trustees, four in number, were the late Messrs. Thaddeus Arathoon, Albert M. Zorab, Thaddeus Paul, and the present Chairman, Mr. S. M. Gregory, known familiarly as "Zavak", the author of *The Land of Ararat*, published in London, in 1920 and dedicated to the late Mr. Thaddeus Stephen.*

With a view to preserve the names of those noble-minded and kind-hearted ex-pupils and others who have subscribed liberally to the "Armenian Education Trust Funds", we give below a list of the donors which we have culled from the Report, prblished in 1920, by Mr. S. M. Gregory, the Chairman of the present Trustees.

LIST NO. 1. (Rangoon)

1910.	Jan. 1.	Mr. S. Balthazar ...	Rs.	10,000-0
1915.	Dec. 31.	Interest at 6% from 1 Jan. 1910 to 31 Dec. 1915 ...	,,	4006-5
			Total Rs.	14,006-5

* The dedication which is an expression of sincere admiration from a grateful pupil towards his master, is as follows:

"Dedicated with affectionate regard to Thaddeus Stephen, Esq. for thirty years the revered Head Master of the Armenian College and Philanthropic Academy, Calcutta, now in retirement amidst the universal respect and veneration of his numerous pupils; to whose tuition and sound practical advice, during his early years, the author attributes whatever success in life he has been able to achieve."

LIST No. 2. (Batavia)

1908.	Sept. 4.	Mrs. Mariamjan Gaspar	Fl. 8000.00
1915.	Dec. 31.	Interest from 4th Sept. 1908 to 31 Dec. 1915 ...	,, 4624.76
		Total Florins	12624.76

LIST No. 3. (Macassar)

		Florins.
1909-1911.	M. Stephens*	21,684.13
,,	Seth Paul*	21,684.13
1909.	Thaddeus Paul*	10,000.00
1911.	Mrs M. Stephens	10,000.00
1908-1912.	M. S., L. S., & H. S. Arathoon	2,000.00
,,	M. A., S. A., & C. A. Edgar ...	1,400.00
,,	S. M., & G. M. Gregory ...	1,136.71
,,	P. C. Paul	768.00
,,	M. S. Martin	720.03
,,	L. C. John	506.00
1910.	Sundry contributors ...	600.00
1909-1915.	Interest at 6% to 31st Dec. 1915	22,186.31
	Total Florins	92,685.31

LIST No. 4. (Calcutta)

		Rs.	As.
1909-1910.	Donations by Messrs. Stephens, Paul & Co.† ...	50,000	0
,,	Thaddeus Arathoon ...	10,000	0
,,	J. C. Galstaun	10,000	0
,,	Seth Paul, Gregory Carapiet & J. C. Galstaun, in memory of Mr. M. J. Galstaun ...	10,000	0
,,	C. L. Philllips	7,000	0

* For further donations, see List No. 4, foot note.

† This amount includes donations of Florins 10,000 each by the late Messrs. M. Stephens, Seth Paul and Thaddeus Paul, and a donation of Florins 5000 by Mr. S. P. Stephens, now residing in London.

		Rs.	AS.
1909-1910.	Mrs. Nanajan J. Sarkies ...	6,000	0
,,	S. T. Creet	5,000	0
,,	A. S. Mackertich ...	3,000	0
,,	P. H. Crete	2,000	0
,,	A. M. Arathoon ...	2,000	0
,,	T. M. Thaddeus ...	1,000	0
,,	S. J. Apcar	1,000	0
,,	M. Mackertich	500	0
,,	Paul Brothers for lights ...	1,020	0
,,	Mrs. A. C. Martin of Rangoon, being one-third share of the bequest of Rs. 1000, left by her father, the late Mr. M. Owen of Rangoon, to the Armenian College ...	333	6
	Total donations Rs.	108,853	6
,,	Interest on Mortgages, Govt. Paper and Bank Deposits from 1909-1916 ...	41,167	2
	Total Rs.	150,020	8

LIST No. 5. (Sourabaya)

		Florins.
1908-1913.	G. L. Apcar	10,000.00
,,	A. M. Zorab	9,100.00
,,	A. P. Hacobian	5,000.00
,,	N. P. Hacobian	3,500.00
,,	S. L. Apcar	1,500.00
,,	M. Johanness	500.00
,,	Arsene Zorab	225.00
,,	Sam Joakim	1,000.00
,,	J. Zorab	100.00
,,	L. M. Zorab	150.00
,,	V. A. Apcar	250.00
,,	S. M. Galstaun	250.00
,,	H. A. Apcar	250.00

		Florins.
1908-1913.	M. N. Galstaun	250.00
,,	J. C. Jordan	250.00
,,	J. E. Arathoon	25.00
,,	Carr, Joakim	250.00
,,	P. N. Galstaun	200.00
,,	Seth Zorab	50.00
,,	A. J. & L. Zorab ...	400.00
,,	S. M. Zorab	75.00
	Total donations Fl.	33,325.00
,,	Interest at 6%, from 13 Feb. 1908 to 31 Dec. 1915 Fl.	12,404.67
	Total Florins	45,729.67

From the Report issued by Mr. S. M. Gregory, in 1920, we find that on the 31st December 1919, the assets of the "Armenian College Trust" amounted to £10,036-19-1, whilst those of the "Education Fund" stood at £13,970-8-2. And in a printed appeal, issued on the 1st January 1912, under the joint signatures of the late Messrs. M. Stephens and Seth Paul, we find the names of the following donors, whose contributions had already been received and invested.

Mr. & Mrs. M. Stephens	Guilders	20,000
Mr. Seth Paul	,,	10,000
Mr. G. L. Apcar	,,	10,000
Mr. A. M. Zorab	,,	10,000
Mr. A. P. Hacobian*	,,	10,000
Mrs. G. E. Gasper	,,	10,000
Mrs. J. S. Sarkies†	Rs.	12,000

*In List No. 5, Mr. A. P. Hacobian's donation is given as Guilders 5000, instead of Guilders 10,0000, as in the above List. We do not know the reason why.

† The donation of Rs. 12,000, given by Mrs. Nanajan Sarkies is shown in List No. 4 as Rs. 6000. Why this discrepancy?

In memory of Mr. M. J. Galstaun,*	...	Rs.	12,000
Mr. S. Balthazar,†	...	... ,,	12,000

The above donations of Guilders 70,000 and Rupees 36,000, were invested at 6% per annum, through different trustees, at Macassar, Sourabaya, Batavia, Rangoon and Calcutta.

As we have seen, the "Education Funds" were formed into Trusts in London in 1916, but no steps have been taken yet to perpetuate the revered memory of the Founders, although twenty years have elapsed since the Funds have been bearing fruit. Has that rare virtue, called *gratitude*, ceased to exist in this age? If departed worth can be appreciated in this materialistic world, tributes should be paid to the noble band of donors, by placing a memorial tablet, in a prominent place in the College, inscribed with the names of the benefactors, to remind the present and the future generations of students of the patriotism of the former alumni of the national institution.

In 1910, some of the ex-pupils of the College, residing in Calcutta, conceived the laudable idea of starting an "Old Boys' Union", and through the strenuous efforts of the late Mr. A. G. Arratoon, the Union was formed, with a large number of Life and Ordinary Members.

---

* The donation given by Mr. J. C. Galstaun and the late Messrs. Seth Paul and Gregory Carapiet, in memory of Mr. M. J. Galstaun, was, according to this List, Rs. 12,000, but in List No. 4, we find it is given as Rs. 10,000.

†The late Mr. Samuel Balthazar's donation of Rs. 12,000 is reduced to Rs. 8000 in List No. 1. We cannot understand how such glaring discrepancies or variations could have taken place when the different Lists of the donors and their donations, as given above, were being compiled by the Trustees in 1916.

We trust the worthy Chairman Mr. S. M. Gregory, who has been actively associated with the "Armenian Education Trust Funds", since their inception in 1909, will be kind enough, with the materials at his disposal, to throw light on the subject, in his next Report. And let it be distinctly understood that in pointing out the above discrepancies, we have no desire to cast aspersions or reflections on anybody, our object being simply to rectify some slight errors that may have crept into the Lists (Nos. 1—5) inadvertently.

The *first* Committee was composed of the following founder-members :—

Messrs. A. G. Arratoon, (President) M. D. Nahapiet, (Honorary Treasurer) Ezras M. Gregory, (Honorary Secretary) A. C. Martin (Representative for Burma) S. J. Apcar, (Representative for Jhalda) M. C. David and Mesrovb J. Seth.

Messrs. A. G. Arratoon and M. D. Nahapiet, the *first* President and the Treasurer who did much for the success of the Union, have departed this life many years ago, but their revered memory is kept green by all the members of the Union.

The present office-bearers of the Union are as follows :

Mr. Mesrovb J. Seth—*President.*

Mr. G. A. Arratoon—*Honorary Secretary.*

Mr. N. P. Hacobian—*Honorary Treasurer.*

On the 30th May 1933, when the last Report was issued, the Union possessed Rs. 18,713-14-4, of which Rs. 18,402-7-7, had been invested in 3½% Government of India Securities of the face value of Rs. 26,000, which are deposited, for safe custody, in the Imperial Bank of India.

Since 1924, the Union has defrayed the expenses of four boys who have, in succession, been educated in different schools, in Calcutta.

The Centenary of the "Armenian College and Philanthropic Academy" was celebrated with great eclat on the 2nd day of April, 1921, when a hundred guests, mostly ex-pupils, sat at a sumptuous banquet, in the big dining Hall*

* The present spacious dining Hall of the College, with a sitting accommodation for 200 persons, was erected in 1896 by subscriptions raised through the ceaseless efforts of the late Mrs. Seth and Mrs. Moss (Moses), the sisters of the late Messrs. Gasper and Chater Gregory. For an account of the origin of this patriotic family, see page 414. The late Mrs. Seth's daughter, Mrs. A. M. Thaddeus, was a social worker in Calcutta, before she went to live in London with her husband. She was the Honorary Lady Superintendent of the "Armenian Refugees Home" some 17 years ago and did much for the alleviation of the sufferings of the large number of refugees, mostly villagers, who had poured into Calcutta from Iraq and Iran. While these pages were going through the press, we heard, with profound regret, of the death of Mr. A. M. Thaddens, which sad event

of the College. Some interesting speeches were made on that occasion and the present writer read a long Paper, in classical Armenian, giving a history of the progress of the venerable institution, since its foundation in 1821. A subscription was then started in aid of the century-old Academy, and Mr. J. C. Galstaun, a worthy alumnus of the College, who presided at the historic function, headed the list with a princely donation of Rs. 30,000.

The following is a list of the subscribers who paid their subscriptions to the "Armenian College Centenary Fund."

	Rs.	A.	P.
Mr. J. C. Galstaun	30,000	0	0
,, A. S. Mackertich	2,500	0	0
,, M. Mackertich	2,000	0	0
,, G. M. Gregory	1,500	0	0
,, G. O. Johanness	530	0	0
,, B. A. Basil	445	0	0
,, M. J. Michael	300	0	0
,, A. S. Gregory	300	0	0
Mrs. Shircore	270	0	0
Mr. V. A. Arathoon	256	8	0
,, G. G. Carapiet	200	0	0
,, G. Velian	150	0	0
,, A. C. Thaddeus	101	0	0
,, H. Apcar	100	0	0
,, C. M. Johaness	200	0	0

---

occurred in London in February 1937. The large two-storyed house in which the refugees were housed, was the property of our public-spirited compatriot Mr. J. C. Galstaun, who with his usual *bonhomie*, charged no rent for the house for the long period that the Home existed. The inmates in the Home were supported entirely at the expense of the Armenian church of Calcutta, and some of them are still in Calcutta having become permanent pensioners of the church.

Miss H. B. Gregory, a cousin of Mrs. Thaddeus and one of the daughters of the late Mr. Chater Gregory, collected, some years ago, subscriptions, amounting to Rs. 37,900, for the clothing of the boys in the Armenian College. This amount was made into a Trust and it appears in the annual Reports of the College as the "Armenian Dorcas Fund, under settlement of Miss H. B. Gregory."

	Rs.	A.	P.
Mr. A. M. Arathoon	100	0	0
,, C. A. Lucas	60	0	0
,, M. G. Mackertich	50	0	0
,, I. Stephen	151	0	0
From the Centenary Fete at Galstaun Park ...	7,916	13	0
From the Centenary Ball, through Mr. A. Stephen	362	0	0
From the Armenian Community, Java ...	3,264	13	4
From the Armenian Community, Sourabaya ...	2,500	0	0
From the Armenian Community, Rangoon ...	2,500	0	0
Total Rs.	55,757	2	4

And there were some, who in the heat of the moment, subscribed liberally, but when the time for honouring their signatures came, they proved defaulters. We refrain from publishing their names in the hope that some day they may perhaps remember their debt of honour to the national institution.

It is sad to reflect that whereas during the first 60 years of its history, the Academy enjoyed a high reputation as a notable seminary for the dissemination of the classical Armenian, it has, during the past 50 years, ceased to be a beacon of national light and learning, and has become, unfortunately, a happy hunting-ground for interlopers, exploiters, impostors and refugees from Turkey who being ignorant of the ancient Armenian have been mainly responsible for the decadence of the national language in the venerable institution, which dates its existence from the year 1821, without any interruption.

We do not wish to be unduly pessimistic and sing jeremiads about the present highly unsatisfactory state of the teaching of Armenian in the College, but we cannot possibly be optimistic and forbearing when we see that the boys who appear for the Matriculation and the higher Examinations of the Calcutta University have no knowledge of the classical Armenian grammar and cannot decline an ordinary noun or conjugate a simple verb. And what shall we say of the bright boy who gave the English definition of the Armenian word *Kherethogh* (a poet) as "one who scratches". We think his asinine brains deserve to be "scratched" for the idiotic definition. In our official capacity as the Examiner in Classical and Modern Armenian to the University of Calcutta, we have ample opportunities of gauging the extent of the knowledge of the boys in Armenian and English and we would be failing in our duty, as an old Member of the national institution and a former Manager if we did not bring the matter to the kind notice of those, who look after the progress of the venerable institution. If the boys are backward in Armenian, it is not their fault, as they have had *no* competent masters to teach them the rudiments of the Armenian grammar, although they have been styled as Professors, Principals, and Head Masters.

Writing of the incompetent Armenian teachers in the College, who have successfully passed themselves off as intellectuals and profound scholars, we are forcibly reminded of the dictum of the divine Master who seeing the incompetency and the worthlessness of the so-called teachers of his day, said, "the scribes and the Pharisees sit on Moses' seat". (Mathew XXIII. 2) In the same way we find that during the past 50 years, Moorats, Asatoorians, Tourians, Mihigians and Moures, have been placed on the chair which had been worthily occupied in the good old days by such eminent educationists and scholars like Kaloos, Thaliadian, Avdall, and Stephen.

History, we are told, repeats itself, for what happened in Jerusalem 1900 years ago, is unfortunately happening in Calcutta at the present day, and yet we are supposed to be living in a highly enlightened and progressive age!

In the last Chapter of the *New Rules and Regulations of the Armenian Philanthropic Academy,* a book of 85 pages, printed in Armenian and English, at the Press of the Academy, in 1843, there are some "Forms of Prayers" for the pupils of the Academy. As they are of special interest, we reproduce the "Morning Prayer", written by Simon, who was the Catholicos of Armenia, from 1763-1780.

"I thank thee, O Lord my God, and bless and glorify thy holy name, who protected thy unworthy and sinful servant, during the night, from all perils and dangers, and brought me in peace to the dawn of the morning, and vouchsafed me to see the light of your mercy.

And now, I beseech thee, O Lord my God, protect me also, during the day, by thy almighty hand, and save me from all hurtful accidents, from visible and invisible enemies, and from all sinful thoughts, words and deeds. Order my steps in thy world: and let not any inquity have dominion over me.

Lead me in good thoughts, in true words, and in deeds free of sin and full of gain.

Be thou the guardian and guide of me, thy erring servant, in all my steps, and save me from the destruction that wasteth at noon-day. And establish thou the work of my hands upon me; yea, the works of my hand establish thou. And do thou provide for the wants of my soul and body. And bring me in peace, without sin and temptation, to the hour of the evening; that I may in that hour also glorify the Holy Trinity, to whom always belongeth glory, for ever and ever, Amen."

There are several other equally interesting Prayers in that chapter, but space will not permit us to reproduce them all. They can however be re-printed for distribution amongst the pupils in the institution, since there are no copies of the original publication extant, with the exception of the one in our possession from which the above prayer is an extract.

In the Calendar for 1872, printed in Armenian at the Press of the Academy, we find there were 46 boys on the Rolls for that year, of whom only one, Mr. Aganoor J. Carapiet, is living to-day in Julfa.

We also find that for teaching this fairly large number of boys, there were two masters only. A Mr. Charles Gillmore was the English teacher, and for his high attainments he was gratefully remembered and spoken of in terms of high praise by all the old boys whom we met in Calcutta, Rangoon and Java thirty years ago. The late Mr. Thaddeus Stephen, a born educationist and a strict disciplinarian, was the teacher in Armenian. And for teaching 46 boys, and they were taught very efficiently, they had in those days, *two* teachers, with perhaps a couple of pupil teachers whose names are not recorded, but for teaching 60 boys, they have now *ten* teachers in the College, the educational staff being composed of Armenians, Eurasians and Bengalees. Although the boys of

1872 and of the subsequent years were not taught Persian, French, Drawing and Boxing, yet they all distinguished themselves as eminent merchants, doctors, architects, Government servants, engineers, builders and contractors. Have the numerous boys who have left the College during the past 50 years, achieved success in the fields of commerce, industry, science, literature and the allied subjects? We regret to say hardly any.

The Press of the Academy was presented by Pogose Jordan, an eminent Armenian merchant of Calcutta in the first quarter of the 19th century. A large number of books, pamphlets and calendars were published in that Press during the Rectorship of Messrs. Johanness Avdall and Thaddeus Stephen, but like the "Araratian Library", it also disappeared after the late Mr. Thaddeus Stephen left the Academy in 1883.

With a view to revive Armenian printing in the venerable national institution, where in 1824 Father Chamchian's monumental work, the *History of Armenia*, known as *Khrakhchan* was re-printed, with great success, we presented, in 1930, a small hand-press to the College, with a good quantity of beautiful Armenian type, which we had imported from the type-foundry of the Mekhitharist Society at Vienna. Unfortunately thieves got into the cottage in the compound, set apart for the Press, and stole some of the type and with the remnants, the Armenian church notices of feasts and festivals are being printed periodically.

The College according to the last Annual Report for 1935, possesses the following assets in the form of landed properties and investments in Government of India Securities.

Premises Nos. 39, 39A & 40A, Free School Street and Nos. 4 & 4A, Kyd Street ...	Rs.	300,000
Investments at face value	,,	352,765

The investments represent the following Funds :—

Legacy of George Manook of Batavia ...	Rs.	32,500
Do. of Gavork* Manook	,,	44,300

* Gavork Manook is the same person as George Manook who by his will left, in 1820, a bequest of Sicca Rupees 30,000 for the Armenian Philanthropic Academy of Calcutta, and a similar sum for the Armenian

Legacy of Mrs. C. E. Lumbruggen of Negapatam	Rs.	18,600
Do. of Mrs. C. J. David of Bombay ...	,,	18,500
Do. of Phillippos Catchick of Calcutta ...	,,	2,765
Trust of John Michael & his wife Mary ...	,,	145,700
College Foundationers' Clothing Fund ...	,,	50,000
Armenian Dorcas Trust Fund under settlement of Miss H. B. Gregory	,,	37,900
A. Stephen's Scholarship Fund ...	,,	1,500
Mary G. Apcar Trust	,,	1,000

The income of the College for the year ending 31st December 1935, was as follows :—

	Rs.	As	P.
Armenian Church, Calcutta, School fees for church and T. M. Thaddeus Foundationers in the College	41,634	12	9
Armenian Education Trust, London ...	5,984	7	1
John Michael Trust	3,640	0	0
Seth Paul Foundation	832	3	0
College Foundationers' Clothing Fund ...	1,750	0	0
Dorcas Trust Fund for Clothing ...	1,326	8	0
John Michael Trust for Clothing ...	1,040	0	0
Interest on investments	4,362	14	0
Scholarship Fund (A. Stephen) ...	52	8	0
Do. (A. S. Mackertich) ...	500	0	0
Rent of garages and open land ...	3,681	0	0
Swimming Bath	195	0	0
Subscriptions for Annual picnic ...	1,205	8	0
Do. for Annual sports ...	575	3	6
Refund of Income Tax on investments ...	336	12	0
Centenary Fund	4	2	2
Total ...	67,084	14	6

School at Madras. The legacy of Rs. 44,300 shown above, is the amount that was transferred from Madras to the Armenian College, Calcutta, some twenty years ago, as stated in the foot note on p. 484.

The expenditure for the same period is as under :—

Establishment charges, such as teachers' salaries, servants' wages and monitors' allowance	24,608	8	0
General charges, such as boarding, clothing and boots, medicines, electricity, swimming Bath, picnic, sports, Municipal Taxes and interest on Loan to Armenian Church	38,013	5	4
	62,621	13	4
Excess of income over expenditure ...	4,463	1	2
Total ...	67,084	14	6

The College pays annually Rs. 5,385 as interest to the Armenian Church of Calcutta on a Loan, amounting to Rs. 107,700. The Loan, originally, was for Rs. 134,000, but a part payment of Rs. 26,300 has been made. The amount was borrowed for the purpose of purchasing a plot of land, on the south of the College, from Mr. J. C. Galstaun.

In conclusion, it may be mentioned that whereas the former Armenian teachers in the institution had a good knowledge of the English language, a highly necessary qualification, the latter day teachers, though highly-paid, have had a very poor knowledge of English, with the result that the boys in the institution, whose vernacular is Armenian, have been very backward in their English translations, and it is through the translations that the boys have to acquire a good knowledge of the English language. But how can the boys be expected to make any progress when one of the Armenian teachers has been heard to threaten a refractory boy by telling him, "I will told to the Principall, not to given to you one medall"! Poor English language, how it is massacred, and in a most ruthless manner, at the hands of idiots, who have the audacity to style themselves as *teachers* !

Shades of Kaloos, Avdall and Stephen ! ! !

CHAPTER XXXVIII.

MESROVB DAVID THALIADIAN.

POET, AUTHOR, JOURNALIST AND EDUCATIONIST.

During the last 400 years since Armenians have formed settlements at the commercial centres in India and founded churches, schools and printing presses, there has not been a scholar possessing the erudition, capacity, tenacity and high purpose like the immortal Mesrovb David Thaliadian, and as coming events cast their shadow forward, there is no likelihood of there being another scholar of his calibre to keep the torch of the ancient language burning in this country hereafter.

He was born unfortunately in an age when literary talents were not appreciated. Had he been born in this enlightened century, he would have earned international fame and reputation, as a poet and a versatile writer of great merit. For his liberal ideas, his consuming patriotism and his unbounded love for light and learning, he was persecuted by the children of darkness, the illiterate and bigoted clergy of his time, who despised light and preferred to live in darkness like the nocturnal mammal, with membranous wings, called a bat.

The Armenian Patriarch* of Constantinople, the spiritual and the temporal head of the Armenians in Turkey at that

---

* It was the narrow-minded, the bigoted and the intolerant Armenian Patriarch of Constantinople, Avietick by name, who in 1701, ruthlessly persecuted the immortal Mekhithar, the Founder of the famous Society which bears his name.

As every Armenian knows, the learned Mekhitharists at Venice and Vienna, have earned the everlasting gratitude of the Armenian nation, for their great zeal and devotion in the cause of the national literature during the past 236 years, for it was in the year 1701 that the "Society of Mekhithar" was founded at Constantinople, by Mekhithar an Armenian monk of blessed memory, with a few devoted disciples. Truly, out of evil cometh good, for through the relentless persecutions of the Armenian Patriarch of Constantinople the immortal Mekhithar, found an asylum and a safe haven at Venice, and through the equally relentless persecutions of another bigoted Patriarch, named James, the immortal time, actuated by a spirit of intolerance, had decided, with the connivance of the Russian ambassador at the Turkish capital, to send Thaliadian, who was a Russian subject, as an exile to Siberia. This was in 1839 when the American missionaries had just established themselves, at Constantinople and the Patriarch had strictly prohibited his flock to have no intercourse with them. Thaliadian, a stranger in a strange place, not aware of the interdict, had accepted employment with the American missionaries as a teacher. The Patriarch was informed that the great Armenian scholar, who was a deacon of the Church of Armenia, had become a Protestant. He was stealthily arrested by the orders of the Patriarch and thrown into a dark dungeon, the "Black Hole" of the Patriarchate where he was detained for the night until he was released by the intervention of kind friends who strongly advised him to leave the city. And but for the kindness of a humane English skipper, who at the request of an American missionary took him to Trebizond disguised, the future *littérateur* of the Armenians in India would have left his bones in the deserts of Siberia, unwept, unhonoured and unsung. Cyrus Hamlin, one of the pioneers of missionary enterprise in Turkey, and the Founder of the famous "Robert College" in Constantinople, has left a vivid account of the incident in his *Among the Turks*, published in London in 1878. His pen-portrait of Thaliadian, giving a correct delineation of the Armenian scholar, is particularly valuable, as there are no portraits of the poet in existence. Hamlin writes :

"After some weeks, a Greek friend, procured a Russian Armenian teacher. Having foreign protection, the Patriarch could not molest him. The teacher, Mr. Mesrobe Taliatine, was most cordially welcomed to our house and home. Rather over than medium size, his beard and eyes intensely black, each with a lustre peculiar to itself, with a quiet ease and grace

---

Thaliadian found a refuge at Calcutta. Both the refugers from Constantinople, as exotic plants, thrived on foreign soil, and bore good fruit.

We shall have occasion to refer to the learned and world-famous Mekhitharist Society again, in a subsequent chapter, as very little seems to be known about them amongst the Armenians in India.

about him and a knowledge "of men and things", not to be looked for, he was for a time a mystery. But his experience had already been a varied one. He had left his Russian home where his father* wished to train him for the priesthood, in order to join a wealthy Armenian relative† in Calcutta. There he had studied for six years in "Bishop's College, established, as he thought, by Bishop Heber, some of whose work, he had translated into Armenian.‡ Hearing in Calcutta of a hopeful movement of reform among his countrymen in Turkey, and his relative having died, he came to Constantinople§ to find the Patriarch and the bankers enemies and persecutors of reform.

His disappointment was very great and he was glad to find a position where he could do something to help forward

---

* This is not correct, for Thaliadian's father died when he was quite young. It was his mother, Zardar, who had her eldest son Mesrovb, admitted into the monastery of Etchmiadzin, the Vatican of Armenia, as a candidate for the priesthood, in fulfilment of a vow.

† This is not correct either, for Thaliadian, who was a native of Erivan in Armenia, had no wealthy relative in Calcutta. He came to Calcutta, in 1823 in quest of knowledge, trusting to Providence only, and he succeeded *par excellence.*

‡ Thaliadian whilst a student in "Bishop's College", Calcutta, translated into elegant classical Armenian verse, Bishop Heber's Prize-poem called *Palestine,* which was printed in the press of the College, with the English text, in 1830, with a very interesting Preface in English.

§ There is an anachnorism here, for Thaliadian did not go to Constantinople direct from Calcutta, after completing his education at "Bishop's College" in 1831. He first went to Erivan, his birthplace, and was engaged as a teacher in the school of the monastery at Etchmiadzin performing the duties of a secretary to the Catholicos' Synod at the same time. He was invited in 1834, by the Armenians of Julfa to go there as the Principal of the school founded by Messrs. Gregory and Seth Sam of Madras. He remained at Julfa till 1837, when owing to some disagreement with the illiterate Managers of the School he proceeded to Tabriz with his wife, who was an aunt of the present writer, Thangkhathoon by. name. At Tabriz, where he was the Principal of the Armenian School, he lost his wife on the 18th November 1837, aged 18 years. After the death of his wife, he went to his native country (Armenia) and being unable to obtain any employment there, he proceeded from thence to Constantinople with the intention of passing on to Europe, as the East, then groping in the dark, could not appreciate his worth, the incident in Constantinople being an eloquent proof of the bigotry of the ecclesiastics of the day.

the movement. Every day he was in our family, our esteem for him increased. We found him a truly refined and cultured Christian gentleman. He had resided for years in some of the best English families in Calcutta. We resolved never to part with him as an associate in our work. His soul kindled with enthusiasm at the thought of being engaged for life in teaching Armenian youth. It was his perfect ideal of a useful and happy life."

Hamlin then goes on to describe how the Russian ambassador in Constantinople at the instigation of the Armenian Patriarch, had ordered him to be seized and sent to Russia and thence to Siberia. An American missionary was providentially on the same ship which was to convey Thaliadian to Trebizond, where he would be received by the Russian bishop and sent to Russia. The missionary arranged with the English captain to land the doomed Armenian at Trebizond, disguised.

Bigotry, fanaticism, religious intolerance and rancour have done incalculable harm to the advancement of learning and science, the "Spanish Inquisition" being a striking example. Why was Galileo persecuted, imprisoned, and his book publicly burnt, because he asserted that the earth moves round the Sun and that the Sun is the centre of the world and not the earth which has a diurnal motion.

Born in 1803, he was a native of Erivan in Armenia, and died at Shiraz in Persia in June 1858. A marble mural tablet, erected in the Armenian church of that city by his devoted friend, the late Thaddeus Catchick Avetoom of Calcutta, bears an inscription in Armenian metrical verse, of which the following is a translation :—

"Here in this dark tomb rests MESROVB DAVID THALIADIAN, an erudite professor, a profound scholar, an eminent poet and an author of great merit. The entire society of Armenian *literati* shall always honour thee with enthusiasm, and neither New Julfa nor Calcutta will forget thee for ever. Died 10th June 1858."

From his youth upwards he had an ardent desire for knowledge, and early distinguished himself as an Armenian scholar. He left his native country and came to India *viâ*

Persia in 1823. Arriving at Calcutta he was soon admitted into Bishop's College as a foundationer by Bishop Heber, whose memory he reverenced throughout his life. The studious youth devoted his days and nights to the acquisition of knowledge, studying English, Latin, Greek and Persian, besides theology and the fine arts; these he mastered in five years, and, at the close of his successful scholastic career, the Board of Education certified him as a Master of Arts. His object in coming to India was to study the cultured languages of classical and modern times, with a view to impart to his countrymen the benefits of occidental education and learning. During the course of his studies at Bishop's College, he translated the learned treatise of Hugo Grotius, on the *Truth of the Christian Religion,* from Latin into classical Armenian. The Armenian translation of the treatise was submitted to the Publication Committee of that College, who unanimously decided to publish the work at their own press for the benefit of the Armenian nation.

Armenian type was cast, and the book was published in 1829, under the direct supervision of Thaliadian. He dedicated it to Messrs. Gregory and Seth Sam, two notable Armenian merchants of Madras. The Armenian community subscribed liberally to that now exceedingly rare publication, for which the late Colonel Jacob of Gwalior gave the handsome donation of Rs. 400. In 1830, he produced a metrical Armenian translation of *Palestine,* a prize-poem by Bishop Heber, whose life he embodied in a biographical sketch that he published as a preface to the translation by way of a tribute to the memory of his patron, who departed this life at Trichinopoly in April 1826. Shortly after, he published at the same press his third publication in the Armenian language on Mythology, which he dedicated to Sarkies Johanness Sarkies, an eminent Armenian merchant of Calcutta. Leaving Bishop's College in 1831, he directed his steps towards his native town in Armenia. After an eventful stay of about ten years in Armenia, Persia and Turkey, and having established several schools in various centres for the education of the Armenian youths, he returned to India in 1840, when he was welcomed at Bishop's College as an inmate, where he published in 1841 the *History of Ancient India* in the high-flown language of ancient Armenia. He dedicated the book to the late Arratoon Apcar, whose portrait formed the frontispiece. He was acquainted with many men of learning and distinguished oriental scholars in Calcutta, and had the good fortune to enjoy the friendship of the late Dr. R. O'Shaughnessy, M.D., Assistant Surgeon in the Bengal Army and Professor of Surgery and Medicine in the Medical College of Calcutta, to whom he dedicated in 1846 an Armenian work of great literary merit, *Annals of the Antiquities of Armenia,* "as a small token of esteem and gratitude by his most obliged servant, M. D. Thaliatin."

In 1845, through his strenuous exertions and with the hearty co-operation of the late Manook Zorab, Thaddeus Catchick Avetoom, and a few other Armenian gentlemen of Calcutta, the Araratian Society was formed for publishing books, &c., in the Armenian language. The Society had for its organ the *Patriot of Ararat,* an Armenian literary journal, ably edited and conducted by Mesrovb David Thaliadian. During the short space of two years (1845-1847), besides editing the journal, superitending the Press and the Seminary of St. Sanduct, that highly-gifted scholar published about ten original works, justly held in high repute, in the classical language of Armenia.

Mesrovb David Thaliadian amid his multifarious literary pursuits, started in 1846 the Armenian Infant Seminary, which he dedicated to the tutelar Saint, Sanduct—an Armenian princess who suffered martyrdom for her Christian faith in the forty-eighth year of the Christian era. This self-supporting school had a boys' as well as a girls' department, where Armenian and English were taught by a staff, superior to that of the Armenian Philanthropic Academy and inferior to no English schools existing in Calcutta in those days. The *Englishman,* in its issue of the 21st January 1850, made the following remarks :—

"THE ARMENIAN INFANT SEMINARY (*dedicated to their tutelar Saint Sanduct*).—The fourth annual examination of this little seminary, of not only boys, but of little girls, took place at the premises near the Armenian church on the 14th instant; and was actually attended by a larger assemblage of respectable ladies and gentlemen than was anticipated. The Armenian history, grammar, &c., was examined by the clergy of that nation, assisted by some lay gentlemen, and the English by the Revs. Messrs. Thompson and Sinclair. Both the boys and the girls acquitted themselves commendably. Their translations from English into Armenian have already appeared in the Armenian newspaper published at the same premises. Specimens of Armenian and English handwriting, arithmetic, as well as ornamental needlework and knittings were laid on the table. Even children of the indigent are taught here, although no donation or bequest is hitherto made to this little institution. After the examination, a short address was made, prizes awarded, and a merited benediction followed by the vicar of the Armenian church. At the close of it, an appropriate hymn was chanted by the children in their own language. As the Philanthropic Academy does not educate *girls,* had this little seminary not been projected by Mr. Mesrop David Taliatin, one of the previous students of the ever-to-be-lamented Bishop Heber's Scholarship (of blessed memory) at the Bishop's College here, assisted by his wife, and other Masters and Mistresses, the little girls of that nation would have remained neglected without their national education."

This seminary was closed after an existence of six years, having been insufficiently supported by the Armenian community, who were indifferent to the study of Armenian, and even pronounced it a *dead language*. It is noteworthy that, during its brief existence, many Armenians of both sexes,* received a sound education in Armenian and English at the feet of Thaliadian. To his efforts the revival of Armenian literature and nationalism in India is mainly due; for, through the medium of his journal, the *Patriot of Ararat,* he revived the dying embers of patriotism amongst the Armenians in this country.

---

* In 1889, when we came to Calcutta, the following ex-pupils of "Saint Sanduct School" were still living. Messrs. John S. Sarkies, Catchick Thaddeus Avetoom, Dr. S. J. Manook, Nicholas Gasper, Mrs. Helen Moses, Mrs. Seth, Mrs. Moss, Mrs. Mesrope Thaddeus and several others.

As has been stated, there are no portraits of Thaliadian in existence, as the art of protography was not known in Calcutta where he lived from 1839-1857 and he was too poor being a struggling author, to possess an oil painting. We are therefore publishing a facsimile of his autograph signature in Armenian, taken from one of his letters written to our revered father, his brother-in-law, in 1837.

If character, can be determined by handwriting, Thaliadian's independence of thought and sublime ideals can be read in the bold signature given below.

A born idealist, Thaliadian was all the days of his stormy life, a confirmed nationalist, a patriotic writer, the zealous standard bearer and the indefatigable champion of the glorious culture and *the nonpareil* literature of ancient Armenia. From his forceful and facile pen, honey and venom flowed alike. Fools were his theme and satire his song.* He castigated the wealthy who were indifferent to national sentiments and pilloried the pedants and the pedagogues for their love of filthy lucre. He paid glowing tributes to those who were imbued with patriotic feelings and exposed the dark deeds of those who, under the garb of piety, imposed upon the credulous. He ridiculed the illiteracy of the clergy and deplored the paucity of educational institutions owing to the apathy and callousness of those who had the power to bless.

* At a well-known Monastery in Armenia, he once saw, to his dismay, an Indian brass spittoon converted into an inkpot. His proud spirit rebelled against the utter bankruptcy of taste in a wealthy institution. He immediately took up a piece of paper and wrote a satire of four lines in classical Armenian verse which can be rendered into English thus: "When you saw in this place the spittoon converted into an inkpot, what hope of happiness there is for you, run away quickly Mesrovb Thaliadian."

CHAPTER XXXIX*

MASSY BABA JOHN

AN ARMENIAN PHILANTHROPIST

Contemporary with Agah Catchick Arakiel, there lived in Calcutta, in the last quarter of the 18th century, another notable Armenian merchant, named Massy Baba John, or Abdul Massy Martyrose, whose name is worthy of record for his philanthropy and patriotism. Not unlike many of his eminent countrymen, he belonged to the 'self-made' class of men. His birthplace was the historical city of Hamadan,† in Persia. Leaving his native town in early life, he came to India and settled permanently in Calcutta, where he was a respectable citizen and an eminent merchant. He became the happy possessor of a large fortune, of which more hereafter. His last will and testament was made out on the 30th day of May 1794, in the Armenian language, and an important codicil, under date the 1st day of April 1795, was added to it, true copies of which we have in our possession. That he was

---

* Chronologically, this chapter should have come immediately after Chapter XXXIV, but it makes no difference historically, as it appears in the section devoted to the "Armenians at Calcutta."

† Hamadan, a town of historical interest in Persia, lies in a low plain at the foot of Mount Elwand in Irak Ajemi on the high road from Bagdad to Teheran and Ispahan. On its site, or near it stood the far-famed Ecbatana, the ancient capital of Media, founded according to Herodotus by Deioces, who delivered the Medes from the yoke of the Assyrians and in 700 B.C. ascended the throne of Media. Ecbatana was the favourite residence of the Persian kings during the summer (Susa during the winter). It is said to have been destroyed by Nebuchadnezdar, king of Nineveh and Babylon, and rebuilt by Darius. Ecbatana is mentioned in the Bible in connection with the patriotic deeds of Esther, the Jewish Queen of the Persian king, Ahaserius (Artaxerxes). The revered shrines of Esther and Mordechai, which are in the custody of the Jews, can be seen to this day at the city of Hamadan, where there are many Jews. The Armenians settled there in the reign of the Great Shah Abbas, the Sefavi king of Persia.

animated by a noble spirit of piety, is evinced by the wording and tone of his will, which commences thus in the original Armenian :—

"Holiest Trinity and one Godhead, the Father, the Son and the Holy Ghost,—Preserve the undersigned Massy, son of Baba John, or otherwise known as Martyrose, who am an orthodox Christian by religion, an Armenian by birth, a native and citizen of Hamadan, a merchant by profession, and a resident of Calcutta under the Britannic Government. . . . "

He had brought his mother from his native town (Hamadan), and she had died and been buried at Calcutta before he made out his last will in 1794, in which he expresses a desire that, after his demise, his body should be interred in the Armenian churchyard of Calcutta, "next to my mother's grave."

Having no heirs, he left his fortune for the benefit of charitable and literary institutions. The clause, with reference to his property, reads :—

"I hereby divide my whole estate into sixteen equal parts and shares; eight parts of which I bequeath and give for the improvements of the Armenian city of New Nakhe Jevan* in the district of Azof, for the following institutions of that place, *viz*., two parts for the national schools, two parts for the orphanage, two parts for the hospital, and the remaining two parts for the benefit of the alms-house,—all which shall remain there in everlasting memory of me and for the remission of my sins and for the benefit of our nation; and out of the remaining eight parts, I bequeath six parts for the relief of

* New Nakhe Jevan, a town of European Russia, under the Government of Ekaterinoslav, is situated on the right bank of the river Don, two miles east of Rostov-on-the-Don. It has a population of 17,000, mostly Armenians, and was founded by the Armenian Archbishop of Russia, Joseph, of the princely house of Dolgorouky Argooteantz, in the reign of Catherine II., Empress of Russia, during the latter part of the eighteenth century. Soon after its foundation, an Armenian priest, a Rev. Stephen Arathoon was deputed by the founder to India to collect donations from the Armenians of this country in aid of that newly-formed Armenian colony. The mission was a success, and it was through the tact of this Armenian priest that the testator was pleased to leave such handsome bequests in aid of the charitable and literary institutions of that place.

civil prisoners in the Court of Requests' prison of Calcutta* and the remaining two parts I bequeath for the relief of poor and itinerant Armenians who may from time to time come to Calcutta from Armenia in search of their livelihood.†

He ratifies the above arrangements and terms in a subsequent clause, *viz.* :—

"My executors shall faithfully and honestly collect all the income accruing from my estate, and of the gross income they shall deduct their annual commission at the rate of five per cent. in December of each and succeeding year, and shall dispose of the nett income in January of each year in the following manner :

"They shall remit eight parts of the nett income to the Trustees in charge of the charitable and literary institutions in the Armenian city of New Nakhe Jevan as aforesaid. They shall also distribute two parts of the nett income amongst poor Armenians from Armenia in the same month of January. And they shall dispose of the remaining six parts of the nett income by relieving Christian civil prisoners in the Court of Requests' prison, paying off the debts of as many as the income in question will suffice, and liberate them during *Passion week;* but should there be no Christian civil prisoners in jail at any time, or there may be few in number, and the amount exceeds the demand, then I desire and enjoin that with the surplus or the whole amount, as the case may be, they shall pay off the debts and relieve Mahomedan and heathen [Hindu] civil prisoners, for *such* shall be my *heirs* after my demise."

The large estate which he left, consisting of landed property and Government securities, is in the hands of the

* The Court of Requests prison having ceased to exist, after the promulgation of the "Insolvent Debtors Act," the annual income from the Estate of the testator left for the relief of debtors, in the Court of Requests prison, was, by an order of the Calcutta High Court, transferred, some years ago, to the District Charitable Society, Calcutta, for the relief of the poor in that city.

† The two parts, or one-eighth of the annual income of the Estate, amounting to Rs. 1,050 and sometimes as much as Rs. 2,000, is paid by the Official Trustee of Bengal, to the wardens of the Armenian Church of Calcutta for the relief of itinerant Armenians who come to Calcutta from Armenia and other places.

Official Trustee of Bengal. The original executors and Trustees according to the Will, were Nierses Johanness, Dionysius Hyrapiet and one of the commissioners of the Court of Requests—the senior judge of that Court for the time being.

The Will is witnessed by Rev. Stephen Arathoon, (the priest from New Nakhe Jevan) Margar Johanness Baboom and Owenjohn Petrus, but in the codicil, which was executed a year after there are two different witnesses, Elias Minas and Moorad Elias.

In the codicil of the 1st April 1795, the testator, takes out of his estate "the newly constructed large two-storyed house adjoining the Armenian church," and bequeaths it entirely to the religious, charitable and educational institutions of New Nakhe Jevan. And it is sad to record that but for the jealousy and the animosity which existed between the then wardens of the Armenian church and the testator, to which there is a veiled allusion in the codicil, Massy Baba John would have left his entire estate to the Armenian church of Calcutta.

In 1861, the grateful Armenian of New Nakhe Jevan erected a memorial over his grave* in the Armenian churchyard, Calcutta, through their representative, Michael Nalbandeantz, a well-known national worker and an Armenian writer of great merit. At the same time, he realised, on their behalf, all the accumulated income from the estate of Massy Baba John, amounting to about Rs. 80,000, which was used to further their literary and charitable institutions, in accordance with the terms of the will, the provisions of which, as far as

---

* The inscription on the marble slab is to the following effect :—

"Sacred to the memory of the late respected patriotic Armenian, Massy Baba John, or, as he was otherwise called, Abdel Massy Martyrose. He bequeathed large legacies in his last will and testament for the intellectual culture of Armenian youths, for the relief of orphans and those imprisoned for debts, as well as for the support of distressed itinerant Armenians. This memorial is erected by the Armenian community of New Nakhe Jevan, in token of their everlasting thankfulness and gratitude.

'Here let me rest on Thee depend,
My God, my hope, my all.
Be Thou my everlasting friend,
And I can never fall.'

Died in Calcutta"

the above institutions were concerned, had up till then been disregarded by the executors. Another omission, an unpardonable one, was that they did not place a tombstone over Massy Baba John's grave, so that the exact date of his death is uncertain; in all probabilitiy it occurred in 1802, for the following reason:—In a valuable list, arranged chronologically from the year 1786 to 1820, which comprises all the donations given at various times by opulent Armenians for the benefit of the Calcutta Armenian church and the poor attached thereto, we find a sum of Rs. 1,300, the amount of the annual income allotted for the relief of poor and itinerant Armenians from Armenia from his estate first mentioned under date of the year 1803. It may therefore be fairly assumed that Massy Baba John had died in the previous year.

There is no record of his death in the "Register of Deaths" kept in the Armenian church of Calcutta, in which the place of burial, either in the churchyard or in the old Armenian cemetery in Collootollah Street, is invariably recorded. He could not have been buried in the churchyard although he had expressed a desire, in his will, to be buried *next* to his mother's grave. The grave in the churchyard, over which a marble slab, without the date of his demise, was placed by the Armenian Community of New Nakhe Jevan in 1861, may therefore be considered as purely problematical and not the last resting place of the great philanthropist. He evidently died "unwept, unhonoured and unsung", like many good men.

There is *no* trace of his mother's grave either in the churchyard, where she was buried, prior to 1794, as stated in the will.

CHAPTER XL

ARRATOON APCAR

An Eminent Armenian Merchant of Calcutta

Among the wealthy Armenian merchants of Calcutta in the last century, the name of Arratoon Apcar stands pre-eminent. He was the founder of the well-known firm of Apcar & Co., of this city. Born in 1779, at Julfa in Ispahan, he was the second son of Apcar, the ancestor of the family, unto whom were born six sons.* At the age of sixteen he found his way to Bombay, where he entered the service of an Armenian merchant named Alexander, with whom he found great favour. Being acquainted with the trade of China and Manilla, the energetic young man began with due circumspection to trade with those countries on his own account, after the merchant's demise. He settled and carried on his business for some time at Bombay† and in 1830, he removed to Calcutta.‡

Apart from being an eminent merchant, Arratoon Apcar possessed all the virtues and characteristics of an exemplary Christian during his useful life. He was a true patriot and a philanthropist. Of a charitable disposition, he was ever ready to help the poor and the needy. He was a true benefactor to those of his countrymen who were obliged, through adverse

---

* The other sons of Apcar, were; Satoor, Thaddeus, George, Gregory and Owenjohn. Their descendants, which are numerous, are to be found in Julfa, Calcutta, Rangoon, Java and England.

†We have in our possession an autograph letter written by Arratoon Apcar from Bombay, dated the 20th February 1915, to his uncle and our grand-father Mackertich Agazar Seth, at Julfa, Ispahan.

‡ The diary of Mesrovb David Thalidian, the Armenian poet, teacher and journalist of India, has the following, under date the 15th day of November 1830 :—

"Sunday to be kept holy; but as it is the custom with our (Armenian) community in India to go visiting on Sundays, so after visiting several of my friends, I went to pay my respects to Mr. Arratoon Apcar, who had just *transferred* his business from Bombay to Calcutta.

circumstances, to leave their homes in Julfa for India. His piety was of an exemplary character; he endowed the church of St. Mary, Julfa, where he had been christened, with munificent gifts, and also left it a handsome legacy, the annual income being remitted to the ministering priests attached to that church for saying prayers for the repose of his soul during service on Holy Thursday night, when prayers are said over the graves of the departed.

In 1843 he established the "Armenian Patriotic School" at Julfa, for the instruction of Armenian youths in their own and the Persian languages, which was more than now a desideratum, when there were no regular schools at Julfa. This school, which was maintained solely by Messrs. Apcar & Co., was about fifty years ago amalgamated with the "Central National Academy" of Julfa, to which institution, now known as the "Shah Abbas School," the annual grant is being remitted.

Arratoon Apcar died on 16th May 1863, aged 85 years. A marble tombstone, in the churchyard at Calcutta, bears the following inscription:—

"Sacred to the memory of ARRATOON APCAR, Esquire, the founder and up to the time of his death, for a period of 54 years, the senior member of the firm of Apcar & Co., of Calcutta. Born at Julfa, in Ispahan, A.D. 1779; departed this life in Calcutta on the 16th May, A.D. 1863. Aged 85 years. '*Requiescat in pace.*'"

He had four sons, *viz.*, Apcar, Seth,* Thomas ,and Alexander† and a daughter, named Sandookth. They were all born in Bombay between the years, 1814 and 1824. Sandookth died in Bombay on the 27th May 1815, aged eight months, and is buried in the old Armenian cemetery at

---

* Seth Apcar was the first Armenian Sheriff of Calcutta. He received from the Shah of Persia the Order of the Lion and the Sun (*Sheer-o-Khorshid*) through the Governor-General of India.

† Alexander Apcar, the father of the late Sir Apcar Alexander Apcar, was the Consul for Siam for many years. After his death, which occurred in 1895, the Siamese Government appointed his son, Sir Apcar Apcar, as their Consular representative in Calcutta.

Girgaum.* Of the four sons, Seth died in London and the others departed this life in Calcutta and were buried in the Armenian churchyard, where the Apcars, who have died in Calcutta during the past hundred years, whether males or females, have found a last resting place.

Gregory Apcar was a younger brother of Arratoon Apcar. He heard from his brother of his successful career, and came to India when quite a youth, in 1808, thirteen years after his brother's departure from home. He joined him while at Bombay, and was a member of the firm of Apcar & Co. until his death, in 1847, at the age of fifty-two. He was buried in the Armenian churchyard of Calcutta. On his marble tombstone the following lines are inscribed :

"Sacred to the memory of GREGORY APCAR, Esquire, an eminent Armenian merchant, highly and deservedly respected for his Christian and moral virtues. Born at Julfa, in Ispahan, A.D. 1795 ; and departed this life at Calcutta on the 23rd June, A.D. 1847. Aged 52 years."

He was succeeded by his son, Arratoon, the late Mr. A. G. Apcar, whose elder son, the late Mr. J. G. Apcar, known as "Father John," was for many years Clerk of the Crown and a Municipal Commissioner. In this connection, we are glad to record that the present Clerk of the Crown, Mr. Owen Moses, is also an Armenian. His father, the late Mr. Catchick Moses, was a popular Pleader of the Calcutta Police Court for many years.

Of the descendants of Gregory Apcar, very few are living in Calcutta to-day. Mr. Walter Gregory, one of the senior advocates of the Calcutta High Court, (being enrolled as far back as 1889) is a grandson of Gregory Apcar, being

* In January 1895, when we first visited the old Armenian cemetery in Bombay, we found the tombstone covering the mortal remains of Sandookth, a millionaire's only daughter, in a dilapidated state and the old tombstone broken in several parts. On our return to Calcutta, we reported the matter to the late Mr. A. G. Apcar, who had a white marble slab immediately made, with an inscription, and despatched to Bombay, to be placed over the grave of his cousin. In 1902, when, at the request of Mr. Apcar, we revisited the old cemetery, we found that the slab had reached its destination safely and was firmly fixed over the grave.

one of the sons of his daughter, Elizabeth, who died at Darjeeling on 4th April 1897 and her body was brought down and buried in the Armenian churchyard at Calcutta. Miss Amy Apcar of No. 44 Chowringhee Road, Calcutta, referred to on pp. 468-69, a highly accomplished lady, is a grand daughter of Gregory Apcar. She has inherited the piety, the benevolence, the nobility and the urbanity of her revered father, the late Mr. A. G. Apcar, whose charities to national institutions, religious, charitable and educational, are without parallel and deserve to be recorded in letters of gold. For his numerous benefactions, his name is inscribed on the Roll of the Immortals.

The late Mr. Thomas Malcolm a storehouse of information, who died an octagenarian in 1918, related to us in 1889, the circumstances which urged young Arratoon Apcar to leave his home, and come to India, in 1795. Relating his youthful reminiscences to Mr. Thomas Malcolm, who was an assistant in his office, Mr. Arratoon Apcar told him that he left Julfa, in sheer disgust, after witnessing the tortures and the indignities which his venerable uncle, Mackertich Agazar Seth,* the collector† of Julfa, was subjected to by the inhuman Persian Revenue officers, who after beating the old man mercilessly, filled his cup of misery by nailing the lobe of one of his ears to a wooden post in the public square, known as "Maidan,"

---

* He was the great-grandfather of the present writer, as stated on pp. 250 and 252.

† In those days and for many years after, the Governor of Ispahan, appointed one of the leading Armenians of Julfa to act as *Khalanthar* or *Khadkhoda* (Mayor) of the place, without any remuneration however, and it was the duty of the Mayor to collect the taxes and pay the same annually to the much dreaded Revenue collectors when they made their appearance.

God alone knows the sufferings of the peaceful and the law-abiding Armenians of Julfa during the 18th century at the hands of the fanatical and rapacious Persians, but thanks to the bull-dog tenacity of the race, they have survived the blood-curdling persecutions, although thousands, nay tens of thousands, have been compelled to seek safety in flight, to the hospitable shores of India. What a contrast to the present enlightened regime of Reza Shah Pehlevi which has brought peace and prosperity to the historic land where in the dim and distant past, mighty monarchs, like Cyrus, Artaxerxes, Jamshid, Ardeshir Babekan, Nooshirwan the Just held indisputable sway and dispensed justice.

in order to extort money from him, but where was the harassed collector to gather taxes from when all the well-to-do Armenian inhabitants of Julfa, had, through incessant persecutions, fled to Russia, Basra and India.

The late Rev. Johanness Catchick, for 50 years the vicar of the Armenian church of Calcutta, who died a nonagenarian in June 1897, in full possession of his faculties, told us in 1890, that he remembered having seen in his younger days, the respected head of the Armenians of Julfa going about with a handkerchief to his nose always, as the Revenue officers, those monsters in human form, had in their savagery and brutality, smashed his nasal bone, with the result that there was a continuous flow of matter from the nose.

The immortal poet, Mesrovb David Thaliadian, who had married one of the granddaughters of Mackertich Agazar Seth, in a beautiful elegy, composed in classical Armenian, after the death of his wife in 1837, pays a high tribute to the memory of the great patriot whose self-sacrifice and unbounded devotion had saved Julfa from the inordinate exactions of the extortionists, who finding that no taxes were forthcoming, despite the tortures they had inflicted on the collector, left him alone and did not demand the usual taxes for some years being fully convinced that the impoverished inhabitants of Julfa were not in a position to pay the annual taxes.

The much persecuted and sorely harassed collector died in his sleep, in 1822, at the ripe old age of ninety, and his grateful compatriots paid him the highest respect they possibly could by burying him, in a very prominent place in the church of St. Mary in the parish of Maidan, where he had worshipped all the days of his stormy life, and on the tombstone which they placed over his hallowed grave, they inscribed the words, "bazmavastak Kathkhodah Mackertich, son of Agazar," which means, "the laborious Kathkhodah (Mayor) Mackertich Agazar." Literally, the Armenian compound word "bazmavastak," means one who labours much. (See p. 252 for the place of his grave.)

Contemporary with Mr. Arratoon Apcar, there lived in Calcutta, a very pious and a highly charitable Armenian, named Agah Owen John Elias, the son of Agah Elias Minas, an eminent merchant and a big *Zemindar* (land owner) of Saidabad in the second-half of the 18th century. Though descended from a family of distinction, his outward bearing was meek and humble. His piety was without ostentation, and his charity knew no bounds; in the words of the poet, he "did good by stealth and blushed to find it fame." A mural tablet inside the Armenian church of Calcutta, has the following inscription, testifying to his genuine worth. It is as follows:

"Sacred to the memory of the late OWEN JOHN ELIAS, Esquire, born 1st November 1786, died 12th March 1860. This, tablet is erected by the Armenian community of this place as a mark of their appreciation of his private and public virtues. His charities to widows and orphans and the poor will not remain unrewarded in heaven. His gifts to Churches, Schools, Asylums and Hospitals, which have made his name to be generally respected, have specially endeared it to his own countrymen."

He was buried, as a mark of great respect, under the belfry on the extreme south, next to the grave of his only son, Joakim, who had died on the 10th September, 1834, aged 15 years, 9 months and 9 days.

It may be mentioned here that after the sad and the untimely death of his only son, the bereaved and disconsolate father, Agah Owen John Elias, distributed a sum of Rupees two hundred thousand to the poor and gave, at the same time, handsome dowries to Armenian orphans and indigent girls as a peace offering for the repose of his son's soul.

There is a long white marble tombstone, with bilingual inscriptions, placed over the grave of Agah Owen John Elias, enumerating his manifold virtues.

The English epitaph is as follows:

"Sacred to the memory of Owen John Elias Esqre., who was born at Sydabad in Bengal on the 1st November 1786 and departed this life on the 12th March 1860, aged 73 years, 4 months and 11 days.

Though descended of an ancient and noble family blessed with opulence, he was poor in spirit and disdained the praise of men and all earthly grandeur, kind, meek and affable in his manners, his soul glowed with the love of his dear Redeemer, and with a longing of his heavenly kingdom. His charities to the orphan, the widow and his gifts to charitable, benevolent and scholastic institutions* knew no bounds. His Christian and moral virtues shall ever endear his memory to his relatives, to his friends and to all his acquaintances."

"Blessed are the poor in spirit, for their's is the kingdom of Heaven". (Mathew V. 3).

In the Armenian inscription, he is called "the bright mirror of piety", and so he was without the least exaggeration. Close to his grave, just near the belfry on the south, his parents are buried side by side. His father, Agah Elias, son of Agah Minas, of the family of Khojah Minas, died on the 16th July, 1825, aged 82 years. His mother Mamar, who was the daughter of Owen John Thomas of the family of Abliath, died on the 10th Ovdan (5th February) 1819, aged 73 years. Agah Owen John's first wife, Mariamjan, died at Benares on the 5th September 1825, aged 29 years and 5 months. She was buried in the English cemetery by Rev. Thomas Morrison. His second wife, Varvar, the daughter of Elias Avdall of Calcutta, died in London some fifty years ago. They had two daughters, one of whom had married Gregory Paul Melitus of Madras, and the other was the wife of Simon Bagram of Calcutta. Both died in London where they had settled with their children. Sir Paul G. Melitus, C.I.E., late of the Indian Civil Service, now living in London, is a grandson of Agah Owen John Elias.

* As can be seen on page 484 Agah Owen John Elias and his father Agah Elias Minas gave donations amounting to Rs. 38,920 to the Armenian Philanthropic Academy from the foundation in 1821 to 1848.

CHAPTER XLI.

ARMENIANS AND THE LEGAL PROFESSION.

About the middle of the last century we find the Armenians in India adopting the legal profession. The late Hon'ble Sir Gregory Charles Paul, K.C.I.E., the learned Advocate-General, who was also a member of the Bengal Legislative Council, was an Armenian. His father, Mr. Peter Jacob Paul, was a prominent member of the Armenian community of Calcutta, by whom he was highly and deservedly respected. He rendered valuable services to the Armenian Church, in his private capacity, as a legal adviser.* up to his death in 1862. His talented son, the learned Advocate-General, was first educated at La Martinière College, Calcutta, where he won the gold medal; and, in 1846, he proceeded to England to complete his education. In due course he graduated at Cambridge, and was called to the bar. He returned to Calcutta in 1855, and commenced practising in what was then the Supreme Court, now known as the High Court. By dint of perseverance, and being gifted with abilities of a high order and commanding an easy flow of language, he rose to his high position.

He died, full of years and honours, on the 1st January, 1900.

The late Mr. M. P. Gasper was one of the leaders of the Calcutta bar during the last quarter of the nineteenth century, having been enrolled in 1872. He was a respected member of the Armenian community of Calcutta, and they paid a tribute to his memory, by erecting a marble mural tablet

---

* On a black marble tablet fixed on the east wall of the belfry in the Armenian church of Calcutta, the following lines are inscribed :—"In memoriam of P. J. Paul Esquire who served the Armenian church gratis for 26 years, as a legal adviser." His grave is in the Armenian churchyard of Calcutta. He died on the 29th September 1862, aged 58 years.

in the Armenian church under the belfry, which bears the following inscription :—

"Sacred to the memory of Malcolm Peter Gasper, Esq. (Barrister-at-Law), eldest son of Peter Malcolm and Madeline Gasper; born at Calcutta 15th June 1848, died at sea off Aden, 3rd August 1890, aged 42 years 1 month and 19 days; who, after taking the medal at the Doveton College, Calcutta, in the year 1863, completed his education in England, where he was the first Armenian student who appeared and successfully competed for the Indian Civil Service Examination in the year 1869; but, his health failing him, he soon after qualified for the bar and came out to India in the year 1872. By his own exertions he attained a prominent position among the leading members of the local bar, in which he distinguished himself by his exceptional talents. The untimely loss of one whose future was so bright and promising has been deeply mourned by a large circle of friends and admirers, who, being members of the Armenian community, have erected this tablet to his memory."

During the second-half of the last century, the following Armenians were enrolled as advocates of the Calcutta High Court, from 1855 to 1893 :—

Inn.	Names.	Year of admission.
L.	Hon'ble Sir Gregory Charles Paul, B.A., K.C.I.E.	1855
I.	J. H. W. Arratoon, B.A.	1864
I.	Gasper Gregory	1868
I.	G. J. Pogose	1869
I.	Aviet Agabeg	1869
I.	Thomas Alexander Apcar	1870
L.	Malcolm Peter Gasper •	1872
L.	Arrakiel Peter Gasper	1872
L.	J. G. Apcar	1874
I.	John A. Apcar	1875
I.	A. Arathoon	1875
I.	A. A. Shircore	1875
I.	St. John Stephen, B.A., LL.B.	1880
I.	J. N. Pogose	1882

Inn.	Names.	Year of Admission.
I.	A. E. Gasper	... 1882
I.	A. T. Apcar, M.A., LL.B. ...	... 1883
M.	A. A. Avetoom	... 1885
I.	Osmond J. Bagram ...	... 1887
M.	M. Zorab	... 1889
I.	Walter Gasper Gregory ...	... 1889
M.	John George Bagram ...	... 1890
I.	G. I. M. Gregory ...	... 1890
I.	C. A. O. T. Gregory ...	... 1891
G.I.	J. Ernest Bagram	... 1893
M.	John Chater Jordan ...	... 1893

The only Armenian, who practised, as a pleader, in the Appellate Side of the Calcutta High Court, was the late Mr. Chater Gregory. He was enrolled in June, 1860. For the origin of his family, see page 414. The following Armenians were enrolled as attorneys and solicitors of the Calcutta High Court, between the years 1856 and 1891.

J. R. Shircore (1856), Martin Camell (1866), L. J. Arathoon (1870), Galstaun Gregory (1870), E. O. Moses (1870),* John Camell (1875), J. A. Apcar (1889); Owen Camell (1891).

Besides these, there were a few pleaders practising in the Police and Small Cause Courts in Calcutta and elsewhere in India.

The Medical Profession, too, had allured some Armenians during the second-half of the last century. There were six Armenians in the Indian Medical Service, (I.M.S.), in the last decade of the 19th century, as below :—

1. Surgeon-Major S. T. Avetoom.
2. Surg. Lieut.-Col. J. M. Zorab.
3. Dr. S. J. Manook, M.R.C.S.
4. Surgeon-Capt. C. J. Sarkies, M.B.

* The late Mr. Elijah Owen Moses, was the father of Lieut.-Colonel O. St. John Moses, I.M.S. (retired) now living in England, and of Mr. G. C. Moses, a well-known solicitor and attorney of the Calcutta High Court and Consul for Portugal.

5. Surgeon-Major S. C. Sarkies.
6. Surgeon-Captain J. G. Jordan.

The first Armenian who joined the Indian Medical Service as far back as 1852, was Dr. J. M. Joseph, M.D., who rose to the rank of Deputy Surgeon-General. (See pp. 299-301.)

In the good old days, the enterprising Armenians, whose love for commerce is proverbial, were solely engaged in commercial pursuits in India. Being first in the field, they had the running entirely to themselves. They have, generally speaking, been ousted from their position as eminent merchants; yet have not shared the fate of their brother-traders, the Dutch, the Danes, and the French. They are now following various avocations in rivalry with Europeans in this country, and their probity has gained for them a world-wide reputation. At Calcutta there are still a few Armenian mercantile houses, and in the following professions and trades they are represented in Calcutta as doctors, barristers, solicitors, authors, school masters, lady teachers, dentists, veterinary surgeons, brokers, house and estate agents, underwriters, chemists and druggists, builders and contractors, cabinet makers, hotel and boarding-house keepers, bakers and confectioners, electricians, mechanics and motor engineers,—all necessary in a civilized community.

Of all places in India, Calcutta contains by far the largest number of influential and well-to-do Armenians. Here they have a church, a college, a day-school for boys and girls, an almshouse, and a club of their own. The Armenians in Calcutta now number about one thousand souls. At other places in India their numbers are but small. In conclusion, it is a noteworthy fact that the early Armenian settlers in India were very conservative in their social habits, and were everywhere recognised by their national costumes; and their ardent love for their Church and national literature have ever been prominent features in their private character. They devoutly performed the various religious rites and ceremonies enjoined by their Church, and instilled into their offspring its dogmas and doctrines. With a praiseworthy zeal they cultivated their national literature, and stimulated its advancement by founding and endowing educational establishments. They were exclusive in their habits. Though engaging freely with their European *confreres* in trade, they did not mix with them socially, and rarely married outside their own nationality. Thereby they preserved their nationalism for many generations; but Time, which brings about wonders, has worked many changes. The national costume has been discarded, except by their clergy; the Armenian language has been almost neglected; and European customs have been generally adopted by the twentieth-century Armenians.

The result of these, changes has been that several Armenians have intermarried with Europeans and Eurasians, and have forsaken their Church for the creed of their wives. But the Armenian community still remains distinct and also somewhat exclusive. It is not likely that they will share the fate of their countrymen at Amsterdam,* Leghorn,† Venice,‡

* Amsterdam at one time contained an influential Armenian colony, and it was here in 1666 that the *first* Armenian Bible was printed by the zealous Woskan, a learned Armenian monk of Etchmiadtzin and a native of Erivan in Armenia. According to the printer's notice, it was published by the hearty co-operation and at the sole expense of Messrs. Stephen, Theodore, and Petrus, three notable Armenian merchants of Julfa, whom he had met at Leghorn on his way to Amsterdam. The printing commenced on 11th March 1666, and was completed on 13th October 1668, the type used in the printing of that and subsequent works having been prepared by the printer's brother, Avetis, who was then an eminent merchant at Amsterdam. This now exceedingly rare Bible is profusely illustrated with fine wood and steel engravings by Dutch artists.

† The Armenian colonists at Leghorn, who were mostly from Julfa and India, were solely engaged in commerce. An Armenian press was also started at Leghorn in 1643 by an Armenian monk named Johanness, a native of Julfa in Ispahan. The first publication issued from it was the Book of Psalms. Other books were subsequently published at that press.

‡ Venice, the Venetik of the Armenians, has played a very prominent part in the history of Armenian literature. The *first* Armenian publication —the Book of Psalms—saw the light there in 1565. It was printed in octavo size by Abgar, surnamed 'the Scribe,' a learned Armenian from Tocat in Armenia. He was a descendant of the former Armenian kings and visited Rome, accompanied by his son, Soolthanshah. From thence they passed to Venice, at that time one of the greatest commercial marts in Europe. There the opulent Armenian merchants, who were chiefly from old Julfa on the Araxes in Armenia, appreciated and encouraged his labours in the cause of the advancement of the national literature.

and at other commercial centres in Europe, where practically they have been absorbed among the people of those countries.

The present Armenian community of Calcutta may be divided into three classes. We give their origin in a chronological order. First, there are those whose ancestors settled in Calcutta during the 18th & 19th centuries. They are called the "Calcutta Armenians", most of whom have had the benefits of English education and there are amongst them, at the present moment, a doctor, a civilian, a solicitor, a foreign Consul, a clerk of the Crown and three barristers and a couple of share and stock brokers. Then come those from Julfa, a fairly large number, who have settled in Calcutta during the past sixty years and are engaged mostly in trade and commerce. They are known as "Julfa Armenians", the present writer being a humble member of that class.

The emigrants who during the past thirty years have come from the Armenian villages of Charmahal in Persia, come next. They are an industrious and a plodding lot, clannish and ambitious, 90 per cent. of the boys in the Armenian College, belong to that class. They are called "Charmahalis."

CHAPTER XLII.

ARMENIANS AND THE NEW CONSTITUTION IN INDIA.

The Armenians of Calcutta, an old minority community that have been socially and commercially connected with the city since its foundation in 1690, being anxious to have their status defined under the New Constitution of India, convened a general meeting for the purpose at the "Davidian School Hall", on the 26th January 1933, under the Presidency of Mr. J. C. Galstaun, O.B.E. After some discussion, it was resolved to send a Memorial to His Excellency the Viceroy, setting forth the past services rendered by the Armenians to the British in this country. A committee, consisting of five members, was appointed to draw up the Memorial. After several meetings, the committee drafted the Memorial which was placed before the community at a general meeting, held at the same place, on the 18th February, 1934. The Memorial met with the warm approval of the community, and it was drawn up and forwarded to His Excellecy the Viceroy, on the 24th March 1934, under the signatures of the members of the committee. The Memorial, which was a document of historical importance, was as follows :—

His Excellency the Right Hon'ble The Earl of Willingdon,
G.C.M.G., G.C.S.I., G.C.I.E., ETC., ETC.
Viceroy & Governor General of India in Council.
New Delhi.

YOUR EXCELLENCY,

1. Your Memorialists beg most respectfully to state that at a General Meeting of the Armenian community of Calcutta held at "Davidian Hall'* on the 26th day of

* "Davidian Hall", an ideal place for holding public meetings and social functions, is in the huge two-storeyed building, known as "Davidian Day School", situated at No. 1, Ashutosh Mookerjee Road, Bhowanipore. The school was founded by the late Mr. D. A. David, some fifteen years

January, 1933, to discuss the future status of the Armenians in India under the new Constitution, a committee was appointed composed of Messrs. J. Camell, G. C. Moses, G. A. Arratoon, N. P. Hacobian and M. J. Seth, to approach your Excellency with the humble request that the status of the Armenians domiciled in British India be defined.

2. Your Memorialists beg to state that the Armenians have been trading with India from very early times and have since the middle of the 16th Century founded colonies in this country, notably at Agra, Delhi, Surat, Bombay, Calcutta, Dacca, Chinsurah, Saidabad and Madras and that when the Honourable East India Company founded commercial settlements in India in the early part of the 17th Century, they found that the Armenians were firmly established at all the important trading centres in the country and with a view to securing their co-operation, as associates in trade, for the furtherance of their commercial pursuits, they entered into an Agreement with them and an important Charter was granted to the Armenians on the 22nd day of June in the year 1688, signed, sealed and delivered in London, in which it is specially stated "that the Armenian nation shall now and at all times hereafter, have equal share and benefit of all indulgences this

---

ago, for imparting free education to poor Armenian girls and little boys, in the Armenian and the English languages. The educational staff is composed entirely of Armenian lady teachers. Free lunch is provided daily for the pupils attending the school whom the school omnibus fetches in the mornings and takes to their homes in the evenings. This philanthropic institution, which supplies a long-felt want, will remain, for ages to be, a glorious and an everlasting monument to the revered memory of that great national benefactor and patron of learning, who left all he died possessed of, for the benefit of education, a blessing he had been sadly deprived of in his younger days, when he first came to Calcutta, in 1875, as a lad of seventeen, as in those days, the Armenian church of Calcutta did not educate poor boys so freely and in such large numbers as it does to-day with very poor results however.

Born at Julfa (Ispahan) on the 17th October 1858, he departed this life in Calcutta on the 7th February, 1936 and was buried in the Armenian churchyard. He lived respected and died regretted.

It may not be out of place to mention here that in response to an urgent appeal from the Armenian National School authorities at Teheran, three years ago, the late Mr. David gave a donation of Rupees fifty thousand to that school for alterations and additional buildings. The

Company have or shall at any time hereafter grant to any of their own Adventurers or other English Merchants whatsoever".

3. *Secondly* :—"That they shall have free liberty at all times hereafter to pass and repass to and from India in any of the Company's ships on as advantageous terms as any freeman whatsoever.

4. *Thirdly* :—"That they shall have liberty to live in any of the Company's cities, garrisons or towns in India and to buy, sell and purchase land and houses and be capable of all Civil Offices and preferments in the same manner as if they were Englishmen born and shall always have the free and undisturbed liberty of the exercise of their own religion. And we hereby declare that we will not continue any Governor in our service that shall in any kind disturb or discountenance them in the full enjoyment of all the privileges hereby granted to them, neither shall they pay any other or greater duty in India than the Company's factors, or any other Englishman born, do or ought to do."

5. *Fourthly* :—"That they may voyage from any of the Company's garrisons to any ports or places in India, the South Seas, China or the Manillas, in any of the Company's ships, or any permissive free ships allowed by the Company and may have liberty to trade with China, the Manillas or any other ports or places within the limits of the Company's Charter upon equal terms, duties and freights with any free Englishman whatsoever."

6. In a second Agreement or Charter bearing the same date as the above, the Honourable East India Company stipulated "that whenever forty or more of the Armenian nation shall become inhabitants of any of the garrisons, cities or towns belonging to the Company in the East Indies, the said Armenians shall not only have and enjoy the free use and exercise of their religion, but there shall also be allotted to them a parcel of ground to erect a church thereon for the

---

Teheran school, is, alas! no more, as it has been closed down and the big house is now being used as a place of divine worship. Alas for the vicissitudes of Time and the irony of Fate!"

worship and service of God in their own way. And that we will also at our own charge, cause a convenient church to be built of timber which afterwards the said Armenians may alter and build with stone and other solid material to their own good liking. And the said Governor and Company will also allow fifty pounds per annum, during the space of seven years, for the maintenance of such priest or minister as they shall choose to officiate therein".

7. These Charters were granted to the Armenians in India, through their representative, the illustrious Khojah Phanoos Kalandar a "merchant of eminency and the head of the Armenians in India" as stated by the Company. The originals of the Charters or Agreements are kept in the archives of the "India House" in London and certified copies of the same were published, *in extenso,* by Mr. M. J. Seth, in a Paper read by him before the "Indian Historical Records Commission" at Lahore, in November, 1925, on the "Armenians and the East India Company" and which was subsequently printed in the "Proceedings" of the Commission for 1925 bearing the imprimatur of the Government of India.

8. Your Memorialists, as members of a minority community beg to gratefully admit that under British rule in India they have always enjoyed perfect freedom and have had the free and untramelled exercise of their religion at all times. They have at the same time held appointments under Government in the Civil and Military services and have been loyal citizens of the British India Empire since the inauguration of British rule in India.

9. It was an Armenian merchant of Bengal, Israel Sarhad, who in July, 1698, acquired letters-patent from the Mogul Emperor allowing the English to purchase from the existing holders the right of renting the three villages of Calcutta, Sutanati and Govindpore for the sum of sixteen thousand rupees, as recorded in the "Chutanutte Diary and Consulations" for 22nd September, 1698.

10. It was the same Armenian who in 1715 accompanied the epoch-making "Surman Embassy" to Delhi and obtained from the Mogul Emperor Farrukh Siyar, the "Grand Farman" for the English which laid the foundations of British rule in India.

11. It was an Armenian again, Petrus Arathoon, who was employed as a confidential agent by Clive to negotiate with the Nawab Mir Jaffir for the overthrow of the Nawab Suraj-ud-doulah, the author of the "Black Hole" tragedy of 1756. It was the same Petrus Arathoon, whom Clive calls the "Armenian Petrus", who at the risk of his life, saved Mr. Watts falling into the hands of the infuriated Nawab Suraj-ud-doulah.

12. It was this Armenian again who at the risk of his life supplied the British fugitives at Fulta, after the sack of Calcutta, with boatloads of provisions, secretly, for a period of six months before the Army of Retribution arrived from Madras on the 20th December, 1756, under Admiral Watson and Colonel Clive.

13. Your Memorialists do not wish to encroach upon your valuable time by enumerating all the services rendered to the British cause in India by the Armenians since the advent of the British into this country in the early part of the 17th Century. They would however crave your indulgence to cite a few outstanding cases. An Armenian Military Officer of the loyal Gwalior Army, Major Owen Jacob, who was commanding the Agra troops against the mutinous Neemuch Brigade near Agra, lost his life on the 6th July, 1857, whilst another Armenian, an eminent merchant of Calcutta, Moses Arakiel, raised a Company of one hundred of his countrymen for the Calcutta Militia when the greater part of the Army of the Presidency was required to act at a distance against Tippoo Sultan of Mysore. The merchant Captain-Commandant of the Armenian Company of volunteers in Calcutta was honoured by the Governor General the Most Noble Marquis Wellesley, for his valuable services, with a sword of honour.

14. In view of the privileges granted by the Honourable East India Company in 1688 to the Armenians in India, and which have never been revoked by the Government or the Crown and in consideration of the services rendered by the Armenians in this country during the past three hundred years, Your Memorialists pray that their future status, as a minority community in India, be favourably considered in the new Constitution for the future Government of India where the

Armenians have large vested interests as loyal citizens of this great Empire.

15. They are anxious for the protection and future security of their churches, educational and charitable foundations and trusts and their vested interests in landed properties and commerce.

16. As a small minority, your Memorialists do not ask for separate communal representation but they humbly pray that all the rights and privileges conferred on the Armenian communities domiciled in India by the Charter above mentioned be confirmed and embodied in the new Constitution for the future Government of India and their special status defined in any way deemed appropriate by Your Excellency.

And Your Memorialists will ever pray.

Dated at Calcutta this the 24th day of March, 1934.

(Sd.) J. CAMELL,
,, G. C. MOSES,
,, G. A. ARRATOON,
,, N. P. HACOBIAN,
,, MESROVB J. SETH.

The Private Secretary to His Excellency the Viceroy, sent the following reply :—

OFFICE OF THE PRIVATE SECRETARY TO HIS EXCELLENCY THE VICEROY.

No. 4783 G.M.

THE VICEROY'S HOUSE,
NEW DELHI.
The 13th April, 1934.

From

THE PRIVATE SECRETARY TO H. E. THE VICEROY.

To

J. CAMELL, ESQUIRE,
Calcutta.

SIR,

I am desired to acknowledge the receipt of the memorial dated the 24th March, 1934, addressed to His Excellency the

Viceroy on behalf of the Armenian community in India over the signatures of yourself and four others.

2. Since the memorial is presumed to be submitted on behalf only of those Armenians who are British subjects, no special definition of the status of the Armenian community is required as that community will enjoy the same privileges as other subjects of His Majesty.

I have the honour to be,
Sir,
Your most obedient servant,
(Sig.),
Private Secretary to the Viceroy.

As one deeply interested in the Memorial, having been closely associated with it from its inception, we were greatly disappointed with the reply, as the Memorial, the objects of which were clearly defined, was not submitted "on behalf only of those Armenians who are British subjects", but on behalf of *all* the Armenians residing in India, whether British subjects or subjects of foreign countries. As a matter of fact, Armenians born in India are, by right of birth, British subjects, and they can therefore have no misgivings as regards their future status in the New India. What we are concerned about is the future status of those Armenians who are domiciled in India, but are not subjects of His Majesty. Are these Armenians, and their number is legion, to be classed differently from their more fortunate brethren? In this connection it may be mentioned that there are a number of Armenians working on the Indian Railways who are most arbitrarily classed with the Eurasians, or as they are now called, Anglo-Indians, with the result that whereas the European employees of the Railways get two months sick leave in the year, with full pay, the Armenian employees are allowed full pay for fifteen days only when they go on sick leave. Why this injustice?

Are the Armenians in any way inferior to the Europeans in purity of blood, colour, physique, intelligence, religion, loyalty, integrity, capability, social habits and mode of living? We think not.

That the Armenians are of European origin can be seen from the following extract taken from an article which appeared in the *Statesman* on the 11th December 1927, under the caption "Armenians in America".

"The testimony of the world's greatest historians, philologists and anthropologists has proved beyond any question of doubt, that the Armenians belong to the Aryan race, which is divided into three main branches.

1. The Nordic.
2. The Alpine.
3. The Mediterranean.

Armenians belong to the Denarian family of the Alpine branch. The original home of the Alpine branch of the Aryan race is Central Europe.

Just as the whiteman supplanted the Indians in America, so the Armenians, centuries before the Christian era, migrated from Europe into Asia Minor in search of better location, and established themselves in and around the region of Mount Ararat where they built the Kingdom of Ararat. The Armenian language, too, in the opinion of world-famous philologists, is Indo-European in origin. It belongs to the Germanic group of Indo-European languages."

In view of the above irrefutable facts, *all* the Armenians, irrespective of their country of origin or place of birth, should be classed with the Europeans under the New Constitution. As a small minority community, the Armenians in India have no separate communal representation, but they have great confidence in British sense of justice and fair play and feel certain that all the rights and privileges conferred on the Armenians domiciled in India by the Charter or Agreement of 1688, will be confirmed. If they are grouped with any community other than the European community, their interests may not be adequately represented. They are anxious for the protection of their churches, educational and charitable foundations and trusts and their vested interests in landed properties and commerce.

With a view to ascertain, through the medium of the public press, the status of the Armenians in the New India, we inserted a query in the *Statesman*, (Calcutta) of the 4th March, 1937, asking for expert opinion in the matter. It elicited an illuminating reply from a well-informed Bengalee gentleman, (a Mr. Dhirendra Nath Sen) which was published in the pages of the same journal on the 23rd March, 1937, from which we extract the following for the information of our compatriots who are not born in India. "An Armenian may be a British subject whether he is born in India or outside. A British subject has been defined in Section 27 of the British Nationality and Status of Aliens Act of 1914, as amended in 1918 and 1922, read with Section I and II. British subjects may be of two classes, namely, (1) natural born British subjects who have been emunerated in Section I of the 1914 Act and (2) naturalised British subjects, who come under Section II of the Imperial Act and also, so far as British India is concerned, under Act No. 7 of 1926 promulgated by the Indian Legislature. Unless an Armenian is a 'British subject' of either description or the subject of a federated State or of a State in respect of which certain concessions have been granted in regard to political rights he cannot be included in the electoral roll for any territorial constituency nor can offer himself for election to the legislatures, Federal or Provincial."

We would therefore strongly advise, nay urge our compatriots, who are not "natural-born British subjects" to take out Certificates of Naturalization, whereby they can be recognised as British Indian subjects. They can then justly claim to be classed with the Europeans on the Indian Railways and enjoy the same rights and privileges as the European employees with regard to allowances for sick leave &c. A Naturalization Certificate does not cost more than a hundred rupees.

CHAPTER XLIII.

SIR CATCHICK PAUL CHATER, C.M.G., LL.D.

THE "GRAND OLD MAN" OF HONG KONG.

The late Sir Catchick Paul Chater, who rose to eminence in Hong Kong, was born in Calcutta on the 8th September, 1846, of respectable Armenian parents, his mother being a grand-daughter of the famous Armenian merchant, Agah Catchick Arakiel of Calcutta, who in 1790 was honoured by King George III with a handsome miniature portrait and a valuable sword for his loyalty and philanthropy in releasing all the prisoners in the Court of Requests jail on the occasion of the happy recovery of that monarch from his unfortunate malady (madness) in 1788, as recorded on p. 450. The history of the Chater family, on his mother's side, goes far back into that of the opening up of India to British commerce. Agah Catchick Arakiel's wife, Begoom, was a great grand-daughter of the renowned Khojah Phanoos Kalandar, the Armenian merchant prince of India, who in 1688 entered into an important commercial understanding with the Honourable East India Company on behalf of the Armenians trading in India.

Sir Paul Chater could therefore justly claim descent from that illustrious representative of the Armenian nation, whom the "Governor and the Directors of the Company of London Merchants trading to the East Indies" justly style, in their several Charters, as a "merchant of eminency."

Having inherited the commercial genius of such eminent and illustrious ancestors, as Khojah Phanoos Kalandar and Agah Catchick Arakiel, the late Sir Catchick Paul Chater of Hong Kong became by dint of perseverance and merit of an exceptionally high order, the architect of his own fortune, having practically risen from the lowest rung of the ladder to the very highest in the commercial world of Hong Kong, being closely connected with all the important civic and commercial activities of that great port—the Gibralter of the East and one of the brighest jewels in the highly resplendent Crown of the Overseas dominions of the wide British Empire on which the sun never sets.

Being a great grandson of that eminent philanthropist, Agah Catchick Arakiel, Sir Catchick Paul Chater, through his princely donations to temples of learning and places of divine worship, in Calcutta, London, Hong Kong and other places in China, secured a prominent niche in the Temple of Fame. During the whole of his life he was a generous giver. The following are some of the amounts he had subscribed to different institutions, religious, educational and benevolent, during the last six years of his life.

La Martiniere College, Calcutta*	... Rs.	1,100,000
Armenian Church, Calcutta† ...	... ,,	300,000
St. John's Cathedral, Hong Kong	... $	250,000
St. Andrew's Church, Kowloon‡	... $	250,000

* A large portrait of the late Sir Catchick Paul Chater, painted in 1925 by an English artist, George Henry, adorns the big hall of the College. The benefactor is depicted, with his decorations, seated on a chair. There is however, no memorial tablet erected in the institution commemorating the princely gift of eleven lakhs of rupees, but we are pleased to see that a day has been set apart, in the second-half of November, every year, known as "Chater's Day". The day is observed as a holiday, and it invariably falls on a Friday.

And a glowing tribute is paid to his memory in the daily "School Prayer", the first portion of which is as follows: O Almighty God, and most merciful Father, who hast taught us to praise Thee as well for the dead as the living: We thank Thee for Claude Martin our Founder, for Paul Chater our Benefactor, and for the lives and examples of all who have served Thee in this School. Pour down Thy blessing, we pray Thee, upon those who are now here." Although Sir Paul Chater's endowment of Rupees eleven lakhs was unconditional, yet, in view of the fact that the golden-hearted benefactor was an Armenian, the Governors of the La Martiniere might have in deference to his nationality, founded a few scholarships, for poor Armenian boys, to be known as "Chater Foundationers". Such a gracious act we are sure, would have greatly pleased the unostentatious Armenian.

† The Armenian community of Calcutta, erected two mural tablets in their church, with appropriate inscriptions, commemorating the donation of Rupees three lakhs to their church. (See pp. 443-444, Nos. 22 and 23).

‡ St. Andrew's Church, the first Anglican church at Kowloon, where Sir Paul Chater attended divine service every Sunday without

University of Hong Kong	$	250,000
Union Church, Kowloon	$	100,000
Union Church, Hong Kong	$	60,000
Ex-Service Mens' Association ...	$	55,000
Missions to Seamen	$	50,000
Masonic Endowment Fund	$	50,000
Dr. Jordan Memorial	$	25,000
War Memorial Nursing Home ...	$	25,000
St. Matthew's Church, London ...	£	2500
Supreme Council 33°	£	2000
Lord Mayor's Armenian Fund ...	£	1500

Sir Paul Chaters' parents died when he was young. His father, Chater Paul Chater, who was born in 1804, was drowned accidently in the river Hughli between Chinsurah and Calcutta, on the 31st January 1853. His body was recovered two days after the sad event and buried in the old Armenian cemetery in Colootollah Street.

His widow Mariam, who was born in 1811, died on the 24th July 1855, and lies buried in the Colootollah cemetery next to her husband. After the death of his parents, young Chater, the youngest of a family of 13 children, was, through the influence of the family physician, admitted into the La Martiniere School as a Foundationer, and it may be mentioned that the grateful pupil, hearing of the financial difficulties into which his old school had fallen, endowed it with a princely donation of Rs. 1,100,000, shortly before his death. A record benefaction indeed, surpassing that of Major-General Claude Martine, the Founder, who had bequeathed a sum of Sicca Rupees 350,000 only for the La Martiniere institution at Calcutta, which was opened on the 1st March 1836.

Leaving the La Martiniere, young Chater, on the advice of one of his sisters, went to try his luck at Hong Kong, where one of his sisters, the mother of the famous Dr. Jordan, was residing with her husband.

---

fail, was erected entirely at his expense, as he gave the land and the building not only for the church but also for the church Hall and the Vicarage.

Soon after his arrival in Hong Kong on the 1st April 1864, young Chater obtained an appoinment, on probation, in the Bank of Hindoostan on a salary of $50 a month. His luggage consisted of a chest of drawers which was up to the last among his most cherished possessions at his palatial residence in Hong Kong known as the "Marble Hall".

He lived with his sister and brother-in-law until they left the Colony toward the end of 1864. His salary was then increased to $100 and he went to live in a cheap boarding house in Wyndham Street.

Young Chater's chief task at the Bank of Hindoostan was the writing up of the clients' pass-books. The Banks' clients, especially the Sassoons, were won by his frank and willing ways and he soon made many friends. One day he plucked up the courage to ask the head of Sassoons' whether they would help him if he started as an Exchange broker. The reply being in the affirmative, Chater tendered his resignation, which was accepted on the condition that he gave so many hours a day to show his successor at the Bank the ropes. With the help of the Sassoons, he started auspiciously, and cleared $600 in the first month as a broker. Thenceforth Fortune smiled on him and he rose to be the greatest financial magnate of the Colony. He had learned something during banking hours which made him confident that much money could be made with careful business methods. He had seen the dollar rise and fall like the ocean tide, now at a level where buying was advantageous and now rising to a point where he could sell with great profit. He therefore set up as an exchange and bullion broker and, with his own savings and with such money, as he could induce friends to invest in his venture, he was very soon on the high road to success.

That prolific and interesting writer, T. P. O' Connor, M.P. who met Sir Paul Chater at Vichy in September, 1924, wrote in the *Sunday Times* (London) as follows :—

"Sir Paul Chater is perhaps the least known and at the same time one of the most powerful and, what is more important, one of the most beneficent figures in the Empire. The young Armenian from Calcutta and everything in Hong Kong have been indissolubly associated. He is at the head of everything there; no enterprise gets on without asking his assistance. Shipping, banking, international companies with their heads in London or in Paris—he is in them all. And he has accumulated one of the largest fortunes in the Empire. He is the father of everything in Hong Kong, by long residence and service. He is the oldest British settler, he is the oldest member of the Executive Council. From his immense wealth he has given most generously to every good cause; he is thus the chief philanthropist as well as he oldest settler in that very prosperous and go-ahead Colony, one of our proudest and best creations in the Empire."

A Shanghai journal wrote of him after his death as follows:

"Sir Catchick Paul Chater's career was in every way a modern romance, for he rose from a poor boy to be the financial king of the Colony, its greatest landowner, one of its most generous benefactors, a leader in its administration, and probably one of the six best known men in all China, with a reputation that had made him famous in many countries".

Speaking at a meeting of the Legislative Council at Hong Kong, on the 27th May, 1926, His Excellency the Governor, (Sir Cecil Clementi, K.C.M.G.) paid the following tribute to the sterling worth and genius of Sir Paul Chater: "This morning Sir Paul Chater passed away at his home in this island. It is difficult for me to speak without emotion of the grievous loss sustained by this Colony through his death When, as a young cadest, I first landed in Hong Kong, I stepped ashore upon ground which under a most successful scheme, devised by Sir Paul, had been newly reclaimed from the sea. Sir Paul was then already a member of both the Executive and Legislative Councils. Indeed it is now forty years since he first sat in this Chamber. My earliest recollections as Clerk of the Executive and Legislative Councils in Hong Kong are associated with memories of Sir Paul, whose sage advice, whose wonderful foresight and breadth of vision, whose remarkable financial skill, and whose unbounded enthusiasm for all that tended to develop the Colony never failed to have a marked influence upon the decisions of both Councils and at all times informed the policy of the Hong Kong

Government. I stood yesterday at Sir Paul's bedside and, as all who knew him would have expected, his last words to me concerned what he might still, even after death, do for the benefit of Hong Kong. He has bequeathed to this Colony his house, his marvelleous collection of porcelain* and his historical series of pictures of Hong Kong from the days of its infancy. But above all he has bequeathed to Hong Kong development schemes of great magnitude, many already completed and some on their way to completion, schemes which have changed the face of the land, which have vastly increased the prosperity of the Colony and which will inure to the comfort and contentment of present and future generations of its inhabitants. While Hong Kong and Kowloon endure, so long will his work remain as his imperishable memorial."

Many were the tributes paid to the memory of Sir Paul Chater by the China papers† after his death. The *Hongkong Sunday Herald* of the 30th May, 1926, in a leading article lamenting the death of the "Father of the Colony", wrote, *inter alia,* as follows:

"It has truly been said that whilst it would require half a dozen volumes adequately to do justice to Sir Paul Chater,

---

* His unique collection of old Chinese porcelain, of which a descriptive catalogue had been compiled by an English expert during his lifetime, was one of the finest in the world. It was valued, some years ago, at $2,500,000. His collection of pictures was considered of such value that Mr. Orange, the well-known architect, spent much time in classifying and co-ordinating it and wrote a very interesting book on it.

† In 1924, we were requested by the late Sir Paul Chater, to draw up the "Geneological Tree" of his mother's family, as he knew very little about his ancestors, having left Calcutta, as we have seen, when quite a young man and lived all his life in Hong Kong (1864 - 1924). And as the geneology would have been incomplete without the family history, we wrote at the same time a history of the family, tracing his descent, through his mother, from the illustrious Khojah Phanoos Kalandar of Surat, whom the East India Company had styled "an Armenian merchant of eminency", in 1688.

Extracts from that work, and from the several articles which we had published about Sir Paul Chater in the Calcutta dailies—the *Statesman,* the *Englishman* and the *New Empire*—in November and December, 1924, appeared in the biographical sketches which were published by the Hong Kong and the Shanghai papers, after his death, which occurred on the 27th May, 1926.

who passed away on Thursday, mere words are inadequate to express the Colony's sense of bereavement. The future historian of Hongkong will find his task as regards the past sixty years a sinecure, for the record of Hongkong will be a replica of the career of Sir Paul Chater. His activities throughout that long period were not only varied—they were wonderful and marvellous. There was simply no limit to his energy, his initiative, his foresight, and his enterprise. He combined the virtues of a Carnegie with those of a Pierpont Morgan. And always Hongkong stood immeasurably to gain by his every stroke of genius, as well as by his magnanimity in every good and charitable cause. Sir Paul has been gathered unto his fathers, but by his works and his greatness of heart he will be held in grateful remembrance so long as Hongkong itself exists."

A few words about the civic achievements of Sir Paul Chater may not be out of place.

In 1887, Sir Paul Chater, then Mr. Paul Chater, was the Treasurer and afterwards the Chairman of the Queen Victoria Jubilee Committee, and ten years after, he was the Chairman of the Diamond Jubilee Committee and it was at this period (1897) that in recognition of his numerous public services, he was created a C. M. G. (Companion of the Order of St. Michael and St. John). In 1902, he received the honour of Knighthood.

At the coronation of the late King Edward, he represented the Colony (Hong Kong), for which service he held the Coronation Medal. He attended all the Royal functions at Buckingham Palace and St. James' Palace, and also at Westminster Abbey. He was also present at the famous review of the British Fleet at Spithead, and was an honoured guest of the Rothschilds and other great families who undertook the entertainment of the representatives from the Colonies.

Sir Paul Chater was also appointed a delegate to represent Hong Kong at the historic ceremony of the Coronation of His Majesty the late King George V.

In 1892, for valuable services rendered to the French Government at Tonkin, he was made a member of that much-coveted order, *Legion d' Honneur*. He became a member of the Legislative Council as long ago as 1887 and a member of the Governor's Executive Council in 1896. He was the Senior Justice of the Peace in the Colony at the time of his death, having been appointed in 1876.

The honorary degree of LL.D. was conferred on him by the University of Hongkong, in January 1923, in recognition of his services as the Honorary Treasurer of the institution for several years and for his magnificent donation of $250,000. And according to an official announcement made by the Governor of Hongkong on the 3rd July 1926, shortly after the death of the G. O. M. of Hongkong, His late Majesty, King George V, would have been pleased to bestow upon the late Sir Catchick Paul Chater, C.M.G. had he lived, a Knight Commandership, Civil Division, of the Most Excellent Order of the British Empire, in recognition of his services to Hongkong.

Ever a staunch Freemason, Sir Paul Chater was installed District Grand Master (English Constitution) of Hongkong and South China in 1882 and continued in office until 1910. He was Past Grand Superintendent of District Grand Royal Arch Chapter of Hongkong, South China and Prior of Provincial Priory of China and a member of the 33rd degree etc.

At the time of his death, Sir Paul Chater was the Consul-General for Siam and a Director of over twenty public Companies in Hongkong.

In his early years, Sir Paul Chater was a keen cricketer and for over ten years, he was a member of the first eleven of Hong Kong, winning his place by consistent good play. His successes on the turf were also a feature of the racing in Hong Kong and his interest in China ponies was maintained until his death. Since 1865, which was the first race meeting he attended in the Colony, Sir Paul did not miss a single meeting. He first began racing in 1874. He was for nearly fifty years a steward of the Hong Kong "Jockey Club" and acted as its Judge and Chairman for many years. He won the Hongkong Derby on 19 different occasions. Sir Paul celebrated his racing jubilee on the 16th February 1925.

He died full of years and honours on the morning of the 27th May, 1926, and was buried, after an impressive service in St. John's Cathedral, in the Protestant cemetery at Happy Valley, next to the grave of his brother, Joseph Theophilus Chater, who died in Hongkong in 1866. Another brother of Sir Paul Chater, named Marcar Chater, died in Calcutta on the 4th April 1909, and is buried in the covered verandah behind the altar of the Armenian church of Nazareth. He was 71 years old.

The funeral, needless to add, was very largely attended. Hundreds of Chinese lined the route from the Cathedral to the cemetery at Happy Valley. The floral tributes, including one from H. E. the Governor, were numerous. Hongkong mourned the death of its "Father" with genuine regret. The mortal remains of the immortal author of its greatness and phenomenal prosperity had been laid to rest, but his munificent princely and catholic benefactions to religious, educational and benevolent institutions in China, Calcutta and London, will, in the words of Horace, remain, for ages to be, "a monument more lasting than brass." (Exegi monumentum aere perennius).

Lady Maria Christine Chater, whom the late Sir Paul Chater married in Hongkong in 1914, died a couple of years ago at "Marble Hall", the palatial residence of Sir Paul Chater in Hongkong, erected in 1911, at a great cost, the beautiful marble used in its construction having been specially quarried in Greece and Italy and polished in Belgium, before being shipped to Hongkong.

Sir Paul Chater had no children. He was survived by his three nephews, one of whom, Mr. Chater Paul Chater is residing in London, another, Mr. Jack Chater, is in Calcutta and the third, Mr. John Theophilus Bagram, is an old and respected resident of Hongkong. As can be seen from the will of Sir Paul Chater, handsome provisions have been made for the nephews.

By his last Will and Testament, dated the 17th legacies, annuities and bequests:

Legacies:—

1. To his wife, Lady Maria Christine Chater, £5000, which was subsequently increased to £10,000 in the first codicil dated the 25th May, 1926.
2. To his sister, Mrs. Sophia Matilda Gunn, residing in London, £2,500.
3. To the "Hong Kong Jockey Club," $50,000, on condition that a Cup to be called the "Chater Cup" be provided annually out of the income thereof.
4. To his grand nephew, Mr. Percy C. Manuk* of Bankipore, Rs. 200,000.

Annuities:—

1. To his wife, Lady Chater, during her life, £10,000 per annum.
2. To his sister, Mrs. Sophia Matilda Gunn, during her life, £2,500 per annum.
3. Mrs. Annie Macpherson, the wife of Rev. Macpherson, during her life, £500 per annum.
4. Mrs. Helen Jordan, the widow of his nephew Paul Jordan, during her life, £1500 per annum.

Bequests:—

1. To his nephew, Chater Paul Chater, residing in London, $400,000.

---

* Mr. Percy Chater Manuk, a favourite grand nephew of the late Sir Paul Chater, is one of the leading barristers practising at the Patna High Court for many years. He possesses a fine collection of old China, Mogul paintings, Persian and Arabic illuminated manuscripts, old Persian enamelled tiles and many rare works of art. His beautiful house at Bankipore, is a miniature museum, frequented by tourists and lovers of art who come to Bankipore annually to see the wonderful collection of rare Persian manuscripts in the world-famous "Oriental Library" founded by the late Mr. Khoda Buksh.

Mr. Manuk is a descendant, through his mother, of the famous Agah Catchick Arrakiel of Calcutta (see p. 468).

2. To his nephew, Jack Chater, residing in Calcutta, $200,000.

3. To his nephew, John Theophilus Bagram, residing in Hong Kong, $300,000, which was subsequently increased to $700,000 in the second codicil, dated the 25th May, 1926.

The above three bequests were to be set apart and invested separately and the income thereof to be paid to the beneficiaries during their life and after their death, to their children.

In the first codicil, dated the 25th May, 1926, he left a legacy of £5000 to Dr. John Cecil Mc. Gown, who had been attending him during his last illness and in the second codicil, bearing the same date, he left a legacy of $50,000 to his clerk, E. Sadick, and a legacy of $25,000 to Dr. Fred Kew.

All the legacies, annuities and bequests were to be paid free of all death duties.

He left his palatial residence, known as the "Márble Hall" to the Government of Hong Kong and the residuary Estate to the Armenian Holy Church of Nazareth, Calcutta, where he had been christened on the 3rd October, 1846.

And if departed worth can be appreciated in this age, we would humbly suggest that when the residue of his estate, which is roughly estimated to be Rupees seventy-five lakhs, is received by the Armenian church of Calcutta, a marble statue of the great benefactor seated on a chair, and facing the altar of the church, be erected under the belfry, on the east of the grave of Mrs. Mary Joseph Emin, with appropiiate inscriptions in the Armenian and English languages, commemorating his munificent bequests, the greatest individual benefaction that has ever been made to that ancient place of divine worship, since its foundation in 1724.

ARMENIANS AT LUCKNOW

CHAPTER XLIV.

ARMENIANS AT LUCKNOW.

Lucknow, the capital of the once-powerful Nawab-Viziers of Oudh* from 1775-1856, had a small Armenian colony during the second-half of the 18th century. There is *inside* the Roman Catholic cathedral at Patna, the grave of an Armenian lady who died at Lucknow on the 29th September, 1796 and her body was brought down to Patna for internment. She was the wife of one Sarkies Johanness and her name was Anna. She was 17 years of age, according to the long Armenian inscription on her tombstone, a facsimile of which was published in 1917, by the late Father H. Hosten, S. J. in his *Record of the inscriptions at the Catholic Church at Patna*.

A son of this lady suffered heavy financial losses during the Indian Mutiny of 1857† which broke out with much fury at Lucknow and shook the British rule in India to its foundations.

In March, 1892 when we first visited Lucknow, we went to see the Residency, which has been immortalised by the poet‡ and the historian, and whose sad, interesting ruins, bear silent, but elequent witness of the past.

---

* On the annexation of Oudh by the British in 1856, the last of these—Wajid Ali Shah—was deposed and deported to Calcutta, where he lived and died a State prisoner at his palatial residence in Garden Reach on the 21st September, 1887, in his sixty-eight year. By the ex-King's death the dynasty founded in 1732 by Saadat Khan, the Persian merchant of Nishapur, became extinct.

† By a strange coincidence the Indian Mutiny broke out exactly a hundred years after the famous victory of the British Army under Clive at Plassey on the 23rd June, 1757, which laid the foundation of the British Empire in India.

‡ Tennyson, in his heart-stirring ode on 'The Defence of Lucknow,' pathetically describes the prolonged siege and the glorious defence of the Residency, which is without parallel in Indian history.

It being the tourist season, there were a large number of visitors who had come from far and wide to see the historic Residency.

The guide, an elderly English gentleman, had been one of the brave juvenile defenders of the "Martiniere Post" which was composed of the masters and the boys of La Martiniere College of that city, named after Claude Martine,* its

---

* Of obscure French parentage and from being a Private in the French Army, Claude Martine rose to the rank of Major-General in the Hon'ble East India Company's service. Through his endowments, his name will be handed down to posterity as an eminent philanthropist. He was born at Lyons on 5th January, 1735 and, after receiving a good mathematical education at a public school, he entered the army at the age of twenty, and landed in India as a common soldier with a French armament under the famous Count de Lally in the eventful year 1757. In January 1761 he was taken a prisoner-of-war by the English at Pondicherry and sent to Bengal, where, after the conclusion of the war, he joined the service of the East India Company. Being strong in mathematics and engineering, he was deputed in 1773 to make a survey of the province of Oudh; and at the request of its ruler, the Nawab-Vizier Sujah-ud-dowlah, he was permitted to attach himself to the Court of Oudh. Sujah-ud-dowlah, with whom Martine had found great favour died at Fyzabad, the former capital, on the 26th January, 1775, and was succeeded by his son Asaf-ud-dowlah, who removed the seat of government to Lucknow. Martine remained in the service of this enlightened prince, whose reign was favourable to foreign art and enterprise. At Lucknow he opened a bank and started other profitable commercial undertakings. A cannon foundry was soon in full swing; not only that, but he made gunpowder, coined rupees, built houses, planted parks, and introduced amongst native lapidaries the Dutch system of cutting diamonds, and succeeded in building up an immense fortune. Besides large landed properties in India and France, he left more than four millions of sicca rupees invested in the Company's Paper, at that time Twelve per cents. After providing for his dependants, and bequeathing £25,000 to his relations at Lyons, and a similar sum to the Lyons Municipality for its poor, he left the greater part of his fortune for the purpose of founding colleges at Lyons. Calcutta, and Lucknow, each to be called after him. He left a large bequest for establishing an *industrial* school at Lyons, of which we have no data. He bequeathed sicca Rs. 3,50,000 for the La Martiniere Institution at Calcutta, which was opened on the 1st March, 1836 and has since held a prominent place as an educational establishment. Out of his estate, the sum of sicca Rs. 8,16,444 was decreed, by the High Court of Judicature, Calcutta, for the support of the college at Lucknow, which was inaugurated

Founder. The various interesting spots within the sacred precincts of the Residency were indicated by him. No visitor can help being affected by the touching epitaphs and the laconic inscriptions in memory of those gallant British soldiers of the beleaguered garrison who fell while upholding British prestige. With a feeling of awe and veneration we looked upon the crumbling walls of the Residency buildings which had been battered by the shot and shell of the rebels. Who cannot but admire the patriotism of those who heroically defended the place, against innumerable odds, for a hundred and forty-seven days, before the arrival of the Relief Party under Generals Outram and Havelock?

Being an Armenian, we were much interested in a square pillar outside the Residency grounds, to which a marble slab was affixed, bearing the simple inscription, 'Johannes House.' The guide informed us that Johannes, who was a well-known Armenian merchant of Lucknow, seeing the dark clouds rising in the horizon of Indian politics, betook himself with his wife and child into the Residency. The building, the site of which the pillar marked, was double storeyed. There Johannes

---

in 1840 at the Constantia Mansion of the founder. In his will he thus refers to his favourite mansion :—"My Constantia House is never to be sold. It is to serve as a monument, or tomb, to deposit my body in, and the house is to serve as a college for educating children and men in the English language and religion." This imposing edifice, one of the architectural ornaments of Lucknow, was designed and built by Claude Martine as a residence for himself during the reign of Asaf-ud-dowlah, who offered Rs. 1,00,000 for it on its completion, but was refused. It is in the Italian style of architecture and highly ornamental. The General's motto, *'Labore et Constantia,'* is inscribed in prominent characters on the front of the building. At the La Martiniere, Lucknow, which in 1869 was affiliated with the University of Calcutta, one hundred foundationers are fed, clothed and educated free of charge. General Martine died, on 13th September 1800 at the Farhat Baksh Palace, also built by him as a residence and his remains were enclosed in a vaulted chamber in the basement of the Constantia House, where his tomb—a simple sarcophagus—stands on the floor, bearing the following literal inscription, which was composed by himself and inserted as a stipulation in his will :—

"Major-General CLAUDE MARTINE, born at Lyons, January 1735, arrived in India as a common soldier, and died at Lucknow, on 13th September, 1800, and he is buried in this tomb. Pray for soul!"

resided and conducted his business. It overlooked the Residency buildings, and the rebels took possession of it, and from its lofty terrace kept up an incessant fire into the compound of the Residency. Ultimately the house was blown up by those besieged, as it was too dangerous a rendezoons for the enemy, "who swarmed in Johannes' house."

Besides Johannes, his wife and child, there was another Armenian, one Carapiet Arathoon, one of the juvenile defenders of the "Martiniere Post". This young man, another victim of the Mutiny, lost his life in the garrison. A son of Johannes was an accomplished scholar and wrote some beautiful poems in the Urdu language. The son of the poet was a photographic artist in Lucknow during the latter part of the 19th century.

As stated on page 100, one of the queens of Ghaziuddin Hyder, the *first* King of Oudh, was the daughter of an Armenian lady named Mary Minas, who had married an English doctor of the Honourable East India Company's service at Patna. The marriage was celebrated by an Armenian bishop, named Arathoon, and the witness to the marriage was a Mr. Carapiet, an Armenian resident of Patna.

The Armenian queen, known as Nawab Sultan Mariam Begum Saheba, or Vilaeti Begum, lived and died a Chirstian, and her grave, can be seen to this day at the deserted cemetery near the Roshan-ud-dowlah's Kothee at Lucknow. She died in 1849. The beautiful marble tombstone that had been placed over her grave, was broken and destroyed by the mutineers in 1857, but there is a marble tablet to her memory in St. Joseph's Roman Catholic church at Hazratganj, erected by her sister-in-law, Amelia Short. Mariam Begum Saheba had no children. The Speirs of Lucknow and Moradabad are the descendants of her younger brother, Joseph Short, and they receive to this day, from the Government Wasika office at Lucknow, the monthly pension of Rs. 833-5-4, that was left to Joseph Short, after the death of Mariam Begum Saheba, who, as we shall see presently, enjoyed a monthly pension of Rs. 2500, left by King Ghaziuddin Hyder*, for her main-

---

* Ghaziuddin Hyder who was raised by the British to the status of King in 1814, died in 1827. He was succeeded by King Nasiruddin

tenance, during her lifetime. It appears from the last Will of Mariam Begum Saheba, which we publish below, that King Ghaziuddin Hyder had given a permanent Loan of a crore of Rupees, bearing interest at 5 per cent. to the East India Company in 1825, with the stipulation that the annual income derived therefrom, amounting to Rupees 5 lakhs, be distributed by the Company's government in charities and pensions, in perpetuity. It was further stipulated that two-thirds of the pension of Mariam Saheba Begum was to go to the high priests in charge of the shrine at Kerbela, after her death.

The Christian queen's Will, which is a translation from the original Persian, is as follows :—

"That whereas it is appointed unto all men to die and all must taste the favour of death and see the face of the Angel of Death, whereof it is most incumbent and necessary for every human being to make an arrangement of his transactions for the future and to make out last Will for his relatives and dependants as directed in the religious precepts, for the guidance on consideration, that after his death no dispute or enmity should take place among his relatives and dependants and in conformity to the instructions laid down in the articles of the Treaties held between both the Governments, that is, the British Government and the King of Oudh, on the 1st Mohurrum, 1241 Hejree, corresponding with the 17th August, 1825 A.D.

Hyder who died of poison in 1837. This easy going King had an English barber in his service whose influence at Court was far greater than that of the native Prime Minister. He was a special favourite of the King and during his stay at the Court of the sensual King, he made a fortune of 24 lakhs of rupees. He was succeeded by his uncle, King Mohammad Ali Shah, who died in 1842 and was succeeded by his second son, King Amjad Ali Shah. He was a weak ruler in whose reign anarchy prevailed throughout Oudh. He died in 1847 and was succeeded by King Wajid Ali Shah whose bad career sealed the fate of the dynasty. He abdicated on the 7th February, 1856. Oudh was annexed and he was sent to Calcutta and allowed a pension of Rs. 12 lakhs per annum. He died at Calcutta on the 21st September, 1887 in his sixty-eighth year. He was a man of literary taste and a poet of some note, but was quite unfit to govern. He spent all his time in the company of eunuchs, musicians and dancing girls, and paid no heed to the wretched condition of the country brought about by his misrule.

The terms of the conditions run as follows :

Article 2nd. This Loan* is made in perpetuity. The Sovereign of the Kingdom of Oudh shall never have the power to take it back, nor shall they exercise any interference with its interest.

Article 3rd. The British Givernment guarantees that it will pay for ever the monthly sums hereafter mentioned, out of the interest of the above Loan, to the persons set down in this Instrument, in the current coin of the place where they may reside, without any deduction whatever.

Article 4th. The Honourable Company will always protect the honour of the stipendiaries who will be paid out of this fund, and it will be the protector of their possessions such as, houses and gardens (whether bestowed by the King of Oudh, or purchased, or built by themselves), from the hands of the sovereigns and their enemies. And in whatever city or country they may be, their allowance will be paid to them there. And it is further inserted in the said Instrument which runs as follows, that "after her demise, one-third of the allowance will be paid to any person or for any purpose she may will it, will be allowed."

Whereas in a state of sound mind and healthy body, I do make and ordain this my last Will and place my legatees under the immediate protection of the authorities of the Honourable Company that after my demise this my last Will to be carried into effect according to the instructions laid down in it. That under the terms of the said Treaty between both Governments, my allowance is Rupees two thousand five hundred per month, one-third of which is Rupees eight hundred and thirty-three, five annas and four English pies, to which sum I hereby give and establish monthly allowance for my younger brother Joseph Short, whom I brought up from his infancy under my care and protection like by own son, and for my other dependants in recompense of their fidelity and good services rendered to me according to which the authorities of the Honourable Company shall regularly pay their monthly allowance generation by generation and womb by womb in perpetuity for ever to the persons set down in this Instrument without any deduction or diminution whatever and in what city or country they may be, their allowance will be paid to them there that they should provide themselves suitably that so they may live independent of any other person's aid for subsistence. If during my existence or after my demise any of my legatee's death had

* The Loan as was for rupees one crore bearing interest at 5 per cent. per annum (vide *Aitchison's Treaties*, Vol. II).

taken place, his allowance shall be continued and divided amongst his heirs according to Divine law. If he had no heirs, his allowance shall be paid to any person according to his Will and if it happens that owing to illness, he should die intestate, then the Resident at the Court of Oudh for the time being shall divide his allowance among his heirs according to the Shuriyat Ghurra (Bright Law). With the exception of this last will no other document or Will should be recognised as genuine or true and it may not be admitted to eradicate the claim of my legatees specified in this my last Will And orders may be given to them when when they chose to proceed in what country they like and regarding their proceeding to other countries,, no other person should be allowed to interfere at all in their affairs. May holy God perfume the grave of blessed memory (His late Majesty Ghazeood-Deen Hyder), who had placed me under the immediate protection of this Honourable Company and in conformity of the said Treaty held between both the Governments. I was always treated and guarded with the greatest attention and respect and honour due to my rank and position under the protection of the Government; in consideration of my privileges from Government, I place all my relatives and dependants under the immediate protection and guardianship of the British Government and trusting that my legatees will be treated in a like manner as myself and the said allowance of Rupees eight hundred and thirty-three, five annas and four pies, I fixed and allowed to them out of my allowance shall be continued on them and regularly paid to them as set forth below.

For my brother Joseph Short, as my own son, the sum of Rupees Eight hundred for the following purpose, *viz.*, for my brother's own expenses and to give maintenance and clothing to my other imbecile brother John Short and my youngest sister Eliza, she is attacked with severe palpitation, if her husband and son may not support her, then my said brother will give her maintenance and clothing Rs. 750. For the purpose of repairs and lighting and charities of the Roman Catholic Chapels, Rs. 50 to be disbursed by my said brother's own hands and discretion, and after the demise of my said brother to be disbursed in the same manner by his heirs. To Lucknow Chapel, Rs. 20; Cawnpore Chapel, Rs. 30; Hakeem Mohammad Ali in recompense of his duties as physician, Rs. 15; Musummat Ghotee Khanum, daughter of Mirza Ashoor Beg, Rs. 18-5-4, in recompense of her fidelity and good services rendered to me.

That regarding the arrangement of my funeral and burial obsequies shall be performed by my brother Joseph Short in whatever place I may be and whatever time it may happen. I have executed this my last Will and recorded in the Residency office with a duplicate. That the monthly allowance fixed by me for the legatees set forth above to be regularly paid to them in perpetuity by their own seals and receipts. If my death should accidently take place at Lucknow, in such case my funeral obsequies should be performed by my brother Joseph Short and my tomb will be erected by his discretion, also and after my demise my brother will become sole proprietor of my whole estate, including jewels, money in cash, Bomind Manzil premises and also of all my personal property whatever is belonging to me, and after my demise my said brother has full power on my male and female, Indian and Abyssinian slaves, either to keep or let them free, and no other person has liberty to interfere regarding them.

I have already examined and adjusted all my accounts from my said legatees not a farthing is due to me from any of them. Therefore, the authorities of the Honourable Company will not allow any one to demand any account from them.

I have executed this my last Will and after impressing my genuine seal recorded it in the Resident's office, with a duplicate of the same, and also delivered one copy of this my last Will to my said brother, and a second copy of it to Hakeem Mahommad Ali, *alias,* Hakeem Nuboo, and a third copy to Musammat Chotee Khanum, daughter of Nusoor Beg for rendering good services, that with the exception of my last Will if any other last Will or deed of gift or any deed may be produced by any of my dismissed servants or those who are in the service, it ought to be recognised a fictitious and forged document and it is most incumbent on the authorities of the British Government to apprehend the said person and to destroy such forged document.

That on the 1st July, 1838 A.D. corresponding with 7th Rubbee, 1254 Hejree. I had executed a separate Will for the performance of my funeral and burial obsequies, impressed my seal, and delivered it to my brother and who will produce the same, and the British Government will give assistance to my said brother to carry out the said Instrument into effect. Dated the 23rd Mohurrum, 1260, Hejree, corresponding with 13th February, 1844 A.D."

The testator, Sultan Mariam Saheba Begum, died a Christian at Lucknow, on the 5th April, 1849, and was buried in a Christian cemetery.

In December, 1926, when we visited Lucknow a second time to attend the Annual Meeting of the "Indian Historical Records Commission", we met an elderly resident of Lucknow, one Mr. William Stephen Speirs, a Government servant, and one of the descendants of Joseph Short, who very kindly took us to the old Christian cemetery where the Armenian queen, Mariam Begum Saheba, was laid to rest on the 5th April, 1849.

We were shocked to see the disgraceful state of the grave, covered with rubbish. May we ask what the Archæological Department for the preservation of "Ancient Tombs and Monuments" is doing? Will not the much-vaunted Department for the preservation of "Ancient Tombs and Monuments" repair and renovate the neglected grave and place a slab over it, thereby justifying its existence? Mr. Speir's told the present writer that both his mother and his maternal grandmother, in accordance with time-honoured Armenian custom, used to burn candles and insence over the grave of Mariam Begum Saheba, on the anniversary of her death.

In 1833, an Armenian bishop from Julfa, who was on a pastoral visit to the Armenians in India, paid a visit to Lucknow where he was accorded a very cordial reception by Mariam Begum Saheba, who had a room in her palace improvised as a chapel where divine service was held. It was attended by Mariam Begum and all her Armenian servants, male and female, who took Holy Commission at the hands of the Armenian bishop. Before the bishop left Luncknow, the devout Armenian queen, presented him with a complete set of very expensive robes and sacred vestments for his use during his Indian tour.

This is related by George Aviet Zachariah, who had accompanied the bishop, as a deacon, from Julfa. After the bishop had completed his tour in India, Burma, the Straits and Java, the deacon left him at Batavia where he settled down in business, married and had two daughters. He was a man of letters and has left some works in classical Armenian. His *History of Java* published at Calcutta, in 1852, is a work of considerable interest.

ARMENIANS AT DACCA

CHAPTER XLV.

ARMENIANS AT DACCA.

Armenians settled and founded a colony at Dacca in the early part of the 18th century when it was one of the principal commercial centres in Bengal, but with the removal of the Viceregal quarters of Bengal from Dacca to Murshidabad, or Maxudabad, as it was then called, ended the distinction of Dacca as a city of metropolitan importance. This was in the beginning of the 18th century.

Inside the Roman Catholic church of "Our Lady of Rosary," at Tezgaon, two and half miles from Dacca, on the Dacca-Mymensingh Road, built in 1677, there are some old graves of Armenians who died at Dacca between the years 1714 and 1795.

They bear inscriptions in ancient Armenian, commemorating the names of the following persons :

1. Avietis, the son of Lazar of Erivan, a merchant, who died on the 17th day of the month of Qamar [16th August], 1714.

   There is also an inscription in Portuguese, in which the date of his death is given, "7 de Junho," (7th June). We cannot account for this discrepancy, but we are inclined to think that the date given in the Armenian inscription is the correct one, as the old Armenians were very particular about dates.
2. Arakiel, the son of Catchick, who died on the 9th Shbath (9th June), 1722.
3. Margar, the son of Balthazar of Julfa, who was a merchant for many years and in his old age came and died at Dacca, on the 4th June, 1736.
4. Michael, the son of Agah Gregory of the family of Khojah Minas of Julfa, who died young in 1740. (There is also an inscription in Portuguese).

5. Khojah Thooman, the son of Mahtesy Bagdseh of Agoolis, who died on the 29th July, 1746.
6. Michael, the son of Gabriel of the Babikian family, who died on the 16th Adam [17th May] in the year 1781, aged 96 years.
7. There is also a grave, inside the church, but the date is obliterated. It is to the memory of . . . . . the son of Rev. Michael.
8. Petrus Mathevosian, a jute merchant, from Hamadan, who died old in 1795.
(This grave is *outside* the church of "Our Lady of Rosary").

We cannot account for the burial of these Armenians in a Roman Catholic church. It may be argued that they belonged to the Roman Catholic faith, but so far as we know, there were no Armenians in Dacca who were members of the Church of Rome. It may be that the early Armenian settlers having no church or cemetery of their own, had their dead buried in that place, it being the only consecrated ground at Dacca, in the earlier part of the 18th century. Can the old Portuguese Records, if any, throw some light on the subject? Prior to the erection of the present Armenian Church, the Armenians of Dacca worshipped at a small chapel which they had built in the locality known to this day as *Armanitola*. In 1781, the present beautiful church of the Holy Resurrection was erected on the site of the old chapel, by subscriptions from Michael Sarkies, Astwasatoor Gavork, (George) Margar Pogose and Khojah Petrus.

In 1837, a beautiful steeple, which was to serve as a clock-tower, was erected on the west of the church, near the belfry, but it fell down during the severe earthquake which damaged many old buildings, in June 1897.* The memorial

* In the earthquake of June, 1897, Mr. Senecherim Highcazony and his wife Catherine, lost their lives under tragic circumstances. They are both buried in the churchyard. Mr. Highcazony was a jute merchant, a nephew of the late Mr. M. Highcazony of Dacca also a jute merchant, and both he and his wife hailed from far-off Alexandrapol, the modern Leninakan, an important city in Soviet Armenia, in the Union of Soviet Republics.

tablet of the steeple, is now fixed on the south-west wall of the belfry. It is a black marble slab and bears the following inscription :

"This magnificent steeple was erected by the means and at the expense of Johanness Carapiet Sarkies Esq., son of the late Carapiet Sarkies Esq., to the honour and glory of our Saviour Jesus Christ and in remembrance of all his ancestors of happy and blessed memory, in the month of July 1837, in the ancient capital of Dacca."

He died in 1874 and on his tombstone in the churchyard the following lines are inscribed :

> "In memory of Johanness Carapiet Sarkies Esq., sincerely and deeply regretted by all who knew him. Born 10th January 1810, died 26th January 1874. Aged 64 years, 16 days. Thy will be done."

His wife Ripsimah, who had died on the 15th February 1837, aged 20 years, lies buried under the belfry, which was likewise erected by Johanness Carapiet Sarkies.

There are, inside and outside the church, some graves which bear dates anterior to the erection of the present church. They are as follows :—

1. Gooltatik, the daughter of Pharsadan of Erivan and the wife of Michael. Died on the 23rd Qamar [22nd August] in the year 1762.
2. Ripsimah, the daughter of Owen of the family of Khojah Minas. Died on the 5th Nadar [3rd September] in the year 1763.
3. Sophie, the daughter of Avag and the wife of Agah Catchick, the son of Agah Emniaz of the family of Khojah Minas of Julfa, who died on the 1st day of Damah [29th October] in the year 149, [1764 A.D.].
4. Dushkho, the daughter of Agah Hovhan, the son of Agah Emniaz of the family of Khojah Minas of Julfa, who departed this life on the 7th day of Damah [4th November] in the year 150 [1765 A.D.].

5. Khathaie, the wife of Agah Hovhanness, the son of Agah Emniaz of Julfa, who departed from this world on the 26th day of Nadar [24th September] in the year 151 [1766 A.D.].
6. Martyrose, the son of Marooth of the family of Khojentz. Died in the year 1767.
7. Woskoom, the daughter of Manuel of Julfa and the wife of Margar of Erivan. Died on the 20th Nakha [20th July] in the year 1768.
8. Hosannah, the daughter of Ephraim and the wife of Petrus, the son of Agazar. Died on the 28th Shams [29th April] in the year 1771.
9. Mahtesy Arathoon, the son of Rev. Gasper. Died on the 16th Damah [13th November] in the year 1773.
10. Vertanness, the son of Anthanes. Died in the year 1780.

From the above it appears that the ground on which the church stands, was used as a cemetery prior to 1781. The extensive ground was the gift of Agah Catchick Minas, whose wife, Sophie, who died in 1764, lies buried *inside* the church. (See inscription No. 3). The church was consecrated by bishop Ephraim who was on a pastoral tour in India at that time, collecting subscriptions for the Holy See of Etchmiadzin, the Vatican of Armenia. This worthy bishop afterwards ascended the throne of St. Gregory the Illuminator as the Catholicos (Pontiff) of all the Armenians. He was consecrated on the 26th December 1809, but resigned on the 6th March 1831, owing to old age. There was an oil painting of this bishop in the Dacca Armenian Church, by a well-known European artist, but it was taken away by the late Archbishop Sahak Ayvadian in 1907, who promised the then Warden, the late Mr. Thaddeus Nahapiet, that he would send it to Etchmiadzin. We would like to know if the valuable painting ever reached its destination. As we protested at the time, the Warden was not at all justified in parting with that priceless art treasure which had adorned the walls of the Dacca church Parsonage for a hundred and twenty-five years! It is to be hoped that the Wardens of the other Armenian churches in India will not be induced to part with such valuable art treasures and relics so easily. The beautiful Altar-pieces in the Dacca church, one showing the Last supper and the other the Crucifixion, were painted by C. Pote, a European artist, in 1849.

As in other commercial centres in India, the Armenians at Dacca flourished for a considerable time in commercial pursuits and amassed great riches, for they had the trade of the place in their hands, and also held considerable lands and *Zemindaries*.

The most eminent Armenian merchant and *Zemindar* of Dacca in the early part of the last century, was the famous Agah Arathoon Michael, of the noble family of Agah Sarkies of Julfa, who died a millionaire on the 20th April 1823, aged 49 years, and was interred *inside* the church, as a mark of great respect. His son Michael had died on the 20th June 1811, aged 18 years and is buried in the churchyard.

Mr. Nicholas Pogose, the founder of the "Dacca Pogose School" now known as Juggernath College, was another rich Armenian *Zemindar* of Dacca, during the last century. That once-flourishing colony is alas reduced now to a few families only, as in the case of Madras and Bombay.

It may be mentioned however that the Armenians at Dacca were the pioneers of the jute trade in the second-half of the 19th century, in the same way that the Armenians of Mirzapore were the pioneers of the Shellac trade.* The well-known Jute Baling firms of M. David & Co., and M. Sarkies & Sons,† both of Narainganj, now owned by Messrs. George Henderson & Co., and James, Finlay & Co. Ld. of this city, respectively, were founded by Armenians, some sixty

---

* The late Mr. Carapiet M. John, known as Carapiet Jambore and Mr. Gregory Carapiet, better known as Gregory Goolzad were the first shallac manufacturers, on a large scale, at Mirzapur some 60 years ago.

† Mr. Herbert M. Shircore, C.I.E., the popular and much esteemed Chairman of the Nǎrainganj Municipality, by whom a road and a girls' school have been named after him, has been the Manager of Messrs. M. Sarkies & Sons of Narainganj for many years. Mr. Shircore is a member of an old and respectable Armenian family of Calcutta.

years ago, the former by the late Margar David* and the latter by Michael Sarkies.

There are a large number of beautiful tombstones in the churchyard, some with pathetic inscriptions† placed over the mortal remains of the Armenians who lived and died at Dacca between the years 1762 and 1929.

Members of the leading Armenian families of Dacca—the Pogoses, the Agacys, the Michaels, the Stephens, the Joakims, the Sarkiess, the Manooks, the Thomass,—with an Archbishop here, an Archimandrite (vardapiet) and a few priests there, a Mutiny veteran‡ yonder, all sleeping the sweet sleep of death and waiting for the trumpet call of the arch angel Gabriel, on the terrible Day of Judgment, when the resurrected, we are told, shall have to render an account of their deeds in this world, before the throne of the Most High.

A new parsonage was built in 1907 at a cost of Rs. 17000, during the wardenship of the late Mr. Thaddeus Nahapiet, and in 1910, the late Mr. A. Stephen of Calcutta, furnished the church with marble flooring, and electric lights and fans, in loving memory of his paternal grandfather, Rev.

---

* Margar David was the maternal uncle of Mr. David Alexander who is the only Armenian jute merchant left in Dacca to-day. Mr. Alexander, the doyen of the Armenian community of Dacca, presented the Armenian church of that city, with a beautiful altar, in pure white marble, in 1915.

† There is amongst many others, an inscription, in ancient Armenian metrical verse, on the tombstone of an Armenian from Tiflis, (Georgia) which can be rendered into English thus: "Oh you gazers at poor me, see the hopes of this vain world, what it promises and what it does, and where it sinks at last, as in the case of poor me. My name is Joseph and I am the son of Catchick. On the completion of my twenty-eighth year, my life was taken away by sad death, and, instead of going to my town which is called Tuphkhis [Tiflis], I was buried under this sepulchre, and my body was placed in the bosom of mother on the 8th day of Damah [5th November] 1811A.D."

‡ One William Harney, a Mutiny veteran, who had married an Armenian wife, has found a last resting place in that ancient cemetery. He was, according to the inscription on his tombstone, born at Belfast, Ireland, on the 23rd March 1830, and died at Dacca on the 16th July 1901. His grand daughter Zenobia, the wife of Mr. V. T. Stephen of Dacca, has erected the memorial over the grave of her "dear grandpa."

Hyrapiet Gregory Bashghoomiantz, who had been the incumbent of the Dacca Armenian church from 1828-1843, and had died on the eve of his departure and lies buried in the compound of the church near the belfry. By an irony of Fate, his son, Rev. Jacob, who had been sent out to succeed his father in the sacerdotal office, performed the funeral service and the obsequies of his sire. The beautiful inscription which can be seen to this day, on the tombstone of Rev. Hyrapiet, a gem in classical Armenian verse, is by the immortal poet, Mesrovb Thaliadian, "the nightingale of the Armenians in India", as he was called by the learned Mekhitharist Society of Armenian *literati* of Venice.

The late Mr. Joseph Lazarus, a successful jute merchant of Dacca, who died some fifteen years ago, endowed the Dacca church with Rs. 100,000, and but for a flaw in his will, which was written in Armenian by the then priest and translated into English by us, the church and other national institutions would have benefited considerably from his large estate. It did not however take long for Nemesis to overtake the ill-advised relatives of the deceased, who had the will of the benefactor declared as null and void, for they very soon lost all their ill-gotten wealth and the person, who acted as their legal adviser, died a terrible death recently, having become a miserable pauper, before his death, so let all those who rob the church and the poor pause and reflect, for sooner or later, retribution must come, Nemesis being an inexorable goddess.

As we have stated above, there are at present very few Armenians at Dacca, but there are some living at Narainganj, engaged in the jute trade, who attend divine service at the Dacca church on feast days and festivals.

And as long as the jute trade exists at Narainganj, and it will exist as long as there is a world demand for the fibre, the Armenian church at Dacca will not share the sad fate of the churches at Saidabad and Chinsurah where no priests are maintained for want of a congregation. We find from the Registers kept in the Dacca church, that since 1831, twenty-five priests have officiated in that church, some of whom have died there, and since 1876, Dacca has been visited by the following Armenian prelates :—

1. Archbishop Gregoris Johannessian, in 1876
2. Archbishop Sahak Ayvadian, in 1907.
3. Archbishop Thorgom Gooshakian, in 1917.
4. Archbishop Sahak Ayvadian, in 1922, (second time).
5. Archbishop Mesrovb Magistros, in 1928.

With the exception of His Grace, the Archbishop Thorgom Gooshakian, now the Armenian Patriarch of Jerusalem, the others were diocesan bishops who had come out to India on a pastoral tour from Julfa. Archbishop Thorgom came from Egypt as a delegate of His Holiness the late Catholicos George V, to collect subscriptions from the benevolent Armenians in India, for the relief of the large number of Armenian refugees who had poured into Armenia, from Turkey, during the Great War. Needless to add his humanitarian mission was a great success for he was able to collect a very large amount from the patriotic Armenians in India, Burmah, the Straits and Java, as it was the "boom" period during the War and everybody was flushed with plenty of cash in those days of unparalleled prosperity, when fortunes were easily made and lost.

There have been some eminent Armenian merchants engaged in the jute trade, at Dacca and Narainganj, during the last sixty years. Their names are as follows :—P. Arathoon, Margar David, Mackertich Abraham George, Michael Sarkies, Abraham Lucas, M. Highcazony, A. S. Mackertich, Tigran Nahapiet, Thaddeus Nahapiet, M. J. Catchatoor and Joseph Lazarus, referred to already on page 577.

ARMENIANS AT MADRAS

CHAPTER XLVI.

Armenians at Madras.

There are no records to show when the Armenians *first* found their way to the Coromandel coast, but there exists authentic evidence which goes to prove that the Armenians were trading on the Madras coast in the early part of the 16th century.

In the *Vestiges of Old Madras*, (Vol. I p. 277) by Henry Davison Love, it is stated :

"In 1507, Dom Francisco de Almeida, the Portuguese Viceroy at Goa, heard from some native Christians of Malabar that the house or Chapel of the Apostle [Thomas] still existed on the Coromandel coast. Of four men whom he sent round by sea to make enquiries, two died, but the survivors brought back a report which was transmitted to the King of Portugal. Ten years later, [1517] two Portuguese, named Diogo Fernandes and Bastiao Fernandes, arriving at Pulicat from Malacca, heard of the Chapel from some Armenian merchants. They all proceeded to the spot, some seven leagues distant, and discovered a very ancient edifice, constructed like a church with nave and aisles, and having timber pillars and roof. Its length was twelve cubits. A sacristy beyond, five cubits long, had a dome surmounted by a dwarf spire rising to the height of thirty cubits. Crosses and peacocks in plaster constituted the decoration. This structure was believed to be the sepulchre of the saint, [Thomas the Apostle]."

The Armenians flourished at Madras during the seventeenth and eighteenth centuries, when they had the trade of the Carnatic in their hands, and carried on a lucrative trade with Europe and the East. From a valuable Armenian manuscript, written at Masulipatam by one Sarkies Johanness in 1790, we find that the Armenians settled *permanently* at Madras in the year 1666. The English had settled there in 1640. These opulent merchants were famous for their piety and true philanthropy, and for the great zeal they evinced in the advancement of Armenian classical literature in India. Their patriotism is perhaps unparalleled. They appealed to Catherine II. of Russia to free Armenia from the galling yoke of the Muhammadans (Persians) and place it under her suzerainty. Two millionaires volunteered to place their millions at the disposal of the Russian Government for the purposes of the projected war, but, somehow or other, the project was not matured.

The *first* Armenian church at Madras was erected as far back as 1712. It was one of the few magnificent edifices in the Esplanade of that city, but the Armenians were obliged to desert it after a time, as the British authorities would not permit so high an edifice to stand in the immediate vicinity of the Fort. The Latin church in the same neighbourhood was objected to for the same reason, and demolished. The present Armenian church, situated in Armenian Street, was erected in 1772, and dedicated to the Holy Virgin Mary, the site being the old Armenian burying-ground, on which, moreover, a chapel stood, where they worshipped while the present church was in course of erection. The ground was the property of the famous Agah Shameer. His wife, Anna, had been buried there in 1765, and a room built to her memory. This room, which is still known as 'Shameer's Room,' was attached to the church that was built seven years afterwards.

KHOJAH PETRUS WOSKAN.

The most eminent Armenian merchant at Madras in the earlier half of the eighteenth century was Khojah Petrus, son of Khojah Woskan, and a grandson of the famous Khojah Pogose of Julfa. He was a true philantropist and an earnest patriot in helping and succouring his countrymen. He was strongly attached to the English,* and was one of the members

* In 1741 presents were sent by the English in Madras to Raghoji Bhonsla, the Mahratta General, and the founder of Nagpur, through Khojah Petrus Woskan. In the same year he was employed by Governor Benyon as political agent in certain negotiations with Imam Sahib of Arcot.

of the Hon'ble East India Company's Council of Madras. He is first alluded to in the Madras Records, in 1724, as "Coderjee [Cojah] Petrus, an Armenian lately arrived from Manilla and an inhabitant of this place [Madras]". At that period, the highly lucrative commerce with Manilla was entirely in the hands of the Armenians, and they were blamed by the President for carrying their merchandise from Europe in Danish ships, and consigning their oriental goods to Pondicherry and other foreign ports in India. They traded in precious stones and rich stuffs with Persia and Europe. They had some fine ships which they officered with Englishmen and sailed under European flags.

It is recorded that, on the occasion of the visit of the Nawab of Arcot to Madras, Khojah Petrus received him with great *éclat*, entertained him for some days, and had all the principal streets through which he had to pass draped in silk. The Nawab, greatly appreciating the loyalty of the Armenian merchant, requested him to name a wish, which would be granted then and there. Khojah Petrus asked for the sole monopoly of the import trade to Madras and into the interior. This request was immediately granted. He thus amassed considerable riches, but sustained heavy losses in the troubled days when the French captured Madras in 1746 under Count Lally and totally demolished all the public buildings. Upwards of forty houses belonging to him in the city were levelled with the ground, besides other houses that he had in the Fort. The French, moreover, seized all that he had in the Fort and carried the spoil to Pondicherry. He took refuge in a Danish town close to Madras, and Count Lally sent him a message to place himself under the protection of the French Government, when the property confiscated by them would be restored. He spurned the overture, replying tersely and sarcastically that whatever riches he had possessed, had been acquired under the auspices of the British Government, to whom he would remain loyal, and that the French were at liberty to confiscate his goods, which would help to replenish their depleted treasury. In spite

In the *Fort St. David Consultations* for the 2nd September, 1749, we find that "Coja Petrus had been very serviceable to the Company by lending them large sums in time of necessity."

of these heavy financial losses, he left, in cash alone, at his death in 1751, the considerable sum of seven lakhs of rupees.

This notable merchant constructed, in 1726, a long bridge of many arches over the river Adyar, which flows through the hills* of St. Thomé and the village of Mamlan at the southern extremity of Madras. It is still standing and is known as the "Marmalong Bridge". He is said to have spent over the bridge the sum of 30,000 hoons, *i.e.*, pagodas (each pagoda being equivalent to Rs. 3-8), and left a fund for the maintenance of the bridge. One of the two tall pillars which flank the south approach, bears a stone tablet, with the following inscription in Latin, in raised letters. "Hunc pontem edificari jassit pro bono publico Coja Petrus Uscan natione Armeni, Anno Salutis, MDCCXXVI". There are also inscriptions in the Armenian and Persian languages. There is another hill, about six miles from Madras, the supposed site of the martyrdom of St. Thomas, the apostle of India. A Christian church has long been in existence at its summit, and is frequently visited by the devout. In 1726 Khojah Petrus caused 160 broad stone steps to be made at his own expense from the foot to the top of the hill, with spacious resting-places at intervals.

Having inherited the piety of his great grandfather, Khojah Petrus Velijanian, who, in 1627, had constructed the beautiful church of St. Bethlehem, at Julfa, Petrus Woskan, built a church at Vepery in Madras, dedicated to Our Lady of Miracles, for the use of the poor Christians of that city. The Capuchin fathers were placed in spiritual charge of that church.

In November 1749, the Capuchins were ordered by the Government to hand over the church to the Danish Missionaries, because they were "suspected of giving the French, before the attack of Madras, intelligence of the strength and condition of the garrison." Petrus Woskan, protested vehemently

---

* There is a church on one of these hills, now in the hands of the Latin clergy, where many tombstones exist to the present day bearing Armenian inscriptions, dating early in the seventeenth century, from which we infer that the church was erected or endowed by the Armenians during that period.

against the high-handedness of the English, but the Council said that, as the Capuchins had claimed a right to it, the orders must stand.

The following is a copy of the letter which he wrote to the Council at Fort St. David on the 1st November 1749.

"I cannot help acquainting Your Honour, &c. of my great surprize to find that there is an Order of Council sent here some days ago to deliver up the Chapel and other buildings at Viparee to the Danish Missionaries, notwithstanding the remonstrances I have made by my Letters to the Honourable Governor Floyer to the contrary, and to which (by the by) his Honour has not yet vouchsafed me an answer hitherto.

It will be great satisfaction to me if Your Honour &c. will please to let me know by what Law of Authority you give away my property at pleasure. It may perhaps be imagined that I have made over Viparee Chappel &c. to the Romish Priests, and of consequence that it is their property; but I declare I have done no such thing. It was originally intended for the poor beggars of Madrass; and how Your Honour &c. can alineate it to other purposes I must own I cannot conceive, as it cost me upwards of four thousand pagodas, which if you will please order to be paid me here, I am ready to deliver it up to the Danish Missionaries or whom else Your Honour &c. thinks fit. But should Your Honour &c. not think proper to do this, nor yet let it remain appropriated to the first use I intended, I, in that case desire the favour I may have the liberty to give it to the Priests of my own Nation, who have had their Church razed to the ground by the French in our late Calamity's.*

I have no ill will to the Danish Missionaries nor to any Christian Missionaries, and have already wrote the Governor I am willing to contribute something towards building a Church for them; but to let them have Viparee Church is what I can never consent to; and therefore I humbly desire Your Honour &c. will not insist on it, upon consideration that

---

* This refers to the first Armenian church at Madras which was erected in *1712. It was demolished when the French, under Count Lally, took Madras in 1746.*

the many troubles I have undergone was with hopes of reaping advantages with Your Nation, and not to be wronged from my right. Your doing me Justice herein will greatly oblige."

The Council ultimately arrived at the conclusion that the Vepery Chapel had really been the property of Petrus Uscan.

In his will, which was in the Armenian language, and dated the 19th January 1750, Petrus Woskan writes about the Vepery Church, as follows:

"After I expire, let my body be buried in the Chappel Nossa Senhora de Milagres, which I got erected at Viparee.

Let 1500 Pagodas be placed in the hands of the Superior, Padre Severini,* to finish the remainder work of the Chappel Nossa Senhora de Milagres (which I begun) and ornamenting the same.

The Superior, Padre Severini, had bought a ground distant from Madrass upon which I got the Chappel erected, and for which Chappel let 1500 Pagodas more be placed in the hands of the said Superior to let them at interest, and with the interest thereof a daily Mass to say for my soul.

I gave Viparee and its ground to Padre Severini to be his prayer Chappel, and no person on my part shall have power to govern them, and the same Padre, being my first executor, shall likewise take all the money I kept for Viparee."

After the death of Petrus Woskan, the Danish Missionaries were put in possession of the Church at Vepery, in November 1752.

His executors, Father Severini, Menatsakan and Johanness Gregory lodged a protest against the transfer, but to no effect, for the *fiat* had gone forth and the decision of the Council was final.

A life-size oil painting, executed at Madras in 1737, of this highly patriotic Armenian, is to be seen at All Saviour's Cathedral at Julfa in Ispahan. The noble and pious Khojah

* Father Severini, a Capuchin Missionary of the Order of St. Francis, was a native of Savoy. He was in spiritual charge of the Portuguese church at Madras as an Apostolic Missionary.

is represented in old-style Armenian garb. With a pen he writes in Armenian, 'The fear of the Lord is the beginning of wisdom.' On one side of the painting is the figure of a heart neatly painted, and beneath it a metrical verse in Armenian, composed by Khojah Petrus himself, the following being a translation :—

"My heart longs for home, where, should I be unable to go, I desire that, when my last day comes, my heart be sent to my native town, so that I, PETRUS WOSKAN, shall have a grave there."

These lines bear strong testimony to his patriotism, which knew no bounds, so much so that he desired that his heart should be taken to the land of his birth for interment. In the Armenian inscription on his tombstone which can be seen to this day in a fine state of preservation in St. Matthias Church at Vepery, it is recorded that in accordance with the wishes of the deceased, his heart was taken out after his death and sent immediately, enclosed in a golden casket, to his birthplace, Julfa, for interment in the church erected there by his great grandfather, the famous Khojah Petrus Velijanian.

This was not the first instance, however, of an Armenian sojourner in India having expressed a fervent desire to be buried at his birthplace after his demise, as will be seen from the following circumstance. Up to a very recent date there was to be seen a solitary tombstone in the ruins of the palatial houses and villas on the banks of the Zenderood river in the city of Julfa, erected by the opulent Armenian merchants of bygone days. The tombstone bore an inscription in the Armenian language, which may thús be rendered into English :—

"Jesus Christ, Lord of all, when Thou sittest on the judgment seat of the Great Tribunal, have Thou mercy on AGAH MAROOTH, on his father THASALY, on his mother KHANPHASHY, on SUGMEER his wife, and on SIMON his son *who died in India*, and whose body was brought from thence and buried in this spot in the year 1706 A.D. May God have mercy on his soul, on his brother APOVEN, and on his sisters AGAHY and GUNGUN."

Khojah Petrus made out his last will and testament in 1750, bequeathing large sums for various places of pilgrimage for Christians, as well as for the establishing of charitable and educational institutions at Julfa, where he was born. He died at Madras on the 15th January 1751, at the age of 70, prior to the erection of the present Armenian church, and his remains were interred at the chapel he had erected in Vepery and on the site of which the present St. Matthias Church was erected in 1823.

The tombstone bears inscriptions in ancient Armenian and Latin testifying to the great virtues of the deceased. The Latin inscription is as follows :—

"Elatus fama in auras, interque nubila caput condens, hic ingressus solo jacet. Discordium conciliator, jurgiorumque placator, Armeniorum fautor, columenque firmum, indigentium præsidium, fervidumque tutamen in publica damna detrimentaque resarciendo impendiosus, largusque refector, in Divina, ædesque sacras propagando haud perparcè strenuus impensor PETRUS USCAN DE COJA POGUS, Armenius, cujus cor Julfæ;

Annos natus 70, e vitta decessit, 15 Januarii 1751."

The English translation which was made for us by the late Fr. H. Hosten, S. J. is as follows :—

"Raised on high by his renown, his head hidden in the clouds, here lies, sunk beneath the sod, one who reconciled discord and appeased strife, the strong support and pillar of the Armenians, the protector and warm defender of the poor, a man generous and liberal in repairing the loss and damage suffered by the public, one who spent his money lavishly and without stint to promote the worship of God and sacred buildings, Petrus Uscan, [grandson] of Coja Pogus, an Armenian, whose heart is at Julfa. Aged 70, he departed this life on January 15, 1751."

Khojah Petrus Woskan had no children. He was survived by his wife, Mamakhathoon, the daughter of Johanness Khalanthar Zachariah of Julfa. She died in 1781, aged 69 years, and is buried in the Armenian church at Madras. She was, according to the inscription on her tombstone, charitable and gave part of her wealth to the poor and also constructed galleries in the Armenian church at Madras. She was, we are told, buried with great pomp.

AGAH SHAMEER SOOLTHANOOMIAN.

Another Armenian merchant who rose to eminence in Madras was Agah Shameer Soolthanoomian. He was born at Julfa in 1723. Coming to India in early life, he settled at Madras, where he flourished during the latter part of the eighteenth century. He was a famous pearl merchant and also carried on a lucrative trade in Persian rose-water and dried fruits imported from his native town. By selling them at immense profit to the Nawab of the Carnatic and to his luxurious household, he amassed considerable riches. He lent large sums to the Nawab of the Carnatic, and the debt was not cleared off when the English took his country. It is recorded that, when the Nawab was being oppressed by his many creditors, Agah Shameer went to pay him his respects, and had the Nawab's promissory note with him. The Nawab asked, "And do *you*, my dearest friend, entertain any fear as to my financial position, and have therefore come to demand your just claims from me?" The noble Agah Shameer replied: "Not so, my lord. I have come as usual to pay my humble respects to Your Highness. My claim against you is but a little dust from your shoes!" And as he spoke he took out the Nawab's promissory note from his breast pocket, tore it up, and threw the pieces at the Nawab's feet. This magnanimous act, which appears little short of a romance, excited the enthusiastic admiration of the Nawab and his courtiers, and the grateful debtor ordered the title-deeds of the village of Noomblee to be brought to him. He then ordered his Private Secretary to write out a *firman,* which he duly signed and sealed, to the effect that he was pleased, of his own free will, to grant the village of Noomblee, with all the lands attached thereto, to his valued and esteemed friend Agah Shameer, as a personal gift, who would be its lawful owner, and could do whatever he liked with the same. Neither his heirs, nor the British Government, were in any way to annul the provisions contained in the deed of gift which was bestowed on Agah Shameer, and he was exempted from paying any taxes thereon.

The village of Noomblee was to remain the property of Agah Shameer and his descendants for ever. This large property was owned by the descendants of the Shameer family of Madras until of late years.

It appears from the Madras Records that Agah Shameer's father, "Coja Sultan David," was a notable merchant of Madras in the first-half of the 18th century. A wealthy Armenian merchant, a "Coja Nazar Jacob Jan," who had been in Madras since 1702, died, date not given, but it must have been shortly after 1740, leaving his large estate at Madras,* and at Julfa, to Coja Sultan David. The estate at Julfa must have been a large one, for the legatee immediately sends his son Shameer to take possession of the properties there. Shameer, then a young man of about twenty, was seized, with his mother Anam, by the "Calantar of Julpha"† and "inhumanly beaten" until they consented to the revocation of Coja Nazar Jacob Jan's will.

The Calantar, according to the Records, suffered for his cruelty, for he was haled before the magistrate, lost his ears, and "dyed a miserable death."

This is not however correct historically, for the Calantar unfortunately died a peaceful death at Shiraz in 1771. Shortly before his death, he had been deputed to Basra by Kherim Khan Zend, the enlightened governor of Fars, to induce the

---

* A fine large house, owned by Coja Nazar Jacob Jan in Charles Street, was at one time occupied by Clive. As the Admiralty House, it eventually became the town residence of the Governor of Madras and the scene of many public entertainments. It is now the office of the Accountant General.

† This was the notorious Khalanthar Sarkies who held the office of Khalanthar or the Mayor of Julfa, (appointed by the Persian Governor of Ispahan), from 1739 to 1752. His memory is held up to execration by the Armenians of Julfa to this day, for his treachery and cruelty. He was a tyrant and surpassed even the tyranny of the lawless Persian Government of that period in oppressing the poor helpless Armenians, many of whom, of the well-to-do class, left Julfa in the dead of night and fled to Basrah, leaving every thing behind.

A son of Khalanthar Sarkies named Bagram, died at Masulipatam in 1816 and is buried in the Bandar Fort St. John Cemetery of that place, where there are other Armenian graves dating from 1784 to 1822.

many well-to-do Armenians who had fled from Julfa, to return to their homes, but his mission was a total failure, as the Armenians at Basra had very painful recollections of the cruelties they had suffered at the hands of the former Persian governors, Azad Khan and Hassan Khan, to say nothing of their accomplice, Khalanthar Sarkies. They had no desire to return to their deserted homes. But we have digressed.

Anam, Shameer's mother at Julfa, acting apparently under pressure, brought to bear on her by the avaricous Calantar, drew bills on her husband for large sums, and forwarded them to Madras, through the Chief and Council of Gombroom (Bandar Abbas) and the Government of Bombay, together with a Power of Attorney to enable the Government of Madras to enforce acceptance, but, as was to be expected, Coja Sultan David protested the bills, and the Madras Council, strongly supported him. This was in 1745.

This Armenian millionaire when at the zenith of his glory, sent some rich presents including a valuable diamond to Heraclius II,* King of Georgia, then a quasi-independent king-

---

* Heraclius II was a Georgian prince educated in the camp of Nadir Shah, King of Persia. He accompanied him on his memorable expedition to India in 1739. In 1733 Georgia had fallen under the sway of Nadir Shah, that obscure soldier of fortune from Khorassan, who had, in 1730, delivered Persia from the Afghans, driven out the Turks and, at the unanimous request of the principal nobles and officers of Persia, ascended the throne on the morning of the 26th February 1735. After Nadir Shah's tragic death in 1747, Heraclius restored the kingdom of Georgia and was proclaimed King at Tiflis. To ensure the safety of his country against his neighbours, who were constantly at war with him, Heraclius declared himself in 1783 a vassal of Russia, but was abandoned by the Russians in 1795, when the Persians, under Agha Muhammad Khan, invaded Georgia, defeated Heraclius, captured and destroyed Tiflis the capital, and led a great number of its inhabitants into captivity. Heraclius II, died in 1798, and was succeeded by his son, George XIII, a weak-minded prince, whose short reign was throughout disturbed by a civil war against his brothers. After his death, in 1800. Georgia was annexed by Russia, and the members of the royal family were carried to the Russian capital. Alexander, another son of Heraclius II, took refuge in Persia; but his wife—the daughter of Melik Sahak (Isaac), an Armenian nobleman of Erivan in Armenia—was taken to St. Petersburg with her son. Alexander ended his days in exile, dying in poverty at Teheran, and lies buried there in the Armenian churchyard.

dom in the Caucasus. In return the king conferred upon him and his male children the city of Loree, near Tiflis, as a mark of royal approbation and invited the esteemed Agah Shameer to go and settle there with his children. This was in 1775.

In 1786, King Heraclius II, by a royal edict, nominates Agah Shameer and his male children as Princes of Georgia and sends him, at the same time, a Coat of Arms. We give below an English translation of the edict or *farman*† from which it appears that Agah Shameer of Madras was held in very high esteem by the sovereign of far-off Georgia.

"By the Grace of God, we of the race of Jesse, David, Solomon, Bagratoony, the son of the anointed Thamraz, King of Georgia and King of Kakh, natural ruler of Samtzkhe, Saathabegoo, lord of Qachakh, lord of Borshaloo, lord of Shamshadin, lord of Kakoo, lord of Shakhoo, lord of Shirwan, conqueror and ruler of Ganja and Erivan, Heraclius the Second.

Be it known to all men that whereas Shameer, the son of Sultan of Julfa, in Ispahan, and his ancestors, have had love and fidelity towards our ancestors and towards us as well, since their coming to Asia in the days of the former kings of Persia and of Nadir Shah. He [Shameer] having now revived the same from the remote country of India, has displayed, in manifold ways, his loyalty and useful suggestions to our kingdom. He is therefore nominated by us as a Prince of Georgia, so that in all places he and his lawful sons may enjoy the same rights and privileges and be honoured with the same honour as the native Princes of Georgia.

And we hereby grant him this Coat of Arms, a round shield with a golden ground, with a ship engraved in the centre

† We are indebted to the late Mr. Gregory Paul Melitus of London, who was descended from Agah Shameer through his mother, for copies of the *farmans,* the originals of which, were in his possession. His maternal grandfather, Seth Sam, had married a grand daughter of Agah Shameer and had come into possession of the original *farmans* and the family documents. With the death of Mr. Melitus, which occurred in 1927, at the ripe old age of ninety-five, the valuable documents were destroyed as the children who had been educated in England, did not know the historical value of the family papers which had been religiously preserved by their revered father, as valuable family relics.

as a symbol of profitableness and permanency towards good works, and in the midst of the ship is placed a rock as a sign of hardest firmness and on the rock is fixed an arm as an emblem of power, and having in the hand a telescope as a sign of careful farsightedness, and on the back of the rock springs an apple tree, full of fruits and leaves, rising above the rock as a mark of honour and fruitful activities.

Having honoured him with all these princely honours, we have, with our own hand, set our special signature to it and sealed with our Royal Seal. Written at our Royal Palace in the Capital city of Tiflis, by the hand of our Secretary, Chancellor Thoomanian, and addressed to [Shmeer] Sultan, the Prince of Goojasp.

In the year of our Saviour, 1786 and in the 43rd year of our reign, on the 22nd day of March and in the year 474 of the Georgian era." The document was translated from the original Georgian into ancient Armenian by Rev. David, the son of Rev. Ohanian, by the order of His Royal Majesty, King Heraclius of Georgia.

In 1790, the heir-apparent, Prince George of Georgia, by order of his august father writes to Agah Shameer, on behalf of himself, his wife Mariam Bagratoony, and his seven sons, David, Ikhane, Bagarat, Thamraz, Michael, Gabriel and Elijah, confirming the grant of the city of Loree, with all the surrounding villages, fields, mountains, forests, waterways, the boundaries of which are minutely defined.

After Georgia had been annexed by Russia in 1800, the Russian government gave notice that if within ten years from that date, no claimants came forward to establish their claim to the city of Loree, it would lapse to Government, and so it did, for the descendants of Agah Shameer at Madras immersed in pleasure-seeking and voluptiousness* did not bestir themselves

* One of the three sons of Agah Shameer, named Johanness, died a poor man in 1834 and is buried in the Armenian churchyard at Madras where all the members of the Shameer family lie interred. A great-grandson of Agah Shameer, Joseph Nazar Jacob Shameer, spent some years in the Madras jail for civil debtors. There are at present no descendants of the Armenian millionaire, in the male line.
—*Sic transit gloria mundi* !

to go and claim their rightful heritage which, as we have seen, had been bestowed upon Agah Shameer by King Heraclius II of Georgia, in 1775.

There exists in the Armenian church at Madras a life-size portrait of this distinguished personage, dressed in Armenian costume and national head-gear, with the following articles arranged before him :—A pair of scissors, a yard measure, a pair of scales with small weights for weighing precious stones, and an ink-pot with a quill pen; in his hand is a row of large pearls which he is offering to a jeweller for sale. This was adopted as the crest of the Shameer family, and it is carved on all the tombstones of the Shameers who lie buried at the Armenian churchyard of Madras. Agah Shameer, the head of the family, died at Madras* in 1797, and an Armenian inscription, of which the following is a translation, appears on his tomb :—

"Here lies interred the body of the noble Shameer Soolthanoomian, an Armenian, who was born at New Julfa on the 4th November 1723, and died here at Madras, on Saturday, the 13th day of June 1797, aged 74 years."

He left three sons, viz., Jacob, Johanness, and Eleazar. Jacob was born at Madras in 1745, and died at *Malacca* in 1774 in the prime of life. He had inherited his father's patriotism. This is clearly illustrated from the pathetic epitaph on his tombstone at *Malacca*.† Naturally studious, he was enthusiastic in the advancement of classical Armenian literature in India. To him is due the honour of having started at Madras in 1772 the *first* Armenian press in India, of which more hereafter. Johanness was born at Madras in 1757, and died a poor man in 1834, leaving only one daughter. He is buried in the Armenian churchyard of Madras. Eleazar was likewise born at Madras, in 1758, and, like his eldest brother, died at the age of 29, in 1787. He is buried in the Armenian churchyard of Madras.

---

* A road in Madras bears Shameer's name.

† See page 251 footnote.

AGAH SAMUEL MOORAT

Agah Samuel Mackertich Moorat, whose noble heart glowed with patriotism, was another Armenian merchant of great wealth at Madras. His name will be handed down to posterity for his benevolence and zeal in the cause of educating indigent Armenian youth and orphans. He died* in 1816 leaving a large bequest for the establishing of a school in Europe for Armenian youth, which should be under the control of the Mekhitharist Fathers† at Venice. They deputed to

* He was a Roman Catholic Armenian and was buried *inside* the Roman Catholic Cathedral in Armenian Street. On his beautiful marble tombstone, in the "Moorat Chapel", the following lines are inscribed:

"Sacred to the memory of Samuel Mucartish Moorat, Esquire, a much respected member of the Armenian community, who departed this life at Madras 20th of April, 1816. By integrity and urbanity in public dealing, by hospitability and benevolence in private life, by exemplary conduct both in moments of difficulty and those of prosperity and by numerous acts of beneficence to the necessitous, he became beloved by all who know him. In token of conjugal and filial affection, this monument is erected by his sorrowing family." His wife, Anna Raphael, who died on the 2nd July, 1828, aged 57 years, is also buried in the Chapel. Their elder son, Edward Samuel Moorat, who died on the 10th October, 1837 is also buried there. Edward Moorat led a most profligate life after his father's death and squandered the large fortune he had inherited from his father. He lived in the beautiful house known as the Old College. He owned "Moorat's Gardens", where the office of the Director of Public Instruction is located now. They were purchased by Government for Rs. 90,000 in 1827 and shortly after, Moorat parted with the "Pantheon," which is the nucleus of the spreading block of buildings that now make up the Madras Museum. His younger brother John, went to live in London where his descendants are still to be found.

† This is a religious band of erudite Armenian monks, leading a monastic life, who are styled 'Adopted Sons of the Virgin, Doctors of Penitence.' For their arms they have a Cross surrounded by the four emblenis of St. Anthony, *viz.*, the Flame, the Bell, the Gospel, and the Staff. The Society is called after its founder, Mekhithar, an Armenian monk from Sebastia (the modern Sivas), whose memory is dear to all lovers of the classical language of ancient Armenia. Endowed with gifts of a high order, Mekhithar saw the deplorable state of neglect into which Armenian literature had sunk owing to the political troubles of Armenia, and conceived the happy idea of founding a monastic order having for its object the advancement of classical Armenian literature and the intellectual welfare of the Armenian nation. After travelling through Armenia and Asia Minor, the missionary priest arrived in 1700 at Con-

40

Madras one of their *confrères*, the Rev. Dr. Sarkies Theodorean, to realise the endowment; and, after a protracted law-suit in the Madras Court, Rs. 640,500 were paid to him on 26th March 1827 by Edward and Johanness, Agah Samuel Moorat's sons and executors.

---

stantinople, a great Armenian centre, where he endeavoured to found his project. At Pera a pleasant suburb of Constantinople, Mekhithar, with three of his disciples, started a printing press and published a few religious and educational works in the Armenian language. His efforts in that direction were frustrated, however, through the machinations of the ignorant clergy of that time, and he had to flee from Constantinople. After encountering many hardships, he and his disciples found a refuge at Modon, a town in Morea, then under the government of the powerful Venetian Republic. For twelve years he remained undisturbed at Modon, and was then obliged to fly before the Turkish invasion of Morea, who took Modon and pillaged and burned the monastery which Mekhithar had established at that place. Thanks to the kindness of the humane Venetian Admiral and the Governor of Morea, they not only sympathised with the destitute monks, but granted them permission to embark in a government vessel bound for Venice. On their arrival there, in April 1715, the twelve hapless Armenian monks were hospitably received by the Republic. The Senate, regarding with favour the great project Mekhithar had in view, was pleased to confer upon him and his followers for ever the Isle of St. Lazarus (San Lazzaro) in the vicinity of Venice, on which there had once been a Leper Asylum. Mekhithar, with his small hand of devoted followers occupied the island, where he erected an Armenian monastery, which was completed in 1740, with a church, school, printing-press and all the accessories of a monastic institution. In that abode of peace, the pious Mekhitharist monks have devoted their lives to study and research. They have rendered valuable services to the literary world in general and the Armenian nation in particular. They have edited and published the Armenian classics and have also rendered into classical Armenian the works of the classical writers of ancient Rome and Greece, for the benefit of the Armenian nation. They have from time to time published many original works of great literary merit on the history, literature, antiquities and archaeology of Armenia. Classical Armenian literature might have sunk into inevitable oblivion, but for the lifelong devotion of the zealous and erudite Mekhitharist Fathers at Venice and Vienna, to whom the entire Armenian nation owes a deep debt of gratitude. Byron, who studied Armenian with the Mekhitharist Fathers, wrote from Venice on 2nd January 1817 :—

"On my arrival at Venice in the year 1816, I found my mind in a state which required study, and study of a nature which should leave little scope for the imagination, and furnish some difficulty in the pursuit. At this period I was struck—in common, I believe, with every other

In 1834, the Mekhitharist Fathers first opened a College in the name of the founder at Padua in Italy; in 1846 it was changed to Paris; and subsequently removed to Venice, where through the bounty of Edward Raphael,* another rich Armenian of Madras, and the father-in-law of Agah Samuel Moorat, a similar institution had been opened in 1836, and named Raphael College, after its patriotic founder. Under the able supervision of the Mekhitharists, the institution continues its useful work in educating Armenian youth in the vernacular and the modern European languages. Some of the former students of the Raphael-Moorat College held high appointments in the Civil and Military services of Persia and Turkey during the second-half of the 19th century, and many other Armenians in humbler position owe their success to the bounty of these patriots of Madras in the early part of the last century. The centenary of the Raphael-Moorat College was celebrated last year (1936) with great *eclat*, by the Mekhitharists of Venice and the numerous grateful ex-pupils of the great national institution.

---

traveller—with the Society of the Convent of St. Lazarus, which appears to unite all the advantages of the monastic institution without any of its vices. The neatness, the comfort, the gentleness, the unaffected devotion, the accomplishments, and the virtues of the brethren of the order, are well-fitted to strike the man of the world with the conviction that there is another and a better even in this life. These men are the priesthood of an oppressed and a noble nation," &c.

* Edward Raphael, a Roman Catholic Armenian, was one of the founders of the Carnatic Bank, the *first* Joint Stock Bank founded in Madras on the 1st June, 1788. He died in 1791, on the voyage to London and was buried at sea. His wife Maria Stephana Raphael, who died in 1790, aged 34 years, lies buried in the Luz (Roman Catholic) Church at Mylapore. Their eldest son, Alexander Raphael, a highly educated person, who had settled in England, succeeded in entering the House of Commons as a Catholic Tory for St. Albans. He was the first Armenian to have a seat in the British Parliament. He had been the Sheriff of London for 1829. As a patron of Armenian literature, he helped the learned Makhitharists fathers of Venice and Vienna to publish some important works in the language of ancient Armenian.

GREGORY AND SETH SAM.

We must not omit to record the names of Gregory and Seth Sam, notable Armenian merchants of Madras in the early part of the 19th century. These two brothers, like Samuel Moorat, were patrons of learning, and in 1834, they founded at Julfa, their birthplace, a school, known as the "All-Saviour's College," under the able Rectorship of that great educationist, Mesrovb David Thaliadian, the future journalist, poet and author of India. The father of the present writer was one of the many pupils who attended that school and he always spoke in terms of the highest praise about the erudite Rector and the sound education imparted by him, but unfortunately the "children of darkness" who controlled the institution, did not appreciate his worth, with the result that he severed his connection with the school in 1836 and went to Tabriz, where his wife, who was the present writer's paternal aunt, named Thangkhathoon, *died on the 18th November, 1837.*

As has been stated in the beginning of this chapter, the Armenians at Madras evinced great zeal in the advancement of the classical Armenian literature in India, by starting printing-presses for the publication of books and journals in the national language.

The first Armenian publication in India, printed at Madras, dates back to the year 1772. The interesting title-page may thus be literally rendered into English :—

"New pamphlet, called *Exhortation,* composed for the awakening of the Armenian youth from the weak and idle drowsiness of the sleep of slothfulness, and with an ardent and tender desire printed at the expense and through the exertions of Jacob Shameer by his tutor Moses Bagram, for the benefit of the tender Armenian youth, in the year of the incarnation of the Word 1772 and in the year 1221 of the Armenian era. *In* India, at the city of Madras, at the press of the said Jacob Shameer."

The works in the Armenian language, published at Madras between the years 1772-1800, possess considerable literary merit.

REV. ARATHOON SHUMAVON

It is a curious fact that the *first* Armenian journal ever printed in any part of the world was published at Madras, a hundred and forty-three years ago, by the Rev. Arathoon Shumavon, an Armenian priest of Shiraz, whose name is dear to all interested in the study of classical Armenian. He started the *Azdarar* (*i.e.* 'Intelligencer') on the 28th October 1794, and published it monthly for eighteen consecutive months until February 1796. Its centenary Jubilee was celebrated, in 1894, by Armenian journalists in Constantinople, Smyrna, Tiflis, Venice, Vienna, Marseilles, and America; and, in commemoration of the event, the religious society of the Armenian *literati* (the Mekhitharists) at Vienna, of the monastic order of the great Mekhithar, published an artistic phototype of the venerable father of Armenian journalism.*

While at Shiraz, the Rev. Arathoon Shumavon had the misfortune to lose his two sons in one week. Overcome by grief, he left his fold and retired from the city. He took up his abode with the Persian *dervishes* (anchorites) in the solitude of Babakoh, 'far from the madding crowd.' This hill, (the Parnassus of the Persians) being within easy distance, however, of the city, was the favourite haunt of the two famous Persian poets, Saadi and Hafez, who frequently resorted thither to invoke their muse. The Armenian cemetery of Shiraz nestles at the foot of this hill, and there sleeps the immortal poet, Mcsrovb David Thaliadian.

For seven long years the bereaved Shumavon remained with the Persian *dervishes* at Babakoh, and studied closely the flowery Persian language—the French of the East,—which he completely mastered, and distinguished himself as a Persian scholar. Yielding eventually to the entreaties of those who were dear and near to him, he returned once more to the city from which he had turned his face. Shortly afterwards he departed from Shiraz, with its melancholy associations, and

---

* In connection with this jubilee, the late Father Dr. Gregoris Galemkharean, a member of the well-known Mekhitharist Society of Armenian monks at Vienna, published in 1893 an opportune work—the first volume of the *History of Armenian Journalism* from 1794-1860—and dedicated it to 'The Armenian journalists of the day.'

came to Madras—which at that time contained an influential Armenian community solely engaged in commerce—as a minister for the Armenian church of that place. The patriotic Armenians of Madras had already shown a praiseworthy zeal for the advancement of classical Armenian literature, and they warmly seconded his endeavours in that direction. About 1789 he started a printing-press at Madras for printing and publishing books in the Armenian language. In the absence of any trained workmen, he acted as compositor and printer. Not only that, but the type used was cast by himself from materials prepared by his own hands and even the paper used was made by him by the primitive method in vogue at that time for making hand-made paper from cotton pulp, a large undertaking, even in the present day, which few would attempt single-handed. The first publication from his press, in 1789-90, was a reprint of *The Martyrology of the Virgin Marianeh*. The interesting title-page may be rendered into English thus :—

"An account of the Holy Virgin Marianeh reprinted from a copy originally printed at Constantinople in the year 1766 A.D., and now printed in India, at this capital of Madras, from type prepared by the Rev. Arathoon, son of Shumavon of Shiraz, for the benefit of the Armenian youths, in the year of our Lord 1789'.

The indefatigable printer adds an interesting notice at the end of the book, dated 30th January 1790, from which it appears that only two hundred copies of it were printed at the expense and through the exertions of the Rev. Arathoon Shumavon, "by the grace of God a priest of Shiraz, in honour of his intimate friend, the noble Agah Marooth Joseph, of the family of Phurnacheantz.

The *Azdarar*, referred to already, gave an impetus to the study of the Armenian language in India amongst the Armenian colonists. At its start it had the modest number of *twenty-eight* subscribers* and the first number was issued on the 30th of

* The price of the *Azdarar* was fixed at one *hoon* per copy. The Madras *hoon* or Pagoda was in those days priced at 3½ Sicca Rupees. It was called the Pagoda by the English traders by reason of its having on the obverse the figure of a Hindoo Pagoda (temple) of Southern India. These interesting coins, both in silver and gold, are still to be found in the Madras Presidency, bearing inscriptions in Tamil.

Thirah (28th October) 1794, "during the patriarchate of His Holiness Lucas, the Catholicos of all the Armenians at Valarshapat, and in the reign of His august Majesty, Heraclius II., King of Tiflis under the protection of the [Armenian] church of the Holy Virgin at Madras, at the press of Rev. Arathoon Shumavon of Shiraz."

With such a humble beginning, Armenian journalism has, during the past 143 years, spread all over the civilized world, and to-day there are over a hundred journals and magazines published in Armenian at all the large cities and capitals of Europe, Asia, Africa and America where Armenians are found in large numbers, but by an irony of fate, India, that gave birth to Armenian journalism, does not possess a single paper to-day in the Armenian language.

Among the contributors of the *Azdarar*, was Seth Sam, who wrote verses under the *nom-de-plume* of "Friend," and the well-known Archbishop Joseph, of the princely house of Dolgorouky Argootheantz, the founder of the Armenian city of New Nakhe Jevan in Russia during the reign of Catherine II. Besides literary articles and contributions, it contained the principal events of the time. Announcements of births, marriages, and deaths amongst the Armenian community of Madras, commercial and shipping intelligence, reviews of books and the advertisements of the Armenian merchants of Madras, are to be found in its pages, and even 'answers to correspondents' were not neglected. Through his profound knowledge of the Persian language, he found great favour in the eyes of Valaji Mahamad Ali Khan, the Nawab of Madras and Arcot, from whom he received permission in 1795 to print and publish books in the Arabic and Persian languages as well. A copy of the Nawab's *firman*, granting him permission, was duly lithographed in fine Persian and Arabic characters and published in the *Azdarar* (pp. 253-254) of that year.

The life of the *first* Armenian journal was however a short one, as it lasted for two years and a half only and died a premature death in 1796, for want of sufficient support, which has unfortunately been the bane of Armenian journalism ever since its foundation in 1794.

Rev. Arathoon Shumavon, the venerable Father of Armenian journalism, died on the 9th February 1824, aged 74 years, and lies buried in the Armenian church at Madras where he had officiated as the vicar for 40 long years. In response to an appeal which we published in the Armenian journals in Europe and the Homeland, the centenary of his death was celebrated at all the Armenian centres, including Calcutta, and at our special request a requiem service was held over his grave, after the celebration of Holy Mass in the Armenian church at Madras, on the morning of Saturday, the 9th day of the February 1924. And in connection with the hundredth anniversary of the death of the Founder of Armenian journalism, we published, in the Calcutta and Madras dailies, an account of the life and the literary activities of the *first* Armenian journalist, who, as we have stated above, was also the compositor, the printer and the publisher of his monthly magazine, the *Azdarar** which had boldly entered the journalistic arena with a modest member of 28 subscribers only! A truly enterprising journalistic feat, never attempted by any journalist, since journalism, that great civilizing factor, came into existence, for whereas in these days of Rotary presses and time-saving Linotype machines, journalism is a real pleasure, it was nothing but a self-imposed task and purely a labour of love in the days when the Rev. Arathoon Shumavon published his *Azdarar* at Madras.

Peace to his soul, rest to his ashes, and may the journalism, which he founded, continue to flourish for the intellectual advancement of a much-persecuted ancient race, which, in the words of Byron "has partaken of the proscription

* There are *three* complete copies of the "Azdarar" extant at the present day. The famous library at Etchmiadzin, the Vatican of Armenia, possesses one. There is a copy in the library of the Armenian monastery of St. James in Jerusalem, and the third copy is in the private library of the present writer. There is also a copy, but incomplete, in the otherwise very rich library of the Mekhitharist Fathers at Vienna, who possess by far the best and the most complete collection of Armenian journals published in the world. It may be noted that since 1794, when Armenian journalism was born, 1586 journals have been published in different parts of the world. There is a collection of 1179 Armenian journals in the National Library of Armenia at Erivan.

and bondage of the Jews and of the Greeks, without the sullenness of the former or the servility of the latter."

ARMENIAN PRESSES AT CALCUTTA

Following the example of Madras, an Armenian press was started at Calcutta in 1797, through the exertions of another Armenian priest, the Rev. Joseph Stephen, incumbent of the Armenian church of Nazareth, Calcutta. The first publication issued from it was a valuable account of a controversy on the Truths of the Christian Religion, which took place between an Armenian monk of Julfa, named Johannes,* deep in theological lore, and the crafty monarch, Shah Safee, otherwise known as Shah Sulaiman I,† who, it may be mentioned, was desirous of converting the Armenians at Julfa to Muhammadanism, but failed in his scheme. According to the printer's preface, it was printed from a manuscript, dated 15th December 1724. We possess a copy of this now exceedingly rare publication, printed in the same year (1797) by the zealous Rev. Joseph Stephen at the newly-started press under the protection of the Armenian church of Nazareth, Calcutta." It was published "at the sole expense of the illustrious Agah Moses, son of the late Agah

* Johanness, a saint and scholar, had, through his profound knowledge of theology, as well as the Persian and Arabic languages, won for himself the honourable title of 'The Theologian of Kings.' He was the author of several theological works in Armenian of great merit, and left a few valuable works—original and translated—in Persian and Arabic, on theology and the Christian religion.

† Sulaiman Shah ascended the throne of Persia in 1665. He was the eldest son of Shah Abbas II, and the grandson of Shah Abbas the Great, the glory of the Sefavi dynasty. After an uneventful reign of twenty-nine years, spent in debauchery, Sulaiman Shah died in 1694 at Ispahan, the former capital of Persia. He was succeeded by his son, the bigoted Shah Sultan Husain; and during the troublous reign of this indolent king, the Afghans invaded Persia in 1722, and laid siege to Ispahan, and, by preventing supplies reaching the besieged, starved it into surrender. The proud Persian king, humiliated at last, with his own hands placed his crown on the head of Mahmud Ghilzai, the Afghan king, and wished him prosperity. Mahmud ascended the throne of Persia, and the Sefavi dynasty, founded by Ismail I. in 1502, was practically at an end. The Afghan rule in Persia lasted for eight years only, from 1722-30, when Nadir Shah drove the Afghans from that country.

Catchick Arrakiel of the Juntloom family of Julfa." The MS., with its pages alternately in Armenian and Persian, remained in the possession of the printer, the Rev. Joseph Stephen, who afterwards presented it, with another valuable MS. in Armenian by the same writer, to the library of Bishop's College, Calcutta.

In 1811, another press was started at Calcutta by Aviet Juntloom. An elementary book, in the Armenian language, was the first publication issued from it. This press was presented, on 1st January 1824, to the Armenian Philanthropic Academy, by the same Aviet Juntloom, and it was at work till 1883. The second Armenian journal started in India, styled the *Mirror*, was published at Calcutta in 1820. After a brief existence, its place was taken by the *Magazine*, which followed the same course. The *Patriot of Ararat*, already referred to on page 520, was the fourth Armenian journal in India. It was published at Calcutta, from 1845-52, under the able editorship of Mesrovb David Thaliadian, the Armenian poet, teacher and journalist of India. This highly instructive journal occupies an honourable place in the history of Armenian journalism.

In 1821, another journal was started in Calcutta but it did not live more than two years. The only journal that enjoyed a fairly long life, was the "Azgasare" (The Patriot) of Calcutta which was ably edited by that profound scholar, poet and educationist, Mesrovb David Thaliadian, than whom a greater Armenian scholar has not been seen in India to this day. But the same fatality—want of sufficient support—sealed the fate of the "Azgasare" in 1852, after an existence of seven years under great difficulties and privations.

Madras tried to revive the "Azdarar" in 1846 but without success, as it did not last a year even. Another attempt was made by Madras in 1848 to resuscitate Armenian journalism, but it shared the sad fate of its predecessors.

Nothing daunted, Calcutta vainly attempted in 1862 to retrieve the fortunes of the moribund national journalism, but it came to a sudden and dramatic end in 1863 by the conviction of the editor for libel with a fine of Rs. 500 and a residence of 3 months in the house of correction.

From 1794-1863, some 11 journals were published at Madras, Calcutta and Bombay, all in the Armenian language, the first five being printed, whilst the remaining six were lithographed, but with the single exception of Mesrovb Thaliadian's *Azgasare* (*The Patriot*) (1845-1852) all the others lacked literary merit and the reason is not far to seek, as all the other Editors, with the exception of the Founder, (Rev. Arathoon Shumavon) were men of business and had no literary attainments or any pretensions to scholarship; nevertheless, they deserve great credit and praise, their shortcomings notwithstanding for having zealously kept the torch of Armenian journalism flickering for 70 years under great difficulties.

We must not omit to mention the journal *Ara* in English, devoted to Armenian politics, literature and history which was ably edited by the late Mr. J. D. Melik-Beglar from 1892-1895 and the *Armenian* of the late Mr. J. Barseghian, who likewise published his journal in English from 1908-1909, and with the death of the *Armenian* which by an irony of fate happened to be the 13th in the list of Armenian journals in India—that unlucky No. 13—Armenian journalism, after a miserable existence of 115 years in this country, died a natural death with the consolation however that it had laid the foundation of the National Press which has achieved great success in Europe and elsewhere where Armenians are found in large numbers.

It is a crying shame however that a wealthy and an advanced community like the Armenians, should not have an organ for the ventilation and the furtherance of communal grievances and affairs in these days of stress and strain when events are moving very fast in the kaleidoscope of India, where the political existence of small communities is in the balance, with "India for the Indians" writ large above.

The following extracts are interesting and of historical value. Under date the 29th February 1779, a Rev. Johanness Ter Nierses wrote to the Armenian Archbishop of Julfa a long letter from Madras, in which, after giving full particulars of the war between the French and the English, he said :—

"At present commerce is at a standstill, and French ships are scouring the seas and capturing every vessel that comes in their way. A Danish ship bound for Batavia from this city of Madras was seized by the French, whereby our [Armenian] merchants sustained a heavy loss." The same clergyman, writing from Madras on 15th January 1784, observed :—

"It is three years now that we are in the midst of a serious war. There was a great scarcity of eatables, and great difficulty was experienced in procuring food, and whatever could be procured was very expensive, owing to which more than half of the population of this city perished through famine, but at the commencement of the war our [Armenian] community were divided into three parts—one part went and settled at Negapatam and Seringapatam, one part settled at Masulipatam, and one part remained at Madras."

From this it will be seen that the increasing Armenian colony of Madras formed three parties about the year 1781. One section settled at Negapatam and Seringapatam; another remained back at Madras; and the third settled at Musulipatam, where they erected a church. A few Armenian families remained at Masulipatam down to the middle of the last century.

There must have been a fairly large number of Armenians living at Hyderabad (Deccan) during and after the 17th century, but we have not yet been able to trace their history.

In January 1895, we copied in an old deserted cemetery at Hyderabad, 19 Armenian inscriptions which were still decipherable, dating from 1640 to 1724. There are two Armenian priests buried there, a Rev. Johanness, the son of Rev. Jacob, who died in 1680, and a Rev. Simon, the son of Rev. Margar, who died in 1724.

ARMENIAN GOVERNOR OF MYLAPORE.

There is near Madras an old Portuguese town of great historical interest, called Mylapore or San Thomé.

Armenians who, as we have seen, were found on the Coromandel Coast in the early part of the 16th century, are known to have lived at Mylapore since the commencement of the 17th century, for the Portuguese voyager, Albert de Mandelslo, who travelled in India from 1638 to 1640, found some Armenian merchants in that place. The town which had been in the occupation of the Portuguese since 1517, was captured in May 1662, by Abdullah Kutub Shah, the King of Golconda, who immediately appointed an Armenian, named Markus Erezad, (Hoorizad) as the Governor of Mylapore.

Early in 1664, we find the Armenian Governor sending a letter to Charles II, King of England, accompanied with some very valuable presents, worthy of the royal recipient. The letter which was brought to light by Mr. S. M. Gregory of London, a few years ago, is exhibited in the Public Records Office Museum in Chancery Lane, London. It is in the Portuguese language, with a translation in Spanish. The English rendering is as follows:

"By that benign spirit which accompanies all Majesties and of which according to reports which has reached me, your own Majesty is possessor thereof through the special grace and disposition of Heaven, I Markus Erezado, Armenian by nationality and Governor in the lands of Meliopor, am convinced in my mind that thuswise I may be permitted, with reliance, to humble myself at the feet of your Majesty, in particular entreating your Merciful Blood to condescend to my petition in subscribing me in the list of your loyal and humble subjects. For, I am deeply anxious that I may be enriched with the possession of such a calling. Although I pass my days in these distant parts, nevertheless, I personally guarantee, in all respects, in the faithfulness of my affections which I bear to the illustrious fame of your Majesty. And, of all those which are most precious in the produce of this land and, similarly, of all other articles which are of value and held in esteem, I, as Governor of this land, place the choicest as an offering under the feet of your Majesty. I do not write these words as a token of my worthiness but rather as the first fruits of my pledge in my faith for the future, being confident that the Royal spirit of your Majesty will not disdain but extend the hospitaliy of its benevolence to those who humbly seek shelter under the protecting care of your Majesty.

A ring with a large blue stone, another ring with an even larger gem of golden hue, a ring with a red stone, smaller than those mentioned above, a pearl of Bahren, a beautiful red stone, delectable to the sight and set in gold, a gem for wearing on the breast and capable of being separated into parts, being a stone with triple blue and white stripes, also a stone of large size and of great value which according to the testimony of natives of this country, is akin to the carbuncle.

All these enclosed in a small golden casket and sealed with the self-same seal which is nigh my signature subscribed below. I offer and deposit at the feet of your Supreme Rulership and request imploringly that whereas, behold, I am now your humble subject and servant, you may, by your graceful announcement, make it known in these Eastern parts, of my devotion to your Majesty. And, now, inasmuch as the work of Ship-building, altogether perfect, is difficult in these parts, I beseech your Majesty to grant me a Ship, by means of which the servants of your servant sailing in Eastern parts may gain products of high quality and value to be offered constantly to your Majesty at your pleasure and as a dutiful recognition on the part of your devoted servant. And confident in my belief in the fulfilment of the object of my petition and no less in the conciliatory spirit of your Majesty, I pray to Jesus Christ to grant your Majesty a triumphant issue, in a multiplied degree, over your seditious subjects who have risen as enemies against the Laws of Christ and all prosperity and happiness to your Majesty according to your desire. Melapor, 4th February in the year 1664.

Your Majesty's
Humble and faithful Servant,
(Signature in Armenian) MARKUS EREZAD

On the back of the letter is the address, as follows :—

"To His Most Gracious and Most Illustrious Majesty Don Carlos, King of England and Supreme Ruler of Great Britain, whom God may keep.

From the Governor of Melapor."

Inside the letter which is folded doubly, is the following endorsement in English :

"Letter from Markus Rezado, Governor of Melapor, addressed to the King, dated 4th February 1664, and duly received in July 1664."

There is nothing in the Public Records to show that the King favoured the Armenian Governor of Mylapore with a reply acknowledging the valuable presents, which were safely received by him, through one James Prince who had brought the letter and the presents from Madras.

Markus Erezad, who fondly hoped to receive the gift of a ship from the King of England, in return for his valuable presents, must have been sadly disappointed and grievously disillusioned.

In the *Vestiges of Old Madras,* Vol. II, p. 107, it is stated that "In 1710, the Armenians were suspected of having designs on San Thomé. They had purchased several houses at the Mount, and Fraser believed that they intended to establish a mercantile centre there and use San Thomé as their Seaport. Special complaint was made of Coja Saffur, 'to prevent which growing evil, it's thought expedient to pull up that insolent weed of ill humour by the root,' so Coja Saffur was confined to the Fort."

In 1749, San Thomé, was granted to the English and it has since remained in their possession. It is now a suburb of Madras containing the historic Little Mount and the Great Mount, otherwise konwn as St. Thomas' Mount. There are Christian churches of great antiquity on these two hills which are now in the hands of the Roman Catholic clergy.

OLD ARMENIAN GRAVES AT MADRAS.

As at Surat, Agra, Calcutta and Dacca, the *oldest* Christian grave at Madras is also that of an Armenian. At the foot of the big flight of stone steps leading up to the facade of the church* on the Little Mount, there is a stone, with a cross inscribed on it, and below there is an inscription of 4 lines in Armenian, which can be translated thus :

> "This is the tomb of Khojah Margar, the son of Khojah David, [died] in the year 1112."

* This church which is dedicated to our Lady of Good Health contains a cave where St. Thomas is said to have suffered martyrdom, and visitors are also shown the print of the footsteps of the Apostle.

The year of his death is given in the Armenian era which corresponds to the year 1663 A.D. In the church of the Expectation of the Blessed Virgin, erected on the summit of St. Thomas' Mount, familiarly known as the Big Mount, there is a stone tablet, let into the outer wall of the church, on the north, bearing a short inscription in Armenian, which can be translated thus :—

> "In memory of Safar, the son of Mahtesy Zachar [Zachariah] 1707."

There is also an inscription, in Portuguese, as follows :

> "Este alpendre com a porta dest a igreja mandon fuzer Coja Safar Zacharias no anno de, 1707."

From the above it appears that Coja Safar Zacharias had the porch, with the door of the church, built in 1707.

He died in 1725, and lies buried *inside* the church at St. Thomas' Mount. There is an Armenian inscription of 7 lines on his tombstone which can be translated thus :

> "This is the tomb of Safar, who was the son of Mahtesy Zachariah of Julfa, [He was] the Elekh fithore of this holy church. Departed this life in the year of the Saviour 1725, on the 5th day of Nirhan [2nd March]."

The words *Elekh fithore,* which occur in the Armenian inscription, are probably Portuguese, denoting the warden of the church. *Elekh* might be corrupt Portuguese for *electo* (elected) and *fithore* might represent *feitor* (a factor).

In front of the original facade of the church, there is an Armenian inscription of 6 lines, but the lettering cannot be deciphered owing to a thick coating of wax from dripping candles.

Near the old flag staff, at the north-east corner of the ground round the church, there is the grave of an Armenian pearl merchant who died at Madras in 1707. There is an inscription of 19 lines, the two last of which, mention in Portuguese, "Gregories Parao, Armenio 1707." We do not know what "Parao" means. The Armenian inscription can be rendered into English thus :

> "This is the tomb of Agah Gregory, the son of Sarkies. He is a native of Erivan, a citizen of a great city, a pearl merchant and an inhabitant of Madras. He is of a meek and humble nature. The Lord seated on a throne of light shall have mercy on his soul and deem him worthy of the Kingdom of heaven. Whoever, shall, on his behalf, say, 'Father I have sinned,' shall be remembered before Christ. Died in the year of the Saviour 1707, on the 22nd day of Thirah [20th October].

Under the portico of the church, lies interred the sister of Agah Shameer, the tombstone bearing inscriptions in Armenian and Latin."

The Armenian inscription can be translated thus :

> "Under this tomb lies Pherenaz, the daughter of the late Soolthanoom and the wife of Johaness of the Armenian nation, much respected by everybody. Born in the city of Ispahan, she lived 33 years and died at Phalighat on the 20th December in the year of our Lord Christ, 1739."

The Latin inscription is as follows :

> "Hic Jacet Domina Perinas filia C. [Coja] Sultan et Dominae, Anam, Conjux C. [Coja] Johanness Marcar, natione Armena, nata Ispan [Ispahan] in Persia diem supremum obiit Paleacot 20 Decembris 1739, trigenta tres annorum nata.

It can be translated thus :

> "Here lies Perinas, daughter of C. [Coja] Sultan and Mrs. Anam, wife of C. [Coja] Joannes Marcar an Armenian by nationality, born at Ispan [Ispahan] in Persia, died at Paleacot on the 20th December 1739, aged thirty-three years."

Under the porch, near the above, is the grave of Agah Shameer's mother, with inscriptions in Armenian and Latin.

The Armenian inscription can be translated thus :

"Under this tomb lies Annakhathoon, the wife of the late Soolthanoom Shameer of the Armenian nation, born at Julfa in the city of Ispahan. She lived in this world 64 years, much respected, and died at Madras on the 20th February, in the year of our Saviour Christ, 1764."

The Latin inscription is as follows :

"Hic sub monumento jacet Anna Jacobyan quæ fuit dilecta conjux Sultani David et carissima nation suæ Armeniæ praecipue suits cognatis, oriunda civitate Julpha in Persia, et agens sexaginta quatuor annos. Obiit in Madrasta 20 Februarii 1764."

It can be translated thus :

"Here under this monument lies Anna Jacobyan, the beloved wife of Sultan David, who was very dear to her Armenian countrymen, and chiefly to her relatives. Born at Julpha in Persia, she died at Madrasta [Madras] on the 20th February 1764, aged 64 years."

On a big old wooden almirah, still in good condition, in the small vaulted building, situated on the north-east of the church, now used as a godown, there are some Armenian letters, in three or four places, which are quite undecipherable. Round the small cross at the top of the reredos of the main altar of the church, there is an Armenian inscription "to the memory of Petrus, the son of Woskan."

And on the wooden support of the pulpit, there is a short inscription in Armenian, "in memory of Agah Allaverdy Sarkies, in the year 1727." There are 14 oil-paintings,* on

* There are 8 Armenian paintings, on cloth, representing Apostles and the scene of their death, in the church of Nossa Senhora da Luz, known as the Luz church, at Mylapore. In the same church, there is a clothed statue of the Infant Jesus, holding the orb of the world, surmounted by a cross, and below it there is an inscription in Armenian, showing it was presented by Khojah Petrus Woskan, the great benefactor of religious institutions at Madras.

cloth, representing our Lord and the Apostles, with their names written below in Armenian, in gilt letters, on a red background. The emblems held by the Apostles are as under :

1. St. Peter holds the keys and a cross.
2. St. Paul, a book and a sword.
3. St. Thaddeus, a book and a club.
4. St. Matthew, a book and a carpenter's rule.
5. St. Andrew, a book and a St. Andrew's cross.
6. St. Thomas, a book and a lance.
7. St. John, a poisoned chalice.
8. St. Philip, a book and a cross.
9. St. Simon, a book and a saw.
10. St. James the Less, a book and a beam.
11. St. Bartholomew, a book and some other object.
12. St. Matthias, a book and a hatchet.
13. St. James the Greater, a pilgrim's staff, a gourd and a scrip.

The background of the pictures shows the form of death of the Apostles.

When we first visited the church in April 1905, we were greatly impressed by the number of Armenian inscriptions in and near the place, which led us to infer that it had been used by the Armenians, as a place of worship, from the commencement of the 18th century, if not earlier. The stone steps leading to the church had been constructed in 1726, by an Armenian, who had also presented the Armenian altar. The pulpit, as we have seen, was the gift of an Armenian. There is the picture of our Lady and child, painted on wood, in Armenian style, and there are the Armenian paintings of our Lord and the Apostles adorning the walls of the church. What further evidence is required to prove that it was at one time an Armenian church?

Armenians have left their mark indelibly in Madras during the 18th century. Built into the east wall of the church of St. Rita, which stands at the south end of San Thome's principal street, is a stone tablet with an inscription in Armenian signifying that it was placed there "In memory of the Armenian nation in the year of the Saviour 1729". It is conjectured that the event commemorated was the opening of the grave of

St. Thomas for the veneration of the faithful, which took place on the 29th April, 1729. During the early ages, the tomb of the saint owed its preservation to the Armenians, from whom the Portuguese learnt the tradition in 1517, as has been stated in the beginning of this chapter.

We have seen in the course of this work how the enterprising Armenians established themselves at all the important commercial centres in India from the commencement of the 16th century, although they are known to have traded with India in the remote past without however forming any permanent settlements in the country.

THE FIRST ARMENIAN IN S. INDIA.

Fully seven centuries prior to the landing of Vasco de Gama on the Malabar Coast, on the 20th of May, 1498, an enterprising Armenian merchant, Thomas Cana by name, landed on the same coast in the year 780 A.D., when one Sheo Ram was the native ruler of Crangamore and in whose eyes he found great favour, which resulted in his amassing considerable riches by trading in muslins and spices, his main object in seeking the Indian shores. He is better known as Mar Thomas. As a trader, he was shrewd and active, as a diplomat, he was tactful and cunning, and we soon read of him as a prosperous merchant at Cranganore and afterwards at Angamale, further inwards the Southern Peninsula. He died in the lap of luxury, basking in the favour of potentates who loved and respected him. According to the traditions of the St. Thomas Christians of Malabar, Mar Thomas or Thomas Cana, founded a commercial town near Cranganore and obtained, by a copper-plate document, from the Emperor of Malabar, several commercial, social and religious privileges for the Christians of that country. The early Portuguese writers call him Thomas Cananeo and give his nationality as Armenian.

He is known to the Malabar Christians of the present day as Knayi Thomman or Kana Tomma, which means the merchant Thomas.

COSTARD, THE GAMALIEL OF JULFA.

A fair idea of the extent of the trade carried on by the Armenian merchants of Julfa with India and the Far East may be gathered from the following valuable and carefully-prepared list of those Indian towns with which the Armenian merchants of Julfa were acquainted and held commercial intercourse in the seventeenth century. This list was prepared in the Armenian language by one Costand, an Armenian schoolmaster at Julfa, at a time when the enterprising Armenian merchants of the commercial city of Julfa were commercially at the zenith of their glory and ventured into the remotest parts of Asia in their commercial pursuits :—

"Cashmere, Peshawar, Mooltan, Attock, Sirhind, Janabad [Shahjehanabad, i.e., Delhi], Akbarabad [Agra], Khurja, Hundwan(?), Bangalah [Bengal], Behar, Phathanah [Patna], Benares, Moven [? Mawana], Ghazipore, Jalalpur, Shahzadpur, Khairabad, Daryabad, Daulatabad, Sirhinj [? Sironj], Berhampore, Surat, Gujerat, Aurungabad, Shahgarh, Hyderabad, Moochleebandar [Masulipatam], and Bhutan."

From India Costand passes on to "Pegu, Ava [Mandalay], Khata(?), Cotta, Cochin, Chirbad(?), Senan(?), Malacca, Batavia, Ternate, Amboyna, Macassar, Timor, Solor, Manilla, and Sharnov(?)." Among Eastern towns, Kabul, Kandahar, Ghaznee, Balkh, Bokhara, and Meshed are mentioned in the list.

The pupils attending Costand's school were the sons of wealthy Armenian merchants, who, trading extensively with foreign countries, paid special attention to the education of their children. They were instructed by Costand in the vernacular and the rudiments of commercial knowledge. Among the many precepts which Costand desired to impress on their minds, were :—

"Do not start on a journey alone. Do not sit and sleep with one whom you have not known and tried; perhaps he may murder you on the way and plunder you of all your goods. Take provisions from your own pantry and a companion from your own house. Keep the paper for writing in your breast [pocket], pen and ink in your coat pocket; the lamp in your luggage; the scales with the weights in its box; the yard measure [iron] in your belt; your senses in your head; and your mind towards God. Be satisfied with what God may give you. Do not trust an unknown person with a parcel. Record all your daily transactions; and do not put off till to-morrow what you can do to-day."

Costand died at Julfa in the year 1702 A.D., and was buried in that part of the cemetery which is allotted to the Armenian monks. A tombstone, bearing a terse inscription in Armenian, the following being a translation, marks his grave :—

"This is the tomb of COSTAND, the scholar, who led a monastic life and died in Christ in 1702 A.D."

Many of the towns enumerated in Costand's list have long since been forsaken by Armenians; but up to the middle of the last century they were to be found in the following towns in India and the Far East, as a pontifical bull from the Holy See of Etchmiadzin, dated 31st December 1850, is addressed to the Armenian residents at "Calcutta, Chinsurah, Saidabad, Dacca, Agra, Gwalior, Cawnpore, Lucknow, Fattihabad, Lahore, Bombay, Surat, Hyderabad, Madras, Masulipatam, Rangoon, Moulmein, Ava [Mandalay], Penang, Singapore, Malacca, Batavia, Semarang, Sourabaya, Thegal, Jeparah," &c.

It is difficult, indeed, to conjecture what India might to-day have been if, coupled with their enterprise and perseverance, the Armenians had adopted an aggressive policy in India.

CHAPTER XLVII.

CONCLUSION.

A GLANCE AT THE PAST AND A PEEP INTO THE FUTURE.

We have seen in the foregoing pages how a handful of Armenians coming from a distant cold country achieved success in tropical India by dint of merit and perseverance. Their racial intelligence, combined with their boundless energy and industry, enabled them to go up the steep ladder of fame and shine, like brilliant stars, in the horizon of India, during the Mogul and the British periods, as able administrators, clever diplomats, military commanders, skilled artisans, renowned poets, eminent lawyers, surgeons and merchants.

The Armenians in India have had no historian in the past and there can be none in the future either, as there will be nothing of interest to chronicle, for gone are the days when an Armenian lad, the son of a merchant, born and bred in India, could rise to be a grandee (Amir) of the Mogul Court and the Governor of important provinces, or for a humble cloth-seller to becomc the Commander-in-Chief of Bengal, Behar and Orissa, the richest jewel in the diadem of the Mogul Government.

With the keen competition that is going on, no Armenian merchant can hereafter earn the fabulous profit of a million rupees on a modest outlay of Rs. 18,500 in fifty years. There will be no diplomats like Khojah Israel Sarhad, Margar Avagsheenentz or Petrus Arathoon—the "Armenian Petrus" of Clive—who by their glorious achievements have found a niche in the history of British India.

Can the future Armenians produce another Gorgin Khan or a Shah Nazar Khan to manufacture huge pieces of ordnance and fire-arms?

There will be no merchant princes like Khojah Phanoos Kalandar of Surat, Khojah Petrus Woskan and Agah Shameer of Madras, or Agah Catchick Arakiel of Calcutta. They are not likely to have an Advocate-General like Sir Gregory Charles Paul, or an advocate of the type and calibre of M. P. Gasper.

There will be no Deputy Surgeon-General like Dr. J. M. Joseph, M.D., nor will there be another Executive Engineer like J. D. M. Beglar. There will be no eminent merchants to occupy the Presidential chair of the Bengal Chamber of Commerce like Sir Apcar Alexander Apcar, a school-mate of Lord Curzon, and a steward of the Royal Calcutta Turf Club. There will no Gregory Sams to occupy the chair of the District Traffic Superintendent of the East Indian Railway.

There will be no Sir Paul Chaters to give princely donations to the Calcutta La Martiniere and the Armenian church. There will be no shipowners, mill-owners or colliery proprietors like Apcar & Co., and there will be no Thaddeus Arathoons and Alexander Apcars to construct jute mills. And lastly there will be no race-horse owners like Mr. J. C. Galstaun and the late Sir Apcar Alexander Apcar and T. M. Thaddeus to carry off the King Emperor's or the Viceroy's Cups on the Calcutta Turf.

These are no jeremiads or the vapourings and the outbursts of a pessimist but they are the sad reflections of one who has spent his life in unearthing the past history of his countrymen in India, and he is therefore in a postition, by reason of his long experience and thorough knowledge of the subject, to make authoritative comparisons between the past and the future status of the Armenians in this country.

The Armenians in India can be proud of a glorious past, but their future, in view of the momentous changes that are taking place in the kaliedoscope of India, is not at all bright.

During the past 400 years, commencing from the halcyon days of the Armenophil Akbar onwards, Armenians have come to India, Burma, Malaya, Java and the Far East in large numbers. If we were to take an average of 50 persons in a year, which is quite a reasonable figure, some 20,000 persons must have found their way to India and the East during that long period. A few thousands may have returned to their homes, after making their pile, but what has become of the rest,

as there are, in the present day, at a fair computation, not more than 4000 Armenians in the whole of India, Burma, Malaya, Java, China and Japan. In the natural order of things, their numbers should have been more than forty thousand to-day, instead of four thousand, and as they rarely married outside their own community in the olden days, they could not therefore have got mixed with Indians or Eurasians. We cannot account for their decadence and gradual decline, in spite of prosperity and affluence in the past.

In former years, many Armenian lads, after leaving school, were able with their limited education, but good physique, to find employment on the Railways as ticket collectors, guards, drivers and firemen, but with the Indianization of the Railways that avenue is practically closed for them. Many used to obtain employment in the jute districts, but the jute trade in Eastern Bengal, of which the Armenians were the pioneers, has now passed into the hands of the Scotch and the ubiquitous Marwaris. What prospects have the poorly-educated young men in this country, with the keen throat-cutting competition on one side and the increasing non-employment on the other.

The boys who after ten or twelve years of free education in the local Armenian College, or other schools, spend another three to five years in gaining technical knowledge in motor or electrical workshops in order to qualify themselves for jobs of Rs. 50 to Rs. 100 per month, without any future prospects, would be well advised to return to Iran, after leaving school, as there are much brighter prospects, for Iranian subjects, in that progressive and regenerated country, than they could possibly expect to have in this country, with the significant words—"India for the Indians"—writ large.

Our pleasant task is finished, under great mental and physical strain, owing to ill-health and old age. The reader will now be able to form his own opinion of what the early Armenians have done in helping the British to inaugurate their rule in India, and what claim Armenians generally have upon English sympathy and help, especially in time of trial and difficulty.

And before we lay down our pen, we must crave the indulgence of our readers for having taxed their patience at times with dry stories of graves, epitaphs, deserted and snake-infested cemeteries, ruined and dilapidated churches and chapels which, we know, will not be of interest to many.

And in recording the names of eminent Armenians who flourished in India during the 17th, 18th and 19th centuries, we have made frequent use of the Persian honorific titles of Agah, Khojah and Khan, which we know, from past experience, are resented by certain narrow-minded people, who imagine that those titles are likely to leave an impression in the minds of the readers that the distinguished holders of the said titles were Persians and not Armenians. We have replied to our would-be critics on page 202 and have therefore, nothing more to add. The lot of the historian is indeed not an enviable one, for he has to record facts which are sometimes unpalatable, but historians, worthy of the name, must be true to their calling always. They cannot be sycophants, for gone are the days when the poor struggling historian had to dedicate his work, with words of adulation, to some rich person, generally a donkey with a golden saddle, in the expectation of pecuniary gain. Filthy lucre, be it noted, is gall and wormwood to the historian who labours ceaselessly and conscientiously in probing the past simply for the sake of an ideal. In fact all literary work to be of any outstanding value, should be a pure labour of love.

We will now make our bow and say *Adieu* to our gentle readers !

APPENDIX

HINDOOS IN ARMENIA*

150 YEARS BEFORE CHRIST.

An Unknown Chapter in the History of Ancient India.

It may not be generally known that the Armenians whose love of commerce has been proverbial, have, from time immemorial, traded with India, whither they were allured from their distant homes in the snow-clad mountains of Armenia, by the glamour of the lucrative trade in spices, muslins and precious stones, which they carried on successfully with Europe by the overland route, through Afghanistan, Persia, and Armenia, *via* Trebizond, long before the advent of any European traders, adventurers and interlopers into the country. And it may be safely mentioned that even before the Mohammedan invasion of India in the 10th century, the Armenians were found at all the principal commercial centres and capitals of India engaged in the peaceful pursuit of commerce.

It would be interesting, however, from a historical point of view, to trace in what period of the world's history Armenians first set foot on Indian soil.

We search in vain the faded pages of Sanskrit writers and Mohammedan chroniclers of ancient times for any reference to this enterprising, commercial people in India. They were hardly interested in politics, and

---

* A Paper read by the present writer at the Ninth Meeting of the Indian Historical Records Commission held at Lucknow in December, 1926. It was published in the Proceedings of the Commission in 1927, and in the "Bengal: Past and Present"—the Journal of the Calcutta Historical Society—for January - March, 1927.

The lecture, by reason of its great historical value, was received with loud acclamations by the large number of Hindoos in the audience, and Professor, now Sir Jadunath Sarkar, M.A. who presided at the Meeting, said that they knew that their remote ancestors had crossed the seas and gone as far as Java, but they never knew that they had gone so far as Armenia. He promised to bring the discovery to the notice of the "Greater India Society", on his return to Calcutta. We hope he did.

We were afterwards informed by some members of the Commission whom we met at the Rangoon Session, in December 1927, that the Paper had been translated and published in the vernacular papers of Gujerat and the Punjab for the information of Hindoos in those parts.

rarely took part in intrigues, their field of action lay, rather, in the bazaars, the commercial marts, and the emporiums of India, over which they exercised vast influence, in the absence of any foreign commercial element, and thereby monopolised the greater portion of the export trade, which they carried on for a considerable period.

The writer ventures to assume, after much careful study and antiquarian research, that they were acquainted with India from remote antiquity, perhaps even when Semiramis, the wife of Ninus, and the warlike queen of the once-powerful Assyrian monarchy, reigned supreme in Babylon. Contemporary as a nation with the Assyrians, it is not improbable that they accompanied Semiramis, as faithful allies, in her invasion of India, which, according to the account given by Ctesias and Diodorus Siculus, was undertaken about the year 2000 B.C., when one Stabrobates (Sthabarpati) held indisputable sway over India of the Vedic times. Armenians, as allies or otherwise, may have accompanied the Greek invasion of India in 327 B.C., under Alexander the Great; for it is a well-known historical fact that he passed through Armenia, *en route* for India, *via.* Persia, where he defeated the famous Darius, the Persian King, who resided at Persepolis, the capital of unparalleled architectural fame at that period.

But it may be asked, what have the Armenian historians to say on the subject. Unfortunately the annals of ancient Armenia which were carefully preserved in the temples of pre-Christian Armenia and which could have thrown light on the subject were destroyed entirely, by St. Gregory, the apostle of Armenia, known as the Illuminator, in the beginning of the 4th Century of the Christian era when by virtue of a royal edict granted to St. Gregory, by that zealous neophyte, King Tiridates, Armenia embraced the Christian faith *en masse,* and the Armenians thus became the *first* Christian nation in the world.

The first authentic record we have of the connection of the Armenians with India is to be found in the work of Zenob, one of the earliest classical writers who flourished in Christian Armenia in the beginning of the 4th Century.

Zenob, or Zenobias, who was a Syrian and one of the *first* disciples of St. Gregory the Illuminator—the Apostle of Armenia—wrote, at the instance of his master, a *History of Taron* (an important province in Armenia) and in that work he refers to the history of a Hindoo colony that had existed in Armenia since the middle of the second century before the commencement of the Christian era till the beginning of the Hindoo colony came to be planted on Armenian soil in the days of remote antiquity. It appears from Zenob's account that two Hindoo Princes of far-famed Kanauj,* named Gissaneh and Demeter, had conspired against Dinakspall, the King of Kanauj, and on the discovery of the plot, which spelt death for the two princes, they had no alternative but to seek refuge in flight, and to far-off Armenia they fled, and there they not only found an asylum, but were accorded a welcome befitting their princely dignity by their royal patron, King Valarsaces (a brother of Arsaces the Great) and the founder of the Arsacidæ dynasty which ruled in Armenia from 149 B.C. to 428 A. D.

This event occurred in 149 B.C. The Armenian King, who was evidently pleased with the Hindoo refugees, allotted them the province of Taron where they built themselves a nice city which they called Veeshap, which in Armenian means a Dragon, since they were of the Takshak House, which, as every student of Hindoo Mythology knows, signifies the Dragon. They then went to the Armenian city of Ashtishat, famous for its temples of the national gods and goddesses of heathen Armenia and there they set up the gods which they had worshipped in India. They were not however destined to enjoy a long period of undisturbed peace and freedom in the land of their adoption, for they were, 15 years after their arrival in Armenia, put to death by the king for which no reasons or motives are assigned by the native historian, perhaps they had, as in India, hatched a conspiracy against their royal patron or abused his hospitality, hence the condign punishment meted out to them by the Armenian king. After their death, these two Hindoo princes, were deified by their descendants, for they must have gone to Armenia with their families and a large retinue, as future events will prove. According to the Armenian historian, these two princes left three sons whose names were Kuars, Meghtes and Horean, and the Armenian king, bestowed on them the Government of the colony and the principality of the province of Taron.

Kuars built a small city and called it Kuar after his own name. Meghtes similarly built a small city and named it Meghti after himself, whilst Horean built his city in the province of Poloonean and called it Horeans.

Being new to the country, they were evidently not satisfied with the first selection of sites for their habitations, so after some time they resolved amongst themselves to find fresh fields and pastures new, so they went to thee mountain called Kharkh and finding it an ideal place by reason of its beautiful and favourable situation, they built themselves 4th century, A. D. or a period of 450 years. And this is how the a city where they put up two gods, and named them Gisaneh and Demeter, after their murdered fathers whom they had deified. These gods were made entirely of brass, the former, according to Zenob, was twelve cubits high, and the latter fifteen cubits and the priests that were appointed for the service of these gods were all Hindoos. Under the auspices of a heathen Government, in whose eyes they had evidently found great favour, the Hindoo colony flourished for a considerable time in Armenia, but with the dawn of Christianity in idolatrous Armenia in the year 301 A.D. the tide of royal kindness began to ebb and ebb very swiftly, for the Indian gods shared the fate of the national gods and goddesses, which were destroyed by that relentless iconoclast. St. Gregory the Illuminator, who had the famous temples of Gisaneh and Demeter razed to the ground, the images broken to pieces whilst the Hindoo priests who offered resistance were murdered on the spot, as faithfully chronicled by Zenob who was an eye-witness of the destruction of the Hindoo temples and the gods. On the site of these two temples, St. Gregory had a monastery erected where he deposited the relics of St. John the Baptist and Athanagineh the martyr which he had brought with him from Ceaseria, and that sacred edifice, which was erected in the year 301 A.D., exists to this day and is known as St. Carapiet of Moosh and has always been a great place of pilgrimage for Armenians from all parts of the world. The Hindoo priests attached to the temples of Gisaneh and Demeter, seeing the destruction of their national gods and their temples, with tears in their eyes entreated the victorious Armenians, their erstwhile brother idolators, to put them to death rather than destroy their mighty god Gisaneh, and for the resistance that they offered to the victors, six of the Hindoo priests were killed on the spot. On the restoration of peace between the Armenians and the Hindoos, the Armenian prince of the house of Siunies proceeded to the Hindoo village of Kuars and succeeded in persuading the inhabitants of that place to renounce idolatry and embrace the Christian faith which had now became the State religion. His efforts were crowned with success and they were duly prepared for baptism, and being conducted to the valley of Ayzasan they were baptised there by St. Gregory. According to Zenob, who as I have said, was a disciple of the Apostle of Armenia, and an eye-witness of the events he narrates, the Hindoos that were baptised on the first day of Navasard, (the ancient Armenian New Years day) numbered 5,050 and these were composed of men and children only, as the females were, it appears, excluded from that number and baptised on another day specially appointed for the occasion.

Some of these converted Hindoos adhered tenaciously to the idolatrous practices of their forefathers, despite the paternal persuasions and the exhortations of St. Gregory. They went even further and taunted the Armenian princes by telling them that if they lived they would retaliate for the harsh treatment they had received at their hands, but if they died, the gods would wreak their vengeance on the Armenians on their behalf. At this the prince of the house of Angegh ordered them to be taken immediately to the city of Phaitakaran where they were incarcerated and their heads shaved as an insult and a sign of degradation. These prisoners numbered four hundred. From the narrative of Zenob, the Syrian, it appears that the Hindoo colony had, since their settlement in Armenian in the year 150 B.C. to the day of that memorable battle in the year 301 A.D. a period of 450 years, multiplied and increased considerably and formed a distinct and an important colony of their own in the fertile province of Taron where in the year 286 A.D. a Chinese colony had also settled under Mamgoon, the founder of the house of Mamikonian which gave a Vardan to Armenia who fought the Sassanians when they wanted to force the religion of Zoroaster on Christian Armenia in the year 451 A.D. The Hindoos, who up to the advent of Christianity in Armenia had remained a distinct community became gradually merged into the native Christian population, as no reference is made to them by any of the Armenian historians who came after Zenob, who, as has been stated before, flourished in the beginning of the 4th century.

Having given a brief out-line of the history of the Hindoo colony in Armenia, we shall now give some interesting extracts from the narrative of Zenob. It may be mentioned that Zenob who was a Syrian wrote his work originally in Syriac, but it must have been translated by him afterwards into Armenian, with Syriac characters of course, as there were no Armenian characters then, for the present Armenian alphabet was invented in the year 413 by St. Mesrovb, who in collaboration with St. Sahak, translated the Holy Bible into Armenian from the original Syriac and Greek texts and which by reason of its faithful rendering and elegant style has justly been pronounced by eminent European savants as the "Queen of all Versions" (*Regina Versionum*).

The Armenian text of Zenob's work in classical Armenian from which the following extracts are translated, was printed first at Venice in 1832 by the learned Mekhitharist Fathers, after a very careful collation with five manuscript copies written at different periods and in different places. The first portion of the narrative gives a description of the Hindoo colony and it is followed by a graphic account of the religious wars that were waged between the Hindoos and the early propagators of the Christian faith in idolatrous Armenia in the beginning of the 4th century. And this is how Zenob, the Syrian, describes the Hindoos whom be sees for the *first* time on his arrival in Armenia, with St. Gregory, the Illuminator, in the year 301 A.D.

"This people had a most extraordinary appearance for they were black, long-haired and unpleasant to the sight, as they were Hindoos by race.

The origin of the idols which were in this place, is this: Demeter and Gisaneh were brothers and they were both Indian princes. They had conspired against Dinaksi, their King, who being apprised, sent troops after them either to put them to death or to banish them from the country. Having narrowly escaped, they fled to King Valarsaces who bestowed on them the principality of the district of Taron where they built a city and called it Veeshap.

They afterwards went to the city of Ashtishat and there set up idols in the names of those which they had worshipped in India. After fifteen years the King put both the brothers to death, I do not know why, and conferred the principality on their three sons, Kuars, Meghtes and Horean. Kuar built the city of Kuars, Meghtes built a village on the plain and called it Meghti, and Horean built a village in the province of Paloonies and called it Horeans.

After some time, Kuar, Meghtes and Horean, resolved to go to the mountain called Kharkhi, and they found the place to be salubrious and beautiful, for it was cool, and abounded in game, grass and wood. There they raised edifices and set up two idols, one in the name of Gisaneh and the other in the name of Demeter and appointed attendants for them from their own race.

Gisaneh had long flowing hair and for that reason its priests allowed the hair of their head to grow, which the King ordered to be cut. This people were not, however, perfect in their faith after their conversion into the Christian faith and as they could not profess the religion of their pagan ancestors openly, they therefore practised the deception of allowing their children to grow a plait of hair on the crown of their heads, so that they may, by seeing that, remember their idolatrous abominations."

In the course of their journey through Armenia, Zenob gives the following account of the war that was waged between the Hindoos and the Armenians in the year 301 A.D.

"And having taken our departure from there (Thordan) we intended to proceed to Karin and Harkh, but some of the Armenian princes informed St. Gregory of the existence of two temples in the province of Taron which still offered sacrifices to the devils, whereupon he resolved to demolish them. Having arrived in the country of the Paloonies, in the extensive village, called Gisaneh, near the village town of Kuars, we met there some of the heathen priests. Having ascertained from the Hindoo prince of Hashtens that the great images of Gisaneh and Demeter were to be levelled to the ground on the following day, they (Hindoos) repaired to the temples in the dead of the night and removed the treasures and filled them into sub-terraneous houses.

They then sent intimation to the heathen priests at Ashtishat urging them to collect warriors and join them early on the morrow as the great Gisaneh was going to give battle to the apostate princes (Armenians). In like manner they put up the inhabitants of Kuars to lie in ambush in the hedges of the gardens and some were sent to waylay Christians in the forests. The head priest whose name was Artzan [Arjun] and his son Demeter took the command of the troops who were stationed at Kuars and numbered 400, and having ascended the hill that was opposite Kuars, they halted there, awaiting the arrival of reinforcements from other places to their aid. On the following day, they descended to the skirts of the mountains to indulge in their usual habit of pillage. St. Gregory accompanied by the prince of Artzroonies, the prince of Andzevatzies and the prince of the house of Angegh and with a small number of troops numbering about three hundred, ascended the mountain in the third hour of the day, where Artzan lay in ambush. They were going carelessly as they never suspected anything and as they approached the acclivity of the mountain, Artzan and Demeter rushed out of their ambuscade when the trumpets of war were sounded and they were attacked most furiously. The princes having heard this, became restless and alarmed, for their horses took fright from the sound of the trumpets and began to neigh and thus excite war, whereupon the prince of the house of Angegh raised his voice and cried, "Prince of Siunies, step forward and see perhaps these are the troops of the prince of the north." He went, but could not ascertain who they were. On his return, the prince of the Siunies said "remove St. Gregory and his companions to a safe place lest they may be captured by the enemy and we will then be disgraced before the King." "Send a trusty person," he added, "to recall our troops, for it is going to be a great war and many are the flags which are seen waving."

The prince of the house of Angegh, then entrusted St. Gregory, into the hands of the prince of Mocks enjoining him to take him immediately to the Castle of Oghkan and await developments, and forthwith sent intimation to the troops. The prince of the Mocks, accompanied by St. Gregory descended the declivity of the hill wishing to go to Kuars, but the people of the place began to block the way. Seeing that there was great danger in the place, St. Gregory hid the relics which he had with him near a spring on the other side of the hill, opposite the village, marking the spot and God covered the relics and nobody could see them till the return of St. Gregory to that spot afterwards. We were, however, pursued by the men of the village, but being mounted on our horses, we took refuge in the Castle of Oghkan where we reached before them as the men of the place came forward and took us in. The villagers (Hindoos) then went to Kuars and informed the people there about us. Hearing this they came and began to besiege the castle. Being seized with apprehensions we immediately despatched a messenger with a letter to the prince of the house of Angegh ,informing him of the state of affairs. He immediately sent four thousand picked men furnished with swords who crossed the river and arrived on the following day. They laid siege to the city of Kuars for three days and having demolished the ramparts, they reduced the place to ruins and the inhabitants were conducted to Meghtes.

The Armenian princes being informed of this, ascended the hill and saw Artzan lying in ambush with about four hundred men. The brave princes made an attack immediately and were putting him to flight when the Armenian troops, hearing the din of the battle, crowded immediately to the mountain whereupon Artzan rallied and began to hurl abuses on the Armenian princes. "Come forward," he said, "O you base apostates who have denied the gods of your ancestors and are the enemies of the glorious Gisaneh. Do you not know that it is Gisaneh who is waging war against you to-day and will betray you into our hands and strike you with blindness and death." At this the prince of the Ardzrunies rushed forward and said "Oh you braggart, if you are fighting for your gods, you are false, and if it is for your country, you are altogether foolish for behold the prince of the house of Angegh and the prince of the house of Siunies and the other nobles whom you know but too well." To which, Demeter, the son of Artzan replied thus. "Listen unto us O you Armenian princes, it is now forty years since we are engaged in the service of the mighty gods and we are aware of their powers, for they fight themselves with the enemies of their servants. We are not, however, able to oppose you in battle for this is the house of the king of Armenia and you are his nobles, but let it be known to you all that although we cannot possibly conquer you, yet it is better for us to die a glorious death to-day in upholding the honour of our gods rather than live and see their temples polluted by you. Death is, therefore, more welcome to us than life. But you, who are the prince of the house of Angegh come forward and let us fight singly."

The prince of the house of Angegh and Artzan having come forward, they commenced going round each other, when Artzan with his spear inflicted hurriedly a wound on his opponent's thigh and well-nigh brought him to the ground. But the prince of the house of Angegh having regained his position, turned towards the antagonist and addressed him thus. "Know you this O Artzan that this place will be called Artzan (the Armenian word for a statue) for you are destined to be fixed here like a statue. And having lifted his arm, he severed his neck together with the left shoulder and leg from the body by a stroke of the sword on the right shoulder. Artzan fell to the ground rolling and they collected a heap over him and he lies buried in the same place and the mount is to this day called Artzan.

Immediately after the action the troops of the priests arrived from the city of Veeshap together with the people of Partukh and Meghti and they all crowded to the field of battle. Others came from Astaghon also and their number was, as they themselves said afterwards, five thousand four hundred and fifty. When they arrived at the summit of the mountain, there was a commotion on both sides and the heathen priests made an attack, *en masse,* on the Armenian troops and putting them to flight made them descend the mountain and fly towards the villages. The villagers who were laying in ambush, opposed our troops and hemming them on both sides began to put them to the sword. But the prince of the house of Angegh, having cut through the ranks of the heathen (Hindoo) priests, directed his course towards the mountain, from the back, where some men were kept in reserve on the top who caused great havoc by flinging stones at our horses. But when Demeter observed the prince of the house of Angegh ascending the hill, he left the troops behind and followed him, so did the other troops who were mounted on horses.

When they went up the hill, the battle was resumed. Our princes were waiting for further re-inforcements since all the troops had not assembled there yet, as four thousand were left in charge of the prisoners at Meghti and three thousand proceeded to Bassean and Harkh. The rest were still in the field pillaging and marauding. And when they were about to commence the battle and exchange decisive blows, night approached and they encamped in the place until the following morning. At dawn, the remaining Armenian troops arrived there and a re-inforcement of about five hundred men from the city of Tirakatar came to the assistance of the heathen priests. The numbers on both sides were thus increased. The heathens numbered six thousand nine hundred and forty six whilst the troops of the Armenian princes were in all five thousand and eighty.

The trumpets were sounded and both sides arranged themselves in battle. At the commencement the Armenians proved victorious over the heathens, but the prince of Hashtens who was now in command of the Armenian troops although of the same (Hindoo) race as Demeter, deserted and joined the heathen priests with seven hundred men and commenced fighting the Armenian princes. When the Armenian troops saw him, they were dismayed and fell to the ground for he was a brave man of extraordinary prowess, of indomitable courage and of vast experience in warfare and military operations which made all the Armenian princes tremble before him. He commenced the onslaught relentlessly and all the troops cried out and appealed to the prince of the Siunies for help whereupon he called out to him (the prince of Hashtens) saying, "you whelp of a wolf! You have remembered the nature of your father and delight in feasting on carrion." The rebel chief retorted by saying tauntingly "You offspring of an eagle, you who boast on the powers of your wings, but if you ever fall into my trap, I shall then show you my strength." The prince of the Siunies could not brook this taunt and rushing on him furiously, struck him on the helmet with his axe and having dislodged him from his troops by driving him to some distance, pursued him to the mountain eastwards. Having chased him to the place known as the Innaknian, (nine springs) he threw him down by a violent shove from his horse and having alighted, he severed his head from the body and dropped it down the mountain saying, "now let the vultures see you and know that the eagle has killed the hare." The prince of the Siunies returned to the army immediately after this and the place where the rebel prince of Hashtens fell, is to this day called the "Eagles."

The prince of the Ardzroonies then attacked the head priest of Ashtishat whose name was Metakes whom he pursued to the summit of the mountain which commanded a view of the battle. When he reached there, Metakes made a violent resistance and struck him on the thigh. The Armenian prince, burning with rage, struck him immediately with his scimitar on the neck which he severed from the body. He then threw down the headless body and the place where the deed was committed was called Metsakogh.

The prince of Arjootz (Hindoo) seeing this, took refuge in flight and concealed himself in the same place which the prince of Ardzoonies pretended not to have observed. He then approached the fugitive and attacked him suddenly but he fled into the forest where a sharp piece of wood from the branch of a tree passed through his heart and liver and he died on the spot. The victor returned with the two horses and the place was called the vale of Arjootz.

After his return, he found that Demeter and the prince of the house of Angegh were wrestling with each other. Having made a rush he cut off the right shoulder of the former and threw him down. He then severed the head and throwing it into his knapsack, went away. The Armenians having attacked the heathen army furiously, put one thousand and thirty eight of them to the sword and the rest were stripped of all they possessed. In this battle Demeter killed the son of the prince of Mocks which caused great sorrow amongst the Armenian princes. When Demeter fell in the battle, the prince of the Siunies sounded the trumpet of peace and both sides stopped slaughtering each other. The surviving heathen priests seeing this, solicited the Armenian princes to give them permission to bury their dead which was readily granted. The killed on both sides were then collected and buried in pits dug for the purpose. Monuments were then raised over their graves bearing the following inscription, in Syrian, Hellenic and Ismaelitish characters.

THE FIRST BATTLE WHICH WAS FOUGHT VERY FIERCELY. ARTZAN [ARJUN] THE HEAD PRIEST, THE CHIEF COMMANDER OF THE BATTLE LIES INTERRED HERE, AND WITH HIM ONE THOUSAND AND THIRTY-EIGHT MEN.

WE WAGED THIS WAR ON ACCOUNT OF THE IDOL GISANEH AND ON BEHALF OF CHRIST.

Note.—Some of the important Hindoo names, as mentioned by Zenob in the course of his narrative, may be identified as follows :—

Gisaneh may have been the corrupt form of Krishna, and Demeter the Hellenised form of Juggernath or Gonesh, which according to Hindoo mythology, are the lords of earth and creation. Similarly, Kuars may be identified with Koilash, Meghtes with Mukti, Horean with Horendra and Artzan with Arjun, all of which are genuine Hindoo names of Ancient India.